Bob Rybica

§ [...t House to do business shall consist of the Deputies of not less than ... States, and all questions ... be decided by the greater number of those which shall be fully represented - but a less number than seven may adjourn from day to day.

Immediately after the President shall have taken the chair, and the members their seats, the minutes of the preceding day shall be read by the Secretary.

Every member, rising to speak, shall address the President; and whilst he shall be speaking, none shall pass between them, or hold discourse with another, or read a book, pamphlet or paper, printed or manuscript - and of two members rising at the same time, the President shall name him who shall be first heard.

A member shall not speak oftener than twice, without special leave, upon the same question; and not the second time, before every other, who had been silent, shall have been heard, if he choose to speak, upon the subject.

A motion made and seconded, shall be repeated, and if written, as it shall be when any member shall so require, read aloud by the Secretary, before it shall be debated; and may be withdrawn at any time, before the vote upon it shall have been declared.

Orders of the day shall be read next after the minutes and either discussed or postponed, before any other business shall be introduced.

When a debate shall arise upon a question, no motion, other than to amend the question, to commit it, or to postpone the debate shall be received.]

---

* Previous to the arrival of a majority of the States, the rule by which they ought to vote had been made a subject of conversation among the members present. It was pressed by Governeur Morris and favored by Robert Morris and others from Pennsylvania that the large States should unite in firmly refusing to the small States an equal vote, as unreasonable and as enabling the small States to negative every good system of government, which must in the nature of things, be founded on a violation of that equality. The members from Virginia, conceiving that such an attempt might beget fatal altercations between the large & small States, and that it would be easier to prevail on the latter, in the course of the deliberations, to give up their equality for the sake of an effective government, than on taking the field of discussion to disarm themselves of the right discountenanced & stifled the project

THE DEMOCRATIC REPUBLIC

THE DEMOCRATIC REPUBLIC
AN INTRODUCTION TO AMERICAN
☆ NATIONAL GOVERNMENT ☆

Martin Diamond
Claremont Men's College

Winston Mills Fisk
Claremont Men's College

Herbert Garfinkel
Michigan State University

RAND McNALLY & COMPANY • *Chicago*

Rand McNally Political Science Series
Morton Grodzins, Advisory Editor

Rand McNally Political Science Series

BARBER, *Power in Committees*
BAYLEY, *Political Liberties in the New States*
BECKER, *Political Behavioralism and Modern Jurisprudence*
BOBROW, ed., *Components of Defense Policy*
CLEMENS, ed., *Toward a Strategy of Peace*
DIAMOND, FISK, and GARFINKEL, *The Democratic Republic: An Introduction to American National Government*
ELDERSVELD, *Political Parties: A Behavioral Analysis*
FROMAN, *Congressmen and Their Constituencies*
GOLDWIN, *Beyond the Cold War*
GOLEMBIEWSKI, GIBSON, and CORNOG, eds., *Public Administration: Readings in Institutions, Processes, Behavior*
GRODZINS, *The American System*
HAIGHT and JOHNSTON, eds., *The President: Roles and Powers*
HANNA, ed., *Independent Black Africa*
MILBRATH, *Political Participation: How and Why Do People Get Involved in Politics?*
—, *The Washington Lobbyists*
PEABODY and POLSBY, eds., *New Perspectives on the House of Representatives*
PRESS AND WILLIAMS, *Democracy in the Fifty States*
Rand McNally Public Affairs Series
ROBERT A. GOLDWIN, ed.
America Armed: Essays on United States Military Policy
A Nation of States: Essays on the American Federal System
Why Foreign Aid?
Political Parties, U.S.A.
100 Years of Emancipation
SCHMIDHAUSER, ed., *Constitutional Law in the Political Process*
SINGER, ed., *Human Behavior and International Politics: Contributions from the Social-Psychological Sciences*
SCHUBERT, ed., *Judicial Behavior: A Reader in Theory and Research*
STRAUSS, *The City and Man*
STRAUSS and CROPSEY, eds., *History of Political Philosophy*
ULMER, ed., *Introductory Reader in Political Behavior*
WILLIAMS and PRESS, eds., *Democracy in Urban America: Readings in Government and Politics*

FOR OUR FAMILIES

Contents

Introduction

IN THIS BOOK WE CONSIDER THE AMERICAN POLITICAL ORDER, OR, IN AN older phrase, the American polity. By the terms 'political order' and 'polity,' we emphasize that American government and politics must be studied within a broad framework, ultimately one that comprehends every activity affecting the common political life by means of which men seek to live their lives well. The task is thus to study the structures and processes of government so as to see the fundamental premises regarding human life which they embody, the organizing facts and principles which make them what they are, and the forces at work within them. Thus conceived, the study of government and politics is worthy of the deepest attention and can generate the most rewarding reflection.

But that is a very tall order indeed. It is enough to make even a small start on such a task. However, how well we succeed is not for an introduction to say but for the whole book to show. But it is proper and useful to indicate some of the distinctive themes, modes of analysis, and purposes which characterize this textbook on American government. We can best begin by emphasizing the significance of its title: *The Democratic Republic*.

Modern conservatives and liberals—scholars and politicians alike—too often pit the *democratic* elements of the American political order against its *republican* elements. The democratic elements they portray as resting upon and exalting majoritarianism and strong national government to achieve "the general welfare." The republican aspects they portray as resting upon and exalting checks and balances, federalism, and limited government to secure "the blessings of liberty," especially for propertied minorities. Both conservatives and liberals thus portray a divided system at war with itself, with the democratic forces gradually overcoming the stubborn republican restraints.

We reject this view, as our title makes clear. We argue instead that the American system is a novel experiment in reconciling the advantages of democracy with the sobering qualities of republicanism. Such reconciliation is the central fact around which nearly all else revolves. American history must be seen as the experience of the successes and failures of that reconciliation. The principles and processes of modern American government and politics, we submit, are best understood when the system is grasped in its essential quality, that is, as a democratic republic. By emphasizing the compatibility of the democratic and republican elements of the system, we hope to open a path away from outworn scholarly and political arguments that stem from the view that these elements are incompatible.

Modern historiography supports our view of the democratic republic. Current historical scholarship has largely supplanted the once dominant view (associated with the name of Charles A. Beard) that the American republic was designed by its framers to further their antidemocratic economic interests and political opinions. While historians have been turning away from this view of the constitutional origins, political scientists have lagged behind; many continue to assume that American democracy has had to overcome a hostile Constitution imposed by the Founding Fathers. This book, in rejecting that view, endeavors to base itself on the most authoritative contemporary historical scholarship regarding American governmental origins and development.

Our view that the Constitution supplied from the outset an essentially democratic 'frame of government' has many important consequences. For example, we relate *constitutional structure* to *political behavior* differently than is done in many other interpretations of American government. Many others sharply separate political processes and behavior from constitutional factors; they believe that the living reality of politics is to be found in political parties and groups, in patterns of voting behavior and public opinion, and not in an archaic and superseded formal Constitution. We seek to show, on the contrary, that questions of both political behavior and of the formal constitutional arrangements are inextricably woven together and are of equal importance. Neither is intelligible without an appreciation of the other. Thus, by showing that American democratic political behavior is the legitimate offspring of the democratic Constitution, we hope to restore constitutional factors to their rightful place as part of political analysis.

Similarly, but for other reasons, many political scientists tend to depreciate the importance of *legal processes* and *formal institutions*. They treat legal and institutional factors as static and derivative, rather than dynamically determinative of actual political behavior. Again, as with the depreciation of constitutional factors, the tendency is to seek reality behind and beneath formal, legal, and institutional arrangements. We agree wholeheartedly with those who do not wish to be deceived by the mere surface of government. A political science that did not reach to the channels, wherever they may be, wherein political authority actually flows would not be worthy of the name. But we hold that legal and institutional analysis (not mere description) is a vital part of dynamic political analysis. Our endeavor is to blend constitutional, legal, and institutional analysis with modern behavioral research in order to give a comprehensive account of the American political order.

Another feature that we believe distinguishes this book is its reliance upon some of the classics of political analysis, especially those dealing directly with the American political order. We use works like *The Federalist* and Tocqueville's *Democracy in America*, not as mere literary embellishments, but as profound teachings which deepen our understanding of political things. And we hope that students will be encouraged to seek out these authors and to find in them more than we can hope to have taught in this book.

Perspective on contemporary American government is needed to appreciate its distinctive modernity as well as its continuity, both with the past and with other nations. This requires both historical and comparative analysis. The historical dimension is especially important in analyzing American government, particularly the founding decade because it contains the master mold in which much of our political development has been cast. More than most other countries we are in the grip of our political history. The comparative dimension is supplied mainly by reference to British government and politics; but some important contrasts are also drawn with other nations to show American students what is striking and problematical in their own system and which familiarity may otherwise cause to seem ordinary and insignificant.

Something should be said for an often denigrated, but we think important, obligation of American government textbooks. What shall it profit a man if he knows a bit about Plato and 'political behavior' but is not quite sure whether there are two or three houses of Congress? In short, students are entitled to find in a textbook a substantial factual account of the essential structures, functions, and powers of American government. We have not feared to be descriptive, but instead have supplied sufficient factual background to make intelligible our analyses of the political-governmental processes, and also such factual information as an educated person might reasonably be expected to possess about American government and politics.

In order to convey a sense of this book as a whole, we indicate briefly the Parts into which it is divided.

Part I discusses the origin of the American Republic. This book in general gives considerable place to the thought of the Founding Fathers. To grasp the principles of any system, it is helpful to see the materials out of which it emerged. As has been suggested, this is especially helpful in the American case. To see *how* and *why* the Framers built is to see *what* they built and to see in the founding of the American regime some of its permanent themes.

Part II discusses the political principles and constitutional bases upon which the American political order rests. We portray the American Republic as a democratic order which has been reconciled with the requirements of liberty and which supports a government reasonably competent to deal with modern problems. Democracy, liberty, and competence— these were the goals at which the Constitution aimed.

Part III turns to the structure and work of the three great branches into which the Constitution divides its government and to the administrative part of that government. It examines the behavior of the people who occupy the offices and exercise the powers within these institutional structures.

Part IV addresses itself to politics—to parties, elections, voters, interest groups—to all the institutions, processes, and people that make up our national political life. We chose to delay the examination of 'politics' until we first examined 'constitutionalism' and 'government.' In the American political order this is reasonable because the constitutional principles and the governmental structures so basically influence the political process. But a warning is appropriate: All the elements of the political order reciprocally affect each other—Congress, the parties; parties, Congress; both, the Supreme Court; and so on. Any division of the subject matter is to some extent merely a necessity of exposition. Building upon the prior analyses of the constitutional principles and the branches of government, Part IV examines the party-group system, membership in the political community, the mechanisms by which government results from political contest, voting behavior, and the dynamics of political campaigning. Finally, an overall evaluation of the American mode of party politics is provided.

Part V shows the polity, in all its components, at work about the business of *governing*. This business is described under three key categories: relationships between the government and the rights of its citizens, relationships between the government and the economy, and relationships between this government and other countries.

A word is in order regarding the division of responsibility among the three authors. This book has been a true collaboration in that each author was deeply involved in the discussion of each chapter. Within that framework, primary responsibility was distributed as follows: Introduction, Garfinkel-Diamond; Chapters 1–3, Diamond; Chapter 4, Fisk-Diamond; Chapters 5–6, Fisk; Chapter 7, Fisk-Garfinkel; Chapter 8, Fisk; Chapters 9–12, Garfinkel; Chapter 13, Fisk-Garfinkel; Chapter 14, Diamond-Fisk-Garfinkel; Chapter 15, Diamond; graphics, Garfinkel; bibliographies, Fisk. The original plan of the book was designed by Diamond and Garfinkel. Diamond supervised the writing of the book as a whole, assuming responsibility for substantial original drafting throughout and for final editing.

For all that is in error or is lacking in this book the authors accept full responsibility. But for all their help in improving the book, the authors gladly acknowledge their indebtedness to the following who examined various portions of the manuscript: Douglass G. Adair, Claremont Graduate School and University Center; Walter F. Berns, Cornell University; Samuel J. Eldersveld, University of Michigan; David Haight, Hunter College; Harry V. Jaffa, Claremont Men's College; Max M. Kampelman, Washington, D.C.; David Minar, Northwestern University; Donald Riddle, Rutgers University; Peter H. Rohn, University of Washington; Victor

G. Rosenblum, Northwestern University; Philip Selznick, University of California at Berkeley; Richard G. Stevens, Santa Clara University; Leo Strauss, University of Chicago; John H. Vanderzell, Franklin and Marshall College; Aaron Wildavsky, University of California at Berkeley; George C. Young, Millersville (Pa.) State College. We also wish to thank Morton Frisch of Northern Illinois University for his assistance in preparing an instructors' manual to accompany this volume. Our special thanks go to Mrs. Virginia A. Barrette and Mrs. Leontine Lawson for competent and cheerful secretarial assistance at all stages of the manuscript. We are extremely grateful as well to Miss Marianne Clark for her patient and skillful editing of the manuscript.

For our families, our dedication records proudly our gratitude for their thoughtful contributions to the book and their kindness in sharing the burdens of writing it.

Finally, with utmost affection, we record our debt to Morton Grodzins, late of the University of Chicago. Professor Grodzins initiated this venture, and supported and guided us through its most important stages. We wish for this book no greater merit than that it be deemed worthy of his memory.

Part One

ORIGIN
OF
THE
REPUBLIC

Chapter 1

The
Formative
Years

> *We hold these truths to be self-evident, that all men are created equal, that they are endowed by their Creator with certain unalienable Rights, that among these are Life, Liberty, and the pursuit of Happiness.—That to secure these rights, Governments are instituted among Men, deriving their just powers from the consent of the governed. . . .*
>
> THE DECLARATION OF INDEPENDENCE[1]

THE DECLARATION OF INDEPENDENCE DID MORE THAN DECLARE THE THIRTEEN colonies independent of Great Britain. Its continuing importance lies in the principles by which it justified independence. The colonies, the Declaration said, "are, and *of right* ought to be, free and independent states." That is, separation from Great Britain was grounded upon principles of just government held to be valid for all men at all times. These principles became the credo of the American political order.

The Declaration: Credo and Problem

The Declaration places two principles at the center of the credo. First, just government must rest upon "the consent of the governed" and, second, just government exists to secure "certain unalienable rights." Four score and seven years later at Gettysburg, Lincoln, who always forced American attention back to the Declaration, restated the two principles when he spoke of the "new nation, conceived in liberty, and dedicated to the proposition that all men are created equal." In Lincoln's formulation, we see the shape the two principles acquired: On the one hand, there is the equality of men from which results the democratic

---

[1] The full text of the Declaration of Independence is reproduced in the Appendix. It is also available in many collections of American documents, among them *The People Shall Judge* mentioned in the bibliographical note at the end of this chapter.

idea of government "by the people"; on the other hand, there is liberty from which results the idea that government may do only certain things and those only in certain ways.

This is all familiar and untroubling until we notice that the Declaration poses a problem which it does not itself solve. The Declaration's two principles are not automatically harmonious. Witness their problematical relationship, for example, in Thomas Jefferson's First Inaugural Address. He spoke of the "sacred principle, that though the will of the majority is in all cases to prevail, that will to be rightful must be reasonable." Jefferson's "sacred principle" is a reformulation of the Declaration's two principles. Consent of the governed has become "majority rule," and by "reasonable," Jefferson refers to the realm of unalienable rights. The two elements, Jefferson rightly implies, may conflict in practice. What if the majority consents to unreasonable or evil things, or indeed demands them? What if men, on the majority rule principle that resulted from the Declaration, vote away the liberty which is its other principle? Or, what if, under the cloak of liberty, a conspiratorial minority endangers the very existence of majority rule?

The Declaration does not offer a solution to this problem posed by its principles. Yet, after all, that was not its job. It sought to rally the colonists—and indeed the world—to the American struggle for independence by declaring the spirit which animated the struggle. But the Declaration's unfinished business—resolving the conflict and incorporating the principles into governmental arrangements—was precisely the task to which the Constitution addressed itself. Indeed, it is the continuing task of the American political order.

The Declaration and the Constitution

Declaration and Constitution—the credo and the frame of American government. Few countries have a national political creed. Fewer have a formal constitution vitally related to the creed. It is no accident, therefore, that much American political debate and scholarship have centered on the relationship between the Declaration and the Constitution. This relationship is at the center of the American political existence. As could be expected, there are conflicting views. For example, many scholars do not view the Constitution as a faithful attempt to solve the Declaration's problem. Rather, they believe that the Framers were so concerned with liberty (or, perhaps, the privileges of the wealthy) that they deliberately retreated from the democratic spirit of the Declaration. This book offers a different view and it suffices at this point simply to assert it. The Constitution is *not* undemocratic and was not a retreat from democracy. Rather, it is a thoroughgoing effort to *constitute democracy*.

In the light of this view, as we consider the formation of the American Republic, we will trace the movement from the credo of the Declaration to the framing of a government incorporating its popular and liberal principles.

The story begins, of course, long before July 4, 1776. There is a colonial history of 170 years, nearly as long as America's subsequent history as a nation. To understand the formation of the American Republic, it is necessary to consider the people, the events, and the principles of the colonial period, which together slowly made up the situation in which the Framers of the American Constitution found themselves.

Colonial Government

The forms of colonial government, which left their stamp upon the later Republic, were in turn deeply influenced by the primarily English origin of the Americans.

The "Anglo-Americans"

Tocqueville called the colonists the "Anglo-Americans,"[2] rightly emphasizing the enormous importance of the English traditions and circumstances from which the Americans sprang. Indeed, to the very eve of the Revolution, they remained *Anglo-*American. They read English authors and engaged in English intellectual controversies. Sons of the well-to-do often went to England for schooling. England supplied wives and husbands to the colonists. Ladies and gentlemen copied English fashions. And most colonial trade was closely linked with England.

But even in their very Englishness, not to say in other ways, the colonists differed from their contemporaries in England. They were imbued only with a certain portion of the English tradition. With the ocean voyage, they left behind much of the aristocratic portion of that tradition. Americans, Tocqueville said, were "born equal." They were cut off, he meant, from the aristocratic and feudal background which weighed so heavily upon Europe. In Europe the new forces of democracy, trade, technology, and religion had to make their way against the claims and the inertia of the feudal past. Modern Europe thus was the outcome of the constant conflict between old and new things. In America there had been a fresh start free from such profound struggle.

Not that aristocratic institutions could never have taken root in the New World. They did in the Spanish colonies. But England was not Spain, and especially seventeenth-century England was in no position to implant aristocracy abroad. It was the English century of revolution. The colonies were launched and took form at a time most conducive to their democratic development. Moreover, the English who came were among those least established in the aristocratic society and least attached to aristocratic traditions. As Burke said, they emigrated from a turbulent England when love of liberty was "most predominant" in the English

---

[2] Alexis de Tocqueville (1805–1859), a French writer and statesman, visited the United States in 1831 and wrote a classic commentary on American society and politics, *Democracy in America*, Phillips Bradley, ed., (New York: Alfred A. Knopf, Inc., 1945). It is an invaluable guide to understanding the American polity.

character; the settlers represented the very "dissidence of dissent, and the protestantism of the Protestant religion."[3]

The colonists built their own institutions, emphasizing the democratic side of the English tradition. This was why, during the Revolutionary conflict, the Americans could proclaim with such conviction that they were only demanding of a defaulting British government rights which were truly British. Of course, quasi-aristocratic practices and habits long continued. For example, the Tories during the Revolution were partly motivated by aristocratic conceptions. But, in a new context, one very much more inclined to democracy, the colonists gave a new direction to English ways. Their very Englishness, as it were, became American.

Charters of Government

The dominant organ of colonial government turned out to be the assemblies which Adam Smith sardonically observed the "Americans were fond of calling parliaments."[4] These legislative bodies became both remarkably democratic and independent. It was the strength of these colonial assemblies, from the very outset, that habituated the colonists to behave more like democratic citizens than the colonial subjects of a king. In the end, their strength, and the loyalty of the people to them, emboldened the "leading men" of America to resist England; and they provided the prototype for the powerful legislature of the Constitution. Like much else in the colonial political arrangements, the assemblies had their origin in the charters on the basis of which the colonies had been founded.

The charters are important first of all because each in some ways resembled a written constitution. Although the charters were issued at the King's discretion, Parliament in fact jealously scrutinized the process. For reasons of its own struggles with the Crown, the seventeenth-century Parliament was much interested in curbing arbitrary government over the colonies. The result was that the charters guaranteed the colonists the "rights of Englishmen" as part of the bargain in going to the New World. Also the charters usually guaranteed that these rights would not be subject to alteration by the ordinary operation of law. This followed the English traditional idea that there was a standard of justice or of liberty to which government had to conform and that a charter (like Magna Carta) somehow had a dignity superior to ordinary legislation. Later American ideas of constitutional government built squarely on this premise. The charter-based constitutionalization of government was an important consequence of the English origin of the colonies.

---

[3] "Speech on Conciliation With the Colonies," March 22, 1775, *The Works of Edmund Burke* (London: Oxford University Press, 1930), II, 187. Burke (1728–1797) was a British statesman and major political thinker.

[4] *The Wealth of Nations* (New York: The Modern Library, 1937), p. 586. Adam Smith (1723–1790) was a Scottish political economist who fathered modern classical economic thought. *The Wealth of Nations* was originally published in 1776.

The Mayflower Compact and the Connecticut and Rhode Island charters are particularly interesting. In the Mayflower Compact (1620) the settlers, going beyond the original royal charter, themselves undertook to spell out the terms by which they agreed to be governed. This introduced a distinctly democratic element into the charter process. The Connecticut (1622) and Rhode Island (1663) charters were wholly written by the settlers themselves and moreover established substantially democratic governments. Consequently, in the 1780s, when the other new states were busily writing constitutions, both Connecticut and Rhode Island were able simply to convert their original colonial charters into state constitutions.

The Colonial Assembly

The colonial assemblies, especially their lower houses, flourished from the outset. Like the English system of a House of Lords and a House of Commons, the colonial assemblies were bicamerally divided into two chambers. However, the influence of the English House of Commons developed only long after the influence of the hereditary nobility surrounding the Crown; the American lower houses developed simultaneously with and then more powerfully than the upper houses. Even in England the Commons came to dominate well before the eighteenth century. In America the dominance of the lower houses was more rapid and complete. The basic reason is simple—the weakness of aristocracy in America. There were, of course, dominant economic classes, clergymen of aristocratic tendencies, families of great wealth and position. But the aristocratic elements in American life were far less rooted and powerful than they were in a genuinely aristocratic society like England. The overwhelming fact was the fundamentally democratic spirit and tilt of the American development. As a result, the decisive legislative authority came into the hands of the lower houses.

The predominance of the democratic lower houses led Edmund Burke to observe that the American "governments are popular in an high degree; some are merely [wholly] popular; in all, the popular representative is the most weighty."[5] All the members of the lower houses were elected, and by a relatively large electorate. It is true that the colonies restricted suffrage. (They also imposed property qualifications as a condition of membership in the assembly.) But the colonial suffrage must be compared with England's, where at the very most 10 per cent of the adult males were entitled to vote. In the colonies the best modern estimate is that from 50 to 75 per cent of colonial adult males were eligible to vote.[6] This

---

[5] *Op. cit.*, pp. 186–87.

[6] The English percentage is computed from data found in the *Encyclopaedia Britannica* (1954), VII, 318; the American colonial percentage is from Chilton Williamson, *American Suffrage* (Princeton: Princeton University Press, 1960), p. 38. See Chapter 10 of the present text for further details.

was an extraordinarily broad electorate for the time. Thus Burke rightly emphasized the "popular" (that is, democratic) character of the American assemblies. They were powerful institutions readying America for independence and a democratic political order.

The Colonial Governor

The colonial governors were the great rivals of the relatively democratic lower houses. Typically, the governor was a royal appointee charged with representing the royal and imperial interests.[7] Increasingly, these interests clashed with those represented in the assembly. Officially, he usually had very great powers: Often he could convene and dissolve the legislative assembly at will, make proposals to the legislature, exercise an absolute veto on legislation, and muster a fair amount of patronage with which to influence the legislature. He also commanded the law enforcement and military forces. But his powers were greater on paper than they were in practice.

The governors' formal powers were limited by the lower houses' power of the purse; they had control over appropriations, including the governors' salaries. As a contemporary observed, "the governor has two masters; one who gives him his commission, and one who gives him his pay." The British Parliament was traditionally stingy, but in this case both Parliament and Crown argued reasonably that the colonists ought to defray their own governmental expenses. The resulting financial dependency of the governors, however, greatly enhanced the power of the assemblies.[8]

The assemblies ultimately took full advantage of their general power over appropriations. Here they were the beneficiaries of the long struggle in England between Crown and Parliament. Over centuries the English Parliament perfected means to keep the Crown in check. The final method was a system of *annual* and *detailed* appropriations. Annual appropriation kept government on a short leash; detailed appropriations (itemizing money grants rather than giving them in a lump sum) gave the legislature the opportunity to examine and influence the executive's conduct in detail. In this respect, the modern American Congress is a recognizable descendant of the colonial assembly. The Constitution forbids that any

---

[7] Two significant exceptions were Rhode Island and Connecticut where the democratic charters written by the colonists themselves provided for annual election of the governor by popular vote.

[8] John Adams, no dewy-eyed democrat, summed up the dominance of the popular assemblies: "The truth is, that the people have ever governed in America; all the force of the royal governors and councils, even backed with fleets and armies, has never been able to get the advantage of them, who have stood by their houses of representatives in every instance, and have always carried their points. No governor ever stood his ground against a representative assembly. So long as he governed by their advice he was happy; so soon as he differed from them he was wretched, and was soon obliged to retire." *Works* (Boston: Charles C. Little and James Brown, 1851), IV, 360.

money be drawn from the Treasury except by congressional appropriation, and Congress insists on detailed annual appropriations for almost all programs. It is interesting also to note that the authority of the lower houses increased especially during the colonial wars when the financial needs of government, and therefore dependence upon the legislatures, was greatest. Governments often become more oppressive during wartime, but it is also the time when a vigorous people can press hard upon the privileges of rulers.

The pattern of assembly-governor conflict had long-lasting effects upon American politics. The first response of the new states was to reduce gubernatorial powers still further. The colonial experience thus worked its way into the new state constitutions and into American political thought more generally. But, as we shall see, despite certain ambiguities, the anti-executive tendency was largely overcome in the federal Constitution.

The Colonial Judiciary

Separation of powers—that basic and perplexing aspect of American government—was not a clearly conceived and supported principle in the early seventeenth century.[9] But the idea of an independent judiciary was clearly developing. Here again the colonists benefited from struggles waged and won in England. English courts and law had long had some substantial independence. During the seventeenth and early eighteenth centuries, this was completely established and eventually became established in the colonies as well. Because colonial life needed rather less governing, the colonial judicial system was of course less complicated, but in general followed the English model. Appointment was by the Crown, but often, as in the case of the governor, the salary was supplied by the colonial lower house. As in England there was a strong system of local courts, an important part of the Anglo-American tradition of localism. Local justices of the peace heard most of the minor criminal and civil cases, and county courts heard and disposed of most of the more important cases. An appellate system carried cases to a colonial court of appeal—sometimes the governor and his council, sometimes separate judicial bodies—and a final appeal sometimes lay to the Judicial Committee of the King's Privy Council in London. The idea and practice of an elaborate and independent judicial system, from the local district up to the Crown, was an important part of the colonial political experience.

The Common Law

As pervasive and influential as any inheritance from the English tradition was the system of common law. The common law had been de-

---

[9] See Benjamin F. Wright, "The Origins of the Separation of Powers in America," *Economica*, No. 40 (May, 1933), 169–85.

veloped, beginning in the twelfth century, by the royal courts to replace the feudal chaos of local legal systems. The materials the courts used and the way they worked with them generated consequences that still influence American law and government. The materials were the common customs of the realm—hence the term 'common law'; the method was a particular style of thinking. This style gives a peculiar importance to precedent, that is, to the reasoning of the judicial determinations in earlier cases.

The common law is thus, above all, judge-made law. It is therefore law that comes not from the arbitrary will of a ruler, nor from the deliberate generalization of a statute, nor from a single codification by legal scholarship. Rather it is law that grows by precedent, from case to case, as judges deal with specific concrete problems in the light of existing custom and what they regard as sense and logic. Hence it is law that grows slowly and with great deference to settled ways and to what has been done in the past. Practice is slowly shaped (and sometimes changed in the process) and applied, and from it the rules of the law are derived. The logic that connects and explains the precedents, plus practical good sense and wisdom, constitutes the logic of the law. This logic of the law, in turn, is the great force in determining the actions of the men who exercise the judicial power.

The common law thus comes to seem the very oracle of experience, speaking in the accents of the settled daily life and judgment of the whole people. Hence it acquires an authority greater than the will of any single ruler, be he the one, the few, or the many. It is a system of law which grips the entire judicial system, which gives peculiar weight to judges and lawyers, and which inclines a people to the belief that all government is somehow under the standard of fundamental law.

From the outset, Americans were accustomed to the common-law emphasis on custom and precedent and attention to regular procedure and regard for property and other rights. Common law profoundly committed the democratic Americans to the idea of liberties placed beyond the reach of rulers, even when those rulers be the people.

Local Government

Tocqueville admired in American democracy what he called "administrative decentralization." This means handling as many merely "administrative" matters as possible at the local level of government. These semi-independent local governments, he thought, become a valuable defense against centralized tyranny. Further, administrative decentralization (that is, vigorous local government) draws thousands of average citizens into the performance of local governmental functions. They learn the skills and habits of independence, and they are saved from both the docility and the sodden absorption in private pursuits that could make them an easily manipulated mass.

English traditions of localism and the physical situation of the colonies inclined the colonial institutions toward decentralization. The perfect example is the New England town meeting, in which nearly the whole body of citizens directly participated. Boards of selectmen were elected for one-year terms. In time, the number of offices multiplied, dividing power among many hands and giving to many the sobering experience of governing. And town government really governed *since it had the final say* on many important matters; relatively little in those circumstances required colony-wide action. The middle colonies and southern colonies, to a lesser degree and in different ways, also developed systems of vigorous local government.

Strong organs and habits of local government grew in all the colonies. The political skills and attitudes bred into the colonists by this experience contributed to resourcefulness during the Revolution and formed the basis of the strong state governments that emerged. Complicated and vigorous local government within the states became—and remains—a distinctive feature of American government and politics.

"The Genius of the American People"

By the time of the Revolution, the colonists had had a long experience with successful self-government and possessed a valuable political tradition. Imbued with a vast sense of achievement, with a dynamic economy and a continent that would sustain further immense employment, and with a sense of political capacity adequate to great ambition,[10] the Americans came from the colonial years to the founding period with a distinctive history and character. During 1776–1789 their lasting "frame of government" was created. It is useful here, before entering upon a brief discussion of the Revolution which opened the founding period, to sum up that history and character.

We may find that summary in two apparently conflicting contemporary statements. Reflecting on the democratic side of the colonial tradition, James Madison said that "the genius of the people of America" requires that "all our political experiments [rest upon] the capacity of mankind for self-government." The "genius" or nature of Americans, Madison is saying, is incompatible with any undemocratic form of government. But that was not the whole story. Bearing in mind the other side of the colonial tradition, the idea of liberty and constitutional restraints, John

---

[10] America's population growth further justified the ambitions. There were 210,000 settlers in 1689. Seventy years later, in 1759, there had been an eight-fold increase to 1,695,000. And by the end of the founding decade, in 1790, the population had grown to 4 million. The astonishing growth rate suggested to many that America might well become the center of the British empire. As Franklin put it, "the greatest number of Englishmen [would] be on this Side of the Water." Dr. Samuel Johnson, Britain's great eighteenth-century literary figure, more tartly observed that the Americans "multiply with the fecundity of their own rattlesnakes, so that every quarter of a century doubles their numbers." *Works* (Troy, N.Y.: Pafraets Book Co., 1903), XIV, 97.

Jay said that "the genius of the American people will not permit a government merely democratic." That is, the American people would not settle for merely majoritarian arrangements, but would insist as well on a set of liberal protections. The two statements disclose again the perennial American commitment to the principles of both popular rule and liberty. That double commitment was the decisive political outcome of the colonial experience. It was the mandate of the colonial history to the founding statesmen. They were compelled to erect a republic resting upon majority rule and yet securing the rights of all, with materials developed during nearly two centuries of colonial experience. But because of the potential conflict between majority rule and liberty and the variety of ways in which a reconciliation may be attempted, the founding generation had an opportunity for inventive statesmanship.

The Impact of Revolution

In 1763, Britain had just vastly extended her empire by winning the Seven Years' War. She promptly began an imperial reorganization. This involved, after a century of "salutary neglect," more stringent administration of old law, and new regulation and taxation of the American colonies. We are not concerned here, however, with the familiar story of the

This cartoon is representative of the extensive criticism of British colonial policy by parliamentary critics at home. The Scottish noble, Lord Bute, had great influence over King George III and was alleged to have filled the government with Scottish 'placemen,' i.e., corrupt appointees—hence the derisive reference to "Sc--h Government." Corruption is further satirized in the figure of King George III holding out a bag of coin.

THE DEPLORABLE STATE of AMERICA or SC--H GOVERNMENT.

This American cartoon of the same era exploits themes and images similar to those of the British cartoon attacking Lord Bute's American policies.

Revolutionary resistance—with details of imperial regulations, with a detailed account of colonial resistance, or even with all the social and economic changes of the period. We are concerned with two great outcomes of the Revolution: the transformation of the colonies into self-governing states and the beginnings of federal union. And we wish to note certain permanently significant political aspects of the process by which these occurred.

Patterns of Resistance

To a considerable extent, the imperial actions that triggered resistance were economic. But the intensity of colonial reactions shows that underlying political factors transformed economic irritation into violent resistance. Consider the linked economic and political aspects of the famous slogan, 'No Taxation Without Representation.' It is possible to understand Dr. Samuel Johnson's suspicion that the Americans did not mean "to exchange solid money for such airy honour."[11] But he partly missed the point; economic hostility to the proposed taxation was linked with intensely held opinions about the limits of Britain's just political authority. It was the *combination* of economic hostility together with deeply held

---

[11] *Op. cit.*, p. 124.

political convictions about "government by consent" that hardened colonial resistance.

The basic pattern of resistance emerged from and utilized the governmental institutions and political skills the colonists had long developed. It is shown in the opposition to the Sugar Act (1764), a revision of an old but hitherto largely uncollected customs duty. Those colonial interests who directly felt the pinch protested the Act first, and they were joined by other commercial interests who looked far enough ahead to what might later be in store for themselves. The legislative assemblies rallied popular opposition to the measure. Experienced colonial politicians and writers ingeniously argued and pamphleteered against the measure. This was the pattern of action.

But it is also necessary to see the pattern of the colonial *argument*. First there was what may be called the British argument; that is, the colonists began with lawyer-like appeals to the rights of all Britons. They argued that, in imposing the sugar duty, Parliament exceeded her authority over the colonies under the British 'constitution.' But, as conflict increased, the colonists moved easily to a still graver and more general line of argument which culminated in the Declaration of Independence. They wound up arguing that Britain was violating not just British rights but rights belonging to all men under the idea of liberty itself. Both arguments reflected a characteristic American tendency. More than most people, Americans were then and are now acutely sensitive to the question: Is government acting within the bounds set to its authority by 'fundamental law'? The appeals to fundamental law increasingly intensified the conflict.

The famous Stamp Act (1765) conflict continued the pattern, but with two significant new developments. Again the legislative assemblies led the protest. But this time political action groups, like the Sons of Liberty, were organized in many localities and took the protest into the streets. In the process, a group of able radical leaders emerged with a formidable popular following. The second important new step was the Stamp Act Congress, the first substantial and American-initiated intercolonial body. The widespread and well organized resistance had its effect; the law became a dead letter.

Despite the efforts of English friends of America and of loyalists in America, no scheme of reconciliation was found acceptable. Edmund Burke wisely urged England to abandon, for all practical purposes, any attempt to impose her will. He proposed treating the Americans as a coequal body of Englishmen, trusting natural bonds between the two people to grow into firmer union in then unimaginable ways. Joseph Galloway, in America, shrewdly urged a new intercolonial body that could mediate between England's needs and the demands of the resisting colonies. But none of this was to be. It was as if an England irresistibly bent on regulation met Americans who were discovering themselves to be immovably unregulatable. A series of maneuvers, aggravations, lulls, and explosive incidents ensued. More and more sections of the population gradually became accustomed to the idea of increasing resistance. Each new irritation or episode was seized upon by the expanding network of radical leaders and fanned into greater consequence. Finally, when England replied to the Boston Tea Party with severely coercive measures, a widespread colonial response erupted in 1774.

In most colonies, a kind of second government was organized, shunting aside the governor, his council, and loyalists in the lower house. The colonists brought into play the skills and habits with which a century and a half of rich political experience had endowed them. Their familiarity with political organization at the local level and their habits of independence meant that they did not have to wait for a national signal to commence resistance. But now a new problem was placing itself on the agenda: the achievement of continental union.

The Revolutionary Beginnings of Union

At the initiative of Virginia and Massachusetts, the two leading colonies, a call went out for an intercolonial body to deal with the crisis. The body styled itself the Continental Congress; the name itself suggests the developing sense of American nationality. The name further suggests how far events had gone beyond the Stamp Act Congress which had been a one-shot, one-grievance affair. The new Congress began to behave like a general government for the continent. In the space of seven weeks, it declared a set of rights and grievances, proposed a stoppage of all commerce with England, announced American readiness to resist with force, and urged the local *committees of correspondence,* those new instruments of local government, to enforce Congress' proposals.

Within less than a year, armed conflict began at Concord on April 18, and a Second Continental Congress convened in Philadelphia on May 10, 1775. All thirteen colonies sent representatives. Delegates were first irregularly chosen by the 'second governments' that had illegally but effectively replaced the old colonial governments and later by the state legislatures after the new state constitutions were adopted. The Congress organized itself as the central body of a loose, federal arrangement. For example, voting was by states; on any given issue, the state's single vote was cast as the majority of its delegation decided. This emphasis upon the states, as we shall see, was continued under the Articles of Confederation and posed a formidable problem when the much more centralized Constitution was proposed. Like England's Long Parliament, the Second Congress found itself a government and was in continuous being (with changing delegations from the states) for six years, when finally the Articles of Confederation went into force. Because of its loose federal foundation, the Congress had to depend upon the voluntary and therefore erratic compliance of the states. Yet the unity and vigor that the Congress lacked as a political structure were partially supplied by the common danger and common cause and by the talents and patriotism of its members. In short, it presided over the Revolution and began a central government as best it could.

The Democratic Effects of the Revolution

Historians still dispute important aspects of the Revolution: Was it fought primarily for economic reasons or for high political principle? Were Americans justly aggrieved or were the British demands fair? Was separation inevitable or could moderate counsel have prevailed? Perhaps the most disputed question is, How much was the War of Independence also a revolution in the modern sense of causing basic social change? The last question alone concerns us here, and it suffices merely to indicate how the Revolution tended to accelerate and strengthen the democratic forces in American life. The strengthening of these forces set the stage for the framing of the Constitution.

Stimulated by wartime needs, commerce and manufacturing expanded. Agriculture prospered, enjoying the competition of both armies for provisions. The western lands were opened to speculation and settlement. Men on the make scrambled for position in the new state governments. Opportunity opened more rapidly in all areas. As soldiers sometimes bitterly have known, war does not necessarily still the energies and opportunities of civilian life. Established social and class patterns changed in another way. Between sixty and one hundred thousand Loyalists, many of them wealthier and more established men, fled the country to Canada or England. Indeed, the American Revolution produced a proportionally greater exodus than the Jacobin repression during the French Revolution. Moreover, nearly as much property was confiscated in America as in France. But the guillotine did not take over the American Revolution, and that alone makes all the difference. Yet the wholesale population and property changes had many consequences—the break-up of great estates through confiscation, more room at the top, a weakening in the conservative influence of older families and institutions.

These changes were important because, despite the generally democratic tone of colonial life, there had also been some contrary tendencies in an aristocratic direction. The colonists were, after all, subjects of a king. Had conciliation succeeded, or especially if the Revolution had been defeated, a more aristocratic society might have developed. Improving transportation and communication might have tightened the connection with aristocratic England. The ambition of leading Americans might have been drawn, as Adam Smith slyly suggested, from "the paltry raffle of colony faction . . . [to] the great state lottery of English politics."[12] Then the seaboard cities would have remained dominant, and the established families would have become more aristocratic. But, at a stroke, the

---

[12] *Op. cit.,* p. 587.

British Crown, nobility, and established church ceased to be forces shoring up aristocratic tendencies in the colonies and became instead hateful things to be opposed.

The revolutionary necessity to draw the populace into the struggle, the philosophy and slogans of the struggle, the severance of British ties, the sudden necessity to institute new organs of government at all levels, all pushed American life far forward in the democratic direction to which it had always been basically inclined.

The New States

The colonies became states and needed governments. A new chapter in American political life opened.

Almost as soon as the Second Congress met in 1775, the Massachusetts Provincial Congress submitted a request for guidance in the ticklish question of what kind of government was proper for a colony in revolt. Congress recommended that Massachusetts elect her lower house as usual, that the lower house then "elect counsellors; which assembly and council should exercise the powers of Government, until a Governor, of his Majesty's appointment, will consent to govern the colony according to its charter." The American posture, notice, was still that of the loyal subject, expecting redress of grievances according to the charter. But after the unequivocal Declaration of Independence, these ad-libbed, ambiguous makeshifts no longer sufficed. Fully legitimate and complete organs of government were required.

Constitution-Making

Congress now urged the states to adopt "such government as shall, in the opinion of the representatives of the people, best conduce to the happiness and safety of their constituents," these representatives to assemble for the purpose of drafting and enacting the state constitutions. Consider the principles implied: The new governments were to be founded upon *written* constitutions; the *people* were to choose *representatives* for the special purpose of *constituting* government; the *end* of these governments was "the happiness and safety" of the constituents, that is, the people. The new constitutions were actually drafted and enacted in a variety of ways, typically by the state legislature itself, and without express popular ratification. But in all the states there was a vivid experience of the basic principle: constitution-making by representatives of the people.

In Massachusetts the process was carried out in remarkable detail and with fullest direct reliance upon popular acceptance. The revolutionary Massachusetts assembly requested the towns to elect new legislative representatives who would be empowered also to sit as a constitutional convention. This body submitted a constitution to the people, but it was overwhelmingly rejected, largely because it lacked a bill of rights. The towns were then asked to elect special representatives solely for a constitutional convention. This special convention adopted a constitution containing a bill of rights, and referred it back to the town meetings. There the required two-thirds of the resident freemen ratified it clause by clause after exhaustive discussion. Interestingly, the only eighteenth-century state constitutions still in force, albeit much amended, are the three (Massachusetts, New Hampshire, and Vermont) that were adopted in this democratic manner.

The State Constitutions

The new state constitutions built upon, but necessarily also departed from, the colonial precedents. The new judicial systems now terminated in the states rather than in the King's Privy Council, but were otherwise little changed. The office of governor, however, was greatly changed in the direction of reduced powers, while legislative powers were correspondingly increased. The anti-monarchical experience of the Revolution had led most Americans to fear the executive as the likeliest source of tyranny, while the legislature had been exalted as the branch closest to popular will. (This view, as we shall see, dramatically did not find its way into the federal Constitution.) Accordingly, in only four states was the governor granted the authority which comes from direct election by the people. In the other nine, running counter to the idea of separation of powers, the governor was selected by and therefore dependent upon the legislature. Conceivably the governor's authority could have grown gradually, even under these arrangements. The possible parallel is the parliamentary system where the prime minister, although completely dependent upon the legislature for his election, has nonetheless frequently emerged as a very powerful executive. But parliamentary executives participate prominently in legislative business and, further, long had the support of still powerful kings. The new state governors, on the contrary, had no such royal support and were largely excluded from the legislative process. Moreover, most were selected for one-year terms, had no veto power, had little appointive power and hence little control over patronage.

Most states adopted bicameral assemblies.[13] They were influenced by colonial custom and by the ancient idea that one portion of the legislative power should belong to the people and another to wealth or birth, so that the many poor and the few rich could protect themselves against each other. But even the appointive colonial upper houses had been but pallid versions of a really aristocratic senate; now both houses were to be directly elected in all states (except Maryland). Further, although not

[13] Georgia had a unicameral legislature until 1789, Pennsylvania until 1790, and Vermont until 1836. So powerful is the bicameral tradition in America, that only one state (Nebraska since 1937) has since experimented with a unicameral legislature.

as broad as for the lower house, there was also a popular suffrage for the senate. The question soon had to arise: What was 'upper' about the upper house? A new kind of upper house—cut off from the old aristocratic roots—was in the making.

One feature of the new senates was the relatively long terms of the members. By contrast, members of the lower house were elected for short terms, typically one year. Acting in the spirit of the Revolutionary maxim, that 'where annual elections end, there tyranny begins,' all the states created a lower branch of the legislature that would be closely dependent upon popular majorities. The lower houses, which had emerged dominant in the colonial period, continued strong in the new states. But a new pattern of democratic bicameralism began to emerge. Authority had now to be shared with the relatively democratized senates.

Suffrage in the States

The strengthened state legislatures rested upon an even more democratic base than the colonial assembly. Yet, although the suffrage was broadened, nearly all the new states maintained some restrictions. Even ardent democrats of that time seldom believed that everyone was entitled to vote by virtue of mere existence; it was still generally assumed that exercise of the vote required some evidence of responsibility. For example, it was widely believed that men with at least some property or who paid taxes, having something to lose, would vote more soberly than those whose votes affected only other people's money. But a clause in the Virginia Bill of Rights reveals what was happening to the idea of suffrage: "All men having sufficient evidence of permanent common interest with, and attachment to the community, have the right of suffrage." The idea of "evidence" persisted but the emphasis was increasingly on the "*all* men" and the "*right* of suffrage." The push was toward a fully democratic suffrage.[14]

The democratizing tendency also affected property qualifications on office-holding, although to a lesser degree. Many states reduced but still maintained some property requirements. South Carolina, for example, which severely restricted the suffrage, had the highest requirements: A senator had to have an estate worth approximately $7,000 and the governor an estate worth the then very great sum of $50,000. (Notice the senatorial qualification; it was an attempt to distinguish the 'upper' from the 'lower' house.) It will readily be seen that it is one thing to allow the people to vote, but quite another if only the wealthy can hold office. But even with regard to office-holding, as with suffrage, most states moved in the democratic direction of reduced qualifications. The federal Constitution, as we shall see, went even further—it places no property qualification on any federal office.

---

[14] See Chapter 10 for a detailed examination of the suffrage.

One other similar change occurred. The rural western areas had long been underrepresented in the colonial assemblies. This was only to be expected. The seaboard areas had been settled first, and men part slowly and reluctantly with initial advantages in government. Wherever they could, the seaboard commercial and plantation interests perpetuated the underrepresentation of the rural western counties. For example, Jefferson complained that "19,000 men, living below the falls of the rivers . . . give law to upwards of 30,000 men living in the western foothills."[15] This is a less glaring example of malapportionment than many that could be cited today. Apportionment has been a perennial issue in American politics and has flared into new significance with recent Supreme Court decisions.[16] The main point here is that, despite the persistence of the colonial pattern, a number of new states began to move toward greater equality of representation.

The Articles of Confederation

We consider now the steps toward union which culminated in the Constitution. To this point, it is useful to state several main themes of the present chapter. The colonies began with a heritage that equipped them for competent self-government. From the outset they were inclined toward a democratic society, yet one in which constitutional scruples would stand against the simple power of majorities. Colonial political institutions developed early and powerfully and became at once a cause of separation from England and also the means by which it was achieved. The Revolution gave a spurt to the democratic tendencies of the new nation, but the Declaration of Independence had eloquently pronounced anew the aim of liberty as well as equality. The new state governments, despite oligarchical features, were experiments in putting the two potentially conflicting aims into concrete governmental form. Meanwhile events were also moving on another plane; the "United Colonies" of the Declaration were becoming the American Republic.

Pre-Revolutionary Experience of Union

Despite considerable experience in colonial government, the Revolutionary leaders of 1776 had very little or no experience in actually governing the whole country. There had been few ventures in intercolonial government. England had not followed a policy of tight imperial control that might have drawn the colonies into a single unit within the broad Empire. Colonies had been formed separately, at different times, and by groups with differing interests or characters. The relatively early achieve-

---

[15] "Notes on the State of Virginia," *The Complete Jefferson,* Saul K. Padover, ed., (New York: Tudor Publishing Co., 1943), p. 649.

[16] For an account of these decisions, and the difficulty of determining and achieving equitable representation, see Chapter 11.

ment of self-government, ironically, had some anti-Union effects. It turned the colonies in upon themselves; politically, Virginia or Massachusetts was the reality, rather than America as a whole, for which no organs of government naturally existed.

Economics and geography added to the separateness. The colonial economies, producing things not chiefly profitable to each other, were more closely linked with England than to each other. The colonies were physically separated in a way now hard to appreciate; water travel to England was cheaper and easier than any considerable inland travel. Insofar as there were any real intercolonial necessities, the colonists depended primarily upon England for their solution. The colonists looked as well to England for art, ideas, and tastes, the other things that might have more actively drawn the colonies together.

Nonetheless there were several experiments in intercolonial government. Although unimportant in themselves, they reveal the kinds of problems that had to be overcome in the framing of the Constitution.

The New England Confederacy. The earliest attempt at intercolonial government was the tiny New England Confederacy (1643). Styling themselves The United Colonies of New England, the colonies of Massachusetts Bay, Plymouth, Connecticut, and New Haven formed a "firm and perpetual league of friendship for offense and defense." So persistent were certain ideas about federal union, as we will see, that 135 years later the same ideas, indeed this very wording, appeared in the Articles of Confederation. The New England Confederacy was merely a *league*, a permanent alliance which did not pretend to set up a general government; its major purpose was to provide joint defense against the Indians, the Dutch, and the French.

Each colony retained full control over its own affairs, but the Confederacy was empowered to deal with all matters of war and peace, and to requisition men and money for this purpose. The Confederacy was also expected to deal with certain boundary problems, and the colonies promised the mutual return of fugitive indentured servants and the extradition of wanted criminals. However, the scheme had a fatal flaw: Each colony was *equally represented* in the central body. Yet Massachusetts' population was more than twice that of the other three colonies combined. By virtue of equal representation, the other three colonies could and did outvote Massachusetts. But, whenever she felt her interests sufficiently touched, Massachusetts violated confederal rulings or went her own way without consulting the confederates. This was the old failing of confederacies which give equal votes to unequal members. It proved a major failing of the Articles of Confederation, and the Framers of the Constitution hammered this fact home repeatedly in arguing for adoption of the Constitution.

The Confederacy was of little practical importance and faded away by 1684. The only other pre-Revolutionary scheme actually employed was England's abortive attempt in 1686 to dissolve the separate New

The Stamp Act required, among other things, that a relatively expensive revenue stamp be affixed to newspapers. The resulting tax burden was a serious,
and in some cases fatal, economic burden. Colonial newspapers were, accordingly, all the more eager to rally resistance against the Stamp Act.

England, New York, and New Jersey governments into a single Dominion
of New England.

Franklin's Albany Plan. Although it failed to be adopted, there was
one intercolonial proposal worth noting. Taking advantage of a unique
nine-colony conference at Albany called by England in 1754 to deal with
Indian affairs, Benjamin Franklin presented a plan of permanent intercolonial government. Of special interest is the fact that Franklin proposed
more than a defensive league; he wanted something more like a *government*. Shrewdly anticipating the looming issues, Franklin empowered his
intercolonial government to deal with defense, trade, and the western
lands—the very matters that shortly appeared on the Revolution's agenda.
Also worth noting is the way Franklin tried to accommodate English and
colonial opposing interests. He proposed a President-General, appointed
and paid by the King, and a Grand Council, composed of two delegates
triennially selected by the colonial assemblies.

Further, Franklin's plan dealt ingeniously with three problems that the Constitution finally had to solve. First, it created a fairly powerful, independent executive. Second, states were represented in the central assembly in proportion to their contributions to the central government. This was an attempt to overcome two failings of confederations. By connecting a state's influence with what it paid, Franklin was trying to overcome the tendency in confederations for member-states to shirk their burdens whenever possible. Further, this arrangement gave more populous, wealthier states the opportunity to have a proportionally greater voice. Franklin hoped thus to avoid the New England Confederacy sort of fiasco, where powerful Massachusetts was utopianly asked to accept absolute equality with much weaker states. Finally, Franklin's plan permitted the central government to levy and collect taxes directly rather than to depend wholly upon collection by the states. This became a key aspect of the Constitution. But Franklin's scheme was ahead of its time. England feared colonial domination of the Grand Council, and the colonies feared English control through the President-General. The plan was rejected.

Adoption of the Articles of Confederation

Yet only two decades later events proved that many underlying forces had prepared Americans for unity. Under the pressure of common conflict with England, the colonists discovered these latent forces: the common English language and legal traditions, the basically common religion, similarities in mode of economy, the essentially democratic character of all the colonial governments and similarity of their political institutions. None of these guaranteed union. But they did open it as a possibility to statesmen who could rise to the occasion.

At the outbreak of the Revolution, the question of formally establishing an American Union was immediately in the foreground. Benjamin Franklin promptly prepared a draft of Articles of Confederation and Perpetual Union. But it took a year of war fully to ready American opinion for so complete a break with England. In June 1776, the Second Continental Congress appointed a thirteen-man committee to draft articles of confederation, and within a month the draft was ready. But there was considerable objection to the degree of centralization which the Articles proposed; the whole enterprise was so novel and tricky as to invite endless discussion, and this wartime Congress had other pressing business. It was not until a year and a half later that Congress submitted a final draft to the states for their unanimous ratification. The requirement of unanimity followed logically from the treaty or contractual character of confederacies. The Framers of the Constitution, as we shall see, maneuvered to avoid this requirement.

The western lands issue. One central issue emerged during the ratification process. Seven of the original colonial charters contained enormous land grants, running from the Atlantic to the Mississippi or the

Pacific. The smaller states without western land claims feared domination by a few giants. This had happened in many other confederacies, and colonial leaders were well read in political history. (It is interesting to note that the vast, vacant western lands, which preoccupied nineteenth-century American politics, e.g., the slavery in the territories issue, presented a problem from the very outset.)

The landless states therefore demanded that the landed states cede their western lands to the central government. Nearly all the states ratified the Articles promptly, but landless New Jersey and Delaware balked and withheld their ratification until 1779. For two more long and perilous years Maryland, immediate neighbor of Virginia (then the largest state and having the best and largest western claims), refused to sign the Articles, and the Union was obliged to limp along under the *ad hoc* Second Continental Congress.

While Maryland was holding out, she and other small states pressed their demands in Congress, where nationally minded men from the larger states also joined them. New York, whose western claims were somewhat shaky legally, early indicated her willingness to cede her claims. Governor Jefferson and others finally got Virginia to agree to cede her claims. They were motivated, in part, by the then common fear that only relatively small areas could maintain a truly republican form of government; they regarded Virginia's western lands, therefore, as a threat to her own republican well being.

The federal solution. Maryland's holdout succeeded.[17] The western lands were finally placed under central control for the common benefit. The states now had a very valuable property in common, insuring the interested attachment of each to the doings of the central government. The western lands gave importance and dignity to the central government, and also a potentially substantial source of independent revenue. But the decision had even further-reaching effects. The Congress resolved that the western lands would in time be "formed into distinct states, which shall become members of the federal union, and have the same rights of sovereignty, freedom and independence, as the other states."

We take this for granted now, but it was extremely novel and important then. The future western states and citizens were guaranteed equality with the first-come seaboard states, who would pay much of the expense for developing the West. Some Americans then and later tried to prevent the equality of the future settlements, wanting their own advantage and fearing a dangerous, boorish western democracy. But it was hard to deny future Americans the benefit of self-government when that was the principle being fought for against England. The decision reveals

---

[17] There is an amusing sidelight to Maryland's conduct. Her adamancy had partly resulted from the pressures of land speculators who had invested heavily in Virginia's western lands. They wanted control to go to the central government where they hoped for a better deal. Aware of what was going on, Virginia insisted that all prior speculative land purchases be invalidated as a condition of her cession. This was not what the Maryland speculators had been fighting for.

the force of political ideas. Both the Revolutionary credo, which exalted equality, and the confederal idea inclined men to think of the West as supplying future equal confederates, not inferior subjects of the original union.

Maryland finally ratified and on March 1, 1781, the Articles went into effect. Despite the long delay this was not an anticlimax. America's enemies had confidently expected what many patriots feared, that the colonies, if they won their freedom at all, would separate into bickering and petty republics, "formidable only to each other." But now, short-comings notwithstanding, at least a formal union had been instituted.

The Nature of the Confederation

The character of the Confederation was the outcome of two contrary things: a desire to retain the full independence of the states *and* a desire to enjoy the blessings of nationhood. The new state governments had become the political realities. Many men had found prestige and position in them. The states had grown in dignity and pride, made the important domestic political decisions, and commanded the loyalty of their citizens. They were loath to part with any of their powers.

A political idea also influenced the determination to preserve the independence and primacy of the states. Many Americans sincerely believed that only the state governments, not some huge central government, could be made effectively free and democratic. In the founding period, this view flourished in the form given to it by the great eighteenth-century French political philosopher, Montesquieu.

The small-republic argument. The argument ran as follows.[18] Large countries tend inevitably toward despotic rule. For one thing, it was thought large countries actually need despotic rule; political authority breaks down in a large, sprawling society if the central government does not ruthlessly gather all power into its hands. Further, large countries, usually wealthy and populous, either are naturally aggressive or are forced to accept military discipline because of harassment by envious neighbors. Their military needs lead them to become bellicose monarchies. Moreover, even when large countries try to stay republican, they cannot succeed. To preserve popular rule, the people must be patriotic, alert, and informed. This requires that people pay more attention to their country than to their personal economic interests, and that the affairs of the country be on a scale commensurate with popular understanding. But in large countries the people turn to private interests, the nation is a vast vagueness, and the people are baffled and rendered apathetic by the complexity of public affairs. Finally, even an alert citizenry of a large country must allow a few men actually to conduct the public business; far removed from the localities, talking the deceiving language of professional

---

[18] Montesquieu, *The Spirit of the Laws; cf.* especially Volume I, Book VIII, chapter 16, and Book IX, chapter 1.

rulers, possessing the instruments of coercion, the trusted representatives will inevitably subvert the republican rule. Thus ran the argument for the small republic.

But keeping republics small had one unfortunate disadvantage: Small republics were regularly defeated in war by large monarchies. The original and traditional reason for confederation, therefore, was defense. By federating, small republics tried to secure themselves against external threats. But the small-republic idea required that nothing be done that subverted the integrity and primacy of the federating states. (For example, they and not the confederal body must directly govern the people.) Hence the *federal idea*: combining for limited purposes into a defensive league which preserves the integrity and primacy of the small republics that compose the league. Thus both the self-interest of men who found advantages in the existing state governments[19] and the persuasive small-republic theory turned men's minds to the idea of a confederation. It took the work of the Constitutional Convention before Americans were ready for a more national form of union.

But although they chose a confederal form, most Americans also wanted an extraordinary amount of benefits from their union. They wanted much more than merely a defensive league, indeed more than the closest knit confederacies of the past had been able to supply. Nearly all wanted some sort of undivided political community with trade among the states, the blessings of a stable national currency, uniform protection of property rights, the development of the West, and complete mutual recognition by the states of each other's legal proceedings. In short a central system was desired that would yield very substantial advantages while all political authority remained with the states.[20] The curious result was that the Articles created not a weak, but a powerful, confederation. It finally failed not because it was a weak confederation but because any confederation would have been too weak to provide the national union Americans really desired.

How the Confederation Worked: "The United States in Congress Assembled"

The Articles built largely upon what the Second Continental Congress had in practice become. The sole organ of government was the Congress of the states. This meant, of course, no separation of powers. Since the

---

[19] John Jay complained that these state leaders "wished to be little kings at home." *The Life of John Jay by his Son William Jay* (New York: J. and J. Harper, 1833), I, 253.

[20] Hamilton later effectively denounced this as a having-your-cake-and-eating-it approach, a contradictory aiming "at things repugnant and irreconcilable." *Federalist* 15, p. 108. This and all subsequent references, are to *The Federalist*, with an introduction by Clinton Rossiter (New York: New American Library Mentor Books, 1961). The student will find particularly valuable the "Index of Ideas" prepared by Rossiter.

power of the states more than guarded against any central tyranny, separation of powers was rightly regarded as unnecessary; the states did not intend to have enough central government to separate the powers of. This Congress met annually for at least six months. On the pure federal principle, all voting in the Congress was by states, one vote to each state. Similarly, the consent of at least nine states was required on all important matters, while the Articles themselves could be amended only by unanimous consent.

States seldom appointed full complements, and delegates were frequently absent. Actual attendance averaged less than thirty, a number more in keeping with a diplomatic parley than a legislative body. Indeed the word Congress should not deceive; this body was in fact more akin to a meeting of ambassadors of the states than to any modern legislature.[21] The delegates were not congressmen in the sense of the members of the present House of Representatives, who are directly elected by and represent the people of their constituencies and whose term of office is constitutionally guaranteed. The confederal delegates were wholly the legal creatures of the state legislatures which chose them, had the power to remove them at any time, and which paid their salaries and expenses.

Nonetheless the delegates proved to be an able lot, and many were deeply concerned with the Union. The most nationally minded men tended to put themselves forward for service in Congress. And congressional experience itself, where national problems presented themselves most visibly, fostered views going beyond parochial state needs. When there, they had some elbowroom to forward their own opinions. Yet, as the years went by, the frustrating powerlessness of the Confederation sapped the quality of the Congress.

A rudimentary executive and judiciary. The Articles permitted a limited development of executive and judicial agencies under the Congress. Least significant is the official who went by the title of President; he was a delegate chosen for a one-year term merely to preside over congressional sessions. A thirteen-member Committee of the States, empowered to act between sessions of Congress on some minor matters, was more important. Further, the Congress established departments of Foreign Affairs, War, Finance, and Marine Affairs. These were rudimentary, but with the employment of permanent secretaries (some were distinguished men like John Jay) to head these departments, the foundations of a federal civil service were laid, and the necessity for regular central administration was thus acknowledged. There was no regular federal judiciary, but the Congress did establish special courts for a few kinds of cases. Traditional regard for judicial independence was observed in the fact that no congressional delegate could serve on these bodies, and the

---

[21] Congress came to mean the legislative branch of government only after the adoption of the Constitution. At the time of the Confederation, the word meant only something like a formal gathering or meeting, as in, say, the Congress of Vienna, a famous diplomatic meeting of 1815.

judges were selected in an extraordinarily complicated way to avoid partiality toward any particular state.

These administrative and judicial bodies had insufficient manpower, their authority did not extend to the most important matters, and they could not impose their decisions in case of state resistance. Yet the Congress was trying to deliver the national benefits that the Articles promised, and the very trying continued the commitment to secure the blessings of Union. The failures taught lessons for future improvement.

Powers of the Confederation. The third article (the 'preamble') shows how much more the Confederation was supposed to achieve than had traditional confederacies. In addition to "common defence," the contracting states sought also "the security of their liberties, and their mutual and general welfare." Pursuant to these great expectations, the Articles assigned numerous and urgent tasks to the Confederation. Naturally, the Congress had the war- and peace-making powers. But it was also empowered to regulate the coinage, establish uniform standards of weights and measures, operate a postal system, superintend trade with the Indian nations, and to admit new states to the Confederation.

The broad national desires are further revealed in the prohibitions laid upon the states. Many aimed primarily at preventing the states from involving themselves with foreign nations. While permitted to maintain land forces, the states were forbidden to maintain peacetime navies, on the belief that naval capacity was likelier to encourage aggression against other states or nations. States were prohibited from making treaties and exchanging diplomatic representatives with any foreign nation. Seeking their own immediate advantage, they might be tempted individually to connive with European powers to the detriment of the Union. Similarly, to prevent dangerous combinations, no two or more states could make any treaty or alliance with each other save by specific consent of Congress. The states also agreed to do certain things on behalf of the common good. They agreed to submit certain matters to central adjudication, keep a militia, extradite criminals, give "full faith and credit" to the judicial proceedings of other states, permit free movement of all citizens, and grant to citizens of other states "all privileges and immunities" of the local citizens.

The Failure of the Confederation

America was 'governed' under the Articles for only eight years. Its failures are familiar. But it is important to acknowledge its achievements because these as well as the failures help explain the Constitution. The Revolutionary War was won, diplomatic relations with major nations were established, and western expansion was begun under the free and equalitarian principles of the Northwest Ordinance of 1787. Above all, the states were held together and remained committed to union. Americans had their first experience of something like a national constitution, and the goal of a liberal democracy persisted. But these things were accomplished largely under the inspiration of the Revolution. As the urgencies became less palpable, the inadequacies and disintegrative tendencies of the Confederation became more and more evident.

Many inadequacies derived from the fact that the Confederation could deal only with the state governments and not citizens.[22] The only government a citizen faced was his own state government. The Confederation, for example, could not tax individual citizens and guarantee collection by prosecution in its own courts. It could only make requisitions of the states and had no way to compel payment. The results were not surprising; during 1781–1786 Congress requested 15 million dollars but received only an inadequate 2.5 million. Circumstances would have made it hard for the infant nation to achieve solvency in any case, but the confederal dependence upon voluntary state compliance made it impossible.

Similar difficulties plagued the enforcement of treaties. For example, the peace treaty with England required some restitution by individuals of confiscated Loyalist property and payment of some debts to English merchants. But noncomplying individuals could be tried only in state courts by judges and juries who were usually on the side of the violators and often operating under state laws which blithely ignored the treaty obligations. Similarly, treaty relations with Indian tribes were supposed to be under central control, but states and communities did as they pleased. This particular problem long persisted under the Constitution, but the Confederation was utterly helpless to hinder the states in any way, or for that matter to supply needed military assistance.

Another vital defect of the Confederation was that it had no power over commerce among the states and with foreign nations. Each state could regulate her trade relations as she pleased. The result was a growing system of competitive state duties, imposts, tariffs, limitations, and controls upon domestic trade that threatened to divide the continent. The states vied with each other for foreign trade by a complicated series of regulatory maneuvers harmful to all in the long run. The deterioration of commerce was threatened by this competition of the states. This economic concern, along with others shortly to be discussed, greatly increased public dissatisfaction.

The weaknesses of the Confederation—the lack of coercive governing power over individuals, of the means to carry out fully national assignments, and of power to regulate trade and thereby create a national economy—became major items on the Constitutional Convention's agenda. For the time, however, public opinion was dominated by the small-republic theory that required a confederal form reserving all real power to the states. But since Americans also contradictorily wanted the broad

---

[22] *Federalist* 15 argued that the "great and radical vice in the construction of the existing Confederation is the principle of LEGISLATION for STATES or GOVERN-MENTS, in their CORPORATE or COLLECTIVE CAPACITIES, and as contra-distinguished from the INDIVIDUALS of which they consist." *Op. cit.*, p. 108.

benefits of close union, radical change in the confederal principle itself was required. While public opinion shied away from that conclusion, dissatisfaction nonetheless mounted until nearly all agreed on the need at least to revise the Articles drastically.

Steps to the Federal Convention

Even before the Articles had been ratified, some men suspected their inadequacy to the national task. Few in number, and with no dramatic evidence yet inclining public opinion their way, they therefore worked loyally for the Confederation and tried fruitlessly to improve the Articles. These efforts were twice killed by the vote of a single state under the requirement of unanimity. They therefore began to seek other ways to revise or replace the Articles and began to consult and correspond on the matter. Newspapers and pamphlets echoed complaints against the Articles. Now in one state and now in another, dissatisfaction flared up; for example, the legislatures of New York (1782) and Massachusetts (1785) called for a convention to reconsider the Articles.

Washington, Madison, Hamilton, and others who were bent on sweeping change, took advantage of the situation. In early 1785, at Washington's urging, delegates from Maryland and Virginia met at Alexandria to settle a dispute over the commercial use of the Potomac River. The meeting soon adjourned to Washington's Mount Vernon home where an intimate discussion produced an amicable settlement. Washington and Madison seized upon this success and persuaded Maryland and Virginia to call a convention of all the states to consider general questions of commercial policy.

This convention met in September, 1786, at Annapolis, Maryland. The Annapolis Convention must be regarded as a remarkably successful failure. Delegates from only five states attended. (Even the host state, Maryland, embarrassingly backed out.) Although some delegates were known to be still en route, the number was insufficient for effective action. On the verge of utter failure, the Annapolis Convention took a remarkable step at Alexander Hamilton's instigation. Despite its own failure as a *trade* convention, it now officially proposed a *constitutional* convention, for general reconsideration of the Articles, to meet in Philadelphia in May, 1787.

The Shays Rebellion

The Annapolis delegates were probably encouraged to this bold move by news they received while sitting—the outbreak of armed rebellion in Massachusetts. Several thousand farmers took up arms, under the leadership of a Revolutionary war veteran, Captain Daniel Shays, and forcibly prevented the courts from carrying out numerous farm mortgage foreclosures. The state government routed the Shaysites in battle and the crisis passed. But the Shays Rebellion was only an extreme expression of difficulties plaguing many of the states. These resulted from a general agricultural depression. State policies were inevitably drawn into question by this economic situation. What governments do or omit to do always affects and is affected by important changes in the economy. Under agrarian pressure, a number of states passed 'stay' laws, literally laws staying or delaying the legal enforcement of mortgage and debt payments on which the depressed farmers were defaulting. It is easy to imagine what creditors thought of these laws.

Inflation was another troubling issue. The then typically indebted farmer liked to pay off his obligations in cheap money. Under debtor pressure, seven states issued inflationary quantities of paper money. Many states passed 'legal tender' laws which permitted payment of debts in the inflated currency, even though, as a lender's hedge against inflation, contracts then usually specified payment in gold. The process went so far that in Rhode Island, for example, the natural order of things was reversed: Debtors hunted down creditors to make them accept cheap paper money.

What seemed simple justice to the indebted farmer seemed outrageous injustice to the merchant creditor. And from a disinterested point of view it was clear that things were getting out of hand, that the long-run interests of all classes were harmed by policies that made the value of money fluctuate wildly and made it impossible for any business to be done on credit. The mercantile interests, who felt the pinch, found attractive the idea of a powerful central government that would be able to stop such state practices. But they were joined by many people not directly involved —and even by some on the other side of the economic fence—because the situation had become so visibly detrimental to everyone's long-run good. When the conflict erupted in violence against government, as in Massachusetts, still more men were ready to scrap the ineffectual Articles.

The anti-Articles men thus found the support they had been seeking. Although the Congress balked, seven states promptly acted on the Annapolis recommendation and appointed delegations. Impressed by this response and by the quality and influence of the men named as delegates, Congress finally issued its own call for the Constitutional Convention.

BIBLIOGRAPHICÁL NOTE

There is no necessity to repeat the references to authors like Tocqueville and Burke who have been cited in this chapter. The reader is reminded of their value for further study. Many of the works suggested here are appropriate as well to the subjects discussed in the next two chapters.

Three works are particularly valuable as general sources of bibliographical suggestions. The *Encyclopedia of the Social Sciences* (1930–1935) contains articles on many subjects treated in this chapter (e.g., common law, constitutionalism) and each article ends with extensive suggestions for further reading. The U.S. Government Printing Office's *Guide to the Study of the*

United States of America (1960) is comprehensive and reliable. Samuel E. Morison and Henry S. Commager, *The Growth of the American Republic* (5th ed., 1962) is a long-established survey of American history; the first volume concludes with a very full bibliography.

Three recent books deal with the origin of the American republic and are useful introductions to the subject: Louis Hartz, *The Liberal Tradition in America* (1953); Edmund S. Morgan, *The Birth of the Republic* (1956); Clinton Rossiter, *Seedtime of the Republic* (1952).

Carl Becker, *The Declaration of Independence* (1922) presents the background of the document. Abraham Lincoln's "Springfield Address of 1857" analyzes the Declaration. Harry V. Jaffa, *Crisis of the House Divided* (1959) includes an excellent discussion of the Declaration.

Charles H. McIlwain, *The American Revolution* (1923) analyzes the colonial legal argument. J. Franklin Jameson, *The American Revolution Considered as a Social Movement* (1926) emphasizes democratic change. Robert Brown, *Middle-class Democracy and the Revolution in Massachusetts* (1955) emphasizes the degree of democracy prior to the Revolution. Charles S. Sydnor, *Gentlemen Freeholders* (1952) emphasizes aristocratic aspects of Virginia politics of the period. Robert R. Palmer, *The Age of the Democratic Revolution* (1959) places the American Revolution within the context of contemporary western European democratic developments.

Edmund C. Burnett, *The Continental Congress* (1941) and Allan Nevins, *The American States during and after the Revolution* (1924) are the standard works on their respective subjects.

Andrew C. McLaughlin, *The Confederation and the Constitution* (1940), John Fiske, *The Critical Period in American History* (1883) which sharply criticizes the Articles, and Merrill Jensen, *The Articles of Confederation* (1940) which defends them, are three important works on this disputed subject.

The Reconstruction of American History (1962), John Higham, ed., contains several essays on conflicting points of view regarding the same matters treated in this chapter.

The People Shall Judge (1949), The Staff, Social Sciences I, The College of the University of Chicago, eds., is an excellent collection of original documents relating to American origins and early political problems.

Chapter 2

Framing the More Perfect Union

> It is new in the history of society to see a great people turn a calm and scrutinizing eye upon itself when apprised by the legislature that the wheels of its government are stopped, to see it carefully examine the extent of the evil, and patiently wait two whole years until a remedy is discovered, to which it voluntarily submitted without its costing a tear or a drop of blood from mankind.
>
> TOCQUEVILLE[1]

WE EXAMINE NOW THE EVENTS OF 1787–1789: THE CONSTITUTIONAL CONvention and the ratification of the Constitution. We will not be studying history as such, but studying the modern constitutional system in the historical setting of its framing. The framing of the Constitution was one of the country's profoundly determinative political events. Major themes of the American polity were there writ large. Often in the history of nations, some single moment or event has enduring significance and consequence. In these moments when the very nature of the regime may hang in the balance, its key forces and issues are peculiarly visible. For example, to understand French politics one must understand the French Revolution; similarly, to understand Soviet Russia one must understand the February and October Revolutions of 1917. Politics itself is grandest and most instructive in these great moments, and the fundamentals of a nation's polity are seen clearly in the historical setting of its decisive event. Moments of political creation disclose what can be obscured by time and the confusion of daily affairs. The framing of the Constitution is such a moment for the American polity.

Moreover, the American past is connected with the American present in a way unlike that of perhaps any other major nation. Many think of 1787 as a rustic America now rendered remote by the changes in Ameri-

---
[1] *Op. cit.*, I, 117–18.

can society. But think how remote 1787 is in other nations. The study of, say, modern Russian, Chinese, or Ghanaian government doubtless profits by some reference to the late eighteenth-century politics of those countries, but in 1787, Catherine the Great ruled in Russia, a Manchu emperor ruled in China, and Ghana did not exist. Catherine and the Manchu would find their countries incomprehensible today; in comparison, James Madison would be practically at his ease in modern America. The Constitution of 1787 is still the fundamental document of the American polity; it still embodies its fundamental principles; it is still the legal source of its basic institutions and powers, and it still influences the politics of their operation. Despite enormous *social* and *economic* change, the constitutional system imparts to America a remarkable *political* continuity.

Preparations

Reflecting the growing support for substantial change of the Articles, every state (except debtor-dominated Rhode Island) sent delegations to the Convention. As under the Articles, there was no thought of direct popular election to this 'confederal' gathering: The state legislatures appointed the delegates.[2] The delegates therefore largely reflected the popular political balance of the moment as it was expressed in the basically democratic state legislatures. Seventy-four men were named (this included numerous alternates), and 55 actually attended. Of these, as many as forty took an active part in the proceedings. The outstanding fact is that more than forty men from all over the country assembled and worked hard and intimately during a long hot summer in Philadelphia.

The Delegates

The intellectual quality of the delegates, especially of the leading men, was extremely high. They were adequate to the very great task our tradition rightly deems them to have performed.[3] Most were intelligent, many were well educated, a few were brilliant, and nearly all were experienced in public and private affairs. Men like Franklin, Madison, Hamilton, Wilson, Livingston, and Mason were scholars, authors of important works, well read in political literature, and accustomed to bring to political matters the style and penetration of their training and intellect. Several had prepared for the Convention by making extensive historical and philosophical studies of problems that would arise. Madison, for example, prepared a long memorandum on the history of confederacies

---

[2] South Carolina, where the governor appointed the delegation, was the sole exception.

[3] The famous observation of William Gladstone, a major British statesman of the nineteenth century, aptly expresses the common opinion: "As the British Constitution is the most subtile organism which has proceeded from the womb and the long gestation of progressive history, so the American Constitution is, so far as I can see, the most wonderful work ever struck off at a given time by the brain and purpose of man." *North American Review* CCLXIV (Sept.-Oct., 1878).

that is still of intrinsic scholarly merit. In short, much of the country's best intelligence, experience, and reputation was at the Convention. We would understand much if we knew why there was then so little separation between power and merit, why the country's best men were called upon or were able to assume such authority.

These able men were (by present-day terms) generally quite young, averaging just over 40 years old. Indeed many of the most important delegates were among the younger men, like Charles Pinckney (29), Alexander Hamilton (30), Edmund Randolph (34), Gouverneur Morris (35), and James Madison (36). George Washington was then only 55. Yet consider the delegates' extensive experience in public service:

  6 signed the Declaration of Independence
24 served in the Continental Congress
21 fought in the Revolutionary War
46 served in colonial or state legislatures
10 helped draft state constitutions
  7 served as state governors
  6 signed the Articles of Confederation
39 served in the Confederal Congress
  3 served as Confederal administrative officers

Clearly they had had ample opportunity to learn what experience could teach about the problems that confronted the Convention. It was no small further advantage that many had come to know each other in public life, making it that much easier for the Convention to achieve profitable discussion.

In addition to possessing intellectual stature and public experience, they also were experienced in business and economic matters. Such combinations of competences, rare today, were more common then. Of the 55 delegates: 40 owned public securities; 14 speculated in land; 24 lent money at interest; 11 had mercantile, manufacturing, or shipping connections; 15 operated plantations. Thus, most were personally involved in the economic interests that would be affected by the Convention's decisions. Of these economic interests, more later; it suffices here merely to observe the fact.

Also nearly two thirds of the delegates were lawyers. Legal education then was sometimes rough and ready, but law practice was no doubt as educative then as now and fostered the same respect for precedent, procedure, and precision which the study and practice of the common law has the capacity to instill. Moreover, some delegates like Mason, Wilson, Dickinson, and Wythe were learned and distinguished lawyers by any standard. The delegates' legal habits deeply influenced the style of the Constitution.[4]

---

[4] Ever since, lawyers have predominated in American legislatures. Tocqueville thought this predominance likely in a democracy: "As the lawyers form the only enlightened class whom the people do not mistrust, they are naturally called upon to occupy most of the public stations." *op. cit.* I, 279. Moreover, the fact that we govern ourselves under a written constitution interpreted by a Supreme Court gives a legalistic framework to our politics, bringing lawyers naturally to the fore.

The Opening of the Convention: Crucial Decisions on Procedure

On the scheduled second Monday in May only the local Pennsylvania and the eager Virginia delegations were in attendance, but by May 25 seven states were adequately represented. The very first action taken was a revealing departure. Under the Articles, congressional action required a majority of nine states. The Convention, however, decided that seven were sufficient for a quorum—with the implication that a majority of four could act. This procedural decision at one stroke increased the likelihood of constructive action. Now no one or two state delegations could deadlock the Convention (as Maryland had held up the Articles). By making action possible, the decision encouraged a readiness to engage in practical compromise.

The Convention then unanimously elected Washington as its presiding officer. His immense personal authority made him a powerful support for the Convention forces pressing for radical change. As behooved the chairman, and perhaps so as not to squander his influence, Washington took little open part in floor controversies. He nonetheless made his opinions known informally and, of course, by the way he voted within the Virginia delegation. His demonstrated ability to combine republican simplicity with the stern conduct of great affairs must have made it hard for delegates to exhibit frivolous or selfish objections in his presence. A Major Jackson was then appointed Secretary. Were his meager minutes all we had, we would know little of what went on. Most of our knowledge is based on the work of James Madison who, by what must have been a prodigious effort, took hundreds of pages of magnificent notes.[5] Several other delegates also kept notes and records. Madison's notes have been checked against these sources, and the story of the Convention has probably been pieced together with great accuracy.

---

[5] "In pursuance of the task . . . I chose a seat in front of the presiding member. . . . I noted in terms . . . intelligible to myself what was read from the Chair or spoken by the members; and losing not a moment unnecessarily between the adjournment and reassembling of the Convention I was enabled to write out my daily notes. . . . In the labor and correctness of this I was not a little aided by practice, and by a familiarity with the style and train of observation and reasoning which characterized the principal speakers. . . . I was not absent a single day, nor more than a casual fraction of an hour in any day, so that I could not have lost a single speech, unless a very short one." Max Farrand, *Records of the Federal Convention* (New Haven, Conn.: Yale University Press, 1911), III, 550. "Mr. Madison [said] that the labor of writing out the debates, added to the confinement to which his attendance in Convention subjected him, almost killed him; but that having undertaken the task he was determined to accomplish it." *Idem.*

Madison's notes and the other sources are all printed in *Documents Illustrative of the Formation of the Union of the American States*, selected, edited, and indexed by Charles C. Tansill (69th Cong., 1st sess.; House Doc. 398, Washington, D.C., 1927), cited hereafter as Tansill. In this chapter all quotations from the Convention proceedings are from Madison's notes and are followed by the date on which they took place.

This almanac cover illustration and accompanying explanation are representative of the sometimes overblown literary and pictorial style of the period. Compare with present-day political cartoons.

The FRONTISPIECE reprefents the truly-patriotick *WASHING-TON* and *FRANKLIN*, triumphantly feated in the FEDERAL CHA-RIOT drawn by 13 FREEMEN, figurative of the happy UNION now form-ing by thefe STATES.—The heroick *WASHINGTON* holds in his hand the grand FABRICK of AMERICAN INDEPENDENCE, the FEDERAL CONSTITUTION, offering it with paternal affection to his *freeborn Bre-thren* the SONS of COLUMBIA;—That ftaunch FRIEND and GUARDIAN of the *Civil* and *Religious* RIGHTS of MANKIND, the fagacious and philofophick *FRANKLIN*, fits attentive with Spectacles on, having juft fcan'd over the GLORIOUS WORK, which will prove the *political* SAL-VATION of his COUNTRY; holding a Staff, on which is affixed a Cap, illufive of AMERICAN FREEDOM, if the CONSTITUTION is adopted.— The Goddefs of FAME flying with a Trumpet in her hand, fpreading the glad Tidings of UNION through the STATES, and founds a Peal to the *immortal Honour* of that *worthy* and *difinterefted* Band of PATRIOTS and HEROES, the 39 MEMBERS of the late FEDERAL CONVENTION, who, with fuch *true Wifdom, found Judgment* and *unbiaffed Patriotifm*, framed the prefent. CONSTITUTION; whofe Names, we truft, will be handed down to ages yet unborn, with the higheft Veneration and Refpect, by every *real Friend* to his *Country*, for their *unfhaken Zeal* in the CAUSE of AMERICAN FREEDOM.—The SUN, entirely clear off the Horizon, fhines refplendently on the AMERICAN FEDERAL UNION, denoting that every ray of light has now burft forth, and beautifully illumes the whole UNITED CONTINENT of AMERICA.

The Basic Agreement on Procedure

Madison's account of the first day ends with this entry: "The appointment of a Committee . . . to prepare *standing rules and orders* was the only remaining step taken on this day" [May 25]. Establishing procedural rules was by no means a merely technical matter. *How* things were done would influence *what* things were done. Indeed, no procedure is so trivially technical that it may not influence a crucial outcome. That is why so many great political fights occur over such procedural matters as the size of a committee, the order of floor discussion, or the method of voting.

There were no such quarrels at the Convention. The rules were adopted with little discussion or amendment. Yet had any delegates—all of whom were connected with conflicting regional, state, economic, and religious interests—been determined to defend those interests at all costs, they would have known how to use the rules question to stall the proceedings. The amicable unity on procedure, therefore, bespeaks a quite general agreement that the fate of union was at stake. It suggests also how much the delegates had in common at the outset, how much they shared the underlying political agreement which was the product of the colonial experience. At times the Convention veered toward grave disagreement, toward what we may call 'regime politics'—almost like the utter cleavage regarding the nature of the regime which characterized the French Revolution. But such cleavage was made unlikely by the basic fact that all the delegates were committed in some significant sense to the credo of the Declaration of Independence. Nearly all accepted that the new government must secure liberty and yet conform to the 'popular genius' of the country. This underlying agreement on 'republican liberty' paved the way for full agreement or, where agreement failed, for practical compromise.

The Issue of Voting Procedure

One procedural dispute, however, was barely averted. It foreshadowed the difficult problem that the Constitution had finally to resolve: the place of the states in the national system. The dispute was over the Convention's method of voting. The Pennsylvania delegation wanted to refuse

> the small states an equal vote, as unreasonable, and as enabling the small states to negative every good system of Government, which must in the nature of things, be founded on a violation of that equality. [But] the members from Virginia, conceiving that such an attempt might beget fatal altercations between the large and small states, and that it would be easier to prevail on the latter, in the course of the deliberations, to give up their equality for the sake of an effective Government, than on taking the field of discussion to disarm themselves of the right and thereby

throw themselves on the mercy of the large states, discountenanced and stifled the project [May 28].

Pennsylvania wanted to base voting on population or wealth; Pennsylvania and Virginia (then the two largest states) would thus have between them nearly one third of the Convention's total vote. Contrarily, equal state voting would give them only one sixth of the vote. These two large state delegations happened to favor a very powerful national government. Voting by population, Pennsylvania and Virginia needed the support of only a few other states to ram through a strongly national constitution. But the "members from Virginia," fearing a "fatal altercation," persuaded Pennsylvania to yield. Virginia saw no permanent advantage in an initial procedural victory that would outrage some of the small states. They would have to be convinced "in the course of the deliberations," not outmaneuvered at the outset.[6]

Organizing the Discussion

The delegates did not consider themselves mere spokesmen for their constituents or instructed agents of interest groups; they also considered themselves *listeners* to the arguments of others. No doubt most arrived with firm opinions, but they also recognized the obligation to defend their opinions rationally and to change them upon conviction. As speaking and listening representatives, they were there to discover the long-run interests of the country as well as serve the immediate interests of their constituents.

For example, one delegate proposed that all votes be officially recorded whenever requested by any member. This was unanimously rejected because "changes of opinion would be frequent" and "such a *recorded* opinion . . . would be an obstacle to a change of them on conviction." Moreover, recording the members' changing opinions would open them to subsequent political attack, "furnishing handles to the adversaries of the result" of the Convention [May 28].

Further, "every member, rising to speak, shall address the President; and whilst he shall be speaking, none shall pass between them, or hold discourse with another, or read a book, pamphlet or paper, printed or manuscript" [May 28]. The Convention was not to degenerate into vain speechmaking, relegating decision to backroom maneuvers: The discussion itself was to be the real center of the Convention. Other rules guar-

---

[6] The Convention's voting procedure problem (but not its solution) is dramatically paralleled in the present conflict between the U.S.S.R. and Red China. Mao Tse-tung had Pennsylvania's idea. At Communist world conferences "each of the 81 Communist parties has had one vote. . . . The Chinese are said to have proposed that the votes of each party be weighted . . . by the size of the party . . . [and] by the size of the population it rules. This would automatically give the Chinese domination of the world Communist movement." *The New York Times*, Western Ed., July 10, 1963, p. 3. The problem is identical, but the Virginians and the Chinese took exactly opposite views of its solution. Mao Tse-tung embittered the conflict by pressing for procedural advantage; Virginia forsook such advantage, believing its objectives could be achieved only by agreement through discussion or compromise.

anteed flexibility in permitting matters to be tabled or brought back to the floor, avoiding procedural rigidity likely to hinder the ripening of agreement through discussion.

The Convention even took the drastic step of closing its doors: no visitors, no journalists, not even out-of-doors discussion within the earshot of non-delegates. Those who suspected the Convention would produce a strong central government naturally complained that only conspirators and evil-doers needed secrecy. Even Jefferson in Paris, who thought the Convention "an assembly of demigods," complained of the "abominable . . . precedent . . . of tying up the tongues" of the delegates.[7] The delegates defended themselves on the ground that they were only making proposals and that a full public debate would subsequently precede action.

The necessity of secrecy to some aspects of governing conflicts with the openness necessary to a liberal democracy. Openness is necessary so that voters can judge issues and persons. Moreover, public debates educate and improve public judgment. But secrecy is frequently better for producing results. One famous, but specialized, form of this problem occurs in diplomacy. For example, President Woodrow Wilson proposed "open covenants of peace, openly arrived at." Others deride this view of treaty negotiation, arguing that nations reach better agreements through closed-door negotiations where real give-and-take can occur. The problem arises in many forms, and democratic statesmanship has frequently to balance the rival claims of secrecy and openness.

In any event, the Convention never wavered from its decision for secrecy, and secrecy achieved its object. Free from daily fear of what enemies back home would make of each position taken in debate, delegates could move more freely toward whatever conclusions the course of the argument dictated. The procedural decision probably had an immense substantive consequence. Had the Convention been open to public and press, it probably would not so radically have abandoned the Articles in favor of the daringly national Constitution.

The Issue of Federalism

The Convention was shortly forced to face its key issue, the one that troubled it longest, most threatened to divide it, and finally was settled by its most ingenious compromise—the issue of federalism.

The Virginia Plan and a Legal-Ethical Question

The issue was precipitated by the presentation of the Virginia Plan, a detailed scheme of government carefully prepared in advance by the Virginia delegation, and especially by James Madison. The outstanding

---

[7] *The Writings of Thomas Jefferson,* H. A. Washington, ed., (New York, 1861), II, 260.

fact about the Virginia Plan is that it proposed a radically *national* government armed with great authority. Indeed the Virginia Plan largely ignored the Articles of Confederation, despite the common expectation that the Convention would merely propose revisions to improve the existing Confederation. This raised a legal and ethical question which troubled the Convention and which has troubled some scholars since. Was the Constitution produced by a body that illegally and unethically exceeded its authority?[8]

The Convention's legal basis lay in the congressional resolution establishing it and in the states' instructions to their delegates. Delegates hostile to the radically national Virginia Plan buttressed their case with an argument drawn from the congressional resolution; it said that the Convention was called "for the sole and express purpose of *revising* the Articles of Confederation." Not only was the Virginia Plan undesirably national, these delegates kept complaining, but it was an illegal proposal in the first place. But the congressional resolution also had wording that the Virginians could use. It said that the *reason* for revision was "to render the federal constitution *adequate* to the exigencies of Government and the preservation of the Union." Virginia could therefore argue that the Convention was justified in going beyond revision, if that was necessary to provide an "adequate" government.

Both sides could make an argument upon the basis of the authorizing documents because they contained an ambiguity, indeed a contradiction. And contradiction cannot command. The contradiction lurked in the double injunction laid upon the Convention: Provide a strong union and also preserve the confederal form. But what if stronger union required abandoning confederation and forming a strongly national government? Which of the two parts of the contradictory command would be binding on the Convention then? The Virginians took advantage of the contradiction to defend the presentation of a plan which ignored the Articles. And the nationalists, as we shall see, throughout the Convention took advantage of the contradictory desire for the blessings of close union while preserving a loose confederal form.

The Constitution as finally adopted greatly departed from the boldly introduced Virginia Plan. But the Virginia Plan became a sort of first draft for the Convention's discussions, and it left its imprint on the final document as first drafts often do. Madison had done his homework. He had prepared a detailed proposal and had organized the support for it. Those least willing to depart from the Articles had failed (or were unable) to organize themselves around a specific set of proposals. From the outset, therefore, the Convention found itself much farther along the road to a national government than would otherwise have been the case.

---

[8] The method by which the Constitution was ratified raised a similar question in somewhat graver form (see below, pp. 55–56).

National or "Merely Federal"?

The Virginia Plan's opening wording made starkly explicit the issue so abruptly placed before the Convention. Resolved: "that a Union of the States *merely federal* will *not* accomplish the objects proposed by the articles of Confederation, namely security of liberty, and general welfare" [May 30]. Therefore "a *national* Government ought to be established consisting of a supreme Legislative, Executive and Judiciary" [May 30]. A "merely federal" union of the states *versus* a national and supreme government—for five weeks this issue held the stage. The detailed work of the Convention, the give and take of compromise from which the Constitution emerged, could not proceed until this issue was somehow settled.

How federalism is understood today. "Merely federal"? Something here confuses the modern ear because it runs counter to a now widely accepted classification of forms of government. Most modern writers regard the United States today as the best example of a fully federal system. These writers have in mind a classification consisting of three basic forms. At one extreme is a *confederation,* a loose association of states (in older times, cities) who, as it were, are the 'citizens' of the central body they create. They retain all the sovereign power, with the central body entirely dependent legally upon their will. In this form, as we saw under the Articles, the states as such and not people are represented in the central body, the states vote there as equal citizens, and central decisions reach real citizens only through the states. Political life therefore centers in the states and not the nation.

At the other extreme is *national* or *unitary* government. Here all sovereign power rests in the central government, with localities legally entirely dependent upon its will. States are legally mere *departments*—the very word used, for example, in France—of the national government, and are its creatures. (In some unitary governments, like Britain, localities nonetheless become politically important, and power is effectively decentralized in practice.)

Federal government is the third form, in this modern typology, standing between the two extremes, and presumably combining the best confederal and national features. This *mixture* is indeed a distinguishing characteristic of American government. But when the Convention opened, there was no thought of the *mixed* form we now call federal. Indeed, the very words federal and confederal had not yet become distinguished; they were used synonymously. Accordingly, the delegates thought of two mutually exclusive alternatives: confederal or federal association versus national government. Gouverneur Morris expressed this general view when he "explained the distinction between a *federal* and *national, supreme* government; the former being a mere compact resting on the good faith of the parties; the latter having a complete and compulsive operation" [May 30].

The small-republic issue. On May 30 the Convention voted six states to one against a federal plan and for the Virginia Plan's "national supreme government." But this drastic decision could not stand. The New York delegation was split over the question and several delegations hotly opposed to a national government were only just arriving. As Madison had seen earlier, there was no point to railroading anything through; a really workable constitution would need the convinced support of nearly all the states. That kind of support could come only after long and thoughtful discussion—the kind the rules provided for—because the federal-national question involved an underlying theoretical issue: the question of the 'small republic.'

The small-republic issue (see pp. 25–26) underlay the controversy over the Virginia Plan. Many delegates strongly opposed radical departure from the Articles because they believed that republicanism was doomed in a large nation. They believed therefore that small-republican states should unite only in the confederal form and primarily for defense against external enemies. Speaking from this small-republic point of view, Sherman of Connecticut argued that "the objects of Union . . . were few." Keeping the peace among the states and defending all of them against foreign enemies, he continued, "alone rendered a confederation of the States necessary. All other matters civil and criminal would be much better in the hands of the States. *The people are more happy* in small than large States" [June 6].

Madison pounced on Sherman's claim that relatively little was wanted from union. On the contrary, he argued, a central government must provide broadly and "effectually for the security of private rights and the steady dispensation of Justice." Madison then compellingly reminded the delegates that

interferences with these were evils which had more perhaps than anything else produced this Convention. Was it to be supposed that republican liberty could long exist under the abuses of it practiced in some of the States [June 6].

Madison was skillfully playing off two sets of fears and thus reaching into a contradiction in his opponents' position. Those who feared strong national government also feared the Shaysite drift of the individual states under the Articles (see pp. 30–31). Like Madison and the nationalists, they too wanted to protect property and achieve political stability. In Chapter 3 we shall see whether these fears and aims affected the place of democracy in the Constitution. Here we are concerned only to see how Madison extorted acquiescence to a relatively strong national government from the reluctant 'small republicans.' He drove them to admit that what they wanted from Union could only be supplied by *an essentially national government*. Madison pointed out that they wanted to have their cake and eat it too, that they wanted all national benefits while retaining all the confederal privileges of state sovereignty.

Madison then presented the 'large-republic' argument for which he is famous. He argued that there was, in a sense, a way to have and also eat the cake—to secure *both* national benefits and republicanism for the country *without* clinging to the purely federal form. A "merely federal" system was necessary only if republics had to be small. If republican liberty could be shown secure in a large country, then there was no longer reason to keep the system purely federal and thus weak. Madison went even further. Largeness was not only compatible with republicanism, he convincingly argued, but it was *necessary* to it. That is, he urged the very converse of the small-republic argument. He argued that smallness and not largeness caused the fatal diseases of republics. The small republics of antiquity were wretched nurseries of destructive conflicts of economic classes. Just such conflict was making liberty unsafe in the 'small' American states; indeed, as all the delegates knew, fear of that conflict was an important reason the Convention had been called. Only a nation as large as the whole thirteen states or larger, Madison argued, would be a safe dwelling place for republican liberty.

The analysis of how the 'large republic' functions is delayed until Chapter 3, where it may be presented more effectively. It suffices for the present discussion of the federal-national issue to state that Madison compellingly suggested ways in which the dangerously concentrated political struggles of small republics would be safely fragmented and dispersed in a large republic.

The New Jersey Plan

The character and fate of what is known as the New Jersey Plan reveals how successfully Madison undermined the "purely federal" position. When the Virginia Plan was on the verge of decisive approval, Patterson of New Jersey presented a plan "purely federal, and contra-distinguished" from the nationalist Virginia Plan [June 14]. The New Jersey Plan shows how far beyond the old Articles the 'antinationalists' were now prepared to go. The New Jersey Plan provided for a kind of federal executive and judiciary; gave Congress authority over foreign and interstate trade; gave the Union an independent revenue source; made all federal laws and treaties "the supreme law of the respective states"; and empowered the federal executive to use the armed might of the Confederacy to compel compliance of recalcitrant states. All this went very far indeed, and the last provision for military coercion was an amazing grant of power. It proved, however, the Achilles heel of the New Jersey Plan.

The fear that a powerful national government would destroy liberty had pushed the Convention close to a gravely divisive issue. But now the long discussion of fundamentals neared its climax and resolution. The 'pure federalists' now admitted how broad the governing powers must be to achieve the blessings of Union, and that legislative, executive, and judicial organs of government were needed for their application. But the

Virginia Plan advocates pointed out that the attempt to achieve these things *by purely federal means* was doomed to failure. It led—in the anti-nationalist New Jersey Plan—to the palpably unacceptable reliance upon military coercion. To coerce a powerful state would be in effect to engage in civil war. The best solution the pure federalists could find required a method that would "bring confusion and ruin upon the whole" [June 19]. This fatal flaw suggested that there was no way to have both firm union and pure federalism.

On June 19 the Convention therefore voted (7–3) against the purely federal New Jersey Plan. It may seem that the Convention had now decided for a purely national plan and that, unaccountably, we have all mistakenly called the United States a federal government. Not so. The Convention *had* once and for all turned against a purely federal system, but it had *not* thereby acquiesced in a purely national government.

Compromise—a mixture of the federal and national principles—now became possible. Political compromise occurs, it is often thought, when each side believes that it has gotten as much as it can get. True, but each side must also believe that 'as much' is enough. If men regard the proposed compromise as morally disgusting or inadequate to safeguard vital interests, they may not settle for it. They may abandon the whole process of peaceful discussion and bargaining and may seek by force to gain their whole end, or may even prefer to go down fighting rather than settle. In short, for both sides to regard a compromise as a good enough settlement, they must not be in great disagreement over a vital issue.

The Convention had originally divided over the question of federalism versus nationalism, the small-republic true federalists regarding nationalism as fatal to liberty, the nationalists regarding a purely federal system as "imbecilically" incompetent. Compromise would have been impossible across this gulf. But by undermining the small-republic theory, Madison had narrowed the conflict. He had lessened the pure federalist fear of a national government. No longer convinced that liberty was at stake, they were less adamantly opposed to nationalism. The Convention now had a different, less grave division. It was now divided between those still advocating a purely national plan and those who, having abandoned a purely federal scheme, were determined only to work *some* federal features into the final outcome. The distance between the two views had become compromisable. In particular, Madison seems to have influenced the Connecticut delegates Ellsworth and Sherman, and it was the Connecticut delegation that helped bring about the key compromise.

The Connecticut Compromise

Once it was agreed that a significantly powerful government had to be formed and could safely be formed, there proved to be broad and immediate agreement on two features of the Virginia Plan: First, that a powerful government necessitated the safeguard of a bicamerally divided legislature; second, it seemed natural and necessary that one house be distinctly national, directly elected by the citizens, and proportioned to population, as were all the state lower houses.

But a fresh crisis broke out over the question of how to constitute the second house. The Virginia Plan's second house was completely unfederal; senatorial representation, like that in the House of Representatives, was based on population and excluded the states as such. All the pure federal fears came to fever pitch again over the question of the second house. The harassed small republicans made their last stand on this issue. Delegations threatened to desert the Convention. Even talk of the sword was heard. One side threatened to unify the country by force; the other threatened that the small states might "find some foreign ally . . . who will take them by the hand and do them justice"[9] [June 30].

At this critical juncture, on the morning of June 29, the respected Dr. Johnson of Connecticut took the floor:

> Those on one side [consider] the States as districts of people composing one political Society; those on the other [consider] them as so many political Societies, *and* a government is to be formed for them in their political capacity, as well as for the individuals composing them. Does it not seem to follow, that if the States as such are to exist they must be armed with some power of self-defense. [Therefore] the two ideas . . . instead of being opposed to each other, ought to be combined; that in *one* branch the *people*, ought to be represented; in the *other* the *States*.

Johnson's Connecticut colleague Ellsworth supported the proposal, hoping "it would become a ground of compromise. . . . We were *partly national; partly federal*. . . . He trusted that on this middle ground a compromise would take place" [June 30].

There was a brief display of adamancy by Virginia and Pennsylvania who genuinely feared that this single federal element—a Senate federally based upon the states—would be enough to ruin the new system. But the Great or Connecticut Compromise was adopted and the crisis of the Convention was overcome. Complex political struggles often come down to some single issue in which all the passions, all the forces find their focus. It is as if, when that single issue is settled, all the passions and forces are spent. Both sides seem somehow obliged fully to accept the outcome and matters move quickly thereafter. In any event, so it was at

---

[9] The situation seemed so grave to Benjamin Franklin that he wrote a pacifying speech (too frail to speak himself, he had it read by a colleague), urging restraint and recommending the Convention thereafter open its daily sessions with prayer. It was immediately objected that to begin praying "at this late day" would arouse public alarm (the ministers would be seen coming and going in the mornings) and perhaps thus injure the Convention. Someone said the real reason for omitting prayers was that "the Convention had no funds" to pay ministers. The story has often been told that Hamilton opposed Franklin's motion on the ground that the Convention needed no "foreign aid." For whatever reason, the Convention evaded the issue by "silently postponing the matter by adjournment." The meetings continued without prayer [June 28].

the Convention. When the pure federalists gained their point on the second branch, they never again waged a general battle on the question of federalism. Indeed they seemed to vie thereafter with the nationalists in granting broad powers to the new government.

The peculiar American brand of federalism could now be created. More accurately, as Madison later put it in *Federalist* 39, the Convention could now create a Constitution which was "in strictness, neither a national nor a federal Constitution, but a composition of both."

A Note on the Small- Large-State Conflict

The delegates were, of course, not disembodied intellects seeking only the light of truth. All had constituents and states with special interests to defend. During the first half of the Convention, the many interests seemed to resolve into two blocs—the large states versus the small. The large states seemed to line up behind the national Virginia Plan, the small states behind the purely federal New Jersey Plan. Indeed, traditionally they are referred to as the large- and small-state plans. Yet almost immediately after the Connecticut Compromise, the two blocs dissolved, and the bitter conflict between large and small states practically vanished. The sudden disappearance of so apparently sharp a conflict has been puzzling. The answer is that the conflict was more apparent than real.

For one thing, the Convention did not in fact divide neatly between large and small states. The Virginia and Pennsylvania delegations, representing the two largest states, did indeed fight for national government, while very small Delaware and New Jersey resisted them. But other states did not fit the pattern. Large Massachusetts wavered; large New York sided with Delaware and New Jersey; small Georgia took the national side; and middling Connecticut and South Carolina were on opposite sides. Moreover, there were men on both sides of the question within nearly every delegation. Further, it was the temporary fortunes of politics, not the size of the states, that gave the nationalists control of the Virginia and Pennsylvania delegations. The *delegations* were nationalist; the two *states* were not. In fact, Virginia later barely ratified the Constitution.

Yet it is true that many small-state delegates vehemently protested that the large states were seeking to dominate. Their protestations were no doubt partly genuine, but were also partly contrived. The cry against the large states was made only by small-state delegations dominated by pure federalists; *nationalist* small state delegates made no such protestations. In short, the cry against large-state domination was partly another argument seized upon by the small-republicans to use against the nationalists.

Despite the inconclusive evidence on which it rested, the idea of a large-small state division has been widely accepted because it was erroneously thought to be the natural division. That is, large states were supposed to want close union (with voting by population), the better to dominate small states, while the latter were supposed to prefer loose confederacy (with voting by states), the better to resist. Scholars neglected Madison's correct observation that history belied this view. In the loose Greek confederacies, he pointed out, "the strongest cities corrupted and awed the weaker," and in the loose German confederacy, the small states were "exceedingly trampled upon" [June 28]. Powerful Virginia could in time better dominate her small neighbors under the ineffectual Articles than under a national government. The small-state complaint at the Convention was untenable because it did not reflect the true interests of the small states. It was produced by the rhetoric of those resisting the formation of a stronger central government on other grounds. Once the national-federal issue was compromised, it naturally evaporated.

"A Bundle of Compromises"?

Besides the great compromise there were many others, the details of which we must turn to shortly. Indeed, Professor Max Farrand once rightly described the Constitution as a "bundle of compromises," and his phrase has won wide usage. But conflicting and erroneous conclusions can be drawn from the compromising spirit of the Convention that lead in turn to erroneous conclusions about the constitutional system.

Some have argued that the delegates' readiness to compromise proves they were really concerned only with their economic interests and thus readily abandoned political principle whenever compromise advanced those interests. On the other hand, some have praised the readiness to compromise as showing a healthy disdain for principle, a sound shying away from doctrinaire philosophizing in favor of hard-headed practicality. Some have argued that, because it embodies so many compromises, the Constitution could not be logical or consistent. And because of this alleged illogicality and inconsistency, still others have tended to treat the Constitution as an obsolete eighteenth-century hodge-podge that cannot be a clear guide for the present.

But the mere fact of compromise is not proof that principle, theory, and consistency were abandoned. Rather, the Framers successfully balanced the rival claims of theory and practical necessity. Despite the compromises which produced it, the Constitution is an essentially logical and consistent document resting upon a political philosophy that remains profoundly relevant.

Men of principle may properly make compromises when the compromises adequately preserve fundamental principle. We have already seen how this worked out in the dramatic Connecticut Compromise. In general, the Convention 'split the difference' only when the difference no longer involved fundamental principles. Under the pressure of necessity, men may honorably settle for less than they believe ideal. Everything depends upon whether fundamental objectives have been attained sufficiently and as completely as possible. Not the mere fact of compromise, but the *kind* of compromise gives the measure of a politician.

Another fact which minimizes the significance of the constitutional compromises is the Convention's underlying agreement on the need for popular and free institutions consistent with the 'genius' or spirit of the country. Once the federal question was settled, that agreement was all the greater. The underlying agreement contributed to the Constitution's coherence. The compromises fit within the basically consistent outlook that made the compromises possible in the first place.

Moreover, most of the compromises were over matters of detail which principle can never wholly settle, for example, the exact length of term for members of the House of Representatives. Those most concerned to keep government responsive to the people wanted a one-year term, others more concerned for stability wanted a three-year term. Yet all agreed on a stable representative body responsible to the electorate, and no one could prove exactly how long the term should be. If only a year, why not a more democratic six months; if three years, why not a more stable four years? This could reasonably be settled by compromise as could the age requirements for various offices, the ratio of representatives to inhabitants, and other like matters. Such splitting the difference does not render the Constitution a patchwork of inconsistent items.

This is not to say, however, that the Constitution is the perfectly consistent expression of complete agreement on political and legal theory. The Convention had followed Franklin's advice: when the "planks" had not fit, a little was taken from both to make "a good joint" [June 30]. And some of the joints are rough. But compromise is the creature of necessity and of men able to recognize necessity. Not blinded by a conviction of their own infallibility, and driven by a sense of urgency, the delegates compromised and were entitled rationally to hope that the Union was being made sufficiently more perfect. They demonstrated, to modify an old expression, that politics is the art of the *best* possible.

The Sectional Problem

Skill at compromise was especially needed for problems arising from sectional differences. The differences that had plagued the Confederation did not disappear at the Convention in a burst of patriotic zeal. All other things being equal, delegates still preferred that *their* interests, *their* constituents, *their* state or section enjoy any benefits available, and they coolly considered each clause with an eye to its effect upon interests with which they were immediately connected. Among these, sectional interests were especially important.

For example, Madison belittled the large-small state conflict, pointing out the greater importance of sectional conflict:

States were divided into different interests not by their difference of size, but by other circumstances; the most material of which resulted partly from climate, but principally from the effects of their having or not having slaves. These causes concurred in forming the great division of interests in the United States. It did not lie between the large and small states: *It lay between the Northern & Southern* [June 30].

The new government and its policies could affect the sections very differently indeed. The Constitution's procedures—as with voting by states versus voting according to population—would give influence to one or another section. The North and the South engaged in a kind of jockeying for position at the start of the race. But at the Convention the sectional issue involved only limited economic matters. Bitter moral and political differences came to the fore only later, leading to the "irrepressible conflict" of the Civil War. Therefore, sectionalism kept the Convention busy but not profoundly agitated. Since only limited economic matters—who would get a bit more or less—and not fundamental principles were involved, the conflicts were readily compromisable. Yet these were the very compromises that could not be achieved under the Articles. Daily political behavior, under the influence of the Confederation's centrifugal tendencies, steadily worsened conflicts. But here at the Convention, faced with the task of founding a government, the delegates took a less narrow view of what Franklin called their "little partial local interests" [June 28].

Slavery and the Three-Fifths Compromise

The Convention was not divided on the merits of slavery. All agreed that it was an unhappy inheritance from the colonial period. North and South alike hoped and expected that, as the South became more diversified agriculturally and more commercial, slavery would gradually die out. (For example, George Washington had sponsored a Potomac Canal company in order to open Virginia to the western trade. A more commercialized Virginia, he hoped, would then find slavery unprofitable and sensibly get rid of it.) The Convention knew that slavery would ultimately cause a divided nation because, perhaps immoral anywhere, it was peculiarly undesirable in a republic; slavery fostered political attitudes and habits of mastery inimical to republicanism.

The Constitution strikingly but subtly reveals the Convention's hostile view of slavery: The word slave never appears in it. Fugitive slaves are euphemistically referred to as "Persons held to Service or Labour" (Art. IV, sec. 2). Imported slaves are described as "such Persons as any of the states now existing shall think proper to admit" (Art. I, sec. 9). As Patterson of New Jersey said, in another connection, they "had been ashamed to use the term 'slaves' and had substituted a description" [July 9]. The Convention did not want the Constitution stained with the word after the thing itself had long disappeared. And when the thing did not disappear, when the South had become more extensively and passionately committed to slavery, what the Convention did still had consequences. In the great debate of 1850, Daniel Webster was able to brandish the Constitution's shamed avoidance of the word as a rebuke to defenders of slavery.

But however much the delegates thought slavery likely to disappear in the future and however much they disapproved of it, substantial economic interests had grown out of its long existence. Most southern delegates were briskly determined to protect those interests temporarily. Many northern delegates either recognized a kind of justice in the claim for protection, or accepted the necessity to accommodate some southern demands. The famous Three-Fifths Compromise was one such accommodation.

Were Negro slaves part of the population or not? It is easy to see what was at stake in this 'procedural' question. If slaves were counted as whole persons, the South would have roughly half the seats in the population-based House of Representatives; if they were not counted at all, the North would dominate the House. Many view the Three-Fifths Compromise, by which the Convention settled the matter, as a particularly crass example of splitting the difference. But the Convention had in fact little alternative. The three-fifths formula had been used in several important instances under the Articles and was included almost as a matter of course in the New Jersey Plan and in one version of the Virginia Plan. The Convention accepted this familiar formula as the basis for calculating both House representation and direct taxation.[10]

Further, it did not seem as brazen to the Convention as it does now that the South should insist that slaves were property and yet should be represented in Congress. In fact, the South did not want the slaves represented, but wanted white representation to reflect the economic value of the slaves. Because slave labor displaced free labor, the southern states had fewer free citizens than their northern counterparts and yet were as wealthy. This fact combined with the idea (then still prevalent, albeit weakening) that property was intermixed with political rights led some northern delegates to see justice in the South's demand for greater representation than its free population warranted.

Besides, northern reluctance over counting slaves toward representation disappeared when it came to counting them in matters of taxation. The Three-Fifths Compromise can cynically be considered a bargain struck by buyers and sellers: The South bought votes with tax money, and the North sold votes for tax relief. But it was a defensible bargain, necessary to make. The South would have yielded to stronger national

---

[10] Article I, section 2, states that "representatives and direct taxes shall be apportioned among the several States . . . according to their respective numbers, which shall be determined by adding the whole number of free persons . . . and excluding Indians not taxed, three fifths of all other persons." Notice the avoidance of the word "slave" and that free Negroes were to be counted as equal to whites.

government on no other terms. Some delegates, as we saw, deemed the southern demand just. In any event, the Convention was faced with the same kind of problem that faced Lincoln later: Not striking the bargain would have freed not a single slave while it would have destroyed the possibility of union. Finally, the general expectation that slavery would ultimately wither away must have rendered the compromise more palatable as a temporary expedient.

The Balance of the Sectional 'Package'

Five other features of the Constitution resulted from the accommodation of southern-northern differences: the delayed ban on importing slaves, the fugitive slave clause, the prohibition against export duties, provision for passage of commercial regulations by ordinary majorities, and the requirement that treaties be ratified by a two-thirds vote in the Senate.

The African slave trade was widely regarded as the most repellent single feature of slavery. Moreover, if slavery were gradually to be extinguished, stopping the slave trade was a logical first step. It was also a first step that would meet least resistance in some southern states, like Virginia, which may have profited from the domestic breeding and selling of slaves. The Convention therefore fairly easily agreed to empower Congress to forbid the importation of slaves. The only question was when to make the ban effective. The states most in need of slave imports won the concession that Congress could not enact such a prohibition for twenty years (Art. I, sec. 9).

The fugitive slave clause was hardly challenged. A system of slavery is precarious if there is a place for slaves to escape to. (Compare today the Berlin Wall and Communist bitterness over West Berlin.) While slavery lasted, slave states had to be granted some method for the return of fugitive slaves. Article IV, section 2 provided that an escaped "Person held to Service or Labour . . . shall be delivered up on Claim of the Party to whom such Service or Labour may be due." It was not clear whether the national government or the state to which the slave had fled was responsible for the delivery, but Congress early assumed the responsibility and maintained fugitive slave legislation. As northern antislavery sentiment mounted, the inevitably dramatic enforcement of this legislation provoked increasing bitterness.

The three remaining features—the banning of export duties and the voting procedures on commercial regulation and on treaties—resulted from sectional economic and geographic differences not necessarily connected with slavery. The North was developing rapidly in commerce, industry, and population, while the South was likely for some time to remain agricultural. The manufactured goods the South needed to import would surely be subject to duties. The South feared that its agricultural exports might be made subject to duties as well. As part of the general settlement of sectional differences, the Convention agreed to an absolute prohibition against the imposition of export duties by the national government (Art. I, sec. 9).

The South similarly feared prejudicial use of the new power to regulate commerce among the states. For example, a northern-dominated government might copy the old British navigation acts and require that southern exports be carried in American-built and -manned merchant vessels, profitably owned and operated by New Englanders. Yet the southern delegates shared the strong general conviction that the national economy had to be freed from limitations imposed by the states. They therefore sought protection in a procedural device—requiring a two-thirds majority for the passage of commercial regulations. This would then have given the southern section a veto over such regulation. But the Convention was determined to keep unimpaired the new government's power over the national economy. The interstate commerce power was accordingly placed among the congressional powers subject to action by ordinary majority vote (Art. I, sec. 8).

However, the Convention did accede to the South's companion demand regarding treaties. The South had vital interests in the then Spanish-controlled Mississippi and Gulf of Mexico which the North might ignore or even deliberately sacrifice. Indeed an earlier proposed treaty with England had gravely alarmed the South in just this connection. Article II, section 2, therefore, requires that treaties be made with the "Advice and Consent of the Senate," provided that "two-thirds of the Senators present concur."

The Convention Concludes its Business

On July 26, 23 resolutions were sent to a specially appointed "committee of detail." After a ten-day recess (the only long break in the summer's proceedings), the Convention labored for a month on this committee's draft of the Constitution. Finally, with all controversial matters settled, only a last literary task remained. "A Committee was then appointed . . . to revise the stile of and arrange the articles which had been agreed to by the House." Hamilton, Madison, and the equally nationalist Rufus King and Gouverneur Morris were named to the committee. That the Convention's final task was confided to the leading nationalists testifies to their predominance at the Convention's close.

This strongly nationalist five-man committee left the major writing chores to Gouverneur Morris who took advantage of the opportunity to add still further nationalist touches to the final product. His performance shows how the opportunity to commit political decision to its final verbal form can be used by a skilled individual personally to influence the event. As Madison observed, "the finish fairly belongs to the pen of Mr. Morris. . . . It is true that the state of the materials . . . was a good preparation . . . but there was sufficient room for the talents and tastes stamped by the author on the face of it."[11]

Maneuvering for the Ratification Campaign

It was one thing to prepare a good constitution; it was another to get it adopted. The question of future approval had hung over the Convention throughout. Nationalists had worried about how far they could go, and their opponents had repeatedly invoked the probable opposition of the public. The outcome was genuinely in doubt. The Constitution's sweeping changes excited powerful opposition. Presently advantaged economic interests feared new national fiscal and commercial policy. State-based politicians feared they would be downgraded by the creation of a powerful national government. The old small-republic sentiment excited popular alarm that a remote and powerful central government would crush the people's liberties. We shall see how the Constitution now revered was then reviled and by what a narrow margin it was ratified.

Shrewd politicians always try to launch controversial projects under the most favorable auspices. In preparing for the ratification campaign, the Framers adopted two main tactical devices: to achieve the maximum appearance of unanimity at the Convention and to tilt the ratifying procedure in favor of adoption.

Achieving 'unanimity'. Broad agreement had resulted from the initial underlying agreement of the delegates, the sense of national urgency, the exhaustive discussion, the brilliant leadership, the awareness that what the Convention could not wholeheartedly agree to the country would never agree to, and the give and take of practical compromise. Now every maneuver was employed in the closing hours to persuade the few unpersuaded and hold in line the wavering delegates.

Three influential delegates, Randolph and Mason of Virginia, and Gerry of Massachusetts, had developed strong objections to the Constitution. Aware that "a few characters of consequence . . . might do infinite mischief" by rallying popular opposition, Hamilton offered himself as a good example:

> No man's ideas were more remote from the plan than his were known to be; but is it possible to deliberate between anarchy and Convulsion on one side, and the chance of good to be expected by the plan on the other [Sept. 17].

Randolph, Mason, and Gerry were not persuaded. But it happened that majorities in all eleven state delegations still in attendance were in favor of the Constitution. This suggested a ploy. The delegates were not asked to sign the document in their individual capacities, as the Declaration of Independence was signed. Rather it was adopted "by the unanimous

---

[11] Max Farrand, *The Framing of the Constitution* (New Haven, Conn.: Yale University Press, 1914), p. 181.

consent of the States present. . . . In Witness whereof we have hereunto subscribed our names" (Art. VII). In this form, the Constitution went to the people with the useful appearance of unanimity stamped upon its face.[12]

The ratification procedure. The second tactical device, choosing a loaded ratifying procedure, was far more important. Here the Convention skirted illegality. Was not a Convention which had been called to "revise the Articles" obliged to use the prescribed method of unanimous amendment? But fidelity to the Articles' procedure—approval first by Congress and then by all the state legislatures—would have doomed the Constitution. The legislatures, dominated by politicians with a personal stake in the old arrangements, would be more hostile to the Constitution than the people. Several legislatures would surely balk at the sweeping changes proposed. The Convention decided to short-circuit these difficulties; it proposed to go directly to the people, over the heads of all the existing organs of government. Further, it made approval in only nine states sufficient for ratification.

Not only tactics but a question of principle were involved. Even if all the state legislatures ratified the Constitution, the new government would be the creature of the preexisting state sovereignties. Legislative ratification would suggest that the new Constitution was but a treaty (in the old federal sense) of sovereign states, subject to the higher legal authority of the state governments which created it. What the state legislatures had joined together they could claim the authority to put asunder. In short, ratification by state governments would tend to make the system merely 'federal,' precisely what the Convention had struggled to avoid.

For bypassing the legislatures, there was excellent precedent in the way some state constitutions had been adopted—the specially and popularly elected ratifying convention.[13] The Convention directed Congress to submit the Constitution "to a Convention of Delegates, chosen in each State by the People thereof." This was a deft stroke for a body about to be denounced from one end of the country to the other for its highhanded and undemocratic manner and views. Opponents of the Constitution found it hard to convince their fellow-citizens that there was anything highhanded or undemocratic in letting the people and not the state legislatures make the decision.

But there was no such precedent for ignoring the Articles' requirement for unanimity or providing for ratification by only nine states. Indeed, a few have argued that the adoption of the Constitution was a kind of *coup d' état* or usurpation. Yet, although the legal status of the action was ambiguous, the free and democratic ratification debate sufficiently exonerates the Constitution from the charge.

---

[12] In addition, George Washington's personal authority was prominently placed behind the Constitution. As chairman, he submitted the document to the confederal Congress with an impressive message that bore weight (as it was intended to do) in the subsequent public debates.

[13] See especially the Massachusetts example, pp. 17–18.

Moreover, not *any* nine states would have sufficed for ratification in practice. Geography and political power dictated that abstention by key states like Virginia or New York would render impractical a union of the remaining states. But the nine-state requirement prevented any single small state from obstructing the plan. (Remember how long Maryland had delayed the Articles, and remember that Rhode Island had not even been willing to participate in the Convention.) Moreover, a kind of bandwagon effect might occur: After a number of states had ratified, the recalcitrants might feel it futile to resist since solitary resistance could not automatically kill the Constitution.

The Campaign for the Constitution

"The business being thus closed, the members adjourned to the City Tavern, dined together and took a cordial leave of each other."[14] But politics had not waited politely for the Convention to conclude its business. Martin of Maryland, and Yates and Lansing of New York had long since left Philadelphia to raise up an opposition. And, secrecy notwithstanding, nationalist delegates had discreetly kept associates back home aware of what was afoot. The ratification campaign began long before there was even a draft of the Constitution.

Like other great political struggles, the campaign over the Constitution was a compound of many things that are difficult to disentangle. Four kinds of factors were predominant: state political alliances forged in earlier conflicts; economic, social, and geographic interests; the issues and arguments; the rival leaderships and maneuvers. In examining these, we continue our examination of what was writ large in this formative period of American politics. The political patterns we see here are of the kind that continue in modern American politics. And in seeing how the Constitution was fought over, we see further into its character.

Old Political Alignments in the States

Old loyalties and obligations (and enmities) carry over into new disputes. When new issues arise, division tends inertially to occur along old party lines. So it was in the ratification campaign. The Convention itself was brought about by a loose national political coalition of men who had worked together earlier on a variety of problems. These same men led the campaign for the Constitution, while opposition to the Constitution rallied round traditional state rivals of the nationalist leaders. In Virginia, Patrick Henry and Richard Henry Lee again battled Washington, Madison, and Randolph; in New York, Schuylers and Livingstons again joined Hamilton against Governor Clinton's powerful following. To a degree, then, the ratification campaign was a continuation of old political wars by new means.

---

[14] *Diaries of George Washington*, John C. Fitzpatrick, ed., (Boston: Houghton Mifflin, 1925).

Interest Groups: *Cui Bono?*

Mystery story readers ask an ancient Latin political question when they ask of a crime: *cui bono?*—roughly translated, *who benefits?* The question is almost always pertinent in politics: Who benefits from this law, that form of taxation, that method of letting defense contracts, the decision to convert this street and not that one into a throughway? This is not cynically to suggest that politics is exclusively a clash of selfish private interests. Politics also involves the deliberate pursuit of the public good. But some men do selfishly seek private advantage from politics, and most men often confuse their private interests with the public interest, unwittingly making the latter a flattering rationalization of the former. Moreover, the most disinterested justice sometimes requires special benefits for special groups. In short, such considerations of group interest are deeply and inherently involved in the subject matter of political science.

Even more than ordinary legislation, the framing of an effective constitution—the fundamental law and the basic procedures by which later law is to be made—affects the broad private interests of the community. Inevitably, therefore, it calls into play these powerful forces, and their conflict sheds light on the meaning of the constitution over which they struggle. We turn now to one aspect of the ratification on which much has been written—the extent to which private economic interests entered the conflict.

Charles Beard's "Economic Interpretation." The founding generation's motives and interests have frequently become a political issue. A recent example is the New Deal controversy in the 1930s, but the classical example occurred during 1880–1914. The rising reform and radical movements of that period resented the constitutional impediments to majority rule. Hoping for success in the popular House, they feared frustration by the restraining devices of the Constitution. At just this time, late nineteenth-century scholarship had virtually converted the Constitution into a divine code received at Sinai, and had deified the Founders. Such scholarship enabled the dominant conservative leadership of that period to parade as the Mosaic guardians of the constitutional tablets. 'Constitution-worship' and veneration of the Founding Fathers had become a powerful support of the status quo. Inevitably, reformers began to search about for feet of clay, to show that the Founders were not disinterested patriots but men rigging a constitution to protect their own interests. Debunking the Founders would emancipate the present from the moral claim of the past and open the way for drastic reform proposals. Charles A. Beard's *An Economic Interpretation of the Constitution*[15] became the classic formulation of the debunking attack. The title conveys the book's thesis: Nearly every important thing connected with the Constitution—the Convention, the provisions of the Constitution, the way it was ratified—is alleged to have an economic basis. Beard portrayed the Framers as "hard-fisted conservatives," protecting "their own interests and those of their

---

[15] (New York: The Macmillan Company, 1913).

class," by constitutionally hamstringing the democratic masses.[16] First, he dug out of neglected archives information on the *personal* economic holdings and interests of the Convention delegates. Second, he argued that those personal interests revealed a *class* pattern, that the delegates represented the wealthy classes, in particular the securities-holding, creditor, hard-money, mercantile, and large landholder interests. Finally, he argued that they deliberately designed an undemocratic Constitution to protect these privileged economic classes. Surely, this was dethroning the Founders with a vengeance.

While Beard valuably reintroduced economic reality into the contemplation of the constitutional period, his evidence and inferences were faulty. Indeed, he himself came nearly to deny, and others tried to moderate, the book's implications. But for a half-century, the Constitution was studied with undue emphasis on its alleged antidemocratic tendencies and on economic determinism. New studies are refuting Beard's main contentions and undermining their influence (see bibliographic note for this chapter). The main historical refutation is that leading *opponents* of the Constitution had in fact roughly the same kinds and degrees of property as the leading *proponents*. That is, the wealthy were not unified as a class in support of the Constitution. Moreover, whatever the economic factors, Beard's main argument falls on one major point: The Constitution is not, as he was obliged to claim, undemocratic. But this subject we examine in the next chapter.

Five main interest-group factors. If economic factors did not divide the country between rich and poor or along clear class lines, still they figured prominently in the ratification process. Five main conclusions are emerging in modern historical scholarship. First, hard-money creditors tended to favor the Constitution while soft-money debtors tended to oppose it. Debtors had obtained favorable state legislation and therefore feared transfer of effective fiscal power to the national government. (Remember that debtors are not necessarily poor; wealthy speculators are often the greatest borrowers.) Second, rich or poor, merchant or artisan, persons intimately connected with commerce probably favored the Constitution more than any other group. This followed from one obvious and great advantage of the new government: It would support a flourishing interstate commerce. Thus, everyone connected with commerce had a potential economic interest in the ratification of the Constitution. This is the key point: *everyone*—rich merchant *and* poor artisan. Rather than being divided along class lines by the Constitution (Beard's erroneous implication), all classes involved in commerce tended to be drawn together in support of it. This foreshadowed a truly vital feature of the American polity—the minimizing of class political warfare.

Third, townspeople favored the Constitution more than did countryfolk. Fourth, the more settled coastal areas favored it more than did the

---

[16] Stanley Elkins and Eric McKittrick, *The Founding Fathers: Young Men of the Revolution,* American Historical Association Service Center for Teachers of History Series (New York: The Macmillan Company, 1961).

western backcountry areas. But these two factors are probably closely correlated with the commercial factor, commerce being strongest in the towns and these chiefly located in the coastal areas. Fifth, important noneconomic interest groups, like army officers, newspaper publishers, and clergymen, probably tended to favor the Constitution.

Yet many of these tendencies were frequently reversed. Many hard-money, rich, eastern townsmen bitterly opposed, while many soft-money, poor, western farmers ardently supported, the Constitution. Local or individual tendencies sometimes overcame more general economic, social or geographic factors. Indeed, the ratification campaign resembles the complicated fragmenting and interweaving of interest groups in a modern presidential campaign. And many individuals were primarily moved by the sheer force of political ideas, to some extent haphazardly and regard-less of their socioeconomic situations.

The Issues and the Arguments

Naturally, many arguments made at the Convention reappeared in the ratification campaign, but with greater partisan vehemence in the context of a popular campaign. Above all, the pure-federalist qualms and doubts, allayed by Madison at the Convention, flared up in the form of two related charges. First, the Constitution violated state sovereignty and created a "consolidated" national government; it was insufficiently *federal*. Second, it had undemocratic, "dangerously oligarchic" tendencies; it was insufficiently *republican*. The two charges were connected by the belief that, *because* the new system was insufficiently federal, it *must* be insufficiently republican. In short, the small-republic belief underlay the ratification debates. The prevalence of this idea becomes understandable when we remember that there was no empirical evidence yet of the feasibility of a large republic. America became the first large republic that ever was.

The small-republic suspicions were at the bottom of many specific complaints. Three typical charges, each with lively modern reverbera-tions, illustrate this. First, members of the new House of Representatives would be insufficiently sympathetic with the interests of their constituents because, in so large a republic, each representative had to represent many thousands of citizens. (The new House was to have only 55 members, fewer even than some state legislatures.) Such a representative, accord-ing to the small-republic view, was too remote from his constituents faithfully to represent their wishes. Second, the President would employ the standing army as an 'engine of despotism' against the people. A state governor, the reasoning ran, could be safely controlled but the remote national executive could not. Third, the new national courts would gradually displace the state courts, and national judges would be indif-ferent to local needs and interests. In short, every power of the new government seemed threatening when viewed through the magnifying lens of the small-republic view.

"all of us little folks". An often-quoted statement of a delegate in the Massachusetts ratifying convention conveys the overall suspicion that the new government would become undemocratic:

> These lawyers, and men of learning, and moneyed men, that talk so finely, and gloss over matters so smoothly, to make us poor illiterate people swallow down the pill, expect to get into Congress themselves; they expect to be the managers of this Constitution, and get all the power and all the money into their own hands, and then they will swallow up all of us little folks, like the great *Leviathan* . . . yes, just as the whale swallowed up *Jonah.*[17]

Unmistakably, then, the issue of democracy entered the ratification campaign. Opponents of the Constitution spoke the language of embattled defenders of popular rights, and supporters of the Constitution warned about the dangers of democracy. But to understand exactly how the question of democracy figured in the campaign, it helps to hear a fellow delegate's seldom quoted reply:

> I am a plain man, and get my living by the plough. . . . [I want] to say a few words to my brother ploughjoggers. . . . I had been a member of the Convention to form our own state constitution, and had learnt something of the checks and balances of power, and I found them all here. . . . I don't think the worse of the Constitution because lawyers, and men of learning, and moneyed men, are fond of it. I don't suspect that they want to get into Congress *and abuse their power.* . . . I think those gentlemen, who are so very suspicious that as soon as a man gets into power he turns rogue, had better look at home.[18]

This reply makes three important points. First, some supporters of the Constitution were ploughjoggers too, just as poor and plain as any of its opponents. Second, the Constitution was no unchecked Leviathan of power; it has all the checks and balances of the Massachusetts constitution, and these are enough. Finally, men are not necessarily all rogues, and power is not necessarily always abused. In short, this delegate argued, the dispute over the Constitution was not a struggle between classes over whether to have democratic government or not. Rather, it was a dispute over the place and purposes of political authority and power in a democratic system. How the American constitutional system grapples with this perennially relevant problem is explicitly a theme of the next chapter and implicitly of the entire book.

Campaign Leadership and Maneuvers

Nationalist leaders pressed for action, believed that time (for doubts to multiply) would work against the Constitution. For example, several Pennsylvania state legislators opposed to the Constitution stalled pro-

---

[17] Jonathan Elliot, *Debates in the Several State Conventions on the Adoption of the Federal Constitution* (Philadelphia: J. B. Lippincott, 1907), II, 102.
[18] *Ibid.*, p. 103.

ceedings by absenting themselves from the legislative session; this left the legislature two members shy of a quorum. The next day, a town mob hunted down two opposition legislators and literally carried them to their seats. The legislature promptly scheduled an election of delegates for a ratifying convention. The maneuver succeeded. Pro-Constitution delegates won in sufficient number to ratify the Constitution. Within five months, the early tide of pro-Constitution sentiment produced ratification by large majorities in five states.

The promise of a Bill of Rights. The Constitution met its first severe test in Massachusetts. The agreement that finally pulled it through helped to produce an immense consequence—the Bill of Rights.

The Massachusetts Convention was closely divided. The still influential Revolutionary leaders Sam Adams and John Hancock wavered or were unsympathetic. Shrewd political pressure by the Constitution's convention managers in time brought the two around. But more than manipulation of a few leaders was required. One of the ratification campaign's major tactical issues came to a head here. Just as pro-Constitution men sought quick action, anti-Constitution men sought to avoid a showdown vote. Their most powerful argument for delay was to propose a second constitutional convention; such delay, they argued, would result in a better constitution, incorporating the improvements suggested by the present public discussion. The Massachusetts pro-Constitution men produced an imaginative solution: ratify now and amend later. That is, Massachusetts ratified the Constitution (by a bare 187–168), but simultaneously recommended a series of amendments to be added later. The idea caught on and a number of states ratified in the same manner. It is entirely possible that without this understanding the Constitution would have failed in several key states. An ill-assorted mass of amendments was proposed, variously aimed at protecting the democratic liberties so many feared the Constitution endangered. Three years later these were reduced to and adopted as the first ten amendments now known as the Bill of Rights.

The Federalist. The two most dramatic conventions were in New York and Virginia, states without which no other group of states could hope to launch a general government. The New York campaign produced one especially significant result—*The Federalist*.[19] This was a series of 85 essays published in the New York press and then brought out as a kind of campaign handbook. It was written, under the pseudonym *Publius*, by Hamilton, Madison, and John Jay. A campaign document, written

---

[19] The title is confusing: Why should nationalists like Hamilton and Madison call themselves 'federalists'? The title was a theft. In order to take advantage of a popular political label, these leading proponents of a "supreme, national government," simply styled themselves 'federalists.' The 'pure federalists,' like Richard Henry Lee who signed his criticisms of the Constitution "Letters of a *Federal* Farmer" (italics supplied), angrily denounced the rhetorical device. But the theft was so successful that generations of scholars have since called the opponents of the Constitution the antifederalists.

under extreme pressure of time ("with the printer's devil ever at my elbow," Madison said), *The Federalist* is, nonetheless, perhaps the finest American writing on politics. Moreover, it has the additional merit of contemporaneity with the formative events; it is the writing of men who were there when the enduring American political themes were being shaped. We draw freely in this book from this intellectual resource.

But the brilliance of *The Federalist* notwithstanding, the Constitution seemed doomed in the hostile New York convention. It took Hamilton's performance on the floor, a threat that New York City would secede and join the Union alone, word that New Hampshire and Virginia had become the ninth and tenth states to ratify, and a pledge to secure a Bill of Rights, before the Constitution finally squeaked through 30–27 against the powerful local political opposition.

Ratification had involved rough and tumble maneuvering and, as Hamilton said, the play of "ambition, avarice, personal animosity, party opposition, and many other motives not more laudable than these."[20] But

In this excerpt from Alexander Hamilton's working notes for the Federalist, *note especially Hamilton's view that democracy exists when "the whole power of government is in the people . . . whether operated by themselves or . . . by their representatives chosen by them whether mediately or immediately and legally accountable to them."*

[20] *Federalist* 1, p. 4.

"*Well, I certainly didn't know this. James Madison only weighed a hundred and twenty-five pounds!*"

Drawing by Saxon; © 1964 The New Yorker Magazine, Inc.

the Constitution had nonetheless been ratified by a high and solemn democratic procedure after a full, free, and intelligent debate. The fullness of the debate contributed much to its rapid and complete acceptance by virtually all parties and groups within a generation.

Tocqueville eloquently characterized that debate:

> If America ever approached (for however brief a time) that lofty pinnacle of glory to which the proud imagination of its inhabitants is wont to point, it was at this solemn moment, when the national power abdicated, as it were, its authority. All ages have furnished the spectacle of a people struggling with energy to win its independence; and the efforts of the Americans in throwing off the English yoke have been considerably exaggerated. . . . [Indeed] it would be ridiculous to compare the American war to the wars of the French Revolution. . . . But it is new in the history of society to see a great people turn a calm and scrutinizing eye upon itself when apprised by the legislature that the wheels of its government are stopped, to see it carefully examine the extent of the evil, and patiently wait two whole years until a remedy is discovered, to which it voluntarily submitted without its costing a tear or a drop of blood from mankind.[21]

The debate over the Constitution was a climactic encounter between two rival political theories of how the ends of democratic consent, liberty, and competent government can best be attained. Despite the broad agreement reached on political fundamentals, deep cleavage was always a possibility. Men of all kinds and classes were drawn into the conflict, adhering to one variation or another of the two theories. Opponents of the Constitution held to the old view that political power had to be tied down close to home. Its supporters urged the new view that great power could safely (if carefully) be assigned to the government of an extended

---

[21] *Op. cit.*, I, 117–18.

republic. The conflict of these views and kinds of interests—revealed so dramatically during the formative decade—is always just beneath the surface of American politics.

BIBLIOGRAPHICAL NOTE

The major sources on the Convention are available in Max Farrand, *The Records of the Federal Convention of 1787* (1911–1937); this definitive four-volume work is a careful collection of all the major notes and papers on the proceedings of the Convention. Another valuable collection is Charles C. Tansill, *Documents Illustrative of the Formation of the Union of the American States* (1927). Arthur T. Prescott, *Drafting the Federal Constitution* (1941) is a handy topical rearrangement of Madison's notes. The major source on the state ratifying conventions is Jonathan Elliot, *Debates in the Several State Conventions on the Adoption of the Federal Constitution* (1836–1845). Max Farrand, *The Framing of the Constitution* (1913), and Charles Warren, *The Making of the Constitution* (1928) are useful accounts of the Convention. A. C. McLaughlin, *A Constitutional History of the United States* (1935) is a general account of the constitutional background.

Charles Beard, *An Economic Interpretation of the Constitution* (1913) has been discussed in the chapter. For an early questioning of Beard's interpretation, see Douglass G. Adair, "Tenth *Federalist* Revisited," *William and Mary Quarterly* (January, 1951), and " 'That Politics May Be Reduced to a Science': David Hume, James Madison and the Tenth *Federalist*," *The Huntington Library Quarterly* (August, 1957). A number of books reexamining Beard's work and freshly investigating the problems have appeared recently: Robert Brown, *Charles Beard and the Constitution* (1956), Forrest McDonald, *We the People: The Economic Origins of the Constitution* (1958), *E Pluribus Unum* (1965); Lee Benson, *Turner and Beard: American Historical Writing Reconsidered* (1960); Cushing Strout, *The Pragmatic Revolt in American History* (1958).

Much less has been written on the pure federalists who have gone down in history as the 'antifederalists.' Jackson T. Main, *The Antifederalists* (1961) is a careful new study, and speaks to the Beard controversy as well. The original writings of the antifederalists have generally been neglected. Indeed, they are available only in the two long-out-of-print editions of Paul L. Ford, *Essays on the Constitution* (1892), and *Pamphlets on the Constitution* (1888).

The modern view of federalism is presented in Kenneth C. Wheare, *Federal Government* (1947) and in "Federalism," by Arthur W. MacMahon, in *Encyclopedia of the Social Sciences*. The 1787 debate on federalism is discussed in essays by Walter Berns, Martin Diamond, Russell Kirk, and Herbert Storing in *A Nation of States* (Robert A. Goldwin, ed., 1963). See also "The Federalist's View of Federalism," by Martin Diamond, in George C. S. Benson, *et al.*, *Essays in Federalism* (1961).

The collected writings of the leading Framers, an indispensable source, are available in a number of editions. There are also many good biographies of the leading figures; the outstanding and most pertinent one is Irving Brant, *James Madison the Nationalist, 1780–1787* (1948).

Part Two

CONSTITUTING
DEMOCRACY

Chapter 3

The
Fundamental
Political Principles

I am therefore of the opinion, that social power superior to all others must always be placed somewhere; but I think that liberty is endangered when this power finds no obstacle which can retard its course, and give it time to moderate its own vehemence.

TOCQUEVILLE[1]

This was the only defence against the inconveniencies of democracy *consistent with the* democratic form of Government.

MADISON[2]

SEPARATION OF POWERS, BICAMERALISM, JUDICIAL REVIEW, THE BILL OF Rights, federalism. How splendid, how familiar, how dull! Let us acknowledge the secret ennui that greets these words. Understandably bored by well-meant but unthoughtful repetition, most of us turn off a kind of psychic hearing aid when these constitutional principles and devices are discussed yet once again. In this chapter we describe their relationship and the underlying political ideas which they embody. When their pattern and meaning are seen, cynical boredom or unthinking acceptance may give way to the rational appreciation the constitutional principles and devices deserve.

Their meaning must be seen in terms of the basic aim of the political order. This basic aim we have suggested in the preceding chapters on the origins of the American Republic. To summarize: The American political order is now, and has been from the outset, an attempt to achieve a free and competent "democratic form of Government." This view of the polity's fundamental aim determines this chapter's inquiries. For example: Does separation of powers actually protect liberty? and if it does, Is the price a fragmented government, incompetent

---

[1] *Op. cit.*, I, 270.
[2] June 6 at the Constitutional Convention (emphasis added).

to its modern tasks? Does separation of powers hinder the expression of democratic will? More generally, we shall investigate whether the familiar fundamentals of the Constitution somehow substantially satisfy all three aspirations of the system—free, competent, democratic government.

"The democratic form of Government"

Most Americans believe, though somewhat vaguely, that their government is democratic. They believe theirs to be "the democratic way of life," for the sake of which they fought in two world wars. They regard America now as defending democracy in the Cold War. But behind vague suppositions about democracy dwell disagreements. By making some of the underlying issues explicit, we will be better prepared to understand the democratic features of the system and their relationship to its constitutional devices.

An Undemocratic Constitution?

We have already encountered one major dispute concerning the place of democracy in the American political order—the dispute resulting from the view that the original Constitution frustrated majority rule (see pp. 57–58). This view has a corollary—the belief that despite the undemocratic Constitution the political system gradually became democratized. According to this view, the dominating feature of American history has been the steady overcoming of the constitutional restraints upon majority rule. The transformation is thought to have been wrought by the process of politics. The *political process* is thus treated as radically distinct from and in conflict with *constitutional forms*. This view contends that underlying social and economic factors (e.g., the effects of the frontier, industrialization, and urbanization) weakened the Constitution by making it in some degree obsolete; and that then the informal political process (e.g., the development of mass political parties and presidential popular leadership) short-circuited the resistance to democracy of the eighteenth-century Constitution.

On this view, history has to repeat itself every day. The Constitution is seen as still the undemocratic document of 1787. Accordingly, the political short-circuiting must occur daily to permit the modern democratic system to function. The student of American government is therefore told that he must constantly penetrate the undemocratic constitutional facade to find the democratic political reality behind it, and political science generally must emphasize a perennial tension between legal forms and changing political reality.

Ironically, this view of the Constitution as undemocratic is shared by some modern conservatives and liberals alike. Indeed, the farther to the right or left one goes, the more likely one is to encounter it. Both believe that the original constitutional system deliberately hamstrung majority rule, but has been radically democratized by the political process. They differ, of course, in that the one disapproves and the other approves the change.[3]

This book rejects the view of the Constitution as undemocratic. It holds that the Constitution is now, has been, and was intended by its Framers to be fundamentally democratic. The constitutional forms, therefore, need not constantly be evaded or warped to permit democracy to function. Rather, the constitutional forms help to generate the political system and are in harmony with it. To study American government, we believe, is to study the complex but compatible relationship of the jointly democratic constitutional and political aspects of the American polity.

The Original Intention Regarding Democracy

The question whether the original Constitution was undemocratic requires examining what its Framers thought about democracy. Here and throughout the chapter we must consider their opinions in order to understand their handiwork. At first glance, the evidence suggests to the modern student that the founding generation feared democracy and hence must have rejected it and framed a nondemocratic government. It is unmistakable that most of the framers had great fears regarding democracy. However, whether they took the step from *fear* to *rejection* is precisely the question.

All the leading Framers were familiar with the political writings of antiquity and accepted much of the classical criticism of democracy. Consider how Socrates challenged the idea of democracy. What, he asked, was the people's claim to rule? Governing or ruling, he argued, was an art like the arts of medicine or navigation. Yet in illness or peril at sea, it made no sense to take a poll of all the patients or passengers. The sensible thing, he suggested, was to seek and follow expert guidance in such matters. Why then in government, in the most important art of all, should power be given to the inexpert many instead of the expert few? The question is acute. Every supporter of democracy is obliged to supply some sort of answer. Indeed the history of the democratic idea can be seen as a series of responses to the Socratic challenge. But the important point here is that the Framers accepted much of the classical critique. They agreed that the generality of men tended to be foolish or worse. Moreover, the Framers did not need ancient writers to teach them the dangers. We have seen with what alarm and disapproval they regarded some of the things majorities had done in the states; for them, Shays' Rebellion was a frightening portent of what enraged masses might do. Thus it is easy to find quotations vividly demonstrating that the Framers had fears regarding democracy. For example, in the 1787 Convention, Elbridge Gerry warned that "the evils we experience flow from the excess

---

[3] Martin Diamond, "Conservatives, Liberals and The Constitution," *The Public Interest*, I, September, 1965), 96–109.

of democracy" [May 31], and Edmund Randolph complained of "the turbulence and follies of democracy" [May 31].

It must be granted, therefore, that the Framers wanted to get rid of democratic "excess" and "turbulence and follies." But did they do it by getting rid of democracy? The careless inference has been that the Framers—like most statesmen and writers until that time—rejected democracy as vicious or unworkable. But this misses the whole point of what distinguished the Framers from such predecessors. They did agree with the antidemocrats on democracy's weaknesses and dangerous tendencies. But they did not reject democracy. Indeed, they almost could not. They knew that whether they liked it or not they had to conform (as we saw in Chapter I) to the "popular genius" of American institutions. They accepted democracy and sought to guard against its "turbulence and follies." James Madison stated their view perfectly in the passage quoted at the beginning of this chapter: They wanted to eliminate or lessen "the inconveniencies of democracy," but only in a manner "consistent with the democratic form of Government." Their candid appraisal of the faults to which democracy is prone must not obscure the central fact: They sought solutions *within a democratic framework*. This is the simple but vital truth in the old-fashioned view that the American constitutional system was "an experiment in democracy." The Framers wanted to "make *démocratie* safe for the world."[4]

What Democratic Government Is

But it does not settle the matter to say that the Framers intended a democratic form of government. We need ourselves to know what democracy is to judge whether the intention was fulfilled. Then we can judge whether separation of powers, for example, is compatible with democracy and, if it is, how it nonetheless guards against democracy's "inconveniencies."

It is not easy to define democracy. To know what the democratic form of government is requires knowing what the other forms of government are. Unfortunately, distinguishing the forms or kinds of government is a central and difficult task of political science. It is the frustrating and fascinating fact that the beginning student of American government must grapple with the very difficulties that bedevil mature scholarship.

Who rules? Forms of government may best be distinguished according to two factors: who rules, and with what characteristic consequences, problems, and weaknesses. Let us deal first with the factor of rule. The harsh fact is that the rule of some men over others is intrinsic to governing. Government is all about the question: What is to be done that will be binding upon the entire community? Conflicting answers arise and a

---

[4] This is to apply to the Framers the fine phrase used to describe the aim of Tocqueville's book. See G. W. Pierson, *Tocqueville in America* (New York: Anchor Books, 1959), p. 112.

decision must be made among them. Every form of government must therefore assign to some person or persons the final say, the authority to give the binding answer. That is what Tocqueville means in the passage quoted at the beginning of this chapter: "social power superior to all others must always be placed somewhere." He warns that, if liberty is to be preserved, this power's course must be retarded so it may have "time to moderate its own vehemence." As we shall see, this is exactly what the Constitution does. But as Tocqueville makes clear, to retard the course cannot mean failing to designate a final social power.

The cracy of the demos. Who is and must be the final "social power" in the democratic form of government? The early use of the word democracy suggests the answer. Democracy is a word of Greek origin. There is little difficulty with the *cracy*. It derives from *kratein*, meaning to rule. However, a difficulty arises with *demo*. It derives from the Greek *demos* and is usually translated as the people. Thus democracy is usually said to have meant originally rule of or by the people. But that is, so to speak, a soft translation, obscuring the fact that rule means rule by some over others. As Plato and Aristotle, for example, used the term, the *demos* were not the whole people. Rather they thought that two groups made up the people—the *demos* and the *aristoi*. *Demos* meant the many. *Aristoi* meant the best. More fully, as the philosophers used the words, *aristoi* came to mean the few who are best. *Demos* came to mean the many who are not best; that is, the great majority of men who are poor, and thus uneducated (and perhaps uneducable), and thus unfit to rule well.

The vital point here is contained in the Greek philosophers' emphasis that democracy means the rule of the majority over everybody, including any dissident minority. Democratic government necessarily operates by majority rule. Abraham Lincoln made the point with compelling logic in his First Inaugural Address: "Unanimity is impossible; the rule of a minority, as a permanent arrangement, is wholly inadmissible; so that, rejecting the majority principle, anarchy or despotism in some form is all that is left." In short, the inference from government by consent is that the greater number of consenting equals rules the lesser. As Jefferson said in his First Inaugural Address, "the will of the majority is in all cases to prevail."

The characteristics of majority rule. But there is more to democracy than merely numerical majority rule. Democracy's nature further consists in the characteristic problems that arise when the majority rules and in the characteristic ends for which the majority strives. Each form of government has peculiar strengths and weaknesses and peculiar ends or purposes. These differ with the differences in the 'personality,' so to speak, of the rulers. In each form of government the ruling element tends to seek its own advantage, or to pursue the common good according to its own characteristic view of that good. Monarchs, aristocrats, and popular majorities tend to have very different ideas of what the national interest is and how to achieve it. Each regime is the bundle of behavior that results from this central fact.

A famous passage from Tocqueville on the propensities of democracy is an excellent example of reasoning in this manner:

> If you hold it expedient to divert the moral and intellectual activity of man to the production of comfort and the promotion of general well-being; . . . [if you] are content to meet with fewer noble deeds, provided offenses be diminished in the same proportion; if, instead of living in the midst of a brilliant society, you are contented to have prosperity around you; if, in short you are of the opinion that the principal object of a government is not to confer the greatest possible power and glory upon the body of the nation, but to ensure the greatest enjoyment and to avoid the most misery to each of the individuals who compose it— if such be your desire, then . . . establish democratic institutions.[5]

But the question of democracy's nature and propensities is a much disputed matter, and we cannot fully settle it here. For our purposes it is sufficient to define democratic government as that form which operates by majority rule and pursues the national interest in the manner characteristic of the majority. This was the way the Constitution's Framers regarded democracy. And, having accepted the democratic form, they set about guarding their system against the follies and evils democracies had hitherto exhibited. In their view, the typical folly to be avoided was the inability of the short-sighted majority to sustain a government and policies competent to serve the long-run national interest and the typical evil was suppression by a tyrannical majority of the rights of minorities.

Democracy and liberty? *Democratic* suppression of *liberty?* Are democracy and liberty separable and indeed capable of opposing each other? This manner of viewing them is easy to derive from the Declaration's two principles—consent and rights. The Framers, and writers like Tocqueville, viewed the problem in this manner. They emphasize the majority rule aspect of democracy and the potential conflict with liberty. But many modern political scientists argue that liberty and democracy are inseparable and, therefore, that democracy, by very definition, includes liberty.[6] They grant that majority rule is essential to democracy. But they insist that *liberty is essential to majority rule* and thus to democracy: Who the true majority is and what it wants cannot be known until everybody has been freely heard from and a fair election held. In this view, democracy requires the continuous formation and reformation of majorities, a process that requires freedom of discussion and political organization.

For the sake of simplicity and clarity, in this book the idea of liberty is considered separately from the idea of democracy. Accordingly, we emphasize majority rule as the root of the democratic idea, the better

---

[5] *Op. cit.,* I, 262.

[6] See a discussion of this question by Hans J. Morgenthau and Howard B. White in the *American Political Science Review,* LI, No. 3 (September, 1957), 714–33.

to be able to see whether American majorities rule competently and with due regard to liberty.

Democracy or republic? But is America not a republic rather than a democracy? We conclude our consideration of democracy by looking at these two frequently contrasted terms.[7] In determining whether these are indeed radically different forms of government, we see more clearly the place of majority rule in the American constitutional system.

The single source most relied upon by those who make the republic-democracy distinction is *Federalist* 10. Countless references to the alleged radical distinction have been drawn from that essay. This is, ironically, a blunder. Actually *Federalist* 10 narrows the difference between the two terms and draws them more closely together than they had ever before been. It makes a republic simply a particular kind of democracy. The word republic comes from the Latin *respublica, res* meaning thing or affair, and *publica* meaning public as against private. For two thousand years, a republic usually simply meant any kind of nonmonarchical government; that is, any government in which politics was a public affair and not the personal prerogative of a king. Thus there were aristocratic republics, oligarchical republics, democratic republics, all kinds of republics. But Publius used the word to mean only a *democratic* republic.[8]

The modern confusion arises in part from neglecting to notice that *Federalist* 10 contrasts a republic with a *pure* democracy. That is, for Publius, republics differ not from democracy in general, but only from a pure democracy. For him a pure democracy is one in which "citizens . . . assemble and administer the government in person." A republic, he says, differs from this in only one way. It is "a government in which the scheme of representation takes place." Now this single difference is extremely important because, as we shall see, it is the basis of the Constitution's "cure" for democracy's "turbulence and follies." But for Publius a republic is simply a representative form of democracy. Accordingly, the best modern synonym for what the founding generation meant by republic is what Hamilton indeed called the new government—a "representative democracy."[9]

But this is not to depreciate the utility of the word republic. It has a valuable rhetorical ring. Unlike the word democracy, it conjures up worthy old-fashioned ideas of restraint and sobriety, of competence and liberty—that is, the very qualities democratic government needs to be its best self. Conservatives are therefore right in favoring the word, as they do; but they are wrong in thinking that the word republic of itself will somehow exorcise the social and economic policies that they detest. Whatever its rhetorical utility, it is impossible to read majority rule out of the American republic, as some have wished to do. This is confirmed by a

[7] See, e.g., Felix Morley, *Freedom and Federalism* (Chicago: Henry Regnery Co., 1959), especially Chapter 1.

[8] See also *Federalist* 39, pp. 240–41.

[9] Alexander Hamilton, *Writings,* H. C. Lodge, ed. (12 vols.; New York: Putnam, 1904), II, 92 (italics omitted).

" *GIVE ME YOUR TIRED, YOUR POOR, YOUR BUSINESSMEN, YOUR UNIONS, YOUR....* "

The cartoonist is suggesting that President Johnson's idea of a "coalition of a majority" is one which includes nearly every important element in the electorate.

simple verbal test. Suppose we say that America is a republic and not a democracy. Does not the question immediately arise: What *kind* of republic? And must the answer not be: a *democratic* republic?

In the very essay from which the misuse of the word stems, Publius makes clear how very democratic that republic is. He states bluntly that there is nothing that a determined, compact majority cannot constitutionally do.

> [A minority] will be unable to execute and mask its violence under the forms of the Constitution. [But] when a majority is included in a faction, the form of popular government . . . enables it to sacrifice to its ruling passion or interest both the public good and the rights of other citizens.

In short, in the American democratic republic—because it is democratic— the majority may commit its excesses *legally,* that is, "under the forms of the Constitution." The majority is the "final social power" designated by the Constitution. Appreciating the fullness of majority power under the Constitution is thus prerequisite to understanding the constitutional system. With that power acknowledged, we can proceed to consider how the system nonetheless guards liberty and supplies reasonably competent government.

The Extended Republic: "A Multiplicity of Interests"

The "cure" for irresponsible majority power, *The Federalist* argued, lies above all in a potentiality of the representative principle: It makes possible an extended republic. Without representative institutions, democracy must confine itself to a small area; a representative democracy, however, may embrace a "greater number of citizens and greater sphere of country." This extension is the indispensable basis of the American constitutional design. To grasp this we must examine in detail James Madison's famous argument that democratic remedies for the defects of democratic government are made possible in a very large republic.[10]

What Size Makes Possible: "A coalition of a majority"

In the extended republic of the United States, and among the great variety of interests, parties, and sects which it embraces, a coalition of a majority of the whole society could seldom take place on any other principles than those of justice and the general good.

Note that nothing in the large republic solution prevents majorities from forming; that would be undemocratic and is thus excluded. Nor is the formation of factions in general discouraged, either by denying groups the freedom to organize or by reducing all men to an undifferentiated mass. On the contrary, the large republic engenders the formation of a very great number of factions. In turn this sheer multiplicity of factions will stifle the formation of the only majority to be feared, the one that would be adverse to "justice and the general good." Madison believed that, because it would be large enough, the American republic would have a great variety of groupings, no single one of which would comprise a majority of the people. Majorities would therefore have to form by coalition, a deliberate association of the smaller groups. The process of coalition would moderate these majorities so that free and competent government would result democratically from them. This concept of majority-by-coalition is crucial to Madison's theory and to the American political system which embodies it.

"The most common and durable source of factions"

What are these factions, coalitions of which form safe majorities? Madison knew the many forces that separate men into conflicting factions. He knew that men divide over religious and political opinions, that they

---

[10] All quotations in this section, unless otherwise identified, are from *Federalist* 10, the major presentation of the extended-republic theory. Notice that, in its argument, extension is based exclusively on the representative principle and not on federalism.

flock to rival ambitious leaders and that, when there is no serious divisive issue, "the most frivolous and fanciful distinctions" (perhaps like the struggle of Gulliver's Lilliputians over which end of a soft-boiled egg to open) may cause violent conflict.

> But the most common and durable source of factions has been the *various and unequal* distribution of property. Those who hold and those who are without property have ever formed distinct interests in society. Those who are creditors, and those who are debtors, fall under a like discrimination. A landed interest, a manufacturing interest, a mercantile interest, a moneyed interest, with many lesser interests, grow up of necessity in civilized nations, and divide them into different classes, actuated by different sentiments and views [Italics supplied].

Madison put the same thought another way: From "the possession of different degrees and kinds of property . . . ensues a division of the society into different interests and parties." No pussy-footing here about economics as a prime factor in political conflict; the Framers believed that political conflict occurs most commonly and durably over economic interests. But notice that economic factors operate in two ways. Men possess "unequal" amounts or "degrees" of property and may divide accordingly. Or they can conflict over the "varieties" or "kinds" of property. The first way, division over *amount* of wealth, leads to the class struggles that destroyed so many older democracies—the mortal combat of the few rich against the many poor. Here is the key: This blunt class struggle is precisely what can be minimized or forestalled in the extended republic. There men will organize the second way, according to diversity in *kinds* of property. And conflict over kinds of property provides the context for free and competent democratic government.

Madison versus Marx. The contrast between the two forms of economic conflict is seen by contrasting Madison and Karl Marx. First, it should be clear from Madison's emphasis on economics that Karl Marx (1818–83) did not invent the idea that economics has something to do with politics, or even the idea that rich and poor tend to be natural political enemies. Indeed all political thinkers knew that. Plato said that there is always "the city of the poor and the city of the rich."[11] Similarly, the nineteenth-century Tory prime minister of England Benjamin Disraeli spoke of "The Two Nations."[12] Thus, Marxism must be seen more precisely, as a specific view of the economic factor. Marxism is based on an historical theory that the perennial rich-poor conflict was reaching a final climax in the advanced industrial nations. It was taking the final form of the capitalist-proletarian class struggle and would end with the triumph of the proletariat. Thus would be ushered in the socialist utopia, wherein the human condition itself would be transformed.

---

[11] *Plato's Republic,* Paul Shorey, trans. (Cambridge, Mass.: Harvard University Press, 1946), p. 327, 423–423a.

[12] He used the phrase in the title of his interesting novel, *Sybil, Or the Two Nations* (London: Penguin Books, 1954).

The key point is that Marxism depends upon the first sort of economic conflict—class conflict over inequality of amounts of property. Madison's strategy is precisely opposed; it seeks to subordinate this to the conflict between kinds of property. That is, in the extended republic the conflict of limited and specific interests replaces the divisive and general struggle between two great classes. In this sense, Madison anticipated and refuted Marxism. Rather than compacting into two great classes, in his theory, rich and poor are fragmented and jumbled into narrow and particular "factions." Accordingly, no single owning class oppresses the masses; and the masses do not organize as a class, but rather fragment and factionally advance specialized, immediate interests.

This is just what has happened. One of the remarkable features of American politics is the absence of powerful Marxian movements like those in Western Europe. American trade unions have never been as influenced by socialism as their European counterparts. Friedrich Engels, Marx's great colleague, commented in 1892 on the unique absence of a major socialist party in America:

> There is no place yet in America for a *third* party, I believe. The divergence of interests even in the *same* class group is so great in that tremendous area that wholly different groups and interests are represented in each of the two big parties.[13]

There has been no such powerful third party since. The "divergence of interests . . . in that tremendous area"—Madison's theory of the extended republic—was built into the constitutional system. And that system has consistently operated, as he intended and as Engels noted, to help the American democracy avert the fatal politics of class struggle.

The Large Commercial Republic

"Tremendous area" does not of itself produce the "divergence of interests" of which Engels complained and upon which the constitutional system depends. We can see precisely what kind of extended republic alone does that by analyzing the defect of small republics. The smaller the republic, "the fewer probably will be the distinct parties and interests composing it; the fewer the distinct parties and interests, the more frequently will a majority be found of the same party." The underlying assumption is that small countries tend to have fewer interests because they have "small," relatively simple and undifferentiated economies.[14] This is an idea straight out of Adam Smith, who showed that a modern, highly differentiated economy depends upon a *large market area*. (Note

---

[13] Quoted in Daniel Bell, *The End of Ideology* (New York: Collier Books, 1961), p. 67 (italics in original).

[14] Small countries with dense population and an active foreign commerce can have advanced economies and achieve the useful multiplicity, and large countries can have agricultural, undifferentiated economies. Consider the vast Asian countries until recent years. But in general, largeness is correlated with variety of economic activity.

The FŒDERALIST, No. 10.

To the People of the State of New-York.

AMONG the numerous advantages promised by a well conftructed Union, none deferves to be more accurately developed than its tendency to break and control the violence of faction. The friend of popular governments, never finds himfelf fo much alarmed for their character and fate, as when he contemplates their propenfity to this dan- gerous vice. He will not fail therefore to fet a due value on any plan which, without violating the principles to which he is attached, provides a pro- per cure for it. The inftability, injuftice and con- fufion introduced into the public councils, have in truth been the mortal difeafes under which popular governments have every where perifhed; as they continue to be the favorite and fruitful topics from which the adverfaries to liberty derive their moft fpecious declamations. The valuable improvements made by the American Conftitutions on the popular modals, b⁻⁻ ⁻cient ⁻⁻d modern can⁻⁻ ⁻⁻⁻ainly

The influence of factious leaders may kindle a flame within their particular States, but will be un- able to fpread a general conflagration through the other States: A religious fect, may degenerate into a political faction in a part of the confederacy; but the variety of fects difperfed over the entire face of it, muft fecure the national Councils againft any danger from that fource: A rage for paper money, for an abolition of debts, for an equal divifion of property, or for any other improper or wicked pro- ject, will be lefs apt to pervade the whole body of the Union, than a particular member of it; in the fame proportion as fuch a malady is more likely to taint a particular county or diftrict, than an entire State.

In the extent and proper ftructure of the Union, therefore, we behold a republican remedy for the difeafes moft incident to republican Government. And according to the degree of pleafure and pride, we feel in being Republicans, ought to be our zeal in cherifhing the fpirit and fupporting the character of Foederalifts.

P U B L I U S.

Madison's Federalist 10 as it first appeared in The New York Packet, Novem- ber 23, 1787.

that this is an important aim of the developing European Common Market.) Mass markets make mass production possible. And mass pro- duction is highly specialized production—the division of labor into many specialized industries and specialized occupations and hence specialized interests. Thus, largeness is valuable because it makes possible the large *commercial* republic which proliferates economic interests. This prolifera- tion is the "variety" of property which produces the moderate conflict upon which the constitutional system depends.

Let us sum up the utility of the extended commercial republic. The 'have-nots' (or 'have-lesses') everywhere outnumber the 'haves.' Democ- racy enables the have-not majority to vote themselves the wealth of the haves. This may go to such lengths as to cause mortal civil strife. One great task of the constitutional system is to prevent the "poor majority" and the "rich minority" from thinking of themselves as such and acting as such. This cannot be done in small countries with undifferentiated economies, where the mass of people are divided into but a few industries and occupations. These few differences seem trivial as compared with the great difference between all the poor, on one side, and all the rich on the other.[15] In a small republic, because the ways of being poor are so few,

---

[15] Although there are important differences regarding size and kind of economy envisaged, a passage in Aristotle may suggestively be compared with Madison:

Where the middle class is large, there is least likelihood of faction and dissension among the citizens. Large states are generally more free from faction just because they have a large middle class. In small states, on the other hand, it is easy for the whole population to be divided into only two classes; nothing is left in the middle, and all—or almost all—are either poor or rich.

Aristotle's Politics, Ernest Barker, trans. (New York: Oxford University Press, 1962), Book IV, Chapter 11, p. 182.

the mass unites in mortal combat with the rich, who similarly are compacted into a class because the ways of being rich are few and relatively noncompetitive. Only in the extended commercial republic can the mass be fragmented into a great variety of interests. When thus fragmented, men seek immediate gains for their particular industries or occupations and not the advantage of their class.

As an example of the process, consider only a single sector of the complex American economy—the transportation industry. There is in fact no single transportation industry. Instead there are the bus, truck, train, aircraft and maritime industries, each with dozens of subdivisions. And within each industry there are literally hundreds of specialized crafts and occupations. What pattern emerges? *Not* "transport magnates" ranged against the "transport proletariat." Railroad and truck owners compete very much more than they collaborate. Railroad unions and teamster unions bitterly compete with each other. True, unions and owners conflict *within* their industries, but they frequently close ranks against other industries. Thus railroad owners and railroad unions cooperate *against* cooperating truck owners and truck unions, each seeking preferential treatment from legislatures and administrative agencies. Even within this single sector of the economy there is no basic class division but rather a welter of conflicting interests. It is from thousands of such interests that the moderating "coalition of a majority" must be formed.

Prerequisites: Democracy and Prosperity

It can be inferred that two basic conditions are required if the moderating consequences of multiplicity are to result. First, the society must be profoundly democratic. As we have seen, a major aim of the extended republic is to prevent the formation of both desperate majorities and ruthless minorities. But if there are social class barriers to limited gains, what difference will economic differentiation make? No matter how diverse the economy, an undemocratic social and political structure negates the desired political effects of economic diversity. Germany was long a case in point—large, diverse, commercial, yet torn by bitter political warfare. The reason is simple: Germany was persistently undemocratic in decisive respects. Only when a country is genuinely democratic will the diverse economic interests adopt the moderate political views and methods of those who confidently seek immediate, limited advantage. The case of the Soviet Union is similarly instructive. It is surely as large and possessed of as many diverse interests and sects as anything Madison had in mind. Yet, for all its *social* and *economic* diversity, the Soviet Union lacks the *political* factors necessary to make the Madisonian scheme work: It lacks a legal-political structure that summons up the socioeconomic diversity and makes it politically significant. Without that structure, mere socioeconomic pluralism may be rendered a nullity and useless for liberty, as the case of the Soviet Union suggests.

Second, the society must have an economy that is relatively prosperous, has some give in it, and, perhaps, is growing. If total quantity of wealth is limited, the distribution of wealth tends to become rigidly fixed on the existing class lines. Economic scarcity exacerbates the political struggle of the rich and poor. In a fixed and limited economy, the poor have in practice little hope of improving their situation save by an assault upon the wealthy few. Accordingly, only a relatively prosperous economy, where patterns of distribution can easily change, encourages diverse economic groups to focus their energies on increasing their immediate share, rather than on politically fatal economic class warfare.

Religious Diversity: "the multiplicity of sects"

But even economic diversity plus democracy and prosperity, Madison observed, was not quite sufficient to secure the full range of liberties. He therefore also stressed another noneconomic aspect of the extended republic—religious diversity. He and the other leading Framers shared the eighteenth century's revulsion against religious fanaticism and tyranny. During the devastating religious struggles of the preceding two centuries, dominantly Catholic or Protestant governments had extinguished domestic liberties and warred with countries of the opposing creed. Other countries, where the two sects were more evenly divided, had been torn by bitter internal struggles. Madison saw in the extended republic a defense against such religiously provoked tyranny and domestic convulsion:

> In a free government the security for civil rights must be the same as that for religious rights. It consists in the one case in the multiplicity of interests, and in the other in the multiplicity of sects. The degree of security in both cases will depend on the number of interests and sects; and this may be presumed to depend on the extent of country and number of people comprehended under the same government.[16]

He argued that so strong was the human propensity to religious domination, only sectarian fragmentation would effectively prevent waves of fanaticism from sweeping across a nation. This fragmentation or multiplicity is likelier in extended republics, as was clear in the case of America. (Consider the greater likelihood of religious dominance and conflict had America broken into several independent nations; a single sect might well have emerged as a domineering majority in each.) Religious multiplicity is thus immensely important in the American polity. It is a vital part of that multiplicity which necessitates the moderating process of coalition, and it offers all religious sects ultimate national protection against oppressive local majorities.

---

[16] *Federalist* 51, p. 324. On the relationship of religious multiplicity to a modern commercial society, it is useful to compare Adam Smith, with whose work Madison was familiar. See especially pp. 744–46 in *The Wealth of Nations* (New York: The Modern Library, 1937).

Representation and the Process of Coalition

The representative principle makes the extended republic and its multiplicity possible. Moreover, it is at the level of the representative that much of the moderating process of coalition occurs. Often the spokesman for the interest groups dominant in his state or district, the representative may be loyally prepared to sacrifice the national interest on behalf of their extreme demands. But he and those he represents soon learn that they simply do not have the votes. In order to secure congressional majorities for desired legislation or to win the Presidency, cooperation with other groups proves necessary. Thus ensues the coalescing process. As the coalition enlarges to form the necessary majority, an enormous number of conflicting selfish interests must be taken into account. The groups within the emerging coalition must at least make concessions to each other's needs. In the process, the grossest demands of each tend to be moderated. It becomes difficult to formulate laws and policies favoring the coalition members that are not at the same time roughly compatible with "justice and the general good."

Thus, even in terms of the narrowest selfishness, multiplicity and the coalition process tend to moderate the worst effects of that selfishness. But something more valuable than that can happen. The discovery that one's grossest demands are absurdly impossible of achievement can lead to an enlightened kind of self-interest, a habitual recognition of the indisputable needs of others and a sobriety about the general requirements of society. And something still worthier can happen. As the extremes of selfishness are moderated, the representative can become free to consider questions affecting the national interest on their merits. The jostling of innumerable interests gives him a margin of freedom from any single interest group. He is thereby enabled, to some extent, to pursue the national interest as he comes to see it in the instructive national arena.

Representative Government

The aim of every political constitution is, or ought to be, first to obtain for rulers men who possess most wisdom to discern, and most virtue to pursue, the common good of the society; and in the next place, to take the most effectual precautions for keeping them virtuous whilst they continue to hold their public trust.[17]

A major problem in the American Republic, therefore, is the democratic choice of this wisdom and virtue—democratic choice because the whole system rests upon choice by majority rule; wise and virtuous representatives because of the republican belief that government of and for the people more competently solves problems and protects liberties when it is conducted by such representatives rather than by the people themselves. The representative is thus viewed as more than a mere mouthpiece

---

[17] *Federalist* 57, p. 350.

for his electors. The presumption is that the representatives will be able men who, in congress assembled, will deliberate and judge wisely on behalf of the people. The Constitution conduces to the choice of such representatives in three main ways: by the nature of the public offices; by the size and variety of the electoral district; and by indirect election and appointment.

Constitutional Bases of Capable Representation

The first way the Constitution contributes to achieving able representation lies in the nature of the offices. Men of the requisite capacity seek office only when the office offers opportunities adequate to their abilities and ambitions. The Constitution creates such national offices— offices that are independent, powerful, honorific, and of sufficient duration. Precisely because national office constitutionally affords great power and honor, able and ambitious men can pursue political careers within the constitutional framework rather than by unconstitutional adventurism. Nor does all of this assume that thirst for high office is merely a lust for power. Rather, as modern corporation executives, for example, tell us, the ablest men gravitate to posts where authority is sufficient for accomplishing great tasks. Further, the terms of the national offices are constitutionally fixed, preventing arbitrary removal, and are of sufficient duration to attract able men. The 4-year President, 6-year senators, and life-tenure judges have sufficient time to pursue long-range plans and achieve important goals. The possibility of reelection (especially relevant to the House of Representatives) increases the prospective time. (The Twenty-second Amendment, which limits Presidents to two terms, departs radically from this original constitutional principle.) Finally, Congress sets the pay for national offices. Although tending to the low side, national compensation has usually been sufficient for almost anyone to try a political career, and it has usually been higher than that of comparable office in most Western European countries.

The second constitutional factor lies in the size and variety of district to be represented in an extended republic. Since the number of offices does not increase proportionally with the size of the republic, each district tends to possess a "greater number of citizens and extent of territory." Further, the more complex and varied the national economy, the more each large district is likely to reproduce the valuable multiplicity. Thus not only Presidents and senators but even representatives are elected from districts where the multiplicity-coalition process is at work. Consequently, candidates must appeal to diverse interests and win wide popular support. Capacity to win such elections is correlated to capacity to govern fairly and ably in office. The kinds of policies, natural ability and training, and experience that it takes to win in such districts and from such a varied electorate approximate the kinds of policies, ability and training, and experience a good office-holder needs. Moreover, representatives from such districts need not be the captive of any one group but, rather, can find some elbow-room for statesmanship in the very confusion of factions.

The third constitutional strategy for securing able representation lies in the original constitutional reliance on *indirect election* and *appointment*. This has often been attributed to distrust of the electorate. In fact, indirect election of President and Senate was as much the result of compromises on the federal-national question as it was of concern about democracy. That is, indirect election was in part a concession to the 'pure federalists' who wanted the states as such to have a place in the electoral process. However, it was also unmistakably thought that both indirect election and appointment might secure better qualified office-holders than direct popular election. For example, Madison favored "the policy of refining the popular appointments by successive filtrations." The Seventeenth Amendment and political custom have since made both Senate and Presidency popularly elective for all practical purposes. The original constitutional preference of an appointive judiciary has, however, remained unchanged. Unlike many state judiciaries which are elective, the entire national judiciary is appointive.

Representation and Majority Rule

By nature of office, size of constituency, and mode of election or appointment, the Constitution encourages merit in the representatives. But is this all compatible with the idea of *democratic* representation? Especially, were not indirect election and judicial appointment constitutional dodges to prevent majority rule? Actually, reflection reveals how a determined and sustained majority, from the outset, has always been, as it now is, able constitutionally to impose its will despite indirect election and appointment.

For example, the state legislatures which appointed the senators were themselves wholly popular bodies. Contests for election to the state legislature early and frequently became in effect popular contests over rival candidates for the Senate. Besides, as early as 1800, candidates for state legislatures typically were identified with political parties. Thus, in voting for the legislative candidate, the citizen knew that he was choosing between two parties and, therefore, between the rival senatorial favorites of the two parties. For example, the Lincoln-Douglas contest of 1858 was surely a profoundly democratic canvass of popular opinion. But this famous election was indirect; no one voted for Lincoln or Douglas, only for state legislative candidates committed to one or the other. Indirect election was undoubtedly less purely democratic than direct election. Indeed, Lincoln and his party had a slight majority in the popular vote, but lost in the number of legislators elected. But more often than not popular opinion prevailed; the method was not decisively undemocratic. The case was the same with the Presidency. Indirect election almost immediately became subject to the same popular controls. As Jefferson pointed out, election via the Electoral College was nonetheless "election by the people, in *practice* (for they vote for [elector] A only on an assurance that he will vote for [candidate] B.)"[18] Nothing in the Constitution impeded this development.

The case of the judiciary is somewhat different but, by putting the hypothetical extreme case, the same ultimate power of the popular majority may be discerned. At its pleasure and by simple majority, the popularly elected Congress has the constitutional power to remove some matters from the jurisdiction of the inferior courts and even of the Supreme Court. Congress also has power to create new courts and (probably) to terminate old ones. These new courts may be filled with docile appointees. Finally, Congress by ordinary majority may constitutionally enlarge the Supreme Court to any size desired. Then the popularly elected President, with the consent of the Senate, may constitutionally pack the Court with 'tame' judges until the will of the Court is broken. No decision by the judicial representatives—that is, those to whom the judicial function is delegated—could long withstand a sustained and determined majority expressing itself through the political branches.

Granted then that majorities can constitutionally overcome these express "retarding" obstacles, but are there hidden barriers to democracy? A representative system may be made undemocratic either by suffrage qualifications (limiting voters) or by representative qualifications (limiting those who may be elected). The suffrage question is extensively treated in Chapter 10. It suffices here to give the main conclusions: There was a very broad electorate in 1787; it was expected to broaden steadily; it was sufficiently broad to be deemed a democratic suffrage then and has broadened steadily and profoundly ever since. As to qualifications upon the representatives, "no qualification of wealth, of birth, of religious faith, or of civil profession is permitted to fetter the judgment or disappoint the inclination of the people."[19] The national system totally excluded undemocratic qualifications although these lingered on in some states. Regardless of origin or previous condition, anyone could aspire to national office. This legal fact immediately and profoundly democratized the political process. Finally, note the relatively generous provisions admitting citizens of foreign origin to public office in a country where immigration reached unprecedented proportions. No hidden barrier here to the influence of the newly arriving immigrants.

The constitutional system of representation is thus thoroughly compatible with "the spirit and the form of popular government." Yet to demonstrate the legal power of majorities under the Constitution is not to suggest that a tyrannically-minded majority can readily break through the constitutional barriers. It certainly does not suggest that it should. But what must be understood to appreciate the restraining constitutional

---

[18] Letter to John Taylor, May 28, 1816, *The Works of Thomas Jefferson*, P. L. Ford, ed. (New York: G. P. Putnam's Sons, 1905), XI, 531.
[19] *Federalist* 57, p. 351.

devices is that majorities *can* rule under the "forms of the Constitution." It is to these forms or devices that we now turn.

Separation of Powers

Separation of the legislative, executive, and judicial powers of government into separate branches of government is the most fundamental institutional feature of the national government. Two ideas underlying the concept of separation of powers are immediately familiar:

> The accumulation of all powers, legislative, executive, and judiciary, in the same hands, whether of one, a few, or many and whether hereditary, self-appointed, or elective, may justly be pronounced the very definition of tyranny. . . . [T]he preservation of liberty requires that the three great departments of power should be separate. . . .[20]

First, the mere "accumulation" or concentration of power is tantamount to tyranny because any such monopoly of power will inevitably be abused. Second, salvation lies in distributing power among three branches of government. All this seems so familiar and natural that Americans cannot imagine sensible men looking at the matter in any other light. But this was an essentially novel idea when the American system was created, and it is not an universally accepted idea today. It gives American government a strongly distinctive character.

It is indeed natural to regard government as divisible into various functions, perhaps even into the modern trio: legislative—law-making; executive—carrying out law and actually conducting the public business; judicial—applying law in particular cases. But not until the seventeenth and eighteenth centuries did men (like John Locke and Montesquieu) begin to think that these three *functions* should be distributed among different *branches* of government. The new thought was that the difference in functions should become the principle of government structure. The various functions of government had existed in earlier systems (and had been recognized by political theorists). But either they were not distributed at all or else were not distributed according to any principle. That is, either a monarch, an aristocratic body, or a popular assembly singly performed all the functions; or else the functions were haphazardly and overlappingly performed by the various organs of government. The systematic assignment of the legislative, executive, and judicial functions to separate branches of government is the novel and striking feature of separation of powers.

As we saw in Chapter 1, the colonial governments from the outset had some separation of powers. Conflict between legislative assemblies and royal governors hardened the separation. By 1776, separation of powers in some form was almost automatically written into the first state

---

[20] *Federalist* 47, p. 301.

constitutions.[21] In the Articles of Confederation, there was none because there was not enough power worth separating; that is, federalism was regarded as a sufficient barrier to central tyranny. But in forming a powerful "federal and national" government, the Constitutional Convention almost unquestioningly based it upon separation of powers. We inquire now into the reasoning upon which the doctrine of separation of powers rests.

A Barrier to Tyranny over the People

Separation of powers has three aims, two dealing with tyranny and one with achieving competent government. The simplest of the three aims is to protect the people from tyrannical government. The idea is that power divided is power less likely to be used oppressively. In a more elegant eighteenth-century phrase—popular liberty is better secured when three distinct bodies must concur in schemes of usurpation and perfidy. The separate functions are thus entrusted to separate branches so that each may be a check upon the others. But the Framers knew that it was not enough to enshrine separation of powers merely in the "parchment provisions" of the Constitution. The danger was that one branch might in reality overwhelm the others and concentrate all power within itself, behind the facade of the Constitution. Accordingly, for separation of powers to be a barrier to tyranny, it must neutralize not governmental tyranny in general, but tyranny in the various forms it can take—legislative, executive, or judicial tyrannies in particular.

Danger from the executive branch. Executive tyranny would appear to have been the chief fear. Did not the Declaration of Independence strike the basic and permanent note when it tied American independence to a struggle against executive tyranny in the person of King George III? Yet the leading Framers had reasons for not regarding the executive as the greatest danger in the new system they were devising. On the contrary, they thought that the outstanding lesson of the post-Revolutionary decade was the tendency to executive feebleness. The legislatures, they believed, had become dangerously dominant in the new state governments; they believed also that this legislative predominance was the natural tendency of representative democracies. And, of course, the Articles of Confederation, for 'pure federal' reasons, had necessarily lacked a strong national executive. Thus, far from being concerned to hamstring the executive, the Framers wanted to create a strong executive branch, confident that the other elements of the constitutional system would sufficiently guard against executive tyranny over the people.

Their confidence rested upon two main checks provided by the system,

---

[21] The Constitution makes no provision for separation of powers in the state governments. This was naturally left to the state constitutions. However, the doctrine has been so completely accepted that all the state governments have always maintained some form of separation of powers.

as well as, of course, upon separation of powers. First, the Presidency is basically a democratic elective office. As we have seen, the citizenry from the outset, despite indirect election by the Electoral College, decisively influenced the outcome. Presidential power, like all political power under the Constitution, results primarily from winning majorities in free, popular elections. Second, although a very powerful office, the executive still lacks one supremely dangerous ingredient—the prerogative. This was the British king's area of personal and independent authority, a vast region of little-defined discretionary power, relatively free from parliamentary control, the king's to exercise as he desired; it was thus always a threat in the background to law and to constitutional government. The President is constitutionally vested with the very broad "executive power" and thus has in truth a "touch of the prerogative". But his powers must derive from the Constitution; he can appeal to no source, like the prerogative, beyond it. (E.g., he cannot, as the executive can in many countries, independently declare a national emergency and suspend "the ordinary processes of government.")

Of course, separation of powers itself profoundly restrains the Presidency. The bulk of governing powers are constitutionally granted to a Congress; and the senators and representatives—close to popular opinion, closely allied with local interest groups, rooted in state politics, and vividly aware of their legislative dignities—are a strong check upon the executive. Finally, the President has to deal with a powerful and independent judiciary which has broad authority to set boundaries and give meanings to the laws he enforces and to his means of enforcing them.

These restraints which made the leading Framers little fearful of executive tyranny have worked. Election, limited discretionary power, and the necessity for more or less peaceful coexistence with Congress and the courts result in an executive safely kept—thus far at least—from tyrannizing over the people.

Danger from the legislative branch. What the constitutional designers really feared was legislative dominance. The representative legislature is the very essence of the republican idea. Possessing most of the great powers of government and intimately connected with the interests and opinions of local constituencies, the lawmaking body was thought to have the advantage in conflicts with the other branches. The Framers regarded it as the branch likeliest to succeed in deceiving and dominating the people; this was the "elective despotism" Jefferson warned of. The Constitution's main institutional protection against the danger of legislative tyranny is separation of powers. Because of the separation, the legislature needs the concurrence of the other two branches before its laws become effective, and the executive and judiciary are given additional means to resist it. Further, the executive and judiciary can alert the people to the danger and rally them against any usurping movement in the legislative branch. The constitutional design thus depends on an executive and judiciary capable of combatting the legislature.

Danger from the Majority Itself

Thus far we have considered only the first aim of separation of powers —preventing tyranny *over* the people, from whatever branch the tyranny originates. But it has a second and subtler aim. It also seeks to thwart tyranny *by* the people, that is, tyranny of the majority over minorities. Nothing in the structure of 'unseparated' democratic governments slows down majority action; whatever Demos wants, Demos promptly gets. Separation of powers seeks to introduce a retarding factor. But separation of powers obstructs a tyrannizing majority differently and more subtly than it obstructs tyranny by government over the people. Against the latter, separation of powers relies upon and cooperates with majority rule. That is, the majority can rally behind a befriending branch or branches and in time can subdue the tyrannical branch. The problem is obviously different when the tyranny is supported by the majority itself. The legislative branch, for the same sort of reasons that it was deemed likeliest to tyrannize over the people, was deemed likeliest also to become the vehicle for tyranny by the majority. As a brake on majority tyranny, as we shall see, the aim of separation of powers is to create an executive and judiciary capable of temporarily blocking popular will as expressed through a compliant or demagogic legislature.

Separation of Powers and Competent Government?

But separation of powers does not function solely to forestall tyranny, whether over or by the people. That is how it is usually conceived. Indeed, many modern observers believe that the Framers were so excessively fearful of political power that they dangerously fragmented the government; that they set the separate branches against each other and thus encouraged stalemate and inefficiency—potentially disastrous in the modern world.[22] But, ironically, this was not at all how the leading Framers understood what they were doing. On the contrary, they saw a third aim of separation of powers: It was the only practicable way then to strengthen government in general and assure some substantial coherence and effectiveness.

The modern critics blame stalemate on the ability of the separated Congress to frustrate presidential leadership. They contrast the 'obstructive' American Congress with the legislative body in an idealized parliamentary system where there is no separation of powers. There the executive is drawn from the legislature and functions within it with the support of tractable party majorities. The modern critics suggest that something like this would have provided stronger, more effective government in America.

But what kind of parliamentary system would in fact have been

---

[22] See, for example, James MacGregor Burns, *The Deadlock of Democracy* (Englewood Cliffs, N.J.: Prentice-Hall, Inc., 1963).

created in 1787? The best guess is one with the kind of weak executive then typical in the states and, moreover, one in which the centrifugal tendencies of American federalism would have had dangerously free play. Apart from the factors tending to executive feebleness in a representative democracy, the divisive tendencies of the states would probably have been fatal to any American parliamentary system. These divisive tendencies, so crippling under the Confederation, would probably have produced a Congress unwilling to create the strong executive a parliamentary system needs. (The same would probably be true today. Would the proud and suspicious states really be willing to submerge their identities in an all-powerful Parliament?) By contrast, under the Constitution the separate executive served from the outset as an integrating and nationalizing force. In any event, this was precisely what the leading Framers wanted. They saw separation of powers not as a way to create a legislature capable of resisting the executive, but just the other way around. Accordingly, by virtue of separation of powers, the Constitution makes possible an independent and powerful executive, capable of curbing legislative anarchy or tyranny and of supplying leadership to the American polity.

In Part III of this book we examine closely the relations of President and Congress. Here it suffices to emphasize that the original aim was to create the basis for a powerful executive. Tocqueville noted this constitutional power and foresaw its development.

> The President . . . possesses almost royal prerogative, which he has no opportunity of exercising; and the privileges which he can at present use are very circumscribed. The laws allow him to be strong, but circumstances keep him weak.[23]

Tocqueville predicted the circumstances which would conjure presidential power into being from its constitutional basis—the immensely complicated and dangerous problems of war and domestic crisis from which the modern Presidency has in fact developed. But this development rests upon the constitutional basis of 1787. The Framers knew that Congress could not of itself cope with such problems. By separating the executive from Congress, they made possible a powerful executive and thus deliberately laid the foundations of the modern Presidency.

Branches Capable of Retarding and Leading

In the American democratic republic there is no problem that Congress will not be a powerful and assertive body. That is easily provided for. But precisely how does the constitutional system provide an executive and judiciary capable of retarding threats to liberty from either the legislature or the people and of supplying long-range leadership? The first step is obvious: The executive and judiciary must be independent branches of

---

[23] *Op. cit.*, I, 131.

government. Accordingly, the Constitution itself establishes as firmly as possible their jurisdictions, appointment processes, and financial bases; these matters are not left at the mercy of the legislature. But much more is required even than this.

The "mixture" of powers. Further to give the executive and judiciary the constitutional wherewithal to retard and lead, the Constitution partially *mixes* or *blends* as well as separates the powers of government. It does not treat each function of government as having exact boundaries, with each branch assigned exclusive jurisdiction over all aspects of its function. On the contrary, the executive and the judiciary are each constitutionally assigned *shares in the legislative power*.[24] For example, the President's veto gives him, so to speak, one sixth of the legislative power. That is, it takes one sixth more (the difference between an ordinary and a two-thirds majority) of the vote of each house to override his veto. The President is also empowered, indeed required, to propose legislation and report to Congress on the "state of the Union." That is, he is constitutionally obliged to spend part of his time thinking as a legislator. An immense output of modern legislation is executive-originated and rests upon this constitutional base. As to the judiciary, the judges touch on the legislative realm quite specifically in reviewing the constitutionality of laws and other official acts, and they have a broad range of discretion in interpreting and applying the laws Congress makes. One aim of this mixture of powers, paradoxically, is to achieve the maximum separation of powers practicable. The belief here is that the executive and judiciary can maintain their independence as checks upon the popular legislature only when they are strengthened by sharing in the legislative power.

The "personal motives" to retard and lead. Checks upon power, however, are not automatically and invariably good things. Thus the doctrine of separation of powers does not intend that the branches should constantly obstruct each other. That would bring government, imbecilically, to a halt. Similarly, it is senseless if the separate branches prevent each other from acting justly or usefully. In short, separation of powers makes sense only if it restrains what should be restrained while permitting efficient government otherwise. It makes sense, for example, only if Presidents and judges typically restrain not majorities, but only foolish or tyrannical majorities. This is precisely the belief upon which the leading Framers acted: Separation would tend to forestall foolish and tyrannical measures, while the separate branches would ordinarily collaborate efficiently in proper measures. A famous passage from *The Federalist* states the underlying argument:

> The great security . . . consists in giving to those who administer each
> department the necessary constitutional means and personal motives to

---

[24] The legislature also inevitably shares in this mixture of powers. For example, the Senate shares in the presidential powers of appointing federal officers and making treaties; Congress as a whole creates, supports, and to a degree controls the executive departmental organizations and controls important aspects of judicial organization and jurisdiction.

resist encroachments of the others . . . . Ambition must be made to counteract ambition. The interest of the man must be connected with the constitutional rights of the place . . . . This policy of supplying, by opposite and rival interests, the defect of better motives, might be traced through the whole system of human affairs, private as well as public.[25]

It is not enough, the argument runs, to equip the executive and judicial branches with the constitutional means to check each other. They must also have the motives, that is, the will to resist and lead popular opinion. But why in a democratic society will they too not pander to popular favor? The answer is *not* that Presidents and judges would always be men of outstanding virtue and wisdom. Rather, the constitutional system relies heavily on their *"personal* motives": The private passions and interests of Presidents and judges are expected to lead them to protect liberty and advance long-run national interests.

But what personal motives will perform this remarkable task? Only a very long excursion into political philosophy would lead to the answer. But the enigmatic passage just quoted supplies the main clue in the word ambition. Truly ambitious men do not readily yield to *momentary* popular clamor because thus yielding produces little *lasting* fame or power. Ambitious Presidents and judges know that the dignity and privileges of their offices will be diminished in the long run if they make themselves mere puppets of popular opinion. They will not want these offices made foolish or servile. The constitutional belief is that Presidents and judges will stand firm for reasons of self-interest. They will gamble that their own power and prestige will be greater than ever when the majority comes to its senses. In this way, separation of powers seeks to supply democracy with officers who, because they hold important and powerful offices and because they can satisfy their ambitions in those offices, will tend to oppose momentary follies and self-destructive errors on the part of the democracy.

But the system does not depend entirely upon selfish personal interest. It relies also on the sense and decency of the office-holder and seeks to enhance that sense and decency. The executive and judiciary, as we have seen, are great offices, are based upon the broadest national constituency, are given tasks where the national interest most vividly presents itself, and are given terms of office sufficient to kindle their best ambitions. Under such circumstances they are expected to strive to be as big and national as the offices they hold, and to execute and adjudicate in the national interest skillfully, as it were, out of a sense of professional honor. Indeed, the constitutional system depends generally upon a certain portion of decency in the citizenry and their representatives. No constitutional scheme can indefinitely save a corrupt or utterly foolish people from disaster or tyranny. The Constitution presupposes a citizenry that appreciates liberty and is capable of pursuing its self-interest in an enlightened

---

[25] *Federalist* 51, pp. 321–22.

way. And it assumes an equal or greater portion of decency in the three branches of government, and that they will ordinarily cooperate efficiently under a properly arranged Constitution.

In short, separation of powers is a rather fragile device, requiring good sense and moderation. The public generally, and Presidents, judges, and legislators in particular, must respect the separate jurisdictions of the branches despite, indeed because of, the difficulty of drawing boundary lines. It must also be remembered that separation of powers is an organic part of a subtle constitutional system, needing other parts of the system for its own operation and itself in turn necessary to their functioning. For example, separation of powers is closely linked to judicial review (see pp. 229–30), whereby the Supreme Court pronounces on the boundaries of the three branches. Similarly, separation of powers depends upon the "multiplicity of interests" which lessens the likelihood of majority "factions." (Of what use would separation of powers be if a determined Communist majority formed in this country? Would a Communist President, Communist Court, and Communist Congress check and

Two 'upper' houses: medieval and modern. In the picture of the British House of Lords under Edward I, whose reign was noted for its "Model Parliament" (1295), note presence of the King and evidences of aristocratic authority. The United States Senate is shown during their vote ratifying the 1963 atomic test ban treaty. The President is not permitted to attend a Senate Session without an invitation.

balance each other?) At the same time, the very existence of the independent branches tends to foster the necessary "multiplicity." The forming and reforming of diverse groups for immediate, limited purposes is encouraged by the differences in times and manner of election, sizes of constituencies, and kinds of power that characterize separation of powers.

Bicameralism

Bicameralism (from the Latin *bi*, meaning two, and *camera*, meaning a chamber) is the division of the legislature into two houses. It may be understood essentially as a variant of separation of powers. This suggests that there is more to bicameralism than the familiar opinion that Congress was divided simply so that the states might be equally represented in one house. Bicameralism is not limited to federal systems; it is also appropriate and is used in unitary systems. Indeed, the American Senate is organized as a separate house in part for a guiding and restraining purpose entirely unconnected with federalism. Its origins suggest that purpose.

Precursors of Bicameralism

The American Senate can be understood in contrast with the ancient Roman Senate, the remote forebear from which it takes its name. The Roman Senate (from *senex*, meaning old and, presumably, wise) was supposed to guide and restrain the popular will as expressed through other governing organs. In practice, the Roman Senate was selected by the aristocratic patricians; that is, it represented a social and economic class. The second house in the English system, the Lords, functioned similarly; it was an hereditary noble body counterbalancing the commoners. Medieval France had what could be called a tricameral system, consisting of the three estates (from the Latin *status*); the different bodies represented distinct classes within the society. These three earlier systems all presupposed aristocratic society, a society radically divided into different classes or stations in life. The divided legislative bodies were to represent these different classes in the society. Early bicameralism, if it can be called that, was thus part of the ancient idea of the mixed regime. This was the theory that the best practical government was one that blended the three pure forms of monarchy, aristocracy, and democracy. A king would superintend the general interests of society, separate bodies would represent the aristocracy and the general citizenry, and all three would be checks upon each other. The mixture was supposed to yield the best and avoid the worst aspects of each pure form.

Modern Democratic Bicameralism

The American version of bicameralism is fundamentally different because the American society is overwhelmingly democratic. The American Senate does not and cannot have the aristocratic foundation of the roughly comparable bodies in the earlier systems. It is designed to fit into a democratic system that rests upon ultimate majority rule. But the contrast with the earlier systems reveals a distinctive feature of the American Senate. The constitutional scheme is that, within a democratic polity, the Senate is in some ways to be the upper house, supplying some of the advantages of the old mixed regime idea. Rather like the separate executive and judiciary, the Senate is devised to prevent the dominance of the popular house:

> When the people . . . call for measures which they themselves will afterward . . . lament and condemn . . . how salutary will be the interference of some temperate and respectable body of citizens . . . to check . . . the blow meditated by the people against themselves, until reason, justice, and truth can regain their authority over the public mind.[26]

As the most directly popular organ of the government, the House has

---

[26] *Federalist* 63, p. 384.

to be a large and, potentially, frequently changing body. But this, it was reasoned, makes it subject to erratic and ill-considered gusts in popular opinion. Accordingly, the Senate is made a much smaller body with greater continuity, the better to be able to check the presumably rash House, and to supply positive leadership as well. Competent government, especially in matters of foreign policy, requires "system," long-range planning of "well-chosen and well-connected measures."[27] The popular House is less likely to supply such legislative leadership because its members serve shorter terms, are more often removed from office, and are more likely to be neglectful of national and long-run interests in favor of the wishes of the constituents they face every two years. The Senate is constructed to secure experience, stability, and a national outlook. Senators ordinarily come from large and hence more diversified constituencies. Their six-year term gives greater time for statesmanship. The system of staggered elections, by which only one third of the Senate can change during a given election, encourages continuity of policy. Further, the Senate is given greater responsibility than the House in the sobering areas of foreign affairs, appointing national officers, and judging impeachments.

Constitutionalism: The Question of Limited Government

Constitutionalism can be understood as the opposite of unlimited and arbitrary political power. That is, a constitution is designed to limit government so that government may not do whatever it pleases whenever and however it pleases. Constitutionalism assumes various forms depending upon the standard and the methods of limitation employed. But in its simplest sense, all constitutionalism involves the very idea of law itself, as in the familiar maxim: 'A government of laws and not of men.' Of course, this maxim cannot be understood literally since in fact laws cannot govern of themselves, but always require men to make and execute them, and adjudicate issues arising under them. What is intended is the rule of men *bound* by law, that is, an actual government of men like an ideal government of laws—regular, rational, and aimed at the public interest, rather than arbitrary and based merely upon desire and power. The rule of law entails many things: The network of law constrains all government action, those who govern are also subject to the laws they make, government acts according to known and established procedures and through general laws and policies rather than by specific acts of favoritism or harshness directed against specific individuals. A vital supposition underlies the principle of rule of law: If government follows these procedures, it will tend to do what is intrinsically fair and just. It is believed that procedural regularity somehow tends to yield substantive justice.

But American constitutionalism goes beyond the general idea of a

---

[27] *Ibid.*, p. 383.

government of laws. It includes specific concepts of limited government and, accordingly, specific kinds and techniques of limitation. It holds that these are essentially embodied in the written Constitution, which is the fundamental law that limits ordinary government. This primacy of the Constitution reflects the two major principles of the Declaration of Independence. First, the Constitution is regarded as fundamental, and thus supreme, law because it embodies the basic will of the people, expressed in their constitutive capacity. That is, the Constitution is instituted by the *consent of the governed*. Second, Americans believe that the Constitution provides the major and adequate arrangements necessary to liberty; that is, the Constitution adequately secures the *inalienable rights* of the people. From the force of these two principles the Constitution acquires an immense force in American political opinion, so immense that American government and politics have a peculiarly constitution-alized character. We examine in detail in Chapter 4 the kinds of limitations that flow from this constitutionalization of government. Here we are concerned only with the broad principles involved in the American concept of limited government.

Limiting the Scope of Government: "The Pursuit of Happiness"

What the Declaration of Independence means by "the pursuit of happiness" indicates an important (and controversial) aspect of the American concept of constitutionally limited government. At a minimum, the Declaration means that men themselves have the right largely to determine wherein their happiness lies rather than have government and the public authorities determine it for them. This involved a great change from traditional political thought. Until the seventeenth century, most political philosophies rested upon conceptions of natural or divine justice. In these philosophies government's function was to secure justice (not rights) and to assist mankind to achieve the closest possible approxima-tion to what nature or the divine will intended. From this it tended to follow that, in principle, government properly could control every aspect of human behavior. Official authority and not private judgment was made the arbiter of how happiness should be pursued. Above all, this meant a close connection between the political and religious spheres. For example, in the Middle Ages, governmental and quasi-governmental institutions tended to regulate minutely the moral and economic life of the people. In the sixteenth and seventeenth centuries, these practices had culminated either in corruption or in extreme religious tyranny and savage religious wars.

In revulsion, philosophers like Hobbes, Locke, and Montesquieu shifted the emphasis of government from the achievement of justice (which opened the door to the excesses) to the securing of rights. These new views were reflected in the Declaration's emphasis on rights and thus on the private pursuit of happiness. In the religious sphere, this means tolerance of differences and separation of church and state. In the economic sphere, this means the continuous process of an essentially free play of economic forces. Unquestionably, the American constitutional system presupposes a free, private, commercial society. But this does not mean that it requires laissez-faire capitalism, nor is it to say precisely what kinds and degrees of governmental regulation and control are compatible with the constitutional system. There has never been a time when American economic theory and practice required the absence of governmental regulation. But it is, of course, immensely difficult to draw the line between what may and what may not be regulated. Each generation works out its own balance in these matters. But this much must be emphasized: While the Constitution is compatible with a broad range of economic and social practice, it embodies that principle of limited government which rests upon a bias in favor of the primarily *private* pursuit of happiness. Some fundamental limitations on the scope of government are indispensable to the constitutional system.

Limiting the Power of Government: Federalism and the Specific Protections of Liberty

The American constitutional system employs two other major modes of limitation: the federal division of power between the central and state governments, and the many specific prohibitions and procedural requirements in the original Constitution and the Bill of Rights. These are efforts, not to reduce the scope or reach of government, but to limit or constrain the power by means of which government performs the tasks assigned to it. These are of such importance, and have generated so many aspects of the American political order, that they are reserved for separate consideration in Chapter 4, which is focused on the powers of the national government.

The Constitution: Fixed or Flexible?

A written constitution designed to limit the powers of government is subject to two opposite dangers. It may be interpreted so narrowly that it is converted, say, into a fixed and rigid eighteenth-century legal code, doomed to disregard because government cannot then deal with changing political problems. Or it may be interpreted so flexibly that it becomes a mere facade behind which politics operates as it pleases. The two extremes to be avoided are easily stated. But it is difficult in practice to adhere to the mean between the extremes.

Adapting the Constitution

We may find a guide in John Marshall, an early and great Chief Justice of the Supreme Court:

[This is] a constitution intended to endure for ages to come, and consequently, to be adapted to the various crises of human affairs. To have prescribed the means by which government should, in all future time, execute its powers, would have been to change entirely, the character of the instrument, and give it the properties of a legal code. It would have been an unwise attempt to provide, by immutable rules, for exigencies which . . . can be best provided for as they occur.[28]

In his view the Constitution consists of fundamental principles and arrangements which give the American polity its essential character. These principles and arrangements are so designed as to be capable of guiding conduct in varying circumstances. In any given decade, new institutions, new practices, and new judicial interpretations must be inferred and developed from the constitutional principles for dealing with the problems of that decade. But the Constitution is not those particular institutions, practices, and interpretations; it remains the source of fundamentals from which they are derived. Thus it is adaptable but firm in its essential character. In this lies the strength of the constitutional system. Yet at the same time there is the unavoidable risk that under guise of adaptation to changing circumstances the Constitution may in effect be distorted and ultimately scrapped. The task is always to judge whether a proposed innovation is consistent with the basic constitutional order. This depends upon whether the innovation conforms to the essential principles of the order. To judge wisely requires of each generation a renewed understanding of the constitutional design.

Changing the Constitution

The Constitution is "adapted to the various crises of human affairs" by judicial interpretation, by executive and legislative actions that go unchallenged and become constitutional custom, by shifting public opinion and the forces that mold opinion. But it is not enough that the Constitution may be *adapted;* it is also capable of *change.* The Framers were aware that time might disclose basic inadequacies in the original design which it would be impossible or dangerous to try to interpret away. Accordingly, they provided for amendments to the Constitution.

Some have argued that the amending process was rigged to prevent any real change by enabling a tiny minority to block an amendment. Since three quarters of the states must ratify an amendment, opposition by one quarter of the states plus one kills an amendment. Thus, *bare* majorities in the 13 *least populous* states could block an amendment desired by overwhelming majorities in the 37 most populous states. Conceivably, then, a tiny fraction of the national popular vote would prevail against the democratic majority. This 'scare arithmetic' has been an important argument for those who have regarded the Constitution as undemocratic. But turn the arithmetic around. Bare majorities in the

---

[28] *McCulloch* v. *Maryland*, 4 Wheat. U.S. 316 (1819).

38 least populous states can *pass* amendments against the opposition of overwhelming majorities in the 12 most populous states. A national minority can pass an amendment. In short, the requirement of an extraordinary numerical majority of states does not mean an extraordinary national popular majority.

The real aim and practical effect of the complicated amending procedure is not to give power to minorities, but to require *nationally distributed* majorities. It is only accidental that the procedure contains the possibility of a minority blocking (or passing) an amendment. The aim of requiring nationally distributed majorities is to insure that no amendment could be passed simply with the support of a few populous states or sections. In this sense, it was another concession to the 'pure federalists' who feared dominance by the great states. And, harking back to "multiplicity of interests," it was also hoped that a nationally distributed majority, engaged in the solemn process of constitutional amendment, would favor only necessary and useful amendments. The solemn process also prevents, as was hoped, such a proliferation of amendments as would make the Constitution the patchwork of carelessly conceived amendments which many state constitutions have become. There have been only 24 amendments in nearly two centuries, indeed only 14 if the original Bill of Rights is subtracted. Adaptation rather than change has been the system's main mode of adjustment to changing circumstance.

In short, the amending process is another example of a device, compatible with democracy, that tends to preserve constitutionalism while empowering government competently to face its problems.

To sum up: The underlying aim of the constitutional system is, upon the basis of democracy, to render government adequately powerful and competent to its tasks, and yet to guard effectually against perversion of the power that has to be granted. We have been examining the principal elements of that power and that effectual guard. *Democracy:* "Final social power" rests with majorities. *Multiplicity of interests and sects:* Majorities emerge only by coalition from a special kind of social diversity. *Representation:* Government is conducted by representatives, selected in ways that foster judgment and skill. *Separation of powers* and *bicameralism:* Government offices are arranged so as to retard, guide, and thereby moderate democratic will. *Constitutionalism and limited government:* The scope of government and the exercise of its political power are constrained by the constitutional system.

BIBLIOGRAPHICAL NOTE

The two most important works on the American political order, as the frequent references to them attest, are *The Federalist* and Tocqueville's *Democracy in America*. Many readings suggested at the end of the previous two chapters are, as their titles indicate, relevant here as well.

The subjects dealt with in this chapter are major themes in political philosophy. Accordingly, any number of the great political philosophers may be recommended here for further reading. Aristotle's *Politics* is perhaps at once the most difficult and the most comprehensive and profound. The writings of Hobbes, Locke, and Montesquieu, are among those most relevant to the study of American problems. Introductory essays on them (and on other writers mentioned in this book) may be found in *History of Political Philosophy*, Leo Strauss and Joseph Cropsey eds. (1963).

Readings on the "undemocratic Constitution" are given at the end of Chapter 2. Regarding problems of democracy more generally, a variety of points of view are presented in: Henry Steele Commager, *Majority Rule and Minority Rights* (1944); Robert A. Dahl, *A Preface to Democratic Theory* (1956); Martin Diamond, "Democracy and *The Federalist:* A Reconsideration of the Framers' Intent," in the *American Political Science Review* (March, 1959); Willmoore Kendall, *John Locke and the Doctrine of Majority Rule* (1941); and Yves Simon, *Philosophy of Democratic Government* (1951). The student will find in these works many suggestions for additional readings.

Two famous studies of representative government are: Edmund Burke, "Speech to the Electorate at Bristol" (1774) and John Stuart Mill, *Considerations on Representative Government* (1861). C. H. McIlwain, *Constitutionalism, Ancient and Modern* (1947) is a useful introduction to problems of constitutionalism.

Arthur N. Holcombe, *Our More Perfect Union* (1950) analyzes the American political system in terms of the principles of the Framers. Conyers Read, ed., *The Constitution Reconsidered* (1938) is a collection of essays that deal with many of the subjects of this chapter.

Chapter 4

The American Constitutional System: Powers and Constraints

WE NOW EXAMINE THE CONSTITUTIONAL POWERS OF THE NATIONAL GOVERN-ment together with the constitutional constraints upon them. These matters lie within the field of study known as *constitutional law*. In America, constitutional law is the study of the legal problems arising when power is constitutionally allocated among separate branches and levels of government, all of which are accountable to those whom they affect, and when law and the judicial branch are the arbiters of the limits of national and state power.[1] This chapter pursues, primarily from the constitutional-law point of view, the basic inquiry: Do the constitutional powers render the national government competent to achieve the public interest without subverting either the democratic authority or the individual liberties which the government was designed to secure?

This concentration on law and constitutional power is significant. The study of government requires the study of political power in all its manifold aspects. But the *constitutionalization* of power and giving a special primacy to law are peculiarly important in the American polity. The concentration on the legal would be inappropriate in studying countries (e.g., some in Latin America and the Middle East) where the official constitution is ineffective and the political realities lie in simple force; it would only be somewhat less inappropriate in studying countries (e.g., France) where many of the political processes flow in channels not decisively affected by the official constitution. In America, however, the official constitution and its law very deeply affect the style and substance of government and politics.

For example, citizens in America usually ask two questions about public policy, while those of many other countries ask only one: Others simply ask *should* their national government do this or that; we also ask *may* ours do it under the Constitution. Thus, many Americans who

---

[1] The definition is paraphrased from the description in the Harvard Law School 1963–64 Catalogue of the school's famous course in constitutional law.

genuinely oppose racial discrimination believe that the national government's powers do not extend to general legislation on the subject and, therefore, that only the states have constitutional authority to deal with many aspects of discrimination. That is, their answer to the 'should' question regarding racial discrimination is offset by their answer to the constitutional 'may' question. And it goes without saying that some Americans, who favor racial discrimination quite apart from constitutional considerations, nonetheless effectively employ constitutional arguments to support their preference. The important point is that no such constitutional complication of both substance and rhetoric exists in, say, the French political system.

A peculiar American word usage reveals another aspect of the American constitutionalization of government. We usually speak of the power*s* of government, not, as a European might, of its power. This word usage indicates the extent to which we differ from many other polities in our conception of governing power. They tend to conceive of governing power as a single undifferentiated mass; we tend to conceive of our national government at least as depending upon particular powers constitutionally allocated to it.[2] This effort to govern ourselves according to particular grants and limitations contributes greatly to the unique importance we give to law and to legal modes of thought.

Indeed, in almost every aspect of our government and politics and in almost every episode of our history, disputes over the law of the Constitution have been somewhere near the center of our political stage. The Louisiana Purchase, the Civil War, the rise of industrialism, the New Deal and the welfare state, and strife over racial discrimination are a few of the instances that come readily to mind. A witty and informed English periodical commented on this quality of American politics as it was manifested in the very political collision between President Truman and Congress in 1951, when the President seized the steel mills during the Korean war:

> At the first sound of a new argument over the United States Constitution and its interpretation, the hearts of Americans leap with a fearful joy. The blood stirs powerfully in their veins and a new lustre brightens their eyes. Like King Harry's men before Harfleur, they stand like greyhounds in the slips, straining upon the start. Last week, the old buglenote rang out, clear and thrilling . . . .[3]

All of this is of course not in any way to suggest that the only power in the American system is what the Constitution formally distributes. For example, we do not find in the document any mention of congressional committee chairmen, of the great interest groups and their lobbyists, of

---

[2] The Tenth Amendment supports this view of the national government. In contrast, we tend to conceive of the state governments as (subject to whatever limits the state constitutions impose) the repositories of the general reservoir of governing power as distinguished from the national government's particular powers.

[3] The London *Economist,* May 10, 1952, quoted in Alan F. Westin, *The Anatomy of a Constitutional Law Case* (New York: The Macmillan Company, 1958).

state and city political bosses and machines, or of party leaders and organizations—all bearers of vital power. But to an important extent the main kinds of American governmental and political power (including those just named) emerge from, rest upon, and are shaped by the official constitutional grants and constraints. Accordingly, these are one key to the whole American governmental and political reality.

We shall proceed in this chapter under four headings. First, a look at the bare bones of the Constitution as a *legal* document, to see its characteristics, content, and design; second, the grants of the national powers in and of themselves, to learn in general what they are and what sense and unity they have; third, the national government in the context of the whole federal system, to see how everything the national government does influences, and is influenced by, the presence of constitutionally and politically powerful states; fourth, the specific constitutional limitations (such as those of the Bill of Rights) upon the granted powers; like the federal factor, these limitations affect every aspect of the national powers.

The Document

Three general characteristics of the constitutional document illuminate the whole.

First, the comprehensive political principles which we examined in Chapter 3 are fitted together in it into a tightly knit entity, a careful piece of legal draftsmanship. As such, the document encourages—and responds to—the American attempt to find prescriptions for all manner of public problems through analysis and explication of its words—through *construction,* to use the lawyer's technical term.[4] This characteristic of the document helps explain why American debates over policy issues so often tend to be conducted as debates over the meaning of these words. Out of this meaningfulness has grown the lively tradition and the immense literature of American constitutional law.

Second, the document itself was in turn created out of other traditions, those of Anglo-American common law and Anglo-American governmental practice. (Indeed the first sentence of its first article makes significant use of a common-law property term, "vested,"[5] and one of its most famous phrases, "by and with the advice and consent" [of the Senate], is the same as one in the traditional enacting clause of British statutes.)[6] The experienced lawyer-politicians who drafted the document understandably used the materials that they knew and that lay near at hand. And ever since then men trained in the same traditions have been leaders in the

---

[4] Thus one speaks of 'construing' a provision in a legal document in order to discover its full and correct significance.

[5] At common law a vested right is one that is immediate and fixed, fully and presently held.

[6] "Be it enacted by the King's most Excellent Majesty, by and with the advice and consent of the Lords Spiritual and Temporal, and Commons, in this present Parliament assembled, and by the authority of the same." See, e.g., Christopher Hughes, *The British Statute Book* (London: Hutchison University Library, 1957).

operation of the national government. In a profoundly important way the Constitution is a common-law and a common-law lawyers' constitution.

Third, the document has a decisively legal quality in still another sense. Some constitutions are purely *political;* they provide for the effectuation of their institutions and processes only through politics and the decisions of political bodies like legislatures. The American Constitution acquires a legal quality because it is in part effectuated through law, the courts, and legal processes as well. (This is one great reason for the vast influence of the American judiciary.[7]) Two constitutional provisions illustrate the difference. Article IV requires that "full faith and credit shall be given in each State to the public acts, records, and judicial proceedings of every other State." This is a legal provision; the courts recognize and give effect to it. Article IV also requires that "the United States shall guarantee to every State in this Union a republican form of government." This is a political provision; the Supreme Court has refused to allow it any judicial application. When the clause is given effect, it has to be voluntarily by Congress or the President.

The Preamble

The constitutional document begins with one of its few flourishes, a brief and eloquent statement of purpose traditionally called the Preamble.[8] It is settled law that the Preamble grants no powers and imposes no limitations.[9] However, attempts are occasionally made to extract concrete legal implications from it by construction. For example, some commentators argue that its opening phrase, "We, the people of the United States," implies that the national government was created by the people directly, and not by the states; this construction tends to reduce the stature of the states in the system. Others have tried to support broad views of the national powers by emphasis on the Preamble's broad statements of the objects of the Union.

After the Preamble, the Constitution proper, exclusive of amendments, is divided into seven parts, called articles. Each deals with one general subject.

The First Three Articles: Separate Organs of Government and Basic National Powers

The first three articles deal with Congress, the Presidency, and the judiciary respectively, and are hence commonly called the legislative, executive, and judicial articles. Here the fundamental powers are granted

---

[7] Compare Tocqueville, *op. cit.,* I, 102–109.

[8] The word preamble does not appear on the paper the Convention delegates signed in Philadelphia in 1787.

[9] For a remarkable, although considered by most scholars ultimately unsound, argument that the Preamble had great legal significance see William W. Crosskey, *Politics and the Constitution in the History of the United States* (Chicago: University of Chicago Press, 1953), I, 363–379.

and the three great branches constituted.[10] All three articles follow the same general pattern. Each confers its branch's powers, indicates the mode of their exercise, and sets some restrictions on them. Each decrees the structure of its branch, lists its principal offices, and provides for the selection of persons to fill them. Aristotle remarks that a constitution is an arrangement of offices; that is, the way "a citizen body distributes office"—the kinds of authority it establishes and those to whom it gives that authority—determines the characteristics of that country's regime or polity.[11] Thus when the three articles have made their arrangements, the basic frame of government is already seen emerging.

Article I: the legislative branch. Article I is the longest and most detailed of all, because of its necessarily complex provisions on organization and procedure and because it also contains the bulk of the whole government's grants and many of the limitations. Section 8 is an enumeration of most of the grants, and section 9 of the limitations. Section 10 is devoted to numerous limitations upon the states, mostly ones designed to protect the national powers from state interference.

Article II: the executive power and the Presidency. Article II begins with words that lead immediately into some of the numerous mysteries of the American Presidency: "The executive power shall be vested in a President. . . ." This is often compared with what may be an artful difference in the words of Article I, "All legislative powers *herein granted* . . . ." The President thus appears to possess "the executive power," general and undefined, while Congress possesses only those "powers herein granted." The latter formulation, at least on its face, seems more restrictive. Some experts, pointing to the preciseness of the Constitution's drafting, claim that the difference is deliberate. They see in the term "the executive power" a descendant of the powerful British executive, a distant but clear and intended echo of the common-law tradition and the prerogative power of the British crown. This view thus asserts that the draftsmen deliberately laid the basis for a broadly powerful Presidency. Other experts disagree, often on the ground that, intended or not, so important a constitutional—and political—conclusion should not be based on such delicate verbal nuances. The question has run through all the long history of political struggles over a strong executive versus legislative supremacy.

Article III: the judicial power and the judiciary. This article plainly builds with common-law materials—"during good behavior,"[12] "law and

---

[10] The term separation of powers does not appear in the Constitution. But even in the very form of the document each branch has a separate article and is separately empowered, and is thus given equal dignity with the others. Here, as so often, the practical lawyer-draftsmen do not state or discuss a principle, but simply use it.

[11] Aristotle's *Politics*, trans. E. Barker (New York: Oxford University Press, 1962), Book IV, Chapter 3, section 5, p. 161.

[12] A proper reading of the Constitution frequently requires that such general-seeming phrases be given their precise significance at common law. For example, "good behavior" meant simply not being convicted in the courts of an 'indictable' crime, i.e., a serious crime like murder, rape, or robbery. That is, good behavior did not refer to the realm of political misdeeds; hence the constitutional illegitimacy of many recent proposals to impeach the Chief Justice.

equity," "cases," "original jurisdiction," "appellate jurisdiction"—and is fully intelligible only when these are recognized and understood.

In conception and drafting, the article maneuvers skillfully both between judicial independence for the courts and control of them by the democratic legislature and also between the federal and national principles. It creates the Supreme Court, authorizes creation of lower courts, vests "the judicial power" in them—safely beyond the reach of Congress and President, specifies the jurisdictions these courts may exercise, and gives all judges what amounts to life tenure. But then it counterbalances this independence with Congress's broad powers over the jurisdictions. And the "judicial power" granted is itself not general. For example, it is clearly limited by federal considerations; it extends only to a list of cases where some national interest is involved—a range broad enough to protect national authority but narrow enough not to invade the ordinary administration of justice by the states.

The Last Four Articles

The last four articles complete the 'frame of government' established in the first three.

Article IV: the 'federal' article. This article contains the Constitution's principal express statements on the place of the states in the system.

Article V: amendment of the Constitution. This article grants the power to amend, but provides that it may be exercised only by a blend of congressional action and two forms of state (or popular) action. Thus states and nation—both parties to the federal bond—each have some voice in the amending process, and democratic provision is also made for popular participation as well. The article places only one express limitation on what can be done by amendment: No state may be deprived of its equal suffrage in the Senate without its consent. The argument has sometimes been made, however, that an amendment might be so contrary to the rest of the Constitution as to be void—unconstitutional. The question has not been settled, either by practice and agreement or by Supreme Court decision.

Article VI: the question of supremacy. Article VI contains the famous supremacy clause, whereby the Constitution and all national laws "made in pursuance thereof" are declared to be "the supreme law of the land." The clause establishes two kinds of supremacy, and the constitutional answers to all questions about the federal bond start from these neat, economical, and very legal arrangements. One kind is the supremacy of the Constitution itself over both national and state government. The Constitution is thus made "superior paramount law, unchangeable by ordinary means."[13] The second kind of supremacy is directed at the federal-national question and decrees national supremacy. Thus, it requires all state judges to uphold the "Constitution and the Laws of the

---

[13] *Marbury v. Madison*, 1 Cranch (U.S.) 137 (1803). In this case the Supreme Court made the Constitution's paramountcy the basis of the doctrine of judicial review.

United States," anything in their own state constitutions and laws to the contrary notwithstanding.

Article VII deals briefly with the means by which the Constitution is to be ratified (see pp. 55–56), and need not be considered here.

The Amendments

We need not examine the amendments in this brief overview of the Constitution as a document. Important as some are to the system, none is a central structural member of the framework of government. Some in fact are minor or obsolete, and two (the Eleventh and Twelfth) are early corrections of apparently unintended consequences of the original document. But, of course, some—like the Bill of Rights and the post-Civil War Fourteenth Amendment—are highly important in constraining governmental power, and are discussed in detail elsewhere.

The Powers of the National Government: Patterns and Characteristics

Two doctrines have conditioned the exercise of the national government's powers and therefore require notice before we examine the powers' patterns and characteristics. These are, first, the doctrine of delegated and enumerated powers and, second, the doctrine of separation of powers.

Analysis begins with the traditional statement that the national government is created by the Constitution, by which the sovereign people have *delegated* to this government certain powers therein *enumerated,* and have *reserved* to themselves or the states all powers not so delegated. These formulations sound old-fashioned, even trite. But vital constitutional fact and political reality lie behind their well-worn words.

The judgment that Lord Bryce, the eminent British analyst of American institutions, expressed in the 1880s remains sound:

> The subjection of all the ordinary authorities and organs of government to a supreme instrument expressing the will of the people, and capable of being altered by them only, has been usually deemed the most remarkable novelty of the American system.[14]

This "most remarkable novelty"—the concept of a paramount Constitution, as laid down in its supremacy clause—is rooted in the idea that the source of the supremacy is "the will of the people" (in the language of the Declaration of Independence, "the consent of the governed"). Next is the idea that the people have made the written Constitution their "supreme instrument." Finally there is the idea that by enumeration in this instrument they have delegated to the national government not an undifferentiated mass of governing power, but only those powers they have deemed proper ones for it to have. The result: a democratic system,

---

[14] James Bryce, *The American Commonwealth* (2 vols.; 3rd ed.; New York: The Macmillan Company, 1899), I, 37.

controlled by the specifications of a fundamental document. All the complicated granting, dividing, and limiting of the government's powers —so characteristic of the American system—is to operate within this doctrinal context. And the "ordinary authorities and organs of government," because they are in "subjection" to the supreme Constitution, are to exercise in their functions only such authority as reaches them through this series of narrow gates.

For many reasons, these ideas are sometimes more ignored than followed. But American political conflicts over what the government's powers are and how they are to be employed are always affected by the environment the ideas create. And—as we shall repeatedly see—so are American political processes generally.

Separation of powers similarly conditions politics and the exercise of the national powers. In Part Three, when we study the branches of the national government and their work, we shall examine some of the innumerable problems and difficulties separation of powers entails. Especially we shall need to see whether, as many fear, the separation stultifies or paralyzes the machinery of government. At present we need only note that the distribution of powers within the national government is in general accord with the principle of democratic responsibility; the great bulk of the main powers are granted to Congress, the representative and most directly popular branch. But the subtle blending and intermingling of powers causes the other branches to interact continuously with Congress in the actual process of governing. Later we shall study in detail the roles that are played in this process by the President, the administration, and the courts. Nonetheless, Congress and its powers are the center and the place to start.

The Patterns of the Grants: National Functions

At first glance (e.g., Art. I, sec. 8) the powers granted to Congress seem to be a very diverse collection, almost a jumble, with few links among the individual items and little apparent reason for some of them. For example, what relationship—if any—is there between the obviously vast and vital power to "regulate commerce . . . among the several states" and the seemingly trivial power to "fix the standard of weights and measures"? And why should the national government be concerned with the latter anyway?

Actually there is an underlying order. This is an order based on a calculated division of functions between nation and states. From it there emerges a national government that is sufficiently empowered to cope with the functions assigned to it and, further, that has some flexibility for development and adaptation as history and politics require. Of the national functions two stand out.

External affairs. One of these two concerns external affairs: relations with foreign nations and security against foreign dangers. Separation of powers operates revealingly. Congress is given the principal substantive powers, e.g., to provide and regulate an army and navy; to tax and borrow "to provide for the common defense"; to declare war. But the President's broad executive power is given full play; moreover he has related specific powers (to command the army and navy, to send and receive ambassadors —and hence to control diplomacy—and to negotiate treaties). He *conducts* all the external affairs over which Congress has substantive authority. His are the powers and duties of management and action and, as we shall see, of leadership.

In Chapter 15 we shall consider the complexities of the conduct of foreign affairs. Here the important points are, first, the pattern in the national powers and, second, the persistence of this pattern. War and diplomacy have changed mightily since the Framers' day, and the function has now become a gigantic enterprise that pervades the country's life and consumes perhaps a tenth of the national product. But the function is still in the same constitutional hands, and largely in the same form in which the Framers put it there, and still is carried out by means of the same grants of power. (And, we may add, is still subject to the same clashes between President and congressional groups as it was in John Adams's time.)

A national economy. The second function concerns the nation's economy. We have seen already how important the fostering of an "extended" and "commercial" republic was for the creation of the diverse society of a "multiplicity of interests." The proper extent of government control over the economy has been and is debatable; that the economy should be adequately national and unfragmented is not. The Constitution therefore gives the national government a set of powers appropriate to the task of fostering—and regulating—the requisite truly national economy, a nationwide area in which commerce can freely operate and diverse economic processes and groupings proliferate.

First, Congress has the great power to regulate interstate and foreign commerce. This power constitutional law has long held to be decisive, and able within its sphere to override any contrary or obstructive or limiting state regulation. It is the cornerstone. To it are added other substantial powers to create and protect the nationwide monetary system that a nationwide economy needs, e.g., the powers to create a national postal system and—not so trivial after all—to "fix the standard of weights and measures." Imagine the difficulties for nationwide business if the pound and inch varied from state to state; the Constitution has its acute and precise sense of the practical.

Correlatively, the states are placed under limitations to prevent them from interfering with this national economy. They may not coin money, "emit bills of credit" (that is, issue paper money), or make anything but gold and silver legal tender; the national monetary system is to be safe from them. And, crucially, they cannot cripple that legal enforceability of debts and obligations which lies at the root of a commercial economy.

The prohibition is neatly put, in common-law legal terms: They may not "pass any law impairing the obligation of contracts."

Like war and diplomacy, the national economy has been transformed since 1787. But note the very modern way in which the Constitution envisaged a national economy. This helps explain the basic continuity of the constitutional system. The vast developments of 175 years in government and the economy have not required that the Constitution be superseded. Rather, the developments were able to take place within the constitutional setting, by adaptation, and mediated by the system's own creative traditions.

The Characteristics of the Grants: Fullness of Power

The national powers all have some important common characteristics. The theme which organizes these characteristics is that though the powers have boundaries, within these boundaries they are full and sweeping; the grants are not made with a timid or a grudging hand.

First, the national government is *master of its own affairs;* it is not constrained by any compelled dependence on the states. This was, of course, the vital principle for which the Framers had contended, when they rejected a "merely federal" system (see pp. 40 *ff*). Thus, the national government does not have to act through the agency of the states. It appoints, pays, and controls its own officials, and enforces its laws in its own courts directly on individual citizens. And—an obvious but vital point—it rules its own seat of government.

Second, reflecting the tightly-knit logical structure of the constitutional document, the powers *reinforce* and *complement* each other. Thus, the national government does not have just the power to regulate commerce in a general way; it also has powers to regulate the money in which commerce is conducted, the mail on which it depends, the bankruptcies which may disturb, and the patents and copyrights which may stimulate or clog it, and so on. Similarly the commercial powers interlock with the war powers, each strengthening the other both in specifics and in the broad implications.

Third, the major granted powers are supported by some express auxiliaries (e.g., the power to coin money is supported by the power to punish counterfeiting) and in addition numerous further auxiliaries have been found to be implied. One of the most famous and most central of the express auxiliaries is the "necessary and proper" clause. The sweep of the language is notable; it empowers Congress to make

> *all* laws which shall be necessary and proper for carrying into execution the foregoing powers, and all other powers vested by this Constitution in the government of the United States, or in any department or officer thereof.[15]

---

[15] Art. I, sec. 8. Emphasis added.

This power's significance, and the significance of the idea of *implied powers,* is revealed in a contrast with the Articles of Confederation. The second of the Articles limited the Confederation to the exercise of its *"expressly"* delegated powers. That is, what was not said in so many words, the Confederation could not do; it could not derive any powers from the express grants by construction. The Constitution pointedly avoids limiting the national government in this way. Indeed, when the first Congress was considering the Tenth Amendment, some states' rights advocates tried to get the word "expressly" put in; this was rejected by Congress. The national government is therefore not limited to the exact letter of its express powers; it has as well whatever implied powers a reasonable construction of the constitutional document adds.

The wish to confine government within expressly and precisely stated limits is frequently based upon a utopian belief that government can somehow be given enough power to do necessary things but not enough to do harm. Were it that easy to place power under lock and key, liberty would not come at so great a cost in eternal vigilance. *Federalist* 31 deals persuasively with this futile hope:

> A government ought to contain in itself every power requisite to the full accomplishment of the objects committed to its care.

Further,

> there ought to be no limitation of a power destined to effect a purpose which is itself incapable of limitation.

The national government has such purposes; certain objects committed to its care, like national defense, involve

> dangers to which no possible limits can be assigned.

Accordingly, the national government's capacity to accomplish such objects

> ought to know no other bounds than the exigencies of the nation and the resources of the community.

In short, the characteristics of the national powers display a thrust toward *plenary* powers, toward authority fully commensurate with the responsibility.

The National Government and the States

So far we have discussed the national government's powers with almost no reference to the states. With the states off the stage, we have seen a powerful national government. But this government lives constantly in the presence of active and powerful state governments. The two tower up as the overwhelmingly dominant structures in the country's political landscape, and together they largely cause that immense complexity which startles and at first bewilders the student of American institutions . . . . There are two governments, covering the same ground, commanding with equally direct authority, the obedience of the same citizen.[16]

No single fact of American political life is more complex or more productive of the peculiar qualities of American constitutionalism and American politics than the fact of these two governments "covering the same ground."

Conflict and Resolution in the "Federal and National Compound"

This presence of two powerful governments in the constitutional system is the inevitable consequence of the compromise upon which the system is based. The system is a compound one which tries to fit together the national and federal principles. A distinctive characteristic of the compound is a constant jostling between the two governments and an equally constant necessity both for collaboration and also for resolution of conflicts.

The source of conflict is the clash between the national and federal principles: Both the national government, on the national principle, and the state government, on the federal principle, can and do claim final legal authority over the same citizens. But clearly there cannot be two final legal authorities on the same subjects. The American system attempts to resolve the conflict by means of a constitutional *division of subjects* over which the two governments have the final say. This is the familiar idea that each government is final and supreme within its constitutionally assigned sphere.

Dividing authority into two autonomous spheres encounters difficulty, however. Indeed, it may not be improper to compare the difficulty with a still more familiar one: rendering unto Caesar the things that are Caesar's and unto God the things that are God's. That there are two dominions may well be unchallenged. But three problems arise, problems that provide us with a basic outline for considering conflict and resolution in the American federal system. First, the two authorities inevitably tend, despite any agreed-upon division, to have overlapping concerns. Second, even reasonable men can and do disagree profoundly over what belongs to each dominion. Third, when there is collision between the two dominions, a method is needed for the final resolution of these overlaps, disagreements, and collisions.

The problem of overlapping concerns. Whatever the constitutional division of authority, in performing their respective functions both the national and state governments tend in practice to expand beyond any strict boundaries. It is a natural fact of our style of life and governing that the national and state governments often have concerns that overlap, and therefore sometimes clash. The ominous troubles that arise over

---

[16] Bryce, *op. cit.*, I, 17–18.

segregation of Negroes in public education is one painfully real example. Given its indubitable constitutional authority over defense, the national government is inevitably concerned that its citizens be educated (if for no other reason than that they be sufficiently literate to qualify for the draft), that the nation not be torn by internal strife, and that in the age of the Cold War America's international reputation not be tarnished by racial injustice. The state on the other hand is concerned to preserve its established social customs and to run its schools in ways it thinks best. And both governments are under intense political pressures to act, because belief and desire run high in this matter. Both governments are thus drawn into the same areas of activity and consequently into overlapping—and possibly conflicting—regulation.

The problem of boundaries: "the question . . . perpetually arising." Even when each government tries faithfully to stay within its sphere and no serious overlap of concerns occurs, there remains the sheer difficulty of deciding what matters have been assigned to the respective spheres. For example, it is settled constitutional law that only economic activities that involve or affect interstate commerce are subject to national regulation under the commerce power. But in practice where exactly does purely *intra*state commerce leave off and *inter*state commerce begin? Or consider again the problem of desegregation. A state university's policy on admitting students unquestionably comes under the authority of that state. But there is also a national power (and obligation) under the Fourteenth Amendment to see that all citizens receive "the equal protection of the laws." Where is the line to be drawn?

The problem was given a classic formulation by Chief Justice Marshall in the famous case of *McCulloch* v. *Maryland*. No one disagrees, he said, that there are two spheres and that the national government is limited to its granted powers. "But the question respecting the *extent of the powers actually granted*, is perpetually arising, and will probably continue to arise, as long as our system shall exist."[17] One classic pair of responses to the question dates from the earliest years of the Republic and is still current: *strict construction* versus *liberal construction* of the grants. Strict construction reads the grants narrowly and literally and is reluctant to see in them more than the express meanings. Liberal construction reads them broadly and with a readiness to see implied meanings in them. Thus, strict constructionists read the "necessary and proper" clause as granting no more than the power to enact laws *indispensably* necessary to carrying out the expressly granted powers. Liberal constructionists, on the other hand, read it as a broad aid to all the national powers, authorizing any and all means, not otherwise prohibited by the Constitution, that are *reasonably* adapted to effectuate the national powers.

The two schools of construction arose out of the first great political conflict under the Constitution, that between Jefferson's political forces

---

[17] *McCulloch* v. *Maryland*, 4 Wheat. (U.S.) 316 (1819). Emphasis added.

and the Federalist party led by Hamilton. The Jeffersonians were strict constructionists, the Hamiltonians, liberal. As is often the case, these constitutional views were linked to basic political and economic positions and interests. All this emerges clearly in their famous struggle over the establishment of the first Bank of the United States. The Hamiltonians strongly supported the project of a national financial institution, incorporated by the national government, as a means to further their basic policies; it would help the national element in the constitutional system to predominate, and would help create a truly national and commercial economy. The Jeffersonians as strongly opposed it; they saw the Bank as a possible instrument of monopoly and of political and economic influence for financial and commercial interests, and as likely to undermine the agrarian economy they favored. Above all, they saw in the Bank a threat to the powers of the states over local economic affairs. Still somewhat influenced by the small-republic idea, the Jeffersonians wanted to defend the federal element and to keep the national powers narrowly confined.

In the American style, the battle was fought as much in the language of constitutional law as in that of economics and politics. Both sides agreed that the national government had no express constitutional power to incorporate a bank. The constitutional issue therefore turned on the proper construction of the "necessary and proper" clause: Was the Bank a necessary and proper means to effectuate the express financial, commercial, and other powers of the national government? What precisely does "necessary" mean? Jefferson, as a strict constructionist, argued that the Bank "does not stand on that degree of *necessity* which can honestly justify it." As a liberal constructionist, Hamilton replied that "*necessary* often means no more than *needful, requisite, incidental, useful,* or *conducive to*."[18] In the end the liberal-construction view prevailed; President Washington supported Hamilton, Congress chartered the Bank, and the Supreme Court, on Hamiltonian grounds, upheld the act as constitutional.[19]

Similar disputes over the extent of the national powers are a perennial part of American politics. For example, those who oppose foreign economic aid often believe that the national government has no constitutional power to spend money for at least some of the program's purposes.[20] Supporters of the program contend that the power is clearly implied in the expressly granted powers over defense and foreign relations and also, as they read the constitutional language, in the power "to . . . collect taxes . . . to pay the debts and provide for the common defense and general welfare of the United States." In truth, the strict-construction and liberal-construction arguments are almost always available, and

---

[18] Quoted in The Staff, Social Sciences I, The College of the University of Chicago, ed., *The People Shall Judge: Readings in the Formation of American Policy* (2 vols.; Chicago: The University of Chicago Press, 1949), I, 420, 422. Emphasis in original.

[19] In *McCulloch* v. *Maryland.*

[20] E.g., Barry Goldwater, *The Conscience of a Conservative* (New York: Hillman Books, 1960), p. 98.

useful, political weapons. In many (though not by any means all) concrete situations there is some uncertainty and room for argument about constitutional meanings. However, liberal construction has been and continues to be the dominant view. Indeed, the country has never actually been governed under the strict construction.[21]

The problem of resolving conflict. Given the inevitability of conflict between nation and state, an official method for resolving conflict became indispensably necessary; it had to be settled who has the final power to pass upon the constitutional boundaries of state and national authority. The method adopted is characteristic of the American polity. The issue is treated as one of *law;* that is, the conflict is made to arise in the form of specific *cases* which come to the courts, and finally the Supreme Court, to decide. The Supreme Court is the "arbiter of the federal system."

The predominant principle which has guided the Court in resolving such conflicts can be well seen in Chief Justice John Marshall's opinion in *Gibbons* v. *Ogden*,[22] a famous case involving the Robert Fulton steamboats.

The state of New York granted a steamboat monopoly to Ogden. This barred the port of New York City to Gibbons, a New Jersey steamboat operator, and thus excluded him from the developing New Jersey–New York trade. There was no real quarrel here about the respective spheres of authority. No one denied that, if the national power over interstate commerce had not existed, New York could grant the monopoly and regulate New York harbor under her authority over *intra*state commerce. But on the other hand the New Jersey–New York trade was part of *inter*state commerce over which the national government unquestionably had authority. The question therefore was: When conflicting exercises of legitimate national and state power put the two governments on collision courses which of the two must yield the right of way? The Supreme Court's principle of resolution—and it has been the predominant American answer ever since—was ultimate national supremacy; no matter how well justified otherwise, "the acts of New York must yield to the law of Congress."

The rise and fall of one constitutional doctrine, usually called the doctrine of *dual federalism,* particularly illuminates the nature of the principle of national supremacy.

American states, subject to whatever limitations their own constitutions impose, have a general authority, commonly called the *police power*,[23] to govern their populations. Dual federalism commenced in a new answer that came to be given after Marshall's time to an old question

---

[21] See, e.g., Harry V. Jaffa, "The Case for a Stronger National Government," in Robert A. Goldwin, ed., *A Nation of States: Essays on the American Federal System* (Chicago: Rand McNally & Company, 1963), p. 119. But see Alfred H. Kelly and Winfred A. Harbison, *The American Constitution: Its Origins and Development* (3rd ed.; New York: W. W. Norton & Company, 1963), pp. 332–35.

[22] 9 Wheat (U.S.) 1 (1824).

[23] The term is only cognately related to policeman. It signifies the general power of internal government and regulation, and is ultimately from the Greek *polis,* city.

about the nation-state relationship: Does the state police power in and of itself limit the national powers? Originally, following the kind of logic we have seen in *Gibbons* v. *Ogden,* the Supreme Court, and authorities on constitutional law, emphasized national supremacy and held that the police power was not such a limitation. But gradually, beginning rather late in the nineteenth century, the Court began to indicate that it was. A well-known example will illustrate this.

In 1916 the national government, acting under the commerce power, forbade by law the shipment in interstate commerce of goods manufactured in factories employing child labor. The law undoubtedly had— and was intended to have—some repressive effect on the employment of child labor. But employment and working conditions are undoubtedly a local matter, subject to regulation by the police power of the state. Here was a clear collision. The Supreme Court held the national law unconstitutional, ruling that the national government could not so exercise the commerce power because the exercise reached into the domain of the state.[24] This was dual federalism; the powers and spheres of the nation and the states were to be kept entirely separate and distinct, by means of the rigid *exclusion* of the national from regulating any matter that was subject to the state power. In a sense this reversed the supremacy clause; that is, when the national authority collided with the state police power, the former was to yield. To say the least, this was a grave constriction of national ability to regulate nationwide problems (and a happy situation for large interests that would otherwise have been subject to national regulation).

But dual federalism met its downfall in the 1930s. The vast and dangerous problems of the Great Depression clearly exceeded state competence and clearly were appropriate subjects for the full exercise of the national powers. The dual-federalism notion of an automatic mechanical limit on these powers irrespective of the facts of the situation began to seem less and less reasonable and more and more a distortion of the Constitution. The Supreme Court returned to a modern form of its earlier view, that the national powers are indeed plenary and not limited in the dual-federalism fashion.[25]

The lesson learned has been heeded ever since. Today the national government may use its powers fully and freely on any subject they reach, even though such use may affect matters falling within the spheres of the powers of the states.

Some graver aspects of the states' rights arguments. The usual arguments for states' rights suggest merely that although the national powers are ultimately supreme they should be somewhat more narrowly interpreted or less energetically exercised than they now are. But at various times in American history, including the present, some voices

---

[24] *Hammer* v. *Dagenhart,* 247 U.S. 251 (1918).
[25] See Edward S. Corwin, "The Passing of Dual Federalism," 36 *Va. L. Rev.* 1 (1950).

have argued that much more drastic potentialities of state sovereignty and states' rights exist as against the national government. These have challenged the very principle of national supremacy.

Thus some pre-Civil War advocates of states' rights claimed that a state had a constitutional right to nullify any federal law affecting it— that is, a right to declare such a law null and void as it affected that state. It has also been argued, and is today argued in a few quarters that, similarly, the state has a right to interpose when the national government attempts an exercise of powers that the state believes to be unconstitutional and thus to prevent such an exercise within that state.[26]

Both the doctrine of *nullification* and that of *interposition* are based on the view that the states are fully sovereign and the Union a "merely federal" compact of states, with the national authority ultimately subordinate to them. The two doctrines are not, and never have been, accepted, either by scholarship or by the courts, as part of American constitutional law. The American Union is no doubt one of indestructible states. These states possess, and are free to exercise, broad powers of government on their own authority and independently of the national powers. But perhaps the oldest and still best-established principle of the Union is that the national government is not a mere agent or subordinate of the states. The great statement is that of Chief Justice John Marshall in *McCulloch* v. *Maryland:*

> If any one proposition could command the universal assent of mankind we might expect it to be this—that the government of the Union, though limited in its powers, is supreme within its sphere of action. This would seem to result, necessarily, from its nature. It is the government of all; its powers are delegated by all; it represents all and acts for all. Though any one state may be willing to control its operations, no state is willing to allow others to control them. The nation, on those subjects on which it can act, must necessarily bind its component parts.

Strict construction, dual federalism, interposition, and nullification are all attempts to make the purely federal aspects of the constitutional system dominant. But the decision of the Constitutional Convention, the basic tradition, and the present tendency are decisively against those attempts.

Law, politics—and ambiguities. That the principal of national supremacy can have harsh applications is apparent in the desegregation problem. Witness the bitter conflict in 1962 over the admission of a Negro student to the University of Mississippi. On the basis of nearly 25 years of gradual development of precedent in education cases, a federal court found that under the Fourteenth Amendment the student was entitled to admission, and directed the university officials to admit him. The state, exercising its many powers over its university and over the peace of its cities, flatly refused to comply. The student's admission was finally ac-

---

[26] See, e.g., James Jackson Kilpatrick, *The Sovereign States: Notes of a Citizen of Virginia* (Chicago: Henry Regnery Company, 1957).

complished and the court order carried out, but only through a display by the national government of physical force. Bitter rioting followed during which two lives were lost and many persons were injured.

But such stark confrontations of national and state powers, resolved by rigid judicial (and if necessary executive) enforcement of the principle of ultimate national supremacy, are the dramatic exceptions. At least equally important is an undramatic continuous process of conflict resolution through ordinary law and politics. The two great American legal traditions, constitutional law and common law, are both traditions of dialogue, of the working out, through common sense and the reasoned application and adaptation of doctrine, of practical solutions for specific problems. And American politics is adept and experienced in compromise, brokerage, and the gradual creation of genuine agreement or negotiated settlements.

The processes of resolution—in both their dramatic and their undramatic aspects—struggle with two central difficulties. The first is that nation-state issues can touch the political nerve and can summon up all

A cartoon of 1833 attacking the doctrine of nullification as the first step toward disunion and despotism. The figure in the center is John C. Calhoun, the South Carolina statesman most closely associated with the nullification doctrine.

the forces of the nation's political life, because these issues can involve vital questions of who shall rule what and how. As they always have and no doubt always will, regions, states, social classes, interest groups, factions, parties, politicians, all struggle for survival and advantage—and quote the Constitution to their purposes.

The second difficulty is that the Constitution permits, even invites, this use and abuse. There can be differing interpretations of the nation-state balance and differing views of just where boundaries between national and state powers lie, because the constitutional compound does combine the potentially conflicting national and federal principles.[27] That is, there are some real ambiguities in the Constitution, in the strict sense of points having double or dubious meaning or of being open to more than one interpretation. There are still more points where, although the general principle is fairly clear, room exists for flexibility and judg-

This 1960 cartoon shows the judiciary rejecting the doctrine of interposition, a recently revived version of nullification which holds that state governments should interpose their authority between their citizens and supposed unconstitutional encroachments of federal power.

---

[27] A famous historical example is John Calhoun and Daniel Webster, both able and learned men, and both firmly and sincerely convinced—of direct opposites. See, e.g., Kelly and Harbison, *op. cit.*, ch. 14.

ment in the application. These ambiguities and flexibilities lead to clashes. But they also give law and politics their opportunity. If everything were clear and simple there could be no solutions, only victories and defeats. The potentially conflicting national and federal elements of the system have through law and politics found, and will continue to find, new constitutional and practical resolutions that somehow maintain the essential character of the system's "compound." As a matter of governmental and political practice we can see compelling needs for a large, powerful, and vigorous national government, but we can also see some countervailing needs and forces. Regional economic and political interests, fear of centralization, and the tradition of liberty through local autonomy will continue to sustain the federal and decentralized aspects of the system. There is no doubt that the national government is larger, more active, and a more pervasive influence in American life than it was some years ago. But state and local government has also become steadily larger, more active, and more pervasive.[28] We must now examine the practical governing arrangements which arise from the interplay of these powerful national and state governments.

Federalism in Action

As we have seen, the distribution of powers and responsibilities between nation and states produces conflict—doctrinal disputes, clashes of government authority, intense political struggles by various interests, and intricate litigation over its formal and legal aspects. It also produces a vast complex of workaday governing in the innumerable tasks carried on by the various levels and agencies of government in forming public policy and administering public affairs.

Every area in the United States (other than the District of Columbia) is governed by both the national government and a state government. Further, each of these governments is divided into separate departments, agencies, and authorities. State government is elaborated into counties, cities, districts, and other subgovernments. All of these subdivisions may (and most do) have their own purposes, programs, officers, offices, funds, exactions, regulations, requirements, prohibitions, pecularities, ways of doing or not doing things, and all the other trappings of rule. And each

---

[28] According to a standard text, state and local government expenditures (which are a useful rough measure) have been moving quite steadily upward. In 1957 they stood at about 11 per cent of Gross National Product; in 1948 the figure was about 7.9 per cent, and in 1929 about 7.3 per cent. The rate of increase has been considerably higher than that of domestic program expenditures of the federal government; federal expenditures on such programs (i.e., exclusive of national security and military and foreign aid programs) increased about 50 per cent and state and local ones about 60 per cent in the 1948–1957 period. And, surprisingly in view of the often-expressed feeling that the federal bureaucracy is overwhelming, state and local expenditures on such programs are consistently over five times as large as the federal. Charles R. Adrian, *State and Local Governments* (New York: McGraw-Hill Book Company, Inc., 1960), ch. 5.

may be acting upon the individual inhabitant directly and more or less independently, in a very welter of governing. How is this busy confusion organized, and how does it work?

Separate or intermixed? The conventional view is that national and state functions are quite separable in principle and typically separated in practice, with each government doing its own jobs.

> . . . like a great factory wherein two sets of machinery are at work, their revolving wheels apparently intermixed, their bands crossing one another, yet each set doing its own work without touching or hampering the other.[29]

On this view, each function is to be performed entirely by only one government—for example, defense by the national government, public education by the state, regulation of the instrumentalities of interstate transportation by the national government, regulation of the manufacture of goods (even for interstate commerce) by the state. Further, this view holds that any national participation in state and local functions is improper and undesirable; such participation is regarded as contrary to the spirit of the Constitution and as tending toward dangerous concentration of power in the hands of the national government, toward undermining the independence of the states, and toward destruction of the American tradition of local autonomy and self-help.

But some experts take a very different view. They see the various functions not only as "apparently intermixed," but as actually intermixed—and properly so. They believe that the typical situation is an actual sharing of functions and an endless process of collaboration in innumerable ways. Indeed, they sometimes urge that the true image of the federal system is not a layer cake, with national, state, and local government functions in separate and distinct layers, but rather a marble cake, with all of the components interspersed throughout.[30] They offer as an example of their view the health officer of a rural county. He is appointed by the state, but under national standards of qualification. His salary comes in part from both state and federal funds, the county supplies an office and some expense money, and a city pays a further part of his salary because he serves as its plumbing inspector. He acts as a federal officer when, acting under federal law, he impounds impure drugs shipped from a neighboring state, as a state officer when, acting under state law, he inspects locally produced foods, and as a local officer when, acting under local ordinances, he inspects local butcher shops.

But the marble cake image can be misleading. Despite their constant and indispensable collaboration, the three levels of government do in fact have important elements of separateness and autonomy. They are legally

---

[29] Bryce, *op. cit.*, I., 325.
[30] See Morton Grodzins, "The Federal System," in *Goals for Americans: The Report of the President's Commission on National Goals* (New York: Prentice-Hall, Inc., 1960).

and structurally separate entities; they respond ultimately to different constituencies; they can pursue sharply separate policies. This separateness remains an important feature of the system even today when the cooperative sharing and intermingling of functions has increased. The cooperation, no matter how habitual, is essentially voluntary. The national and state governments always retain the capacity—legal and practical—to pull in opposing directions or to function separately. But the separateness was no doubt more pronounced in the nineteenth century. Like Lord Bryce in the 1890s, Tocqueville, in the 1830s, had seen considerable separateness:

> two governments, completely separate and almost independent, the one fulfilling the ordinary duties and responding to the daily and indefinite calls of a community, the other circumscribed within certain limits and only exercising an exceptional authority over the general interests of the country.[31]

However, there was some sharing and intermingling of functions even in the nineteenth century. For example, the national government granted land for state public schools and colleges and supplied money and engineering help for roads and canals built by the states; national and state agencies cooperated on banking and fiscal matters, and national and state law-enforcement officers sometimes worked together.[32]

The rise of cooperation. During the twentieth century, however, there has been a massive (though not entirely uniform or uninterrupted) increase in such intermingling. National regulation of business and industry began at least in the 1880s and has developed ever since, just as industrialization and nationwide business and a national economy have developed, and it has always involved interactions with state and local regulation.

Beginning even earlier and reaching large proportions by 1900 and gigantic ones today, national and state programs of aid to farmers and agriculture and to other special groups have moved almost in step, though most of the money has usually come from the national government. Vast programs of waterway, rail, and road building, social welfare services, education, housing construction, and the conservation and development of natural resources, to name but a few, have been cooperatively developed. Indeed, the number is so great that a complete inventory of all the activities in which the states and the nation are jointly engaged would be almost impossible to make.[33] It is even difficult to obtain any firm figures on their magnitudes. The best-known figure covers only amounts of

---

[31] Tocqueville, I, 61.

[32] See Daniel J. Elazar, *The American Partnership: Intergovernmental Co-operation in the Nineteenth Century United States* (Chicago: The University of Chicago Press, 1962).

[33] A general survey as of 1955 may be found in the 1955 *Report to the President* of the U.S. Commission on Intergovernmental Relations, ch. 3. See also the continuing reports and studies published by the present Advisory Commission on Intergovernmental Relations.

money actually granted to state and local governments by the national government to aid programs of these governments in which the national government has some interest. These are termed grants-in-aid. In 1902 regular grants to major programs totalled about 3 million dollars; by fiscal 1963 they had grown to over 7 billion. In recent years the largest programs have been (in descending order of size) highway construction, assistance to needy aged persons, assistance to dependent and needy children, public health research and services, distribution of food through school lunches and otherwise, and aid to education.[34]

Through the remarkably wide range of the grant-in-aid programs and through innumerable other forms of cooperation, we see nation-state-local relationships in virtually every aspect of governing America. These federal relationships must be continually borne in mind as part of the workaday process of governing.

The Constitutional Limitations

A fundamental characteristic of the American constitutional system is its complex effort to constrain—to channel, control, regulate, limit, and hem in—the powers of government. We have already encountered several such constraints in pursuing our inquiries thus far. In Chapter 3, as we dealt with underlying political principles, we saw how a constitutional system is in itself an overall constraint and how the separation of powers and other constitutional devices are general guards against abuses of power. We have seen also that the common-law tradition is another important and pervasive constraint.[35] We have just considered in some detail the constraints that result from the federal element in the system. To complete our survey of the system we must now turn to the specific constraints the Constitution places upon the powers of government. These are traditionally designated the 'constitutional limitations.' These limitations are numerous and diverse, and it will be helpful to identify a few categories and to define a few terms used in connection with them.

Some limitations are *substantive*. These are directed against the substance of government powers and bar government from doing certain things. For example, the First Amendment forbids any national legislation abridging freedom of speech. Some are *procedural*. These are directed against the methods, the procedures, by which powers are exercised. For example, the national government's powers to forbid and punish crime are subject to the procedural limitation that trials must be by jury. Some limitations, such as those of the Bill of Rights, apply *only to the national government*. Others, such as those of the Fourteenth Amendment, apply

---

[34] See the Commission's *Report*, and for recent years *Congressional Quarterly Weekly Report*, August 20, 1963, pp. 1507–14.

[35] Examples of general common-law concepts implicit in the system are that all official actions are subject to law, and that the law is a rational and integrated body of ideas and doctrine "broadening down from precedent to precedent" and not simply a creature of the ruler's fiat.

only to the states. Some limitations are *absolute* and exclude any qualifications or exceptions. Some are *conditional* and allow exceptions or come into operation only when a condition or prerequisite is satisfied. Thus, no ex post facto law whatever may be passed, but private property may be taken for public use if just compensation is paid. Some are (as we have seen) *legal* in nature, suited for enforcement in the courts; some are *political*, suited for enforcement only by political means and processes. The limitations in the Bill of Rights are legal; the procedural limitations imposed on Congress in section 5 of Article I are almost entirely political.[36]

It would be possible to proceed with a full analysis of the constitutional limitations and of their place in the system. But a familiar difficulty of presentation arises. Often one must know *A* before he can know *B*; yet at the same time he needs to know at least something of *B* before he can really understand *A*. This is especially a problem with the constitutional limitations. It is indispensable that we have them in mind as we study the branches of government and the political processes in the chapters that follow. But their full legal and political consequences cannot really be grasped until we understand, say, the judiciary, the practical problems involved in regulating the economy, and the relationships between the President and Congress. Accordingly, our presentation of the limitations is in two sections: a brief guide to them here and an extended consideration of them in Chapter 13.

Those we consider here we divide into three groups: those in the Constitution proper; those added by the Bill of Rights; and those added by the Fourteenth Amendment. This division is not for convenience only. As will be seen, it also reflects the pattern of the limitations as well. While there is overlap, the limitations within each group tend to share a distinctive character or thrust.

Limitations in the Constitution Proper

Limitations in the Constitution proper are placed wherever in the instrument they are relevant for the original draftsmen's purposes. Since they are therefore scattered, an impression of their overall characteristics is somewhat hard to get at first. On closer inspection, however, pattern and purpose emerge.

Some apply to the internal workings of the government, and are intended to protect these against some specific danger or abuse. An example is the set of requirements (Art. I, sec. 5) designed to foster orderly procedure and effective debate in Congress and to assure some public record of congressional proceedings. Another has been developed

---

[36] For example, this section requires that Congress keep a journal of its proceedings and record the votes of its members. If Congress failed to follow these procedural requirements it seems unlikely that citizens could seek their enforcement in the courts. The only recourse would be to political means, such as 'throwing the rascals out' at the next election.

by construction of Article III; the "judicial power" can be exercised only in "cases or controversies." The courts thus hold themselves forbidden to give general advisory opinions to Congress or the President. This helps to maintain the desirable degree of judicial detachment from direct policy making.[37]

Many are addressed to preserving some political characteristic of the system. The prohibition against grants of titles of nobility is a precaution against the creation of a formal aristocracy, inimical to the republican nature of the regime. The prohibition of bills of attainder and ex post facto laws arose from considerations of political liberty, since these had frequently been used in England against political opponents of a regime. The prohibitions of tax preferences or disadvantages for any state are aimed at preserving the federal independence and equality of the states.

There are (e.g., Art. I, sec. 10) limitations applied to the states. Many of these are obviously correlatives to powers granted the national government and are aimed at preventing various possible kinds of nation-state clashes. Others apply to the states some specific protections of political interests and freedoms applied against national action; for example, the states also may not pass ex post facto laws or bills of attainder, nor may they grant titles of nobility.

Some personal rights and freedoms are protected, but not in the systematic way that we shall see in the Bill of Rights, and most of those protected are ones having a political aspect. Thus, jury trial and habeas corpus are in part examples; violations of these rights in England had often been aimed at political opponents of a regime. When one is told that the Constitution is an ancient and legalistic eighteenth-century curiosity surviving only because it is preserved in the amber of patriotic piety, it is instructive to reflect that all modern totalitarian regimes tamper with or wipe out just such rights as these. Tyranny does not die and some of its basic methods do not change much.

The Bill of Rights

In the debates over ratification, an insistent demand emerged for further limitations that would go beyond the political orientation of those in the Constitution proper and that would systematically protect more personal rights and freedoms. Ten amendments were therefore added shortly after ratification. The first eight are the Bill of Rights proper.

Understanding of them begins with their background in eighteenth-century Anglo-American legal and political ideas. Perhaps the most fertile sources both of their general principles and of their specifics were the

---

[37] The first prominent instance of this judicial self-restraint occurred in 1793. President Washington, through Secretary of State Thomas Jefferson, asked the Supreme Court to answer a number of questions on international law arising out of the war that was beginning in Europe. The justices politely declined to do so, mentioning the separation of powers and the fact that they were "judges of a court." The correspondence is quoted in Harold J. Berman, *The Nature and Functions of Law* (Brooklyn: The Foundation Press, Inc., 1958), pp. 65–68.

views Americans then held of the "rights of freeborn Englishmen." But understanding cannot stop with this history. Since their adoption, and especially in the last thirty or forty years, the provisions of the Bill of Rights have almost all been the subject of many judicial decisions, much debate, and a great deal of voluminous and detailed analysis. Their meaning and application have hence been greatly developed and painstakingly expounded.

The major contents of the Bill can be roughly grouped under four headings: (1) the freedoms covered by the First Amendment; (2) the restraints on procedure in criminal prosecutions and in some other kinds of legal proceedings; (3) the protections for property; and (4) the very extensive and complex subject bound up in the phrase "due process of law."

The First Amendment freedoms clearly aim in part at protecting a free and democratic political process. But they also protect from governmental repression freedom of religion and a broad range of nonpolitical speech and writing—protections appropriate to a society in which happiness is to be privately, and thus freely, pursued.

Detailed restraints on criminal procedure are found in several amendments, e.g., the provisions for grand jury indictment, jury trial, assistance of counsel, etc. Some aspects of these protections have effects far beyond criminal cases, however. Thus the Fourth Amendment's interdiction of "unreasonable searches and seizures" is broadly protective of personal privacy against many other kinds of governmental action as well.

The main explicit protection for property—so central, as we have seen, to the whole system—is found in the provision of the Fifth Amendment that "No person shall . . . be deprived of life, liberty, or property, without due process of law; nor shall private property be taken for public use, without just compensation." Short though this clause is, it is broader than it may look. For example, it protects certain kinds of contract rights as well as ordinary tangible property—another example, be it noted, of the legal aspect of the Constitution. The Amendment's protection of property is thus understood to be general and has had an extensive and important history.

Due process of law contains some elements of each of the above three categories and much else besides and has very numerous applications. It began as a procedural protection. This function continues and has been developed by the courts into a powerful and wide-ranging weapon against almost any kinds of official procedures by the police, by government agencies, by Congress, or by any official authority, which the courts regard as seriously unjust or oppressive. In addition, however, due process acquired a substantive aspect. In this aspect it is concerned with the substantive content and effect of laws and other official actions. A statute which is excessively arbitrary, or unfair, or an unjust deprivation of freedom or property, may be held to be a violation of due process even though scrupulously fair procedures are used in its administration and enforcement. An immense body of constitutional law, which we shall look at later, has grown out of this single clause.

Constitutional Limitations on the States: The Fourteenth Amendment

The Bill of Rights has been held by the Supreme Court to apply only to the national government. Its protections are therefore not available against the state governments. The Fourteenth Amendment however has become, in the hands of the Supreme Court, a very copious source of limitations on the states, similar to those of the Bill of Rights.[38]

The Amendment contains two principal protective clauses: the due process clause and the equal protection clause.[39] Each has its own meaning and effect, although the courts do not always distinguish sharply between them. The due process clause here has at least as broad a meaning as that of the due process clause in the Bill of Rights. Further, the equal protection clause is construed as a sweeping prohibition against many kinds of state action which the courts conclude are arbitrary, or seriously discriminatory, or clearly unreasonable. But the two clauses do much more as well, in that through them many of the same protective principles are applied against the states as are applied against the national government through the Bill of Rights. These include the First Amendment freedoms, protection against the taking of property for public use without just compensation, and many that protect persons from unfair or oppressive official procedures.

Taken together, the various constitutional limitations are a broad armory of protections against oppressive government. Most can be and are formally enforced by the judiciary on occasion; this vastly strengthens the general judicial constraint upon the operations of government. But the influence of the constitutional limitations goes far beyond the court-room. They are a standard by which government is judged. As such, they profoundly influence public opinion and through it the political process and official conduct. This influence is dramatically illustrated in the civil-rights controversy. The Negro and other civil-rights organizations combatting segregation or seeking to register voters have no greater weapon than the simple force of these constitutional limitations. Their very phrases—"the equal protection of the laws," "the right of the people peaceably to assemble," and the like—are impressive statements of American ideals, and make powerful slogans in political struggles.

---

[38] In *Barron v. Baltimore*, 7 Peters (U.S.) 243 (1833), Chief Justice Marshall held for the Court that the Bill of Rights applied only against the national government and not against the states. This remains the technical legal situation. But in a long series of important cases, the Court has construed the Fourteenth Amendment as "incorporating" many protections of the Bill of Rights, and hence in effect has made them applicable against the states. For a detailed discussion, see pp. 428–29.

[39] The third protective clause, that relating to privileges and immunities has in effect been construed out of existence by the Supreme Court, beginning with the Slaughterhouse Cases, 16 Wall. (U.S.) 36 (1873).

How these limitations operate in politics and in constitutional law will be considered in detail in Chapter 13. It suffices here to emphasize that they are vital to the constitutional system. Like the other principles of that system which Part II has discussed, they are among the principles that inspirit the institutions and processes of government to which we now turn.

BIBLIOGRAPHICAL NOTE

The decisions of the U.S. Supreme Court are published in the official edition, the *United States Reports* (now amounting to over 370 volumes), and in two commercial editions, the *Lawyers' Edition* and the *Supreme Court Reporter*. The decisions of the lower federal courts are published only in commercial editions, the *Federal Reporter* for the Courts of Appeals and the *Federal Supplement* for the district courts. Decisions are referred to ('cited') by volume number, the abbreviated title of the edition of reports, the page where the decision begins, and, usually, the year of the decision (and where necessary the specific court) given in parentheses. Thus, 123 F.2d 456 (C.A. 2d 1961) is the citation of a decision which might appear in the 123rd volume of the second series of the *Federal Reporter* beginning at page 456 and rendered by the Court of Appeals for the Second Circuit in 1961.

Citations and brief analyses of the decisions of the Supreme Court construing the Constitution are found in Edward S. Corwin (ed.), *The Constitution of the United States: Analysis and Interpretation* (1953). This work is often referred to as *The Annotated Constitution;* the citations and analyses are arranged as annotations to the clauses of the Constitution. Professor Corwin also prepared a much briefer annotation, *The Constitution and What It Means Today* (12th ed., 1958).

A standard history of the Supreme Court is Charles Warren, *The Supreme Court in United States History* (rev. ed., 2 vols., 1937). A definitive history is now being prepared under official auspices by a group of distinguished scholars. Two standard histories of American constitutional law are Alfred H. Kelly and Winfred A. Harbison, *The American Constitution: Its Origins and Development* (3rd ed., 1963), and Carl Brent Swisher, *American Constitutional Development* (2nd ed., 1954). A brief history of the Court is Robert G. McCloskey, *The American Supreme Court* (1960). This and Kelly and Harbison contain valuable bibliographical essays. Studies of episodes and periods in the history of the Court and of the law abound, as do biographies of individual justices.

There is no standard general treatise on American constitutional law. However, a useful one by a political scientist is C. Herman Pritchett, *The American Constitution* (1959). Again, specialized studies of particular doctrines abound. Pritchett and the bibliographical essays just mentioned cite a large proportion of these.

Much of the best writing on American constitutional law is found in the scholarly journals, especially in the law reviews published by most of the major American law schools. This literature is indexed generally in the *Public Affairs*

Information Service index. The law reviews are indexed exhaustively in the *Index to Legal Periodicals*.

The casebooks prepared for use in law school courses on constitutional law, civil liberties, federal jurisdiction, and allied subjects often contain quantities of valuable information and exceedingly penetrating analysis. A leading example of a constitutional law casebook is William B. Lockhart, Yale Kamisar, and Jesse H. Choper, *Constitutional Law: Cases, Comments & Questions* (1964, with 1965 *Supplement*). A casebook on federal jurisdiction, Henry M. Hart, Jr., and Herbert Wechsler, *The Federal Courts and the Federal System* (1953), is an excellent work that is too little known to students of government.

Most major newspapers carry accounts of the current work of the Supreme Court. The *New York Times* is outstanding among these.

Part Three

THE
BRANCHES
OF
GOVERNMENT

Chapter 5

The Legislative Branch: Congress

IT IS USUALLY SAID THAT PARLIAMENTS, CONGRESSES, AND SIMILAR LEGISLATIVE assemblies have three basic functions. One is *representation;* they represent their constituents in their governments. Another is *policy-making;* by legislation and other means they participate in determining the policies of their governments upon the various public questions they confront. The third is *oversight;* by various means they oversee and criticize, perhaps supervise and direct, the activities of their governments. The American Congress performs all three of these functions with an authority and vigor unusual among legislative bodies.

Seven characteristics do much to give this complex branch its nature and to make it a unique feature of the American system.[1]

First, Congress is partly federal and partly national. This is most apparent in the *federally equal* representation of states in the Senate and the *national* representation of people in the House. But there are further subtleties in the blend. (1) A federal touch: No state can be excluded from the House; each state must have at least one representative. (But for this provision Alaska, Nevada, Vermont, and Wyoming would today not be entitled to even one representative.) (2) A national touch: Each house itself, and not the states, has the sweeping constitutional powers over the elections of members and over their conduct. (3) The Senate is not so federal as it at first glance looks, apart from the equal suffrages of the states. Once elected, senators are free from official control by their electors. Thus, they need not vote jointly, or as agents of their state, as delegations did under the Articles; senators vote as individuals, each as he pleases. A state is hardly represented in a really federal way when its senators are free to vote on opposite sides of an issue. Similarly, a state cannot remove its senators, and thus effectively control them, as it could

---

[1] Note as we go along how vitally these characteristics are connected with the provisions of the Constitution concerning Congress. For convenience, the most important of these, drawn from Articles I and VI, are given in continuous form in the box on p. 134.

All legislative powers herein granted shall be vested in a Congress of the United States, which shall consist of a Senate and a House of Representatives. . . . The House . . . shall be composed of members chosen every second year by the people of the several states, and the electors in each State shall have the qualifications requisite for electors of the most numerous branch of the State legislature. . . . Representatives . . . shall be apportioned among the several States according to their respective numbers . . . but each state shall have at least one representative. . . . The Senate shall be composed of two senators from each State, chosen . . . for six years; and each senator shall have one vote . . . . The times, places, and manner of holding elections for senators and representatives shall be prescribed in each State by the legislature thereof; but the Congress may at any time . . . make or alter such regulations. . . . Each house shall be the judge of the elections, returns, and qualifications of its own members. . . . Each house may, . . . with the concurrence of two-thirds, expel a member. . . . The senators and representatives shall receive a compensation for their services, to be ascertained by law and paid out of the Treasury of the United States. . . . The Congress shall have power . . . . [Here follows a statement of the powers of Congress and of limitations on the powers of the states.] This Constitution, and the laws of the United States which shall be made in pursuance thereof, . . . shall be the supreme law of the land. . . . The senators and representatives before mentioned, and the members of the several State legislatures, and all executive and judicial officers, both of the United States and of the several states, shall be bound by oath or affirmation to support this Constitution. . . .

its delegates under the Articles.[2] Moreover, a senator can be protected by his brother senators, through their constitutional power over senatorial elections, from locally rigged elections; and because there is a fixed time for elections he cannot be snatched back to face reelection at the will of his local political foes. (4) A very practical national touch: Senators and representatives are secure in their pay, which is determined by national law and paid by the national government.

Second, Congress is also a compound of the national and the *local*. A congressman may on the same day help make important national policy, spend hours getting a $10,000 flood control project for his district over some petty hurdle, and spend other hours talking large policy—or petty politics—with visitors from home.[3] Senators and representatives have their independence of their state governments. But their political positions— even their political lives—usually depend significantly on local issues that affect the interest groups and voters at home. Compare a British member of parliament; his career, and hence his time and effort, lie almost entirely

[2] See William H. Riker, "The Senate and American Federalism," *Amer. Pol. Sci. Rev.*, 49, (June 1955), 452–469. See also George H. Haynes, *The Senate of the United States* (2 vols.; Boston: Houghton Mifflin Co., 1938).

[3] See, e.g., Stephen K. Bailey and Howard D. Samuel, *Congress at Work* (New York: Henry Holt & Co., 1952).

in the House of Commons and in his national party organization, and though he may often work hard for his constituency he is often not even a resident of it.

Third, Congress is deeply and inextricably involved with virtually all the innumerable groupings of American political life: parties, factions, interest groups, lobbies, public service associations, and all the rest. In this, as in its federal and local aspects, it is truly the broad and diverse *parliament*[4] of the extended republic, where the "multiplicity of interests" meet and contend, and in contending keep each other from single supreme power. From that diversity and contention there results the most characteristic process in Congress, the moderating and unifying process of compromise and coalition. Interest must usually accommodate to interest, region to region, party group to party group; seldom can any one hope to get the necessary votes by itself. Congress is not the complete, ideal solution to the problem presented by Madisonian factions; it is in some respects both a vehicle for them and crippled by them. But it is a significant part of the large solution the American constitutional system attempts, and this is a prominent and pervasive part of its life.

Fourth, Congress is a compound of the democratic and the undemocratic. It responds—sometimes too readily—to small eddies and shifts in the winds of politics. And in the long run all strong movements in the popular will usually get their way. But there is much that is strikingly undemocratic. Two examples from among many illustrate. The Senate is sometimes limited by the power of senators to inhibit action by filibusters and parliamentary maneuver. In the House an old committee chairman, who represents only a few rural counties in one state, has in the recent past greatly influenced and often nearly controlled what matters the House could even consider.[5]

Fifth, Congress is intensely and inevitably political. Democratic election contests are the decisive American political event. Seats in Congress are major prizes in these contests. Elections in turn mean politics, and the typical member of Congress is a politician through and through; he may also be a statesman and a great public servant, but usually only if he is a pretty effective and successful politician as well. And Congress itself is the very embodiment of the political system.

Sixth, in its work Congress functions by a complex tangle of institutions and processes. These operate in what often looks like a most haphazard and unsatisfactory fashion. Congress is not a tightly organized and efficient machine, brisk, prompt, and rational. Sometimes it fumbles and stalls. Sometimes it does nothing, sometimes too much. Sometimes it accomplishes prodigies in a few hours (e.g., during some emergencies and during the adjournment rush at the end of a session). Sometimes it is paralyzed in deadlock. Sometimes it quite literally does not know what

---

[4] 'Parliament' is derived from Old French *parler*, to speak; it is a place where people talk.

[5] The chairman of the famous House Rules Committee. See James A. Robinson, *The House Rules Committee* (Indianapolis: Bobbs-Merrill Co., 1963).

it is going to work on next. This mode of life and work results largely from two basic features, each springing from Congress's nature. First, there is a mixture of petty scheming and grand strategy, of the trivial and the profoundly important. There is thus the making and unmaking of small cabals and of great coalitions, much windy oratory and much careful study, much heedless time-wasting and much hard work, the settling of immense conflicts and the airing of trivial grievances, and—out of it all—a good part of the development and effectuation of the great structures of the public policy of the nation. Second, there is the almost incredible volume of business, some of it quite incredibly abstruse and complex, that comes to Congress as the center of American government. Given these two features, the complex tangle of institutions and processes is inevitable.

Seventh, we have so far spoken of Congress by itself. But Congress is affected in everything by its great rival and partner, the Presidency. And both are affected by the great administrative system where the actual daily work of governing is done and where much of the rivalry and partnership operates. We shall talk here mainly about Congress, with both the Presidency and the administrative system kept off stage, so to speak. This is necessary for simplicity in exposition, but we must never forget them.

The Structure and Organization of Congress

The Constitutional Elements

As so often in the American system, constitutional elements are important. Congress is the subject of the first and longest article of the Constitution and is the chief grantee of the national powers. And, by its authority over its members and its internal affairs, it has much independence of the other parts of the political order. But this constitutionally endowed preeminence and autonomy is qualified by the constitutional limitations, and, under the system of separation of powers, by the courts and by the rivalry of the Presidency.

Bicameralism is a second important constitutional determinant. The two houses of Congress are about equal in power (unlike the British Parliament where the Lords are the distinctly weaker body), although they are constitutionally designed to be as unlike as is practicable in a democracy. The Senate, though in part the result of federalism, is also designed to be an 'upper' house. That is, it is to be a "select and stable member of the government," a "temperate and respectable body of citizens" capable of supplying competent leadership and of restraining the momentary passions of the people and a possibly too-responsive House.[6] The result is a Congress of two distinctly separate houses, with differing terms and constituencies and even differing powers and interests,

---

[6] See *Federalist* 63, pp. 407, 410.

tending to check each other and thus to give less direct and immediate—but also more accurate because more complex—expression to popular opinion. The division of Congress into two coequal but greatly different houses deeply affects virtually all of congressional structure and organization.

Another vital element is the constitutionally fixed term for members. Fixed terms assure the member some scope and elbow room. He is guaranteed some time (though in the House, with its two-year terms, not much) to become—and then to be—a competent legislator, time to manipulate his situation to advantage, time to carry through substantial pieces of legislative work both for the public interest and for his own reputation and influence in his constituency. Thus he has the chance to establish a personal record of achievement, and to make himself partially independent of political circumstances. The fixed term has another consequence; it tends to make him independent of his party and party leaders. A British prime minister may dissolve Parliament any time his party members get restive, forcing every member to face a new election. This gives him, and through him the national party organization, a strong disciplinary weapon which helps to produce remarkable party discipline and regularity in the House of Commons. Constitutionally fixed terms deprive the congressional leadership of this weapon. Party commands can sit pretty lightly on the shoulders of a senator or congressman who keeps his relationships with the interest groups, voters, and party back home in good order. This independence is reflected throughout congressional structure and organization and throughout congressional functioning.

The Constitution adds further to the members' independence by granting legal immunities to them. First, they are free from arrest for other than certain designated reasons while attending sessions, and these reasons can be regulated by *legislation*. This is a small thing in quiet times. But there have been many occasions when kings and tyrants—including modern dictators—have assailed the freedom of legislatures; the principle of legal immunities was then not a small thing at all. Second, of more obvious modern significance, the members have immunity from legal proceedings, including slander suits, for anything they say in their house; there is absolute legal freedom of congressional speech.

But the constitutional elements that have the greatest immediate bearing on congressional structure and organization are Congress's sweeping powers of self-rule. Each house has almost unlimited and exclusive power to create its own internal arrangements: "each house may determine the rules of its proceedings." To insure that these rules are obeyed, it can discipline its members, even expel them. Moreover, the powers of self-rule are beyond any control by the states, by the voters, or by the President (who has no veto here), and almost completely beyond any control by the courts. Congressional self-rule is another example of how the Constitution aims at competent government by declining to fetter the men who have to govern. Congress is constitutionally free to do its work by pretty much whatever internal procedures it sees fit to use.

Within this constitutional framework Congress has been largely the creation of its own nature, as that nature has responded to the forces and events of American political life. It settled into a rather stable general pattern of structure and organization, and even of functioning, comparatively early—in many respects by, say, the 1840s or 1850s. Part of its genius is a flexibility, and it is never quite the same as it was ten years before or will be ten years later. But these are mostly slow, small, elusive changes within a stable pattern. Indeed, a great public question today is whether Congress has moved, or will move, sufficiently in step with time and events.

Congress in short has turned out to have a strong institutional personality, with marked characteristics. There is nothing quite like it in the American political order (even in those state legislatures that have been patterned on it) and certainly nothing like it in any other political order. It leaves its impress on everything it touches, and it has in almost every aspect of its existence its own distinctive style. This style is deeply affected by the constitutional design. The Constitution apparently wants a legislature that is, though held within constitutional boundaries, a strong and fully independent branch of government. It gets one. But is Congress also (because of federalism, separation of powers, and its own stiff bicameralism, self-rule, and fixed terms) so encumbered and so independent that neither it nor the Presidency can be *competent* agencies of government?[7] We shall have to see.

The Internal System of Authority[8]

The Constitution and the political order give Congress the potentiality of independence and great power. But to realize this potentiality, Congress requires an effective internal system of authority. It must have such a system if it is to be a functioning entity and not a mere formless assemblage neither organized for nor capable of the orderly and effective handling of its business. Such a system is generated principally by four features.

The parties. When an observer visits Congress what he first notices turn out to be party things. Each of the two chambers is divided physically by an aisle, with all Republicans sitting on the presiding officer's left and all Democrats on his right; indeed, in the Senate they have

---

[7] Many experts think so. See, e.g., James MacGregor Burns, *The Deadlock of Democracy* (Englewood Cliffs, N.J.: Prentice-Hall, 1963). So does a prominent Senator, Joseph Clark, *The Senate Establishment* (New York: Hill and Wang, 1963). But compare William S. White, *Citadel: The Story of the U.S. Senate* (New York: Harper & Brothers, 1956). White and others of his school of thought find very little wrong. For further discussion of the problem see pp. 270–73.

[8] The phrase is borrowed from Roland Young, *The American Congress* (New York: Harper & Brothers, 1958), but is here given a somewhat different meaning.

separate cloakrooms, and in the House they have different doors and separate lobbies.[9] In committees similar separation prevails; Republicans and Democrats sit on opposite sides of the chairman. And as our observer reads about Congress he notices more of the same; newspapers identify senators and representatives as Republicans or Democrats and speak of Congress as being 'controlled' by one party or the other.

Yet our observer almost equally soon discovers that we do not have *party government*[10] in anything resembling the sense in which Britain, for example, has it. In Britain general elections are contests over which party is to govern. A party 'wins' an election when it wins a majority in the House of Commons. Its leaders in Commons then form the Cabinet, the head of the executive. They propose a program of legislation along the lines of their party's policies. This is dutifully voted for, usually in its entirety, by the party's M.P.s, and is put into effect by the executive. And at the next election the party and all of its candidates campaign largely on this program and the party's administration of it.

Almost none of this kind of party *government* exists in Congress. Nonetheless the *influence* of party is vital and pervasive. However, both the degree of this influence and the mode of its operation differ widely in various aspects of congressional functioning; party influence in formal organization is overwhelming, in formal policy-making slight, in informal organization always considerable, and in the informal parts of policy-making sometimes great and sometimes slight. Some concrete instances will illustrate this complexity.

On the day a new Congress first meets, we might think we are seeing party government. The formal organizational steps (e.g., election of the Speaker of the House) are commonly taken by strict party votes, all Republicans voting one way and all Democrats another. Much the same separateness and party unity prevail in several other aspects of formal organization. Each house of Congress has a "majority leader" and a "minority leader" who head their parties and are dominant figures in that house. Committees, the most permanent and most important official sub-organizations of each house, are organized on rigid party lines. The chairman of each committee is a member of the majority party in that house; seniority on committees is calculated separately for Republicans and Democrats; appointment to committees is by action of the parties; and membership is proportioned roughly to party strength in the parent house.

So far this looks like party government; the parties *acting as parties* have assumed the responsibility for managing governmental matters. But we soon reach the end of these rigid clarities. A good example is found in

---

[9] This is ingeniously used; congressmen are numerous and busy, and a convenient way for a party group to pass the word on what vote it suggests is to station spokesmen at the door when a roll call occurs.

[10] That is to say, a system in which a political party bears formal responsibility for conducting the government.

the official party groups—usually called 'conferences' by the Republicans and 'caucuses' by the Democrats—made up of all the members of a house that are of the party; in party government these official party groups would formally make policy. Not so in Congress. They are not only not real sources or determiners of policy; nowadays they almost never even try to bind their members to specific stands on even minor policy issues. Indeed, the Democrats customarily seldom meet in caucus. It is true that some of the party 'policy' and 'steering' committees (but not, for example, that of the House Democrats) frequently influence policy as well as legislative strategy and tactics. But, significantly, on surprisingly few things is there really a firm party position. Unlike parties in many other national legislatures the parties in Congress do not have, or even claim to have, fully developed and comprehensive programs, binding on all members, that include positions on all significant policy issues.[11] Such programs, and such discipline, are necessary in party government systems. They are unknown in the American system.

Yet if the formal participation of the parties as such in formal policy determination has distinct limits, their informal, unofficial influence on congressional life and functioning is nonetheless vast. A glance at a senator or representative shows this. He always has a party label and very rarely changes it. His closest working associations and strongest

---

[11] Members of Congress frequently state that when they came to Congress they found much less party discipline and pressure on votes and issues than they had expected. See, e.g., Charles L. Clapp, *The Congressman: His Work as He Sees It* (Washington, D.C.: The Brookings Institution, 1964), pp. 313–20.

political ties in Congress are in most cases with members of his own party, and he usually looks first to them for aid in his legislative projects. He may belong to 'factions' and other groups that are economic or regional or ideological. But these are more often within his party than across party lines. Indeed, even his personal and social relations around Congress are usually closer with members of his own party than with members of the other.[12] Through party channels flows much of the communication and interaction of political life and of government. For example, it is through party channels and as a party leader that the President exercises much of his formidable influence over Congress. Further, the members of Congress have connections with the national, state, and local party organizations and party chiefs; it is through these party channels that many of the influences from the society and from other parts of government and politics are transmitted to Congress. This duality, of being both parties *in Congress* and of not being solely in Congress, is a central fact about the Congressional parties.

The overall influence the parties have is well revealed, in its complexity and diversity, in the way members of Congress vote. Strict party votes are uncommon, but they do exist. Votes in which all but a few members line up with their parties are common. Votes in which very large numbers vote against a definite policy of their party are rare; a member apparently thinks a good deal before going contrary to the urging of his party leadership. He may in the end do so, but the gravitational pull is strongly against it.[13] (It must also be remembered that the occasions are rather rare when the urging is really intense; as we have mentioned, the parties do not normally take strong formal positions on many issues.)

Departures from party regularity do occur, however. Indeed, they are a distinguishing characteristic of the American Congress because they are more common and important in it than they are in the legislatures of party government systems. Individuals, state delegations, regional groups, factions, and ideological groups on occasion do diverge from party norms, if not so often from the parties' rare express commands. Coalitions do form across or independent of party lines; Southern members are an example on regional and civil-rights issues, as has been the "Conservative Coalition" of conservative Southern Democrats and conservative Republicans on

---

[12] See Clapp, pp. 14–17. A congressman writing to his constituents remarked frequently on how distant personal relationships with members of the opposite party tended to be; Clem Miller, *Member of the House: Letters of a Congressman*, ed., John W. Baker (New York: Charles Scribner's Sons, 1962). The same apparently is true, though perhaps to a lesser degree, in the Senate; see Donald R. Matthews, *United States Senators and Their World* (Chapel Hill, N.C.: University of North Carolina Press, 1960).

[13] E.g., in the second session of the Eighty-eighth Congress, the average Democrat voted with his party majority in disagreement with the other party's majority 69 per cent of the time, the average Republican 71 per cent of the time. These figures are taken from the article "On Party Unity," *Congressional Quarterly Almanac*, XX, 740–41 (Washington, D.C.: Congressional Quarterly Service, 1964).

issues of spending, social welfare legislation, and the scope of federal power.[14] But such coalitions are sufficiently untypical as to attract attention, and to be thought to require some explanation; the more usual and natural 'coalition' is generally felt to be one within the party, despite all the looseness of its bonds. And although there are rather few rigid party stands and doctrines, there are certainly sufficient general party tendencies and orientations to make it possible to speak of the parties' philosophies as basic outlooks. Indeed, if we are looking for the single best predictor of the voting behavior of members of Congress, and their policy positions generally, it is party affiliation.[15]

Some observers, spellbound by the comparison with party government, dwell exclusively on the looseness of congressional party organization and the weakness of party influence. They thus understate how much party unity and influence there actually is in Congress. Moreover, they thus miss a vital fact: There is more party unity in Congress than in the party system generally. Such organizational looseness and weakness as exist within Congress result from basic traits of the American party system generally—for example, its decentralized and federal structures as these respond to the centrifugal forces of American politics. But Congress and its traits tend to restrain and stifle the centrifugal forces. Much more centrality and discipline exist in congressional party life than in the national parties generally, because Congress does in truth *nationalize*. The 'national touches' of which we have spoken really do work; it is a *national* legislature.

We can therefore see in the parties in Congress the first great agency of the internal system of authority that makes Congress at least in part an entity, and a functioning entity.

Officers, leaders, and 'the leadership.'

[In] all legislative assemblies the greater the number composing them may be, the fewer will be the men who will in fact direct their proceedings. . . . [Enlarge them and] the countenance of the government may become more democratic, but the soul that animates it will be more oligarchic. The machine will be enlarged, but the fewer, and often the more secret, will be the springs by which its motions are directed.[16]

Congress of course cannot operate simply as a body of equals, working solely by general debate. Assemblies as large as the House, or even as large as the Senate, must organize themselves and must be led; their work must be planned and structured and to an extent guided and controlled. The question therefore is: How is this done in Congress, with what effect upon its function of being a democratically representative and

---

[14] *Ibid.*, pp. 745–48.
[15] See, e.g., David B. Truman, *The Congressional Party: A Case Study* (New York: John Wiley & Sons, 1959), pp. vi–vii.
[16] *Federalist* 58, pp. 381–82.

competent legislature, and with what guards against the inevitable danger of oligarchic control that Publius points out?

In each house of Congress there are constitutional officers; there are party potentates; there are members who occupy important committee posts; and there are members who have power because of political influence, or personal prestige, or specialized knowledge, or important connections. The leadership of Congress is a complicated blend of these. The blend is conditioned by the constitutional arrangements and affected by all the multifarious forces of politics, and the leadership blend shifts as members rise and fall in official and personal power and as the subjects of congressional attention change.

The principal constitutional officer of the House is the Speaker. He is elected by the House (i.e., by the majority party). In the Senate there are the constitutional "President of the Senate," who is the Vice President of the United States, and the "President pro tempore of the Senate," who is elected by the Senate.[17]

The Speaker is the center of the leadership in his house; the two Senate officers are not in theirs. This arises from differences between the houses and from the nature of the Speakership. Senators are fewer in number than representatives, and they are elected for longer terms and from constituencies that are in nearly all cases larger and more diversified, and in all cases more independent political entities. Senators are therefore generally more powerful, more important, and prouder individual figures, and so less amenable to discipline. Further, the smaller Senate can get its business done with somewhat less strong official leadership. Hence, for example, the famous freedom of debate in the Senate while House proceedings are rigidly regulated by the rules and by the presiding officer.

The House Speakership itself is a remarkable office. First, different though it has become, it still stands in the tradition of the great Speakership of the British House of Commons, whose occupant's independence and power as the leader and official spokesman of the House were made the palladium of the democratic rights of the Commons against nobles and monarchs, at least since Stuart times. Further, the American Speaker is elected by his house, as the President of the Senate is not, and this in itself vastly enhances his status; he has the moral authority that derives from the consent of his peers.

The Speaker's official powers are now small compared to what they were before the House overthrew a tyrannical Speaker in 1910. Before this revolt, the Speaker appointed all committees, controlled absolutely what matters came before the House and who spoke in debate, and otherwise ruled the House nearly completely. Today he can only influence, not determine, the business of the House and the course of debate,[18] and has

---

[17] See Article I, sections 2, 3.

[18] Some 1965 changes appear to have considerably strengthened his hand; however, it is too early to tell what the long-run consequences of these will be, and whether they signal a trend.

no official power over committee appointments. Even so, his actual powers plus the prestige and status of the Speakership are sufficient to make the office a very powerful one *in the hands of the right man*. This qualification is important; as with the Presidency, the Speakership depends for much of its effectiveness on the personal qualities and skills of its holder. The Presidency pro tempore of the Senate might have developed along the same lines but, for whatever reasons, it did not and the Speakership now stands unique in the American Congress, and is often spoken of as the second most powerful elective office in the country. There have been only twelve Speakers since 1900, and they have had an average of 23 years of service in Congress before their election. The Speaker is always a senior and highly respected member of the majority party in the House, and his party standing is an integral part of his influence.

Around the Speaker there is a small group of congressmen of his party, a group of somewhat uncertain and changing membership. Together with him and their opposite numbers of the minority party, they make up 'the leadership of the House.' The group always includes the formal majority party leadership structure. The majority leader is usually its most important member, ranking next to the Speaker and often rising to that office. He is invariably an important party figure, elected by his party's conference or caucus. His assistant, the majority whip, is also normally a part of the leadership. These men are the core, and it is around them that the key committee chairmen and key individuals—the rest of the blend of leadership elements—assemble.

The House is of course by no means exclusively ruled by the majority party. The minority party is led by a more or less parallel leadership group. It too elects a floor leader and a whip, around whom also cluster a shifting group of that party's principal figures having bases of power equivalent to those of the corresponding members of the majority leadership. The minority leader is usually his party's chief House spokesman, and ordinarily becomes Speaker when his party wins a majority. The minority party leadership conducts its party's floor opposition to the majority party. But to some degree the two leadership groups cooperate—or at least negotiate—and the business of the House is largely managed between them.

In the Senate somewhat the same state of affairs prevails, with two leadership groups composed of important committee chairmen or ranking members and other key senators centered around the party leaders. In the Senate the majority and minority floor leaders are in a sense even more important, since they have no Speaker to rival or overshadow them. However in the Senate—smaller, less tightly organized, and more individualistic than the House—senators' personal qualities generally count for more, and formal or official posts for less. The actual power of the formal leaders thus varies greatly with the specific leader's personal influence.[19] And

---

[19] It is commonly said that President Lyndon B. Johnson, when he was Senate majority leader, was the great modern example of power based on personal influence.

hence, even more than in the House, matters are generally conducted by informal conferences and negotiations, depending on circumstances, personalities, and politics.

The committees and 'the committee system.' Just as any large and busy assembly needs leaders, it also needs a means of dividing and delegating some of its tasks. Especially needed are means for the preliminary study, selection, and preparation of matters for its attention. Some legislatures—e.g., the British House of Commons—have this done for them by a party acting through a cabinet. Others have it done for them by the executive. But Congress is not part of a system of party government, nor will it accept much direction by the executive branch in general or the President in particular. It therefore has to do this work itself. (This insistence upon doing its own work and thus participating fully in the legislative process is one of the most distinguishing features of the American Congress and one of the most important determinants of its behavior.) It does this work by a system that reflects Congress's own nature —a loose, diverse, decentralized organization within which the multiplicities of interests and groupings of the American political order are continuously manifested. This is the famous 'committee system.' By committee system is meant both the committees themselves and the practice of handling congressional business this way.

The committees do the preliminary and preparatory tasks, but they do much more as well. Indeed, the bulk of the real work of Congress is done by them and within them, rather than on the floor. The committees are in fact "little legislatures"[20]—distinct entities, with much independence, great powers, and characteristic individual personalities. The most immediately striking fact about the system is that (subject to the familiar caveat that there are exceptions to almost every statement that can be made about Congress) the committees are a gateway through which all legislation must pass. In general, only legislation that has been recommended by a committee is even debated by either house, let alone enacted. But what of a proposal that does not pass the gateway? What if the committee disapproves of it, or does not get around to it amid the turmoil of the typical session of Congress, or even obstinately refuses to act on it at all? The short answer is that the proposal is dead. There are exceptions, but they are exceptions; the general rule is committee approval or oblivion.

The fundamental device by which the committee system operates is *reference of bills*. The fundamental idea underlying the device is that the committee is to be a permanent and responsible agent of its house. Reference of bills is as old as the committee system. However, its present statutory basis is the Legislative Reorganization Act of 1946, which is the fundamental statute governing the organization and procedure of Congress. This act provides that "all proposed legislation . . . relating to the subjects listed under the standing committees . . . shall be referred

---

[20] This celebrated phrase is from Woodrow Wilson's famous book, *Congressional Government*.

to such committees, respectively. . . ."[21] Thus, when a bill is introduced it usually is immediately and automatically referred to a particular committee. The Act's lists of subjects cover virtually everything Congress legislates on. They give to each committee a field—its *jurisdiction*, as these fields are called—over which it reigns, since normally all bills in that field must pass through its hands. Committees usually defend their territories fiercely against any encroachment and oppose any efforts to send to another committee any bills that 'belong' to them. They are usually upheld in doing so by the parent house. There are of course some overlaps of jurisdictions and some cases of doubt; modern government and its concerns cannot be divided into watertight compartments. But in most cases jurisdiction is readily determined and is exclusive.[22]

Thus secured in both their function and their territories, the committees (and especially the *standing* committees)[23] are the basic working groups of Congress. In the main it is by them that proposals and controversies are considered, evidence and arguments on facts and issues shaped and collected, bargains and the reconciliations of competing interests developed, the actual statutes drafted or revised, the highly important 'reports' to the houses made,[24] and floor debates conducted. Legislators, executive officials, lobbying groups, and interested citizens do much—often most—of their planning, advocating, struggling, and negotiating on legislative measures at the committee stage of the legislative process. Accordingly, we need to look closely at these formidable institutions.

As to membership,[25] each house has a full set of committees (there are also some additional ones composed of members from both houses). They vary in size from the House Appropriations Committee with fifty members to some Senate committees with a mere handful of members. Each representative belongs to at least one committee and often to both a 'major' and a 'minor' committee. Each senator belongs to two major committees, and sometimes more. The rule, departed from only rarely and under unusual circumstances, is that every committee is to have both Republican and Democratic members, and in numbers roughly proportional to the parties' numbers in the house concerned. The system thus

---

[21] Sections 102 and 121 of the Legislative Reorganization Act of 1946, 60 Stat. 812 (1946).

[22] Committee jurisdiction was one of several subjects put on the agenda of the joint House-Senate Committee on the Organization of Congress, established in March 1965.

[23] There are other kinds of committees besides standing committees, e.g., *special* and *select* committees, created for a particular task and expiring when that task is completed.

[24] The report is the formal written statement made by a committee to its parent house when it returns a bill to the house. A report usually contains a description of the bill and of its intended effect, of what the committee did, and of what the committee recommends; see the bibliographical note to this chapter.

[25] There are numerous studies of congressional practice on committee assignments. See for example Nicholas A. Masters, "House Committee Assignments," *American Political Science Review*, LV (June, 1961), 345–57.

contemplates that partisanship and party strife is to go on *within* the committee, rather than in struggles for access to it, and that all the confrontations of democratic politics can freely take place there. The committee can be a microcosm of American political life, especially of those parts of it concerned with the committee's subjects.

As to internal organization, the dominant principle is *seniority*,[26] which is length of continuous service *on the committee*. A member of a committee ranks (on his side, Republican or Democratic) in accordance with his seniority. The chairman is the member who has most seniority on his side, and the 'ranking minority member,' the highest position on the minority side, is the minority party member with the most on his.[27] Status on the committee, and perquisites, and often authority, are in vital respects the product of seniority. Further, there is an associated principle that a member once appointed to a committee is entitled to stay on it as long as his party has space available on it for him. (When a party loses seats in a house in an election, its committee seats are correspondingly reduced.) The immediate result is that service on a committee tends to become a *career* and *a route to power;* the typical member, when he gets on a committee whose field is a satisfactory one for him, often stays on it for his whole career in Congress. Whether seniority and the stability in committee membership that it produces are good or bad, is a question we shall explore later. Here we only note the cohesiveness and separateness they tend to give the committees as self-contained functioning entities.

As to internal distribution of power, the dominant principle of the committee system is despotism—despotism tempered or limited here and there but despotism nonetheless. The chairman is the despot. This is the more remarkable because his position is due almost solely to seniority, not to ability, or support, or achievements, or external influence. But it is the case. The rules of Congress provide few constraints on him, and custom and the committees' self-adopted rules do not generally provide many more. He is controlled, to the extent that he is, by politics and by personal pressures, not by official requirements.

The result is that, within broad limits and barring rather exceptional circumstances, the chairman rules the committee. He calls meetings or he does not call them much as he sees fit. He largely controls the agenda and proceedings at meetings he does call. And he usually has in practice a near-veto over committee action; it is difficult, especially on the House side, to get a bill to the floor over really determined opposition by the chairman. Even when a bill reaches the floor, he is entitled to a leading and powerful role in debate. And his powers over the committee staff

---

[26] See George Goodwin, Jr., "The Seniority System in Congress," *American Political Science Review,* LIII (June, 1959), 412–36.

[27] For the very few exceptions to this rule in the House in the modern era, see George B. Galloway, *History of the House of Representatives* (New York: Thomas Y. Crowell Company, 1961), pp. 68–9. Exceptions in the Senate are few, and usually arise only when the more senior member elects to decline the post.

and even over the functions and fates of junior members of the committee are not much less than absolute.

The committee system, and the band of veteran potentates who preside over it as chairmen and ranking minority members (positions of similar status), can already be seen to be an extremely important part of the legislative process. But even so the whole tale is not told. These powers and this importance are increased—indeed, literally multiplied—by the *sub*committees established by most committees in recent years. These, modeling themselves on their parents, have often acquired great power of their own, and at times permanence and independence as well. This has greatly increased both the amount of work the committees can do and also the effects of both the virtues and the vices of the committee system. We shall return to these later.

The procedural framework and the standing rules. "Lawmakers must themselves be governed by law, else they would in confusion worse confounded quickly come to grief."[28]

Almost everybody has heard about 'the rules' of the House and Senate and of seeming abuses of them: Filibusters by a few determined senators often successfully obstructing legislation the majority strongly favors; the Rules Committee doing the same in the House; legislation being passed or defeated by procedural tricks and wily parliamentary maneuvers rather than by fair debate and free vote, and so on. We therefore tend automatically to be suspicious of the rules and of the whole procedural framework of which they are a part. Real abuses do exist— perhaps inevitably. But some system is indispensable, and the actual procedural system is a vital and useful part of the internal system of authority in Congress.

The procedural system is old. Indeed, the necessity for a procedural system was already well known in the Founders' day. The manual Thomas Jefferson prepared, when as Vice President he presided over the Senate, was based on the traditional procedure of the House of Commons, and is to this day part of the rules of both House and Senate.

The procedural system is complex. Jefferson's manual and the other sources have been elaborated and developed over the years, and now cover in detail virtually every conceivable aspect of procedure. This

---

[28] Robert Luce, *Legislative Procedure: Parliamentary Practices and the Course of Business in the Framing of Statutes* (Boston: Houghton Mifflin Company, 1922), p. 1. The passage goes on:

> It is agreed that 'the bad mode of deliberating' by the National Assembly was one of the chief causes leading to the catastrophes of the French Revolution. A hundred members might be seen trying to address the House at the same time. . . . No rules were observed in the conduct of business. . . . 'If one single rule had been adopted, namely that every motion should be reduced to writing . . . it is astonishing how great an influence it would have had on their debates and on their measures.'

(The passage is quoting a distinguished member of the British House of Commons, who witnessed the tumultuous collapse of the first French assembly after the upheaval of 1789.)

growth has taken place in the common-law manner, partly by formal adoption of new rules but mainly by the gradual case-by-case accretion of custom and 'precedents'—decisions in specific cases by the two houses and their officers. The precedents of the House of Representatives alone now fill several stout volumes.[29] The system thus answers not only the obvious procedural questions we are all familiar with but also deals with the most remarkable tangles and intricacies. How bills are introduced, the jurisdictions and powers of committees, the way in which committees report, the various avenues whereby reported bills reach the floor, the regulation of debate, the scope of permissible amendments, all these things and many more are subject to it. Here, to illustrate the technicality of the procedural problems Congress faces, is a sample passage from the *briefest* and *simplest* of the authoritative treatises:

> A motion to strike out the enacting clause is, in effect, a preferential amendment, and in order at any time recognition is secured to offer it during the reading of the bill for amendment (VII, 787) but is not in order until after the first section of the bill has been read. (V. 5327; VIII, 2619). . . . The reading of a bill for amendment in the Committee of the Whole being concluded, a motion to strike out the enacting clause is not in order (IV, 4782; VIII, 2368). . . . [but] where a bill contained but one paragraph the motion was entertained at the conclusion of the reading of the bill. (VIII, 2618). . . . [it] takes precedence of the motion to amend (§875; V, 5326; VIII, 2622, 2626, 2627), and may be offered while an amendment is pending (V, 5328–5331; VIII, 2624), but like other motions to amend, yields to the motion to refer when reported to the House from the Committee of the Whole (VIII, 2634).[30]

The procedural system tries to do two often contradictory things at once. It tries to get the business of Congress dealt with in an orderly, precise, and decisive fashion so that majority action may be taken, and it also tries to hear and record dissents and minority stands. In this latter it is in harmony with an underlying goal of the American polity, securing agreement by free debate and bargaining among diverse groups.

The procedural system is strict. But it can be manipulated. Nothing is more common under it than that something must be done at the exact time, and in the exact manner, and under the exact circumstances as the rules provide, or else it cannot be done at all. But learned parliamentarians can often, on the proper occasion and with the requisite support in the house, get around many restrictions. Indeed, the Senate often proceeds "under suspension of the rules," a device which makes many of the restrictions inapplicable and can be adopted "by the unanimous consent of the Senators present." Suspension is resorted to for convenience in

---

[29] *Hinds' and Cannon's Precedents of the House of Representatives of the United States,* published by the U.S. Government Printing Office.

[30] Clarence Cannon, *Cannon's Procedure in the House of Representatives* (Washington, D.C.: Government Printing Office, 1953). The references in parentheses are to volume and page of *Hinds' and Cannon's Precedents.*

dealing with routine, minor, or noncontroverted matters by agreement among the various leaderships and other influential members concerned.

The system in fact rests on consent entirely. This is not only as to its details and as to minor circumventions of its rigors, but also as to its very existence. That is to say, it rests upon the self-restraint of Congress itself. Congress makes the rules, and Congress can unmake them or simply disregard them. Thus, if a bare majority in each house should choose to enact a statute in total disregard of each and every rule and procedural restriction, nobody could stop them, and the resulting statute (a few constitutional questions aside) would be perfectly valid.[31] Yet such exercises of blunt majoritarian power are virtually unknown; fidelity to the rules is in truth the rule. This tells us something about Congress and about the procedural system. What produces such self-restraint in a great and stormy legislature, where matters of absolutely first importance for the nation—and for all the parties, interests, and factions involved—are constantly under consideration, and where ambitions and convictions flame at the highest intensity? Why do majorities thus restrain themselves, even when convinced of the rightness and crucial importance of their cause?

The personal virtues of the members, an enlightened general awareness that in the long run self-restraint works to everybody's advantage, and respect for the authority that the tradition of substantial compliance since the Founders' time has conferred upon the procedural system—all play their parts.

But there is a more basic reason: simple necessity. As we have seen, some of the deepest forces of the American political and constitutional order drive Congress toward being a competent and independent entity. It could not be one without a procedural framework deeply built into its internal system of authority. It must have what any successful procedural system for a legislative assembly provides: a process which enables the assembly to identify problems of public policy, formulate the issues these involve, develop and consider proposed courses of action to deal with them, act upon the proposals, and observe and review the results of its actions.

In short, the procedural framework of the legislative process in Congress is a remarkable machine, sometimes stiff and cumbersome, sometimes baffling, sometimes startlingly powerful, but always complex and always important. It does much, as do the other elements of the internal system of authority, to condition Congress's operation, the subject to which we now turn.

The Operation of Congress: The Legislative Branch at Work

What we have said so far can, if taken by itself, give a false impression; it can make Congress appear simpler and more orderly than it is.

---

[31] See Luce, Ch. 1.

In reality Congress is the center of a veritable maelstrom of activity, activity that is not only confused and intense but also made up of myriads of foci of conflict, a maelstrom of innumerable struggles.[32] Congressional actions create, destroy, or vitally affect interests of enormous magnitude and of the most diverse sorts. Consequently, all manner of groups and factions, public officials, and agencies (and Congress itself) pour almost unbelievable quantities of effort and thought into eliciting, forestalling, and influencing congressional action on issues that literally every day of every session press upon Congress in far greater numbers than it can possibly consider. Congress represents its constituents, makes public policy, oversees government, and performs its other functions under conditions that often involve much confusion and almost always involve intense struggles.

The idea of the legislative struggle must be made precise, however, because it can obscure important distinctions and be delusively dramatic. In Congress 'struggle' ranges broadly, from mere trivial jostlings for petty advantage up through the real conflicts of Madisonian factions. But we seldom have seen there what the term also conjures up, the grand and ominous confrontations of the Red and the Black, where in a riven society, two great sides, locked in a final conflict, battle to the death.[33] Such confrontations make for a grimly simple legislative scene, grimly easy to understand, with everything polarized on the single dimension. This is not the American scene; the American polity has solved or repressed these fundamental divisions, and its Congress is engaged not with one or two of these, but rather with a confused and tumultuous horde of lesser divisions.

The result is the maelstrom, unintelligible unless we have some method of surveying and interpreting it. One useful method is to look first for some pattern, or rhythm, in a hypothetical average session of Congress.

The Pattern of the Session

Each 'Congress'[34] is elected in an even-numbered year and convenes for the first time in January of the following year. Its first session usually lasts until late summer or early fall. It then adjourns until the following January, when it convenes for its second and last regular session. It may recess for varying lengths of time during a session, and the President may call either or both houses into extraordinary or 'special' session at any time.

---

[32] Indeed, the title of a highly regarded book, Bertram Gross, *The Legislative Struggle: A Study in Social Combat* (New York: McGraw-Hill Book Company, Inc., 1953), is a vivid formulation of the author's central point, which is that the key to the functioning of Congress lies in the fact of struggle among competing interests and interest groups.

[33] The great exceptions are the period just before the Civil War and the Reconstruction Era after it.

[34] Congresses are numbered consecutively; the First Congress first convened in 1789 and the Eighty-ninth in 1965.

The convening of a session, and especially the first session of a new Congress, usually takes place in an atmosphere of considerable public interest and often of some suspense. In this first dramatic stage the central presence of the Presidency is manifest; after Congress is organized the first important formal event is the receiving of the President's first messages. The two principal ones are his State of the Union Message, which outlines his 'legislative program' for the session, and his Budget Message, which accompanies and discusses the Administration's proposed budget for the fiscal year beginning on the ensuing July 1. These two messages are generally delivered in the first few days, and several other messages on specialized topics not much later.[35] Congress thus early has before it the main body of the President's proposals for legislation and major statements by him on other aspects of public policy, and these usually dominate the session in this stage. (We shall also see that the President has been active in the congressional arena before this and that he continues to be active throughout the session.)

Before the session convened, however, less formal and less visible but exceedingly vital processes have been going on. First, all the numerous parts of the congressional complex have been making their own plans for the session. The congressional parties, the state delegations, the regional and ideological blocs, the leaderships, the committees and subcommittees, and all the rest of the groups in Congress have been busy for weeks, each from its own viewpoint. Second, all the interest groups and government agencies have been doing the same—reviewing, planning, calculating, sounding out sentiment 'on the Hill'[36] and among their friends and foes, and devising their own legislative programs and strategies. From these and other presession and early-session activities, the outlines of the first agenda for the session begin to emerge.

The materials for the session. The legislative process is a continuous one. Each session encounters some new problems and goes off on some unexpected enterprises. However, many things are either left over from earlier sessions or else recur session after session. The striking examples are the great long-term federal programs, such as national defense, foreign aid, regulation of agriculture, and the construction of public works. But there are literally hundreds of less conspicuous leftover or recurring matters. In short, there must be early in every session a sorting and organizing of a mass of materials, old and new, that make up the grist for the congressional mills.

The grist can to some extent be classified. The early stages of the legislative process usually disclose a half dozen or so major issues, some

---

[35] See Article I, section 3: "He shall from time to time give to the Congress Information on the State of the Union. . . ."

[36] 'The Hill' is Capitol Hill, the slight eminence where the Capitol and the Congressional Office buildings stand. The White House is about a mile and a half to the northwest. In between, 'downtown,' are a number of the principal government buildings. So on the Hill means in and around Congress and downtown means in the departments and agencies.

old and some new, the headline-makers, that seem likely to dominate the session. Behind these march at least three other principal groups. One is matters of lesser but still major importance and controversiality. A second is the very large group that are minor compared to the other two but are still of some general public importance. A third is the vast bulk of minutiae, including matters of petty or merely local interest, housekeeping chores, the never-ending task of overhauling, revising, and updating existing legislation, and the like. Striking facts of the congressional workload are its sheer size and the high proportion of seemingly insignificant matters.

The preparatory—or quiescent?—stages. After the excitement of the President's messages and the identification of the expected headline-makers, and the general whir and bustle of the early stages of the session, the next several weeks often seem to be a time of quiescence. Few bills are passed, floor activity is desultory, nothing much seems to be happening, and criticisms that Congress is wasting time and accomplishing nothing begin to be heard. In truth, a good deal of time is being wasted. But two activities are going on that are inconspicuously laying the groundwork for the hectic doings and spectacular developments of the later parts of the session.

One is a continuation of the process, already mentioned, of surveying, planning, exploring, and organizing. It is now especially concentrated on what might be called the diplomatic aspect of the legislative struggle, that of the politicking, negotiating, and bargaining among the participants; alliances are being made and unmade, deals and arrangements set in motion, and campaigns of influence and persuasion conducted.

The second is the legislative work of committees and subcommittees and their staffs. The various bills are in their hands; the fortunate ones are being actively worked on. This work involves extensive study and inquiry, delays while the views of the departments and agencies concerned are collected, and innumerable conferences and discussions. Then *hearings*, normally the next stage in the committee process, require considerable preparation and generate voluminous records of testimony and documentation which must be dealt with, even if often in cursory fashion.

These two procedures have to be pretty nearly completed before bills are ready for the floor. A 'stage wait' is therefore almost built into the legislative process, and a session may be weeks or even months old before much legislation introduced in January, or even legislation left over from the preceding session, is ready for consideration on the floor.

At full flow. At some point however, perhaps well along in the spring or in the early summer, all the machinery is started and turning; politics, the preliminary and preparatory processes, and the committees are working so that legislation in quantity is emerging and ready for floor action. The mills are now going at their full standard pace. Several currents are evident.

A good deal of legislation is either noncontroversial or else controversy about it has been settled off-stage. For such legislation, once the committee work is done, passage comes without substantial debate and by means of various 'consent' procedures. Congress protects its precious floor time jealously from matters it is not really interested in—in part to be able to squander it on things it is. It is these latter, and there are a few every session and not always the supposed headline-makers, that inspire most intense debate and consume most floor time.

In between the extremes lie the run-of-the-mine matters that make up the bulk of the work of Congress. These come up by regular channels, are debated in the ordinary course and for the expected time (which often strikes the outsider as surprisingly short), and are briskly 'voted up' or 'voted down,' as the Capitol Hill phrase goes.

Among the regular features of every session are the appropriations bills. These are bills that appropriate—i.e., allow or direct the actual spending of—money. Twelve or thirteen regular appropriations bills, and two or three supplemental ones, are enacted each session. They must be; money has to be provided because the government has to go on, and only appropriations can legally provide it.[37] But all of them contain some keenly controversial points. Accordingly, the legislative process here has stormy passages. The Appropriations Committees of both houses, and their networks of subcommittees, largely dominate because the vast amounts of money, and the incredibly complex accounting, financial, and policy problems involved, are so hard to handle. Many of the tempests, accommodations, and compromises therefore take place within the committee procedures. But there is plenty left to provide fiery debates, especially when the committee itself had doubts (although it often closes ranks on the floor even when it has been sharply divided), or when some members of its house refuse to accept its verdicts. For years a feature of every session has been the lively episode when the appropriations bill for foreign aid came to the floor of the House. The chairman of the Appropriations subcommittee that handles it has been very suspicious of the program and has striven to cut its funds drastically, which the Administration's supporters have opposed.

The adjournment rush. The regular appropriations bills come up for debate at different times during the session, after the first two months or so. When most have been enacted, a fair number of the major and controversial measures debated, the necessary routine and housekeeping business dealt with, and some dent made in the eternal flood of minor or specific matters—say about mid-June—speculation begins over when the session will adjourn. Sessions generally run longer than predicted,

---

[37] Article I, section 9, provides that "No money shall be drawn from the Treasury, but in Consequence of Appropriations made by Law." There are occasions when Congress does not get the appropriations bill passed by July 1, the start of the fiscal year, and only resort to makeshifts enables government to go on until passage of the bill.

well on into August or September or even later. And often there arise parliamentary or political impasses that cause the by-then weary and fretful denizens of Capitol Hill to wonder whether the end will ever come.

It always does, however, and it is always preceded by the adjournment rush, a period of some days of febrile activity and great confusion during which vast numbers of matters are acted upon with extraordinary speed. The rush is natural, perhaps inevitable, in congressional life. Some of the participants in it are making a last try to get their projects acted upon. Some have deliberately held theirs back to try to slip them through—unnoticed in the confusion and, hence, unopposed. And often it is only the pressure of impending adjournment that forces compromise and agreement on matters that have been in deadlock.

Adjournment ends only the session, not the work of Congress. And of course planning and politicking never cease.

The Sources and Handling of Legislation

Representative assemblies do make laws—witness our custom of calling them *legislatures*.[38] But not all legislate in the fullest sense. For example, British statutes are usually prepared by the government departments; selected, introduced, and managed in Parliament by the Cabinet; and passed automatically, after at most some parliamentary revision, by the disciplined votes of the majority party. And for some assemblies, legislation—indeed, policy-making generally—is actually only a minor concern, with representation, oversight, or other functions the important ones. Not so with Congress. It does many other important things besides legislating but legislation is in truth one of its central and principal functions, and it legislates in a very full sense; and its other functions are in the main closely related to this one.

The sources. The flow of legislation proposed to Congress is immense, a gigantic river. Furthermore, this river flows continuously, day after day and year after year, huge, turbulent, muddy, and unending. At least ten or twelve thousand bills, many minor or eccentric or repetitive but many not, are introduced in an average session. Yet even this figure is an inadequate measure; often a great array of separate proposals and vast amounts of effort, planning, and activity eventuate in a single bill— a final proposal agreed upon by a whole throng of individuals and groups that have been working on it. And the actual output of completed legislation, though minute compared to this input, annually fills immense volumes, thousands of pages of intricate and technical law.[39]

---

[38] The word is from the Latin *legislato* (*lex*, *legis*, law, and *latio–nem*—bringing or proposing).

[39] The laws are published each year in the *U.S. Statutes at Large*. The public laws for 1962 fill nearly two thousand pages. The volumes since the First Congress fill about thirty feet of shelf space. The public laws of general importance that are currently in effect are codified by subject matter in the *United States Code*, which fills about three feet of shelf space with very large and very closely printed pages.

A Bill

To enforce the 15th Amendment

S. Cities as the Voting Rights Act of 1965

Sec. 2- Many States and, allowing any
State or political subdivision to institute...
every federal, State or local election...
in which any person of any other race or color...
is permitted to vote.

Sec. 3

An every part and all of any article in which...
(a) [and where shall test] upon part
of A G [are needed of null of voting] by the...

AN ACT

To enforce the Fifteenth Amendment to the
Constitution of the United States

Be it enacted by the Senate and House of

Representatives of the United States of America in

Congress assembled

That the Congress finds—

In many areas large numbers of qualified

citizens have been and continue to be denied the right

to vote on account of race or color, in violation of

the Fifteenth Amendment.

The most significant means of denying the

right to vote on account of race or color is the

racially discriminatory administration of tests and

AN ACT

To Enforce the Fifteenth Amendment to the Constitution of the United States

Be it enacted by the Senate and the House of Representatives of the United

States of America in Congress assembled.

That this Act may be cited as the Voting Rights Act of 1965.

Section 2. In any State or political subdivision thereof which has citizens

of different races or colors and as to which the Director of the Census certifies

---

89TH CONGRESS
1ST SESSION

S. 1564

IN THE SENATE OF THE UNITED STATES

MARCH 18, 1965

Mr. MANSFIELD (for himself, Mr. DIRKSEN, Mr. KUCHEL, Mr. AIKEN, Mr.
ALLOTT, Mr. ANDERSON, Mr. BARTLETT, Mr. BASS, Mr. BAYH, Mr. BENNETT,
Mr. BOGGS, Mr. BREWSTER, Mr. BURDICK, Mr. CASE, Mr. CHURCH, Mr.
CLARK, Mr. COOPER, Mr. COTTON, Mr. DODD, Mr. DOMINICK, Mr. DOUGLAS,
Mr. FONG, Mr. GRUENING, Mr. HARRIS, Mr. HART, Mr. HARTKE, Mr. INOUYE,
Mr. JACKSON, Mr. JAVITS, Mr. JORDAN of Idaho, Mr. KENNEDY of Massa-
chusetts, Mr. KENNEDY of New York, Mr. LAUSCHE, Mr. LONG of Missouri,
Mr. MAGNUSON, Mr. McCARTHY, Mr. McGEE, Mr. McGOVERN, Mr. Mc-
INTYRE, Mr. McNAMARA, Mr. METCALF, Mr. MONDALE, Mr. MONRONEY,
Mr. MONTOYA, Mr. MORSE, Mr. MORTON, Mr. MOSS, Mr. MUNDT, Mr.
MURPHY, Mr. MUSKIE, Mr. NELSON, Mrs. NEUBERGER, Mr. PASTORE, Mr.
PEARSON, Mr. PELL, Mr. PROUTY, Mr. PROXMIRE, Mr. RANDOLPH, Mr. RIBI-
COFF, Mr. SALTONSTALL, Mr. SCOTT, Mr. SYMINGTON, Mr. TYDINGS, Mr.
WILLIAMS of New Jersey, Mr. YARBOROUGH, and Mr. YOUNG of Ohio)
introduced the following bill; which was read twice and referred to the
Committee on the Judiciary

A BILL

To enforce the fifteenth amendment to the Constitution of the
United States.

A BILL
To enforce the Fifteenth Amendment to the
Constitution of the United States

Be it enacted by the Senate and House of
Representatives of the United States of America in
Congress assembled, That this Act shall be known as
the "Voting Rights Act of 1965."

SEC. 2. No voting qualification or procedure shall be imposed on or applied to persons of
one race or color which is not applied equally to
persons of any other race or color.

the Voting Rights Act signed into law on August 6, 1965. First are some of the sketchy notes made by one draftsman at an early stage in the session. The next exhibit is far less rough but still a draft, typed on plain paper in a busy legislative office. Another draft reflects a different approach; drafts piled up thick and fast, so much so that they not only had to be dated but also labeled in hasty longhand, "A.M." or "P.M." At last, a preliminary agreement is reached between Congress and the White House. On March 15, the President delivered his message on the subject, and on March 18 a bill based on the agreement was introduced as S. 1564. Despite its finished look, S. 1564 was a long way from adoption. Indeed, as things turned out, it was not the bill Congress finally acted upon. Analysis, pressures, private negotiations, redrafting, subcommittee meetings, public hearings, amendments, further redrafting—the legislative process ground on. Senator Everett Dirksen (R. Ill.), leader of the Republican minority, favored a strong provision authorizing federal court supervision of the casting (and counting) of ballots. Here is an excerpt from an early proposal of his, with longhand revisions. Others preferred a purely administrative procedure rather than court enforcement, and also objected to Dirksen's proposal of what they termed an 'escape hatch.' A compromise was accepted whereby Senator Dirksen relinquished the escape provisions but secured an important element of judicial supervision. Here is part of the minority leader's press release on this crucial compromise. Finally, after numerous similar episodes, a statute was enacted.

General that all such persons have been placed on the rolls of persons eligible to vote, the Attorney General may institute an action ~~in the appropriate district~~ to protect the rights of such persons secured by Secs. 4, 5, 7, 9, 10 and 11, and for an order requiring that such persons be permitted to vote. Such action shall be filed in the appropriate district court, which shall have jurisdiction thereover, ~~and~~ upon request of the Attorney General shall be determined by a court of three judges in accordance with the provisions of section 2284 of Title 28, U. S. Code. The relief in such action may include the appointment by the court of such persons as may be necessary to observe at such places as the court may order, whether persons entitled to vote are permitted to vote and have their votes counted. The court may in its discretion impound all ballots cast in such election until such time as

Public Law 89-110
89th Congress, S. 1564
August 6, 1965

An Act

To enforce the fifteenth amendment to the Constitution of the United States, and for other purposes.

Be it enacted by the Senate and House of Representatives of the United States of America in Congress assembled, That this Act shall be known as the "Voting Rights Act of 1965".

SEC. 2. No voting qualification or prerequisite to voting, or standard, practice, or procedure shall be imposed or applied by any State or political subdivision to deny or abridge the right of any citizen of the United States to vote on account of race or color.

SEC. 3. (a) Whenever the Attorney General institutes a proceeding under any statute to enforce the guarantees of the fifteenth amendment in any State or political subdivision the court shall authorize the appointment of Federal examiners by the United States Civil

Voting Rights
Act of 1965.

Judicial remedies.

For Immediate Release

STATEMENT BY SENATOR DIRKSEN

I have not been deeply wedded to the so-called escape provisions in the pending Voting Rights Bill, namely, the 60% provision. Applying to registrants and the national voting average as the springboard from which states and subdivisions can take themselves out from in under the Voting Rights Bill. I have only one concern and that is that the bill be in truth and in fact a Voting Rights Bill which will actually achieve the right to vote rather than to be content with punishment for those who impede this right.

Accordingly, I am quite willing to relinquish my position on the so-called escape provisions provided the bill contains both some provision for a state or subdivision which has effectively cleansed itself to prove this to a court and a section mandating the Attorney General to go into court on receipt of 20 or more written complaints from persons whose names have not been placed on the official voting list. Under this provision the Attorney

Proposed legislation comes from many sources, as we might expect from the decentralization both of Congress and of the American political system generally.

One source is the obvious and traditional one, the individual senator or representative. However (though measurement is difficult), this source probably has been for some time comparatively minor.[40]

Probably the largest and in many ways most important source is the executive branch. The White House supplies many of the major proposals dealing with great issues affecting the nation as a whole. In addition masses of other proposals, many narrow and specialized but also many of substantial importance, come from the departments and agencies; each has its 'legislative program,' the proposals it would like to see enacted. Indeed, to some extent Congress expects them to make recommendations about improving and adding to the statutes they administer.

A third source is the interest groups. Most have legislative programs, and a great deal of proposed legislation, and a substantial part of that which is finally enacted, originates with them, directly or indirectly.

A fourth source is the committees. They regard themselves as having continuing power over everything within their jurisdictions. This includes matters on which new legislative action appears desirable, all legislation they have handled in the past, and all aspects of its administration. Committees and subcommittees therefore often initiate legislation quite on their own. Also they often do so because of suggestions from individual senators and representatives, from the departments and agencies, from the White House, or from interest groups. Indeed, it is misleading to think of the sources as really separate. The true picture is one of interaction—sometimes cooperation, sometimes rivalry, sometimes the closest teamwork—centered usually in and around the committee because of the committee system of handling legislation.

The handling of legislation. It is easy to state the formal steps a piece of proposed legislation usually goes through on its way to enactment: introduction as a bill or resolution in one house; reference to the proper committee; reference by it to a subcommittee; staff study; solicitation of comments from the departments and agencies concerned; hearings by the subcommittee; subcommittee consideration and 'mark-up' of it; report on it by the subcommittee; hearings, consideration and 'mark-up' by the full committee; report by the full committee to the parent house; placing on a 'calendar'; determination by the house to debate it; debate, amendment, and passage; the same process, with virtually all the same steps, in the other house; settlement of differences between the two

---

[40] There are few recent instances of a major statute largely originated and carried through primarily by an individual legislator. See Emmette S. Redford, *Congress Passes the Federal Aviation Act of 1958* (University, Ala.: The University of Alabama Press for the Inter-University Case Program, 1961) for a near-instance. Most individual undertakings deal with very minor or narrow matters, however.

houses' versions by a conference committee; final passage by both houses in identical form; submission to the President; reference of it by his office to the interested departments and agencies for their advice to him on whether to veto or sign it; reports by them to him; signature by the President.

Of these steps four especially require notice. Not all are important in the history of every statute. Indeed some can on occasion be very simple and *pro forma* and all can take many different shapes. But they give us the main landmarks in the complex turmoil of the legislative process.

The birth of a proposal. Should legislation be sought? is a question that can get asked at nearly every turn of every part of governing, and by everybody concerned with governing—legislators, the President and his men, officials in the departments and agencies, committee staffs, interest groups.

In late 1954 a group of union leaders decided to seek federal legislation raising the minimum wage in the first session of the new Eighty-fourth Congress, convening in January 1955. The resulting campaign was an important event in that session. In December 1957 Senator Monroney of Oklahoma, chairman of the Subcommittee on Aviation of the Senate Commerce Committee, decided, after many discussions with government aviation officials and officials of the commercial airlines' trade association and lobbying organization, that a new federal statute regulating commercial aviation was needed. Out of this emerged the Federal Aviation Act of 1958.[41] In both cases the decision might have been *not* to seek legislation, but to pursue some other approach, or to work on some quite different project. Behind every legislative proposal there is such a decision, often made by some informal, unofficial, group.

Committee handling. Committee procedures often assume the air and trappings of an impartial, nonpartisan, almost judicial inquiry. This can be misleading; seldom is committee work that much insulated from politics, interest-group activities, and the other processes of government. But it is equally misleading to suppose that committee work is merely a facade, with all the studies, hearings, and deliberations serving merely to give plausibility and an appearance of procedural legitimacy to ends determined off stage by scheming and politicking. There are rigged hearings and predetermined results. But there are also many instances of responsible judgment based on genuine inquiry. The typical situation is a blend. We must recognize that politics, interest groups, publicity, partisanship, domineering chairmen, and all the rest bulk large in the handling of legislation by congressional committees. But congressional fidelity to the institutional arrangements, and a congressional sense of

---

[41] See Gus Tyler, *A Campaign for a Federal Minimum Wage* (Case Studies in Practical Politics; New York: Henry Holt and Co., Inc., 1959), and Redford (see note 40).

independence, responsibility, and craftsmanship, also bulk large. Four important aspects of the committee process should be noted here.

First, access to the committee process is limited, and narrows at each successive stage. Many proposals do not get committee attention at all. Of those that do, many are abandoned or rejected at each stage.

Second, development of the facts, issues, and contentions may be stage-managed but it is usually fairly extensive. On occasion some sides to a question may be neglected or even suppressed, and sometimes inquiry is cursory. But, although often not sharply focused and precise, the development in the typical case is pretty thorough, within limits set by the nature of the situation.

Third, seldom does a proposal that is at all controverted get through without a great deal of bargaining and concession, perhaps especially in the final, closed mark-up session, when both supporters and critics are hardheadedly calculating the chances of getting it enacted. The final vote on the floor yields—or at least records—clear and simple results, Yes or No. The intermediate processes do not deal so much in the clean-cut.

Fourth, many people other than the legislators participate in the process. At virtually every turn not only staff members but also outsiders such as representatives of interest groups and administrative agencies are on hand and exerting influence. The roles of staff members are often particularly complex. Sometimes they act as technicians, professional experts in the committee's subjects or experts in law and government; sometimes as experienced veterans of service with the committee, with vast knowledge of what has been done and not done and what can and cannot be done; sometimes as specialists in the politics and group interactions that surround and color everything; and sometimes as recognized representatives of the interest groups and factions concerned.

The struggle for consideration on the floor. A fair number of bills that have been thoroughly studied by a subcommittee and its committee, reported by the committee with strong recommendations that they be passed, and are important and powerfully-supported legislation, either never appear on the floor, never even get the chance to be debated, and quietly die in the shadows, or are debated only in most limited and cursory fashion. This is because both houses are swamped with proposed legislation, more than they can ever consider properly—or even at all. Consequently there are many parliamentary, procedural, and political obstructions on the path to the floor.

These obstructions are to be found in House and Senate alike but they are most visible on the House side. In the House a legislative proposal must in most cases be approved for consideration on the floor by the Rules Committee.[42] And even when a proposal has gotten to

---

[42] Unless its supporters try to get it on the floor by one of the uncertain and seldom-successful devices that circumvent the Rules Committee. For example, by means of the 'discharge petition' a majority of the House members can force a bill to the floor.

the floor it may find itself being debated in violently limited time (say an hour for complex legislation), or under circumstances where amendments and technical objections that will cut it to bits are easy to make, or where it is squeezed by other and greater events and its friends are powerless or far away. And all these things work in reverse too; a bill that has the right backing and comes at the right combination of time and circumstance flashes through with dazzling ease. A great deal, a very great deal—indeed, much of the bill's chances for life—depends on circumstances, on the intricate interplay of forces in the congressional arena, and most of all on the skill, prestige, determination, and support its friends can muster.

The conference committee. It is very common for a piece of proposed legislation to be passed in differing forms by the two houses. The differences must be eliminated if it is to become law. If this cannot be achieved by ready agreement or by informal means it becomes the task of a conference committee. A conference committee is made up of members of both parties and both houses, appointed for the specific purpose by the leaderships of the two houses, normally from among the more senior members concerned. A representative once wrote to his constituents back home:

> For those who have followed these newsletters from the beginning I have sought to trace the interplay of forces at work here. There is cooperation. There is contention: the ins versus the outs, the old boys versus the new boys. Through it all we have been trying to perceive the locus of power. The conference committee is the central core of that power.[43]

The conference committee always has a broad range of discretion; its proceedings and recommendations cannot be effectively reviewed by anybody, and each house is very much inclined in most cases to accept the recommendations of its conferees. The conference committee members are always senior and usually very senior indeed—ten, twenty, thirty years in Congress. They usually are acknowledged experts on the subject of the bill, as high-ranking members of the committees that considered it. They usually are thoroughly familiar with the bill itself and responsible for it. They meet in secret and no record is kept of what is said or done. How do they decide?

The evidence is necessarily scanty and uncertain, but it suggests the following. There is sometimes rancorous ugly partisanship. There is sometimes duplicity; members who supported a provision in public debate oppose it in secret conference. There is pride, stubbornness, crass bargaining. There is also much careful and responsible work, away from the glare of publicity. Republicans and Democrats, representatives and senators, conservatives and liberals, the conferees have worked and struggled with each other for many years over just such issues and problems as they now have before them, and expect to do so for many years more. In the typical case they know well that work-

---

[43] Miller, *op. cit.,* p. 114.

able agreements between diverse views must be reached, some sort of decision taken, the machinery of government kept turning. So, usually a quiet settlement is reached, by negotiation and compromise. The houses usually accept the settlement immediately and without demur; it becomes the will of Congress, and the formal work of legislating is done.[44]

The Process of "Legislative Oversight"[45]

A second major function of Congress grows naturally out of its function of handling proposed legislation. Any legislative body is naturally and properly concerned that the laws it makes "be faithfully executed"; at a minimum it wants to be sure that its mandates are not ignored or perverted. Equally naturally and properly, it wants to follow and appraise the working out of its policies in the actual application and to inform itself of emerging policy issues that may one day require legislative attention. And, equally naturally but not always quite so properly, it wants to exercise some continuing control over administration.

Congress does all this by a group of processes commonly given the somewhat odd title of 'legislative oversight.' We have already seen in general how Congress is organized and operates so we can describe this second major function in less space.

The tools and methods. The essence of these processes of legislative oversight is a continuous cycle of interrelationships between Congress and the Presidency, the administrative system, the interest groups, and the public. In this cycle every major element of congressional operation— committee work, floor action, and the work of individual members— comes into play. Normally, however, the processes take place mainly in and by means of the committee system, Congress's basic working machinery.

The committees operate here mainly with their authority over subjects, programs, and agencies within their jurisdictions. The informal is important. Each committee is usually in continuous informal contact with the sectors of the executive and administrative relevant to its jurisdiction. The chairman, or an important committee member, or an influential staff expert, inquires, comments, suggests—on occasion orders or threatens or forbids. The agency or administrator, well aware of the significance of the committee's authority, is inclined to obey or at least to respond, perhaps even to clear proposed action with the committee in advance.

This authority, congressional interest, and informality can breed

---

[44] See Clapp *op. cit.*, pp. 244–54, and Gilbert Y. Steiner, *The Congressional Conference Committee* (Urbana: University of Illinois Press, 1951).

[45] The phrase "legislative oversight" comes from the Legislative Reorganization Act (Section 136). The language of the Act suggests that it involves "continuous watchfulness." It has to do with overseeing rather than with overlooking.

dangers. The situation can develop to the point where the committee is running the agency, without either the formal legal right to do so or the responsibility for the results. This can offend against both separation of powers and the requirements of good management. But because the powers behind the authority are so flexible and so great, such dangers seem inevitable.[46] Four important powers upon which the legislative oversight is based are the following.

The general power to legislate. Congress is the creator of the departments and agencies of the government, and also of the statutes under which they operate and which they enforce. It can pass legislation in pretty much any form it likes, and containing pretty much any directions and requirements it likes, and can create a wide variety of agencies to administer it. It can include in the legislation detailed instructions on what is to be done, and how; it can require reports from the administrators (indeed, it has sometimes required that they get the approval of Congress or a congressional committee before they act); it can keep the administrators on a short tether by providing that the statute will remain in effect only for a short period, often only a year or two, and will thereafter have to be renewed by a new act if the program is to continue.

The power of the purse. Only Congress can order government funds to be spent. From this base it can, and does, exercise many controls. It may specify in great detail just what the money is to be spent for, and how. It may review in great detail just what has been done and not done before granting any further funds to a program, and make very clear to the administrators what it thinks should have been done in the past and now should be done in the future. Indeed, it has created a special agency, the General Accounting Office, responsible only to Congress, to carry out detailed surveillance and audit of expenditures, and of various aspects of administrative performance that can be related to expenditures.

The power over personnel. Congress must authorize offices before they can be filled, and in so doing can set the qualifications for them and the duties and authority they are to have. Also, the Senate has explicit constitutional power to pass upon the appointment of major officers of the government. So Congress can by these means control to some degree what is to be done and how it is to be done, and review it when it has been done by administrators.

The subpoena power. Finally, Congress has the basic power of compulsion upon which its investigatory activities ultimately rest. This is the power to compel by subpoena the testimony of witnesses and the production of documents. The power is subject to some constitutional limitations. The President has the right to order that matters close to what he asserts is his personal domain not be revealed; this right is

---

[46] A recent study of the subject is Joseph P. Harris, *Congressional Control of Administration* (Washington, D.C.: The Brookings Institution, 1964).

Activities in Congress

THE WASHINGTON POST
Thursday, Sept. 16, 1965   A 21

TODAY

Senate

Meets at 11 a.m.

Committees:

Commerce. 10 a.m. Open. On P.L. 88-108, work rules dispute. To hear James J. Reynolds, Assistant Secretary of Labor. Rm. 5110, New Bldg.

Commerce. 10 a.m. Exec. On committee business. Rm. 5112, New Bldg.

Finance. 10 a.m. Open. On H.R. 9042, implementing agreement between the U.S. and Canada relating to trade in automotive products. To hear Sen. Gaylord Nelson (D-Wis.); industry witnesses. Rm. 2221, New Bldg

Interior. Parks and Recreation Subcommittee. 10 a.m. Open. On S. 622, administration and protection of the Appalachian Trail. To hear Interior Department. Rm. 3110, New Bldg.

Labor and Public Welfare. Special Subcommittee. 10 a.m. Exec. On H.R. 7042, amend section 402(d) of the Federal Food, Drug and Cosmetic Act. Rm. 4232, New Bldg.

Public Works. 10 a.m. Open. On S. 2309, U.S. participation in the statewide exposition to be held in Alaska during 1967. To hear Alaska Centennial Commission and other Alaska witnesses. Rm. 4200, New Bldg.

Judiciary. Antitrust and Monopoly Subcommittee. 10:30 a.m. Open. On dual distribution. To hear Norman Geller, Republic Wire Corporation; Allan Levine, Automotive Service Independent Association; Ralph Bryson, Independent Garage Owners of America Association. Rm. 1318, New Bldg.

Labor and Public Welfare. 10:30 a.m. Exec. On nominations and other committee business. Rm. 4232, New Bldg.

Conferees. 2 p.m. Exec. On H.R. 728, amend vessel exchange provisions of the Merchant Marine Act. Rm. EF-100, Capitol.

House

Meets at noon to consider S. 2042.

relating to Atomic Energy Act, and conference reports.

Committees:

Agriculture: 10 a.m. Exec. To continue on sugar legislation. Rm. 1301, Longworth Bldg.

Banking and Currency. Domestic Finance Subcommittee. 10 a.m. Open. To continue hearings on S. 1698 and related bank merger bills. To hear Comptroller of the Currency James J. Saxon and K. A. Randall, Chairman, Federal Deposit Insurance Corp. Rm. 2128, Rayburn Bldg.

Foreign Affairs. Subcommittee on Foreign Economic Policy. 10 a.m. Open. Subcommittee on Foreign Economic Policy. On utilization of excess U.S.-owned foreign currency. To hear Rep. Lester L. Wolff (D-N.Y.). Rm. 2255, Rayburn Bldg.

Foreign Affairs. Subcommittee on State Department Organization and Foreign Operations. 10:30 a.m. Exec. Further consideration of Foreign Buildings Act amendments. Rm. 2200, Rayburn Bldg.

Interstate and Foreign Commerce. 10 a.m. Exec. On pending legislation. Rm. 2125, Rayburn Bldg.

Judiciary. 10 a.m. Open. Subcommittee No. 1. On Private Immigration bills. Rm. 2237, Rayburn Bldg.

Judiciary. Subcommittee No. 1. 10 a.m. Open. On Private Immigration 2141, Rayburn Bldg.

Merchant Marine and Fisheries. 10 a.m. Exec. On S. 944, to provide for expanded research and development in the marine environment of the U.S., to establish a National Council on

Marine Sciences, Engineering and Resources. Rm. 1334, Longworth Bldg.

Post Office and Civil Service. Subcommittee on Postal Operations. 9:30 a.m. Exec. Pending legislation. Rm. 215, Cannon Bldg.

Post Office and Civil Service. 10 a.m. Exec. On pending legislation. Rm. 215, Cannon Bldg.

Public Works. 10 a.m. Exec. On pending legislation. Rm. 2167, Rayburn Bldg.

Rules. 10:30 a.m. Open. Meeting on H.R. 3140, to assist in combating heart disease, cancer and stroke; S. 2300, omnibus rivers and harbors bill; and S. 306, Clean Air Act. Gallery Floor, Capitol.

Education and Labor. 9:45 a.m. Open. Hearing on the administration of the National Labor Relations Act of 1935, as amended, by the National Labor Relations Board. To hear representatives from AFL-CIO, United Mine Workers of America, U.S. Chamber of Commerce, and International Brotherhood of Teamsters. Rm. 2175, Rayburn Bldg.

Education and Labor. 10 a.m. Open. Ad hoc subcommittee on poverty. On United Planning Organization.

Education and Labor. Select Subcommittee on Labor. 9 a.m. Open. To continue on H.R. 10721, to amend the Federal Employees' Compensation Act. To hear public witnesses. Rm. 2261, Rayburn Bldg.

Appropriations. Interior Subcommittee. 10 a.m. Exec. Rm. H-307, Capitol.

Appropriations. State, Justice, Commerce and Judiciary Subcommittee. 10:30 a.m. Exec. Rm. H-310, Capitol.

Appropriations. District Subcommittee. 1:30 p.m. Exec. Rm. H-302, Capitol.

This illustrates a routine day in the life of Congress: While general sessions are important (e.g., the House met to consider the Atomic Energy Act), the basic work is performed by the committees in both houses.

termed 'executive privilege.' Some of the internal processes of the judiciary are sacrosanct. And the Supreme Court has limited some inquiries into the affairs of private individuals. But these are exceptions; by and large the power is sweeping. It is the immediate foundation of the most spectacular form of legislative oversight, the congressional investigation.

Congressional investigations. The congressional investigation is old; the first one took place in 1792 and concerned a disastrous military defeat. Investigations have been conducted by most if not all Congresses ever since. But not until the last few years have they become the massive industry they are today. Only about 285 were conducted from

1792 to 1925, about 100 of these after World War I. Today Congress conducts over one hundred in *every session.*[47]

As government has grown there has been more to investigate. As the executive and administrative have risen in importance, Congress has had more motive to investigate them, in order to maintain its own position. As government programs have gotten more complicated and difficult to grasp and understand, Congress has needed to investigate more. Congressional investigations are a natural—and necessary and often desirable—concomitant of big government.

The boom in investigations really began with the Legislative Reorganization Act of 1946; by it all standing committees were for the first time granted authority to conduct investigations. Investigations have now become commonplace, instead of the special and somewhat unusual things they formerly were. Today they are usually simply part of the more ordinary processes of legislative oversight—of inquiry and hearings by a committee. But while thus absorbed into the general processes of legislative oversight, the investigative tool is still likeliest to be used by committees in situations that are, so to speak, pathological; hence a congressional investigation often has an explosive potential.

They have shown Congress at very nearly its best, and at very nearly its worst. Among the best most authorities list at least two well-known ones. One of these is the Teapot Dome investigation of the 1920s. It uncovered extensive corruption and misconduct in the Harding Administration, including the Cabinet, which in all likelihood would have gone undetected without the investigation. Another is the Pujo investigation, conducted shortly before World War I, of the financial and banking industries of the country; valuable in itself for producing a vast amount of information and a new understanding of these industries, it also has been a model for most subsequent investigations of economic matters.

Investigations often have immense effects on individual reputations and on public opinion about issues. The investigations during the 1930s of the munitions industry (which portrayed the industry as profiteering provokers of war) had much to do with the strong desire for isolation that nearly dominated American foreign policy until World War II. The Temporary National Economic Committee, a congressionally sponsored investigation in the late 1930s of the structure and functioning of the national economy, effected a permanent and important change in public attitudes. Senator Harry Truman made a national reputation which started him on the road to the White House in the investigation, over which he presided, into the conduct of the American war effort in World War II. Senator Joseph McCarthy also made a national reputation, though of a different kind, with his investigations of questions of subversion and disloyalty during the early 1950s.

---

[47] *Congressional Quarterly* (see bibliographical note) customarily collects the data on them in each session.

Indeed, probably the greatest function of the investigation is to influence public opinion. This is a fact that members of Congress seeking personal publicity have turned to advantage, as have members seeking to build up public support for some policy. And it is fundamental both to the great achievements of which the investigation is capable and also to the equally great abuses to which it is subject.

Other Functions: 'Grand Inquest,' Ultimate Tribunal, and Political Forum

In addition to the two great functions of legislating and overseeing, there are others, less familiar, less visible, sometimes less explicit, but important nonetheless. They are often intertwined in the legislating, overseeing, and representing functions, and are correspondingly difficult to describe separately. But it is important to be aware of these more elusive functions and to be able to sense them being performed in all the other aspects of congressional activity. Brief mention of three especially significant and illustrative ones is made here.

Congress is the "grand inquest of the nation," the chief instrument whereby great inquiries into all the affairs of the polity may be made. By its committee proceedings and investigations and also by its debates and its many other means it informs itself and the nation at large on public matters—and indeed on many things that touch only rather remotely on public matters.

On various grave public matters Congress serves as the ultimate constitutional tribunal. It impeaches officers of government, passes on constitutional amendments, and admits new states.

Finally, Congress is a great political forum, the parliament where political things are talked about and an arena where political struggles are carried on.

The Members and Their Two Constituencies

So far, we have talked about Congress with little reference to its individual members. In a sense this is wrong; people make institutions. But in a more important sense the members cannot be understood without some preliminary understanding of Congress, because their characteristics and behavior as individuals are decisively influenced by what Congress is and does. Now we can with profit turn to the members, their characteristics, the work they do, and how they do it. Here, among other things, we see with special clarity the representative function in action.

The Effects of the Election System

Senators and representatives are influenced by the totality of American political life. However, election arrangements are particularly in-

fluential. These arrangements affect the members in two major ways: through the influence states and localities have within the national legislature and through the extent to which Congress is unrepresentative.
The influence of locality. The House is elected by the *single-member district system.* Any state entitled to more than one representative divides itself into districts and elects its representatives from these, one to a district. (See pp. 351–55.) This tends to introduce a strong *local* element into the resulting representation. Indeed, the influence of locality in the House is a fine instance of the localizing—and thus decentralizing—tendency in American politics.

Thus, a representative is not only, say, a Democrat from California; he is also the representative from San Francisco—indeed, from a specific part of San Francisco. He is therefore more involved with narrowly local problems and issues, and with local pressures and local politics, than if he were elected 'at large'—from the state as a whole and by the state electorate as a whole. For example, he is likely to be more concerned with the maritime industries, with foreign trade, with matters affecting industrial labor, business, and commerce, and with urban problems, than a representative from the great farming area of the Central Valley of California, who is likely to be more concerned with farm prices, water supply, and farm labor.

In short, the representative is likely to be quite strongly tied to the interests of his district. But with this dependence may go a compensating *in*dependence. He may be politically independent of all but that district; if he builds personal followings and satisfies the dominant political forces there he may not have much need for support by wider groups or by his state or national party. Such a representative is not very amenable to general party control. Also his independence has another important consequence. He may have to serve almost slavishly the narrow specific interests of his district but can be perfectly free to be an independent statesman regarding all other questions. Some of the most valuable and most national-minded representatives have been products of just such situations.

Localism also helps create the bargaining that is so distinctive a feature of Congress. The individual member must be ever alert to wishes and needs from the constituency whence comes his political lifeblood. However he is free, within limits set by conviction and by political constraints, to swap his support on other issues in return for consideration of his local problems. Congressional leadership depends a great deal on such bargains; the leadership often wins support on great national policy matters by helping members on their local problems.

Regional and national interests and forces, including the national political parties, moderate these localizing, decentralizing influences to varying extents. But when to these influences there is added the federal aspect of the Senate, the localizing effects are very great indeed.

The effect of unrepresentativeness. Influenced by party considerations and the wishes of incumbent representatives, the states often (1) neglect to rearrange district boundaries to reflect population changes and (2) 'gerrymander,' that is, draw district boundaries to the advantage of incumbents or the party or group dominant in the state. An example of the first is Georgia in 1964. The legislature had not redistricted the state since 1931. By the 1960 census one congressional district contained only 272,154 people while another contained 823,680. An example of the second is Los Angeles County, California, after the 1951 redistricting. The county had twelve congressional districts. Democratic candidates got almost half the votes for representatives in 1952, but only four were elected, so thoroughly had Democratic votes been concentrated in a few districts by artful drawing of district lines.

Both refusals to redistrict and gerrymandering have long been widespread. In most states the districting power is in the hands of the state legislature. The legislatures have been disinclined to redistrict *themselves* to the disadvantage of their senior incumbents, especially those of the party in power. They therefore have tended to be controlled by senior legislators from rural areas (because long neglect to redistrict means they do not reflect the growth of cities). Their bias therefore inclines to favor overrepresentation of rural voters and of whichever party has been in control. Further, the practices have similarly aided individual congressmen who become well-established and senior. These have strong influence with their state legislatures. The upshot is that the House tends to be overloaded with representatives of long seniority from rural districts, as compared with more junior ones from urban and the newer suburban districts. The situation is changing, in large part because the Supreme Court has held that malapportionment is in some cases unconstitutional, and is requiring that it be remedied. But change is slow.[48]

The federal effect of the Senate. To all this must be added some federal characteristics of the Senate. These include the traditional status of a senator as embodying the dignity, independence, and power of his state, the state's own traditional status as a quasi-sovereign principality, and the federal aspect of senatorial representation that makes the least populous state the equal of the most populous. Add to this the great personal power of a senator and the importance of seniority. It follows that many states, especially the southern ones, quite accurately see the Senate, and their senators' power and seniority in it, as their principal defense against the rest of the nation. Together with other forces they tend to make the Senate an assembly where some proud and formidable potentates, very senior, many from the South, are grimly dedicated to maintaining the Senate and Congress in the old ways and the federal bond loose.

---

[48] The leading case on congressional malapportionment is *Wesberry* v. *Sanders*, 376 U.S. 1 (1964). For further discussion, see pp. 354–55.

Personal Characteristics

What of the personal characteristics of senators and representatives? The diversities are very great, in age, occupation, experience, personal background, and virtually every other dimension. But there is some clustering, so that it is possible to speak of a typical, or average, member: He is a man of middle-class family background, college- or university-educated, middle-aged, with a good deal of experience in politics and several years' seniority in Congress, of considerable prominence in his home state or district, strongly conscious of the dignity and power of his office but also keenly aware of how easily and abruptly he can be turned out of it, originally a lawyer or businessman but now devoted pretty much full-time to politics.

This last characteristic is crucial. Some senators and more representatives are political amateurs, in politics only temporarily, with their real interests lying elsewhere. And a few do actually maintain separate careers outside politics. But for most, politics has become their profession. Service in Congress is demanding. The sessions require nearly continuous attendance in Washington, and today always take up over half of the year. The intervals between sessions are fairly well-filled with committee work and work for constituents. Legislative and policy issues are complex and time-consuming. And much time is required by political activity, either for personal reelection or on behalf of the party (or both)—especially for those who plan to stay in political life. The day is gone, if it ever really existed, when a man could maintain wide business or professional activities and go to Washington for a few months a year for a term or two and effectively represent his state or locality in Congress.

The difficulties are reinforced by the seniority system and the traditions of Congress; both reserve real power and effectiveness for members of considerable length of service. Indeed, in some states, notably in the South, an incumbent of considerable seniority has a great advantage over challengers for his office because the importance of his seniority to local interests is generally recognized by the key local political groups and by the voters.

As a consequence, both Senate and House tend to be assemblies of professionals, experienced, informed, and fully dedicated to politics.

A Congressman's Work and His World

What is the member's job like and how does he do it, and what is the world of Congress like and what is his life like in that world? These are, even more than most questions about Congress, complex and difficult, so only a bare sketch can be given in brief space. For convenience we begin with a newly elected representative, a 'freshman congressman,' and follow some of his adventures, with some indication of differences that are found on the Senate side.

When he arrives he finds himself much on his own. Neither Congress nor his party particularly welcomes newcomers, and he is expected to manage his own affairs and find his own place, and meanwhile be inconspicuous. New senators receive more attention, but even they are impressed with how low they are in a hierarchy—and it takes a good deal to impress even a brand-new senator with that.

His first problems are getting desirable committee assignments, organizing an effective office and staff, and orienting himself in the flood of business. The committee assignment procedures are tricky and full of subtleties, and he often is dissatisfied with what he gets and changes once or more in his early years. He discovers that the prime function of his office and staff is service to his constituents and constituency, and that he must see that this is well and diligently attended to if he wants to be reelected. Senators have a greater bulk of this work; they are not expected to do as much personally but it is even more of an administrative burden to them and their staffs, and they are equally concerned by it.

In his legislative work he usually feels, from his first days on throughout his career, that he has neither the time nor the equipment to comprehend or deal effectively with anywhere near all the problems that come before Congress. He therefore tends to specialize, usually in some aspects of his committee work. He has three main possibilities, and he usually tries to achieve a blend of them (senators have more flexibility in doing so): (1) a specialty directly useful to his constituents (e.g., for a member from San Francisco, the maritime industries); (2) a specialty that will enable him to rise in his house (Congress gives much status and authority to members who become respected experts on some difficult and important part of Congress's responsibilities, e.g., taxation); and (3) a tempting but risky course, to try to become a public figure by being active on large and publicized issues (senators have by far the better hope of this).

Whatever his choice, time—often years—must pass before he learns his job and understands Congress, and before the slow lift (faster in the Senate) of experience and seniority carries him to positions of power and importance. He usually develops a considerable regard for his function and a strong pride in his place. Indeed, especially if he is a senator, he often acquires a harsh arrogance and egoism that are only in part defenses against the incessant demands and pressures that beat upon him and against the perennial strife and conflict in which he is involved. More attractively, he also usually develops a devotion to Congress and a camaraderie with his fellow members based on common experiences—in particular the troubles of politics and of elections and campaigning. These troubles never really leave him. Some districts are said to be 'safe,' especially for an incumbent, and senators have the comparative insulation of a six-year term. But few members ever feel really and permanently safe.

Much of his job revolves around committee work. He serves on one major committee, sometimes two, and on one minor one (a senator typically serves on more). Each parent committee may have active subcommittees. During the session, especially after the first few weeks, he spends several hours almost daily in hearings and meetings, and studying legislation and other committee business. Committee work may fill much of the time between sessions, especially if he becomes chairman or ranking minority member of a committee or of an important subcommittee, or becomes involved in an important study or investigation, or goes in for committee travel.

Further, as he advances in standing on his committee he is called upon more and more to do floor work, to report committee bills to the floor and to 'manage' them during debate, or at least to participate in debate, and to share in the often protracted and complex negotiating within the committee and between the committee and other groups. Other tasks and responsibilities will also begin to crowd in. He may become something of a national figure, an entrancing but time-consuming role. His party, which gave him little guidance and less support in his early days, may start to call on him—to speak, campaign, help lead. So, sooner or later, he is likely to have difficulty with the competing demands (and not just demands on his time) of his legislative work and his work for his constituents.

Of these, the 'casework' is the least troublesome. It deals with problems of individuals seeking some specific action from the federal government—a veteran whose benefit rights are being determined; an alien or naturalized citizen having trouble with the Immigration and Naturalization Service; a businessman seeking help with a government contract, and the like. With some experience the member can delegate most of this to his staff.

Another part is more complex, much more difficult, and of broader significance. In virtually every district, and certainly in every state, there are federal activities. The member must be the Washington emissary for his constituents concerned with these—military installations, industries dependent on government contracts, federal water projects, federal housing developments, national parks and forests, and so on. Each is a continuous problem (and opportunity) for the member. He should be always at work, seeking new installations or contracts or projects or the expansion of old ones or some change in their management, repelling raids by other states, urging entire new legislative programs which will have some local effects, and so on unendingly. All this takes his time and energy. Worse, it presents dilemmas. He finds he has conflicting responsibilities—two 'constituencies,' so to speak. He must be at once a *local* man and a *national* man. He must represent and serve both the voters back home *and* also the general public, the national interest. He should not just 'vote the mail,' on every public issue and devote himself to serving his own people. He must represent them, but he must do more, if he is to be true to his office. For example, he must get for his local people their proper share of federal projects *and* must also play his part as a national legislator in deciding whether the national interest requires more projects or fewer. The success of the constitutional system and of representative popular government depends upon his—and Congress's—representing both constituencies well.

Conclusion

This brings us full circle. This chapter began with the large subjects of Congress's place and purpose in the constitutional system. It then moved to the narrower and more specific subjects of congressional structure and congressional functioning, and finally reached the most specific subject of all, the individual member. But with this subject we encounter again the grand subjects of constitutional place and purpose. Are we, then, now ready to evaluate? Unfortunately, no. Congress cannot be soundly evaluated without taking account of the Presidency and the departments and agencies, the administrative system. However, many of the problems and issues are already suggested in the present chapter, and the reader may profitably glance ahead to the end of Chapter 8, where they and others are brought together and dealt with.

BIBLIOGRAPHICAL NOTE

Congress and its committees generate a great many documents and receive many more from other governmental sources. The authoritative guide to all government documents is Lawrence F. Schmeckebier and Roy B. Eastin, *Government Publications and Their Use* (2nd ed., 1961). Congressional and related documents and the bibliographical aspects of congressional procedures are dealt with from the legal standpoint in most books on legal bibliography; of these Erwin H. Pollack, *Fundamentals of Legal Research* (2nd ed., 1962), is recent and standard. There is a useful 'Research Guide' for the use of political science students in Roland Young, *The American Congress* (1958), pp. 281–324; it covers not only documents but also much of the reference material and scholarly literature on Congress.

The statutes and other enactments of Congress are printed, in the form and chronological order in which they were enacted, in the annual volumes of the *U.S. Statutes at Large;* citation may be by volume number, abbreviated title, page, and date: for example, the Civil Rights Act of 1964 is 78 Stat. 241 (1964). Before the annual volumes of the *Statutes at Large* come out enactments are published in 'slip law' form—i.e., as separate sheets or pamphlets. Each statute is given an identifying number reflecting its nature, the chronological order of its enactment, and, in recent years, the number of the Congress which enacted it. Thus, the Civil Rights Act of 1964 is P.L. 88–352, meaning the 352nd general statute (P.L. means *public law*) enacted by the Eighty-eighth Congress. A statute is usually divided into sections, more or less consecutively numbered.

Public statutes of general importance are also published in the *U.S. Code* in codified form; that is, their sections are classified by subject and distributed by subject through the *U.S. Code*. The *Code* is composed of a number of subject-matter titles, e.g., Agriculture, comprising more or less all statutory provisions falling into the title's category. Citation is by title number and *Code* section number (not the statute's own section number). Thus, 5 U.S.C. 1009 is section 1009 of Title 5. The *U.S. Code* is published in an official edition every six years and kept up to date by annual supplement volumes. An annotated version by a commercial publisher (*U.S. Code Annotated,* or *U.S.C.A.*) also exists. Very conveniently, this is kept up to date by annual 'pocket parts' and by fortnightly pamphlets during sessions and is supplemented by an additional service (*U.S.C.A. Congressional and Administrative News*) giving the texts of most important executive orders and administrative regulations and of the committee reports on most important statutes.

When a bill or resolution is introduced it is given a number indicating its type, the house where introduced, and its chronological order. Thus, H.R. 1 of the Eighty-eighth Congress is the first bill introduced in the House in the Eighty-eighth Congress, and H.J.R. 1 the first joint resolution. Congressional committee hearings, on a bill or otherwise, are usually published, but there is no simple general index or guide to them. When a committee reports a bill to its house, its report is numberd chronologically. Thus H. Rep. 1 of the Eighty-eighth Congress designates the first House committee report filed during the Congress. Reports and various other documents originated by or received by Congress are published more or less chronologically in the *Serial Set;* publication began in 1817 and has reached well over ten thousand large volumes.

The Senate and House *Journals* are the official records of the actions and proceedings on the floor. They are highly technical and usually of little general interest. They are also published in the *Serial Set. The Congressional Record* purports to be a transcript of what takes place on the floor, including verbatim reports of debates; actually it is not quite this, being subject to revision and expurgation, but when used with understanding is an invaluable source. It is published daily in pamphlet form during sessions, and thereafter in bound volumes. Pagination of the bound edition differs from that of the daily edition.

The great unofficial current reference on Congress is *Congressional Quarterly,* a commercial publication which appears first in *Weekly Report* pamphlets and thereafter in annual bound *Almanacs.* It is almost indispensable for any substantial work on congressional affairs. There are numerous historical reference works, such as the *Biographical Directory of the American Congress, 1774–1949.*

Some of the scholarly books on various aspects of Congress have been cited in the footnotes to the present chapter. The scholarly journals of political science publish many articles, and are indexed in the Public Affairs Information Service index. Most books and articles contain bibliographies.

Chapter 6

The
Executive Branch:
The Presidency

> Energy in the Executive is a leading character in the defini-
> tion of good government.
>
> Publius

> The American Presidency is a formidable, exposed, and some-
> what mysterious institution. It is formidable because it repre-
> sents the point of ultimate decision in the American political
> system. It is exposed because decision cannot take place in a
> vacuum: the Presidency is the center of the play of pressure,
> interest, and idea in the nation; and the presidential office is the
> vortex into which all the elements of national decision are ir-
> resistibly drawn. And it is mysterious because the essence of
> ultimate decision remains impenetrable to the observer—often,
> indeed, to the decider himself.
>
> John F. Kennedy

> Central to the system is the office that is most political and
> also most above politics, the Presidency.
>
> Denis W. Brogan[1]

The Outlines of the Presidency

The most important single fact about the American executive
branch is that the President is *the* central personage of the national government and of the entire country.

Few people can name many members of Congress or of the Supreme
Court, or follow the activities of these bodies very closely, or pay great
attention to many of their pronouncements, or are much concerned if
either or both adjourn for several months. Not so with the President. He

---

[1] The quotations are from: *Federalist 70*; a foreword by the late President in
Theodore C. Sorensen, *Decision-Making in the White House* (New York: Columbia
University Press, 1963); and *Politics in America* (Anchor Books; Garden City, New
York: Doubleday & Company, Inc., 1960), p. 230.

is every day under the keenest and most unremitting scrutiny. If he is out of action, say with illness, even for a few days, most people know of it and many are deeply concerned. Every major statement by him is heard widely and with attention, and nobody doubts that he had the right—perhaps even the duty—to make it and the right to have it heard. Indeed, we often feel that debate on any significant public issue is not even well launched, let alone complete, until the President has spoken. A tragic instance evokes this centralness: When President Kennedy was assassinated in November 1963, American life almost literally stood still in suspense and anxiety until it was clear that President Johnson had firmly and fully taken charge.

Some incidents from an ordinary week of presidential activities (February 4–11, 1963) suggest the range and importance of this remarkable office and also summon back to mind many things all of us already know about it:

* The Comptroller of the Currency, a Treasury Department official who by statutory authority "exercises general supervision over the operations of national banks," announced somewhat suddenly that he was changing the date for certain reports these banks must submit to him. The banking industry was reported to be considerably upset.

* The President confirmed rumors that he would reappoint for another term the chairman of the Federal Reserve Board, the independent regulatory authority that supervises the Federal Reserve Banks and the Federal Reserve System. Ever since the President took office in 1961 there had been speculation that he and the chairman might clash over the latter's rather conservative views on monetary policy.

* The President expressed concern over the continued presence of Soviet military forces in Cuba and indicated he was exerting pressure for their removal, but denied they were a present offensive threat to the Western hemisphere. A Republican senator stated he had given the Administration information on these forces and his recommendations for action. This was a senator who previously had bitterly criticized the Administration and asserted that the Soviet forces were much larger than the Administration said they were and did constitute a serious offensive threat.

* The Commandant of the U.S. Marine Corps sent to the President a recently rediscovered executive order originally issued by President Theodore Roosevelt in 1908. It required 50-mile marches by Marine Corps officers as tests of their physical fitness. The President suggested that the commandant "find out how well present-day officers perform the test."[2]

---

[2] The Marine Corps responded as vigorously as might be expected. Fifty-mile hikes became a national fad, so much so that *Life* magazine devoted a major story in its Feb. 22, 1963, issue to them. It reported, among other things, that a ten-year-old boy of Bloomington, Indiana, covered 50 miles in 18 hours and 45 minutes of walking time in weather so cold that it froze his peanut-butter-and-jelly sandwiches.

* The White House sent to Congress in a special presidential message a detailed proposal for a $5.3 billion program of federal aid to the nation's schools. The Secretary of Health, Education, and Welfare testified before a congressional committee on the proposal. It was hotly attacked by committee members because it put the whole program in a single package instead of in several separate proposals. Some commentators felt the Administration had done this for the publicity and tactical advantages of making the message a complete statement of its views on the total needs of American education. The White House also sent to Congress another special message, proposing a comprehensive long-range program of federal aid to research on and treatment of all forms of mental illness, and the President briefed Democratic congressional leaders on the message at their regular Tuesday breakfast meeting at the White House.

* The President, in his news conference, criticized all parties involved in a strike, then over two months old, which had shut down all the New York newspapers, for failing to negotiate responsibly with each other.

* In yet another special message to Congress he urged appropriation of half a billion dollars to accelerate public works by the federal government in economically depressed areas of the country, "to provide jobs and encourage economic expansion in areas of high unemployment and low income."

* A 14-year-old Pennsylvania girl won a school competition for posters promoting National Dental Health Week. Her poster contained a cartoon of the President and a legend, "Brush with great vigah," spoofing his characteristic accent and one of his favorite turns of speech.

* The President met with his Committee on Traffic Safety, made a brief speech at the showing of the Mona Lisa, then on loan from France, at the National Gallery of Art in Washington, and had lunch with a group of Georgia newspaper editors and publishers.

* The President received the Foreign Minister of Costa Rica, presented the Distinguished Service Medal to an American general retiring from command of the NATO forces, and held a prayer breakfast attended by over a thousand persons from Congress, the diplomatic corps, the federal departments and agencies, and private life. In his remarks at the breakfast he stated that both the perils and the opportunities America faces are the greatest in history and that "in such a time the limits of mere human endeavor become more apparent than ever."

Nine Major Presidential Functions

How to make sense of this vast bustle of variegated activities? One way is to notice in them the 'roles,' or functions, scholars customarily identify in the President's work. At least five of these functions are more or less explicitly imposed on him by the Constitution.[3]

* He is the chief executive, the officer to whom it grants "the executive power" and who is required by it to "take care that the laws be faithfully executed." Thus, it is he who is ultimately responsible if a Comptroller of the Currency—in the first of our examples of presidential activities—fails in his statutory duty of exercising the appropriate degree of "general supervision" of the banking industry.

* He is the chief of the Administration and of all the officers of the executive branch. He appoints them, even those who head the great independent agencies like the Federal Reserve Board; and it is in his name and subject to his general direction that they and their innumerable subordinates work, sign orders, testify before congressional committees, and manage their organizations.

* He has charge of the foreign relations of the United States. This emphatically includes the problem of Soviet troops in Cuba. Congress can declare war, the Senate can pass on treaties, and individual senators can investigate and speak. But the final power—and the real responsibility —both lie with him.

* He is commander-in-chief of the armed forces, and in all things, large and small. For example, the ultimate blame for the disastrous surprise at Pearl Harbor in 1941 is properly laid at his door. So is the ultimate credit for the triumph of American arms in 1945. And nobody doubts he can reinstate a presidential order issued by a famous predecessor who had pronounced ideas about physical fitness in the armed services.

* He is a leader—indeed, by far the chief leader—in legislation. Legislative proposals for federal aid for education and for campaigns against mental illness, and against joblessness and want, and on a thousand other subjects come in their original form from 'the White House' and get their original impetus from his support.

He also has other functions as well, less explicitly constitutional but hardly less important.

* He is the official chief, and usually the actual leader, of a major political party. Even the proudly independent congressional potentates of that party recognize him as their chief and come to his party breakfasts, and indeed usually feel obligated to give him and his policies more than merely token support.

* He is in a real sense the general manager of the economic welfare of the country; strikes, threats of depression, questions of economic opportunity, all are demands upon his leadership.

---

[3] For the constitutional roles see Edward S. Corwin, *The President: Office and Powers 1787–1957* (4th rev. ed.; New York: New York University Press, 1957). For the roles generally see Clinton Rossiter, *The American Presidency* (rev. ed.; Harvest Books; New York: Harcourt, Brace & World, Inc., 1960).

As discussed on pages 176–80, the office of President of the United States is made up of a multitude of functions.

° Perhaps most important of all, he is the preeminent voice of public opinion on virtually every conceivable issue—including dental health.

° And, finally, he is *chief of state*. He is ceremonial head of government and principal representative of the nation, the figure who confers honors, receives visiting eminences, and otherwise embodies our national dignity and national values. He is not a crowned king, but there is more than an echo of royal precedence about him.

The Unifying Themes

Truly, the President wears many hats. But three important themes, or characteristics, unify his functions and give qualities in common to everything he does.

First, the Presidency is a profoundly *political* office. It is very much a part of the political order, of party politics in the ordinary sense, and of the political processes within government.

Second, the Presidency is not a fixed thing; it changes with the circumstances of the times and the attributes of its holders. Mr. Kennedy's Presidency was strikingly different from Mr. Eisenhower's, as his was from Truman's and Roosevelt's, and as Mr. Johnson's is from all four. This is only partly because of differences in the policies of the men; the personal capacities, habits, and style of each holder also transform the office independently of policy differences.

Third, the Presidency is *national* and *democratic*. The President is democratically elected by the nation at large and is responsible to the nation at large as no other official is. He is therefore deeply alone at the pinnacle of the American democracy. He is its greatest officer and greatest politician. At the same time, because he is the man who sits where Washington, Jefferson, Jackson, Lincoln, and the two Roosevelts once sat, he is also the heir, and the present-day representative, of a great people's most honored heroes.

The Rise of the Modern Presidency

"There is an idea, which is not without its advocates, that a vigorous executive is inconsistent with the genius of republican government."[4]

Is this vast modern Presidency a distortion of the office's proper place in the system, and at odds with its proper nature? Is it a result of persistent usurpation of power by ambitious Presidents and their followers? Is it a growing despotism, capable unless checked of swallowing up American constitutional freedom?

Or is it a natural, healthy, and desirable growth, a harmonious development from the original foundations as these have responded to circumstances? Is it in fact a crowning achievement of the American

---

[4] *Federalist* 70, p. 423.

political order, an office whose powers are so skilfully arranged and so fortunate in their development that great responsibilities can be carried by their holder with a very minimum of danger to freedom and democracy?

Or is it—a third possibility—simply a recent accident, neither a distortion nor a natural evolution but something new not rooted either in history or in the basic structure of the system, purely a product of modern times?

The Constitutional Framework

Distortion, healthy growth, or modern accident—where does the truth lie? Inquiry must begin with the constitutional framework and the decided ideas it embodies; this is because the framework and the ideas constantly exert a vital and pervasive influence on the office. Both the framework and the ideas can be most readily approached if for a moment we look through the eyes of the draftsmen of 1787 at the issue they saw themselves confronting, and which we will always confront: What kind of executive is likely to be best suited, now and as times change, to a free democracy in which the executive and legislative are separated? The thought of 1787 offered two conflicting views.[5]

One was that the great danger lay in *executive* predominance or usurpation. This position had in mind the tyrants of classical Greece, the fall of the Roman Republic, the despotic George III and his subservient Parliament, and the royal governors of the colonies. The royal governors had been tamed, the Declaration of Independence's denunciation of the king written, and the 'executive' (such as it was) of the Articles of Confederation devised, under this sign in the zodiac of political ideas. The other view was that equal or greater dangers lay in *legislative* predominance or usurpation, either in itself or as a vehicle for tyrannical popular movements. This view read the decline of classical Greek democracy as an example, arguing that there unchecked assemblies had made government first incapable and finally unfree.

The second view had less support at first, but the 1787 Convention finally rejected the first view, that of the executive kept weak to be safe, and concluded instead that "a vigorous Executive" is indeed consistent with "the genius of republican government." This is important; the Constitution has to be read in the light of this final decision that "energy in the executive is a leading character in the definition of good government." Indeed, what emerged from the Convention was an office that some alarmed opponents of the Constitution saw as almost an elective monarchy.

Its central features are the constitutional bedrock of the Presidency of today: (1) He is a single person; he is not encumbered by a council.

---

[5] See Chapter 3, pp. 86–87.

(This is a device always appealing as a means of bridling an executive, and in 1787 was popular in the state governments.) (2) He has his own national and democratic mode of election, independent of the legislature; hence he can have and cultivate his own constituency. (3) This independence is reinforced; he has a fixed term of office, an irreducible salary, an explicitly granted set of powers of his own, freedom from removal except by the difficult process of impeachment, and is eligible for reelection. (4) He is the holder of "the executive power." Whatever that somewhat enigmatic power may be or may become, he shares it with nobody; it is his alone. (5) He is pretty much master in his own house. He has substantial controls over his subordinates; he alone nominates them to office and he can require their opinions "in writing." He can, if he is able, take a commanding place in several fields of vital national concern—for example, war and diplomacy—that are constitutionally entrusted to him.

These are the basic elements of what the Framers gave him, and what their Constitution gives him today. To grasp their meaning we need to look at the ways in which the Presidency has been used and developed by its various holders. This is particularly necessary because the constitutional arrangements stay away from detailed and rigid specificity. Perhaps the draftsmen thought that constitution-makers often fail by trying to do too much, instead of stopping with general placing of the big members in the structure.[6] They did not attempt explicit full resolutions of all the complex and subtle relations of power, separated and shared, that their Constitution creates between its executive and legislative. Much was properly left for history.

A Hundred and Seventy-Five Years of History

The central tendency of this history has been the development of the potentialities and resources of the office. This tendency appeared at the outset; Washington added permanently to the office some of his own immense personal reputation, and it has remained ever since profoundly dignified and respected even when in the hands of its feeblest and least admired holders. A weak or foolish President disgraces himself, not the office.

Washington also gave to the office a strand of restraint and republican moderation. He could, perhaps, have been some kind of monarch, but though he acted with vigor and independence he also kept severely within strict limits of republican constitutionalism. He required that as President he be accorded proper deference, but he regarded himself personally as simply an American gentleman. He firmly rejected, as an invasion of the executive sphere, the House's demand to see the execu-

---

[6] Recall Napoleon's cynical but shrewd aphorism that a constitution should be short and obscure.

tive papers regarding the hotly debated Jay Treaty, but he treated the constitutional rights of the Senate in the same matter with full respect.

The *political* potentialities of the office began to emerge under the third President, Thomas Jefferson. Washington and Adams had certainly participated fully in policy formation and the legislative process, and Adams was never above the party battle to the extent Washington was. However, Jefferson first fully attached to the Presidency the active leadership of a major political party; indeed he may on occasion have actually presided over his party's congressional caucus.

After Jefferson the Presidency became for a time almost a council, closely linked with the Cabinet and the leadership in Congress, with the President himself hardly more than first among equals. Even so it remained, in part because of its irreducible constitutional stature, the principal office in the government. And late in the period an important development began; the nomination of presidential candidates began to pass from the congressional party caucuses (see pp. 357–58) to the forerunners of the modern national party conventions. Thus the Presidency began to disentangle its political underpinnings from Congress, and to connect these directly with the people and a national constituency. This was a significant step in developing the democratic and national potentialities of the office.

This development progressed greatly under Andrew Jackson. He was very much one of the strong Presidents, and because of the political situation of the time and his own qualities he was able to become a champion and embodiment of the popular will. With him the office began fully to acquire the democratic character which has become one of its greatest strengths and most valuable resources. Thus, in his long war with the Bank of the United States he appealed to the people over the heads of Congress—the first President to do so—and became the voice of the people of the nation.[7]

Important further aspects of presidential strength emerged vividly under Lincoln, the next undoubtedly strong President. Strong Presidents explore and develop new resources of the office, and these, though they fall into disuse during quiet times or in less active hands, remain available, awaiting the next President who can employ them. Lincoln therefore had available to him the dignified Presidency of Washington, the political Presidency of Jefferson, and the democratic Presidency of Jackson. In dealing with the crisis of the Union, Lincoln added vastly to these resources of the office by a new view of its constitutional authority. First, he claimed the fullest scope both for specific presidential powers like that of commander-in-chief and also for the general presidential duty to "take care that the laws shall be faithfully executed." Then, by combining these so that they enhanced each other, he in effect created new presidential

---

[7] See, e.g., Wilfred E. Binkley, *President and Congress* (3rd ed.; New York: Vintage Books, 1962), chs. IV and V.

powers, including the great, almost boundless, "war power." Second, in the first days of secession, he exercised powers that *perhaps* belonged to Congress or the government generally; e.g., he suspended the writ of habeas corpus. Third, in those early days, he exercised powers that *clearly* did not belong to the Presidency; e.g., he raised troops without authorization and spent money without appropriations. Indeed, in his struggles to save the Union when Congress was divided or half-hearted, he was by far the closest approach to a presidential dictator this country has ever seen.

No subsequent President has ever gone so far as Lincoln did. (Nor has any ever had to govern so divided a nation.) But the capacities he gave to the Presidency as an instrument of crisis government and of national leadership have remained a permanent part of the office, accepted by constitutional law, by government practice, and by public opinion. These capacities were called upon by President Wilson in World War I and by Franklin D. Roosevelt in the Great Depression and in World War II, and they may save the country in some future nuclear catastrophe.[8] But they have also made presidential tyranny a genuine danger as well as ever-present spectre in the American political tradition. It was part of Lincoln's genius that he employed dangerous power without being corrupted by it, and it is part of the genius of the American political system that it has always been able to recover its constitutional balance after crisis—at least so far.

Every strong President since Lincoln has added to the office. Some of these additions have been in constitutional doctrine, some in the more elusive realms of accepted practice concerning the office and of its status in public opinion. Examples abound. Theodore Roosevelt added the role of vigorous *doer* in any and all phases of national life, from natural resources to physical fitness, that may catch a President's fancy. Woodrow Wilson added the role of *spokesman* for the aspirations of the peoples of the world for freedom, democracy, and peace. Franklin D. Roosevelt added the role of magical *popular leader* taking his nation along the path of sweeping social reform and great adventures. And every President since World War II has been—has had to be—the leader of the free world in the Cold War.

After 175 years of development, and in a time when the demands upon the office seem to increase almost daily, the Presidency is today more central than ever in the American political system, and more awesome, more political, more democratic, and more resourceful than ever. Further, as this brief survey suggests, the rise of the modern Presidency seems in the main to have been very much a natural growth upon wisely laid foundations.

---

[8] On this possibility see Charles Fairman, "Government Under Law in Time of Crisis," in Arthur E. Sutherland, ed., *Government Under Law* (Cambridge: Harvard University Press, 1956), p. 232.

The Modern Presidency: Powers, Duties, and Functions

The modern Presidency is in general a product of its constitutional framework, of the evolution of the American political system and political ideas, and of the personalities and actions of the men who have held the office. So too in particular are its constitutional powers. These powers are central to everything about the office. Around them cluster the complex of duties and functions of the Presidency.[9] Powers, duties, and functions have all developed in relationship to each other through nearly two centuries of presidential politics and presidential governing. A good way to examine the development and relationship of the presidential powers, duties, and functions, is to examine them in terms of the Presidency's great areas of governing. The three areas we shall study are the executive-administrative, the legislative process, and foreign affairs. A view of these will lead us to the heart of the Presidency.

Executive and Administrative Aspects

We naturally think first of the President as an executive and administrator, in charge of the executive branch and engaged in carrying out laws and policies ordained by Congress. And undoubtedly he is an executive and administrator. But what precisely does that mean? The situation is not so simple as might seem, partly because of one of the Delphic utterances of the Constitution.

Article II begins: "The executive power shall be vested in a President of the United States." This is cryptic. Is it a grant of power? Or does it simply designate the office? If the latter, does the President have any executive powers other than the specific ones explicitly granted, plus such auxiliary ones as may reasonably be inferred from these? If on the other hand the sentence is a grant of power, then what is this "executive power" that it grants, and why are there in the Article the later express grants of specific executive powers? And if "the" executive power is granted to him, does he therefore have a monopoly of executing law and policy, so that any attempts by Congress either to participate in execution or to set up executive agencies free from his control are alike unconstitutional? Around these and similar technical legal-constitutional questions have swirled the perennial American debates over the role of the Presidency; Americans do tend to talk politics and political philosophy in the language of constitutional law.

A broad view of the cryptic "executive power" is supported by the President's constitutional oath (Art. II, sec. 1). He does not promise, as many think, to "take care that the laws be faithfully executed."

---

[9] Corwin is the standard work on the constitutional and legal aspects of the powers of the Presidency. A fascinating account of the problems of the early days of the office is James Hart, *The American Presidency in Action: 1789* (New York: The Macmillan Company, 1948).

That is a specific duty, and perhaps power, established by Article II, section 3. His oath is not so narrow. He promises to execute, not merely the laws, but *"the office of President of the United States,"* and, further, to "preserve, protect, and defend the Constitution." These two obligations go beyond those of the only other oath provided by the Constitution (Art. VI). This latter oath, required of all legislators and executive and judicial officers, state and federal, merely obliges the taker to "support this Constitution." Does the difference import some special powers inherent in the Presidency to go with the additional obligations? Advocates of a strong Presidency urge that it does, and, indeed, that the faithful-execution clause does also. And strong Presidents, at least from Lincoln's time, have acted vigorously on this belief.

Presidential views. Lincoln certainly took the broad view, and felt free to act beyond his explicit constitutional powers when he believed that he could not otherwise preserve the Constitution and execute the laws. Theodore Roosevelt asserted (though, perhaps prudently, only after he had left office) a somewhat similar position in his famous 'stewardship' theory of the office:

> My view was that every executive officer, and above all every executive officer in high position, was a steward of the people, bound actively and affirmatively to do all he could for the people, and not to content himself with the negative merit of keeping his talents undamaged in a napkin. I declined to adopt the view that what was imperatively necessary for the Nation could not be done by the President unless he could find some specific authorization to do it. My belief was that it was not only his right but his duty to do anything that the needs of the Nation demanded unless such action was forbidden by the Constitution or by the laws.[10]

In this spirit T.R. did many novel things; for example, he intervened dramatically in the great coal strike of 1902. Presidents now intervene in major industrial conflicts as a matter of course and, by now, usually under statutory authority to do so. But Roosevelt was not executing any particular law or policy of Congress; he was on his own. President Franklin D. Roosevelt similarly acted on a broad view of the presidential powers. For example, at the height of World War II he became convinced that further price-control legislation was needed to enable him to carry out the nation's wartime economic policies. Congress was slow to respond. With his confidence as a popular leader, and drawing upon his functions as war chieftain, he thereupon announced in effect that he would legislate if they did not. After some confusion they did.[11]

Other Presidents either from constitutional conviction, dislike of responsibility, or practical or political necessity, have bounded their

---

[10] Quoted in Corwin, p. 153.
[11] See Binkley, p. 325ff., and Corwin, pp. 250–52.

activities more narrowly. For example, Taft and Hoover took the position that when a President has carried out the explicit mandates Congress gives him, he has done his whole duty, and that his powers extend no further than this. But the pressures of the modern situation seem to incline the Presidency toward the expanded, positive, view of the executive-administrative function. Three of the four Presidents since Franklin Roosevelt have accepted the positive view. President Eisenhower apparently opposed it. In 1954, when the Supreme Court declared racial segregation in public schools unconstitutional, a Roosevelt would have felt free to move actively into the situation and to bring the whole executive and administrative establishment into play to effectuate the new principle. Eisenhower did not; indeed, he declined even to use powers explicitly given him by the Constitution and by Congress. Nonetheless, when the governor of Arkansas obstructed a federal court order requiring admission of Negro students to a high school in Little Rock, Eisenhower ordered troops into the city and exercised all necessary executive power to defeat him. Even in the hands of a President reluctant to act on the 'stewardship' theory, the modern Presidency is an office of formidable executive and administrative capacity.

The Supreme Court has never fully and formally accepted the positive and broad view as sound constitutional law. Indeed, the Steel Seizure Case of 1952, one of its main recent pronouncements, seemingly opposes it. That year an industrial dispute threatened to shut off steel production and, in President Truman's opinion, to endanger the nation's entire war effort and the safety of the American troops fighting in Korea. As a last resort, after mediation had failed, he 'seized' the steel plants and put them under temporary government control. The device of seizure had been used occasionally in World War II, but Truman had no express statutory authority to use it as he did. The Supreme Court held that his act was beyond his constitutional powers, express or implied, including "the executive power."[12] Over the years, however, public opinion and government practice have accepted a good deal of presidential authority, akin to the traditional prerogative power of the English crown, to meet emergencies and to see that public policy in general is carried out. Indeed, public opinion often delights in Presidents who execute and administer with a strong and bold hand. And in numerous other decisions the Court has approved such vigor and exercises of such authority.

There can be reasonable doubts about the extent of presidential power, and there certainly must be limits to it. But a safe and pretty accurate summary is the following: In the constitutional framework, in history, and in the logic of the American system, there is much support for the belief that the nature of the system requires a genuinely powerful and independent 'chief executive' and 'chief administrator.'

---

[12] *Youngstown Sheet & Tube Co.* v. *Sawyer*, 343 (U.S.) 579 (1952).

Congressional views. The belief has not been a popular one with Congress. As we have seen, Congress inevitably seeks to exercise some control over execution and administration; in this as in other things it and the President are natural rivals. In times of crisis Congress often cannot successfully compete for mastery against a determined and talented President. In quieter times, and when a crisis is over and reaction against presidential dominance is flowing, the contest is very much more even.

The most dramatic clash of presidential and congressional views was the case of President Andrew Johnson, during the Reconstruction Era following the Civil War. Johnson attempted to continue Lincoln's moderate reconstruction policies, in part using the independent presidential powers and without statutory authorization. The Radical Republicans who dominated Congress attempted to get control of the executive branch to enforce more severe policies. Johnson opposed both the policies and the attempts to undermine his executive authority. But he was not the master politician and leader that Lincoln was, nor did he have the democratic and national support Lincoln had. Matters came to issue when Congress passed the Tenure of Office Act, explicitly aimed at crippling the Presidency. It forbade him to remove from office any executive official, even members of his own Cabinet; this was to destroy the President's control over the executive branch. Johnson removed a Secretary of War who was conspiring with the Radicals against him. The House, led by the Radicals, thereupon impeached him. The impeachment failed in the Senate—but by only one vote.

Removal of executive officials puts one fundamental question of the President's executive power neatly. He has explicit constitutional power to appoint them, with Senate consent. But if he cannot also remove them he is indeed crippled as executive and administrator; his nominal subordinates are then beyond his effective control. Presidents have strongly resisted this because the issue is nothing less than the grand issue of the executive power: Who is to rule the executive and administrative machinery of government, with all the influence over policy this entails, Congress or the President?

The Supreme Court has inevitably been drawn into the conflict between Congress and the Presidency over the removal power. Its answers have been that the President can remove any "purely executive officer," or any officer who is "part of the Executive establishment," but that Congress can limit his removal power over officers (like those in the independent regulatory commissions) whose functions are 'quasi-legislative' or 'quasi-judicial.' These terms obviously can be difficult and slippery, and the removal question may well find its way into the Court again someday. Moreover, Congress by its nature is not likely to cease intervening in the executive establishment. Barred from any particular intervention by the Court, Congress will seek some other way to weaken presidential control over the executive-administrative function.

Legislative Aspects

The President is often called the national government's chief legislator and chief legislative leader. Indeed, when President Eisenhower seemed at first to be declining to act as such, his conduct was regarded by many as unusual and perhaps a bit dubious. We judge our chief executives very largely by their legislative achievements.[13] At first glance, from the standpoint of the conventional view of separation of powers, this seems odd; and some people in fact applauded Eisenhower as returning to constitutionally more proper ways. Were they right and is the modern positive presidential role in the legislative sphere a distortion or usurpation? Whatever it is, what does the role mean for contemporary American government and politics?

Presidents have always been interested in legislation. President Washington might have been surprised to be described as chief legislator, but his Secretary of the Treasury, Alexander Hamilton, initiated legislation of vast importance and Washington himself vigorously expressed his views on many legislative matters. And the actual title fits President Jefferson, the active leader of his party in Congress. Since then some Presidents, by political skill or personal influence or because crises caused Congress to submit, have actually dominated the legislative process on occasion. At other times Congress has been able to exclude the President almost entirely. Today we stand somewhere in between. We expect the President to present a complete legislative program to Congress at each session and to work energetically to get it enacted, and we regard him as 'weak' or ineffectual if he fails, especially if his party controls Congress. But we are a little alarmed if he succeeds too well, and we have never been willing to equip him with the tools (e.g., the power to dissolve Congress and call special elections as the British executive does) that would likely assure his success. We seem not to want unambiguous locations of power; we want a balance between the President and Congress that shifts with circumstances and men. Characteristically, we seem to want, and our system supplies, a diffusion of the power and opportunity to make policy. The President shares policy-making in execution and administration with Congress and Congress shares legislative policy-making with him.

The constitutional situation is much simpler and clearer here than in the executive-administrative sphere. The President has two major legislative powers that are constantly important: the positive power to recommend legislation and the negative power to veto. The two are vitally linked. Without the veto power the power to recommend would be ineffective, because Congress would be free to disregard the recommendations. Without the positive power—and duty—to formulate legislative programs, the veto would be less respected by both parties. Combined, however, the two powers give the President the constitutional

---

[13] See Rossiter, p. 110.

Two views of the relationship between the execu-
tive and the legislative
branches of government.

position of full partnership in the legislative process. The uses he can
make of this position depend, as always, on the specific situation and on
his personal capacities.

The veto power. The veto power is in the Constitution for two purposes. One is to enable the President to defend himself and his branch
against legislative invasions, that is, against violations of separation of
powers. The other is to provide a presidential check upon undesirable
legislation in general. Thus the *Federalist:*

> The primary inducement to conferring the power in question upon the
> Executive is to enable him to defend himself; the secondary one is to
> increase the chances in favor of the community against the passing of bad
> laws, through haste, inadvertence, or design. The oftener the measure is
> brought under examination, the greater the diversity in the situations of
> those who are to examine it, the less must be the danger of those errors
> which flow from want of due deliberation, or of those missteps which
> proceed from the contagion of some common passion or interest.[14]

One vice of a certain type of American political thought is that it

---

[14] *Federalist* 73, p. 443.

"*I HEAR WE'RE SETTING ALL KINDS OF RECORDS*"

imagines constitutional limitations out of thin air. Thus some early supporters of congressional dominance claimed that the President could only veto laws that invaded his sphere or were otherwise unconstitutional. Some of the quasi-collegial Presidents before Jackson, perhaps because they had less independent status or less capacity than their great predecessors, seemed to acquiesce in this limitation, though there is no warrant for it in either the constitutional language or constitutional history. But beginning in Jackson's time, as the Presidency gained independence, confidence, and greater resources, the general claim has been rejected. The final recent episode involved the specific assertion that revenue bills could not be vetoed; Truman vetoed one in 1947, and was upheld.

Presidents now feel free to veto any kind of bill and for any reason. As this passage from the *Federalist* indicates this is how the veto power was originally intended to be used. Naturally Presidents have varied greatly in how much they used the power and for what reasons. Recently its use has increased as the volume of legislation has increased and as Presidents have taken a more active part in the legislative process. The high water mark so far was reached by President Eisenhower. He faced a Congress controlled by the opposition party during most of his administration, and in any event favored limited and less active government rather than positive government of the New Deal and welfare type. In his last term he vetoed more bills than in any other presidential term, and, with his great personal popularity and considerable political skills, was consistently successful in doing so.

The veto is an effective tool. First, it is seldom overridden; one authority remarks that, "Altogether, it seems just to say that the President's veto is normally effective in nine cases out of ten."[15] But this is only part of the tale; the veto's greatest effect lies in threats of its use, made by the President or on his behalf, while a bill is still in Congress. The threat is probably used, and with substantial effect—say, to protect some key provision from drastic alteration in committee—at some time during the legislative careers of most major bills on which the White House has strong feelings.

The power to recommend legislation. This power is not so clear and specific a tool as the veto. To begin with, the Constitution is not even clear whether it is a power or duty; the actual language is: "He *shall* . . . recommend to their consideration such measures as he shall judge necessary and expedient. . . ." No doubt the legally correct understanding is that it is a duty but that the President has a right to perform it, a combination that is in practice equivalent to a power. This opens the door for him. He is thereby authorized to concern himself in any matter that may be the subject of congressional legislation; and he may use all the immense resources of inquiry, study, politicking, and publicity at his disposal to forward his views on the subject. The opportunity is virtually unlimited, and modern Presidents exploit it vigorously. Indeed, an adroit President can on the right occasion set the tone, and nearly determine the agenda, for a session of Congress.

The right—or duty, or opportunity, whatever we call it—is magnified in importance by the nature of Congress. Congress is seldom able to take the initiative, to develop extensive programs of positive legislation; it functions best when it is appraising what has been proposed or has already been done. Hence developing such legislative programs and moving them through the labyrinthine congressional mills is an opportunity and a challenge for the President. In short, leadership escapes Congress and can be seized by him; he can often be in truth chief legislator and legislative leader if he is able.

War and Diplomacy

During World War I it was said of Admiral Jellicoe, who commanded the British Grand Fleet, that he was the only man who could lose the war in an afternoon. The President, like his opposite number in the Kremlin, today can probably cause the destruction of the civilized world in much less time than that. The terrible truth is that the President has,

---

[15] Corwin, p. 282. The veto takes two forms. In one the President returns the bill to Congress, with the constitutionally required, and politically very useful, statement of his reasons for disapproving it. The other is the 'pocket veto.' If Congress adjourns within ten days after a bill is presented to him without his signing or returning it, it does not become law. Such a veto of course cannot be overridden. It has peculiar significance in view of the fact that Congress passes a great deal of legislation in the adjournment rush.

and must have, the *right* to set the American system of nuclear weapon attack in motion, even though the results of an error, a misjudgment, or a fit of madness on his part, would probably be both unpreventable and irretrievable. In the modern world every major nation must have arrangements whereby its fate is in the hands of one man or a few men for instant military action, and for speedy and complex military-diplomatic action, when these are necessary. In the American system the men can be only the President and his immediate subordinates and advisors.

This rests ultimately on the fact that the President heads the executive. In any system, war and the urgent diplomacy related to war must lie mainly with the executive because they cannot be handled by a representative assembly, especially one as complex and cumbersome as Congress.

> Of all the cares or concerns of government, the direction of war most peculiarly demands those qualities which distinguish the exercise of power by a single hand. The direction of war implies the direction of the common strength . . . a usual and essential part of the definition of the executive authority.[16]

The American constitutional and political systems build on this. But such ominous authority in "a single hand" has dangers. We hardly need to be reminded of how many times in history, including recent history, free government has been lost under such circumstances. The American system therefore provides safeguards, contraints upon this necessary "single hand," and does so in characteristic ways. So far at least in our national life these have proven effectual; our crisis Presidencies have not turned into permanent tyrannies.

The President as commander-in-chief. Many constitutional systems give their executive sweeping extraordinary powers for wars and crises, sometimes including power to suspend regular government and rule by unchallengeable decree.[17] Strikingly, the American system does not. The only special authority the President has for such times is that entailed in his constitutional position of commander-in-chief. Thus, the constitutional intent is that in American wars and crises regular government and constitutional government are to *remain largely intact,* as is the web of constraints they impose on presidential power. The President is not only denied the opportunities (and temptations) of discretionary, extra-constitutional rule; the powers he can exercise, though necessarily and properly full, are bounded because he must justify his actions, both logically and politically, within regular and constitutional government.

Today, when war and peace are hard to distinguish, when the Cold War is ever present, and when war in its most extreme form could come

---

[16] *Federalist* 74, p. 447.

[17] See, e.g., E. Drexel Godfrey, Jr., *The Government of France* (2nd ed.; New York: Thomas Y. Crowell, 1963), and generally Clinton Rossiter, *Constitutional Dictatorship* (Princeton: Princeton University Press, 1948).

in minutes, the commandership-in-chief has reached its fullest development. The responsibility resting upon its holder is awesome. However,
it has always been a great power; recall, for example, the uses Lincoln
put it to. And beyond the enormous range of the war and military
aspects of the power there are other major implications as well. One is
that it supports and supplements the general executive power. For
example, President Cleveland relied upon it in his use of troops to break
the Pullman strike of 1894; so did Eisenhower in his use of troops in the
struggle over racial integration of the schools of Little Rock.

But the commandership-in-chief, great though it is as a power, also
is a device whereby the system sets a limit on presidential claims. This is
an instance of the artfulness of the constitutional design. In giving him
this power, the system tells him that this is all he has, that he is to do
his war and crisis governing with it; this repels any suggestion that he
has or should have any *inherent* extraordinary powers.

Related to this restraining aspect of the commandership-in-chief on
the President is the vital fact that it is one of the system's great constraints upon *military* power. The commander-in-chief is a *civil* officer,
politically responsible and the head of the civilian executive branch.
This has profound consequences, though these are seldom noticed, and
the issue of civilian control of the military has seldom come up—which
may be a measure of the effectiveness of the constitutional arrangements.
The role of the military in government is a problem, and often a danger,
in every system. The problem is not just bluntly unconstitutional seizures
of power in the Latin American style. There have been countries in
which the military has claimed to be *legitimately* independent of civilian
authority, and has in crises defied or superseded the latter on this
ground. Germany in World War I and Japan before and during World
War II are examples; in both the military professed to owe allegiance to
the emperor only and not to the regular government. In France (e.g., in
the Dreyfus affair, around 1900) the army has claimed that it represents
the French nation as much as or more than do the republican governmental institutions; accordingly, the army further claimed that it was
somehow directly responsible to the French nation and not to the government. Some shadow of this claim exists in France today.

The American solution is simple: the highest *military* authority is
the *civilian* President. President Truman removed General MacArthur
from command in Korea in 1951 because the general refused to accept
Truman's policies. From the constitutional point of view this was not a
clash between civilian and military; the commander-in-chief can remove
a disobedient general just as the general might remove a disobedient
subordinate commander. The civilian and political authority is thus
made unchallengeably supreme, by being made the top of the military
chain of command. The solution has been politically effective; the subordination of military to civilian authority has seldom been breached and
never been denied, and we have not had ambitious politicians, civilian

or military, claiming to represent an autonomous military interest, or presence, in politics and government.

Foreign affairs. When we come to diplomacy and foreign affairs things are not quite so clear. As so often, separation of powers leaves doubts about just what the respective powers and functions, both constitutional and political, of Congress and the President are. Many such doubts have been settled by history and necessity. But there is enough uncertainty and overlap left so that circumstances and politics can move the boundaries now this way and now that.

The President has undoubted constitutional power to make treaties and appoint diplomatic representatives. Further, it is natural that day-to-day diplomacy be in the hands of the executive-administrative rather than the legislative. The Constitution so provides, giving the President power to send and receive ambassadors. But Congress is nonetheless firmly present throughout the whole field. So the question usually is: How far can Congress, whether as a matter of constitutional law, or good governmental practice, or political feasibility, either participate in these daily affairs or otherwise exercise some authority in foreign policy on its own? As usual, this depends a great deal on the specific situation and on the President. The outlines are about as follows.

The Senate exercises very substantial influence. This derives in part from its powers to ratify or reject treaties and to confirm or refuse appointments (e.g., ambassadorial), but also from the whole complex of powers and capacities that make it so formidable a body. Presidents generally feel they need at least the support of some leading senators not only on treaties but also on all important foreign policy steps, and regard broader Senate support as very desirable. Indeed, probably no legislative assembly in the world rivals the Senate in its influence on foreign relations.[18]

In addition, every aspect is greatly affected by both House and Senate ideas because of Congress's power over legislation and money; these are indispensables, and Congress freely uses its monopoly over them to get its desires respected. Further, the other powers of Congress, such as the power to investigate, are fully available; Presidents have never been able to establish the view, though some have tried, that their authority in the foreign policy area means that Congress must give up the use of these powers.

However, the influence of Congress tends to be a negative rather than a positive one. It is a capacity to check, veto, limit, discourage, and revise, rather than a positive capacity to create, originate, and lead. And this is especially true when the President is an active and 'strong' one. The Senate can reject treaties, or require changes as the price of its consent; it cannot negotiate them, and it cannot administer the multitudinous affairs that arise after treaty arrangements are established.

---

[18] Harold J. Laski, *The American Presidency* (London: George Allen & Unwin, Ltd., 1940), p. 172. The judgment seems still true today.

Congress can refuse enabling legislation or money for a presidential policy; it can seldom create a policy of its own. Occasionally an individual senator or representative will play a creative part, but usually only because of cooperation with the President. Even the power of legislative oversight does not really give Congress anything resembling the policy-making and policy-controlling capacity that it does in some other areas. The President is truly the leader and chief agent of American foreign policy. And as foreign affairs become more important, so also does the Presidency.[19]

The Chief Magistrate

The Presidency has inevitably risen in authority and importance as its great tasks have expanded: foreign affairs, legislative leadership, and the executive and administrative side of government. The modern Presidency is vast largely because these tasks are vast. But the nature of the office readies the Presidency for expansion of its authority. Presidential powers, duties, and functions, when in the hands of effective Presidents, have a way of strengthening—almost multiplying—each other. For example, the President is stronger as a legislative leader because he is also the chief executive and administrator, and stronger as a diplomat because he is both of these. The Presidency aptly illustrates situations in which the whole is greater—or less—than the sum of its parts. If he does well in one area this tends to strengthen him in others, and weakness in one tends to weaken him in all.

It is striking that the actual constitutional powers of the office, looked at one by one and in their strictly legal aspect, are not great. Indeed, they are small compared with those of the President of the Fifth French Republic and even as compared with those of the British Cabinet. But they are strategic powers and they are strategically related. The constitutional design of the office opens to the President the multiplicity of roles from which his overall strength derives. And not least are the *political* roles of party leader, popular spokesman, and ceremonial chief of state.

Thus we come back to the point with which we started, that the President is the central personage of the government and nation. The title by which he is often known, chief magistrate, is revealing. Magistrate is from the Latin *magister*, which contains the meanings of master, ruler, chief, head, director, and leader. This is the real key to understanding the Presidency: It is an office of leadership. Indeed, the familiar names for its roles or functions contain this connotation. The President is a leader in each of his functions and in his office as a whole. The real measure of the power of a leader is found in his followers, in the energy he can draw forth and direct. The President's power is

---

[19] See Tocqueville, I, 130–31 for a vivid account of this process.

measured precisely by the degree to which he can rally support, can galvanize some or many of the innumerable sectors of public opinion behind him, can persuade or manipulate the interest groups and the party factions, and can do all the other things out of which political influence can be made. His opportunities to do so are at times meager, but at other times almost illimitable. There is a remark by a man who when he himself became President provided the classic example of the truth of what he had said: "The President is at liberty, both in law and in conscience, to be as big a man as he can be."[20]

Presidential Leadership: Means and Methods

The purpose here is to explore the power problem of the man inside the White House. This is the classic problem of the man on top in any political system: how to be on top in fact as well as in name. It is a problem common to Prime Ministers and Premiers, and to dictators, however styled, and to those kings who rule as well as reign. It is a problem also for the heads of "private governments," for corporation presidents, trade union leaders, churchmen. . . . The search for personal influence is at the center of the job of being President.[21]

What must come through is a picture of the President—always faced with the hostility of some members of the Congress, of some population groups, and of some of his own administration (Dawes said that Cabinet members were the natural enemies of the President)—working to move the nation from one point to another on those few issues on which he feels, or is forced to feel, strongly, using the stature and prestige of his office where possible, and always shoving, cajoling, reasoning, pleading, and politicking.[22]

If the Presidency is in its essence an office of leadership, then how does the President lead, what means does he have to help him, and what can he achieve? For enlightenment we must look closely at the actual activities of the Presidency and of the President himself.

These activities have vastly increased since Washington's time. In 1789, a busy year when the new government was being created, President Washington approved 54 public laws and issued three executive orders. In 1939 the figures were 502 and 287. By 1949 the increases had been such that the President probably often signed his name not less than *six hundred times a day*, and to a bewildering variety of documents. In a quiet, almost inactive, three-month period in 1948 he approved 193 orders, proclamations, and bills, sent to Congress or government officials 185 messages and letters; issued 52 press statements; appointed 71

[20] Woodrow Wilson, *Constitutional Government in the United States* (New York: Columbia University Press, 1908 and 1961), p. 70.

[21] Richard E. Neustadt, *Presidential Power: The Politics of Leadership* (New York: John Wiley & Sons, Inc., 1960), p. viii.

[22] From a letter by the late Professor Morton Grodzins to the authors of this book, criticizing an early draft. The quotation is but one example of the learning and judgment of a distinguished political scientist to whom this book owes much.

EXECUTIVE OFFICE OF THE PRESIDENT

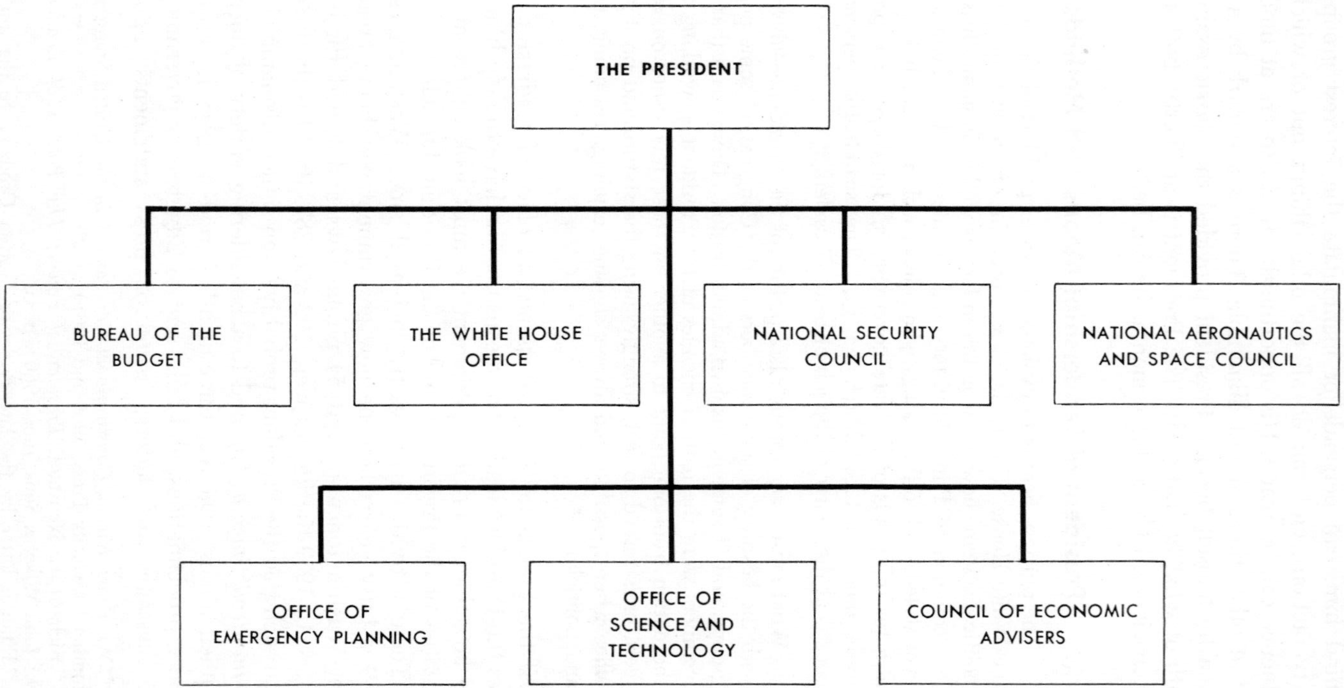

THE PRESIDENT
BUREAU OF THE BUDGET
THE WHITE HOUSE OFFICE
NATIONAL SECURITY COUNCIL
NATIONAL AERONAUTICS AND SPACE COUNCIL
OFFICE OF EMERGENCY PLANNING
OFFICE OF SCIENCE AND TECHNOLOGY
COUNCIL OF ECONOMIC ADVISERS

Source: U.S. Government Organization Manual

officials; received visits from 321 persons, and held ten Cabinet meetings and nine press conferences. Today virtually all these figures are undoubtedly much greater.[23]

The Presidency has therefore had to expand and transform its physical equipment. In Washington's time, in Lincoln's, and even in Hoover's, the *immediate staff* of the President was astonishingly small; in Hoover's time it was still only a dozen or so persons. Today it is over three thousand, organized as the Executive Office of the President with at least a dozen major official bodies and many more minor or unofficial ones, occupying extensive offices in the White House and nearby buildings. In simple size of staff and extent of organization the Presidency is now an *institution*.

It has also become institutionalized in another and more subtle sense. Washington, Lincoln, and even Hoover had few regular tasks outside the great constitutional duties of the Presidency, few services they had to perform for other parts of government and political life; they could pretty much concentrate on matters important to *them as Presidents*. Today the President's assistance, participation, support, and services are subject to thousands of calls throughout government and throughout the nation. It has been well said that the President now has to be a tirelessly busy chief clerk for literally hundreds of matters, governmental and otherwise, and that one of his greatest problems is to find the means and opportunity, amid all these chores, to do his own central job for himself. And that job is to find, develop, and wisely use sufficient effective personal influence on those affairs of government and politics which he, as the only man at the very top of the pyramid, sees as crucial to the Presidency and to the nation, and in which he as President can play some unique and vital part. Yet he cannot neglect the clerkly chores either; effective performance of the right chores, for the right people, in the right way, and at the right time can be an immense source of this personal influence for him.

He faces another new problem as well. Until recently the President functioned in a limited circle of politicians and officials, or if in public then in formal settings and at a remove. Today the office is infinitely more public and popular. Drastic change began at least with Franklin D. Roosevelt's informal press conferences and his famous 'fireside chats' by radio. Now, with omnipresent television, intense news coverage, innumerable personal appearances, and with jet travel taking him everywhere and everybody to Washington, the skills that used to be practiced mainly in the privacy of the Oval Office and the Cabinet Room now have to be practiced before the whole world, and are the more crucially important because of that.

Despite all this, the office depends as much as ever on the President's own personal abilities, as statesman and leader, as shover, cajoler, rea-

---

[23] Edward H. Hobbs, *Behind the President: A Study of Executive Office Agencies* (Washington, D.C.: Public Affairs Press, 1954), pp. 4–5.

soner, persuader, politician, and all the rest. The President as a personal doer does not disappear into the institutionalized Presidency; he remains paramount and vital, and as a person, not a bundle of functions. However, he must today largely act through that Presidency, by means of it, and in a sense as a part of it. Gone are the days when Polk could literally substitute for a large part of his Cabinet and day by day run most of the governmental machinery by himself. Gone are the days when Lincoln could transact all the significant business (and much of the trivial business) of the presidential office in his own person and by his own hand. Gone are the days when a Grover Cleveland could go off on a long summer's vacation without even a secretary and answer his mail himself. Today's President must do his own job—nobody else either can or will—but he can do it only *in the context* of the institutionalized Presidency. So we must turn now to the organizations and procedures that make it up. In examining these we must keep in mind the crucial duality we have identified—the institutionalized Presidency *and* the actual President's problem of personal influence.

The Cabinet and its Uses

> The Cabinet is a creation of custom and tradition, going back to the First President, and functions at the pleasure of the President. Its purpose is to advise the President on any matter concerning which he wishes such advice (pursuant to Art. II, sec. 2, of the Constitution).[24]

The Cabinet is the principal organization we all associate with the Presidency. The usual view is that it and the President are a team, a band of brothers, that the Cabinet contains the President's principal advisors and administrators and is—or at least should be—his chief instrument in his work. This view misses much, and is often quite wrong. The Cabinet looks from the outside very settled and formal. Actually it is the uneasy product of strong conflicting forces that swirl around the Presidency, and hence is a complex and constantly changing phenomenon, with much of its reality concealed from view. Above all it is the reflection of the wishes, habits, and situation of each particular President.

The nature of the Cabinet. Any President needs advisors and trusted chief subordinates. Volunteers are always plentiful because, among other reasons, factions and individuals are always struggling to get close to the great office and its power and prestige. But they often want to share it or control it, in their own interest. This is a price the President is seldom willing to pay; by his nature he wants as much freedom, flexibility, and undiluted primacy as he can get.

He can get a great deal if he is able. The Cabinet came into being simply because Washington found it useful and natural to meet with his

---

[24] From the official description of the Cabinet in the *U.S. Government Organization Manual 1962–63*, p. 51.

official family,' and later Presidents followed his example. The Constitution does not even mention the Cabinet, let alone establish it; as we have seen, the Framers rejected any plural executive and even any council that the President would be obliged to consult, still less to obey. To this day the Cabinet has no constitutional, and little statutory, foundation. Further, history has settled that the President has the right to dismiss any Cabinet member at pleasure and that he has a fairly free hand in his appointments. Within the Cabinet he can make himself the unchallenged chief. The famous story about Lincoln (that his Cabinet voted unanimously against a proposal of his, whereupon he remarked, "Seven Noes, one Aye; the Ayes have it.") is apocryphal, but it states the *constitutional* possibility—for the right President.

But the President's *political* position vis-à-vis his Cabinet is not as secure. As always much depends upon the President and the circumstances. Some Presidents (Monroe, Pierce, and Buchanan, for example) were little more than first among equals, and submitted to Cabinet decisions. And all Presidents have sometimes found themselves unable to cope with some particular Cabinet member on some particular matter. An important variable is the independent political power the Cabinet member possesses. However, in general and in the long run, few Cabinets or Cabinet members can be really independent. Seldom can they stand up to the holder of the presidential office, to the man who carries the constitutional responsibility and possesses the constitutional powers, who is chief of so many things—and who got all those votes.

The nature of the Cabinet itself further militates against its being an independently powerful entity. Cabinet appointments are often made to pay political debts, or to give representation to an interest group or a political faction, or to draw into the administration some individual who is specifically useful or too powerful to ignore.[25] The resultant divergences in the backgrounds and constituencies of the Cabinet members inevitably give rise to disunities and rivalries. These are reinforced by rivalries inherent in the situation. Each member is responsible for the success of his department upon which, in turn, his political future depends. For success he needs the President's support and aid. But the President has only a limited supply of these, and in a sense what one member gets the others do not, so Cabinet members are natural rivals for presidential favor. And they have few official or personal interests in common to counterbalance the disunities. The British Cabinet bears a constitutional *collective* responsibility, so that each member has a stake in the success of his colleagues, and personal political success in Britain consists largely in moving upward through a series of Cabinet offices. None of this obtains in the American situation. The individual Cabinet member stands or falls on his own, on his own success with (or against) the President, with Congress, with powerful interests, and with the public.

[25] See Richard F. Fenno, Jr., *The President's Cabinet* (Cambridge: Harvard University Press, 1959, and New York: Vintage Books, n.d.).

The upshot is that the American Cabinet is distinctly not a weighty, unified council. It does not *as a body* mold broad policy or coordinate administration; nor does it by authoritative advice participate *as a body* in the presidential office. America has presidential government, not cabinet government.

The uses of the Cabinet. Nonetheless Presidents have found many uses for the Cabinet; if they had not, it would not have endured. And because the Cabinet is so variable an institution and so complexly involved in the complexities of the presidential job, many classifications of these uses are possible. One is based on how they affect the 'roles' of the President; this is illuminating and useful.[26] But the Presidency is one job, done by one man, not a bundle of separate roles, and too much emphasis on roles obscures this sovereign fact. Instead, we shall use a classification that groups the Cabinet's uses under three main headings: managerial, congressional, and political.

One of the modern President's great problems is to master and *manage* the immense executive-administrative machine—simply to make it run, and run *for him* and not too much at cross-purposes. The Cabinet can help here. It cannot solve his really crucial problems of coordination. Most of these involve divergences or clashes in which Cabinet members are likely to act as interested parties rather than on behalf of the President.[27] But a President can make the Cabinet meeting a place for getting and exchanging information and for discussion of less intensely charged matters. And it can be one means whereby he can conveniently get his general view and specific wishes known in the individual departmental hierarchies, and can give some sense of central purpose and coherence to them all.

He can also occasionally use the Cabinet and its individual members in executive-administrative tasks involving more than one department. Some reformers in fact propose that the Cabinet be made *the* central structure for Presidential control of administration, around which all specialized executive-administrative groups and activities would be arrayed. But the idea is not popular with Presidents, who do not seem to like being constrained within neat and logical structural arrangements, or to be limited to presiding over an expanded and more powerful Cabinet. They prefer flexibility and freedom, and they may be right. Franklin D. Roosevelt was the least systematic presidential executive-administrator of recent times and Eisenhower one of the most. But Roosevelt was by far the more successful of the two. Eisenhower himself ultimately moved away from organizational tidiness built on the Cabinet toward a more personal and flexible style—and became a more effective President when he did so.

---

[26] See, e.g., Fenno as an excellent example.

[27] As one reads the writings of often-disgruntled ex-Cabinet members one becomes filled with their side of this. But finally one begins to think of them as they must have looked when seen through the eyes of the solitary man at the head of the table.

Second, the Cabinet can be useful to the President in his relations with Congress. It would be simple and perhaps comforting if the Cabinet were his main instrument here, and Cabinet members his principal agents in legislative matters, with everything operating in a coordinated fashion under his direction. But this seldom occurs, and probably cannot occur very often. One reason is that congressional groups want to deal directly with the chief. Another arises from the conflict of interest already noted. Cabinet members are department heads, and the departments are territories over which President and Congress contest. The Cabinet member is always tempted to seek with Congress advantage for himself and his department at the expense, if necessary, of single-minded service to the President's overall national aims. The legislative uses of a Cabinet member are therefore limited to those where his special or departmental interests can be reconciled with the President's larger ones. One task of Presidential leadership is to work out such reconciliations. But within these limits the uses are considerable. Cabinet members can advocate his positions on the Hill, perform indispensable liaison, help keep lower departmental officials in line behind 'the President's program,' and bring their personal influence and expert knowledge to bear on the endless and sensitive intricacies of executive-legislative relations. In this last Secretary Dulles and Secretary Humphrey were of great value to President Eisenhower, as Secretary Dillon and Secretary McNamara were to President Kennedy and President Johnson.

However, the Cabinet can be of greatest use to a President in the broad realm of the *political*—and since the Presidency is so profoundly political this can be very important. Cabinet appointments are patronage of high prestige and value with which he can reward supporters. They also enable him to bring into his Administration, and hence get a hold on, important interest groups and political factions. A dramatic case of this use is when he brings in members of the opposite party in times of crisis; e.g., Franklin Roosevelt appointed two distinguished Republicans to the secretaryships of Navy and War in the threatening days of 1940. Cabinet members can supply information and advice on feeling in all the various sectors of public opinion their personal connections and departmental powers give them contact with. They can make speeches, influence people, generate publicity for the Administration, campaign for Administration programs, and in general work for the Administration in all the vast obscure webs of American politics. A President can also use Cabinet members to protect himself politically. He can never fully escape the blame for mistakes. (The sign Truman put on his desk, "The buck stops here," is basically correct, although Eisenhower was almost an exception.) But Cabinet members can be lightning rods, shields, and scapegoats.

Finally, closely related to its specific political uses, the Cabinet affects the general quality and standing of an administration. Although the Cabinet is not a true executive council, the posts in it are among the great offices in American government, and a President can in them partially compensate for his own limitations. Harding was almost shockingly unqualified for the Presidency himself, but by getting some distinguished men into his Cabinet he obscured and perhaps partly overcame this—at least until some other Cabinet members were exposed as crooked and corrupt. And at a much higher level of presidential quality, Truman's appointments of Acheson, Marshall, and Lovett, and Eisenhower's of Dulles, and Kennedy's of Dillon greatly strengthened their respective administrations.

But all this does not add up to enough to give the Cabinet a consistently vital and major share in the Presidency. The Cabinet is a source of tools and support for the President sometimes, an encumbrance and annoyance for him sometimes, an administrative necessity and sometimes an administrative convenience, and a cipher sometimes. Although to some extent the President governs with it or through it, the Cabinet never governs. The system is always presidential government.

Specialized 'Cabinets' and Councils

The National Security Council. The idea of constraining or supplementing the President by equipping him with a council or some other body of determined membership and functions he would be required to consult is perennial. Rejected as a general proposition by presidential treatment of the Cabinet, the idea comes forward in more specialized forms—and Presidents have turned it to their own uses.

The history of the National Security Council is a good example. There has long been agreement on the desirability of some means for better planning and coordinating of national defense and security policy.[28] The National Security Council, established by legislation in 1947, was expected to be such a means. Apparently its proponents also hoped that it would be a source of semi-compulsory advice for the President, a *de facto* holder of his powers and responsibilities concerning national security. These hopes were speedily and decisively disappointed; no President has permitted it. Indeed, Truman for three years did not even attend NSC meetings, so as to quash any implication that he was required to do so or that he was bound by its decisions.

With this subordination clearly established, Presidents have made considerable use of the NSC. For example, President Eisenhower did so, and in a characteristic way. He felt that in the Presidency as in the military the chief should rely extensively on a staff and—at least at first—hoped to decentralize many tasks and activities out of his own personal hands. So he required for a time that national security matters reach him through the NSC, and that if at all possible the NSC dispose of them

---

[28] Much of the following is derived from Paul Y. Hammond, "The National Security Council as a Device for Interdepartmental Coordination," *American Political Science Review*, 54 (Dec. 1960), 899–910.

itself. This changed before long, partly because of a factor basic to the Presidency. A President's major subordinates want direct private access to him, and they dislike transacting their business with him in open meeting with their colleague-rivals present.

The usefulness of the genuine *advisory* function however, where there is no attempt to *decide* for the President or to *confine* him to set organizational channels, appeared in the work of the executive committee of the NSC during the grim crisis of October 1962 over the presence of Soviet missiles in Cuba.

> . . . It is true in the White House, as in the Congress, that fewer votes are changed by open debate than quiet negotiation among the debaters. But in the White House, unlike the Congress, only one man's vote is decisive, and thorough and thoughtful debate *before* he has to make up his mind can assist him in that task.
>
> That meetings can sometimes be useful was proven by the deliberations of the NSC executive committee after the discovery of offensive weapons in Cuba. The unprecedented nature of the Soviet move, the manner in which it cut across so many departmental jurisdictions, the limited amount of information available, and the security regulations which inhibited staff work, all tended to have a leveling effect on the principals taking part in these discussions, so each felt free to challenge the assumptions and assertions of all others.
>
> Everyone in that group altered his views as the give-and-take talk continued. Every solution or combination of solutions was coldly examined, and its disadvantages weighed. The fact that we started out with a sharp divergence of views, the President has said, was "very valuable" in hammering out a policy.[29]

But note that the committee did not seek to share in the Presidency but simply to assist the President as he wished, and to tender advice which he was free to take or not take.

The Council of Economic Advisers. Part of the President's job since the Great Depression of the 1930s is some general responsibility for the country's economic prosperity. This was given formal recognition in the Full Employment Act of 1946, which makes it national policy to foster full employment and directs the President to stay in touch with economic conditions and to make recommendations to Congress about them.

The President could probably have carried out this task pretty well with his existing resources. However the Act created the Council of Economic Advisers as a small agency in the Executive Office of the President to help him. It has been composed of economists from leading universities. There was at first some suggestion that it should be completely neutral and nonpartisan, and, even further, that it should be a bit distant from and independent of the President. As we would expect, the Presidents have not permitted this, and the Council is today very much an arm of the Presidency, deeply engaged in the political processes

---

[29] Sorensen, pp. 59–60.

of forming and effectuating policy. Indeed, some now fear that the Council is too presidential and too political, and that its judgments are sometimes not purely professional ones but rather simply cloak with scholarly respectability positions reached on other grounds. Such fears may or may not be valid, but they do illustrate the widely held and quite sound intuitive realization that anything that gets near the Presidency is likely to become presidential and political.

Presidential Agencies for Executive-Administrative Management

Today's President needs means, in his own hands and responsible to him alone, to help him in actually managing the immense executive-administrative machinery; only then can he perform his various roles and functions, and only then can he really exploit the potentialities of the office. The Cabinet availing little, he has developed other means.

The Bureau of the Budget. One of these, the Bureau of the Budget, is an important means for this in itself. It also reveals, in a presidential transformation and utilization of rather unpromising materials, something of how Presidents do their work.

In 1921 the budgetary and accounting procedures of the national government were overhauled by statute, and Congress, though not entirely happily, gave up its traditional initiative in proposing expenditures and charged the President with the duty of preparing a general annual budget for the whole government. (There had been no such budget till then, merely a tangle of more or less unrelated spending proposals.) The statute created the Bureau of the Budget to aid in this task, originally pretty much just as a clerical and accounting unit, not an important management tool for the President. The importance of budget-making, and its influence on policy and on management, have since increased vastly. By parallel steps beginning at least early in Franklin D. Roosevelt's time, the Presidents have made it a powerful and much-used agency of the President, especially in two functions.

One function is executive and administrative: The Bureau serves as the President's principal agent in the general management of his branch. This has been largely built on its budget function. The Bureau not only assembles and handles the actual budget figures, it also reviews for the President all requests the departments and agencies make for appropriations. Further, it supervises the administration of the budget, i.e., the actual spending of the money, and apportions general appropriations among specific functions.

The other function relates to legislation and to the always delicate relations between Congress and the executive: the Bureau serves as the President's agent for 'legislative reference,' or 'legislative clearance,' and for handling departmental advice on whether to sign or veto enacted legislation. For example, all proposals for legislation and comments on proposed legislation that the departments and agencies want to transmit to Congress must be submitted to the Bureau and cleared by it as 'in accord with the President's program' before they can go forward.[30]

In short, by means of the Bureau the President can supervise and control the executive establishments—the departments and agencies—infinitely more effectively and thoroughly than he otherwise could. He must always fear, and seek to forestall, their establishing independent relationships with Congress and getting out of step with his policies and activities; the Bureau helps him. He must equally fear and seek to forestall congressional encroachments on them; the Bureau helps him here also by reducing the grounds on which Congress can claim justification to do so.

The Bureau started as a modest technical aid. It has been taken over and expanded by the President into virtually *the* instrument of general presidential management, and into a major tool in some of the endless legislative and political aspects of his job as well.

Agencies for planning and for emergencies. But even this does not end the executive-administrative tale and ever-related tasks of policy-making and politicking. The President needs other kinds of help, different from any that the Bureau, an established, operating, management agency, can give him. He lives today always in the shadow of possible emergencies, especially those—all urgent and terrifying and some almost unimaginably so—of thermonuclear weaponry and of today's desperate international conflicts. As the nation's leader he therefore needs plans for coping with them; and he needs means of making these plans, keeping them up to date, and for creating and maintaining arrangements in the executive branch (and relations with the legislative branch) so they can be put into effect if necessary.

Some of this help he can get from the established departments and agencies, but this is likely to come to him entangled in their own special concerns. He therefore needs an agency of his own to put this help together and orient it to his own views and to the general national interest. This agency, as it existed in the mid-sixties, was called the Office of Emergency Planning.

Special presidential agencies concerned with planning for emergencies and for crisis government have a long history. In World War I much of the administration of mobilization and of wartime economic controls was done by special temporary presidential agencies created for the purpose and abolished at the end of the war. Similar uses of such occurred in the Great Depression and in World War II. Presidents seem to think (and to get more or less grudging congressional agreement) that they must have such agencies in such times to get the presidential job done.

---

[30] For the legislation and clearance functions of the Bureau see Richard E. Neustadt, "The Presidency and Legislation: The Growth of Central Clearance," *American Political Science Review*, 48, (Sept. 1954), 656, and "Presidency and Legislation: Planning the President's Program," *American Political Review* 49, (Dec. 1955), 990.

Personal Assistants and Presidential Commissions

So far we have described Executive Office organizations that are or have become quite formal, with identified official positions, duties, and responsibilities. But these are only the outer battlements of the Presidency. Presidents also need to work independently of formal organizations and formal channels, with adaptable and unofficial instruments and processes that they can shape and change freely. A President can seldom allow himself to be without alternative channels of action and sources of information and influence. If he does not maintain these he becomes the prisoner of the existing organizations. Since Washington's time Presidents have had close, personal, unofficial assistants and advisors for these informal uses. As the Presidency has grown, so also has this inner circle around the President grown and in some ways replaced in personal relations with the President the organizations that have become formal and institutionalized.

Today much of this inner circle is loosely organized in the White House Office.[31] Its basic function is to provide direct and informal personal assistance to the President himself, in any or all of his activities, official or otherwise, and entirely as he sees fit. The White House Office has neither legal duties nor legal powers; its authority comes from closeness to the President and to presidential power. Its chiefs are not subject to Senate confirmation, as the principal members of the Executive Office often are, and the official description of the White House Office is exceedingly brief and general. It answers the President's phone, attends to his personal schedule, manages his press relations, runs his confidential errands, makes his secret inquiries, helps in his personal politicking, arranges his appointments, writes his speeches—and, perhaps most importantly, advises him personally on many vital public matters. This last is obviously highly significant.

The inner circle turns, so far as we can see from the outside, around the 'special assistants to the President' and similar officials. Traditionally these people have functioned informally and unofficially, without titles or pay. In recent years things have been institutionalized considerably. Thus in 1963 there were nine or ten officially recognized special assistants to the President, still without specific *statutory* duties and powers but each more or less permanent and each assigned to pretty clear, though informally defined and somewhat variable, spheres of activity.

The high point of structuring in the White House Office system occurred under Eisenhower, when Mr. Sherman Adams as The Assistant to The President was made a genuine chief of staff to the President, with extensive personal power. We have not seen anything like this since and

---

[31] The *Government Organization Manual* says that "this office serves the President in the performance of the many detailed activities incident to his immediate office," and that its principal figures "assist the President in such matters as he may direct."

may not for a long time. But the White House Office, or something like it, is likely always to be a potent force at the heart of the Presidency.

Just as Presidents have used personal advisers and assistants, so have they felt free to call on prominent citizens, singly or in groups, for advice and assistance in more public but often still personal ways. Thus there have been many committees, commissions, councils, and conferences, of many kinds and on many subjects, created by the President or under his name, to bring him a consensus of informed judgment on some problem or to handle some hot issue, or to focus public thinking on some policy. These have been remarkably varied: individuals, small groups, 'brains trusts,' 'kitchen cabinets,' outside experts, governmental experts, large loosely knit assemblages, and so on. Some recent titles that got into official publications are illustrative: the President's Committees on Traffic Safety, on Employment of the Handicapped, on Equal Employment Opportunities, on the Implementation of the Federal Employee-Management Relations Program, on Migratory Labor, and on Juvenile Delinquency and Youth Crime; the President's Councils on Aging, and on Youth Fitness; the President's Commissions on Internal Security and Individual Rights, and on the Status of Women; and the President's Advisory Committees on Government Organization, on Labor-Management Policy, and on Presidential Office Space.[32] A few of these have had great permanent influence; a famous example is the President's Committee on Administrative Management, whose recommendations in 1939 led to the creation of the Executive Office of the President. Some have amounted to little or nothing. Some have done substantial jobs or have dealt with some important problem. All have had their relationships to the President's powers, duties, and functions. All of them have added to the complexities, dimensions, and resources of the Presidency.

BIBLIOGRAPHICAL NOTE

The Presidency is extensively discussed in histories of the United States and general studies of American government. In addition there are many separate studies of the office, and every President has been the subject of one or more biographies. Brief standard biographies of all the Presidents are found in the *Dictionary of American Biography*. The papers of most Presidents have been published in individual publications, and many of them are also to be found in James D. Richardson ed., *The Messages and Papers of the Presidents* (1896–1899), and successor publications. Executive orders, and numerous presidential proclamations and similar documents since 1936, are found in the *Federal Register*, an official daily publication issued in Washington. Most newspapers cover the Presidency thoroughly and some, notably the *New York Times*, publish all substantial public statements by the President. These are now also

---

[32] From the *Government Organization Manual*.

published in *CQ Weekly Report* (see biographical note to Ch. 5 on *Congressional Quarterly* publications).

The standard treatise on the legal and constitutional aspects of the Presidency is Edward S. Corwin, *The President: Office and Powers 1787–1957* (4th rev. ed., 1957); it also contains extensive notes and bibliographical materials. A brief treatment of the Presidency is Clinton Rossiter, *The American Presidency* (rev. ed., 1960); it contains a useful bibliography. A study that still is valuable is Harold J. Laski, *The American Presidency* (1940).

A recent study of the Cabinet is Richard F. Fenno, Jr., *The President's Cabinet* (1959). A well-known account of relationships between President and Congress is Wilfred E. Binkley, *President and Congress* (3rd rev. ed., 1962). A description of the Executive Office of the President is found in Edward H. Hobbs, *Behind the President* (1954).

Many specialized studies of various aspects of the Presidency can be found in the notes and bibliographies referred to above.

Chapter 7

The Judicial Branch:
Courts for the American
Constitutional System

> *Whoever attentively considers the different departments of*
> *power must perceive that . . . the judiciary, from the nature*
> *of its functions, will always be the least dangerous. . . . The*
> *judiciary . . . has no influence over either the sword or the*
> *purse. . . . It may truly be said to have neither FORCE nor*
> *WILL but merely judgment. . . .*

PUBLIUS[1]

> *The least dangerous branch of the American government is*
> *the most extraordinarily powerful court of law the world has*
> *ever known.*

ALEXANDER M. BICKEL[2]

THE AMERICAN POLITICAL ORDER, IN ITS QUEST FOR A SYSTEM OF GOVERN-ment that is at once democratic, effective, and free, gives an extraordinary place to its judiciary. The American Supreme Court is in truth the most extraordinarily powerful court of law the world has ever known. A few historical examples readily call this to mind.

Very early, the Court asserted the power of *judicial review* over statutes (that is, the power to declare them unconstitutional); as to state statutes in 1796, and as to federal in 1803. In the early decades of the nineteenth century the Court, vigorously exercising this power and others, established its own authority and the constitutional supremacy of the national government in the American system.

In 1857, in its catastrophic Dred Scott decision,[3] the Court in effect destroyed any real possibility of compromise of the slavery issue, and pressed the nation another step toward the Civil War.

After the Civil War, the Court virtually rewrote the Fourteenth Amendment, cancelling it as a protection of the Negroes, which it was intended to be, and making it into a protection of business against state

---

[1] *Federalist* 78 (emphasis in original).
[2] *The Least Dangerous Branch: The Supreme Court at the Bar of Politics* (Indianapolis: The Bobbs-Merrill Company, Inc., 1962) p. 1.
[3] *Dred Scott* v. *Sandford,* 19 How. 393 (1857).

regulation, which it was not intended to be. In the twentieth century, up to about 1937, the Court put rigidly laissez-faire economics into American constitutional law, and, since 1937, has taken it out.

In a series of modern decisions, the most famous being *Brown* v. *Board of Education*, a case involving segregated schools decided in 1954,[4] the Court has not only restored the Fourteenth Amendment as a protection for the Negro, but has also launched the nation on the fateful course toward nationally enforced equality of legal rights for Negro and white.

Beginning in 1962, the Court has started to use its powers to rescue underrepresented citizens from one of the oldest and most pervasive problems of American politics, gross denials of equal representation through malapportioned legislative election districts.[5]

No other court in any major country can claim to have influenced the course of politics and of public policy so clearly or on such a scale.

Nor does the power of the federal judiciary stop with what the Supreme Court can do singlehanded.[6] The federal district and circuit courts in the South have since 1954 acted to great effect in literally hundreds of situations where Negroes were denied constitutional rights.[7] Following the Supreme Court's lead, courts throughout the nation have brought about significant reapportionment of legislative representation in a substantial number of states. One federal court, the Court of Appeals for the District of Columbia circuit, is the greatest single authority holding the procedures of the federal government's departments and agencies to standards of legality and fairness.[8] Examples could be multiplied.

The familiar statement that the American judiciary is *a branch of government* and an *equal* branch is thus indeed true, though it is a statement that can be made of very few judiciaries in the world. How did the American federal judiciary come to have such extraordinary authority? Does the Constitution intend it? What are the consequences of this authority for American government and politics? Can such authority in the hands of judges—appointed for life rather than popularly elected for fixed terms and hence largely immune from any direct control by the people or their representatives—be consistent with American ideas of liberty and democracy? What are the relationships between this

---

[4] 347 U.S. 483 (1954).

[5] *Baker* v. *Carr*, 369 U.S. 186 (1962). The Court confirmed and expanded the principle in *Reynolds* v. *Sims*, 377 U.S. 533 (1964), and other subsequent cases.

[6] The Supreme Court is the head of the federal judicial system. It deals almost entirely with cases appealed from other courts. The general trial courts of the system are the district courts. There are one or more district courts in each state. They are presided over by about three hundred district judges. Above the district courts are the courts of appeals, one in each of the eleven judicial 'circuits' into which the country is divided. There are also various courts of specialized jurisdiction, such as the Court of Claims and the Court of Military Appeals.

[7] One interesting account is Jack W. Peltason, *Fifty-eight Lonely Men* (New York: Harcourt, Brace & World, 1961).

[8] The statutes provide for judicial review and enforcement of the actions of many of the departments and agencies by this court.

potent judiciary and the other parts of the system—Congress, Presidency, administrative machinery, states, and voters? Why has this seemingly 'aristocratic' branch in recent years been so far ahead of the democratic and popular branches in so many seemingly democratic enterprises, such as protecting civil and voting rights? These are questions that govern the work of this chapter.

The Judicial Function in Government

Law and judicial processes apparently exist in all societies. All societies seem to seek means whereby at least some disputes can be settled according to some rule and by authority rather than by direct struggle. In advanced societies, where the political order and the governmental system are highly developed, law is elaborated in complex bodies of rules governing both substantive rights and duties and procedural methods; and the judicial process is institutionalized in independent judiciaries which bring their own special competences to the pursuit of justice and freedom. Typically such advanced societies entrust substantial parts of actual government and politics to their judiciaries and do much of the work of governing by legal and judicial modes. America is simply an extreme case in carrying this to the point where the judiciary becomes a full-scale, equal, branch of government.

This entrusting of governing authority to the judiciary takes many forms, of which judicial review is simply the best-known and most spectacular, the visible peak of the iceberg. There are at least three other important ways in which the American judiciary governs or profoundly affects government and which will help show why the American judiciary is entitled to be called a branch of government. The ultimate question posed in this chapter is that of the compatibility of this judicial governing with democracy.

First, the American courts make much substantive law. Indeed, perhaps in the final analysis, they make more substantive law than does the legislative branch. Part of this comes about in the traditional common-law fashion, by gradually developing bodies of case-law through precedents. Part the courts make in the seemingly subordinate task of applying statutes in cases they decide. This latter they do in two ways. One way is that they fill in gaps Congress left in the statute or supply details and specifics Congress omitted, here making law 'interstitially' and at Congress's request, so to speak. The other way is that by construction they give statutory provisions meanings and applications; this is a more independent mode than the other and a profoundly important one. Antitrust law is a good example of all of these modes of judicial law-making. The basic provisions of the principal statute comprise less than a hundred words. The case-law, however, fills scores of thousands of pages. The statute itself was based on a large body of already existing common-law precedent. The subsequent cases, building on both the new statute and the old case-law, have developed a detailed code of law from the brief and general statutory language. Further, they have given the statute a wealth of contemporary relevances and impacts undreamt of by its draftsmen, while remaining faithful to the statute's fundamental policies. The courts are certainly far more the creators of antitrust law and the actual governing power in antitrust policy than Congress is.

Second, the American courts exercise powerful and pervasive control and influence over practically all the executive and administrative processes and organizations, and consequently over the actual work of government.

Third, even the mere deciding of private litigation by the courts has governmental and political consequences. For example, in some parts of the American South, Negroes not only have been subject to savagely discriminatory treatment by law and the courts in public matters, but also have always been at a serious disadvantage in private lawsuits with whites, the disadvantage usually being greater in the state courts than in the federal courts. This substantially affects government and politics. It has helped the dominant whites to maintain their hegemony, it has embittered the Negro protest, and it has fostered a tinge of lawlessness and deceit in Southern governing. And on the national scene it has weakened the Southern states' claim to be treated as just and responsible polities, thus weakening the whole states' rights position.

In short, the judiciary is very deeply involved in all the processes of determining and effectuating public policy. Neither the courts' influence nor government and politics stop at the courthouse door; both flow freely between courthouse and world. But the judiciary, although a branch of government, is by no means simply a political entity like any other, functioning in the ordinary political ways. It is also a system of *courts of law* and therefore has special characteristics and special roles. Although the political aspect of the judiciary and its function in governing must be fully recognized, nonetheless judges are not simply politicians in black robes.

The American Judiciary: Independence and Responsiveness

To be true to its nature, a judiciary must have independence in actually deciding its cases. If its decisions in specific cases are controlled by popular pressure, or by interest groups, or by other government agencies—that is, by political considerations in the ordinary sense—it is hardly a court at all, but rather a disguised tool of these outside forces. The American national judiciary needs this independence as much as any other judiciary. At the same time, because it is fully a branch of democratic government, it must also be responsive in some ultimate way to the community it helps govern. These opposing pulls of judicial independence and democratic responsiveness must perennially be balanced.

Constitutional Arrangements and Constitutional Customs

The Declaration of Independence complained of King George that "He has made judges dependent on his will alone for the tenure of their offices and the amount and payment of their salaries." This was thought to be contrary to the rights of freeborn Englishmen and to common-law tradition, and, ultimately, to the natural rights of all men. The Constitution therefore provides emphatically to the contrary: Judicial salaries are irreducible and judges hold office "during good behavior" (see p. 105, n. 12) and can be removed only by impeachment.

The question of impeachment. The narrow scope of even this limited means of removal soon appeared. When the Jeffersonian party came to power in 1801, it confronted a judiciary manned in part by judges whom it regarded—not entirely without reason—as malignantly partisan Federalists who were using judicial powers for party purpose. This was the first great confrontation between the judiciary and the political branches; much depended on the precedent it set. There was speculation that impeachment might be useful to remove some of the more activist of these judges and to intimidate the rest. Impeachment proceedings were in fact brought against one Supreme Court justice. But it could not be proven that he had committed any actually criminal acts, and the Senate did not convict. The experiment has never been repeated. On various occasions, factions in Congress have talked of impeaching Supreme Court justices whose views or decisions they disliked, but nothing has ever come of it and the idea has never been accepted as constitutionally proper.[9] The judges are as a result constitutionally very independent indeed. But perhaps the lesson was learned; they have seldom again been so blatantly partisan as the judges who gave Federalist party speeches from the bench.

Other constitutional provisions secure independence to the courts and the judicial function. The judiciary has its own separate article in the Constitution (Art. III). It is the vestee of a constitutionally distinct and separate power, "the judicial power of the United States." The principal court is explicitly provided for by name. Important parts of the jurisdictions of the courts are expressly spelled out. The whole judicial article—indeed much of the whole Constitution—talks in legal language, in the language of the common-law courts themselves, and so heightens the aura of judiciality and independence.

Devices to ensure responsiveness. The American constitutional system does not put its separated powers in watertight compartments. Accordingly, there are means by which the political branches of government and the political processes can affect courts and in some degree ensure their ultimate responsiveness, an essential democratic requirement.

One such means concerns jurisdiction. Under Article III, Congress is free to give or withhold all the jurisdiction of the lower federal courts, and it has on occasion made some use of this freedom. Further, though the Article grants the Supreme Court original jurisdiction in certain

[9] One constitutional difficulty with it is the very restricted common-law meaning of "during good behavior." This is reinforced by Article II, section 4, the language of which suggests that impeachment may only be for crime. For history and a general discussion see Walter F. Murphy, *Congress and the Court: A Case Study in the American Political Process* (Chicago: The University of Chicago Press, 1962).

cases, and provides that "in all the other Cases before mentioned" the Supreme Court has appellate jurisdiction, this latter provision is "with such Exceptions, and under such Regulations as the Congress shall make." In theory, then, Congress could cripple or dominate the Court by manipulating its appellate jurisdiction. In fact, however, Congress has never really attempted this, although on a few occasions Congress has altered jurisdictional rules for limited political purposes.[10]

Another limit on judicial power is ordinary law-making. The courts can, and do, make law. But congressional statutes can replace or revise any body of (nonconstitutional) law the courts have developed by precedent, and can alter interpretations they have given to statutes.[11] But this is a normal exercise of the legislative power and not an encroachment on proper judicial independence. However it can effectively restrain judicial abuses of that independence.

A third means of ensuring judicial responsiveness is constitutional amendment. In two famous instances,[12] the Constitution has been amended to overcome Supreme Court decisions. But this process is usually too slow and too uncertain to be a very promising means of ordinary control over the judiciary.

Neither Congress's power of the purse nor its power of investigation have been much used against judicial independence. At times the judges have been underpaid and the lower courts left understaffed. But this has usually been as much from neglect or economy as from any special purpose of controlling the judiciary. There have also been some congressional investigations and threats of investigations, but on the whole without much real effect.[13]

Presidents have on some occasions, chiefly in time of war, used their powers to pressure or constrain the courts. The extreme instance is Lincoln during the Civil War. He acted very high-handedly; repeatedly he refused to recognize or enforce court orders, refused to allow the courts to sit in areas he wanted subject to military government, and took cases away from them by force. No other President has ever come even

---

[10] The best-known example is *Ex parte McCardle*, 7 Wall. 506 (1869). While the case was before the Court and ready for decision, Congress repealed the statute upon which the Court's jurisdiction of the case was based, and the Court thereupon dismissed it.

[11] See for example "Congressional Reversal of Supreme Court Decisions: 1945–1957," *Harvard Law Review*, LXXI (May 1958), 1324–37.

[12] In 1793 the Court held that a state could be sued in the federal courts by a citizen of another state without its consent. *Chisholm* v. *Georgia*, 2 Dall. 419 (1793). In 1795 the Eleventh Amendment was adopted, negativing this. In 1895 the Court held that the federal government could not constitutionally impose an income tax. *Pollock* v. *Farmers' Loan & Trust Co.*, 157 U.S. 429 (1895). This led to the Sixteenth Amendment.

[13] See Murphy generally. One instance occurred in 1949, when the first trial of Alger Hiss ended in a hung jury. Members of the House Committee on Un-American Activities asserted that the trial judge had been biased against the prosecution, and threatened an investigation. The episode is described, somewhat polemically, in A. J. Liebling, *The Press* (New York: Ballantine Books, Inc., 1961), pp. 144–62. See also the news stories of the affair in the *New York Times*, July 9–15, 1949.

close to such practices. But no other President has had to confront the dreadful challenge of civil war. And in peaceful times the executive has seemed able, or at least inclined, to do little.

Judicial Appointments and Judicial Responsiveness

By far the most important and most used constitutional channel whereby the President and Congress can influence the judiciary is through appointments to judgeships and through control over the sizes of the courts as a means to affect appointments.

The Supreme Court. On at least two occasions, Congress reduced the size of the Supreme Court to forestall presidential appointments it expected to dislike. In neither instance was the device really successful. In 1801 the outgoing Federalists provided by statute that at the next vacancy the Court would be reduced from six members to five; this was to deprive newly elected President Jefferson of the chance to make the appointment. The Jeffersonian majority in the next Congress promptly repealed the statute before a vacancy occurred. As a part of its battle with President Johnson after the Civil War, Congress in 1866 reduced the size of the Court from ten to seven. But it was soon raised to nine, where it has remained ever since.

Some increases in the Court's membership (it began with five members) were intended to allow appointments designed to change its course of decision, and some were successful in this. But for a century, however, such efforts have been unsuccessful. The most recent and best-known failure occurred in 1937, when President Franklin D. Roosevelt, though he was at the height of his fame and power, was unable to convince a Congress controlled by his own party to agree to enlarge the court.

However, the normal appointment process, rather than manipulation of size, is the great means whereby the political branches exercise control over the courts and over the general course of judicial decision.

On the average, Presidents have made two Supreme Court appointments per presidential term. Most go to members of the President's own party. (Out of twenty-odd appointments since 1933 only two have not, one by Truman and one by Eisenhower.) This obviously has implications for political control, not so much of specific case decisions as of the general governmental-political tenor of judicial action. Further, knowing that American party labels are uncertain indicators, Presidents have often tried to get behind a potential nominee's party label to his real views.[14] But these presidential efforts often fail. A leading historian of the Court

---

[14] Thus, President Theodore Roosevelt wrote to a leading Republican senator concerning a prospective appointee: ". . . the nominal politics of the man has nothing to do with his actions on the bench. His *real* politics are all important. . . . He is right on the Negro question; he is right on the Insular business; he is right about corporations; he is right about labor. On every question that would come before the bench, he has shown himself to be in close touch with the policies in which you and I believe. . . ." Letter to Henry Cabot Lodge, quoted in Henry J. Abraham, *Courts and Judges: An Introduction to the Judicial Process* (New York: Oxford University Press, 1959), p. 7.

concluded years ago that "Nothing is more striking in the history of the Court than the manner in which those who expect a judge to follow the views of the President who appointed him have been disappointed." Modern research supports this; one study concludes that "The partisan political affiliations of the justices appear to have been irrelevant to the group behavior of the United States Supreme Court. . . . There may, after all, be validity to the assumption that life tenure makes for independence of judges."[15]

There are a few instances in which a President, by appointments, succeeded in getting a Supreme Court decision he desired. In 1870 the Court held the Civil War statute making 'greenbacks' legal tender unconstitutional, three justices dissenting. Very shortly thereafter President Grant was able to appoint two new justices. A little over a year later the Court reversed itself by a five-to-four vote; the majority was composed of the three dissenters in the first case plus the two new justices. But such instances are few.

Over the long run, the general political, economic, and—obviously— the constitutional views of the sitting justices profoundly influence the Court's decisions. And, of course, appointments reflect these considerations. But influencing the Court is a slow, uncertain, and sometimes perverse task. At best, Presidents and senators (and the interests that stand behind them) who seek by appointments to influence the Court in directions they prefer can reasonably expect to get only general and often unreliable results, and then only over long periods of time. Once appointed, a man tends to assume the robe and habits of his great and independent constitutional office, where no one is his master.

The lower federal courts. Similar forces operate in the lower courts, though less visibly—partly because these courts are themselves less visible than the Supreme Court. On occasion, the political branches have used their powers over court size and judicial appointments in attempts to influence the general course of the judiciary's decisions. In the earliest instance, the defeated and outgoing Federalist party in 1800–1801 enacted statutes creating new judgeships and then appointed Federalists to virtually all of them. (The Jeffersonians promptly repealed the principal statute.)

Control of the lower courts has probably been greater than of the Supreme Court. But, on the other hand, the influence that a judge in the lower courts can have on the policy aspects of the law is much less. And the freedom of choice in appointments that the President and the Senate together have is lessened by the custom of 'senatorial courtesy.' Senatorial courtesy is the senatorial practice of refusing under certain circumstances to approve nominations to the judiciary (and to federal office generally) unless the senators from the state involved approve. This means that often the real choice tends to be less by the President or the whole Senate

---

[15] Charles Warren, *The Supreme Court in United States History* (3 vols.; Boston: Little, Brown and Company, 1923), I, 21–22; and Glendon A. Schubert, *Quantitative Analysis of Judicial Behavior* (Glencoe: The Free Press, 1959), p. 142.

than by the senators of the President's party from the state where the judge is to sit, or that of other local leaders of that party. The influence on the judiciary then tends to be haphazard and based on idiosyncratic local considerations, rather than on any grand strategy by the political branches acting as a unit.

Public Opinion, Interest Groups, and Politics

So far, we have talked about judicial independence and responsiveness mainly in terms of the constitutional arrangements and the practices that have grown up around them. However, we must go beyond the constitutional arrangements to look also at the more explicitly political side of the matter, at what politicians, interest groups, and sectors of the public do regarding the courts through other channels.

Nominally the judiciary is supposed to be almost entirely removed, by virtue of its constitutional independence, from direct influence by any of these. Yet judges are people and are influenced by their backgrounds and associations, by their surroundings, by the events and pressures of the times, by their political outlooks, by their views of the public interest, and by the tides of history and politics. Indeed, judges themselves have often told us so.[16] But our concern is with much more *immediate* and *direct* kinds of influence.

Evidence of effective direct influence is slight. A few lower-court judges have been bribed and a few have acted blatantly as the servants of an interest or a group. But these have been remarkably few. Some justices of the Supreme Court have had presidential ambitions, and some lower-court judges have sought promotion or political preferment. These have on occasion been charged with shaping their judicial actions to these ends. But there appears to be little evidence to show that judicial decision-making has been substantially influenced in this way.

There is however another problem besides these very immediate and direct influences. The Supreme Court is sometimes said to 'follow the election returns,' and there are instances in which it has seemed to shift toward or away from doctrines or viewpoints in response to changes in their general popularity. But clear instances of even this less direct kind of influence are not numerous and probably do not outnumber the instances in which the Court clearly resisted popular trends. Certainly they are vastly outnumbered by the instances of shifts the Court has made on its own, little influenced by public opinion. In the last few years the Court has entered on some strikingly new paths certainly not urged on it by general public opinion.[17] (It must be borne in mind that under the right circumstances a single pertinacious litigant can force the Court to a decision.)

---

[16] E.g., Benjamin N. Cardozo, a distinguished member first of the New York Court of Appeals and later of the U.S. Supreme Court, *The Nature of the Judicial Process* (New Haven: Yale University Press, 1921), and *The Growth of the Law* (New Haven: Yale University Press, 1927).

[17] E.g., its interdiction of prayers in public schools and its extensions of the constitutional rights of defendants in criminal cases.

Congressional groups and Presidents now and then, and outside interest groups fairly frequently, have carried out intense attacks on the courts, especially the Supreme Court, by political means—speeches, public statements, backstage political maneuvering, appeals to public opinion, offers of support or threats of opposition, etc.[18] And there have been instances of quiet lobbying forays into the judicial precincts. (Biographies of Supreme Court justices, for example, relate instances in which leading political and legal figures privately warned members of the Court of the political consequences of possible decisions.) Occasionally these enterprises have apparently gotten identifiable results. The effects, however, have seldom been long-lived, and in most cases it is difficult to show that the enterprise had any real effect at all. It seems probable that the courts often try to give some consideration to what they feel to be legitimate and sound public and political opinion on specific matters but are not often really governed by it.

The most popular means today of attempting to get effective 'access'[19] to the courts are developed and expanded forms of traditional, orthodox, and quite legitimate modes of approach rather than the use of political devices.

Amicus curiae briefs[20] have always been permitted. Over the last half-century use of them has greatly increased, and they have become an important part of the judicial process. They provide an entirely proper means for groups to put before the court their views on legal and policy matters involved in cases under litigation.

Interest groups and other agencies have also always planned litigation with strategic considerations in mind. A well-known example was the concerted effort of several industrial groups to discredit or obstruct by collaborative litigation various New Deal measures and agencies in the 1930s.

Similarly, interest groups and other agencies have always attempted to influence the judicial mind by influencing (or claiming to voice) professional legal and scholarly opinion. The long campaign of the National Association for the Advancement of Colored People embodies striking examples of both litigation strategy and professional influence. The NAACP planned a program of litigation well, and carried it out with dedication. And, by persistent and persuasive advocacy of its cause, it helped apparently to produce a great volume of favorable authoritative comment in the legal and scholarly journals.[21]

---

[18] President Franklin Roosevelt's Court-packing plan was part of one major political conflict that centered around the Court. In the 1960s the Court has come under similar political attack, but now from the other end of the political spectrum.

[19] Access in the sense of opportunity to influence them.

[20] Literally, briefs by a 'friend of the court.' That is, briefs filed by permission of the court, and sometimes at its invitation, by persons who are not parties to the actual case involved but who seek to assist the court with additional argument and counsel.

[21] See Clement E. Vose, *Caucasians Only: The Supreme Court, the NAACP, and the Restrictive Covenant Cases* (Berkeley: University of California Press, 1959). See also Herbert Garfinkel, "Social Science Evidence in the School Segregation Cases," *Journal of Politics* (February, 1959).

Such efforts probably do not convince courts from a standing start. More likely they only aid them along ways they are already beginning to be disposed to go. In short, the judiciary (like any other agency of government) can always use public support and professional assistance and is generally willing to take into account what seems to it to be the best opinion of its time. But its independence is real. The decisions of the Supreme Court, for example, seem to flow mostly from the convictions of the justices that on the law, the facts, and the policy considerations involved, the decisions are the right ones. The Court is a great political-governmental institution. But it is also a court of law.

"The judicial Power of the United States"

The American judiciary is decisively independent both of the other branches of government and of at least the more immediate pressures of politics. But a judiciary may be independent and even play a vital and extensive role in governing, and yet not rank, as the American certainly does, as a co-equal branch of government. The British judiciary is an example. It is thoroughly independent and exceedingly important in the British system. But nobody would regard it as parallel with Parliament. What accounts for the American situation?

A good part of the answer lies in the unusual and strategically arranged powers over the American constitutional system that the American judiciary is granted and exercises. These powers all have their constitutional roots in "The judicial Power of the United States," which by Article III of the Constitution is vested in the federal courts. We therefore start with the fount from which they flow—the language of Article III, as construed by nearly 180 years of law and custom.

'the federal jurisdiction'

Article III opens by vesting the judicial power, and then establishes its basic coverage by providing that "The judicial Power shall extend to all Cases, in Law and Equity" and to "Controversies," falling into certain classes, and listing these classes. The Article has to be read against the common-law background. Thus read, it allows the courts nearly the broadest sweep of authority possible under the Anglo-American judicial tradition. "*All* cases" and "controversies" means that the courts are limited in their competence, if the matter involved falls within one of the listed classes, only by the necessity that the matter comes before them as a "case" or "controversy." Within those limits they can lawfully hear and decide anything that strikes their fancy. This is a broad authority to begin with. Moreover, its limits are largely given to the courts themselves to construe, and they have generally construed it to the advantage of their own authority.[22]

---

[22] There is one principal exception. The courts have held that the judicial power does not "extend" automatically by virtue of the constitutional grant, but rather that they have jurisdiction in any particular class only if it has been granted by congressional statute. The congressional grants have, however, been broad.

Judicial regulation of the federal bond. Two classes of cases or controversies are of special importance in our present inquiry. The first class concerns *vindication of national authority:* (1) cases arising under the Constitution, the laws of the United States, and treaties made by the United States; and (2) cases to which the United States is a party. An immense range of business is thus opened to the national judiciary. The national laws and the national Constitution are enforceable in the national courts, and the national government can sue in its own courts; all nationally created rights and duties are put in the hands of national courts. This obviously has vast consequences for federalism. And when taken together with the broad 'case or controversy' rule, it puts the national courts into a vital place in the system; all these crucial things are to come before them. It is rightly and revealingly called the 'federal-question jurisdiction' of the national courts.

The second class is of nearly equal ultimate importance, though the cases are not so common. This is the class of cases involving *interstate umpiring.* These are principally cases between states but also between a state and citizens of another state. Again, taken together with the case or controversy rule, this puts a broad range of governmentally and politically significant matters within the reach of the national judiciary. Cases between states are often especially striking. For example, California and Arizona have waged a long struggle over their respective rights in the water of the Colorado River. These rights are vital to both states. This struggle between quasi-sovereign political entities, so different from what we ordinarily think of as the normal subject-matter of lawsuits, has been given judicial determination by the Supreme Court.

The national powers: the judiciary speaks. These alone are broad powers for a political order to grant its judiciary, even leaving judicial review aside for later consideration—far broader, for example, than those the British courts had in the Framers' time or have today. But the peculiarities of the American system and other aspects of the American judiciary add still more authority, especially in connection with the powers of the national government and the constitutional limitations on these powers. Moreover, Americans have been especially inclined to leave many things to law, litigation, and the courts; Burke, Tocqueville, Bryce, and many other commentators all remark on this. Americans seem to be naturally litigious. They also seem to be, of themselves or because of the system, naturally *legislative.* Americans are prone to say, 'There ought to be a law,' whenever they want to change things, and Congress is inclined to oblige. Much that would be done in other systems by custom, fiat, or administrative arrangements leads, in democratic, Congress-minded America, to bulky and detailed statutes. Bulky and detailed statutes are perfect grist for the judicial mills. The judges deal with this mass of legislation in the vigorous and enterprising style of common-law courts, firmly blending new statutes into existing law as judges have interpreted and applied it. The whole becomes a blend of law in which it is difficult to tell the intention and influence of the judge from that of the legislator.

There is also a strong American tradition of giving great weight in government to the legal and judicial. Partly this derives from the common-law principle that no official act is completely beyond the reach of the law, and perhaps of some kind of judicial process. The legal-minded Americans expand this rather moderate principle into a much broader one and tend to subject fully to the law and to the courts virtually everything governmental. We are inclined to think, and to make our institutions and processes provide, that pretty much everything in government should be subject to surveillance and correction by the courts.

The great volume of detailed statutes engenders complex administrative institutions and processes to carry the statutes out. What powers and duties do the statutes give the administering agencies? In what way are these applicable to the fact situation at hand? Has the administrative process complied with procedural requirements? Have any constitutional principles been transgressed or any rights violated? The questions are endless and omnipresent, and, in the American system, the courts are entitled to answer them.

On many counts, therefore, the courts are able to affect governing under the national powers and to introduce their views of policy into it. But a mere listing of even these broad interventions does not really convey a full sense of the judiciary's opportunities under its constitutional powers in the American setting. For example, because we have separation of powers, the judiciary can greatly affect the relative positions of the political branches. Thus by 'liberal' or 'strict' construction of statutes and the Constitution, it can throw its influence—often decisively—now to the side of the President, now to the side of Congress. And we have not yet considered the greatest source of the judiciary's political authority. Standing behind each of its other powers and operating through them is the grandest power of all, the power of judicial review. Judicial review is the power whereby any court—and ultimately the Supreme Court—may declare any federal or state statute or executive action unconstitutional, on the ground that what is "repugnant to the Constitution is void."[23] This extraordinary power strengthens and sharpens each of the other judicial powers manyfold.

Judicial Review

Let us imagine an extreme and hypothetical case. A statute is passed almost unanimously by both houses of Congress. It is signed happily by the President and acclaimed both by a majority of public opinion and by expert judgment as a fine and desirable piece of legislation, fully in accord with the letter and spirit of the Constitution and greatly in the public interest. Then it comes before the Supreme Court. By a narrow margin of five votes to four, and on the basis of reasoning and of views of the Constitution that an overwhelming majority of all respected legal scholars regard as completely wrong, the Court declares the statute unconstitutional. What is the result? Barring the special and quite

---

[23] *Marbury* v. *Madison*, 2 L. Ed. 60 (1803).

unusual, the result, at least for a time, is simple and final: The statute is legally dead, dead almost as if it had never been born, never been passed, never been signed. "It is, in legal contemplation, as inoperative as though it had never been signed."[24] All the statute's virtues and all its support will not save it. Congress is powerless. The President is powerless. The voters of the United States are powerless. The Supreme Court has spoken and, so far as the law is concerned, the matter is at an end—unless some other constitutional avenue can be found and the occasion is one to call forth an exceptional effort. And the same thing can happen with a state statute and other legislative and executive actions.

This is an extreme and hypothetical case. But it could happen and has happened in principle, indeed in most details. Yet we have said that the American polity is based on the principle of popular sovereignty, of representative democracy, under a well-designed and effective Constitution. Were we wrong? Or has something *gone* wrong? Has there been usurpation by the Supreme Court? Or was there a blunder by the Constitution's draftsmen? Can such arrangements possibly work and work well? How has it come about that the Supreme Court—a legal tribunal, appointive, beyond direct control by ordinary democratic processes—has become the special guardian of the Constitution? Why does not this position go to the elected and representative legislature, or to the great popular leader, the President? Why is the *Court* given the last word on constitutionality, binding upon Congress and President when these latter also are sworn to uphold the Constitution and in any event can be disciplined by the voters (who are presumably the final sovereign) if they go beyond their powers? And what consequences flow from all this for liberty, for competence in government, and most of all for democracy?

The historical background. The idea of judicial review has its roots in the general idea of a higher law binding on governments. The idea of a standard of justice superior to the mere will of rulers is an old one; it appears in most of the great political philosophies throughout history and in many traditional lines of political thought. In various forms it was common among Americans during the Founding Decade.

The oldest form of the idea in the Anglo-American tradition lay in a view of Magna Carta and the principles of the common law as the authoritative embodiment of ancient English custom and wisdom. Magna Carta and the common law were thus held to be in some sense superior to ordinary laws whether royal or parliamentary, immune to change by them, and a standard by which their legitimacy could be judged. This view had given rise to some resounding rhetoric and imposing legal-political theorizing. For example, in one English case, the great seventeenth-century exponent of the common law, Chief Justice Sir Edward Coke, claimed that

---

[24] *Norton v. Shelby County*, 118 U.S. 425 (1886). Actually even an invalidated statute can have some legal consequences; see Oliver Field, *The Effect of an Unconstitutional Statute* (Minneapolis: University of Minnesota Press, 1935).

it appears in our books, that in many cases the common law will controul Acts of Parliament, and sometimes adjudge them to be utterly void: for when an Act of Parliament is against common right or reason, or repugnant, or impossible to be performed, the common law will controul it and adjudge such Act to be void.[25]

The statement did not survive as an authoritative legal precedent, and is probably inaccurate, but it was widely used in argument. The view it embodied was popular with the rebellious American colonists, particularly when broad philosophical ideas of natural rights were blended into it.

Even more directly foreshadowing the unique American institution of judicial review were some specific practices in both colonial times and the Founding Decade. For example, written fundamental documents (charters, constitutions, etc.) were common in the colonies, and these were sometimes explicitly regarded as standards against which to measure ordinary orders and legislation (see Chapter 1). There were clear precedents involving judicial review in the British Privy Council and possible precedents in some colonial courts. And in several states, various courts or 'Councils of Revision' had apparently exercised something like the power of judicial review. In short, there was a tradition and material whence the Framers could draw the idea of a fundamental law and of some sort of enforcement of it against the ordinary authority of government.

Nonetheless the full institution of judicial review was an immense American innovation. The novelty lay in combining two things: first, embodying fundamental law in a written document, the authority of which derived directly from the explicit consent of the governed; second, and above all, providing for constitutionally legitimate enforcement of the written fundamental law by the judicial branch.

The establishment of the power. There is some uncertainty about the constitutional status of judicial review. The power did not spring fully grown from the Constitution but, rather, had to be established or vindicated by the judiciary itself. The steps along this road, as the Supreme Court was, so to speak, establishing itself, illuminate the significance of judicial review and illustrate how the judiciary functions in the work of governing.

The Supreme Court began in 1790 as a tribunal of precarious status and uncertain jurisdiction; two of the six justices first appointed declined to serve, and in its first year or two it got only a handful of cases, and those not very substantial ones. By, say, 1800 it had become not only a powerful court but also a powerful branch of government. Yet before 1803 no federal court had unequivocally held a national law unconstitutional. But between 1789 and 1803 foundations for much of what came later were laid, partly in the Supreme Court and partly in the federal circuit courts by Supreme Court justices sitting there (as was the

---

[25] *Dr. Bonham's Case*, 8 Co. Rep. 114a (1610). And again, Coke in a debate in Parliament, "Magna Carta is such a fellow that he will have no sovereign."

arrangement at that time). And part of it was done in cases involving state rather than national legislation.[26]

Beginning in 1791 federal circuit courts held several state statutes void, the first ones as being contrary to national treaties and later ones as contrary to the Constitution itself. There seems to have been little protest; the cases were perhaps too scattered, too much of merely local interest, and the grounds of invalidity were in the main pretty clear. But in these state cases the first step had been taken: The national courts were beginning to claim to be arbiters of constitutionality.

Preliminary developments were also occurring concerning national legislation. In 1792 one circuit court refused on constitutional grounds to undertake some nonjudicial duties (settling veterans' claims) assigned them by an act of Congress.[27] This suggested, though by quiet implication rather than overt decision, that the judiciary was not bound by federal statutes encroaching on its judicial prerogatives. The Supreme Court itself hinted at a similar view in cases it decided under the same act a few years later. And in 1796, in a very prominent case, the Court *upheld* a federal statute as constitutional.[28] In upholding a statute, the Court is perhaps less likely to bring upon itself powerful political opposition than when it invalidates a statute. But the power of judicial review is equally asserted in both instances. When it upholds a statute, no less than when it invalidates one, the Court tests the statute against the Constitution and thus clearly asserts its authority to do so.

In other developments, the Supreme Court itself held in 1796 that a treaty prevailed over a conflicting state law.[29] Before that, in 1793, in a dramatic step, it had taken jurisdiction of a suit by private citizens against the state of Georgia. The language of the Constitution seemed to justify this—but not clearly, and so positive a judicial action was something of a surprise.[30] The holding was speedily reversed by the Eleventh Amendment, but it was a large claim of authority by the Court. Finally, of great importance though less obvious, the national courts, and especially the Supreme Court, were steadily developing a substantial body of important case-law. In it both state and national statutes were interpreted and applied, and not always with humility and deference and unquestioning obedience to whatever the letter of the statute seemed to require. Rather, it was on occasion done with independence, a critical eye, and a plain regard for what the judges thought reasonable and desirable. Thus, in this way too, the federal courts were quietly moving toward broad authority.

Marbury v. *Madison,* decided in 1803 and the great landmark case claiming the right of judicial review, was itself a masterpiece of indirect

---

[26] The cases and historical accounts are surveyed in Walter F. Dodd, *Cases and Materials on Constitutional Law* (5th ed.; shorter selection; St. Paul: West Publishing Co., 1954), pp. 11–12.

[27] See *Hayburn's Case*, 2 Dall. 409 (1792).

[28] *Hylton* v. *U.S.*, 3 Dall. 171 (1796).

[29] *Ware* v. *Hylton*, 3 Dall. 199 (1796).

[30] *Chisholm* v. *Georgia*, 2 Dall. 419 (1793).

advance. It held an act of Congress unconstitutional—but on the modest ground that the act attempted unconstitutionally to give a new power to the Court. After this landmark case, slow and undrastic steps continued, each one adding a bit to the judiciary's assertions of authority and status but each unlikely to attract much dangerous opposition or to inspire drastic counteraction by the political branches. Finally, in 1810, the Supreme Court moved decisively into the federal-national field and explicitly held unconstitutional an important and much discussed state statute.[31] And a few years later, to clinch matters, the Court asserted, as against the state courts, a final power of judicial review; it asserted power to review decisions of the highest state courts regarding the federal constitutionality of acts of their own legislatures, in this case the highest court of proud Virginia.[32]

The judiciary's delicate work of twenty-odd years had been well done. By those slow steps the Supreme Court had emerged as fully independent—both of the states and of the other branches of the national government—as the possessor of the power of judicial review, and as entitled to exercise some measure of judgment and statesmanship as well as the technical arts of law. By the end of these crucial formative stages, the essential characteristics of the national judiciary are before us. It is not just a system of courts performing the customary judicial functions of adjudicating disputes between citizens and presiding over the *private* law of the polity. It also takes part in government and politics, adjudicating disputes between government and citizens, between the multiple governments of federalism, and between the other branches and agencies, and presiding over the *public* law of the polity.

In participating in these processes of governing and politics, it has developed an array of tools. The most striking of these is judicial review. Judicial review is not only extraordinarily powerful in itself; it also increases the power of other tools—such as those of statutory construction, of the supervision of administration, and of others that arise out of the judiciary's federal-question jurisdiction—because it is always the heavy club behind the door.

But is judicial review constitutional? The federal courts' power of judicial review was established early and has remained firmly a part of the American system ever since. But the power is a drastic and difficult one, and the Constitution gives here, as it occasionally does to other delicate issues, an answer containing a tinge of ultimate ambiguity to the question: Is it constitutional?

In view of its importance, it is ironical that some irreducible uncertainty clings around the question: Did the Framers really intend judicial review? This question is the subject of a large and once hotly controverted literature.[33] The strongest evidence supports the view that judicial review

---

[31] *Fletcher* v. *Peck*, 6 Cranch 87 (1810).
[32] See, e.g., *Martin* v. *Hunter's Lessee*, 1 Wheat. 304 (1816).
[33] The classic studies include Charles A. Beard, *The Supreme Court and the Constitution* (New York: The Macmillan Company, 1912), Max Farrand, *The Records of the Federal Convention* (3 vols.; New Haven: Yale University Press, 1911), and

was intended. The records of the Constitutional Convention show that some delegates favored it. The *Federalist*, propagandizing for the Constitution, contains in the seventy-eighth essay an explicit defense of it as a valuable feature of the proposed constitution. Many members of the First Congress had been at the Convention, and that Congress passed the 1789 Judiciary Act which specifically refers to judicial review. As with many other controverted features of the Constitution, the situation seems to be this: The most highly influential Framers knew what they were doing and clearly intended some kind of judicial review, while many others more or less vaguely expected it to develop, and the specifics were left for the future to work out.

But apart from external evidence of the Framers' intention regarding the Constitution, what is the status of judicial review in the *language and logic of the constitutional document itself?* The classic defense of the constitutionality of judicial review, based upon the actual language of the Constitution, is found in *Marbury v. Madison*.

The case turned on an amusing set of facts. The outgoing Adams Administration in early 1801 made numerous last-minute judicial appointments, most minor but some important. For some reason, a commission officially appointing one William Marbury to be a District of Columbia justice of the peace was not delivered to him. It seems to have been found, signed and sealed but still undelivered, in the office of the Secretary of State. Furious at what he deemed a packing of the judiciary with "midnight judges," newly-inaugurated Jefferson believed that the Federalists "had retired into the judiciary as a stronghold" from which to batter down his new administration. Thus, trivial though the Marbury appointment was in itself, Jefferson apparently instructed his Secretary of State, James Madison, not to deliver the commission. Marbury applied to the Supreme Court, under a provision of the 1789 Judiciary Act, for a writ of mandamus whereby the Court would require Madison (hence the name of the case: *Marbury v. Madison*) to deliver the commission.

The issue was now serious. It was generally understood that, if the Court issued the writ Jefferson would have Madison defy it, thereby challenging the Court's authority. From the point of view of tactics, Chief Justice Marshall's opinion in the case was superb. He rendered a decision which at once asserted the Court's authority, permitted him to rebuke the Jeffersonians, and at the same time gave Jefferson no opportunity to defy the Court. The Court held that Marbury was indeed entitled to his commission and thus in effect rebuked Jefferson for high-handed partisanship. But here the opinion veered. The Court held that it was powerless to issue Marbury the writ for which he petitioned because the federal statute granting the Court power to issue such writs was unconstitutional (because it attempted to add to the "original jurisdiction" of the Court, which is granted only by Article III).

Marshall's holding that the statute was unconstitutional and other

Charles Grove Haines, *The American Doctrine of Judicial Supremacy* (2d ed.; Berkeley: University of California Press, 1932).

technical aspects of the case have been severely criticized by scholars. But far transcending all the details of the case was Marshall's justification of the power of judicial review. His argument and his rhetoric became solid rock upon which the traditions of the Court have since been based. His argument was in substantial part based on *Federalist* 78. He starts from the undoubted premise that the Constitution, as expressing the fundamental will of the people in their constitutive capacity, is intended to be superior to statutes, and, accordingly, statutes in conflict with it are void. Further, the Constitution is put into writing so that the limitations it imposes will be explicitly stated. But who is to determine when the limitations have been exceeded? Here Chief Justice Marshall's argument begins to get into some difficulties. He asserts that the Constitution is law, and that "it is emphatically the province and duty of the judicial department to say what the law is." Critics contend that this simply assumes the conclusion, that the Constitution may not necessarily be intended to be "law" in this sense. Marshall's implicit response is that it would be absurd to leave the decision as to limitations in the hands of Congress since one of the great purposes of the Constitution is precisely to restrict the legislative branch.

This is the basic outline of Marshall's argument, that the whole logic or very nature of the Constitution requires judicial review. But he then proceeds to more detailed arguments resting on the constitutional language. Marshall gives examples of provisions of the Constitution (e.g., the requirement of two witnesses to convict of treason) that are obviously addressed directly to the courts, and points out that it would be absurd to require the courts to close their eyes to this and to obey a statute allowing conviction on the testimony of only one witness. Critics usually admit this. But they say that at most it gives the courts the power of judicial review only over such provisions, and that there are not very many of these in the Constitution nor are they very important on the really great questions such as federalism, national power, and separation of powers. Further, the critics argue, it is not obvious that even here the courts are entitled to make decisions that are binding on the *other* branches, and still less clear when the issue concerns a provision (e.g., the commerce power) not addressed directly to the courts.

Finally, there is Marshall's contention that since "the judicial power" extends to "all cases arising under" the Constitution, it would be absurd to require the judges to decide such cases without applying the Constitution as the *supreme* law. Critics respond that this again assumes the conclusion, that it is simply an assumption that "the judicial power" includes the power of judicial review—which is the point to be proven.

The classic Marshallian justification of judicial review from the logic and the actual language of the Constitution thus turns out to be less than entirely satisfactory. Yet most critics admit that at least some degree and some kinds of judicial review are legitimate and not a usurpation. Most also agree it is desirable. Some have attempted to construct more satisfactory textual justifications of it. One such is the following.

The Supremacy Clause of the Constitution requires that state court judges be bound by the Constitution as "the supreme law of the land" over, for example, the laws of their own states. Therefore they must refuse to enforce any *state* statutes in conflict with the Constitution, else how would they be "bound" by that "supreme law"? Having thus to decide the compatibility of state statutes with the Constitution, state courts seem obliged by the Constitution to exercise the power of judicial review as to such statutes.

But such authority in the state courts can hardly be final. Article III, section 2 provides that the federal judicial power extends to all cases "arising under" the Constitution, and that the Supreme Court may have appellate jurisdiction over them. The Constitution therefore seems to contemplate that, when cases involving the Constitution occur in the state courts, they may be appealed to the Supreme Court. When such a case comes to the Supreme Court for review, the review must be able to cover the constitutional issues decided by the state court, else how could there be said to be an effective appeal? That is, when state courts exercise a preliminary power of judicial review, the Supreme Court must be empowered to exercise a final power of judicial review when it considers on appeal the constitutional findings of the state courts. The necessity—or perhaps simply the propriety—of at least this much judicial review appears as soon as the constitutional language is unfolded in this way. If courts are to be courts, and appeals appeals, and if judges are to be "bound" by the "supreme law," the conclusion seems to flow.

Does the same line of analysis apply also to *federal* statutes? Not quite so clearly; hence, partly for this reason, the existence of a general power over state statutes is usually regarded as somewhat more firmly based than that over federal. (It is also more vital for the sheer preservation of the Union.) But the application is still strongly persuasive. The analysis further draws upon the language of the Supremacy Clause. State courts are bound not only by "this Constitution," but also by "the laws of the United States which shall be made in pursuance thereof." This must mean that they are *not* to be bound by federal laws not made "in pursuance" of the Constitution, else the phrase "in pursuance thereof" is meaningless surplus. Now "in pursuance thereof" may be read merely to require that the federal statute in question have been duly passed by Congress, and to empower the state court merely to decide this, not to go further and also decide whether the statute was within Congress's constitutional power to enact. But since they are to make this latter decision as to state statutes and the Constitution, it does not seem unreasonable that they should do the same with federal statutes as well. If it thus be granted that state courts may judge the constitutionality of federal statutes, then the Supreme Court likewise may be deemed to have this power. The reasoning is the same as outlined above regarding state legislation. That is, cases in which state courts have considered the constitutionality of federal legislation may be appealed to the Supreme Court. Hearing such appeals necessitates that the Supreme Court exercise the final power of judicial review over the federal legislation that is disputed in the state case.[34]

Excessively complicated and refined though such reasoning may seem, it has an underlying strength, a strength that derives from the peculiar American federal-national compound. The Supreme Court—by force of such reasoning and by force of events—has come to have enormous influence over both state and national government, because the complexities of the federal-national bond invite a final authority in the Court.

The Judicial Resources

The Administrative Arm, the Hierarchy, and the Constituency

Any organization, including a judiciary, that aspires to participate in the processes of actually governing must possess an *administrative arm* that can handle the routine of ordinary governmental life. We have seen this in both Congress and Presidency. First, the courts need methods and procedures to get the daily work done. Multitudes of detailed affairs must be coped with. Records must be kept. Orders and instructions of unassailable precision and completeness must be issued. Second, the organization also needs experienced and devoted assistants to perform quietly discreet auxiliary functions so that the judges may more effectively perform their major functions. The American judiciary is well served by an administrative arm adapted to these two kinds of tasks by a history that goes back at least to the royal chancery of thirteenth-century England. Modern office equipment has arrived, but the basic procedures are much the same as in Marshall's day. For example, a modern lawyer is still at home with the 'record'—that is, the formal file—in *Marbury* v. *Madison*, and it still tells him economically the full technical story of that case. Such case records are perhaps the main method of organizing the judicial work. The office of the clerk of the court (the ancient and still-used title) is the head of a court's administrative staff.[35] Case records and the office of the clerk together are the bones of judicial functioning, and bear well the heavy burdens put on them by the judiciary's large role in American government.

Besides an adequate administrative arm, a governing organization needs internal order and cohesion so that the machinery works. The judiciary achieves this very effectively through carefully arranged *hierarchical relationships*. Complexities exist in the relationships between the upper and lower courts, and the upper do not by any means attempt to dictate all the views of the lower. Lower courts have much independent discretion and flexibility. Indeed, there are examples of outright resistance.

---

[34] For a review of this whole line of reasoning and an ingenious criticism of it, see Bickel (Note 2).

[35] Probably almost anybody who has ever had any dealings with the office of the Clerk of the U.S. Supreme Court, for example, would praise the accomplishments of that remarkable office.

But on crucial matters concerning the system as a whole, the central and typical fact is discipline, mutual loyalty, and cooperation. Heads of big government agencies, great business corporations, and the national political parties, all struggling with the recalcitrance of far-flung organizations, must often envy the hierarchical authority of the U.S. Supreme Court.

Further, a governing agency almost always has—and needs—a *constituency*, people and groups involved in its work, seeking its favors, and concerned in bending its activities toward their goals and wishes. This assembly of clienteles, interest groups, and supporters is often—perhaps even usually—the organization's principal source of political support, its principal means of communication with public opinion, and an important force mediating between it and the general public and groups it deals with. Here also the judiciary is well off; it has a constituency that any government organization might well envy.

The heart of this constituency is the legal profession. Lawyers and judges are close to each other for many reasons. First, they have the social bond of membership in the same guild or brotherhood. In England, from medieval times until recently, the higher judges and the upper stratum of the bar were in fact members of an actual brotherhood (known as serjeants-at-law). In America, all federal judges were once lawyers, many in active private practice. Second, lawyers and judges share the economic bond of the same stock-in-trade and the same profession. Third, they share the intellectual bond of a common guild language, a common mode of professional thought, the same communication network, and similar ideas, values, linked roles, and expectations.

Lawyers as a class tend to be influential, articulate, and politically active—an excellent lobbying group. Not all lawyers support everything the federal judiciary does, but they usually support the judiciary itself, and they almost always support the ideas of the rule of law and of an independent, powerful, and respected judiciary.

Tradition and Doctrine

A governmental organization's public position is strengthened if it is part of a respected tradition and expounds a characteristic doctrine. Here again, the federal judiciary is well equipped. In America the tradition of law is highly respected, and associated with the American master tradition of freedom, justice, and personal rights. The American pantheon of heroes certainly includes the great justices of the Supreme Court, for example, John Marshall and Oliver Wendell Holmes. Many ideas and phrases from the common law are established in American thought and speech. Many struggles for American values are associated with law and the courts.

Within the general tradition of regard for the law, there is an inner legal tradition as well. Judges and lawyers tend rather proudly to think of themselves as the present members of a continuing institution, the common law, whose pattern of function and thought has, they believe, a noble history of many centuries and has created the doctrine the judiciary expounds. The judge derives from this tradition a special independence and a special inclination to do a share of governing by independent lights—and methods—of his own.

This doctrine—'the law'—organizes the legally authoritative rules of the national polity, and does so in a way that makes it both the influential language of the rules and also a principal means for their creation, development, and concrete application. This is bound up with the common-law idea of *precedent*, the idea that the true essence of law lies not in any specific and explicitly formulated dogmas or rules but rather in the inner logic of the principles by which cases have been decided by the courts in the past. In the eyes of the common law, statutes fundamentally are a secondary source of law. A specific statute prevails over any specific rule of the common law that conflicts with it, of course, but as a whole it is 'the law' which is the more important, and a statute acquires its full and true meaning only when it is placed in the context of 'the law.' And this law is to be discovered and applied by judicial analysis of the inner logic and meaning of the judicial precedents.

The common-law tradition acknowledges the supremacy of the legislative power. But it does so with a certain coolness and reserve that inevitably arise from this view of the independent and judicial nature of the law. This view, originally developed in common-law struggles against British Tudor and Stuart despotism, the American judiciary has fully applied to the legislative and executive branches. The result is that the law grips and infuses the political order's whole corpus of legal rights and duties and official powers; and the position and authority of the judiciary, as the final source and expounder of the law, are enlarged and strengthened accordingly. One of the many striking aspects of the American judicial branch is that among its chief weapons in the political struggle is this, a tradition that has medieval roots but has been transformed and adapted for use in modern governing.

Procedure

A governing organization must be able to some extent to control its own activities. It must be able, within reasonable limits, to act or not act as it sees fit, able to evade being forced into pitfalls and snares set by its opponents, able to seize opportunities, and able to make the most of its strengths and minimize its weaknesses. We have seen the devices Congress and the Presidency use for these purposes. The judiciary has developed, in the often-denounced complexities of legal procedure, some devices of its own.

First, it acts only when actual cases are actually brought before it. For example, it does not give 'advisory' opinions on general legal or constitutional problems merely on the request of President or Congress. And it requires that the cases it hears be actual adversary contests arising out of real facts and real controversies. Thus it cannot be compelled to commit itself on broad abstract propositions or in specially con-

THE NEW YORK TIMES, TUESDAY, MARCH 9, 1965.

Summary of Supreme Court's Action

Special to The New York Times

WASHINGTON, *March* 8 — The Supreme Court took the following actions today:

AERONAUTICS

Reversed an earlier decision to review two Second Circuit decisions against the Hughes Tool Company in its tangled dispute with Trans World Airlines, thereby allowing the Appeals Court decisions to stand (Nos. 443 and 501, Hughes Tool Co. v. Trans World Airlines).

ANTITRUST

Held unanimously that Section 10 of the Clayton Antitrust Act, which prohibits a common carrier from making contracts without competitive bids with other concerns in which its directors or top officers have "any substantial interest," must be interpreted strictly (No. 232, U.S. v. Boston & Maine R.R.).

ARMED FORCES

Held unanimously that the beliefs of three conscientious objectors met the religious test laid down by Congress, as interpreted by the Court, and that they should be exempt from combatant training and service (No. 50, U.S. v. Seeger; No. 51, U.S. v. Jakobson; No. 29, Peter vs. U.S.).

Agreed to hear two cases raising the question of whether the Soldiers' and Sailors' Civil

Relief Act prohibits states from imposing a motor vehicle license fee on nonresident servicemen whose cars and house trailers are registered in other states (No. 632, Snapp v. Neal; No. 803, California v. Buzard).

CRIMINAL LAW

Affirming convictions of a Negro for rape in a case in which the death sentence was imposed, held 6 to 3 that purposeful exclusion by the state of Negroes from juries in Talladega County, Ala., because of their race had not been satisfactorily proved (No. 64, Swain v. Alabama).

ELECTIONS

Held unanimously that the Attorney General has the power to bring a suit against a state and its officials to protect the voting rights of Negroes guaranteed by Federal law and the Constitution (No. 73, U.S. v. Mississippi).

Affirmed unanimously a District Court ruling that Louisiana's old constitutional interpretation test for prospective voters was unconstitutional and held that the court correct in ordering a complete reregistration in counties where it was used and the state's new citizenship test is being used (No. 67, Louisiana v. U.S.).

Agreed to review a case raising the issue of whether

it is constitutional for ginia to require payment poll tax by voters in s and local elections (No. Harper v. Virginia State Bo of Elections).

GAS

Agreed to review four ca presenting important iss as to scope and proper e cise of the Federal Po Commission's right to imp price conditions when grants a natural gas produ authority to sell gas in in state commerce (No. ♦ United Gas Improvement v. Callery Properties, I No. 678, Public Service Co mission of New York v. C lery Properties, Inc.; No. 7 Ocean Drilling & Explorat Co. v. F. P. C.; No. 756, P. C. v. Callery Propert Inc.).

PARENT AND CHILD

Remanded for clarificat of whether it rested on F eral grounds the Califor Supreme Court's ruling th the state could not com close relatives of the menta ill to pay for their care state institutions (No. 1 Department of Mental Hygi of California v. Kirchner).

———

The detailed proceedings the Supreme Court yester appear on Page 42.

This Supreme Court calendar illustrates the wide range of legal and constitutional issues which regularly come before the Court.

trived cases. This insistence on actual cases obtains for the courts the benefits of full debate on all the issues and implications, and full disclosure of the facts. Hence it can decide on the basis of materials that have been passed through its own rigorous testing and verifying procedural processes of pleading, trial, argument, decision, and appeal.

In addition there are the most basic procedural facts of all. The judiciary, though it in general must decide cases that are properly brought before it, nevertheless can to a considerable extent determine the timing and scope of its decisions. Further, the Supreme Court has developed a quite wide freedom of choice as to what appellate cases it will hear at all, and has other means of declining to deal with issues until it feels ready to do so. And every court can almost completely determine for itself what its *opinion*—its explanation of its decision—will contain. It can if it chooses say no more than is formally necessary, which can be very little. Or it can, when it thinks the right case and right time is at hand that its voice will be heard and be effective, speak as fully as it wants and as eloquently as it is able. The courts have very substantial strategic and tactical advantages in the political dialogue.

Finally, to all the foregoing discussion of judicial powers and resources there must be added a further central fact that gives the judicial branch a unique quality: Judges do their own work. A member of Congress is deeply dependent on his colleagues, on staff people, and on administrators. The President, vital though his personal capacities are, is part of a vast organization. The votes and opinions of a justice of the Supreme Court, however, are almost entirely his own product. He himself reads the record, studies the law, hears the oral argument, and makes up his own mind, and, finally, does his own writing. The judicial process comes to focus in individual men.

The Judiciary in Action

The Scope and Effects of the Judicial Powers

An official compilation records 73 acts of Congress declared unconstitutional in whole or part by the Supreme Court up to June 1952; a dozen or so have been added since then. Between 1890 and 1938 it declared unconstitutional no less than 228 state statutes.[36] There have been ever more occasions (1) on which various national or state actions, other than statutes, were held unconstitutional by the Supreme Court and by the lower national courts,[37] and (2) on which a court has indicated, with significant effect, that a statute or official action or policy was getting near the edge of constitutionality.[38] More imporant still—and here no tabulation can be made—are the almost literally innumerable occasions when the courts have made effective use of their power of statutory construction and their other powers to declare and enforce 'the law.'

And in any event, figures could give only slight indications of the actual importance of these exercises of the powers of the courts, since they merely count and do not measure the impacts. There can be no doubt that the impacts have been enormous.

---

[36] Robert H. Jackson, *The Struggle for Judicial Supremacy* (New York: Vintage Books, n.d.), p. 50, gives the figure for state legislation. The official compilation is in *The Annotated Constitution* (see Bibliographical Note to ch. 4).

[37] E.g., executive orders by the President, activities of congressional committees, interventions by state governors in labor-management disputes, and injunctions issued in such disputes by state courts.

[38] Federal administrative law, for example, provides many instances in which such indications were given and Congress or the agencies concerned thereupon retreated from the debatable ground. See, *passim*, Kenneth Culp Davis, *Administrative Law Treatise* (4 vols.; St. Paul: West Publishing Company, 1958).

The scope and effects of the judiciary's powers are always great but they are not always the same. The judicial branch's use of its powers can be identified as falling into distinctive historical periods. For example, from the time that judicial review was fully established until after the Civil War, the courts actually declared few state and fewer national actions unconstitutional. During John Marshall's long tenure as Chief Justice (1801–1835) the Supreme Court's central preoccupation was with energetic and active vindication and expansion of the national authority. This was done through liberal constructions of national statutes and constitutional powers. Next, under Chief Justice Taney (1835–1864) the Court passed through a somewhat less clearly focused phase, a period principally of consolidation and gradual development broken chiefly by its ill-starred efforts to deal with the slavery question more decisively than the situation permitted and in a grievously untenable way.

For several decades after the Civil War, during the age of industrialization, the judiciary moved again, though irregularly, into activism. In this period, judicial review and all the other powers were chiefly addressed, as they always are, to the great question of the times: the question of national constitutional power over business and industry and the labor movement. Gradually, the Supreme Court came to a drastic position, almost completely unfavorable to any kind of government regulation. Hundreds of state (and some national) regulatory and welfare statutes and actions were either held unconstitutional or else crippled by limiting construction. By 1900 a vast structure of constitutional and legal doctrine had been developed by the courts which forbade any substantial regulatory and welfare programs. Despite a few bitter attacks on these views, the courts achieved a position of extraordinary political power and public regard as almost godlike expounders of true justice and wisdom on public policy. The judiciary had succeeded in getting itself accepted not only as a fully independent branch of government but as the *superior* one. For thirty-odd years after 1900 the courts were engaged principally in applying their restrictive doctrine from the almost unchallengeable eminence of this position. The period marked the high tide of judicial influence in American government and politics.

Beginning in the middle 1930s, a profound change occurred. At its heart was a substantial withdrawal of judicial control over the substantive policy aspects of economic regulation. The judiciary abandoned much of the doctrine against government intervention in economic and social matters, and began to apply the remainder not with the activism of former days but rather with self-restraint and with conscious regard for the policies of the political branches. The 'judicial supremacy' about which the New Deal reformers justly complained all but disappeared. Judicial review is now rarely used to forbid economic and social measures, although the courts continue to use their other powers to police some of the doings of the political branches in these fields.

Finally, in the last few years, there has opened what appears to be

206. UNITED STATES SUPREME COURT. BY AL HIRSCHFELD, 1937.

This 1937 cartoon emphasizes, from the liberal point of view, the age and weariness of the "nine old men" who were then turning thumbs down on New Deal measures.

In the 1960s, as these two cartoons on the apportionment question show, it was the conservative turn to attack the Court.

"Change the legislature? Let's change the Constitution!"

"That bull's back in again!"

another distinctive era in the judiciary's history, an era whose central concern is judicial effectuation of the civil and political rights and liberties of individuals. In all periods the judicial branch has been profoundly involved with the great questions of government and liberty. The current period is thus marked not by a new basic interest but simply a change in direction and emphasis from the preceding period when economic liberty as against government regulation occupied the center of the judicial stage.

Judicial Policy-Making and the Democratic Principle

The courts are thus seen from many aspects as a true branch of government, deeply involved in actually governing. How legitimate, from the standpoint of the goal of democracy in government, is this involvement? What, if any, are the proper limits to this functioning by a judicial *branch* and to the directions in which it may operate?

Views of judicial policy-making. Whether judicial power and democracy are thought to clash depends largely upon one's view of the extent to which the judiciary makes political policy. Views of judicial policy-making have changed over time. These changes result both from the way the Supreme Court itself changes from one historical period to another and also from the way scholars change their view of the nature of judicial policy-making.

There is a distinct difference, for example, between the Marshall Court and the late nineteenth-century Court with regard to judicial policy-making. Few of Marshall's contemporaries doubted that the judicial branch was deeply involved in public policy. This lay partly in what his Court did but also partly in how it did it. When it ruled on the constitutionality of legislation it did so upon broad principle, and when it construed a statute or a governmental power it spoke not just the language of technical legal analysis but also that of policy judgment, of statesmanship, of what appeared to it desirable and reasonable. It advanced toward authority slowly and prudently, but when the authority was in hand it did not hesitate to use it undisguisedly.

Later in the nineteenth century the judiciary changed its style. The official view became what has been called the 'mechanical,' or 'phonograph,' theory of the nature of the judicial function; that is, the courts asserted that they were merely spokesmen for an impersonal higher entity, embodied in the law and the Constitution. In its periods of most drastic judicial activism, when it was most radically opposing government regulation, the Supreme Court typically was saying that it had itself no will, no choice, no independent authority, but was merely a phonograph through which the pronouncements of the higher entity were heard. Further, it generally insisted, the views of this entity were fixed and immutable; they might be imperfectly known at any particular time but they had always existed, were only *discovered* by the Court, and would never change.

This claim—that the judiciary was merely the Constitution's phono-graph—had the effect of making the question of whether judicial power conflicts with democracy seem irrelevant, because it denied that the judiciary was governing at all. One could talk about the policies and policy-making of the Marshall Court and hence of its relationships to popular sovereignty and to the political branches. It was clearly govern-ing, so the question of whether it was substituting judicial for popular rule could more readily be asked. But what could one say about a Court that was merely a recording device? Ultimately, however, the claim became pretty clearly inconsistent with reality as judicial activism be-came more and more vigorous and creative. The late nineteenth-century Court was obviously governing, and it was doing so in some respects in conflict with the national will and national needs. (By contrast, the Marshall Court, though activist, had been in basic accord with these.) Perhaps inevitably, there was a reaction against the Court's mechanical theory.

According to the mechanical theory, there was no conflict at all between democracy and judicial power. There later emerged a group of new scholarly views that had the opposite effect of making judicial power seem deeply inimical to popular rule. These new views of law and the judicial function, made up of several not entirely consistent elements, belong to what may be called the 'sociological' school of jurisprudence. This school argued that, contrary to the mechanical theory, the judiciary in actuality exercised very great policy-making powers. It further argued that the courts' decisions, and hence their policies, were determined only to a small degree by the law and the Constitution. Rather, this school argued, judicial policies were determined principally, perhaps almost exclusively, by the judges' personal wishes, interests, psychologies, and social and political ideas. Those who held this view in effect claimed that, in the guise of legal reasoning and falsely pretending to an objectivity implied by their black robes and the whole rigamarole of the law, the judges were simply imposing their personal policy preferences upon the American people.

In the 1890s, the Supreme Court is accused of having imposed laissez-faire economics, in the 1960s of imposing its own arbitrary theory of race relations. But in all its extreme forms, this 'sociological' view suggests that at the very center of American government, exercising an extensive, uncontrolled, and almost purely discretionary power over the doings of elected representatives, Presidents, state governments, and people alike, there sits a tiny group of powerful and irresponsible judicial oligarchs, ruling under false credentials.

An important variant of this view regards judicial decisions as policy-making but attributes them to a different determinant. The courts, and the Supreme Court especially, are alleged to 'follow the election returns.' That is, the judges are said to respond not so much to their own wishes but to tides in public opinion and to the wishes of President and Congress out of fear of reprisal by the people or the political branches.

In this variant the judiciary obviously is not held to be a barrier to democracy; but, as in all such sociological views of the judiciary, it is still contended that judiciality and the judicial mode have none of the merits long attributed to them and are little more than a sham.

What then is the legitimacy of an extensive judicial power in a democracy? The answer, we have seen, depends upon how far the judiciary is thought to be involved in policy-making *and* whether the judiciary, in making policy, merely arbitrarily follows its own preferences or whether it operates in a distinctively judicial mode upon the foundation of law and the Constitution. This chapter, while regarding the judiciary as indeed deeply involved in governing and hence in policy-making, has also emphasized that there is an authentic judicial mode that greatly lessens the conflict between judicial policy-making and the democratic principle. Out of this judicial mode there develop important constraints on, and determinants of, judicial policy-making other than political pressures and the judges' predilections.

Some constraints. There is first of all what is commonly termed *judicial self-restraint.* The courts frequently decline to make policy or to govern as fully as they could because they feel it would be improper or impolitic, or beyond their capacities, or contrary to the spirit of the democratic constitutional system to do so. But this is not all.

Judges are members of a guild, of a profession, and they tend to be influenced and controlled by its methods, standards, and requirements. Their very professionalism as guild members is a force tending to constrain them in policy-making as individuals.

This is greatly reinforced by the long tradition, now having almost compulsory force, that requires that a court's decisions be explained and justified in reasoned written opinions. Formally, a federal judge is free to decide any case any way he likes and for any reason, subject only to two controls. One control is loose: He can be reversed by a higher court on appeal. One is extremely loose and very seldom applicable: He can be impeached. But even justices of the Supreme Court, who are beyond the reach of control by appeal and who are officially entitled to more discretion and freedom than inferior judges anyway, are not all that free. They write opinions, and these are subject to scrutiny, especially by the profession. A judge or justice determined to follow his own predilections in defiance of what he believes the law requires might not mind being thought a knave by those who disagree with him on the issue of public policy involved. But he might well hesitate to give in his opinion either a frank avowal of his determination, and so be thought a traitor to the tradition, or else try to fob off a specious argument by way of cover, and so risk being thought a fool by his professional brethren. And if a judge mistakenly believes the law coincides with his predilections, his opinion will reveal his error and he may then perhaps be persuaded to abandon it.

But this all means that much depends on how certain and clear, and how *determinative* of issues and cases, the law is. Laymen are inclined to think either that the law is a bundle of categorical rules that produce flat answers to all questions or else, cynically, that it is simply mumbo-jumbo out of which lawyers—and judges—can artfully get any answers they like. Lawyers and judges insist that it is neither. They argue that there are some areas of uncertainty, and even ambiguity, in the law. But they say that as to questions that can properly be put to it, the law answers most quite positively and indicates a narrow range or group of possible answers to many more; and on only a few does it give hopelessly conflicting guidance or no guidance at all. The cynical layman's view is no doubt justified in some instances, but as a general thesis the weight of the evidence is against it. The nets of the law constrain the judges more closely than the layman (or the 'sociological' theory) realizes.

A final point is implicit in the entire viewpoint of the present book. It is that the constitutional system is *itself* a central constraint. It constrains and shapes the courts, and in substantial part determines cases, just as it constrains and shapes most other elements in the American political order. The Contitution is flexible, but not limp. Some parts are more flexible, more open to varying interpretations, than others. But many are a good deal less than flexible, and all are more determinative of judicial behavior than a simple 'realistic' view would lead one to suppose.

Conclusion. Thus, upon analysis, the problem of the relationship between the democratic principle and governing by the judicial branch narrows considerably. Both the constraints imposed by the judicial mode itself and the ultimate authority of the political branches over it make the power of the judicial branch compatible with democracy. But some difficulties remain, and the present book does not attempt a final solution of them. Instead, since any solution emerges from its proponent's total knowledge and philosophy of government, we set forth some of the main themes to be found in the modern scholarly literature on the subject.

One position popular with many political scientists is that judicial review and most other aspects of judicial policy-making are an anomaly in our democratic system and that, although the judiciary has legitimate and important functions in other realms, any real policy-making in social, economic, and political matters should be done by the democratically responsible organs of government.[39]

Another view widely held by political scientists is less uncompromising. It points out that, in a sense, judicial review and judicial policy-making have been democratically approved by the American people because they have accepted it for so long; that while it is a restraint or limitation on full democratic rule, it is not democratically illegitimate because it is imposed by democratic self-restraint.[40]

---

[39] See, e.g., John P. Roche, *Courts and Rights* (New York: Random House, 1961), p. 105.

[40] See, e.g., Loren P. Beth, *Politics, the Constitution, and the Supreme Court* (Evanston, Illinois: Row, Petersen & Company, 1962), p. 23.

Some legal scholars have concluded that judicial review and policy-making are probably essential to make the American system work, but that they are justified only by this necessity, and are otherwise both illegitimate because they are antidemocratic in nature and unintended by the Framers in fact, and also dangerous because they damage the spirit and effectiveness of self-rule.[41]

Other legal scholars have agreed that judicial review and judicial policy-making are necessary to the operation of the system as a reasonable and very successful means of deciding what actions of government in the complex American system are constitutionally proper, but believe that they were in fact intended and hence are not matters of judicial usurpation, and that the nation has democratically approved them and today democratically supports them.[42]

Still other legal scholars find them thoroughly democratic, on the ground that, in the end, they limit only the powers of the other branches, not the ultimate power of the people.[43]

Some political scientists and some legal scholars hold that no society is properly and legitimately democratic unless it accepts some limitations on democratic power in the interest of liberty and justice, and that the courts are well adapted to develop and apply these limitations, acting in the light of sound political philosophy. To put the thought somewhat differently and in the style of the *Federalist:* It is the genius of the American polity to develop institutions which, "as far as republican principles admit,"[44] supply to the American democracy the competences and restraints it itself acknowledges to be necessary. The powerful American judicial branch—deeply and properly involved in governing and yet self-restrained and ultimately responsive to sober and determined popular authority—is such an institution.

BIBLIOGRAPHICAL NOTE

Most of the materials mentioned in the Bibliographical Note to Chapter 4 are also relevant here.

There are various books by political scientists introducing the student to the work of the federal judiciary, especially the Supreme Court, e.g., Beth and Roche, cited in the notes in this chapter. Others, by legal scholars, include Charles Black, *Perspective in Constitutional Law* (1963), and Paul A. Freund, *The Supreme Court of the United States* (1961). An effort to study the federal judiciary comparatively with some European ones, and a lengthy bibliography,

---

[41] See, e.g., the discussion of this view in Bickel.

[42] See, e.g., Charles L. Black, Jr., *The People and the Court* (New York: The Macmillan Company, 1960).

[43] See, e.g., Eugene V. Rostow, *The Sovereign Prerogative* (New Haven: Yale University Press, 1962).

[44] *Federalist* 77, p. 463.

are found in Henry J. Abraham, *The Judicial Process* (1962). A survey of all of the American court systems is found in Lewis Mayers, *The American Legal System* (2d ed., 1964).

There are many books on aspects of the place of the federal judiciary in American government. Those likely to be helpful to the nonspecialist reader include Charles P. Curtis, *Lions Under the Throne* (1947) and Wesley Mc-Cune, *The Nine Young Men* (1947).

The history of the actual caseload of the federal judiciary, especially the Supreme Court, is described in the classic and still authoritative Felix Frankfurter and James M. Landis, *The Business of the Supreme Court* (1927). Perhaps the most useful single account of the development of the idea of judicial review is Charles Grove Haines, *The American Doctrine of Judicial Supremacy* (2d. ed., 1932). A brilliant account of the Supreme Court's early years is the same author's *The Role of the Supreme Court in American Government and Politics 1789–1835* (1944).

There are biographies of most of the better-known justices. Personal relationships among the justices of the Court in the crucial period of the 1930s are described with great frankness in Alpheus Thomas Mason, *Harlan Fiske Stone: Pillar of the Law* (1956). The mechanics of the Court's operations are fascinatingly described in a lawyer's handbook, Robert L. Stern and Eugene Gressman, *Supreme Court Practice* (3rd ed., 1962). A recent book on the Court by a political scientist is John R. Schmidhauser, *The Supreme Court: Its Politics, Personalities, and Procedures* (1960).

Relationships between the Supreme Court, the lower federal courts, and other government authorities in the application of Supreme Court decisions are most often described in connection with specific episodes. One recent work is Jack Peltason, *Fifty-eight Lonely Men: Southern Federal Judges and School Desegregation* (1961). The development of policy by the Court in a specific area and its relations to government in that area is analyzed in Victor G. Rosenblum, *Law As a Political Instrument* (1955). A study of the development of constitutional doctrine by the courts as a result of the efforts of lawyers in litigation is Benjamin Twiss, *Lawyers and the Constitution* (1942).

In recent years some political scientists have been energetically exploring research on law and the judiciary by methods drawn from those of the behavioral sciences, such as psychology and sociology. The literature is surveyed in Glendon Schubert,"Behavioral Research in Public Law," *American Political Science Review* (June 1963). The Winter 1963 issue of the periodical *Law and Contemporary Problems* is devoted to a symposium on the subject.

Chapter 8

The
Administrative
System

CONGRESS, THE PRESIDENCY, AND THE JUDICIARY GOVERN, BUT THEY CANNOT govern alone. They cannot do the actual daily work of governing. This is done, as it must be done in any modern government, by the departments and agencies—the *administrative system*. Nor can the branches function separately and in isolation. They interact intricately with each other, with the states and localities, and with interest groups, private individuals, and the public generally. And much of this complicated interaction —so distinctive an aspect of the American political order—takes place in the administrative system.

Efforts to equip the American government to deal more competently with the modern world without impairing either liberty or effective democratic control must take these facts into account. Such efforts must also take into account the fact that a modern administrative system, though it is a remarkable and indispensable agency of government, can, when it goes wrong, produce its own special evils: red tape, waste, officiousness, bureaucratic muddle, bureaucratic tyranny, and the like.

The Nature of Modern Government

The Administrative System: The Core

Government today must be big government, because there are almost overwhelming amounts of work it must do. It must be in large part administrative government, because the administrative system is the only means whereby this mass of work can be done, whereby the necessary money can be collected and spent, the polity's controls on the economy and the society operated, the great modern war machine built, the innumerable governmental services rendered, the detailed rules and orders issued, and all the rest. All these activities are beyond the capacities of legislatures and unaided executives. So a large, powerful, and effective administrative system is in truth the core of modern government.[1] The purposes for which government exists today are accomplished largely through this system.

Accordingly, the American administrative system is almost incredibly vast and complex. It has about two and one-half million civilian employees, spends about a hundred billion dollars a year (nearly a sixth of the Gross National Product), and carries on literally thousands of major programs and functions—almost endless labyrinths of organizations and activities.[2] Most public policy in fact is carried out through the administrative system. In important respects, Congress, the Presidency, and the courts are in effect small groups of men clustered around this behemoth, trying to guide it, train it, prod it this way and that.

Gigantic though it is, the system would be of little importance in the study of government if administrators were simply clerks and production hands, carrying efficiently into execution the unambiguous designs of others. But the system is not just a simple machine, a neutral and automatic instrument without life or will of its own, with which the two great political branches can do wholly as they please and which simply transmits, unaffected and undistorted, all impulses flowing into it from them. Inevitably it *makes* much public policy and *affects* more. Indeed, both Congress and Presidency frequently invite or compel it to make policy and to exercise much independent judgment and discretion.

In at least two other vital respects the system is not a simple machine. First, its official structures and formal relationships, the 'tables of organization,' are important, the vital framework, but they are not the whole story. Administrative organization is not just a pyramid with commands flowing down and obedience rising dutifully up; a great deal is involved in complex and pervasive webs of informal, often unofficial, relationships, so that decisions are made in unexpected places and things are done outside official channels.[3] Second, the system is never still; there is much stability and continuity but also everything, formal and informal alike, is subject to unceasing development, flux, and change.

A Meeting Ground

An erroneous conventional picture of the administrative system is that the President directs it through his Cabinet and other senior officials, and

[1] Cf. Carl J. Friedrich, *Constitutional Government and Democracy* (Boston: Little, Brown and Company, 1941), ch. 2, "The Core of Modern Government: Bureaucracy." Note that Friedrich uses the term *bureaucracy* as we use *administration*. We reserve 'bureaucracy' to describe administration when it has become, so to speak, pathological.

[2] See *The Budget of the United States,* including its section on personnel, and the *U.S. Government Organization Manual 1964–65* (Washington: Government Printing Office, 1964), *passim* (hereafter *Government Organization Manual 1964–65*).

[3] Cf. David B. Truman, *The Governmental Process* (New York: Alfred A. Knopf, Inc., 1951), ch. 14, "The Web of Relationships in the Administrative Process," and, e.g., Herbert A. Simon, Donald W. Smithburg, and Victor A. Thompson, *Public Administration* (New York: Alfred A. Knopf, 1956).

THE GOVERNMENT OF THE UNITED STATES

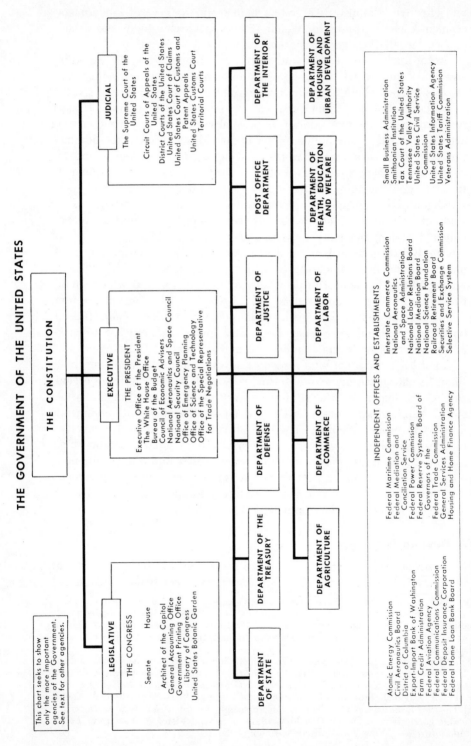

THE CONSTITUTION

This chart seeks to show only the more important agencies of the Government. See text for other agencies.

LEGISLATIVE

THE CONGRESS

Senate   House

Architect of the Capitol
General Accounting Office
Government Printing Office
Library of Congress
United States Botanic Garden

EXECUTIVE

THE PRESIDENT

Executive Office of the President
The White House Office
Bureau of the Budget
Council of Economic Advisers
National Aeronautics and Space Council
National Security Council
Office of Emergency Planning
Office of Science and Technology
Office of the Special Representative
for Trade Negotiations

JUDICIAL

The Supreme Court of the
United States

Circuit Courts of Appeals of the
United States
District Courts of the United States
United States Court of Claims
United States Court of Customs and
Patent Appeals
United States Customs Court
Territorial Courts

DEPARTMENT OF STATE

DEPARTMENT OF THE TREASURY

DEPARTMENT OF DEFENSE

DEPARTMENT OF JUSTICE

POST OFFICE DEPARTMENT

DEPARTMENT OF THE INTERIOR

DEPARTMENT OF AGRICULTURE

DEPARTMENT OF COMMERCE

DEPARTMENT OF LABOR

DEPARTMENT OF HEALTH, EDUCATION AND WELFARE

DEPARTMENT OF HOUSING AND URBAN DEVELOPMENT

INDEPENDENT OFFICES AND ESTABLISHMENTS

Atomic Energy Commission
Civil Aeronautics Board
District of Columbia
Export-Import Bank of Washington
Farm Credit Administration
Federal Aviation Agency
Federal Communications Commission
Federal Deposit Insurance Corporation
Federal Home Loan Bank Board

Federal Maritime Commission
Federal Mediation and
Conciliation Service
Federal Power Commission
Federal Reserve System, Board of
Governors of the
Federal Trade Commission
General Services Administration
Housing and Home Finance Agency

Interstate Commerce Commission
National Aeronautics
and Space Administration
National Labor Relations Board
National Mediation Board
National Science Foundation
Railroad Retirement Board
Securities and Exchange Commission
Selective Service System

Small Business Administration
Smithsonian Institution
Tax Court of the United States
Tennessee Valley Authority
United States Civil Service
Commission
United States Information Agency
United States Tariff Commission
Veterans Administration

Source: adapted from U.S. Government Organization Manual

that Congress's main activity with respect to it is to pass laws for the system to carry out and to appropriate the money needed to do so, with some occasional legislative oversight. In Britain the administrative system is in fact firmly under the control of the executive, and Parliament has little access to it. But American separation of powers requires a more even division between President and Congress.[4] The American constitutional and political systems irrevocably separate and yet indissolubly link the two great political branches with separated but shared powers and concerns. The webs of relationships that run through this administrative system link together all the separated elements of the American polity, and provide a meeting ground for all of these elements in the processes of governing. The branches meet there, sometimes as rivals and sometimes as partners, in virtually every aspect of the business of actually governing.

American federalism and political decentralization also play their roles. We require that every part of the national government be responsive to pressures from regions, states, and localities. This applies to the administrative system.[5] An American administrator managing, say, a national soil conservation program affecting State *A* does not listen just to the Presidency, Congress as a whole, and his hierarchical superiors in the system. He must also, much more than his British opposite number, consider and work with the senators and representatives from State *A* appearing in their capacities of emissaries of *A*, with the office of its governor, with its administrative officials, with its local farm organizations and their Washington agents, with its politics and political personages, and so on. The administrative system is a meeting ground for the branches. It is also a meeting ground for the states and national government.

Indeed it is also a meeting ground for the people and their government. Individuals and groups have more of their encounters with actual government here than in any other place, and the struggles for access and influence are probably more extensive and continuous here than in any other place. Probably more lobbying, manipulating, advising, arguing, and petitioning is done here than around Congress and the White House put together. Such processes as these must exist *in some degree* in any free democratic polity; the administrative process in such a polity always contains some popular participation. But the American emphasis on democratic controls and decentralized responsiveness adds to this. Neither American politics, nor American interest groups, nor American public opinion would tolerate the independence, professionalism, and rigor that

---

[4] Parliament's principal and almost sole access is through the responsible ministers; the freedom of American congressional committees to question administrative officials and see their files, for example, is unknown in Britain.

[5] Cf. Morton Grodzins, "The Federal System," in *Goals for Americans: The Report of the President's Commission on National Goals* (New York: Prentice-Hall, Inc., 1960), and "American Political Parties and the American System," *Western Political Quarterly*, XIII (December 1960), 974.

characterize some European administrative systems and make them often highly rational and highly efficient but also often oppressively authoritative.

These, then, are the conditions within which the specifically administrative aspects of modern large-scale government in America must be approached. They are the givens, the constraints, that any efforts to adapt our government to today's world will encounter, and they suggest the characteristic problems any modern administrative system necessarily entails. It must be large and complex if it is to perform effectively its various functions of instrument, policy-maker, and meeting-ground. It must be powerful, with a broad range of discretion and authority, if it is to perform them well. But size means expense, cumbersomeness, and possible waste; complexity means possible muddle and red tape; and power, discretion, and authority mean possible officiousness and bureaucratic tyranny.

The Rise of the Administrative System[6]

The Departments

The great features of the system are the eleven executive departments, headed by the Cabinet members.

The classic functions: the three original departments. Congress and the Presidency opened for business in the spring of 1789. By fall three executive departments, the Departments of State, Treasury, and War, had been created and staffed by them and were in operation. In these opening episodes things appeared that have been important in American government and administration ever since. Even in 1789 Congress and President did not attempt to govern by themselves, without any administrative structures; they have never attempted to do so since. The complexity and delicacy of the relationships of the administrative system to the branches appeared. So did the partnership-rivalry of Presidency and Congress and the close connections between structure, administration, the constitutional system, policy-making, and politics.

State was designed as a very *presidential* department, reflecting congressional recognition of the President's constitutional primacy in foreign affairs. Its organic act (i.e., the basic statute constituting it) thus

---

[6] A careful history up to about 1920 is Lloyd M. Short, *The Development of National Administrative Organization in the United States* (Urbana, Illinois: Institute for Government Research, 1923). See also the four volumes of Leonard D. White's fascinating administrative history, *The Federalists, The Jeffersonians, The Jacksonians,* and *The Republican Era: 1869–1901* (New York: The Macmillan Company, 1948–1958). A thought-provoking account of the first year (the book's coverage is broader than its title indicates) is James Hart, *The American Presidency in Action 1789* (New York: The Macmillan Company, 1948). There is no standard single general history for recent times though there are many studies of specific agencies.

said little about its internal organization or the duties of the Secretary; he was expected to function flexibly as an especially close advisor and deputy to the President. He has done so ever since. Treasury on the other hand was made much closer to Congress, in view of Congress's constitutional powers to tax, to regulate the monetary system, and the like. In Treasury's organic act Congress therefore felt free to assign it duties and give it instructions, and to impose responsibilities to Congress. For example, the Secretary of the Treasury was required to report directly to Congress whenever requested. Administration, and any policy-making, by the department were to be kept on a short congressional leash; Congress has been intermittently trying to achieve this with executive departments ever since.

The two functions of State and Treasury, foreign affairs and finance, were obviously national. But what of another classic function of government, the maintenance of internal order and the regulation of domestic affairs: Should the national government take some administrative share in it under a broad reading of its constitutional powers over domestic matters? Further, what of the miscellany of minor national tasks that did not fit very obviously into either State or Treasury? And should not the President be given some organized assistance in his job of taking "care that the laws be faithfully executed"? This all raised the question of creating a general domestic affairs department, a 'home' department. Congress decided not to, for reasons still familiar today. The states were then the main governmental agencies of the American people; many feared that a home department might encroach on the states and their rights. Further, such a department would cost money, and politicians —then as now—resisted spending money in a fashion so open to possible criticism. And in any event there was congressional fear that another department would both aggrandize the President and his executive branch and also put some further patronage in his hands.

So the department was not created, and the miscellaneous tasks were parcelled out as best they could be. State was put to work keeping the archives, taking the constitutionally required census, and so on. (It did not get rid of the last of such chores until about 1950.) Treasury was given the Lighthouse Establishment and the Coast Survey, functions bearing on commerce, because it was the more congressional department and Congress has the constitutional power to "regulate . . . commerce." It was given the General Land Office because Congress has constitutional power to make regulations concerning the territory and other property of the United States. (Treasury still contains the U.S. Coast Guard, the descendant of the Revenue Cutter Service that Congress as the taxing body created in the early days to prevent smuggling and other evasions of customs.)

The early history of War, the third of the 1789 departments, provides an excellent example of a phenomenon that has been typical ever since: An important interest group, with strong sectional roots and strong representation in one of the major parties, succeeds, after a bitter struggle in which both Congress and the Presidency are deeply involved, in getting both a major program adopted and also a major administrative unit set up to look especially after the group's concerns with the program.

The Federalist party was greatly influenced by the Eastern mercantile and shipping interests which wanted naval protection and by related groups that expected to profit from building and maintaining a navy. As created, War included the scanty naval forces the nation then had. But the department was dominated by the army, which naturally opposed any naval expansion because that might jeopardize both the army's primacy and also its budget. This was unsatisfactory to the Federalists and their groups, so they pressed energetically for the creation of a separate Department of the Navy. The Jeffersonian party on the other hand was influenced by agricultural interests and by the West and the South. These were less involved in trade and shipping and did not want to help pay for warships they felt little need for. Also they were anxious that support for the army, a form of military power much more useful to frontiersmen and land speculators, not be compromised. After prolonged wrangles, the Federalists won a double victory. They not only got a navy. They also got it put into a separate department, free from army control, able to manage its own affairs as its supporting interest groups would want, and separated out so that they could the more readily watch over it.

Developing functions: Postoffice, Justice, Interior. Even under the Articles of Confederation a Postmaster General and basic postal services were provided, and from 1789 on a Postoffice existed in the federal administrative system, although it did not reach full status as a department headed by a Cabinet member until 1829. An effective nationwide postal service had to exist if the nation was to be a nation, and of course Congress had the explicit constitutional authority to create it. It appealed to virtually everybody and was especially vital to the emerging national economy. Further, it provided a tempting vista to Congress of pork barrel, patronage, and useful favors for constituents.

But that vista was equally tempting to the Presidency. And the Presidency had some advantages in the struggle for control. The postal service, necessarily a very large and intricate administrative operation, would require detailed management and supervision which the Presidency was better able to give than Congress. The history of the Postoffice has therefore been altogether too much one of struggle between the two branches and between politics and professionalization. These struggles were unfortunate for the efficiency of the service, and were resolved finally only by making the department substantially independent of both President and Congress. Its administration is now greatly professionalized. Postal service jobs were long the staple of party patronage and the Postmaster General's office itself frequently the preserve of the chief political manager of the President's party. But the 'pork barrel' and patronage aspects have now disappeared into civil service or else are more or less mechanically divided between Presidency and Congress by longstanding agreements. Neither the Presidency nor Congress now seriously attempts to administer or to lead in the development of Postoffice policy; in effect they tinker with, but ultimately ratify, policies and administrative arrangements developed by the department itself. There are many ways of performing a function of governing; for some functions one way is to have it done almost completely by a professional administrative apparatus with little control or intervention by the political branches. But this is probably most possible when the function tends to be politically neutral, like the postal function, and thus summons up little of the conflicts of interest and opinion that characterize politics.

The Attorney Generalship also was created in 1789; from the outset the new government had to have a lawyer. For a long time the Attorney General was simply a lawyer in private practice who served as counsel and legal advisor to the executive branch, with no staff or official office. But in the American government, deeply rooted in law and constitutionalism, high policy and high politics involve law constantly; so from the beginning Washington had the Attorney General meet with the Cabinet. Gradually, also, the legal problems and legal business of the national government increased, and the Attorney General inevitably became an administrator as well. Today the Department of Justice is a very substantial organization, and the Attorney General functions fully as an administrator, politician, and presidential advisor, as well as the head of the government's legal services.

The first Attorney General was a trusted advisor to the first President; administration came later. In contrast, the Department of the Interior began, reluctantly created by a doubtful Congress, as a low-level administrative catch-all for several comparatively unrelated functions that, whatever they might have been, were not very high policy or very high politics.

The idea of a home department had been rejected in 1789. It was reproposed by Presidents, Cabinet officers, or congressional groups at least in 1812, 1816, 1817, 1825, 1826, 1829, 1845, and 1848, as the clutter of miscellaneous domestic tasks remorselessly grew. However Congress continued to refuse to act, so the miscellaneous tasks continued to be done by various bureaus scattered among the existing departments.

But the departments became increasingly unhappy, and urged with rising vehemence that efficiency required these tasks be taken away from them and put in a separate department. This unusual desire on the part of administrators to diminish their domain may well have been prompted by motives other than a love of efficiency; the vehemence was no doubt enhanced by departmental desires to be rid of these awkwardly extraneous activities and of the jealously independent and troublesome bureaus that performed them. Finally, in 1849 the Department of Interior was created, and four programs were moved into it, bureaus and all: patents from State, public lands from Treasury, pensions and Indian affairs from War. This obvious miscellany was made still more troublesome by the continuing natural tendencies of these bureaus, aided by their client groups and friends around Congress and the White House, to keep as much independence and freedom of action as possible.

The Secretary of Interior has had to preside over such uneasy miscellanies ever since, made the more so by the addition of more functions, their increased complexity, and the keen congressional, presidential, and interest-group politicking characteristic of most of them. Only fairly recently has administrative orderliness sufficiently prevailed so that the Department can now say, after listing some of the odd jobs it has gotten rid of, that its role has changed "from that of general housekeeper for the Federal Government to that of custodian of the Nation's natural resources."[7]

Clienteles and departments: Agriculture, Commerce, and Labor. Of the three departments next created, Agriculture, Commerce, and Labor, it is sometimes rather cynically said that each is pretty much just an interest group writ large and embodied in a governmental organization of Cabinet rank. This oversimplifies things and overstates interest group significance. Government is not as plain as all that, and government administrative organizations have wills and purposes of their own. However, the three departments are in fact engaged primarily with the federal programs affecting these three great sectors of the economy, and the groups concerned are inevitably active and deeply involved not only in the large politics but also in the detailed operations.

The Department of Agriculture was created first of the three, in 1862, because agriculture was the first of the three sectors to develop both the necessary kind of interest group representation in politics and also the kinds of needs for which possible federal programs seemed appropriate. The department's history strikingly illustrates how an agency may change as its clientele's situation changes. It began life as a research center, applying to farming the scientific discoveries then beginning to attract attention. Later it became a benefit-granting agency, and then in part a regulatory agency as the national government began to regulate economic activity and enforce rules on commercial practices and standards of product quality. Still later it was organized around specific problems in the economics of agriculture, first farm management and later the marketing of agricultural products. Today Agriculture has emerged as the administrator of broad government policies aimed at the great general economic problems of the industry. It still provides immense benefit and service programs, but it is now also deep in stormy and controverted issues of more general national policy as agriculture has become a general national problem.

A Department of Commerce and Labor was established in 1903. Business had virtually dominated American society and government for

---

[7] *Government Organization Manual 1962–63*, p. 224.

decades, and the new department was principally a consolidation of agencies engaged in already developed programs of government assistance and benefits to business. Some labor programs were involved in the new department, but these were largely limited to research, advice, and encouragement (but not much concrete support) on the improvement of labor conditions. The labor programs were so dwarfed by the business programs that the double departmental title was a sham. This accurately reflected the status of American labor and labor organizations at the time. After a long campaign by the trade unions, the split into two departments took place in 1913. However, Labor has always remained the smaller and weaker of the two, and has never possessed the sweeping and full-blooded programs of assistance, benefits, and spending that Agriculture and Commerce can offer to their constituencies. The successes of labor interest groups with government have not been in achieving a potent department of their own. In contrast, the Commerce Department has always been substantial, although it has fluctuated in size and importance with the political standing of business and its interest groups. For example, when Herbert Hoover was Secretary during the Harding and Coolidge administrations in the 1920's and the status of business was once more unrivalled, Commerce was the most active department in the entire government.

HEW and the question of new departments. We have described nine departments. (War and Navy were merged into the Department of Defense in 1947.) In 1953 one new one was added—the Department of Health, Education and Welfare (HEW), and in 1965, still another—the Department of Housing and Urban Development. Is it likely that any more new departments will be created? Proposals have recently been made for a department of transportation. The history of HEW sheds some light on the kinds of forces that will be involved if and when any new department is formed.

The national government has had from its beginning programs to benefit national health, education, and welfare. Such programs have fluctuated in size and importance, but they have been almost continuous and there seems little doubt they will continue, and in fact probably expand considerably. And they have developed diverse and well established supporting groups.

The thrust toward departmental status came because such status has advantages for both administration and interest groups. It entails Cabinet rank; it insures permanence, status, and independence; it gives useful political visibility. And it can improve organizational order and rationality by bringing together related agencies and programs. On the other hand, it can be a somewhat empty achievement as in the case of the Labor Department. It is often a danger to existing agencies; they may lose independence if they are included, or encounter new competition if they are left out. And it often involves political difficulties. All these forces were present in the case of HEW.

The Republican party and conservative groups had campaigned for many years against the 'welfare state'; they understandably feared that HEW would expand federal health, education, and welfare programs of precisely the kind they opposed. Congress was in the main opposed, conservative congressmen being joined by others whose prime concern was probably traditional congressional reluctance to strengthen executive establishments; HEW as a department would probably have greater resources in coping with Congress than the existing scattered administrative units. On the other side, some interest groups, especially educational organizations, warmly supported HEW. Although not all the existing agencies concerned were enthusiastic, the lure of departmental status persuaded most of the administrators, and the administrative good sense of better centralized control won out in the end.

Probably the decisive step was taken in 1939, when the Federal Security Agency was created. It collected most of the then-existing agencies in the fields, including both long-established ones like the Public Health Service and the Office of Education and also vast new depression-born welfare agencies like the Social Security Board. In government as in other organizations, administrative rationality and integration once launched are hard to stop.

The Agencies

From the beginning there have been various national administrative establishments not attached to any department; the first was created in 1790 to deal with claims between the United States and the individual states. The usual term for such nondepartmental establishments is 'agencies,' though they bear a variety of individual titles.

Virtually throughout the development of the administrative system the agencies have been on the increase. In the beginning they were few and often impermanent, but by 1860 four, possibly five, existed. The National Academy of Sciences was established in 1863, and agencies concerned with military and veterans' affairs a few years later. Throughout the rest of the nineteenth century one was established every few years. Examples are the Civil Service Commission in 1883, as part of the great movement for reform of the federal civil service, and the Interstate Commerce Commission in 1887, the first of the regulatory commissions. In the era of Progressivism and reform in the early twentieth century, temporary investigatory agencies were created, then several major permanent agencies such as the Federal Reserve Board and the Federal Trade Commission. Many agencies—most temporary but a few permanent—were created during World War I in connection with war, mobilization, and foreign affairs, and the form became accepted as a normal and widely used resource of government. In the 1920s, several important ones were established, including the General Accounting Office, the Bureau of the Budget, and the Federal Power Commission. Many were created during the period of the Great Depression, the New Deal, and World War II.

Many of these were temporary, but a good many became permanent. Today the agency form is very prominent in government; there are at least thirty-odd that are substantially important. Of these some are of very great importance indeed, overshadowing several departments.

Why agencies? What is the meaning of this aspect of the development of the administrative system? Why agencies rather than more departments? What place do agencies have in the system?

For many situations in government, the agency form can be adapted more readily than the department form. It can be closely attached to the President, or closely to Congress, or made largely independent of either. It can be useful in performing a new function that does not fit readily into an existing department; examples are the development of atomic energy by the Atomic Energy Commission and of space exploration by the National Aeronautics and Space Administration. An agency can be temporary, exploratory, and tentative, or subject to frequent review and revamping; emergency and wartime agencies are examples. It is useful for functions which are so urgent, or so crucial, or so sensitive, as to need the direct and constant supervision of the President or of Congress; the National Aeronautics and Space Administration and the Central Intelligence Agency are in some respects examples. It is often especially appealing to Congress in that it may be insulated from presidential control and brought closer to congressional. Similarly it is often especially appealing to interest groups, whether in or out of government; they often want the program or function they are concerned with to be in the hands of a separate agency, which may be more independent or more single-minded or more easily watched—or perhaps more manageable—than some established department.

The rise of the agencies and their place and uses in the administrative system are made clearer if we look at the major categories of jobs they do.

Regulation. A number of agencies, including some of the oldest, are engaged primarily in general regulation. Some regulate an industry, e.g., the Civil Aeronautics Board regulates commercial aviation. Some regulate a sphere of economic activity, e.g., the Securities and Exchange Commission regulates the stock markets and the issuance of securities by corporations. There are many others, including some whose functions are not solely regulatory.

Monetary and financial affairs. The national government has long been deeply involved in the monetary and financial affairs of the nation. The great agency instance is the Board of Governors of the Federal Reserve System. The Board handles some of the government's own financial affairs and exercises some broad and general powers of regulation and supervision over the banking industry, but its most important concern is with general economic and monetary conditions.

Grants, benefits, and services. The national government operates immense programs that distribute services and benefits in money and other forms. Many of these programs are in the executive departments; Agriculture and HEW are familiar examples. However, many programs have been given to agencies. One example is the Veterans Administration. Another was the Housing and Home Finance Agency, before it was placed within the Department of Housing and Urban Development, which operated an extensive group of programs involving slum clearance and urban renewal, the development of community and public facilities, and the guaranteeing of mortgages on residential construction.

The new science and technology. The national government has always had agencies dealing with scientific and technological matters. In recent years the agency form has been very much used in the government's vast new scientific and technological programs and functions. The Atomic Energy Commission and the National Aeronautics and Space Administration are well known. Less well known but exceedingly important is the National Science Foundation, established in 1950. It conducts basic scientific research, coordinates various scientific research programs both in and outside government, and serves as the channel for much financial support of private research by government.

Housekeeping: things and personnel. Much of the enormous and complicated task of keeping house, so to speak, for the national government is done by specialized agencies created for the purpose. One is the General Services Administration which deals with buildings, supplies, records, equipment, transportation, and communication for all the departments and agencies. Another is the Civil Service Commission. It deals with personnel and is concerned with recruiting, with testing applicants for employment, with some aspects of employee training, and with administering most of the statutes and regulations that affect government employees.

The varieties in form and organization. So far we have distinguished simply between departments and agencies, with no regard to varieties of external form and internal organization. However these are of importance for the functions the units perform and how they perform these, and for the units' places in government.

The traditional and best-known pattern is that of the executive department. It is headed by a Cabinet member and is divided into several major units usually called bureaus, offices, or services, and engaged in carrying out several programs or functions, each assigned to a specific bureau. Thus the Department of the Interior today includes a dozen or so major bureaus. Bureaus with related programs are often grouped into larger units within the department, often headed by an assistant secretary. Interior for example has four such groups: Fish and Wild Life, Mineral Resources, Public Land Management, and Water and Power Development. Bureaus are often divided into smaller units, commonly called divisions and sections.

Some of the major agencies (or administrations as several are called) differ from departments in form and organization chiefly in that their

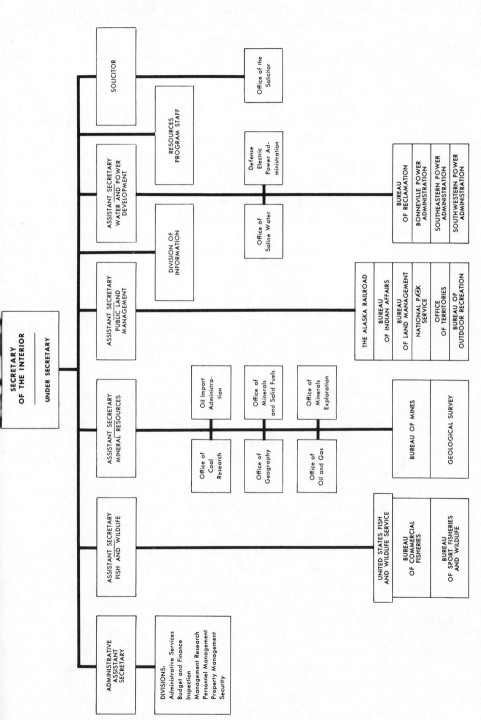

SECRETARY OF THE INTERIOR

UNDER SECRETARY

ADMINISTRATIVE ASSISTANT SECRETARY

DIVISIONS:
Administrative Services
Budget and Finance
Inspection
Management Research
Personnel Management
Property Management
Security

ASSISTANT SECRETARY FISH AND WILDLIFE

UNITED STATES FISH AND WILDLIFE SERVICE
BUREAU OF COMMERCIAL FISHERIES
BUREAU OF SPORT FISHERIES AND WILDLIFE

ASSISTANT SECRETARY MINERAL RESOURCES

Office of Coal Research
Oil Import Administration
Office of Geography
Office of Minerals and Solid Fuels
Office of Oil and Gas
Office of Minerals Exploration

BUREAU OF MINES
GEOLOGICAL SURVEY

ASSISTANT SECRETARY PUBLIC LAND MANAGEMENT

DIVISION OF INFORMATION

THE ALASKA RAILROAD
BUREAU OF INDIAN AFFAIRS
BUREAU OF LAND MANAGEMENT
NATIONAL PARK SERVICE
OFFICE OF TERRITORIES
BUREAU OF OUTDOOR RECREATION

ASSISTANT SECRETARY WATER AND POWER DEVELOPMENT

RESOURCES PROGRAM STAFF

Office of Saline Water
Defense Electric Power Administration

BUREAU OF RECLAMATION
BONNEVILLE POWER ADMINISTRATION
SOUTHEASTERN POWER ADMINISTRATION
SOUTHWESTERN POWER ADMINISTRATION

SOLICITOR

Office of the Solicitor

Source: U.S. Government Organization Manual

heads do not have Cabinet rank. The Veterans Administration is a large agency of this kind. There are numerous smaller establishments that also follow in general the department pattern.

Within an establishment the organization varies greatly. It may be rigidly hierarchical or it may be a loose confederation of nearly sovereign principalities, depending largely on the degrees of political power the units have. And it may be completely centralized in a few hands in the Washington office or it may be diffused and decentralized into field offices and by broad delegations of power to subordinate officials.

The most striking, and in some respects most interesting, variation from the standard pattern is the administrative establishment headed by a commission or board. This multi-head form is frequently found where the function is 'quasi-judicial'—deciding specific individual cases—or 'quasi-legislative'—making broad policy under circumstances where representation of a variety of viewpoints seems desirable. Thus the five-member Federal Trade Commission decides, somewhat in the fashion of an appellate court, cases involving the enforcement by agency officials of the statutes the agency administers. The Federal Reserve Board determines the broad lines of the monetary and banking policies to be followed by the Federal Reserve System. It is argued that the same reasons that appellate courts and legislatures are composed of more than one person recommend the multi-member commission rather than the usual single administrative head for the performance of these quasi-judicial or quasi-legislative functions. An administrative establishment that has judicial or legislative tinges recognized in its very organization seems odd from the standpoint of strict separation of powers. But such establishments have become an inescapable part of modern government, of which the administrative system is the core and in which the separated powers of governing are blended in the daily process of governing. The use of the commission form is an effort to minimize dangers arising from that blending.

An even more striking departure from separation of powers is a special variant of the commission form—the commission that by law is made "independent," that is, not formally responsible to or under the control of the President. The classic example is the Interstate Commerce Commission; its members hold office for long, fixed terms, are in effect irremovable, and are (at least formally) free from control by either President or Congress concerning their policies and their decisions in specific cases. The best-known of these 'independent regulatory commissions,' as they are often called, are those engaged primarily in regulation of business. The usual justification is that by combining independence with multi-membership these commissions take regulation 'out of politics' and achieve expertness, continuity, balanced and moderate policy, and wide representation of interests.

Congress has often liked the independent commissions because they can be congressionally created outposts in presidential territory; anything that weakens presidential control over the administrative establishment opens new political opportunities to Congress in its perennial jostling with the Executive. Regulated groups have often liked them as being more sympathetic to the groups' problems and more amenable to the groups' influence. And Presidents have not always disliked being thus freed by them from the vexatious (and often unrewarding and usually politically risky) tasks of regulation. Critics however have asserted that, isolated and specialized as they are, independent commissions are vulnerable to undue influence by the regulated industries; that, divorced from the protection and support of the Presidency, they are vulnerable to undue congressional pressures and are prone to be passive and over-cautious in their policies; and that, upon occasion, they are capable of independently following policies at odds with a general policy both Congress and the President may favor.[8]

Other variations from the standard departmental pattern range from agencies almost indistinguishable from a judicial tribunal (e.g., the Tax Court and the Indian Claims Commission) to ones almost indistinguishable from a private business corporation (e.g., the Panama Canal Company and the Export-Import Bank) with the government as the principal or sole stockholder.

The use of the judicial type is easily explained. Some policy or program gives rise to a large number of cases (e.g., claims by Indians against the government respecting lands said to have been unlawfully taken from the tribes) that are appropriate for determination by essentially judicial methods, but for various reasons (that the cases are too numerous or too specialized, or are nonrecurring) should not be given to the regular courts.

The reasons for use of 'quasi-business' types are more complex. The most familiar one is a wish to apply business methods and a businesslike atmosphere to government activities of a business enterprise nature. A more elusive and probably more significant reason is a wish to insulate the establishment from the usual controls on the administrative system, especially the control involved in annual congressional budgets and appropriations. The typical government corporation provides its own funds by selling its services or product and thus eludes some congressional fiscal controls. The importance of this wish to insulate is revealed in the facts that many government corporations were created by presidential order rather than legislation, and that the form has become less popular since Congress asserted authority over them by the Government Corporation Control Act of 1945. President–Congress rivalry lies just beneath the surface of many aspects of government.[9]

---

[8] The standard treatise on the independent regulatory commissions is still Robert E. Cushman, *The Independent Regulatory Commissions* (New York: Oxford University Press, 1941). See also Marver H. Bernstein, *Regulating Business by Independent Commission* (Princeton: Princeton University Press, 1955).

[9] See Merle Fainsod, Lincoln Gordon, and Joseph C. Palamountain, Jr., *Government and the American Economy* (3d ed.; New York: W. W. Norton & Company, Inc., 1959), ch. 24, for an account of government corporations.

How the Administrative System Works

We have now seen something of the functions of an administrative system in modern government and its general place in American governmental processes. We turn now to a closer-range study of the actual workings of the system as seen in the behavior of the legislators, congressional staff people, administrators, employees, White House officials, state and local emissaries, interest group representatives, courts, and private individuals whose interactions make up the administrative system.

Patterns of Interaction: The Life History of a 'Program'

Much of the activity typically revolves around *programs*,[10] existing or proposed, and around the arrangements for carrying out programs. Indeed, these are frequently the two things to look for first in examining the busy confusion of a government office or an episode of governing. Further, programs and arrangements, whether formal or informal, have a common characteristic: Their roots are deeply entangled in statutes, executive orders, court decisions, directives, regulations—in law and the official. These define the program, authorize the administrative establishment's existence, determine its form and position, grant its powers and its money, and impose its duties and responsibilities. An old, large, and complicated department will have a mass of them. A small, new, one-job agency may have only a few. But they always exist, performing their vital functions as, so to speak, the charter and framework of the program and the establishment, and are useful preliminary guidelines for the inquirer.

Another guideline consists in the recognition that the great driving forces behind the activity entail political struggle. The administrative system and all the people and activities connected with it, like all of government, respond to pressures, to events, to "the felt necessities of the time,"[11] to the efforts of all the various groups and constituencies involved, to the tides and eddies of public opinion and of political life, and to the system's own internal needs and drives. The life history of any program can therefore be elusive and complex, and we can seldom be sure we have found it all. Even so, an oversimplified and hypothetical life history such as the following can convey a good deal.

The first steps. The typical program gets at least its start toward establishment through the work of a small and often quite informal alliance of influential people. This is so even when there appears to be

---

[10] 'Program' is a term commonly used to refer to any identifiable governmental undertaking, large or small; e.g., the saline water conversion program, the commercial airline subsidy program, the FTC trade conference program, the foreign aid program, the moonshot program, the mailhandling automation program.

[11] Oliver Wendell Holmes, *The Common Law* (39th printing; Boston: Little, Brown and Company, 1946), p. 1.

a sweeping and general movement for the program in public opinion; interested activists take the lead. They may be found anywhere. In the establishment of federal regulation of civil aviation they were found among the leaders of the air transport industry itself and among people in or near the White House who were concerned over some alarming difficulties the industry was having; Congress played little part. The saline water conversion program on the other hand largely originated with a few Western congressmen and some officials in the Department of the Interior. The activists are not always political men; the federal soil conservation program was largely started by a small group of scientists, some in and some out of government. Sometimes one resourceful man, combining various groups into a winning coalition and building the necessary support, is all-important, e.g., Senator George Norris can be properly described as the father of the Tennessee Valley Authority. There are innumerable examples, and they may be found in the White House, in the civil service, in the Cabinet, in the interest groups, among congressmen and senators, among committee staff members, and wherever talent and interest combine to provide an impulse toward innovation.

But wherever the first impulse comes from, the process of establishing the program is always complex, and usually involves people in all the other places. After some preliminary canvassing of the possibilities of the proposal and of potential support and opposition, the proponents usually seek a general route to follow through all these places. Some proposals can be put into effect simply by decision of a department or agency on its own, or by an executive order issued by the President; others need legislation; many need both. Some are radically new proposals, others slight modifications of existing programs. Some need broad propaganda efforts; others are best pursued by stealth. But seldom can the project, if it is of any magnitude or significance at all, avoid involving the White House, some parts of Congress, and one or more existing departments or agencies.

Usually the moving parties find themselves in a complex situation in which they have to do many things—perhaps all at the same time. They must first of all gather support for their proposal. Support usually must come from both inside and outside of government. A dilemma is often encountered: Inside support may not be easy to get until there is evidence of some public demand for the proposal, this public demand being manifested by outside support. And the outside support may not be easy to get until the appearance of inside support makes the proposal look feasible.

Whatever general route is adopted, along which the activists seek to guide their proposals, there is next the problem of clearances. For example, the proposal may not need an executive order, or even explicit presidential or White House approval or support. But its proponents, unless they are so overwhelmingly strong in the relevant congressional circles as to be unconcerned about White House and agency opposition (a rare situation), must at the very least get the proposal accepted by the Budget Bureau as "consistent with the President's program" and also by somebody in authority in the White House Office as not objectionable to the White House on other grounds. This may involve some very delicate negotiations and multiple clearances with agencies and influential groups. On the other hand, the proposal may not require legislation. But its supporters must make fairly sure—and this may be very hard indeed to do—that there will be no serious congressional opposition, that any necessary requests for appropriations will be at least entertained, and that no influential member or committee staff person in Congress who wants to participate is being left out.

Further, there is the problem of location. The proponents must pick a suitable spot within the administrative system for their proposed program. This normally involves interesting some people in some appropriate agency; even if the proponents are already entrenched in an appropriate agency their colleagues will want to have a word to say. It also normally involves careful and tactful checking to see if other departments and agencies (and their clienteles and supporters in the interest groups and on Capitol Hill) object to the program or its proposed location as an invasion of their provinces or an interference with their own schemes. Many a fine proposal dies because somebody has already preempted the field.

Nor can the proponents ever hope to get any of these things finally arranged and put at rest. As the processes go on they must modify their proposal endlessly to meet objections, but without suffering decisive loss of support already gained. They must *organize* support; mere spontaneous waves of favorable sentiment are seldom enough. They must keep the supports flowing and keep them organized through all the usual endless dispiriting delays and setbacks. And perhaps most difficult and most crucial of all, they must find some way to move their proposal through the vast traffic jams surrounding the various parts of Congress, the White House, and all the other decision-making areas through which it must pass. The costs in time, money, effort, patience, determination, and talent can be enormous—an effective, through perhaps not just, rationing or screening system.

After establishment. Success does not by any means always crown their endeavors; for every proposal that is adopted, hundreds of serious proposals are developed and pushed. But let us assume the proposal's proponents do succeed. All the requisite clearances and affirmative approvals are finally obtained; Congress or the President issues the required legal authority establishing the program; and Congress grants the initial appropriation, the crucial 'first money.' Let us even assume that the organization that is to run the program is set up in the agency involved, the chief administrators are selected (often only after intense bargaining within the supporting groups) a staff is collected, and the people go to work.

This is still only the beginning. The new enterprise must make its way in the teeming and competitive jungle world of government. It must maintain and replenish its supports and keep its opposition within bounds. It must diligently pursue at all times the ever-delicate task of maintaining sufficiently harmonious relations with the Executive Office and with the relevant congressional committees. It must strive to build some permanent organization, both formal and informal and both inside government and out, and a permanent constituency. And it must do all this under built-in handicaps. Compromises had to be made and limitations accepted to get the program adopted. The authorization is seldom just what was hoped for. Indeed, the legislative process being what it is, the product may seem almost unworkable.

Nor can difficulties be overcome once and for all. There is always the annual crisis of getting the appropriation. Recurrently there is the crisis of getting the program's authorization extended. And there are other woes. The immediate urgencies which helped launch the program pass away and supports consequently fade. Other urgencies come to the fore and the program has to compete with them for public, presidential, and congressional interest. Every now and then things go spectacularly wrong, as they inevitably will; then an angry White House or a marauding congressional committee (often both) comes down with fire and sword. The administrative organization itself begins to get a bit tired and apathetic and confused, after perhaps starting out with crusading zeal and great efficiency. Problems show up in the statute or executive order with which the program started, and the tortuous process of getting the requisite changes must be undertaken. Litigation arising under the program begins to reach the courts, which often take alarmingly different views from the program's managers and supporters on what the program can legally do, what it must not do, and how it is to proceed (if at all), and the managers and the supporters are made painfully aware of just how independent and just how much a coequal branch of government the judiciary is. A new President comes in, and consequent moving and shaking take place throughout every part of the administrative system, no matter how meritorious and nonpolitical that part may claim to be. And so on; life in the higher levels of government is seldom tranquil, and then not for long. And not only does everybody, in the famous old phrase, 'want to get into the act'; almost everybody does.

The Tools of Governing

The picture which now begins to emerge of governing, as seen from the standpoint of the administrative system, is that of an immense field of varied and complex activities, functioning through many different organizations and processes, and characterized by complexity, struggle, and change. We are now much closer to the daily work of governing than we were when studying the great commanding features of the government: the constitutional order and the three great branches. Let us move still one step closer and look at some of the principal tools used by the organizations and processes in this daily work.

Many of these tools resemble those used in any managerial or operating task: Money, people, words, and things are common to all. Indeed it is sometimes said that there is but one basic process of policy-making and administration, whether public or private and whether done in a government bureau or in a private business corporation. There are, no doubt, some common elements, but government has its important peculiarities. One of the most striking of these we have already mentioned: Basic to everything is *law*—statutes, congressional resolutions, judicial decisions, executive orders, administrative rules, and administrative orders. Law literally is the framework and a vital part of every tool of the administrative system. We must not fall into the legalistic error of seeing nothing else, but law is truly omnipresent.

Judicial enforcement of the law. Law is most obvious in the classic administrative tool. This is simply enforcement of Congress's statute by litigation brought by the administrative authorities in the ordinary courts. The federal antitrust laws forbid conspiracies "in restraint of trade or commerce among the several states." The Antitrust Division of the Department of Justice brings actions in the federal courts against business firms thought to be involved in such conspiracies. The Internal Revenue Service collects taxes, and sometimes sues delinquent taxpayers to get its money.

Purchases, gifts, subsidies, and benefits. An equally familiar tool is the direct use of money and other benefits. The government wants something done; it pays people to do it. It wants farmers not to grow too much wheat; it pays them not to. It wants a vigorous and developing air transportation system in the country; it provides technical services and subsidies to the airlines so they can progress and expand. It wants needy children cared for; it contributes to their support. Here we are fully into the administrative process. Congress and the President can make policy, and the Attorney General, even more or less single-handed as he was in 1789, could carry out a considerable program of litigation to enforce it. But it takes literally thousands of people literally thousands of man-hours to devise and carry out means to spend the thronging billions of the national budget.

Procurement and contracting. A special form of this last tool, and one especially adapted to the administrative process, is of vast importance today: Through its gigantic expenditures, government can greatly influence whole industries and indeed whole regions, not only by the general level of spending but also by specific procurement and contracting policies and their administrative details. For example, when country-wide dispersal of defense industry is proposed, Southern California congressmen oppose it vigorously; Southern California is the center of the missile and aerospace industries. When a policy requiring equal employment opportunities in defense plants for Negroes was adopted the whole social picture of the nation was affected. Indeed, the influence the national government can exercise in these ways can become one of the greatest of its tools. Both Congress generally and its individual members supervise the uses of the tool as closely as possible; here is one of the closest current linkages between Congress and administration, and one of the President's great aids in dealing with Congress—a powerful modern variant of the old-fashioned pork barrel and patronage.[12]

Rule-making: administrative legislation. Laws must be made before there can be enforcement and spending. Indeed the chief voice of public policy is legislation. The average person ordinarily and rightly thinks of Congress as the law-making body in government. He would admit that administrative authorities no doubt make specific and additional supplementary rules. But from his view of Congress's legislative preeminence, he would probably feel that very much of this rule-making, especially if the rules are at all important, would be bureaucratic usurpation, certainly illegitimate, possibly illegal, probably improper, and beyond doubt something that Congress should not agree to, if Congress is doing its job. In this he would be greatly mistaken.

Administrative authorities enact a great volume of rules, and ordinarily these are almost as fully law as congressional statutes. Such administrative legislation is not illegal or unconstitutional except in unusual circumstances. It has been agreed to, and in fact usually authorized, by Congress for many years. It is almost inevitable and usually desirable; Congress often must and should enact statutes that are general and undetailed, deliberately designed to be supplemented by rules devised by the administrative system. An example is the Treasury Regulations issued by the Internal Revenue Service; these are much bulkier than the Internal Revenue Code, the compendium of the statutory tax law. The Code of Federal Regulations, a very incomplete codification of administrative legislation, is bulkier than the *U.S. Code.*

The processes of administrative legislation or rule-making vary greatly. Some administrative rule-making follows procedures nearly as formal and public as congressional law-making. Some rule-making may be very informal; e.g., the head of an agency makes a speech or writes a letter in which he enunciates some new agency policy. To some extent administrative legislation is regulated by statutes and by the courts. Various devices for systematic congressional, or presidential, supervision have been tried but without great success, perhaps because the processes of administrative rule-making are simply too numerous and varied. At

---

[12] For example, the White House and the agencies customarily arrange things so that the legislator can make the first public announcement of government contracts affecting his district.

best Congress and President can influence general directions and examine a few instances in detail. But this is still a great deal. Administrators must live with the knowledge that at any moment some interest group, some professional association, some White House aide, some interested congressional subcommittee, may turn a quiet administrative nook into a scene of political turbulence.

Administrative adjudication. Besides acting like legislatures, administrative authorities sometimes act like courts, deciding cases arising under congressional or administrative legislation.

Some of this administrative adjudication is *formal*, with hearings and with written decisions based upon the record made at the hearing. For example, in the Federal Trade Commission a suspicion that a business firm is seeking an unlawful monopoly is first investigated by a unit of the agency staff. A prosecuting unit may thereafter file a complaint; a hearing may then be held before an impartial hearing officer and a 'cease and desist order' (which is rather like an injunction issued by a court) may be forthcoming if the hearing officer decides, and on appeal the members of the Commission agree with him, that the charge has been sustained. Much more common is the *informal* type: An official of the Department of Agriculture decides a dispute between the buyer and the seller of a perishable farm commodity over the quality of the shipment; an official of the Veterans Administration decides whether an applicant is entitled to some benefit he is seeking; and so on.

Administrative adjudication is subject to many controls by the courts. For example, many administrative cases, though by no means all, are reviewable by the courts. Indeed, administrative adjudication has been very largely shaped under the supervision of the courts. But administrative judging is nonetheless real; not all judging by government is done in the courts. And although it does not have constitutional guarantees like the regular courts, administrative judging, especially that of the formal type, is independent. Not only is presidential and congressional intervention regarded as improper and often illegal; so is off-stage intervention by other officials of the agency.[13]

Licensing and inspection. Administrative authorities, in the course of carrying out their programs, grant and withhold many kinds of certificates, licenses, and other authorizations. Indeed, much administrative legislation and adjudication concerns these. Some are immensely valuable and hotly competed for; examples are a certificate authorizing an airline to operate on the lucrative route between New York and Los Angeles, a license to be the sole TV station on a particular channel in a major metropolitan area, and a permit to graze large numbers of cattle on public land.

Licensing blends almost unnoticeably into inspection. In determining

---

[13] See section 5(c) of the Administrative Procedure Act of 1946, 60 Stat. 237 (1946), 5 U.S.C. 1001 (1958), and Kenneth Culp Davis, *Administrative Law Treatise* (4 vols.; St. Paul: West Publishing Company, 1958), ch. 13.

whether to issue or renew a license, the government must necessarily raise questions: Is this vessel seaworthy? Is this food pure? Is this atomic energy installation producing power for a private utility being safely operated? What grade is this beef? Is the state of California, as it spends the several million dollars granted it annually by the national government for aid to needy children, living up to the requirements set by the statute under which it is entrusted with the national taxpayers' money?

In short, legislation by Congress and by the administrative authorities establishes standards, norms, requirements. Administrative authorities issue licenses under these, inspect to see if they are being followed, and enforce them if they are not. The courts give the legislation its authoritative construction, supervise the fairness of the procedures used, and ultimately pass on the rationality of the decisions reached. Presidential, congressional, and interest-group pressures swirl about the licensing and inspecting process, now influencing it, now being repelled by agency independence or legal requirements.

Advising, informing, educating, suggesting, supervising, managing, assisting, coaxing, counseling, threatening, urging . . . . Government means ruling, so the administrative system uses compulsion. But government is more than this, and the system does at least all the noncompulsive things listed in the above title, and many more besides. Indeed, here in these areas of noncompulsion are to be found some of the subtlest interactions among the branches, the states, the people, and the other elements of the polity.

The Federal Trade Commission, carrying out its statutes, issues compulsory orders that are enforceable in the courts and by all the weapons of the law. But it also conducts 'trade practice conferences' to get the members of an industry to agree on, for example, what competitive practices are feasible for that industry, so that orders will be less necessary. And it engages in extensive campaigns of discussions, speeches, conferences, and pamphleteering to explain what it thinks the law requires and to help everybody concerned to keep out of trouble with it. The Department of Agriculture's Soil Conservation Service provides advice and assistance to farmers on how to conserve their soils. The Department of Commerce's Business and Defense Services Administration provides a broad range of help and advice to business in many fields—including getting defense contracts. The list could go on almost indefinitely; nearly every department and agency does things falling under the present heading.

Investigations and the power to inquire. Much is heard about the congressional power of investigation. But the administrative system has powers of investigation that are almost as broad, are vastly more extensively used, affect many, many more people, and probably have a greater total impact. Some of these investigative powers are indispensable if modern government is to exist. But they present many grave problems. An agency need not limit its investigations to persons and subjects within its statutory jurisdiction or its power to regulate; it can investigate anybody and anything remotely connected with its official concerns, and for any purpose (including, apparently, mere "official curiosity"— *U.S.* v *Morton Salt Co.*, 338 U.S. 632 [1950]). It need not have any real grounds for investigating; "fishing expeditions" are all right (*Ibid.*). Investigations can be too broad and sweeping to be lawful, but the lawful scope is enormous. The Fourth Amendment's prohibition against "unreasonable searches and seizures" is seldom applied, and the Fifth Amendment's protection against self-incrimination is not always available because numerous ways around it exist.[14]

American Big Government: Issues and Proposals

We now have completed the survey of the organizations and processes of American government to which all of Part Three of this book has been devoted. With that survey before us, we can conclude by considering some of the great issues the American system of government presents and some proposals made for its improvement. We begin with issues concerning the system as a whole. We then turn to the relationships among the branches, and then to the branches individually. We conclude with the grand issue of 'big government.'

Nation and States: The Issues of American Federalism

Is the national government, by exploiting modern crises and the extraordinary potentialities of a modern administrative system, becoming too large and powerful? In particular, is it usurping functions which should be performed by the states, if at all, thereby reducing the powers and significance of the states? Is the balance of power in the American federal system being wrongly shifted in favor of the national government and against the states? The issue is not new; it has been argued since the first days of the republic. Modern debate on it, however, dates from the days of the New Deal when the federal government dramatically began to increase the size and scope of its activities. But there is doubt that in recent years there has been any serious unnecessary tipping of the balance against the states. State government, e.g., in money spent and programs carried on, has been increasing in size and scope much more rapidly than the federal government. In recent years the federal government has undertaken comparatively few new programs of any great size touching the states' spheres, except in cooperation with the state governments. The key fact is that state and local government expenditures are today much greater than the federal government's domestic expenditures and even approach total national expenditures including national security.[15]

---

[14] See generally Davis, ch. 3.

[15] See, e.g., Charles R. Adrian, *State and Local Governments* (New York: McGraw-Hill Book Company, Inc., 1960), ch. 5.

Some rise in federal power has been inevitable as more national problems have developed; the country is now largely a national society and a national economy, and the states are hence not the social, or economic, or political entities that they were before this became so. Another factor has been that the states have been less responsive to public demands for new governmental services, or less able to perform them; if this changes, many activities may shift to the states. Indeed, some experts predict that this shift may well soon occur. They argue that the establishment of the 'welfare state' in all the industrialized nations, including the United States, required considerable governmental centralization for the new and controversial social services to be instituted successfully. But, now that these services are widely accepted, they believe that there will be less need for centralization and that power is likely to be devolved down to smaller, and in some cases nongovernmental, authorities.[16]

The American system contemplates independent and powerful states, and there are forces in the system that tend to keep them so. This is unquestionably desirable; although the traditional arguments for the usefulness of the states require some revision today, they have a core of truth.[17] But the vitality of the states in the system cannot contravene the fundamental preeminence and potency of the national government. The national element in the compound national-federal system was designed by its leading Framers to be preeminent and potent. The central government is constitutionally supreme in its fields; these in turn are constitutionally broad and vital, and in the modern world are likely to get more and more vital. The governmental arrangements for effectuating the national element are too skillfully designed and too successful to fade away. Congress is a great national legislature as well as a great federal forum, and even when most affected by states' rights ideas it has never abandoned this national greatness. The Presidency is a great national office, and its holders tend to use it as such. And the Supreme Court did perhaps as much as either Congress or the Presidency to make a nation of the country in the early nineteenth century, and it has the same capacity today to uphold the national authority.

But even giving all these nationalizing forces their full weight and adding to them the vast potential nationalizing force of the national administrative system, there are countervailing *federalizing* forces as well. The states are constitutionally represented as such in the Senate and local communities in effect in the House, and through these representatives they make themselves strongly felt *as states and communities* there, in the White House, and in the administrative system.

---

[16] See, e.g., Gunnar Myrdal, *Beyond the Welfare State* (New Haven: Yale University Press, 1960).

[17] See, e.g., for discussions of these subjects the report of the Commission on Intergovernmental Relations in 1955.

State and local governments and groups also speak directly and influentially to—indeed, *in*—the administrative system.[18] And the President needs state and local elements, both in the coalitions he needs to win his elections and also as allies in his struggles with Congress. Least of all is the Supreme Court bound to the purely national. Austerely independent, it can—and does—hold what it deems the constitutional balance between nation and states, and the states are neither more nor less free than the nation to convince it of the justice of their causes. And, as we shall see, the states as states are immensely important in the political party system.

The Separated Powers: Dominance or Deadlock?[19]

Next in scope to the problems of nation-state relationships are those of the general structure of the national government itself.

Conservative and right-wing spokesmen frequently assert that not only are the states being swallowed up by a national Leviathan but also that, within the national government, the Leviathan is the executive and the administrative system which acting together are gaining a crushing dominance over Congress. Liberal and left-wing spokesmen on the other hand do not see this dominance; instead they see deadlock. They see Congress as the villain; in their view, Congress nearly paralyzes executive and administrative policy-making while it cannot make creative, integrated, and comprehensive policy of its own. Hence, they argue, decisions are not taken, futile stalemate prevails, and governing goes by default.

The issue of deadlock. The liberal charge that Congress causes the deadlock of government usually rests upon the belief that some form of cabinet or parliamentary government would have advantages over the American scheme of radical separation of powers. It is argued that cabinet government, in which the executive in effect controls the legislature, is more flexible, more responsive to the popular will, and more able to carry through a program. It is said that the American system fosters deadlock between Congress and President and irresponsibility in both, and is rescued from complete impotence only by the party system, which bridges some of the gaps created by separation of powers. Liberals generally see a solution to the problem in increasing the executive's legislative authority and responsibility. Proposals have ranged from a complete constitutional overhaul and the installation of full-fledged cabinet government to various minor tinkerings with the existing machinery.

---

[18] See, e.g., Grodzins.

[19] A detailed and highly-regarded recent statement of the "deadlock" viewpoint is James MacGregor Burns, *The Deadlock of Democracy* (Englewood Cliffs, N.J.: Prentice-Hall, Inc., 1963).

The vital point is that liberal critics thus regard the American system as intrinsically and radically defective because the system itself produces dangerous deadlocks that otherwise could be avoided. But could they? Deadlock or failure to act in time (or wisely) is a human failing not peculiar to the American system. In British history, for example, there have been parliamentary stalemates perhaps as serious as any in the American experience. Moreover, many alleged deadlocks have not been due to the system at all. Rather they have arisen from fundamental policy disagreements among the American people, and these could not (or should not) be eliminated by any changes in governmental arrangements. For example, congressional slowness or failure to act on welfare and civil rights often reflects the absence of a firm majority opinion behind the proposals. Failure of action at such times is not deadlock produced by the system but rather the natural inability of a democracy to act when its people are fairly evenly divided.

The issue of executive–administrative dominance. Commentators of a more conservative persuasion, less favorable to active, positive government and affirmative policy-making, think that the trouble is not deadlock but dominance by the Presidency and the administration. Far from seeing the system as deadlocked and doing too little, conservative critics see the system as executive-dominated and doing too much. Their proposals for reform range from exhortations to Congress to exert itself and recapture its lost authority to proposals for constitutional amendments aimed at reducing presidential or administrative powers or both.[20]

Actually, it is difficult to see much real dominance of Congress by the Presidency or by the administrative system. The Presidency is more active and more powerful today than it was in Harding's time, and so is the administrative system; but so is Congress. In most political systems the executive tends to gain over the legislative in times of war or other crisis. But by the same token it tends to lose ground when the crisis is over, and the American Presidency today is far back from where it was in 1933 or 1943. Power relations between the two branches are never stationary, but in recent years movement seems to have been around some point of fundamental equilibrium.

As to the administrative system, there is paradox in the alarmist views. The system is indeed powerful. But this very power casts doubt on the claim that the Presidency is overpowerful. As we have seen, the President cannot manipulate the administrative system at will. This being so, its power is in some measure a counterpoise to his, and we cannot simply add presidential and administrative powers together and

---

[20] Many are discussed in Ernest S. Griffith, *Congress: Its Contemporary Role* (3d ed.; New York: New York University Press, 1961), Bertram H. Gross, *The Legislative Struggle* (New York: McGraw-Hill Book Company, 1953), and other books on Congress.

A cartoon attacking the spoils system (from Puck, September 18, 1889): The slave is President Harrison being forced by state party bosses to grind out patronage for their local political machines. President Lincoln is said to have remarked while ill with smallpox: "Tell all the office-seekers to come at once, for now I have something I can give them."

get an alarming total. Further, Congress is a partner and rival of the Presidency in the administrative system, and nearly a full participant in it with him. The powers it has Congress shares—perhaps one reason why despite much urging to do so Congress has not seriously undertaken to prune these powers drastically. Thus the rise of the administrative system has not simply swelled the President's powers over Congress; that enormous administrative system, as we have seen, is also an arena in which Congress can successfully compete with the President.

The successes of the Madisonian scheme. The liberal critics of supposed executive-legislative deadlock and the conservative critics of supposed executive dominance agree in opposing the existing system. But there is much continuing vitality and soundness in this Madisonian scheme of separation of powers which they jointly oppose. The system is perhaps not sufficiently fully and quickly responsive to national presidential majorities, not sufficiently plebiscitary and populist, to satisfy the more extreme liberal critics. Nor is it sufficiently obstructive of popular majorities, sufficiently reactionary, to satisfy the more extreme conservative critics. However, it does seem still to be providing the country with a pretty good representative system. Democracy, liberty, and competence of the American style still exist. There is orderly, democratic reference to the people and the responsive movement—too slow for the liberal critics and too full for the conservative critics—of broad coalition majorities. There is certainly liberty, though further protections of personal freedoms, as against some congressional committees and especially as against some aspects of the administrative system, do seem needed. There is competence; the level of statesmanship and effectiveness in the three

As part of a Federal Civil Service examination, candidates discuss a topic presented by the examiners (here shown at opposite ends of the table) who evaluate each candidate's performance.

branches compares favorably in most respects with any country. Americans have no ground for complacency, but none for undue concern either.

Reforms in the Branches

Congress. Both the deadlock and dominance views of the system give rise to many sweeping proposals regarding Congress. Liberal proposals for changing Congress arise out of the belief that Congress is not sufficiently creative, unified, and effective, that it does not develop full and integrated programs of public policy, carry these through to enactment, or effectively direct their actual execution. Conservative proposals spring from an opposite view that the whole national government including Congress is already much too active and powerful, and that the inactive and federal aspects should be strengthened rather than the active and national.

Judging between these opposites is a large question, involving the whole of one's political philosophy, including whether one wants more, and more positive, national government or less. But one significant point is that Congress is a stubborn organism, firmly settled in its ways and very resistant to change because it has been made what it is by a multitude of forces in the whole of the American system. Therefore any drastic attempts to overhaul it would hardly be successful unless they also overhauled the constitutional system itself—a large order.

Many less sweeping but still substantial proposed changes also have their doubtful aspects. Two are illustrative.

It is sometimes suggested that Cabinet members be given seats in the House or Senate so they could appear in person to advocate their programs and answer questions.[21] It is contended this would improve understanding and cooperation between executive and legislative and increase the purposefulness and unity of congressional proceedings. It might—and it might increase Cabinet unity as well. But it might also have undesirable effects. For example, Cabinet members might thereby develop such independent political strength in Congress as dangerously to undermine the President's authority over them, already shaky enough at times. Further, rivalries which already exist in the Cabinet might sharpen and become dangerously institutionalized. Further still, it might undesirably strengthen the lesser administrative officials; on specialized departmental matters the typical Cabinet member could seldom be expert enough to be more than their spokesman, and they could then in effect deal directly with Congress, free from much executive control.

Another proposal addresses itself to pork-barrel spending and the like. It would give the President an *item veto*. In appropriations bills, for example, he could cut out specific undesirable items without having to veto the whole bill. But this might also give the President an all-too-powerful weapon over individual senators and representatives through threatening local projects politically indispensable to them.

Other substantial proposals for changes seem similarly vulnerable. But could not some useful modest changes be made in the intricate—and often creaky—internal structures and processes of Congress? Some could, but few specific proposals would do much good without also risking considerable harm or at least unacceptable uncertainty.

The committee system is another favorite target. On occasion, selection of chairmen by seniority brings to power men who are incapable and irresponsible, and keeps others there though they become senile, lazy, or downright malicious. But what other mode would be better? For many years, selection in the House was by the party potentates with no regard to seniority; this had the flaws of rule by unrepresentative political machine, because the congressional parties were not then (and because Congress so jealously guards its independence are never likely to be) broadly-based, responsible national parties. Later, selection was by the Speaker, then virtual czar of the House; this had the flaws of tyranny. Other alternatives seem open to other objections.

Well then, what about curtailing the powers of committees to bottle up bills and frustrate open and democratic legislative processes? Here effective reform possibilities seem greater. For example, means can be

---

[21] Although Cabinet members frequently appear before congressional committees, the constitutional separation of powers has always been understood to bar their appearance on the floor of either house. Of the executive branch, only the President has been permitted to appear before Congress and then only to address it and never to participate in its debate or to answer questions.

devised to assure that bills can be gotten more readily to the floor despite opposition by committee chairmen. But will this alone do much? The enormous legislative business of Congress will still have to be divided among committees, and these will cherish their jurisdictions, and will develop their expertness and vested rights. And Congress needs such committees, not only to manage its legislative business, but also to be able to cope at all with the Presidency and with the administrative system. So committees will inevitably have substantial control over legislation within their provinces no matter what formal methods are devised to get bills to the floor.

The same mixture of modest possibilities of improvement coupled with substantial risk meets us on other issues. Larger and better committee staffs might improve internal performance and also Congress's ability to compete with the Presidency and the administrative system; but they might also put Congress too much in the hands of its own staff aids. More resources, staff and otherwise, for individual members of Congress might help them do better jobs; but these also give them an undue advantage over their opponents in elections, and foster more undesirable interventions by the individual members in the administrative process. The members might be better legislators if errand running and case work for constituents were cut down; but perhaps the ordinary citizen should have someone as potent as a member of Congress to help him fight his battles with the national government and its vast and powerful administrative system, and every state and district should have its advocate in Washington to further its interests.

The Presidency.[22] Many reform proposals concerning the Presidency seek to divide the office up, to spread its powers and responsibilities out to more than one man. The arguments are usually that the Presidency is too big a job for one man, and that so much depends on it that it should not be entrusted to the judgment and capacities of one man.

One proposal is to provide the President with some chief colleague, either elected and thus politically responsibile *with* him, such as an 'executive vice president for administration,' or else appointed and thus administratively responsible *to* him, such as a 'first secretary for government.' This colleague would share some of his responsibilities or relieve him of some of his burden. At first these proposals sound reasonable. They might, for example, usefully strengthen him in his dealing with the administrative system (it is doubtful they could be much help to him with Congress). But on closer examination they go against the grain of the office. Presidents want—and need—flexibility, independence, and freedom to select and change their advisors and their methods and channels for doing business. Further, there is a dilemma. If this new

---

[22] Most books on the Presidency contain materials on proposed changes. A thorough survey, and a set of proposals, may be found in Herman Finer, *The Presidency: Crisis and Regeneration* (Chicago: The University of Chicago Press, 1960).

official is an administrator, with little independent power and discretion of his own, he will be an additional organizational layer interposed between the President and the Cabinet, of doubtful help either politically or administratively. If he is a politician, a public figure in his own right, perhaps elected with the President, he will be a potential rival; the President is then likely to keep him firmly in the background, and the office will turn out to amount to as little as the President can make it amount to.

More drastic proposals for dividing the office up embody the idea of a presidential council. One such proposal is for a joint Cabinet, the regular Cabinet plus the principal members of Congress. This joint Cabinet would take some initiative in policy development and have some authority over policy coordination and execution. At first glance this seems reasonable, especially if one is concerned over the clashes and stalemates between President and Congress and with their doubtful and divided control over the administrative system. But there is a basic difficulty. Congress and the Presidency are irremediably separate centers of power; as such they inevitably clash unless one abdicates or is cut down. A joint Cabinet would drastically cut down the power of either Congress or the Presidency.

Some who propose to divide the office up have no intention of thereby cutting the office down. Rather, they hope that an administrative chief colleague or some form of joint Cabinet would actually increase the ability of the executive to cope with modern problems. But others who press for these changes do want to cut down presidential power. They hope to strengthen Congress at the expense of the Presidency and they hope that by weakening the Presidency they will halt the growth of big government. In addition, they usually also seek specific reductions in the President's constitutional powers, such as limiting his power to make international executive agreements and to limit the treaty-making power of the government as a whole.[23] But such limitations upon the Presidency are in fact limitations upon the government as a whole. And a government constitutionally incapable of coping with any problem of its time is as much a political cripple today as Hamilton in 1787 thought it would be. Diminishing the Presidency—either by new constitutional limitations or by weakening the office relative to Congress—is to diminish the strength of government, and is thus to commit the error the Framers most sought to prevent. Significantly, diminishing "our one truly national political institution,"[24] would increase the force of localism in American politics. And perhaps the desire to increase this force and to hinder broad national programs is the motivation at the bottom of both sets of proposals.

---

[23] See discussion of Bricker amendment, pp. 514–15.

[24] The Supreme Court is of course a vitally national and in some ways political institution. But what is here meant is that the Presidency is the sole elective summoner-up of America's national political life.

Big Government—and Bureaucracy?[25]

We come now to the hard and basic final question: Suppose that the federal balance of nation and states, the three branches,[26] and their relationships, and all the other elements of the polity are in—or can by reform be brought to—a reasonably satisfactory state, but that the demands upon the national government continue to be great and hence its size and power continue to be vast; can the American system cope with the modern big government that thus arises, without grave distortion or loss of its traditional values of democracy and freedom? The question can be put another way: Can American representative democracy really survive and function, not just in name and form only, or is necessity inevitably driving us away from full self-government toward a substantial degree of bureaucracy, rule by the executive-administrative apparatus?

Many reforms can be effected in this apparatus that will both improve its performance and also ameliorate the problems. Administrative legislation needs more public participation in its enacting processes. Administrative adjudication needs to be disentangled from some official red tape and to acquire more of the virtues of its judicial counterpart without loss of appropriate flexibility. The whole administrative process needs to be more open to critical public inspection and less cloaked in official secrecy. And actual administration—rational and efficient management—can be improved in many places.

But the core of the question remains. So far it seems possible to give a favorable answer to it: American big government has so far been politically responsible. However, the terms of the problems change constantly. Andrew Jackson could reasonably say that almost any job in government could readily be mastered by any intelligent man; since the different kinds of jobs then numbered only a few hundred, political control by President, Congress, and public was comparatively easy. Today neither the citizen, nor the member of Congress, nor the President can personally operate a moonshot, regulate the civil air transportation industry, manage the economy, devise programs for conservation of natural resources, conduct America's relations with a hundred nations, and so on, nor even have a really full grasp of the subjects.[27] And no doubt things will get bigger and more complicated.

To this point, the American constitutional system has stood the

---

[25] We here use 'bureaucracy' in the pejorative sense of rule not by the democratic many or the aristocratic best but by the government bureaus, wherein their powers are pathologically magnified.

[26] Discussion of issues and proposals concerning the judiciary was for convenience located in Chapter 7.

[27] An illuminating experience is to look at a random selection of pages in the *Government Organization Manual* and speculate as to what proportion of the programs described there a President or member of Congress could reasonably be expected to understand, let alone to have mastered.

test of big government admirably. But more than ever, it will take skilled statesmanship, decent qualities among the citizenry, and understanding of the nature of the system itself to continue to support the immense burden of big government in a gigantic country of more than two hundred million.

BIBLIOGRAPHICAL NOTE

The *Government Organization Manual* and the *Budget* (see note 2) are both storehouses of information on the departments and agencies. Annually the Senate Committee on Government Operations produces a descriptive survey and a wall-chart of the whole administrative system. It and other congressional committees and subcommittees from time to time investigate and produce studies of various parts of the system and its functions; there is a substantial library of these, of varying levels of accurateness and quality. In the late 1940s and again in the 1950s official commissions headed by former President Herbert Hoover studied and reported on "The Organization of the Executive Branch." Most departments and agencies publish annual reports on their activities. There is a vast quantity of other government documents, many touching aspects of our subject; here as with all government documents the invaluable guide is Laurence F. Schmeckebier and Roy B. Eastin, *Government Publications and Their Use* (2nd ed., 1961).

There is an almost unending scholarly literature on the organizations and processes of the administrative system. The works of Leonard D. White, plus the book by Lloyd M. Short, both cited in note 6, are introductions to the history of the subject. Texts on public administration (e.g., Simon et al., note 3) usually supply copious bibliographies, as do occasional issues of the *American Political Science Review*. Writings in the scholarly journals are accessible through the Public Affairs Information Service index and the Index to Legal Periodicals; writings in other periodicals, through the Readers' Guide to Periodical Literature.

Discussions of issues and proposals concerning the problems of modern American government and its reform are found throughout the literature on American government described in the bibliographical notes for Chapters 4–7. Guidance to problems especially connected with the administrative system may be found in Paul H. Appleby, *Policy and Administration* (1949), Charles Hyneman, *Bureaucracy in a Democracy* (1950), and Robert K. Merton, ed., *Reader in Bureaucracy* (1952).

Part Four

POLITICS

Chapter 9

Politics,
Parties,
and Groups

The regulation of these various and interfering interests forms the principal task of modern legislation, and involves the spirit of party and faction in the necessary and ordinary operations of government.

PUBLIUS[1]

POLITICS MEANS MANY THINGS. HERE WE EMPLOY ITS MOST FAMILIAR common-sense meaning: e.g., candidates competing for votes, groups competing to influence the government. Notice that politics involves competition: the clash of rival politicians, parties, and interest groups. At the center of this clash stands government and its great powers. Politicians and groups seek control of government because they want to influence what government will do or will compel others to do. The essence of politics inheres in the question, To which ends will the powers of government be directed? Such policy questions range from the relatively trivial, like a neighborhood zoning conflict, to the profoundest questions involving the fundamental character of the society. And politics—whether over trivial or profound matters—can summon up powerful interests and passions.

Sources of Political Controversy and Association

If everyone agreed on public policy there would be no politics and no politicians. Politics commences in public controversy, that is, in differing opinions regarding public matters. The study of politics centers on these differences of opinion. Accordingly, our examination of Ameri-

---

[1] *Federalist* 10, p. 79.

can political parties and interest groups begins by considering the basic sources of political disagreement out of which the competition of political associations emerges.

Economic Factors

Among the latent causes of faction, "the most common and durable source . . . has been the various and unequal distribution of property."[2] How people make their money and how much they make influences their needs and desires, and thus influences both the *specific demands* they make of government and their *fundamental political viewpoints*. These two effects of the economic factor must be carefully distinguished.

The effect on specific demands. Those in the same occupation or kind of enterprise are both competitors and collaborators. As individual workers or firms they compete for jobs and markets. Butter producers, for example, compete against each other for the consumer dollar. But the general situation of an occupation or enterprise usually also gives all the competitive participants a common interest. Thus butter producers all share a specific common interest against all producers of oleomargarine. The otherwise keenly competitive butter producers unite in the National Dairy Association to advertise their common product and—the politically relevant factor—they collaborate for political purposes. Dairymen long obtained state and national legislation handicapping the sale of oleomargarine. Similarly, individual auto workers compete for jobs, promotions, and bonuses, but combine in their union to represent common interests in collective bargaining with their employers. Yet in turn, these same employers and unions work together on issues affecting the automobile industry as a whole; they jointly seek duties on competitive imports and jointly oppose decreases in government defense contracts.

Such organized economic interests are not automatically and entirely political; they ordinarily become politically involved only when government impinges on their interests. In modern industrial society this impingement is frequent and substantial. Interest groups actively seek ways by which to benefit from the impact of government. Politicians in turn are acutely sensitive to the needs of such groups. Indeed, because leaders need followers and votes, politicians not only respond to group demands, they also may arouse and activate persons with common economic interests, hoping thereby to develop organizational support for political office and influence.

The effect on fundamental political viewpoints. But the way people make their living and the amount of money they make affect more than the immediate and specific demands they make of government. The economic factor also commonly affects their general political view-

---

[2] *Idem.* see pp. 75–80 for an extended discussion of this topic.

point. Rich and poor tend to see things differently. Urban industrial workers tend to think about politics differently than farmers. Those engaged in international commerce tend to have a different general political 'style' than, say, small town merchants. Party identification and voting studies show that some economic groupings vote predominantly Republican, others predominantly Democratic. Unquestionably, economic factors influence fundamental political views and the resulting patterns of political association.

Geographic-Regional Factors

There is a natural overlap between geographic and economic factors. This has always been especially true in agriculture: The Great Plains wheat belt, California and Florida citrus groves, Southern cotton and tobacco, and Western cattle and sheep herding are familiar illustrations of economic geography. True, modern scientific techniques have lessened the dependence of particular crops on the natural characteristics of soil and climate, thus somewhat dissociating economics and geography. Also, modern transport and communication have blurred the distinction between city and country folk in style of dress and speech, kind of schools, homes, entertainment, and political information. There nonetheless remains a substantial distinction between the politics of agricultural regions and those of manufacturing, mining, shipping, and financial regional dominance.

Sectional or regional politics obtains in any territorial unit wherein the inhabitants are linked by some powerful common interest. The region may be as large as the eleven states that made up the Southern Confederacy, or smaller like the flood area portions of the several states served by the Tennessee Valley Authority. Or the region may be a single state whose politics are dominated by the needs of a single industry, like the Michigan automobile industry or West Virginia coal mining. Or the region may be as small as a congressional district or a township and dominated by a single plant; there is even a regional politics of neighborhoods over questions of zoning.

But not all regional politics is economically based. The politics of geographical sections reflects in general their different histories, different heroes, different miseries and triumphs. The distinctiveness of Dixie could easily characterize a separate nation, and indeed one would have resulted from a turn of the fortunes of civil war. Westerners have always seen themselves in a different way from Easterners, and the nominating politics of the Republican party quadrennially confronts that schism, though usually with less virulence than the North-South ruptures within the Democratic party. Regional variations have been diluted by remarkable changes in the quite recent past as jet aircraft and televised popular culture shrink distance and homogenize regional patterns. Nonetheless, there is continuing, albeit diminishing, substance to distinctive regional qualities, and political organizations continue to build on these sources of faction.[3]

Ethnic and Racial Factors

Geographic regions frequently acquire their distinctive character from a common stock. Some communities are long dominated by the original settlers; others have been ethnically transformed by later migrants. New England Yankee-Puritan culture was altered by the Irish who gave Boston politics a new flavor, as did the Italians in Providence and New Haven. Catholics and Jews outnumber white Anglo-Saxon Protestants in the nation's largest city, New York. These ethnic groups tend to have politically relevant common interests.

Undoubtedly, the sharpest cleavage in current American society is along racial lines. Different needs and desires of Negroes and whites give rise to political demands and associations. Organizations supporting Negro demands like the National Association for the Advancement of Colored People (NAACP) are countered by the formation of White Citizens' Councils. Within each of these antagonistic camps are further divisions reflecting a variety of leaders and strategies. The Negro-white problem is the mammoth example of the racial factor in politics, but there are others, such as the longstanding problems of American Indians and Orientals.

Groups based on common national origin have often presented special problems for American foreign policy. Many American citizens have close old-country ties. Isolationist sentiment between the two world wars was strongly affected by Irish-American and German-American antagonism toward Britain. Polish-American hostility to the 1945 Yalta agreement between the United States and the Soviet Union affected the 1952 presidential election. Similarly, United States relations with Israel reflect the political influence of American Jews grouped in several electorally important major cities.

Religious Factors

Again our categories shade into each other; religious upbringing is obviously correlated to ethnic or national origin, and religious factors are also frequently important as a regional characteristic. Thus Utah politics is greatly influenced by the Mormons and big city politics by Catholics, Jews, and in some degree by Black Muslims. And religious considerations obviously affected national politics in 1928 and 1960 when Alfred E. Smith and John F. Kennedy, the only Catholic presidential nominees, ran on the Democratic ticket.

Many political demands and controversies derive from the multiplicity

[3] Cf. Arthur Holcombe, *Political Parties of Today* (New York: Harper and Bros., 1942).

of religious denominations. Roman Catholics have felt put upon by taxation for public schools and now seek aid for their extensive system of parochial schools. Jews and Seventh-Day Adventists oppose Sunday closing laws as imposing a compulsory Sabbath other than their own. Jehovah's Witnesses frequently clash with legal requirements which violate their conscience, as the Supreme Court flag salute cases[4] illustrate. And agnostics are joined by some religionists like Unitarians and Jews in opposition to Bible readings and prayers in the public schools. As the dominant group, Protestants do not ordinarily organize as churchmen for political defense of their general religious interest. However, there is a social teaching, consciously formulated and given organized expression by the National Council of Churches. Also, Protestantism was a major factor in the once powerful prohibition-temperance movement, and Protestant churchmen have been leaders in antiobscenity, civil rights, and other causes.

Nor are Catholics, Mormons, Jews, or Jehovah's Witnesses, to name a few, merely concerned with narrowly conceived group interests. The historic Papal encyclicals on social and political teachings of the Roman Church have always gone far beyond the immediate interests of Catholics. The organized religious faiths teach distinctive moral and social creeds. Opinions formed out of strong religious commitment reflect a fundamental mode of thought which has almost always included a mode of political thought.

Attachment to Leaders

Leadership in one respect is merely instrumental, providing an organizational medium through which primary sources of controversy are actualized. Leaders simply summon up controversy from its basic sources, raising issues where people have interests. But leadership, and the response to it, is also an independent variable, an independent source of political controversy. Within limits, leaders create as well as reflect historical circumstances. The attachment followers develop for leaders conjures into existence political controversy where none would otherwise exist at all, or would not exist in anything like the same way and degree. The bellicose resurgence of post-World War I Germany was in vital respects the product of Hitler's twisted genius; England's courageous resistance in World War II was to some extent the product of the sheer force of Winston Churchill; and thousands were stimulated by Gandhi to practice 'passive resistance,' enduring imprisonment and prolonged fasting in the cause of Indian independence. Sheer attachment to leaders, be they noble or ignoble, has ever been a source of political controversy and of the formation of groups, parties, and movements.

---

[4] *Minersville School District* v. *Gobitis*, 310 U.S. 586 (1940); *West Virginia State Board of Education* v. *Barnette*, 319 U.S. 624 (1943).

'Ins' v. 'Outs' and the Political 'Game'

Political contests are sometimes motivated by little more than the desire of the 'outs' to replace the 'ins.' Apart from substantive issues of public policy, the status, power, and perquisites of governmental office are sufficient inducements for many to undertake the ardors of campaigning. And even if the ins endorse much the same policy, the outs claim they can implement it far better. This rallying cry is enough for most partisans to close ranks and mount the political offensive. And win or lose, as those who know politicians can testify, the political 'game' can be attractive for its own sake. There are duller ways to live!

Indeed, even if all substantial interests over which sensible men fight could somehow be satisfied or eliminated, a divisive tendency would continue. In Madison's words: "So strong is this propensity of mankind to fall into mutual animosities that where no substantial occasion presents itself, the most frivolous and fanciful distinctions have been sufficient to kindle their unfriendly passions and excite their most violent conflicts."[5]

Social-Psychological Factors

Opinions are views about events and issues. Where people have a clear and direct interest at stake their opinions may well be a foregone conclusion—say an American watchmaker's view of tariffs on Swiss-made watches. But the relation between individual interests, political issues, and opinions is generally more complex. Social psychologists explain complex political opinions as filtered through basic attitudes or predispositions. Thus a person's specific opinion of Medicare is thought to reflect broader underlying attitudes to big government, welfare programs for indigent persons, frugality and thrift as virtues, etc. These broad attitudes, in turn, are thought to be organized in more general patterns of political predispositions often called ideologies. Familiar examples are conservatism and liberalism; liberals tend to favor and conservatives to oppose such specific proposals as Medicare.

Psychologists ascribe many political actions and opinions to differences of personality, normal and abnormal. Freud held that psychological frustrations imposed by civilized societies find outlets in political aggression, including rebellion and warfare.[6] Harold Lasswell, a psychoanalytically oriented political scientist, also maintains that neurotic drives often underlie distinctive political roles and behavior.[7] More recently, stimulated by the rise of totalitarian mass movements, psychologists

---

[5] *Federalist* 10, p. 79.
[6] Sigmund Freud, *Civilization and Its Discontents* (London: Hogarth Press, 1930).
[7] Harold D. Lasswell, *Psychopathology and Politics* (New York: Viking Press, 1960).

have probed for personality traits predisposing a type they call "authoritarian personalities" to join such political movements.[8]

But the significance of social-psychological factors for understanding politics is greatly disputed between 'political behavioralists' and traditional political scientists.[9]

Rational Differences of Opinion

Our consideration of the sources of controversy thus far might seem to imply that political opinions are merely rationalizations of individual and group interests, that ideas are merely the prettied-up surface of such underlying interests. In fact, political controversy and organization also stem from human intelligence independently grappling with questions of public policy in the general interest. This will shock only cynics who can conceive of no human act which does not emanate from an ulterior motive. Yet there are always men, identical so far as the eye can see with respect to tangible material interests, ethnic background, or personality traits, who nonetheless hold opposing opinions of the public good. Common interests do not ensure common opinions, and common opinions do not require common interests.

Mankind has a capacity for sympathy and for friendship. Abolitionists did not have to be slaves, or have the interests of slaves, to form their powerful political movement. Empathy—feeling what other people feel—is a particularly human quality. Compassion for those whose interests one does not share in any material sense entails a sense of justice. It leads to a transcending of narrowly conceived self-interest and to a search for enlightened principles of common justice. The sheer play of human intelligence, and intelligence animated by compassion, leads men, apart from any other source of controversy, to form conflicting opinions of the public good. So powerful is this human wish to act justly, and not merely out of selfishness, that there are few political acts which are not at least cloaked in the dress of virtuous principle. If this is merely rationalization it is necessary to ask, why bother? The answer is plain. People respond to such justification; they require it even when fooled by pseudo-principles masquerading as the common good.

Men are indeed fallible in knowing the common good, and immense philosophical difficulties are involved in questions of human rationality.

---

[8] T. W. Adorno, et al. *The Authoritarian Personality* (New York: Harper and Bros., 1950). Cf. the important criticisms in Richard Christie and Marie Jahoda, eds., *Studies in the Scope and Method of "The Authoritarian Personality"* (Glencoe: Free Press, 1954).

[9] See, Robert A. Dahl, *Modern Political Analysis* (Englewood Cliffs, New Jersey: Prentice-Hall, 1963); Heinz Eulau, *The Behavioral Persuasion in Politics* (New York: Random House, 1963); James C. Charlesworth, ed., *The Limits of Behavioralism in Political Science* (Philadelphia: American Academy of Political and Social Science, October 1962); and Herbert J. Storing, ed., *Essays on the Scientific Study of Politics* (New York: Holt, Rinehart and Winston, Inc., 1962).

That is why entirely rational and disinterested consideration of policy questions by perfectly honest and public-spirited citizens can still lead to conflicting views. Such honest differences of opinion are an independent and prolific source of political controversy.

Types of Political Organization

Politics is not a game of solitaire. At the heart of political life are combinations of the politically interested. This tendency to form groups, parties, and movements inheres in the human condition. We have noted that differences in degree and kind of wealth, race, region, attachment to leaders, attitudes, and ideas produce corresponding political combinations. But while combination is natural and universal, its actual manifestations vary with different kinds of government. Under monarchy or dictatorship, factions seek political influence at the royal court or through the ruling clique. Where representative assemblies develop, men combine to influence the policies, nominations, and elections of representatives. Where dissent is suppressed factions go underground, but where liberty is extended, organized groups flourish and multiply. We examine briefly some major forms of such organized groups, culminating in the modern political party.

Juntos and Cliques

Seizure of power and rule by an alliance of leaders, called a junto or clique, is an old but continuing form of political organization. Naturally, this mode of organization flourishes in nondemocratic regimes. Rather than depending upon free popular support, the power of the junto derives from the power of preexisting organizations or institutions controlled by junto participants. The leaders pool their power bases. Thus a military junto rests upon weapons and men commanded by the junto leaders. A broader alliance may unite the military with churchmen, trade union leaders, or others with well established bases. The term junto was often applied pejoratively to intraparliamentary factions in England and America prior to the full development of democracy and the acceptance of parties as legitimate political associations. The dreary succession of coups d'état by juntos in South America and the Middle East are all too familiar modern examples.

Ideological Mass Movements

Ideological mass movements strive to rally 'the masses' through idolized leaders to fervently held social doctrines. Their programs demand radical reform or total replacement of existing institutions and their methods also tend to be radical; often aiming at overthrow of the existing system, they use electoral campaigns more for propaganda than to win office.

Parliamentary parties are denounced as too wedded to the status quo to serve as instruments for sufficiently radical social change. Bargaining, conciliation, and compromise are disparaged as betrayal of principle. Doctrinal dogmatism is coupled with claims to being the sole organizational embodiment of social progress or justice. Opponents are castigated as heretics and a quasi-religious commitment is demanded of followers. Mob-like street demonstrations and gigantic rallies are common means of instilling passionate attachment to the movement and its leaders as well as to foment civil disorder.

The modern ideological mass movement is a post-World War I phenomenon; fascism, nazism, and communism are the outstanding examples. In the United States, on a much smaller scale (the important reasons for which we consider shortly), a number of such movements came into being during the depression of the 1930s. Father Coughlin's National Union for Social Justice was a popular neo-fascist group. Senator Huey Long's near-dictatorial rule of Louisiana politics made use of many devices of mass movement leadership. The German-American Bund and the American Communist Party sought to emulate their European models with some temporary and partial success.

Limited-Issue Parties and Movements

Not all ideological movements are concerned with total social reform. Many come into being to promote more limited causes: prohibitionists, abolitionists, old-age pensionists, single-taxers, racial segregationists, civil rights proponents, etc. Some, like Dr. Townsend's old age pension movement in the 1930s, border on full-scale mass movements. Others, like the women's suffrage movement or the 1932 veterans' Bonus Army march on Washington, utilize militant tactics. Some, like the Greenback and Prohibition parties, have nominated candidates and conducted election campaigns. But the narrow dominant purposes of such limited-issue parties and movements limit their electoral success and distinguish them from major party organizations.

Interest or Pressure Groups

If an interest group is defined as any aggregate of persons "that, on the basis of one or more shared attitudes, makes certain claims upon other groups in the society,"[10] all political groups (including parties) are a kind of interest group. But a narrower meaning is intended here. We refer to that wide range of groupings whose interest is typically limited and specific, which commonly have other than solely political functions, and which function politically by influencing other more wholly political bodies. Typical interest groups are economically based,

[10] David B. Truman, *The Governmental Process* (New York: Alfred A. Knopf, 1951), p. 33.

like labor, business, or farm groups, and are organized primarily for their members' private benefit rather than to promote broader political values. But included among interest groups are others like the reform-minded League of Women Voters and those which advance the general interests of a particular minority like the National Association for the Advancement of Colored People.

Not all interest groups engage continuously in political activity. Rather, they become involved when specific governmental action impinging on the group is feared or desired. This may take the form merely of informing the local congressman of a formal resolution passed by the group concerning a pending bill. More involved organizations employ professional lobbyists and public relations firms to manage extensive pressure campaigns. Fears that lavish expenditures for propaganda, election campaign contributions, and sometimes bribery, obtain special privileges for 'the interests' has led to the pejorative overtone of the term 'pressure groups.'

Some interest groups engage in electoral activity—directly, or through auxiliary organizations, e.g., labor's Committee on Political Education (COPE) of the AFL-CIO. Candidates may be endorsed or singled out for attack, campaign contributions made or withheld, and election workers may be recruited from group members. Characteristically, however, interest group politicking stops short of nominating candidates for public office in the group's own name.

Political Parties

Political parties are the most distinctively political voluntary associations to be found in democratic countries. They are the organizations that form expressly to take over the reins of government by winning electoral contests. No effort need be made here to give their main characteristics in brief. The nature and functioning of the modern political party form the major subject of the balance of this chapter.

Anglo-American Evolution of Party

Modern parties are characterized by their mobilization of votes in the *electorate* on behalf of *candidates*. But such parties did not appear fully formed. They evolved slowly from an older (and continuing) function of parties as mobilizers of votes in *legislatures* on behalf of *proposed bills*. This was a logical evolution from within the legislature outward to the general electorate: The need to line up dependable support within the elected legislature eventuated in electoral campaigns to win seats for copartisans and to defeat opponents.

It is useful to locate within that evolution the moment when the Constitution was framed. To understand the development of American parties, we have to understand what partisan political processes the

Constitution envisaged. And to understand that, we have to know what experienced and educated eighteenth-century statesmen knew about parties as they had emerged from British and American experience.

British Party Origin

Party originated as a synonym for faction. Both were odious terms because they designated divisive groups (party is from the Latin *partire*, meaning to part or divide), seeking their own selfish interest rather than the general good. The word party still has a negative connotation, as when someone is condemned for playing partisan politics. But this is pallid hostility compared to the earlier opprobrium in which parties were held. Opposition party groups were condemned as inherently seditious conspiracies to be forcibly suppressed.

Political parties could not arise as legitimate groups until they escaped from this opprobrium. Factional pursuit of governmental influence had to be accepted as *loyal* to the constitutional order, although organized in *opposition* to particular officials and policies. The idea that *loyal opposition* is not a self-contradiction grew in Britain with the gradual ascendancy of Parliament. When, at least a century before the American republic was founded, the House of Commons became the center of governmental authority in a constitutional monarchy, to rule in Britain meant ruling through Parliament. Factional leaders therefore had to develop tactical skills and organizational forms appropriate to winning votes within the legislative assembly. The triumph of Parliament thus necessitated some form of legitimate party politics.

Seventeenth- and eighteenth-century British parties—Whigs versus Tories—were more divisions within the relative privacy of Parliament than organizations of the electorate. Nonetheless there was an electorate, albeit with a limited suffrage. Getting into Commons required winning elections, and that meant electoral campaigning. It was soon discovered that the same advantage which party organization supplied within Commons applied equally to winning votes in the constituencies. Party electioneering, therefore, did not wait on the achievement of a mass suffrage. British parties as early as 1660—and quite extensively in the eighteenth century—sought to influence the election of incumbent members of Parliament by publicizing their votes on important legislative issues.[11] This was the embryo of the later development of parliamentary party groups into full-scale nominating and mass electioneering party organizations.

Eighteenth-century British politics came to recognize parties as the inescapable outcome of representative government. Edmund Burke, the great conservative political theorist and statesman, had practical experience of party as a leading member of the late eighteenth-century

---

[11] See Cecil S. Emden, *The People and the Constitution* (London: Oxford University Press, 1962), p. 102.

Parliament. He wrote a famous defense of the legitimacy of parties as appropriate and necessary instruments through which to pursue the public good. "Party divisions," he declared, "whether on the whole operating for good or evil, are things inseparable from free government."[12] If those truly devoted to the general interest fail to organize, he argued, the organized special interests will take control. The effective pursuit of good policies in a free representative government necessitates party organization.[13]

Four significant characteristics of party association emerged in eighteenth-century Britain: (1) conscious partisan identifications which distinguished Whigs from Tories; (2) partisan voting blocs within Commons; (3) the growing acceptance of party as a legitimate form of united opposition; and (4) the circulation of lists of legislative supporters and opponents to voters in the electorate as a mode of election campaigning. By the end of the eighteenth century—that is, prior to the drafting of the American Constitution—the modern political party was in process of birth. And this experience of emerging party politics was part of the immediate heritage of eighteenth-century Anglo-Americans.

American Origins

It was not merely a matter of British heritage but also of American experience.[14] The Framers of the Constitution themselves were leading factional-partisan organizers, first in the Revolutionary period and then in the states. American parties were at least as developed (except *nationally*) as their British counterparts, because America had a broad suffrage, was more democratized in general, and had more wholly a system of popular representative government.

As in Britain, rival parties were often designated Whig or Tory; the major division in the colonial assemblies was between a 'court' party, rallying to the royal governor, and a 'country' party seeking to enlarge the authority of the elected assembly.[15] And to a greater extent than

---

[12] "Observations on a Late Publication Intituled The Present State of the Nation," in *The Works of Edmund Burke* (London: Oxford University Press, 1925), I, 229. For a theoretical treatment of Burke on party and of party development generally, see Harvey C. Mansfield, Jr., *Statesmanship and Party Government* (Chicago: University of Chicago Press, 1965).

[13] Cf. Austin Ranney and Willmoore Kendall, *Democracy and the American Party System* (New York: Harcourt, Brace, 1956), pp. 138–40.

[14] "[T]he framers . . . had before their eyes an abundance of examples illustrating the very tendencies which have become so prominent in modern party development." Carl Becker, "The Nomination and Election of Delegates from New York to the First Continental Congress, 1774," *Political Science Quarterly*, XVIII (March, 1903), 18.

[15] "You say 'our divisions began with federalism and anti-federalism'," John Adams wrote to William Keteltas in 1812. "Alas! they began with human nature; they have existed in America from its first plantation. In every colony, divisions have always prevailed. In New York, Pennsylvania, Virginia, Massachusetts, and all the rest, court and country party have always contended." *Works* (Boston, 1851), X, 23.

This partisan attack on the anti-federalists appeared in 1793.

in England, these were not merely *parties in parliament*. Because of the broad suffrage, and because political power came more exclusively from popular consent, they were farther along the road to the modern political party—*parties in the electorate*. The American colonial and state parties had to influence many more voters in order to win elections and successfully pursue their policies in the representative assemblies.

More than an interesting historical question is involved here. An understanding of party development in 1787 speaks to a disputed issue in American political science, one we have encountered earlier—the status of democracy in the American constitutional system. Political scientists who see the Constitution as antidemocratic also believe that the Framers were antiparty. They reason that, since parties are the very embodiment of modern democracy, an antidemocratic Constitution had also to be antiparty. They contend further that parties arose only after the founding decade. As one distinguished political scientist wrote, "parties . . . transformed the American Constitution. . . . they have democratized it."[16]

As has been made clear throughout this book, and especially in Chapter 3, we view the Constitution as neither undemocratic in content

[16] E. E. Schattschneider, *Party Government* (New York: Farrar and Rinehart, Inc., 1942), p. 2.

nor in intent. The Framers had no *antidemocratic* reason for being *anti-party*. But this does not dispose of this vexing question. For, on the other hand, the Framers certainly did not foresee and deliberately design the modern two-party system as we know it. They lived when party institutions, like modern democracy itself, were in process of development. They most certainly were thoroughly familiar with parties. But these were only quasi-modern parties; they were numerous, more ephemeral, and party lines were more easily blurred, degenerating into mere shifting factions. And because prior to the Constitution there was no functioning national government, there were not and could not be *national* parties. The stable national development could only come after 1787.

It must be acknowledged that the leading Framers themselves sharply criticized the 'party spirit.' Washington's Farewell Address, surely the most misquoted of all American speeches, is often used to support the view that the Framers were antiparty. But the essential point is that Washington *took the existence of parties for granted.* He did not seek or hope to eliminate them; rather he threw his weight as Patriot-President only against the "baneful effects of the spirit of party," offering a standard higher than party to which the honorable could repair.[17] As Washington put the criticism, no decent man can disagree. Like Burke, he and other leading Framers hoped for disinterested national leadership above mere partisan animosity. But like Burke and Madison, Washington also accepted party as inevitable: "A fire not to be quenched, it demands a uniform vigilance to prevent its bursting into a flame, lest instead of warming it should consume."

The Framers stood at a midpoint in the emergence of modern parties, when no one could fully predict what their future would be. In any event, their Constitution does not expressly provide for parties. But perhaps constitutions generally ought not to constrain by express provision the living stream of politics. If the political process is formally and legally prescribed, it may well be less capable of constitutional adaptation to the "various crises of human affairs." Our best judgment is that this was the American case. Parties were thus not subversive of the Constitution, but rather grew within its boundaries as a natural and logical outcome of the constitutional system. The task was not to banish parties, but to channel and contain this emerging mode of political organization by the general constitutional restraints upon the "violence of faction."[18]

---

[17] For a view which gives greater emphasis to the idea of a trans-party rule of "the most elevated characters," see "The Nature and Origin of the American Party System," in Harry V. Jaffa, *Equality and Liberty* (New York: Oxford University Press, 1965).

[18] Cf. Madison's mature observations on parties in a letter to Henry Lee, June 25, 1824, in Gaillard Hunt, ed., *The Writings of James Madison,* IX (New York: G. Putnam's Sons, 1910), 190.

The Constitutional Basis of the Party-Group System

The first and crucial fact about the Constitution and the political parties and groups that arose under it is the constitutional protection of *liberty*: Voluntary political associations are *permitted*. Second, the Constitution delegates great power to *popularly elected representatives*: Political group and party organization is thereby *stimulated*. Last, various *constitutional structures* induce parallel extra-legal structures: The party-group system is distinctively *shaped* by the Constitution.

Liberty

Political parties, groups, and movements are latent in the many sources of faction, ready to proliferate when liberated. Thus the Constitution need not create parties in the same way that it establishes formal governmental branches. It has only to liberate them. Indeed, officially established parties or interest groups are as noncharacteristic of political freedom as officially established churches are of religious freedom.[19] The Constitution legally secures the essential tools of voluntary political organization. Political organizers may assemble meetings, petition for redress of grievances, speak and write freely in appeals for popular support. Congressmen may not be prosecuted for speech or debate in Congress. Political activists are protected against bills of attainder (legislative statutes singling out persons for punishment without judicial trial). Age-old restraints on political activity are constitutionally proscribed, and political crime is substantially abolished as a legal category.

The Constitution provides the free and democratic arena; a free and democratic political process consequently ensues.

Elected Representatives

By permitting voluntary political associations, constitutional liberty makes party organization *possible*. By establishing representative institutions and making elections the prime path to governmental power, the Constitution makes party organization a practical *necessity*. Parties are the most effective instruments for organizing voting strength both within representative bodies and in popular elections. Those who neglect or refuse to play the party game are at the mercy of those who do. Even in America, where nonpartisanship is deemed a political virtue more than in most nations, independent candidates are rarely taken seriously. Realistically, the people's choice is a choice among party-endorsed alternatives.

---

[19] It is a clear sign of undemocratic rule that the Soviet Constitution (Articles 126 and 141) officially establishes the primacy of the Communist Party.

All constitutionally created national offices, other than judicial, are elective, and the elected officers appoint the judiciary. The House of Representatives is directly elected by what amounts to the most popular suffrage provided in state elections. This alone would suffice to stimulate the growth of parties, as evidenced in the way parties grew in the British Parliament with its single elective chamber. But in the United States, senators now are also elected directly by the people. Yet parties grew around the Senate even prior to the Seventeenth Amendment; senators were early selected by a party process within the popularly elected state legislatures. The Constitution thus fostered the development of parties from the outset, in the indirectly elected Senate as well as in the directly elected House.

The same is true of the indirect election of the President (see pp. 83–84). There is still no presidential equivalent of the Seventeenth Amendment, but nothing can be plainer than the speed with which the party process brought the selection of the Electoral College and presidential politics under its control. Indeed, many state legislatures, using the flexibility permitted under the Constitution, early turned both the election of senators and presidential electors over to direct popular election. This further stimulated the development of party organization by enlarging the numbers from which pluralities must be formed. Establishment of a strong, elective national executive stimulated *national* political alignments. Federalists and Anti-Federalists, Democrats, Whigs, and Republicans—all sought to organize the nationally distributed majorities needed to control the Electoral College and name the President.

The parties are organizational responses to the power vested in the elective Presidency, Senate, and House of Representatives. Political leaders must influence or control these governmental branches if their views and interests are to prevail. That is the constitutional stimulus underlying the party-group system.

Basic Constitutional Structures: Federalism and Separation of Powers

The Constitution not only legitimates and stimulates the formation of political associations; equally important, it substantially molds their distinctive traits. Schattschneider's metaphor is excellent: "If the parties are the river of American politics, the stream of the living impulse to govern, the Constitution is the river bed, the firm land whose contour shapes the stream."[20] The distinctive "shape" of the political party "stream" occupies the remainder of this chapter. Here we briefly note the influence of two major constitutional "contours"—federalism and the separation of powers.

Federalism continued the preexisting state parties into the new constitutional design by continuing the governmental basis for separate

[20] E. E. Schattschneider, p. 124.

political organization on the state level. The continuing existence of powerful state governments is a constant constitutional influence upon party behavior. Fifty states now separately elect numerous officials who tax, spend, and regulate in ways that vitally affect the peoples' interests and beliefs. The same organizational incentives which liberty and popular elections provide in national politics are thus constitutionally multiplied fiftyfold. Federalism makes American parties far more decentralized—with all the gains of decentralization in local democratic vigor and costs in confusion—than parties in unitary constitutional systems.

Constitutionally established separation of powers—coupled with bicameralism and staggered terms of office for President, senators, and representatives—intensifies the need for political parties. Party organization is stimulated because there are many more offices to be filled and more frequent elections to be contested. Party organization is useful in all political competition; it is indispensable in the welter of American electoral contests. Separation of powers also specifically shapes party character. It multiplies power points within the national government that can be separately controlled. Because they are separate, the governmental branches, even the houses of Congress, can be controlled by different parties. Similarly, even when controlled by the same party, the President's views may be opposed by members of his own party in the separated Congress. The constitutional structure thus molds the structure of party organization in the vital areas of policy, unity, and internal party discipline.

Major Characteristics of the American Party-Group System

American party politics appears as strange and unique to most foreign observers as Lyndon Johnson's Texas drawl or ten-gallon hat. For instance, most Americans see important differences between Republicans and Democrats, but foreigners often find it hard to tell them apart. And they are understandably puzzled by a political system without profoundly differentiated parties, while most Americans take for granted that Republicans and Democrats differ enough. Americans easily pick out detailed differences among their familiar political trees, but fail to see the overall likeness of the forest. Let us begin with the broader perspective of foreign observers and seek out the overall distinguishing characteristics of the American party-group system.

The Two-Party Pattern

The next President of the United States will be a Republican or a Democrat! No doubt this statement does not impress the reader with the predictive powers of political scientists. Yet its very triteness derives from near-perfect reliability. And only somewhat less perfect is the probability that the same two-party alternative will apply at every level—from senators and congressmen, to governors and state legislators, to mayors and city councilmen. It is a fundamental feature of American politics that there are only two major parties.

Although trite to Americans, the two-party pattern is a remarkable phenomenon of political behavior. Its recurrence requires millions of individuals, spread over a vast continent with varied interests and views, to limit their votes to the same two-party alternative. Yet, as the saying goes, 'This is a free country.' Voting is by secret ballot. Millions are legally qualified to hold office. Anyone eligible may become a candidate, organize a new group, and seek the endorsement of thousands of existing groups. The salient fact remains that American voters habitually but voluntarily ignore candidates not nominated by one of the two major political parties.

Minor parties. Nonetheless, numerous minor parties regularly contend for presidential and other elective offices. The strongest presidential bids have been made by temporary split-offs from a major party, like the Progressives who bolted the Republicans in 1912 behind ex-President Theodore Roosevelt, or the Dixiecrat bolters from the Democratic party who ran J. Strom Thurmond, of South Carolina, in 1948. But these were intraparty maneuvers more than serious bids to establish new major parties; by temporary withdrawal the bolters were trying to punish and thus influence the parent party.

Occasionally minor parties attain major party status on a local level. The 1948 Dixiecrats, a national minority, were the majority in some states and localities. Socialist mayors once were common in such cities as Reading, Pennsylvania; Bridgeport and Norwalk, Connecticut; and Milwaukee, Wisconsin. Milwaukee voters even elected a Socialist congressman on occasion. In Wisconsin state elections, during the 1930s, the Progressive party provided the major opposition to the Republicans, the Democrats running third. The Minnesota Farmer-Labor party functioned similarly on the state level about the same time.

Overwhelmingly, however, American minor parties—particularly the programmatically extreme movements—have been electorally impotent. Still they run candidates because their real purpose is not immediate electoral success. Though more imaginative followers may be sustained by the fantasy that a revolutionary change in voting behavior is imminent, most American minor parties typically have other aims than immediate success at the polls. The bolters from major parties seek increased factional power within their home-party organization. The ideological and limited-issue minor parties utilize election campaigns to publicize their teachings and leading spokesmen, some hoping for ultimate electoral success, others building toward victory by extraconstitutional means.[21]

---

[21] The Federal Communications Act requirement that all candidates receive "equal time" on television and radio gives minor parties an immense publicity opportunity. Thus a dozen or more minor parties create difficulties for broadcasters by demanding their "equal time." It took a special act of Congress to exempt the 1960 Kennedy-Nixon television debates from the requirement.

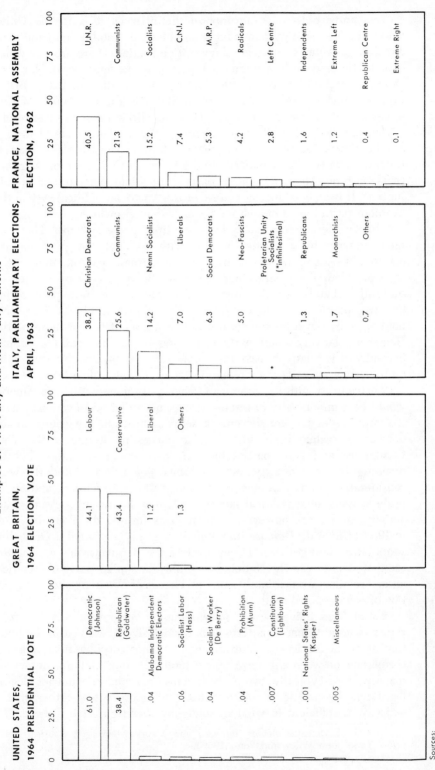

PARTY PERCENTAGES OF POPULAR VOTES
Examples of Two-Party and Multi-Party Patterns

UNITED STATES,
1964 PRESIDENTIAL VOTE

61.0	Democratic (Johnson)
38.4	Republican (Goldwater)
.04	Alabama Independent Democratic Electors
.06	Socialist Labor (Hass)
.04	Socialist Worker (De Berry)
.04	Prohibition (Munn)
.007	Constitution (Lightburn)
.001	National States' Rights (Kasper)
.005	Miscellaneous

GREAT BRITAIN,
1964 ELECTION VOTE

44.1	Labour
43.4	Conservative
11.2	Liberal
1.3	Others

ITALY, PARLIAMENTARY ELECTIONS,
APRIL, 1963

38.2	Christian Democrats
25.6	Communists
14.2	Nenni Socialists
7.0	Liberals
6.3	Social Democrats
5.0	Neo-Fascists
*	Proletarian Unity Socialists (*infinitesimal)
1.3	Republicans
1.7	Monarchists
0.7	Others

FRANCE, NATIONAL ASSEMBLY
ELECTION, 1962

40.5	U.N.R.
21.3	Communists
15.2	Socialists
7.4	C.N.I.
5.3	M.R.P.
4.2	Radicals
2.8	Left Centre
1.6	Independents
1.2	Extreme Left
0.4	Republican Centre
0.1	Extreme Right

Sources:
U.S.: *Congressional Quarterly*, Dec. 16, 1964, p. 2791;
Great Britain: *Keesing's Contemporary Archives* 1963-64, pp. 20, 349;
Italy: *The New York Times*, Nov. 25, 1964;
France: *Keesing's Contemporary Archives* 1963-64, pp. 19, 164.

Two-party pattern is uncommon. Familiar as it is in the United States, the two-party system is far from universal. Totalitarian (and many dictatorial) regimes suppress all opposition parties. There are many such nations—the free world is but a small portion of the total world. Nor is the two-party pattern universal even among democratic countries. Britain supplies a close parallel to the United States in the alternation of Conservative and Labour governments. However, Britain is sometimes termed a "two-and-one-half" party system because of persistent electoral strength for the Liberal party. Once the major alternative to the Conservatives, Liberals have not won a majority in the House of Commons for over forty years. Yet no American minor party can obtain comparable popular support. It is an outstanding feature of the American political system that its minor parties are so much more minor than elsewhere.

Most modern democracies have multiple party systems. There are three or more major parties, usually with no single party obtaining a majority of seats in the legislature. These are usually parliamentary rather than presidential systems, chief executives being elected by the legislature rather than by popular suffrage. Typically, the multiple party system has two notable consequences. The first is cabinet instability. Executives hold office by the sufferance of a fragile coalition of two or more parties. Hence a relatively small party can bring down the coalition cabinet. Secondly, it is relatively easy for a new party, even though representing quite narrow interests or extreme ideologies, to obtain legislative seats.

The contrast with the American system is profound. What in America would be a minor party or interest group, not to be taken seriously as an electoral contender, can become a serious threat to the constitutional-democratic system itself where major parties proliferate easily. Thus, Communist and Nazi parties have their American imitators, but the dynamics of the two-party system inhibits their growth. Similarly, while considerable antitax sentiment exists among American retailers and service trade artisans, their political tactics are largely limited to pressure group activity. In France, however, such interests formed the Poujadist party in 1953 (*Union de Défense du Commerce et de l'Artisanat*). Only three years later, they got over 11 per cent of the popular votes and elected some 40 deputies to the National Assembly. A similar party of American antitax retailers would simply stand no chance of obtaining such a proportion of congressional seats.

Ballot form influence on party number. What produces two-party rather than multi-party patterns is not conclusively resolved in the literature of political science.[22] But among the major considerations is a high correlation between the form of electoral balloting and the number of major parties. Typically, two party systems are found in countries electing legislators by simple *plurality* votes (the most votes, rather than a majority, is sufficient to win) in *single-member* legislative districts. The

---

[22] Cf. E. E. Schattschneider, *op. cit.*; and Maurice Duverger, *Political Parties* (New York: John Wiley and Sons, 1959).

United States and Great Britain are prime examples. By contrast, there is a near-perfect correlation between multi-party systems and balloting by some form of Proportional Representation (P.R.). This entails multi-member legislative districts and a somewhat complicated mode whereby voters indicate relative preferences among a number of candidates. The difference is that the single-member district plurality vote system exaggerates the victory of the winning party at the expense of the losers, whereas P.R. awards every party a number of legislative seats proportionate to its strength in the electorate. Under the former design minor parties are sharply discouraged; under P.R. parties naturally proliferate. In this way, formal ballot structure significantly shapes political behavior in different countries.

The Presidential Focus

The dominance of two major parties is closely related to another distinctive feature of the American party-group system—the centripetal influence of the Presidency. This highest governmental office exerts a powerful pull on everyone concerned with political power. Political leaders synchronize their organizational activity to the quadrennial politics of presidential elections. And the mass communications media reflect the entire citizenry's attention to presidential politics, far overshadowing that given any other governmental, religious, sports or entertainment figure. The Presidency engenders the greatest interest, turnout of voters, and political excitement.

As it tends to be the unifying organ of the governmental branches, the Presidency as the greatest prize in American politics performs a similar function in the party-group system. Despite technicalities of the electoral college system, every politician realistically assumes the practical necessity for obtaining a nationally distributed majority of popular votes to win the Presidency. Only a major party, with at least a minimum degree of internal unity, can put together the combination of voters needed to produce such a national consensus.

The presidential focus of American politics has many important consequences. For one thing, like the single-member district-plurality system, it is another harassment to the minor parties. Minor party candidates always flounder on their potential supporters' fears that they will be throwing away their votes. However friendly to a third party, most voters feel impelled to choose the 'lesser evil,' the less obnoxious of the two major candidates, one of whom undoubtedly will occupy the White House. Because of the constitutional design, minor parties cannot promise their supporters any share of electoral influence: Winning the Presidency is an all-or-none affair. By contrast, in a multi-party parliamentary system, minor party supporters are less discouraged by the 'lesser evil' fear; they know that if their party gets, say, only 10 per cent of the vote it may still be a decisive factor in forming the next government.

The presidential focus of American political life also helps explain the relative absence of local or regional parties unaffiliated with the national major parties. The Democrats and Republicans are the nationally advertised products—the name brands of the political market. These party labels, nationalized by the preeminent presidential candidacies, are too valuable to be ignored by most candidates for lesser office. Overwhelmingly, congressional, state, and local candidates utilize the national Democratic and Republican party labels to designate themselves as the major candidates between whom the real choice lies.

Within the two parties generally, the need to agree upon and work for a presidential candidate is tremendously unifying. When we recall the vast range of local and parochial interests striving for attention and influence, we can more fully appreciate the powerful nationalizing effect supplied by the presidential focus. For even with this great centripetal influence, the major American parties are remarkably decentralized organizations.

Decentralized Party Organization

Official Republican or Democratic organization charts can be misleading. Each seems to depict a hierarchical chain of command, with authority running down from top to bottom as in a business or military organization. But the actual power structure within American major parties is quite different, as Professor Schattschneider has emphasized.

> Decentralization of power is by all odds the most important single characteristic of the American major party; more than anything else this trait distinguishes it from all others. Indeed, once this truth is understood, nearly everything else about American parties is greatly illuminated.[23]

This unique trait is manifested in the simple fact that national major party leaders cannot control local usage of the party label. It is as if local bottling firms could label any beverage Coca-Cola without authorization by the national Coca-Cola Company. Even our most popular Presidents, Franklin D. Roosevelt for example, failed in efforts to withhold their party's nomination from programmatically unreliable legislators. In other nations, where nominations are passed on by central party committees, much stronger disciplinary sanctions restrain successful candidates from opposing their party on important issues. Both aspects of party decentralization—local rather than national power over party nominations and feeble national discipline over the party's elected office-holders—are distinctive elements of American politics. Strikingly, the informal distribution of power within both major parties closely parallels the formal constitutional power structure. We can best consider the complicated blend of formal and informal factors contributing to party decentralization under the

---

[23] Schattschneider, p. 129.

OFFICIAL REPUBLICAN PARTY ORGANIZATIONAL CHART

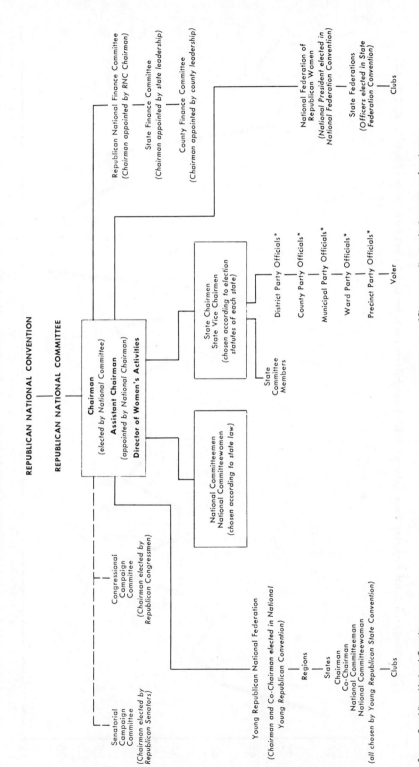

REPUBLICAN NATIONAL CONVENTION

REPUBLICAN NATIONAL COMMITTEE

Chairman
(elected by National Committee)
Assistant Chairman
(appointed by National Chairman)
Director of Women's Activities

Republican National Finance Committee
(Chairman appointed by RNC Chairman)

State Finance Committee
(Chairman appointed by state leadership)

County Finance Committee
(Chairman appointed by county leadership)

National Federation of
Republican Women
(National President elected in
National Federation Convention)

State Federations
(Officers elected in State
Federation Convention)

Clubs

State Chairmen
State Vice Chairmen
(chosen according to election
statutes of each state)

State
Committee
Members

District Party Officials*

County Party Officials*

Municipal Party Officials*

Ward Party Officials*

Precinct Party Officials*

Voter

National Committeemen
National Committeewomen
(chosen according to state law)

Senatorial
Campaign
Committee

(Chairman elected by
Republican Senators)

Congressional
Campaign
Committee

(Chairman elected by
Republican Congressmen)

Young Republican National Federation

(Chairman and Co-Chairman elected in National
Young Republican Convention)

Regions

States
Chairman
Co-Chairman
National Committeeman
National Committeewoman
(all chosen by Young Republican State Convention)

Clubs

*Chosen according to election statutes of each state

Source: Republican National Committee

Percentage of Total Popular Vote Obtained by Republican Presidential Candidate in the South* 1872-1964

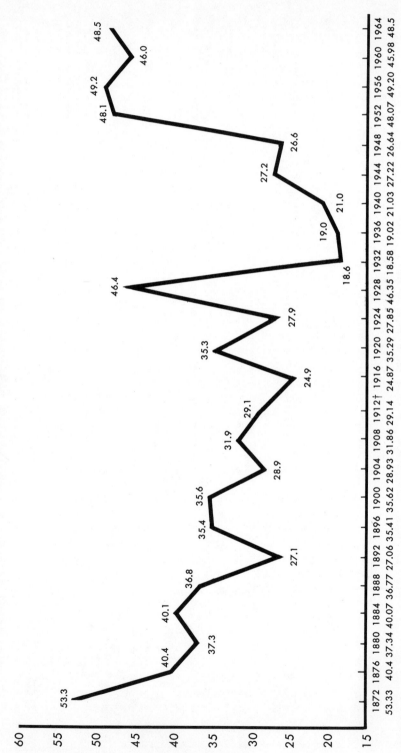

1872 1876 1880 1884 1888 1892 1896 1900 1904 1908 1912† 1916 1920 1924 1928 1932 1936 1940 1944 1948 1952 1956 1960 1964
53.33 40.4 37.34 40.07 36.77 27.06 35.41 35.62 28.93 31.86 29.14 24.87 35.29 27.85 46.35 18.58 19.02 21.03 27.22 26.64 48.07 49.20 45.98 48.5

(*Alabama, Arkansas, Florida, Georgia, Louisiana, Mississippi, N. Carolina, S. Carolina, Tennessee, Texas, Virginia)
†In 1912, Taft (Rep.) 12.45%
Roosevelt (Progressive) 16.70%

headings of the two structures that most affect that decentralization—federalism and separation of powers.

Federalism and party decentralization. The states under the federal Constitution supply fifty separate governmental bases for party organizations to develop. And each separate state party can wax powerful irrespective of national party defeats and independent of national party control. Consequently, the major American parties are often described as loose associations of largely autonomous state parties. President Eisenhower so instructed a news conference questioner on the limits of his position as party leader:

> Now, let's remember, there are no national parties in the United States. There are forty-eight state parties, . . . they are the ones that determine the people that belong to those parties. There is nothing I can do to say that . . . one is not a Republican. The most I can say is that in many things they do not agree with me. . . . We have got to remember that these are state organizations, and there is nothing I can do to say so-and-so is a Republican and so-and-so is not a Republican.[24]

Actually there is much more potential for national control in the Presidency than this suggests. The President's leadership is not lightly rebuffed, and valuable patronage and financial inducements are at his disposal. If he is popular with the voters, lesser candidates will seek to ride into office on his coat-tails. So when a popular President like Eisenhower publicly singles out certain "so-and-sos" to say "that in many things they do not agree with me," it is a burden not to be incurred frivolously.[25]

Nor is responsiveness to national leadership solely a matter of patronage and funds or threats of political reprisal. The President has ready access to state leaders; he will be heard, and he may be persuasive. There is a responsiveness by nationally ambitious men to national interests and issues. The arena of their ambition is broader than their immediate state power base. Presidents can utilize such leadership factors; significant variables are the popularity and competency which each President supplies to his position as chief of party.

The party system, in short, is federative (and national), not anarchic. There are some central controls. Bolters from the national ticket may be refused seats on the party national committee; on occasion too, congressional party caucuses have imposed penalties on bolters such as withdrawal of patronage and seniority rights, undesirable committee assignments, and even expulsion from the caucus.[26] Future combinations of

---

[24] Presidential press conference, October 11, 1956.

[25] Eisenhower brought pressure on the Illinois Republican senatorial candidate in 1954: "In April, I had told him I would not back him until he announced that he would support my program. Consequently, I remained silent on his candidacy until he gave public assurance that 'you can count on my loyalties and my support' as the junior senator from Illinois.'" Dwight D. Eisenhower, *Mandate for Change* (Garden City, N.Y.: Doubleday & Company, 1963), p. 433.

[26] Examples are the rejection of six Dixiecrats by the Democratic national committee in 1949, and the withdrawal of patronage from Congressman Adam Clayton

determined leadership and propitious circumstances could expand these precedents into more centralized organizational practices.

However, the fact of great party decentralization remains. It is one thing to hold the national party together on the basic item that stimulates its formation as a national entity, the national ticket; it is vastly more difficult for national leaders to exert influence on state and local organizations where the Presidency is not directly at stake.

By virtue of federalism, American state governments operate on a scale comparable to full-fledged nations. Many have as much or more territory and inhabitants. Consequently, not only the party organizations, but the whole political process is decentralized by federalism. Interest groups and lobbies, with their campaign contributions and propaganda apparatus, gravitate to these fifty centers of substantial government. The effect is cumulative: The interest groups seek influence by supplying state and local party organizational needs, and the state and local organizations are all the better able to maintain themselves independently of the national party's treasury and patronage.

Party decentralization is more than just a two-level system of national and state organizations. The proliferation of elective units and offices within each state supports considerable *intrastate* decentralization. The gross totals are astonishing: 100,000 local governments (including cities, counties, towns, school and special districts); more than 514,000 elective local officials; plus about 15,000 elective state officials. Even if refined down to an estimated 170,000 *important* state and local separately elected office-holders,[27] the stimulus to decentralization is enormous.

This stimulus to intrastate decentralization works in two ways. First, the existence of important and quasi-autonomous county and city governments has the same effect within each state that the fifty states have within the nation: It causes powerful party organizations to spring up at the level where important matters are being decided. Thus county and city party organizations often become substantially independent of the state party organization. Second, the proliferation of elective offices at the statewide level weakens the governorship as a centralizing factor. In the national government, only the Presidency is elective and all other administrative posts are appointive; this lessens the decentralizing potential of these other posts. But at the state level, numerous administrative officials such as secretaries of state, lieutenant governors, school superintendents, auditors, and the like are separately and independently elected. Access to these independent wielders of governmental authority is eagerly sought by interested groups, and considerable patronage is at their disposal to lubricate their own independently sustained personal and party machinery.

Powell, Jr. by the House Democratic patronage committee after Powell supported Eisenhower in 1956.

[27] These figures and estimates are from Herbert Kaufman, *Politics and Policies in State and Local Government* (Englewood Cliffs, N.J.: Prentice-Hall, 1963), p. 16.

Paradoxically, however, intrastate decentralization *increases* national party influence within the states. The tremendous pace of modern urbanization has resulted in much more important and direct contact between the national government and the cities. In addition to being 'a nation of states,' we are becoming also 'a nation of cities.' Powerful mayors in the larger cities increasingly deal directly with Washington, and many get a friendlier ear there than in their own state capitals. National party connections are useful in obtaining urban renewal programs, federal installations, government contracts for local producers, etc. This has led to some nationalization of the entire political process, including party organizational leadership.

Within each state, centripetal influences similar to the presidential focus at the national level restrain the system from utter fragmentation. The existence of other independently elected state officers has been a handicap, but powerful factors of executive leadership are increasingly provided in the gubernatorial office. Governors are statewide celebrities and in the populous states acquire national prominence as potential presidential candidates. And they provide a central, though far from exclusive, office for dispensing patronage and steering campaign contributions to loyal party candidates.

In summarizing, let us recall the important difference between the American compoundly federal-and-national system and a purely federal system (see pp. 42–46). While the federal elements decentralize the relation between national and state party organizations, the national elements of the system countervailingly pull the state parties into the vortex of national politics. Professor Key forcefully described this dual tendency:

> When considering the problem of organization for the conduct of state politics one fact of fundamental importance must be kept firmly in mind: the American states operate, not as independent and autonomous political entities, but as units of the nation. Within the states public attention cannot be focused sharply on state affairs undistracted by extraneous factors; political divisions cannot occur freely on state questions alone: national issues, national campaigns, and national parties project themselves into the affairs of states. Political parties within the states become at times but the shadow of their national counterparts, and always the states' position in the federal system profoundly affects the form and character of their politics.[28]

Separation of powers and party decentralization. At the outset we noted the lack or feebleness in America of two centralizing controls commonly available to party leaders in other countries: national control over party nominations and programmatic discipline over elected officials. In discussing the influence of federalism on decentralization, we emphasized state control over nominations. Here we emphasize the second

---

[28] V. O. Key, Jr., *American State Politics* (New York: Alfred A. Knopf, 1956), p. 18.

factor, the weakness of American major party leaders in holding national elected officials to the party line on issues.

Four linked constitutional features weaken central party discipline: separation of the executive from the legislature, bicameralism, staggered and fixed terms of office. Their decentralizing effect is best seen in contrast with parliamentary systems where these features are absent. Under a parliamentary form of government, Congress would elect one of its own members President of the United States. The party with a majority of seats would control that choice; hence the President (and his Cabinet) would be comprised of the congressional majority party's leadership. Such a President might seem very weak, beholden for his tenure on the continuing support of the legislature (in comparison with the constitutionally *fixed* four-year term). However, the President and his fellow party leaders would have a powerful inducement for securing that continuing support. The parliamentary congressman's term would also be flexible rather than fixed for a specified period. By parliamentary practice, should Congress defeat a major administration-sponsored bill, the President could dissolve Congress and schedule new elections. Each parliamentary legislator knows that a vote against his party's leadership may well be a vote to send himself back into the labor and expense of a campaign—with the risk of defeat. A majority party in a parliamentary government, therefore, tends towards disciplined unity because continued tenure in office for all is jeopardized by anything that dissolves the 'Administration's' majority.

The actual American Constitution, of course, separates the legislature and executive. Congress does not choose the President (except in the rare absence of an Electoral College majority); nor may the President be concurrently a member of either house. Congress and President are separately elected for constitutionally fixed periods which cannot be altered by strategic decisions of party leaders. Add bicameralism and staggered terms of office, and the relative freedom of elected officials from party discipline on legislative issues increases even more. The upshot of these factors is that each office-holder is constitutionally on his own. The party leadership cannot punish him by altering his term of office no matter how he votes.

The uniquely American mid-term election exemplifies the decentralizing tendency. These are congressional elections—the entire House of Representatives plus one third of the Senate—occurring at the mid-point of every presidential term. This is the low point of the presidential focus when local constituency issues predominate. Despite national party efforts to impart a national theme and to supply organizational aid, each candidate tends to regard his situation individually. Candidates are torn between national loyalties and the requirements of winning election in a state or district during a time of minimal national emphasis.

The relationship between the constitutional structures and the party system is a two-way process: The separation of powers helps decentralize the parties, but decentralized parties also help protect the separation of powers. A dominant, homogeneous, and disciplined party could bring all the separated branches under its centralized control. Without party decentralization, the formal, constitutional separation of powers could thus be nullified in practice. But with decentralized parties, President and Congress retain separate identities and characteristics, and frequently are at odds, even when one party has the Presidency and a majority in both houses of Congress. Yet, while party decentralization makes for conflict between the branches when one party is in power, it has the opposite effect when the branches are divided between the parties. When Republicans control one branch and the Democrats the other, the tendency to deadlock between President and Congress (or between House and Senate) would increase if each party were centralized, homogeneous, and more radically divided on issues. American party decentralization makes it possible for the branches to agree even if the President is a Democrat while the Republicans control one or both houses of Congress.[29]

Diversity and Tenuousness of Major Party Membership

America is called 'a nation of joiners' because so many belong to so many organizations. But there is one organization most people tend *not* to join in any formal sense of the word—'the party of their choice.' People are usually Democrats or Republicans in a vague and loose way that parallels the looseness of party structure. And those who formally join do so in a variety of ways and with minimal obligations. Because of the federative, decentralized, and relatively undisciplined character of the major parties, there is no single way to participate in national party organization. Participation in the national party structures—national conventions, national committees, congressional campaign committees—actually rests on a variety of state and local constituency membership bases. Disciplinary weakness reduces programmatic cohesiveness and partisan obligation among the general membership. Just as congressmen maintain party identity with minimal fidelity to national party leaders or policies, so does the party membership. And beyond the actual members, millions deem themselves faithful party adherents despite programmatic inconsistencies and without undertaking any membership obligations at all.

[29] This combination of separated powers and decentralized and undisciplined parties makes American politics partially resemble multi-party parliamentary systems. The American presidential system, where the majority (presidential) party cannot count on the full support of its own members in the legislature, parallels the multi-party system where the parliamentary majority (executive-cabinet) is a coalition of minority parties. In both cases, support *across* party lines is needed for bills to pass. A Democratic President usually needs, and because of decentralization can obtain, the support of Republican legislators. An Italian coalition Premier similarly needs support from legislators affiliated with other parties to operate the government. In this respect, American government is closer to the Italian or other multi-party systems than it is to the British form of disciplined two-party government.

Becoming a Democrat or a Republican is very different from joining the Girl Scouts, the John Birch Society, the United Automobile Workers union, or pledging oneself to a college fraternity. It is also in striking contrast to membership in minor political parties. The minor parties, like most membership organizations, generally conduct initiation rites, require fidelity to the organization's rules and purposes, and expel those who do not fulfill their responsibilities. Membership responsibilities range from mere dues-payment to acceptance of quasi-military discipline, as in revolutionary and authoritarian movements. Few of the millions calling themselves Democrats or Republicans are party members in any of these ways.

What then is the nature of adherence to the major American parties? Three basic types will be examined: hardcore activists, the party in the government, and the party in the electorate.

Hardcore activists. These are the people who join affiliated party clubs, pay dues, or perform organizational tasks. They do the party's work, from lowly precinct captains to the national chairman. There are some 3,000 counties in the United States, and these are further divided into town, ward, and precinct units for electoral work. Recruiting tens of thousands of party workers to man these units is extremely difficult, and many precincts are poorly organized. Here patronage plays its vital role in obtaining faithful campaign workers. For example, employees of automotive licensing offices may provide a statewide network of party workers. Other public agencies are similarly politically employed. The 'spoils system,' 'machine politics,' and 'boss rule' form the seamy but vital side of this distinctly American mode of professionalized political organization. Because American major parties are not ideological movements, few campaign workers are idealistically motivated enthusiasts. However, idealistic amateurs in some places do much doorbell-ringing, and often advise party leaders on issues and candidates, thereby advancing their policies.[30]

The party in the government. Members of party caucuses within the government are officials elected on the party's ticket. Though membership responsibilities and discipline sometimes sit lightly on congressional shoulders when bills are voted, caucus membership is essential to partake in party legislative decisions and to be eligible for such plums as the speakership, desirable committee assignments, and patronage. Some office-holders are of course also hardcore activists; Senate Majority Leader Mansfield is as deeply Democratic, and Minority Leader Dirksen as deeply Republican, as any precinct captain. Yet the requirement of electoral success, *constituency popularity*, makes it possible for many party office-holders to be less pronouncedly partisan than hardcore activists. A precinct captain or a national chairman is chosen for partisan reliability, not for broad nonpartisan appeal, whereas many party candidates are

[30] James Q. Wilson, *The Amateur Democrat* (Chicago: University of Chicago Press, 1962).

The barricade.

Most Americans greatly admire the country's leading national political figures, but at the same time have a very jaundiced view of the 'typical politician.' This hostile view of politicians may indeed, as the cartoon suggests, deter, some young people from following political careers.

precisely so chosen. The party usually wants a broadly popular candidate, not one known only as a party man. And, where direct primaries are held, it gets such men whether party leaders want them or not; primary laws require the parties to accept as official candidates whomever the primary voters elect, whatever his beliefs or record of party loyalty. Consequently, membership in the American 'party in the government' is quite tenuous, especially by contrast with parties in other governments.

The party in the electorate. At the level of the general electorate, membership becomes very tenuous indeed. Two kinds of party adherents may be distinguished. Some formally register as Democrats or Republicans where state laws require prior party registration in order to vote in the party nominating primary. However, this is not a particularly strong membership bond. Ranney and Kendall estimate that only about 10 to 30 per cent of enrolled Democrats and Republicans turn out to vote in their party's primary contests.[31] Most Americans fall into a second, even more tenuously partisan grouping. These are voters who merely think of themselves as Democrats or Republicans. When asked by survey interviewers most people regularly indicate a clear preference between the major parties, but only one third volunteer a *strong* partisan choice. And a still smaller number participate in any party activities beyond voting.[32] This 'smaller number' of participants in party activities, however, runs into millions—an impressive testimonial to American political

[31] *Op. cit.,* p. 200.
[32] Cf. A. Campbell, P. E. Converse, W. E. Miller and D. E. Stokes, *The American Voter* (New York: John Wiley and Sons, 1960), pp. 91 and 124.

E JOHN BIRCH SOCIETY
INCORPORATED

Belmont, Massachusetts

Local Address:
SUITE 1004
1028 CONNECTICUT AVENUE, N. W.
WASHINGTON, D. C. 20036

ounder

NATIONAL 4-H CLUB FOUND

7100 CONNECTICUT AVENUE   •   WASHINGTON, D.

Telephone: (Code 301) OLiver 6-9000   •   Cable NATFOUR, Washi

LEAGUE OF WOMEN VOTERS
OF THE UNITED STATES

00 SEVENTEENTH STREET, N. W., WASHINGTON, D. C. 20036 TEL. 296-1770
Mrs. Robert J. Stuart, President

Americans
for **D**emocratic
Action

MRS. FRANKLIN D. ROOSEVELT   REINHOLD NIEBUI
1947-1962   Honorary Chairman

DON EDWARDS   EDMOND F. ROVN
National Chairman   Chairman, Executive

REGINALD H. ZALLES   LEON SHULL
Treasurer   National Director

MRS. JANE J. BUCHENHOLZ
Secretary

1223 Connecticut Ave., N.W., Washington, D. C. 20036, Tel. 628-254:

ERICAN FEDERATION OF LABOR AND CONGRESS OF INDUSTRIAL ORGANIZATIONS

EXECUTIVE COUNCIL

GEORGE MEANY   WM. F. SCHNITZLER
PRESIDENT   SECRETARY-TREASURER

WALTER P. REUTHER   GEORGE M. HARRISON   HARRY C. BATES
WM. C. BIRTHRIGHT   JAMES B. CAREY   DAVID DUBINSKY
DAVID J. McDONALD   EMIL RIEVE   WM. L. McFETRIDGE
JOSEPH CURRAN   MAURICE A. HUTCHESON A. J. HAYES
JOSEPH D. KEENAN   JACOB S. POTOFSKY   A. PHILIP RANDOLPH
RICHARD F. WALSH   LEE W. MINTON   JOSEPH A. BEIRNE
JAMES A. SUFFRIDGE O. A. KNIGHT   KARL F. FELLER
PAUL L. PHILLIPS   PETER T. SCHOEMANN L. M. RAFTERY
PAUL HALL   HERMAN D. KENIN   JOHN J. GROGAN

EXECUTIVE COMMITTEE

GEORGE MEANY
WALTER P. REUTHER
GEORGE M. HARRISON
JAMES B. CAREY
HARRY C. BATES
DAVID J. McDONALD
DAVID DUBINSKY
WM. F. SCHNITZLER

815 SIXTEENTH STREET, N.W.
WASHINGTON 6, D. C.   NATIONAL 8-3870

NATIONAL CONFEDERATION of AMERICAN ETHNIC

562 Davis Building   •   Washington, D. C. 20006   •   T

NATIONAL PRESIDENT
Hon. Blair F. Gunther
Former Judge, Pennsylvania
Superior Appellate Court,
Former Board Chairman,
Polish National Alliance

*B'*NAI *B'*RITH *Y*OUTH *O*RGANIZATIO

1640 RHODE ISLAND AVENUE, N.W. • WASHINGTON, D.C.   20036 • EXECUTIVE 3

ational *Education* *Association*
IAL COMMISSION ON TEACHER EDUCATION
AND PROFESSIONAL STANDARDS
STUDENT NATIONAL EDUCATION ASSOCIATION
FUTURE TEACHERS OF AMERICA

1201 SIXTEEI
WASHINGTON,
ADAMS 4-484

socialist party / social democratic feder:

1182 BROADWAY   •   NEW YORK 1, N. Y.   •   LEXINGTON 2

American Temperance Soc

NATIONAL HEADQUARTERS
6840 Eastern Avenue, N.W.
Washington, D.C. 20012

VETERANS OF FOREIGN WARS
OF THE UNITED STATES
FOUNDED 1899

OFFICE OF
EXECUTIVE DIRECTOR
WASHINGTON OFFICE

V. F. W. MEMORIAL BUILDING
200 MARYLAND AVENUE, N. E.
WASHINGTON 2, D. C.

INVESTMENT BANKERS
Association of America

425 Thirteenth Street, N. W., Washington, D. C. 20004
EXecutive 3-3366

PRESIDENT
WENDELL W. WITTER

VICE PRESIDENTS
GEORGE W. ELKINS, JR.
JOHN P. LABOUISSE
WILLIAM F. MORGAN
ALBERT PRATT
FRANCIS R. SCHANCK

GOVERNORS
RUCKER ALEX
A. LOWRIE APPLEGATE
LEO H. BARICH
ROBERT H. B. BALDWIN
WILLIS H. BLAKELY

ALAN K. BROWNE
HARRISON CLARKE
A. HALSEY COOK
J. IAN CROOKSTON
JOHN W. McMILRAU
JACK O. DOERGE
BAYARD DOMINICK
ALLEN C. DuBOIS
HARVEY B. GRAM, JR.
WILLIAM G. HARDING
DAVID J. HARRIS
ELMER G. HASSMAN
CHARLES J. HODGE
ARTHUR HORTON
B. F. HOUSTON
HERBERT D. HUNTER

FRANCIS
JOSEPH
ROBERT
WILLIAM
EDGAR N
SAMPSO
RUSSELL
FREDERI
HERMAN
DAVID B
KENNET
MILTON
FRANK I
RICHARD
WHEELOR
CARLTON

American associations represent a wide variety of interests and views.

involvement, despite the casualness and tenuousness of party 'membership.'

Diversity and Power of Interest Groups

"In no country of the world has the principle of association been more successfully used, or more unsparingly applied to a multitude of different objects, than in America."[33] Tocqueville's observation applies as well today. Interest groups are important in all democracies, but their diversity and power are particularly great in the United States. An authoritative estimate found some twenty thousand national associations plus an even greater number of locally organized groups.[34] Of course, not all are of political interest. Some, like the National Association for the Advancement of Colored People, are almost constantly involved with government; others, like a movie star's fan club, almost never. And circumstances involve groups differently at different times. The American Medical Association (AMA), formed to promote professional standards and uniform licensing practices, became increasingly political in opposition to 'socialized medicine' proposals.

The greatest number of politically concerned groups arises out of economic interests—James Madison's "most common and durable source of factions." The significant characteristic of American economic interest groups is their number, which is in turn the result of their fragmentation and diversity. This diversity is frequently obscured by an oversimplified division of economic groups into business, labor, and farm categories.[35] Yet from the perspective of countries with more homogeneous economic classes, diversity is the salient feature of the American group system. "What surprises the European student of the American political process is the lack of concentration of effort by the important power blocs."[36] Neither capital, nor labor, nor agriculture speak politically with a single authoritative voice.

The American Federation of Labor–Congress of Industrial Organizations (AFL-CIO) does not even speak for all of organized labor, let alone all workers. Only about a third of all nonagricultural workers are union members, and powerful independent unions like the Teamsters feud with the AFL-CIO. And within the AFL-CIO itself, the old-line craft and the newer industrial unions are in frequent conflict. Similarly, only one third of the farmers belong to agricultural associations. These are divided into "a bewildering array"[37] of crop and marketing cooperatives, in addition to the major American Farm Bureau Federation, National

---

[33] Tocqueville, *op. cit.*, I, 191.

[34] Jay Judkins, ed., *National Associations of the United States* (Washington, D.C.: Department of Commerce, 1949).

[35] Cf. David B. Truman on "Classifications of Interest Groups," *op. cit.*, pp. 63–65.

[36] D. W. Brogan and Douglas V. Verney, *Political Patterns in Today's World* (New York: Harcourt, Brace and World, Inc., 1963), p. 34.

[37] Truman, *op. cit.*, p. 87.

JOSEPH F. CARLINO
CHAIRMAN
CIVIL RIGHTS AND IMMIGRATION

Roy Wilkins, executive secretary of the National Association for the Advancement of Colored People, urges a subcommittee of the Republican Party's 1960 Party Platform Committee to draft a strongly pro-civil rights plank.

Grange, and Farmers Union. Here, too, diversity is the rule of American associational life.

Businessmen are better organized,[38] but no more as a homogeneous capitalist class than in the case of workers or farmers. Neither the National Association of Manufacturers nor the Chamber of Commerce of the United States can speak for all businessmen. Each contains highly competitive firms, often on opposing sides of legislative battles. Moreover, about one million firms belong to some fifteen thousand additional national trade associations.[39] This is a staggering statistic; small wonder that British political scientists, Professors Brogan and Verney, find "nothing comparable in weight and influence to the Federation of British Industries or the Swedish Employers' Confederation"[40] in American politics.

The complexity and fluidity of American politics is also increased by the multiplicity of places at which interest groups must exert pressure. "The business community operates at a variety of levels of government, often as individual firms or industries, as well as through a number of organizations. . . ."[41] The same is true for all political groups; they

[38] Cf. E. E. Schattschneider, *The Semisovereign People* (New York: Holt, Rinehart and Winston, 1960), pp. 31–34.
[39] *National Associations of the United States, op. cit.*, p. vii.
[40] Brogan and Verney, *op. cit.*, p. 34.
[41] *Idem.*

gravitate to every level where governmental power affects their interests. Swedish and British political life is highly concentrated in Stockholm and London; American politics is far more kaleidoscopic. The diversity of interest groups, thus, is of a piece with the decentralized and federalized character of American government and parties. Interest groups fragment and specialize, in part, because they have a great variety of fragmented and specialized portions of political power to deal with.

For example, British or Swedish interests, however particularized they might wish to remain, *must* combine because they confront relatively disciplined, centralized party organizations. A British M.P. dares not break party ranks on a significant vote no matter how much pressure the local industrial giant may bring to bear. In the United States, a congressman is far freer to respond to such pressure and, therefore, gets more pressure. The weakness of centralized party power within the legislative chamber entails the increased power of interest groups in the lobby. In sum, American interest groups are both more fragmented into narrowly particularized interests and also more powerful in influencing individual officials than are the organized interests of other democratic countries.

Programmatic Similarities and Differences

Unlike pressure groups that concentrate on their specialized interest, parties campaign to become the government. The major parties necessarily deal with the full range of current national problems. Moreover, they must appeal broadly to greatly divergent interests to weld together an electoral majority. And that must be the *next majority*, not, as for minor parties, a subsequent awakening of a *future majority* for socialism or some other ultimate goal. Major party programs are aimed at winning the coming election and assuming responsibility for governing.

The present distribution of opinion in the United States makes it a practical necessity that a *majority* party be a *moderate* party. Democrats and Republicans fight hard, but not so bitterly as parties do in many other countries (or as Americans did in the years leading to the Civil War). The outstanding characteristic of the American party system is that the parties are not locked in struggle over life and death issues. Contrast the German election of 1932 when Hitler's Nazi party and the opposing parties proclaimed utterly opposed conceptions of the nature of the regime—with jail and death the loser's portion. Professor Duverger points out that "in France and Italy political warfare . . . is not concerned with subsidiary principles but with the very foundations of the state and the nature of the regime."[42] The strong Communist parties contest for election with the democratic parties, but the Communists "do not accept Western democracy, do not agree with a pluralism of parties which they

---

[42] Maurice Duverger, *op. cit.*, p. 419.

would replace by a single party, and do not recognize any right of opposition or of freedom of speech for all."[43] Nations with elections between such deeply antagonistic major parties hover constantly on the verge of constitutional suicide. Religious schism can also cause 'regime-question' politics. In Belgium even the trade unions are organized separately on religious lines, and the perennial struggle between Flemish and Walloon is conducted by each side with the feeling that its very basis as an ethnic and religious community is at stake.

The contest between American Democrats and Republicans is normally pallid by contrast. So pallid, that it is commonly viewed from abroad as no contest at all. Indeed many Americans agree with Lord Bryce that the Republican and Democratic parties are like "two bottles, both empty, but bearing different labels."[44] On this view, whatever historical differences produced the two major parties originally, nothing but the battle between ins and outs distinguishes them now.

Tweedledum and Tweedledee? Up to a point, the claim is well-founded that the dominant American parties have no significant programmatic differences. Republicans and Democrats do agree on the fundamental nature of the regime. They both take for granted constitutional essentials like separation of powers, federalism, judicial review, and representative government. Both parties accept the basic ingredients of a stable democratic political order: popular election, peaceful succession to office, and loyal opposition to the victorious party by the organized minority.

Similarly, though there is a greater likelihood that Protestants (outside the South) will be Republicans and that Catholics and Jews will be Democrats, the parties are not tied to any religious organizations. Both parties endorse the fundamental separation of church and state, thus minimizing the possibility of religiously based political controversy. There is substantial agreement, too, on the essentials of a privately owned and operated economy. Party differences on public regulation are within the framework of predominantly private enterprise.

Lord Bryce's quip is erroneous. The American parties are not "*empty* bottles"; rather, the important bulk of their contents is the *same*. Tocqueville was more perceptive: "In a country like the United States, in which the differences of opinion are mere differences of hue, the right of association may remain unrestrained without evil consequences."[45] Fundamental consensus moderates the fierceness of the party struggle.

Differences between the parties. But, if Democrats and Republicans do not battle in the streets, and if extremist parties with sharp ideological differences are but minor parties under American conditions, there are nonetheless important "differences of hue" between Democrats and Re-

---

[43] *Idem.*

[44] James Bryce, *Modern Democracies*, vol. II (New York: Macmillan, 1927), p. 115.

[45] *Op. cit.*, I, 197.

publicans. We cannot catalog these in detail, but the fact of real difference can be illustrated by examining three areas where partisan stands can be seen: national party platforms, congressional votes on important issues, and public perceptions of party differences.

The national party platforms are too often lightly dismissed as statements of alternative positions. True, much of the language is contrived to blur rather than expose controversial stands; platform writers strive to attract the supporters of a policy with minimal repulsion of its opponents. But the platforms are not written only for the general public, few of whom actually examine them; rather, they are viewed closely by particular groups with interest-sensitized eyes whose support may well be needed in the coming election. Some planks actually originate with interest groups, though modified to suit a more broadly aimed policy statement. Platforms may not firmly bind party office-holders, which is another matter, but they do present discernible alternatives on important issues. Professor Turner reports:

> Analysis of the platforms of 1948 . . . reveals collisions in ideology and differences in emphasis which could hardly escape a serious reader. Democrats advocated repeal of the Taft-Hartley Act; Republicans commended themselves for having passed it. Republicans advocated "prudent conservation of resources" in foreign aid programs; Democrats boasted that "generous sums have been provided." Republicans promised another reduction in taxes, especially to provide an incentive to new industry; Democrats advocated a reduction, when possible, for low-income groups only. Republicans advocated either voluntary cooperation, or state and local control of public policies; Democrats pointed to a long list of federal legislation enacted by their party.[46]

Congressional votes on important issues seldom divide on straight party lines, yet no other factor is more important than party in forming voting alignments. Generalizing the results of a number of empirical studies, Professors Ranney and Kendall offer four major areas of party difference in congressional divisions:

> (1) The Democrats in Congress generally vote for lowering tariffs; the Republicans generally vote for maintaining or increasing them. (2) The Democrats generally favor a tax structure with a narrow base and high surtaxes on large incomes; the Republicans generally favor a tax structure with a broad base and low surtaxes on large incomes. (3) The Democrats generally favor federal regulation of wages and hours; the Republicans generally oppose it. (4) The Democrats generally favor public ownership or regulation of public utilities (particularly electric power); the Republicans generally oppose it. On most other issues— public works, states' rights, armaments, veterans' claims, women's rights, the merit system, etc.—both parties show a low degree of cohesion. . . .[47]

---

[46] Julius Turner, "Responsible Parties: A Dissent From the Floor," *American Political Science Review*, XLV (March 1951), 144.

[47] Ranney and Kendall, *op. cit.*, pp. 396–97.

Public perceptions of party differences reveal the same thing. Between two thirds and three fourths of the electorate believe the parties are markedly different in viewpoint and in the interests favored. The Roper Public Opinion Center at Williams College reports:

> The polls tend to verify the commonly accepted caricature that the Democratic Party is the party of the poor and of labor and the Republican Party is the party of business and of the rich. In the field of foreign policy the public sees little difference between the parties, although at times it has given a slight edge to the Republican Party as the more successful avoider of open combat.[48]

In each of these areas of partisan difference—platforms, congressional voting patterns, and public opinion—the most striking difference is found in those questions of socioeconomic policy which are generally labeled 'left' and 'right,' or 'liberal' and 'conservative.' In America the party struggle is greatly moderated, as we have seen, by constitutional consensus and the fragmentation of economic and other interests. But there remain what may be called 'muted-regime questions'—questions, that is, which in other countries with less consensus and with greater differences between rich and poor produce extreme ideological cleavage between the parties. But these "differences of hue" are real enough, and the bedrock layer of strength within the Republican party can easily be distinguished from the bedrock Democrats on central issues of extending the 'welfare state,' government spending, friendliness to organized labor, etc.

---

[48] Quoted by Clinton Rossiter, *Parties and Politics in America* (Ithaca: Cornell University Press, 1960), p. 150.

At the same time the parties are drawn together by a dynamic consequence of the two-party pattern as it operates within a fundamental
consensus: Where there are only two major parties there is a strong
tendency for them to make overlapping appeals to the electorate. The
precise line separating party supporters in the electorate cannot be known,
and the parties cannot afford to satisfy only their hard-core backers. The
strongest partisans are so firmly committed that, within limits, they have
nowhere else to go. Those in the center of public opinion, however, of
moderate views and tenuous party identifications, are more easily moved
from one to the other party from election to election. (About one fourth
of the eligible voters fit this category.[49]) In the United States and Great
Britain, the two major parties fear to offend this less committed center.
The result is that programmatic differences between the parties tend to be
moderated.

Differences within the parties. The "differences of hue" which dif-
ferentiate hard-core Democrats from rock-ribbed Republicans also exist
within each party: Liberal and conservative wings in each deviate from
the central tendencies previously described. The Republican Old Guard
(including not a few young conservatives) are the bedrock of Republicanism, but the Grand Old Party includes such stalwart liberals as
Governor Rockefeller and Senator Javits of New York. And the Democratic bedrock of New Deal, Fair Deal, and Great Society liberalism is
continually embarrassed and frustrated by Democratic conservatives, like
economy-minded Senator Harry Byrd of Virginia. And when the currently vital civil-rights issue is examined, the Democratic label is torn
and shredded between northern and southern wings.

Geographical distribution of internal party differences is more than
an accidental pattern. Regionally centered programmatic variations developed corresponding with the dominant interest of a geographical section.
The peculiarities of the eleven states making up the Civil War Confederacy produced a distinctive bloc within the Democratic party that
has continuing importance. Similarly, within the Republican party, the
senators from New York and other major industrial and urban regions
have had different political orientations from those of Midwest and Great
Plains Republicans. The northern Great Plains and the Northwest for
some time were the regional basis of Progressive Republicans like La
Follette of Wisconsin, Norris of Nebraska, Borah of Idaho, and Morse of
Oregon (the latter moving from the 'left-wing' of the Republicans to the
'left-wing' of the Democrats, all the while retaining his Senate seat).
However, the center of modern liberal Republicanism seems now to have
shifted to the East.

Sectionalism, at one time a major trait of the American party-group
system, has been a steadily fading phenomenon. Even the South, which

---

[49] Cf. A. Campbell, et al., *op. cit.*, p. 124.

has maintained the greatest sectional homogeneity, is breaking up politically. Not all Southern Democratic organizations can be counted on to bolt the national ticket at the first rebel yell. Southern industrialization and urbanization is causing political transformation. The northward and urban migration of Negroes and their increased organizational power and militancy have changed civil-rights politics from an overwhelmingly Southern problem into a dominant feature of the national political life. Many white southerners now vote Republican for President while adhering to the state Democratic party on other offices. Even the Democratic dominance of state office is giving way. Alabama, Georgia and Mississippi elected Republican congressmen in 1964, and a South Carolina Democratic senator and a congressman 'crossed the aisle' into Republican ranks. And, similarly, the rock-ribbed states of Maine and Vermont, no longer the dependable Republican bastions of years gone by, send Democratic senators to Washington and Democratic governors to their state capitals.

Finally, in the kind of party-group system we have examined, with weak party discipline, decentralized organizational leadership, and decentralized constitutional-legal nomination processes, there is room for considerable insurgency and independence. Individually attractive candidates, such as Dwight D. Eisenhower, can appeal to the public almost without need or benefit of party. Another, Fiorello LaGuardia, was for years the coalition Republican-Fusion mayor of predominantly Democratic New York. Not inaccurately, he boasted that he could be reelected "even on a laundry ticket." (Of course it would have had to be a *liberal* laundry ticket, as LaGuardia well understood but neglected to add.) The independent appeal of popular candidates furthers the possibility that programmatically dissimilar candidates and leaders are found under the same American party banner.

Though we have emphasized the grouping of people into parties and interest-focused organizations, it is well to remember the remarkable extent to which individualism remains as an element of American politics. True, "there are districts in which Benedict Arnold could get elected on the Democratic ticket and others in which Aaron Burr would win if he got the Republican nomination."[50] However, *split-ticket voting* and nonpartisan attitudes are far more widespread than in other nations. Brogan and Verney may again serve as our European observers: "The willingness of the American voter to switch party allegiance or to vote for the man rather than the party is puzzling to a European who takes party loyalty for granted. Americans seem to vote much more as individuals (and for individuals) than Britons or Swedes."[51] A substantial measure of nonpartisan feeling remains, for good or ill, a significant feature of American political life and of great consequence for the character of the party-group system.

---

[50] Brogan and Verney, *op. cit.*, p. 47.
[51] *Ibid.*, p. 34.

BIBLIOGRAPHICAL NOTE

A brief, lively book is Clinton Rossiter, *Parties and Politics in America* (1960). Major textbooks are: V. O. Key, Jr., *Politics, Parties and Pressure Groups* (6th ed., 1964); and Austin Ranney and Willmoore Kendall, *Democracy and the American Party System* (1956). More behavioral are Avery Leiserson, *Parties and Politics* (1958) and Samuel J. Eldersveld, *Political Parties: A Behavioral Analysis* (1964). Comparative perspective is supplied in Sigmund Neumann (ed.), *Modern Political Parties* (1956).

Important works on sources of political controversy include: Karl Marx and Friedrich Engels, *The Communist Manifesto;* F. J. Turner, *The Significance of Sections in American History* (1932); David Truman, *The Governmental Process: Political Interests and Public Opinion* (1951).

For socio-psychological analyses, see: Herbert Hyman, *Political Socialization* (1959); and H. J. Eysenck, *The Psychology of Politics* (1955). Mass movements are examined in Eric Hoffer, *The True Believer* (1961); and in Rudolf Heberle, *Social Movements* (1951).

The origin of modern Anglo-American party organization is traced in Eugene C. Black, *The Association: British Extraparliamentary Political Organization, 1769–1793* (1963). Also see: M. Ostrogorski, *Democracy and the Organization of Political Parties* (2 vols., 1902); Cecil S. Emden, *The People and the Constitution* (1962); Wilfred E. Binkley, *American Political Parties: Their Natural History* (4th ed., 1962); William N. Chambers, *Political Parties in a New Nation: The American Experience 1776–1809* (1963); and Noble E. Cunningham, Jr. (ed.), *The Making of the American Party System 1789–1809* (1965).

The relationship between the Constitution and parties is considered in E. E. Schattschneider, *Party Government* (1942). Comparative analysis of the impact of electoral forms on parties is presented in Maurice Duverger, *Political Parties* (1959). More generally, see D. W. Brogan and D. V. Verney, *Political Patterns in Today's World* (1963); and Herman Finer, *Theory and Practice of Modern Government* (2 vols., 1932), a classic in comparative government texts.

On competitiveness of American parties, see Joseph Schlesinger, "A Two-Dimensional Scheme for Classifying the States According to Degree of Inter-Party Competition," *American Political Science Review* (1955). For minor parties, see Howard P. Nash, Jr., *Gadflies of American Politics: A Short History of Third Parties* (1956). Proportional representation is attacked by Ferdinand Hermens, *Democracy or Anarchy?* (1941); the classic defense is by John Stuart Mill, *Considerations on Representative Government* (1861).

Party organizational structure and leadership are depicted in Hugh A. Bone, *Party Committees and National Politics* (1958). Case studies have been published by the Eagleton Institute of Rutgers University, including: Francis Carney, *The Rise of the Democratic Clubs in California* (Case No. 13, 1958); and Frank Munger, *The Struggle for Republican Leadership in Indiana, 1954* (Case No. 23, 1958). See also, James Q. Wilson, *The Amateur Democrat: Club Politics in Three Cities* (1962); and Stimson Bullitt, *To Be a Politician* (1961).

The relevant literature is surveyed in Harmon Zeigler, *Interest Groups in*

American Society (1964). Also see Donald C. Blaisdell, *American Democracy Under Pressure* (1957); and Henry W. Ehrmann (ed.), *Interest Groups on Four Continents* (1958).

On party viewpoints, see: Kirk Porter and Donald B. Johnson, *National Party Platforms, 1840–1960* (1960); Dean Acheson, *A Democrat Looks at His Party* (1955); and Arthur Larson, *A Republican Looks at His Party* (1956). The effectiveness of party lines in congressional policy votes is revealed in Julius Turner, *Party and Constituency: Pressures on Congress* (1951); Duncan McCrae, Jr., *Dimensions of Congressional Voting* (1958); and David Truman, *The Congressional Party* (1959).

Chapter 10

The Political Community: Suffrage, Immigration, and Citizenship

> Who are to be the electors of the federal representatives? Not the rich, more than the poor; not the learned, more than the ignorant; not the haughty heirs of distinguished names, more than the humble sons of obscure and unpropitious fortune. The electors are to be the great body of the people of the United States.
>
> PUBLIUS[1]

> Give me your tired, your poor,
> Your huddled masses yearning to breathe free,
> The wretched refuse of your teeming shore.
> Send these, the homeless, tempest-tost to me.
> I lift my lamp beside the golden door!
>
> EMMA LAZARUS[2]

DEMOCRATIC POLITICS MEANS SEEKING VOTES FROM MEMBERS OF THE political community. To be counted an equal member of a democratic society means to be taken into account by those who govern. In this chapter, we consider this legal community of persons whose support, or at least whose tolerance, democratic political leaders require if they are to be powerful.

We will consider three aspects of the entry and integration of people into the American political community: First, the suffrage—who may vote? Mere physical presence in a population nowhere suffices to be counted politically equal. Second, the regulations governing the immigration of foreigners into the country. How does this particularly American problem affect the political community? Third, the process by which people—natives as well as immigrants—acquire the right to be counted citizens and thus equal members of the political community.

---

[1] *Federalist* 57, p. 351.
[2] Inscribed on the Statue of Liberty in New York Harbor.

Suffrage

Since democratic government is a system for representing the will of the people in government, progress toward universal suffrage—i.e., enfranchisement of all the people—is one index of democratic achievement. But *universal* suffrage cannot mean literally that *every* human being has the right to vote. Not all limitations on voting eligibility are necessarily dilutions of democracy.

Democratic Suffrage Qualifications

It is surely no limitation of democracy to deny the ballot to infants or to mentally deranged adults. No one can consider them part of the public whose democratic will is to be represented in government. Other qualifications for voters have been urged by theorists of good democratic credentials. John Stuart Mill, for example, advocated much more difficult examinations than contemporary literacy tests.[3] Age, sanity, and literacy are not the only widely accepted modern limitations on the suffrage. Felons are excluded, citizenship is required, and residence and advance registration regulations limit voting. Each of these qualifications is reasonably consistent with enabling the appropriate public to register its will. However, drawing exact boundaries around a particular category is always difficult. Thus, there are contemporary pressures to reduce the voting age due to large-scale military service of teen-agers. English literacy testing was challenged by Spanish-speaking and -writing Puerto Rican citizens of the United States. And, apart from the matter of categories, the actual administration of quite legitimate suffrage qualifications may be corrupt or undemocratic, as in discriminatory use of literacy tests against Negroes.

Progress toward a fully democratic suffrage continues to concern those who strive to eliminate undemocratic vestiges from American political life. Yet, as will be seen, despite continuing difficulties, the modern legal and constitutional provisions governing the suffrage in the United States are unmistakably democratic. Where undemocratic practices persist, they are likely to be *violations* rather than *applications* of contemporary law.

The contemporary suffrage will become more meaningful against the historical background and political dynamics from which universal suffrage has emerged. Frequently, in political analysis, the development of an institution or process helps to reveal its essential characteristics. Moreover, the development of the American suffrage illustrates changing conceptions of membership in the political community, and sheds light on perennial features of the American political system.

---

[3] *Considerations on Representative Government* (New York: Liberal Arts Press, 1958), p. 132.

Early Development of Suffrage Democracy

The essential features of a democratic suffrage developed early in America. True, judged by twentieth century standards, the American suffrage at the outset was indeed limited. Most obvious was the exclusion of half the adult population—women were not enfranchised until this century. However, this was not an issue which distinguished eighteenth-century democrats from their antidemocratic opponents; on grounds basically unconnected with the question of democracy, both democrats and antidemocrats then considered women unsuited for political life. Actually, formal obstacles to female voting were rare; it was not necessary to limit by law what was largely unthinkable. Similarly, while slavery as such was attacked on equalitarian grounds, it was inconceivable to extend the suffrage to other than free men. Judged by eighteenth-century democratic standards, these exclusions from the political community were extraneous to the issue of suffrage democracy.

Representative of the most democratic viewpoint of the time, Jefferson noted that even the purest democracy would necessarily limit its suffrage:

> Were our State a pure democracy in which all its inhabitants should meet together to transact all their business, there would yet be excluded from their deliberations: 1. infants, until arrived at years of discretion; 2. women, who, to prevent depravation of morals and ambiguity of issue, could not mix promiscuously in public meetings of men; 3. slaves, from whom the unfortunate state of things with us takes away the rights of will and of property. Those then who have no will could be permitted to exercise none in the popular assembly, and, of course, could delegate none to an agent in a representative assembly.[4]

The relevant question, therefore, is: Could the mass of *free adult men* vote at the outset of the American republic? Was there a democratic suffrage among those who formed the political community? The evidence leaves little doubt that most persons deemed eligible for a democratic suffrage by Jefferson did possess the franchise in 1789.

Property qualifications. The major doubt that has been cast upon the extent of the early American suffrage arises from the fact of property qualifications—the requirement that voters had to possess a *freehold* (ownership or long-term lease of land) in rural areas, or tangible assets of varying monetary value in the towns and cities. Many have maintained that the suffrage was thereby restricted to a small propertied elite. However, even the most restrictive estimate concluded: "It would probably be safe to say that nowhere were more than one third of the adult males disfranchised by the property qualifications."[5] In most places

---

[4] Edward Dumbauld (ed.), *The Political Writings of Thomas Jefferson* (New York: Liberal Arts Press, 1955), p. 98.

[5] Charles A. Beard, *An Economic Interpretation of the Constitution of the United States* (New York: The Macmillan Company, 1913), p. 242.

far fewer than a third were disfranchised. Researchers now conclude that "probably most free adult men had the vote in 1787"[6]; there were "few who were disfranchised by law."[7] A closer examination of the property qualification will make plausible these higher estimates of the early suffrage.

It requires a deliberate intellectual effort for modern urbanites to overcome the ring of the word 'property' as a qualification for voting. Today it conveys an image of substantial wealth and of a small elite class. This was not the colonial connotation. Possession of property was then practically synonymous with membership in the local community. "Landholders though poor"[8] is the accurate contemporary description of the average colonist's condition.

Eighteenth-century America was overwhelmingly an agricultural society with vast stretches of virgin land. In England, where land was in short supply, property requirements did substantially limit the suffrage. But in America it was easy to acquire a freehold. The essential point was recognized by historian Charles A. Beard:

> When it is remembered that only about 3 per cent of the population dwelt in towns of over 8000 inhabitants in 1790, and that freeholds were widely distributed, especially in New England, it will become apparent that nothing like the same proportion was disfranchised as would be today under similar qualifications.[9]

Nor was this widely based suffrage limited to New England. Southern freeholds were not confined to the wealthy either. A chronicler of the South Carolinians reported: "Everyone upon his arrival obtained his grant of land and sat down upon his freehold. . . ."[10] In Georgia it was said that "the people claimed as a right at least 50 acres of land for every person in a family, whether white or black."[11] Soliciting immigrants from the old world, Benjamin Franklin summed it up: "Land being thus plenty in America, and so cheap as that a labouring man, that understands Husbandry, can in a short time save money enough to purchase a piece of new land sufficient for a plantation, whereon he may subsist a family. . . ."[12]

---

[6] Robert E. Brown, *Charles Beard and the Constitution* (Princeton: Princeton University Press, 1956), p. 38.

[7] Forrest McDonald, *We the People* (Chicago: University of Chicago Press, 1958), p. 359, n. 1. Cf. Lee Benson, *Turner and Beard* (New York: Free Press of Glencoe, 1960) for a criticism of Brown and McDonald, and a defense of Beard's more restrictive interpretation. However, see Chilton Williamson, *American Suffrage, From Property to Democracy, 1760–1860* (Princeton: Princeton University Press, 1960) for convincing evidence that the mass of free adult males could vote by 1789.

[8] Williamson, *op. cit.*, p. 85.

[9] *Op. cit.*, p. 242.

[10] Williamson, *op. cit.*, p. 36.

[11] *Ibid.*, p. 31.

[12] F. L. Mott and C. E. Jorgensen (eds.), *Benjamin Franklin* (New York: American Book Co., 1936), p. 217.

Almost any person with a bare minimum of skill and luck could acquire a freehold, and with the freehold the right to vote. The property qualification did not then have the restrictive effect that the word now conjures up. As staunchly royal Governor Bull of South Carolina, perhaps ruefully, pointed out: "by far the great number of voters are the most Inferior Sort of People."[13] And not only was the freehold qualification not substantially restrictive, but it was not even stringently applied as a formal requirement. Informally, it was frequently overlooked. "It was apparently customary in some, if not all, colonies to allow all adult males, when known to the community and to any degree respected or liked, to vote."[14]

The freehold requirement was not used in towns or cities where it would have been unwarrantedly restrictive. There was a wide variety of substitute requirements. A North Carolina borough enfranchised all—with or without property—within two miles of the borough on the day of election. Possession of property other than land and of modest monetary value was a more common requirement. Such monetary qualifications were curiously 'democratized' by the depreciation of paper currency, and the Revolutionary period witnessed a trend to lowering the face amounts of these requirements as well. But even prior to the Revolution, it was easy for townspeople to qualify simply by swearing that they owned the necessary amount. In Pennsylvania, "every man with a chest of tools, a few implements of husbandry, a few spare clothes, a bed and a few household utensils, a few articles for sale in a window, or almost anything he could call or even think his own supposed himself within the pale of an oath, and made no hesitation of taking it."[15]

By the time of the Revolution, the American colonies already had the broadest suffrage in the world. And the Revolution prodded them on to further liberalization of the right to vote. The central Revolutionary ideas implied liberalization—'No taxation without representation' was the popular rallying cry of the revolutionists. It was not really possible to direct that demand against the British while somehow denying its relevance at home.

Taxpayer qualifications. During the Revolutionary period several states changed the nature of the property requirement; they replaced freehold with taxpayer status as the requirement for voters. Frequently misunderstood by modern students as an effort to restrict voting to the upper classes, the move actually and intentionally extended the suffrage. *All* adult males were normally required to pay these direct taxes. As Williamson points out, when taxation was universal, "a taxpaying suffrage was almost universal suffrage."[16]

---

[13] Williamson, *op. cit.*, p. 31.
[14] *Ibid.*, p. 49.
[15] P. S. Foner (ed.), *The Complete Writings of Thomas Paine* (New York: Citadel Press, 1945), pp. 287–88.
[16] Williamson, *op. cit.*, p. 136.

The democratic direction of this change is revealed by its opponents, feeble though their voices were. For example, the New Hampshire press attacked the substitution of taxpayer voting for property qualifications "as making possible the outvoting of property owners by those with no property, so that a number of transients, some Scotch, some Irish, and 'even French peddlers,' would be able to vote away the assets of the well-to-do."[17] Actually, there was little opposition by the wealthy classes. "Marylanders, irrespective of class, status, or section, were swept along by a movement based upon democratic principles but initiated at the top. Some marvelled at a popular movement led by a number of the substantial citizenry. . . ."[18]

Early religious, ethnic, and other qualifications. Suffrage qualifications were not exclusively economic. A typical colonial requirement for voting was an oath designedly obnoxious to anyone outside the pale of orthodox Protestantism. Some colonial laws were more direct and specifically barred Catholics and Jews, as was done in England. Quakers and other nonconforming groups were also excluded at one time. It was an additional democratic outcome of the Revolutionary period that these *religious* barriers to voting (but not for some time to office-holding) were dropped from the new state constitutions.

However, *racial* discrimination, compounded by its connection with slavery, continued into and beyond the founding decade. Even free Negroes were barred by many state constitutions—North as well as South. The same clauses which limited the suffrage to whites effectively barred American Indians and Orientals as well. However, free Negroes did vote in some states, and were even credited with swinging the balance of power to the Federalist party in the close New York election of 1813.[19] For the most part, Negro suffrage was tied too closely to the slavery issue to be separately resolved prior to the "irrepressible conflict."

Few other qualifications were imposed on the early suffrage. The traditional definition of maturity, twenty-one years, was the common minimum voting age. Oddly enough, citizenship was far from a universal requirement; 22 states and territories once permitted aliens to vote. Freehold and taxpayer requirements insured that voters were resident members of the community, so there was less need for specific legal requirements to exclude transients or the just-arrived. Fear of immigrant group voting power, however, did lead to some residence qualifications. Pennsylvania, for example, directed a two-year residence rule against its numerous German immigrants. But most states were entirely free of special qualifications beyond the basic requirements.

In sum, the early freehold property and taxpaying qualifications

---

[17] *Ibid.*, p. 106.
[18] *Ibid.*, p. 146.
[19] See Dixon R. Fox, "The Negro Vote in Old New York," *Political Science Quarterly*, XXXII (June 1917), 257.

were not nearly as restrictive as they would be in our modern industrial and urban world. The very lowest economic layer was barred, but at the very least more than three fourths of eighteenth-century American free men—the relevant political community—could vote even prior to the elimination of property and taxpayer requirements.[20] By the founding decade the country was committed to a democratic suffrage. The new state and national constitutions continued a political process which speeded the movement to universal suffrage from the outset of American history.

Constitutional Basis of Suffrage

The Constitution wholly embodied the extensive suffrage attained by 1787. The relationship of the Constitution to the suffrage supports the general view of this book that the Constitution establishes a fundamentally democratic regime, subtly arranged to foster certain values. One way to see that relationship is to ask: Did the Constitution facilitate or handicap the further democratization of the suffrage? Although constitutional interpretation is not the simplest of tasks, the answer to our present question is plain enough. The Constitution was, in Jefferson's phrase, "democracy made easy."[21]

The original Constitution establishes only one national requirement for voting: All those who "have the qualifications requisite for electors of the most numerous branch of the State legislature" must be eligible to vote for members of the House of Representatives.[22] The particular qualifications are thus left entirely to each state but with one vital restriction: The most popularly based statewide suffrage must be used in electing national representatives. This had practical consequence in such states as New York and North Carolina which then had a differently based and more restrictive suffrage for their smaller 'upper' houses.

The Framers could have imposed national restrictions on the suffrage, or, yielding most easily to federal necessity, simply have left it to the states. But they chose, rather, to tie the national suffrage to the most democratic element in the state political process. The Constitution applies the widest statewide franchise to the national congressional election. As to the President, the Constitution left matters to the states, where there was every reason to believe further suffrage expansion would occur. And the anticipated democratization early and thoroughly occurred. The presidential suffrage today still derives from the constitutional

---

[20] Benson, *op. cit.*, p. 181, infers this from Beard's figures. By contrast, Brown, *op. cit.*, p. 39, maintains that the figures "should be revised upward to [a percentile in] the high 90's."

[21] Quoted in Williamson, *op. cit.*, p. 299.

[22] Article I, section 2, cl. 1. The Seventeenth Amendment applies precisely the same language to the election of senators.

authority of the state legislatures to select presidential electors at their own discretion. (Congress is now assigned the same authority for choosing the electors of the District of Columbia by the Twenty-third Amendment.)

Four constitutional amendments must be noted. The post-Civil War Fourteenth Amendment, for the first time, explicitly brought universal manhood suffrage into the text of the Constitution. The language is sweeping and applies to both state and national elections. However, the provision failed to create a judicially enforceable individual right, even though the "right to vote" appears as a phrase. States remain constitutionally free, if they are willing to risk the penalty, to deny the ballot to persons qualified by the terms of the Fourteenth Amendment. The prescribed penalty is that the offending state's delegation to Congress shall be diminished proportionately. However, the cumbersome nature of this sanction, and the failure of Congress to implement it, have effectively nullified the provision. The Fifteenth Amendment further proscribes state or national abridgement of the right of citizens to vote "on account of race, color, or previous condition of servitude." Congress has implemented this Amendment by statute in an effort to protect the right of suffrage for Negroes. And there has been much litigation in the courts as Negro citizens have claimed their rights under the Fifteenth Amendment.

Woman suffrage was constitutionally guaranteed by the Nineteenth Amendment—though some states had previously permitted women to vote. Earlier, the "privileges and immunities" clause of the Fourteenth Amendment had been unsuccessfully claimed as the basis for a suit against a New York state law limiting the ballot to men.[23]

For decades reformers campaigned to eliminate poll taxes (direct head taxes) as a requirement for the suffrage. A remote descendant of the early taxpayer qualification, the poll tax was introduced in some southern states to harass the late-nineteenth-century Populists whose support came largely from the poorer whites and Negroes. Under attack, all but five states had eliminated the tax requirement by 1964. Then the Twenty-fourth Amendment was adopted, prohibiting requirement of poll or other taxes as a condition for voting in elections or primaries for national officers. The Amendment does not prohibit such taxes for voting at the state level. However, the subsequent 1965 Civil Rights Act directs the Attorney General to challenge such state requirements in the courts.

In brief, suffrage qualifications are established predominantly by state action. But the Constitution requires the states to extend the same suffrage for electing national congressmen and senators as for electing the larger of their state legislative houses. And citizens may not be denied the ballot for state or national officers on grounds of race, previous

---

[23] *United States* v. *Anthony*, Fed. Cases 14459 (1873). Also see *Minor* v. *Happersett*, 21 Wall. (U.S.) 162 (1875).

enslavement, or sex; nor may citizens be denied the ballot for national officers on grounds of nonpayment of poll taxes. The Constitution has never stood in the way of suffrage reform; it was indeed "democracy made easy."

Political Dynamics of Suffrage

Once nearly universal white manhood suffrage was made a basic part of the political system, it was relatively easy for excluded persons to find the political support needed to obtain the suffrage too. This ease of suffrage expansion had an enormous consequence which is seen by contrast with Europe. Suffrage democracy came much later to Europe where it had feudal inequities to overcome and faced an entrenched aristocracy with the power and will to oppose political equality. In much of Europe the movement for suffrage democracy became a hard-fought class struggle. European socialist parties may have gained more popular support from espousing democratic suffrage equality than from espousing socialist economic equality. The unique failure of American socialists to develop a major political party—powerful socialist parties developed in every other western nation—is significantly attributable to the lack of opportunity to lead a movement for suffrage democracy.[24] No American party of the left could claim the mantle of democratic leadership. No clearcut class or partisan division over suffrage extension developed in the United States.

Even the earliest parties did not divide sharply over the suffrage issue. Jeffersonian Republicans regarded the freehold qualification as entirely democratic; it suited their agrarian orientation perfectly. Disagreements over suffrage reform were more issues within than between the parties. Frequently these differences depended on the partisan outcomes of suffrage extension which affected party fortunes differently in different states. Where Federalists were dominant, as in the North, Republicans favored including certain new groups. The reverse held true in the South—with important exceptions in both sections. For example, one ingredient of New York Federalist strength was the free Negro vote. When Republicans gained control of the state they singled Negro voters out for additional property qualifications.[25] There was, no doubt, a party battle in several states over the continuation of financial qualifications for voting. But that was *partisan-political* warfare (i.e., a battle for state party advantage) more often than it was *economic-class* warfare. There was no sharp dichotomy of democratically inclined Republicans and aristocratically inclined Federalists. "A democratic suffrage philosophy was not the monoply of either of the two great parties,

---

[24] See Louis Hartz, *The Liberal Tradition in America* (New York: Harcourt, Brace & World, 1955).
[25] Dixon R. Fox, *op. cit.*, p. 258.

because they shared a common inheritance of democratic ideas from the Revolutionary period."[26]

The fact that an initially broad suffrage could be expanded easily contributed to the distinctive character of American democratic politics. It removed from the scene an issue that in Europe aggravated the politics of class struggle, and thus opened here the way for the moderate politics of "multiplicity of interests and sects."

The dynamic process by which the suffrage expanded also illustrates distinctive aspects of American politics. Tocqueville stated it well.

> When a nation begins to modify the elective qualification, it may easily be foreseen that, sooner or later, that qualification will be entirely abolished. There is no more invariable rule in the history of society: the further electoral rights are extended, the greater is the need of extending them; for after each concession the strength of the democracy increases, and its demands increase with its strength. The ambition of those who are below the appointed rate is irritated in exact proportion to the great number of those who are above it. The exception at last becomes the rule, concession follows concession, and no stop can be made short of universal suffrage.[27]

Tocqueville's historical rule is implemented by political parties in their search for votes. Nonvoters, by their nature, cannot vote themselves into positions of power from which to change suffrage provisions. Short of a revolution, nonvoters need a substantial number of the already enfranchised to champion their cause.

There is a dynamic reciprocity between parties and suffrage. The initial creation of popularly elective political offices stimulates party organization—the machinery for soliciting votes on a large scale. Politicians then are tempted to expand the suffrage to nonvoting groups likely to support their electoral efforts. Even when a group is apathetic about acquiring the ballot, political leaders will seek out their participation if they are potential supporters. Of course, the identical factors which impel some parties to champion the suffrage for sympathetic groups also repel other parties which fear such groups as potential opponents. However, a party supporting a particular expansion is sooner or later likely to come to power, whereas even after returning to power the opposing party is unlikely to dare launch a frontal campaign to disfranchise a particular group of voters. It is far easier to oppose the *extension* of suffrage in a democratic nation than to propose the *revocation* of existing suffrage; and it is easiest of all to champion the cause of universal suffrage with appeals to the democratic creed. Thus the opponents of universal suffrage have been steadily overwhelmed.

Do not assume that a simple utilitarian calculus places everyone on one side or the other, favoring or opposing an extension of suffrage,

---

[26] Williamson, *op. cit.*, p. 181.
[27] Tocqueville, I, 59.

depending entirely on the anticipated net gain or loss of partisan votes. There are other considerations. A strong commitment to democracy may override a party's fear that a new voting group will favor one's opponents, as we noted in the case of upper class leadership of the Maryland movement for suffrage reform following the Revolution.[28] And party leaders, who may have no strong principled commitment to suffrage extension, sometimes have little choice; the pressures for suffrage reform may come from interest groups which do have such strong principles and whose voting support they need. An example is the civil-rights coalition of liberal, labor, church, and minority groups which has pushed many politicians beyond their own desire for suffrage reform. In this coalition, devotion to democratic values irrespective of narrowly construed group interest is blended with narrow partisan considerations. A mixture of shared interest and idealism is common in politics as in other spheres of life.

The generalized consensus for democracy has become so strong that public opposition to the ideal of universal suffrage is politically imprudent. Even in sections of the country most hostile to civil rights, Negro suffrage is seldom attacked in principle. Far fewer white Americans object to political equality for Negroes than to most other forms of racial integration.[29] Significantly, the first civil-rights legislation enacted by Congress after Reconstruction mainly protects voting rights. Truly, this heralds the culminating triumph of suffrage democracy which Tocqueville predicted.

Integration into the Political Community

Thus far we have considered who comprises the American political community primarily from the point of view of the 'easy case'—the extension of the suffrage to the native, white, Protestant male. In many countries this would be the end of the tale because their population is religiously, ethnically, and racially homogeneous; they have only the easy case, the single homogeneous stock. There, once the suffrage was fully democratized, the political community would be fully formed; there would be no further hindrances to voting and, beyond that, to full membership. But the United States is, of course, not such a homogeneous country. From American diversity have arisen the 'hard cases,' those minorities who have been barred from the suffrage and, even more, from full membership. Three kinds of groups were initially estranged from the community for reasons arising from this diversity: religious minorities, immigrants, and racial minorities. We will examine the process of their integration. In addition, we must consider the absorption into the po-

---

[28] See note 18.
[29] See the "rank order of discriminations" in Gunnar Myrdal, *An American Dilemma* (New York: Harper, 1944), pp. 60 ff.

litical community of one other major group, but one which can hardly be said to result from a diversity peculiar to America—women.

Religious Minorities

We need not add to what has already been said concerning suffrage for religious minorities. Their voting problems were resolved almost entirely by the end of the founding decade. Also, the early constitutional separation of church and state had a profound influence in differentiating American politics from that of some other democracies. As a result, religion was not allowed to take the center of the stage in American politics as divisively as it did in many European countries. This is not in the least to suggest that religious animosities have not persistently and sometimes bitterly affected American politics, nor to suggest that every religious minority fully enjoys the highest privileges of membership in the political community. Catholics, Jews, and Mormons are elected and appointed to high office, but no non-Protestant until John F. Kennedy ever won the Presidency. The famous 'melting pot' conception of America notwithstanding, religious groups retain distinctive identities which significantly affect voting and partisanship. But the overriding fact is nonetheless that all major religious groups share the basic values of the American polity. Accordingly, none of the major religious groups pursues its political ends by radically (and divisively) distinctive political means. They all work within the accepted process of American politics.

Immigrants

An extraordinary aspect of American politics results from the unique role of immigration in American society. Immigrants arrived in huge successive waves over the years. Almost all Americans are derived from this immigrant stock, and American history is practically indistinguishable from the history of its immigrant population. The early Anglo-Americans actively solicited emigration to this country. The Declaration of Independence complained that King George III had "endeavoured to prevent the population of these States; for that purpose obstructing the Laws for Naturalization of Foreigners; refusing to pass others to encourage their migration hither, and raising the conditions of new Appropriations of lands." As late as 1885, millions of American school children collected funds to erect a base for the Statue of Liberty, which still beckons "beside the golden door" of New York harbor. We shall see how much less open that door now is, but for much of American history unrestricted immigration admitted hordes of all manner and description to the new world.

Even before the mid-nineteenth century, when nearly all were 'foreigners' and when most came from northern and western Europe, many nonetheless experienced difficulty: in Pennsylvania, the Germans; in New Hampshire, the "itinerant French peddlers"; the Scandinavians, the Irish —all felt the heavy burden of xenophobia and discrimination. Yet, difficult as it was for the earliest 'greenhorns,' their children and grandchildren so soon became 'native stock' that they greeted with scorn the later waves of immigrants: Italians, Poles, Hungarians, Jews, Greeks, Slavs. And these, in due course, all too frequently passed the burden on to Orientals, Mexicans, Puerto Ricans, and used the slavery-tainted Negroes, more than any others, to support their claim to some degree of higher status.

White immigrants suffered much initial economic and social discrimination, but experienced little difficulty getting the vote. Many states once permitted aliens to vote and, where required, citizenship was only a temporary delay. The dynamics of suffrage expansion operated with a vengeance with the immigrant groups; the suffrage was practically thrust upon them. And of course the native-born second generation was legally the political equal of everyone else. Also, the easily visible foreignness of the ex-Europeans—their accents, dress, mannerisms, even their foreign-sounding names—was rapidly Americanized. They became full-fledged members of the political community, not only as voters but as wielders of power and as statesmen. Indeed the Irish have been so successful that they have impressed their distinctive style onto American politics. There are relatively few areas of political (and economic and social) life where immigrant minorities long remain 'second-class citizens.'

Racial Minorities

Few Negroes could follow this path to complete integration, though more travelled it than may be realized. Many lightly colored mulattoes have 'passed' into white society.[30] This was far less a product of intermarriage than of illicit intercourse dating from two centuries of master-slave concubinage. For most, immediate visibility as Negroes was preserved irrespective of American (including white) ancestry going back farther than that of most other Americans. Unlike the children of white immigrants, foreign ancestry could not be eliminated by substituting American for African culture. American Negroes are altogether Americanized—their names, religion, language, dress, and values are purely American;[31] but the stigma of slavery affects the Negro's still largely segregated situation.

---

[30] It is estimated that 4 to 6 per cent of American "Negroes" assume "white identities" each year. See Myrdal, *op. cit.*, p. 1208, n. 49.

[31] Efforts to reclaim an African heritage as a source of group pride and identity have been recurrent, but have had slight impact on most Negroes. Recent nationalist successes in Africa, however, have reawakened interest and have also spurred American Negro protest activity.

The Constitution specifically forbids exclusion from the ballot on grounds of race, and Congress has at last established administrative machinery for its enforcement. One of the greatest political transformations in history has been the increase in Negro political power as the principle of the Fifteenth Amendment has been implemented—fully in the North and increasingly in the South. In 1965, six Negroes sat in the House of Representatives from primarily Negro districts. Perhaps more important is the pivotal strength of the Negro vote in city, state, and presidential elections. For example, in the extremely close 1960 election Negroes voted overwhelmingly for Kennedy. This developing electoral power, combined with increasing public acceptance of the principle of political equality, has resulted in many Negro appointments to important judicial and administrative offices. Dramatic as the gains have been, nonetheless, politically, economically, and socially, the Negro remains the least fully integrated member of the community.

Racial minorities, in contrast to religious and ethnic groups, have generally suffered the severest and most lasting political disabilities. The oldest group of Americans, the Indian tribes, have long occupied an anomalous situation. Reservation Indians are wards of the government; in the words of the Supreme Court, the nation has a special "duty of protection" for "these remnants of a race once powerful, now weak and diminished in numbers."[32] However, while preserving their tribal rights and special status, Indians are citizens by birth. Although Indians encounter social and economic difficulty, interestingly, partial Indian ancestry is a political asset in many states.

Orientals were the first object of immigration exclusion, were long denied citizenship, and were among those disfranchised by white suffrage qualifications. Nisei, though native-born Americans, and other persons of Japanese origin were victims of an ignominious episode during World War II. After Pearl Harbor, with no effort to distinguish the loyal and the disloyal, those residing on the West Coast were required by military order to relocate in government detention camps. The government subsequently provided financial compensation, and President Eisenhower made formal apology on behalf of the American nation. But it was an episode in which a racial minority, for the most part native-born Americans, was deliberately estranged from the political community.[33]

Latin-Americans, not strictly a racial group though many are of mixed Spanish and Indian ancestry, have long occupied the kind of subordinate situation ordinarily reserved for racial minorities. On the whole, however, the climate of equality is such today that in nearly all cases progress is being made towards fuller integration into the political community.

---

[32] *United States* v. *Kagama*, 118 U.S. 375, 384 (1886).
[33] Cf. Morton Grodzins, *Americans Betrayed* (Chicago: University of Chicago Press, 1949).

Women

The long exclusion of women reflected widely accepted ideas like Jefferson's about the "depravation" of female morals if women mixed "promiscuously in public meetings"; women simply were not deemed part of the body politic. In some respects, although certainly not quantitatively, the situation of women can be likened to that of a minority group. For one thing, they also bore the physical visibility of their inferior status.[34] Negro women bear this doubly, but immigrant white women too could not acquire political equality along with their male relatives merely by adopting American ways. Some hardy suffragettes sought to cloak this easy identification of their political alienation literally and symbolically by affecting male attire.[35] But Negroes and women could not become politically equal to white men until slavery was ended by civil war and an equally revolutionary transformation in the social and economic roles of women was achieved.

Woman suffrage was opposed by the popular slogan, 'A woman's place is in the home.' Naturally, some politicians nonetheless speculated on possible partisan consequences of female voting, but there was little to go on. In Europe, female suffrage tended to be opposed by anticlerical and socialist forces which feared church influence would be extended. In the United States, the liquor interests and others opposing prohibition thought female suffrage would strengthen the 'dry' forces. There were initially few men sufficiently convinced, brave, or interested to champion the woman suffrage cause. Major social changes and intense efforts by women themselves had to come first.

The supporting context of the movement for the Nineteenth Amendment was the vast change which took women out of the home and placed them in factories, retail stores, and offices. Divorce laws were liberalized to change the ancient 'double standard' by which men but not women could escape from unbearable marriages. Suffragette tactics were bold and dramatic. Often they deliberately sought martyrdom to evoke sympathy and support. They noisily picketed the White House, were arrested, refused to pay fines preferring imprisonment, went on hunger strikes, and gained gloriously huge newspaper headlines when they were force-fed by prison officials. This militancy increased the national embarrassment until it became politically unbearable.

Victory came first in the western states. By 1900 women could vote for the President in Wyoming (which led the way), Colorado, Idaho, and Utah. By then, too, they were able to vote for school board officials—where mothers seemed most obviously to have an interest and

---

[34] See Myrdal, *op. cit.*, appendix 5, for a comparison of Negro and female "minority" status problems.

[35] For a history of the suffragettes, see Elizabeth C. Stanton, Susan B. Anthony, and M. J. Gage, *History of Woman Suffrage* (6 vols.; Rochester, N.Y.: National American Woman Suffrage Association, 1900–1920).

This jibe at women's rights movement (Thomas Nast, 1869) was entitled: "Women's Kingdom is at Home;"

Women's suffrage parade, Washington, D.C., 1919;

Senator Margaret Chase Smith (R, Me.) campaigning for the 1964 Republican presidential nomination.

competency—in a great many states. Jubilee day came in 1920 when the Nineteenth Amendment was finally ratified, and the triumphant militant movement for woman suffrage was transformed into the more sedate League of Women *Voters.*

Female suffrage is now totally unchallenged, but women are by no means accepted as full political equals. In the Eighty-ninth Congress, there were but a dozen women: two senators and 10 members of the House of Representatives. However, women do hold many administrative and judicial posts, far more for example than Negroes, and are extremely active in local government. In 1964 Senator Margaret Chase Smith of Maine campaigned for the Republican presidential nomination. This was the first such real bid by a woman, but her candidacy was not taken too seriously. No woman has ever been nominated for either President or Vice President on a major party ticket, nor has any ever served on the Supreme Court. The direction continues to be toward fuller political (and economic) equality, but traditional conceptions have not been wholly overturned, and women generally are much less politically interested than men.

Regulation of Suffrage, Immigration, and Citizenship

Detailed regulation of voting, entry into the country, and citizenship is necessary in all countries. Such regulations are invariably tediously detailed. They are particularly complex in countries like the United States with heterogeneous populations. And the more numerous and complicated the regulations, the greater the range of administrative discretion and possible abuse.

Suffrage

Suffrage regulation remains primarily a state function, subject to constitutional requirements enforced by judicial review, and congressional enactments. State suffrage qualifications vary too greatly to permit complete cataloging. Some are anachronisms such as denying the ballot to persons engaging in duels (Nevada, Virginia, and Wisconsin) or to those who bet on election outcomes (Florida, New York, and Wisconsin). All states since 1926 require citizenship. Most disqualify the insane, prisoners, felons, and vagrants. In addition, there are four significant categories of suffrage regulation:

Age. Only four states depart from the traditional 21 years minimum (Georgia and Kentucky, 18; Alaska, 19; Hawaii, 20). The slogan, 'Old enough to fight, old enough to vote,' recently elicited sympathy when millions of young men were drafted into the armed services. President Eisenhower was among those who supported a proposed constitutional amendment requiring the states to lower the voting age, but Congress demurred. Southern congressmen, concerned with general civil-rights suffrage legislation, argued that the states were the traditionally established and proper jurisdiction for setting suffrage qualifications.

Residence. Membership in a political community strongly implies that one makes one's home there. (This was not always so obvious. Early English practice was for voting rights to go with a freehold, and those with several properties could vote in as many localities.) There are two reasons for limiting the suffrage to actual residents: to ensure that voters have primary attachment to the community of interest represented in the election, and to help prevent fraudulent repeat voting. A difficulty with these otherwise reasonable requirements results from the amazing mobility of the modern American family. Several million votes are annually forfeited by change of residence too close to an election to allow time for qualifying at the new address.[36] Requirements vary from state to state; and within the state, different lengths of residence are commonly required for state, county, and precinct jurisdictions. All states require state residence for a minimal period ranging from six months to two years. Precinct residence requirements are shortest, reflecting their function as purely administrative units rather than as communities of significant interest.

Taxpayer-property. With the Twenty-fourth Amendment the final vestiges of the taxpaying qualification have disappeared from the national suffrage. But six states still limit the suffrage to taxpaying property owners in special local referenda on bond issues and the like. South Carolina accepts property ownership as an alternative to literacy.

Literacy. It would appear that voters should possess at least some capacity to respond intelligently to public affairs. The ability to read and write is widely accepted as a minimal indication of that capacity and as consonant with democratic views. Even so, only 19 states use any sort of literacy test for suffrage. Compulsory education, free public schools, and naturalization literacy requirements for citizenship now practically ensure voter literacy. There is little pressure, therefore, to establish additional literacy testing for voting—except to accomplish ulterior purposes.

Literacy tests, like many aspects of public administration, inevitably leave officials some discretionary authority. Competitive political parties watch carefully to prevent ordinary partisan discrimination, but ethnic and racial discrimination is a special problem. There is a disproportionate preference for literacy testing in the South (seven of the 11 southern states versus 12 of the remaining 39 states) where it has frequently been used to disfranchise Negroes rather than to ensure a competent electorate. For example, a registrar of voters in Forrest County, Mississippi, rejected as failing to meet the literacy requirement "at least nine-

---

[36] One survey found about 3 per cent of the national electorate disfranchised by residence requirements. See Angus Campbell, Converse, Miller and Stokes, *The American Voter* (New York: Wiley, 1960), p. 90, n. 2.

teen qualified Negroes, including three college graduates and the holder of a National Science Foundation Fellowship."[37]

Another misuse of literacy testing was involved in the famous "grandfather clause." The Fifteenth Amendment, barring race and previous servitude as grounds for denying voting rights, was adopted in 1870. Oklahoma proceeded to waive the literacy requirement for descendants of those eligible to vote prior to 1866. In 1915, this "grandfather clause" which patently discriminated against those descended from slaves was declared unconstitutional.[38] Another common form of literacy testing was the oral demonstration, to the registrar's satisfaction, of an applicant's 'understanding' of the state constitution. These would be difficult tests to apply even with the purest intent; they are at best highly subjective, and in practice have been applied unequally to Negroes and whites. The 1965 Civil Rights Act suspends literacy tests where less than 50 per cent of the voting-age population could vote as of November 1, 1964.

New York City presented an interesting problem in the use of English by its literacy testing. There, the requirement was satisfied by a written test administered by public-school teachers. This had been attacked, not on grounds of discriminatory administration, but as unfair to the many Spanish-speaking and -writing Puerto Rican immigrants who meet all other voting qualifications. Consequently, the 1965 Civil Rights Act makes a sixth-grade education completed in an American-territory school, though in a language other than English, sufficient proof of literacy. Prior to this Act, an American precedent for literacy qualifications to be satisfied other than in English had been set in the Hawaiian state constitution which requires that all voters be literate in either Hawaiian or English.

Immigration

The largest wave of immigrants to the United States coincided with the end of easy access to virgin land, the closing of the frontier at the end of the nineteenth century. Pressure mounted to regulate previously unrestricted immigration. Fearful of immigrant competition for jobs, organized labor sought to stop the incoming flow of cheap labor. But there was another major factor. Mostly, the new immigrants did not come from the same 'old country' as those already here. They were not the familiar northwestern Europeans, but came instead from south, central, and eastern Europe. And they arrived in astonishing numbers—an average of a million a year between 1905 and 1914—rekindling old European animosities and evoking strident claims of ethnic superiority from many of the earlier settlers.

Congress directed its first restrictive statutes against the Chinese with the Oriental Exclusion Act of 1882. The same year, trade union pressure helped enact a bill forbidding the importation of foreign con-

[37] *New York Times*, May 1, 1962, pp. 1, 24.
[38] *Guinn v. United States*, 238 U.S. 347.

tract laborers. Various categories of undesirables were added by 1920; for example, anarchists, illiterates, and immoral persons were barred. But the immigrant tide was not stemmed, and new fears were added to old with the 1917 Russian Revolution and the rise of the international Communist movement. The result was the first effective limitation of European entry to the United States.

The Quota Act of 1921 established a 'national origin' system of admissions as the basis for 'old world' immigration policy until 1965. ('New world' Latin-Americans, Canadians, and others born in an independent country of the Western Hemisphere were not subject to immigration quotas.) The vital portion of the 1921 Act was its formula for calculating quotas. This used the 1910 census as the base year and assigned each nation a quota of 3 per cent of the number of Americans who in 1910 were of that national origin. A total of about 355,000 Europeans could come each year by that formula. Subsequent amendments to the act further reduced the total permitted immigration to an annual total of 156,487, including token quotas for Asians and Africans.

During the severe depression of the 1930s, America seemed less the

Jammed together in steerage-class discomfort, millions of hopeful immigrants set sail for America and a new life. In the early 1900s the United States was attracting over one million immigrants a year.

San Francisco Chinese-Americans rally for John F. Kennedy in 1960. Recognition of ethnic groups is a major aspect of American political campaigns.

land of unlimited opportunity and the flow of immigrants slowed to a trickle. More persons actually left the United States than came, and quotas for a time ceased to be barriers. But the dislocations and persecutions of World War II renewed the press of Europeans for visas to America, though very few could be admitted under the quota system. The major problem has been the heart-rending situation of large numbers of displaced persons, refugees first from German Nazi and then from Russian Communist tyranny. Included were the remnants of European Jewry—survivors of an unbelievable holocaust in which six million persons were methodically exterminated by the Nazi genocidal program. Many Czechs, Poles, Hungarians, and others also felt the inhumanity of the self-proclaimed master race.' They were liberated only to flee once more as Soviet occupation brought down an iron curtain of totalitarian rule.

Congress responded with special legislation providing temporary and piecemeal relaxation of quotas. Future quotas were borrowed against; some were mortgaged to the year 2000. Congress also enacted a major overhaul and codification of existing statutes in the Immigration and Nationality Act of 1952. Under this McCarran-Walter Act, quotas were retained much as before; for example, on the national origin basis, the largest quotas were assigned to the United Kingdom and Ireland. However, the 1952 Act removed direct racial prohibitions. Further, reflecting Cold War necessities and politics, Communists and their sympathizers were added to the list of undesirables forbidden entry.

The McCarran-Walter Act was passed over President Truman's veto; and later Presidents Eisenhower, Kennedy, and Johnson, all urged Congress to liberalize its provisions. National origin quotas were attacked as ethnically discriminatory and thus out of keeping with the American heritage. America's claim to leadership of the free world was embarrassed by an implicit doctrine that there are superior racial stocks. Moreover, at a time when many needy refugees besieged our consular offices for visas in countries with exhausted quotas, the quotas of other countries went unused. In short, democratic commitment, Cold War practicality, and humanitarian morality were urged as the basis for a less restrictive policy.

On the other hand, supporters of the limited-quota program argued that the United States has been comparatively generous—no other major nation has admitted so many refugees. The United States cannot hope to solve the displaced persons problem by itself, nor be expected to resettle all the refugees of the world. American unemployment is pointed to as a continuing problem which would be worsened by an influx of immigrant laborers. Finally, it is argued, moral responsibility is satisfied by America's generous food surplus relief contributions and by other forms of foreign aid.

After 41 years, the ethnically discriminatory quota system was repealed by Congress. President Johnson ceremoniously signed the 1965 Immigration Act into law at the Statue of Liberty. Overall limits replace nationality quotas. However, the distinction between 'new' and 'old' worlds is retained. Western Hemisphere nations, as of 1968, have annual immigration quotas totalling 120,000 (previously, there had been no limit on this category). The rest of the world is limited to 170,000. No more than 20,000 persons may come annually from any one nation anywhere. Individual admissions are determined within these limits on the basis of priorities that pay no regard to national origins. Relatives of residents, scientists, professional and skilled workers, needed unskilled laborers, and refugees from Communism have varying claims to preference. (For example, 100,000 refugees from Castro's Cuba have been generously admitted.) But these priorities and the overall national limits are likely to change America's ethnic composition only slightly. Nonetheless, to significant numbers of previously excluded foreigners, America again lifts her "lamp beside the golden door."

Citizenship

The concept of citizenship was developed by the ancient Greeks and Romans, replacing the earlier concept of kinship. Blood-related families and tribes as the basis for community were replaced by the

---

[39] Note should be taken that not all aliens come to the United States as "quota immigrants." Foreign students, businessmen, tourists, government officials, etc., come for temporary stays under special visas issued outside the quota system. Other persons enter permanently as the spouse, offspring, or parent of American citizens. There is also an amorphous category of semi-permanent "nonquota" resident aliens.

citizenry—the free inhabitants of a city. However, modern citizenship concepts still preserve an element of the kinship principle. This is the rule of *jus sanguinis* (law of the blood), which gives children the citizenship of their parents. By the contrasting rule of *jus soli* (law of the soil), citizenship is derived primarily from the country where one is born, even if different from the national allegiance of the parents. American citizenship by birth is governed by a combination of these two principles.

The United States recognizes as citizens nearly all persons born on its soil. This includes not only the states of the Union, but also certain territories and possessions designated by law. Since they are not subject to American jurisdiction, the children of foreign diplomats stationed in the United States are not citizens of the United States even though born on American soil. By this principle, those born abroad in legations or embassies of the United States, on its territorial waters, and on ships of American registry are also native-born citizens of the United States. The rule of *jus soli* even extended American citizenship to a man born in the United States despite the fact that his Chinese alien parents were then themselves legally ineligible for citizenship.[40]

The rule of *jus sanguinis* is applied to children born abroad of American parents. Such children automatically have American citizenship if at least one of the two citizen parents had once resided in the United States or one of its outlying possessions. If only one of the parents is an American citizen, the child is recognized as an American citizen if brought to the United States within twenty-two years and if rather complex residence qualifications are met.

The rules are highly technical and excite the legally inclined to imagine all the possible combinations of parental lineage and places of birth. One of the more interesting complications is the dual citizenship problem that arises in international law when more than one nation claims the same child under varying principles of law. Dual citizenship problems frequently arise from the special status of women; some countries assign married women the citizenship of the husband, a practice once followed in the United States. At one time American women marrying aliens lost their citizenship, and female aliens acquired American citizenship automatically on marrying an American. Organizations seeking equal rights for women were finally successful in removing the dependent citizenship status of women in 1934. Women now are on an equal footing with men, gaining and losing citizenship in the same ways.

Naturalization is the process of acquiring citizenship by legal means rather than by birth. There are two forms of naturalization: collective and individual. Collective naturalization refers to the grant of citizenship to a group of persons by a single act of Congress, or by treaty—in 1803, for example, the people of the Louisiana territory by a treaty with France, and the people of Puerto Rico by statute in 1917.

Individual naturalization is determined by Congress which was ex-

---

[40] *United States* v. *Wong Kim Ark*, 169 U.S. 649 (1898).

plicitly provided the power "to establish an uniform rule of naturalization" by the Constitution (Art. I, sec. 8). The system has always been administered by the courts, mainly the Federal district courts. They are now aided by the Immigration and Naturalization Service of the Department of Justice in fact-finding investigations of an applicant's qualifications and conformity with legal requirements.[41]

Citizenship, whether by birth or naturalization, is not an immutable right, but may be revoked. Certain actions may be deemed, by due process of law, to constitute forfeiture of citizenship—for example, treason, serving in another nation's armed forces without permission, voting in foreign elections or swearing allegiance to another country. For some time revocation of citizenship was more readily applied to naturalized than to native-born citizens. However, increasingly, the Supreme Court has reduced this difference to the near-vanishing point.[42] Importantly, citizenship may be terminated not only as a penalty, but may be voluntarily yielded. Unlike Communist countries—the East Berlin wall comes readily to mind—the United States Congress declared in 1868: "the right of expatriation is a natural and inherent right of all people, indispensable to the enjoyment of the rights of life, liberty and the pursuit of happiness."

The federal aspects of the American constitutional system long raised a special problem concerning citizenship. In unitary nations there is a single national citizenship; subdivision into local governmental units does not affect citizenship. Now all persons born in the United States are citizens, and all American citizens, native-born or naturalized, are thereby citizens of any state of the Union wherein they choose to reside. This national determination of citizenship, both for the states as well as the national community, is established by the Fourteenth Amendment. Until then, the situation was unclear—particularly with respect to the citizenship of Negroes in nonslave states.[43] Although diversity of state citizenship continues to bear on some legal and political problems, the federal complication no longer has any bearing on American citizenship, either natural or naturalized.

The importance of full citizen-membership in the political community can be seen in contrast with the status of aliens. Aliens do possess the

---

[41] The requirements for naturalization are: (1) minimum age of 18; (2) English literacy; (3) understanding of the "fundamentals of the history, and of the principles and form of government, of the United States"; (4) residence in the United States lawfully for at least five continuous years preceding application; (5) of good moral character; (6) within ten years prior to application, petitioner must not have been an advocate, or associate of advocates, of subversive ideas; (7) applicant must support the principles of the Constitution and be loyal to the United States.

[42] "We start from the premise that the rights of citizenship of the native born and of the naturalized person are of the same dignity and are coextensive. The only difference drawn by the Constitution is that only the 'natural born' citizen is eligible to be President." *Angelika L. Schneider v. Dean Rusk, Secretary of State,* 377 U.S. 163 (1964).

[43] The Fourteenth Amendment overruled the important case of *Dred Scott v. Sandford,* 19 How. U.S. 393 (1857) in which native-born Negroes had been held outside the meaning of the term "citizen" whether emancipated or not.

constitutional rights of legal due process and equal protection of the laws, since the Fifth and Fourteenth Amendments provide these protections for all *persons*, citizens or not. And aliens for the most part share citizen burdens like taxpaying, conformity to law, and even military service under some circumstances. But they necessarily remain *in* the community rather than *of* it—subject to its rules and decisions without being politically equal in making those decisions. Aliens may not participate as members of the political community in elections nor hold public office. Certain types of employment are barred, primarily in the federal civil service and in defense plants. They are required to register annually, and may not change their residence without notifying authorities. Finally, for the alien, the omnipresent possibility of deportation differentiates the stranger in the land from the full-fledged member of the American political community.

BIBLIOGRAPHICAL NOTE

The authoritative study of early American suffrage is Chilton Williamson, *American Suffrage, From Property to Democracy, 1760–1860* (1960). Compare the 'Beardian' view in Kirk H. Porter, *A History of Suffrage in the United States* (1918). For other aspects of suffrage, see: Marian K. Sanders, *The Lady and the Vote* (1956); F. D. Ogden, *The Poll Tax in the South* (1958); and Paul Lewinson, *Race, Class and Party* (1932).

Current suffrage regulations are available in an annual publication, *The Book of the States* published by the Council of State Governments. The relation between regulation and nonvoting is considered in, *Report of the President's Commission on Registration and Voting Participation* (1963). Continuing problems of Negro suffrage are surveyed in U.S. Commission on Civil Rights, *Voting* (1961).

Immigration history is surveyed in Oscar Handlin, *The Uprooted* (1951). Also see John F. Kennedy, *A Nation of Immigrants* (1964). The most thorough coverage is Marion T. Bennett, *American Immigration Policies: An Authoritative Survey of Legal, Administrative, and Humanitarian Developments* (1963). A classic among studies of ethnic integration is W. I. Thomas and Florian Znaniecki, *Polish Peasant in Europe and America* (1918). A recent important study is Nathan Glazer and Daniel P. Moynihan, *Beyond the Melting Pot* (1963).

Citizenship theories are examined in Harold F. Gosnell, *Democracy, The Threshold of Freedom* (1948); and John P. Roche, *The Early Development of United States Citizenship* (1949). A psychological study of citizen attachment and alienation is Sebastian de Grazia, *The Political Community: A Study of Anomie* (1948).

Chapter 11

Machinery of Representation: Apportionment, Nominations, and Elections

> The policy of referring the appointment of the House of Representatives to the people . . . supposes that the result will be somewhat influenced by the mode. . . . Whether the electors should vote by ballot, or viva voce, should assemble at this place or that place, should all vote for all the representatives, or all in a district vote for a number allotted to the district—these and many other points . . . might materially affect the appointments. . . .
>
> JAMES MADISON[1]

THIS CHAPTER EXAMINES THE MECHANISMS—THE OFFICIALLY ESTABLISHED formal procedures—by which the American political community achieves its elected representation. These matters are inevitably technical and detailed, but they "materially affect the appointments." As we have noted frequently, mode of procedure affects substance of outcome. That is why politicians struggle over sometimes obscure alternative mechanisms like, say, a particular mode of establishing legislative districts. Similarly, control over nominations is affected differently by party convention than by direct primary systems. And different ballot forms variously facilitate and handicap particular interests and groups. These exemplify the three important processes in our system of popular representation to which we now turn: the mechanisms by which representation is *apportioned*, political party candidates are *nominated*, and *elections* are conducted.

Representation and its Apportionment

The entire political community cannot personally *congress* to make the laws in one gigantic town meeting. Instead the community is rep-

---

[1] In Jonathan Elliott, ed., *Debates of the Several State Conventions on the Adoption of the Federal Constitution* V, 401–402.

resented by elected *congressmen* who legislate in the name of the people. How to assign a small quantity of representatives to a large quantity of people is the technical, but politically vital, problem of legislative apportionment.

Among the important questions that must be answered in apportioning representatives are: How many people shall each district contain? Should each congressman represent the same number of constituents? Is population size the sole criterion for democratic representation or should the physical size of a district and its socioeconomic characteristics be considered? Where precisely shall district boundaries be drawn? By what machinery can fair principles of representation be most fairly administered?

Congressional Apportionment among the States

The Constitution provides that "representatives shall be apportioned among the several states according to their respective number, counting the whole number of persons in each State. . . ."[2] Population has been the predominant basis for representation in the House of Representatives from the outset (Art. I, sec. 2). To maintain the population basis of representation, adjustments must be made to changing population. There can be little doubt that such periodic reapportionment is implied by Article I; Congress is directed to provide machinery for a national "enumeration" (census) every ten years.

The precise formula for determining the number of representatives to be allotted to each state is left to Congress, which also determines the total number of House seats.[3] For most of our history a relatively simple formula was used. The national population was divided by the total number of seats, and the resulting quotient was then used to divide each state's population. The number of times the national quotient went into a state's population was roughly the number of seats awarded that state. Only roughly, however, because of two complications: the federal requirement that each state have at least one seat and the inevitable unevenness of such arithmetical divisions.[4]

If population *numbers* and *characteristics* were uniformly and stably distributed among and within the states, no political problems would

---

[2] This language from the Fourteenth Amendment alters only the 'three-fifths compromise' wording of the original document.

[3] Apportionment of the first Congress was set in the Constitution. There is an additional provision which is outdated, though legally binding. There must be *no more* than one representative for each 30,000 in the electoral base. If 30,000 were the quota applied to the 1960 census it would create a House of 5,977 members!

[4] Changes in the apportionment formula over the years have been in the statistical methods for taking these fractional remainders into account. The statistically inclined will want to read Laurence F. Schmeckebier, "The Method of Equal Proportions" in the symposium on "Legislative Reapportionment," in *Law and Contemporary Problems*, 17 (Spring, 1952), No. 2, 302 ff.

arise. The matter could be relegated to statisticians. But demographic factors display no such tidiness. Immigration affects some areas and not others, and birth and death rates vary by area. There are boom areas and depopulated areas. There are 'silk stocking' districts and those on 'the wrong side of the tracks.' Even age patterns are unevenly distributed— witness retirement meccas like Florida and California.

Changes in population number affect the vital question of number of representatives. Changes in population characteristics vitally affect election outcomes because age, race, economic, and other differences, affect voting behavior. Accordingly, reapportionment to adjust to changing population profoundly affects partisan interests. Yet the remarkable fact is that for the first one hundred and thirty years reapportionment of Congress was accomplished after every census.

Following the 1920 census, however, Congress for the first time failed to agree on a new apportionment. The tremendous population increase on the eastern seaboard, after the greatest ten year influx of immigrants in our history, provoked sharp opposition to including aliens in the enumeration of "persons" as had always been done under the Constitution. Moreover, some argued that the Constitution had been misconstrued and that decennial reapportionment itself was not required. Representatives from states that would have lost seats also attacked the accuracy of the national census figures and proffered alternative statistics of their state's population.

The failure to reapportion after the 1920 census meant that population changes were not reflected in the distribution of representatives for twenty years (1912-1932). The impasse was resolved in 1929 by an act establishing the present automatic reapportionment procedure. The basic feature directs the President to submit a reapportionment plan (prepared by the Census Bureau) following each decennial census. This plan is automatically implemented unless the Congress intervenes within 15 calendar (not legislative) days. Previously, there was no reapportionment unless Congress took the initiative. Another essential feature of the act froze the size of the House at 435 seats.[5] By making the procedure automatic and holding the size of the House constant, Congress sealed itself off from the bitter partisan conflict which apportionment invites.

Automatic reapportionment and professional administration of its "equal proportions" formula[6] have produced a near-perfect distribution of seats *among* the states. But apportionment is a two-stage process,

---

[5] Until 1911 the number of seats had been steadily increased to accommodate states entitled to new seats. This was far easier on representatives from states of declining population which otherwise would have lost seats. Subsequent efforts to increase the number of seats have been beaten back, though the pressure is intense from colleagues whose political lives may be at stake. An exception occurred when Hawaii and Alaska were admitted as states. The House was temporarily increased to 437 seats; with the 1962 election, the 435 seat House was resumed.

[6] See Schmeckebier, cited in note 4.

one at the national and one at the state level. The difficult problems of reapportionment have been mostly at the state level to which we now turn.

Districting within the States

Congress decides how many representatives will be assigned to each state. But the states share in determining how each state's quota of representatives is apportioned *within* the state. By congressional statute each representative must be assigned to a geographically defined district. This function has been mainly performed by the state legislatures, but subject to ultimate congressional regulation. Divided authority over the districting function emanates from the "times, places and manner" clause of the Constitution (Art. I, sec. 4), and is a continuing attribute of the federal power of the states.

Congress has used its ultimate authority over intrastate apportionment very sparingly, but the entire process of districting itself, as a legal requirement, derives from a national statute first enacted in 1842. Until then, several states elected all their congressmen 'at large.' Perhaps that was tolerable where a state had only two representatives. However, as the size of state delegations grew the ballot became intolerably long. Moreover, at-large elections enabled the majority party to win *all* of a state's seats. In contrast, with a state divided into a number of districts, the usual uneven distribution of party supporters is likely to provide the statewide minority party with a majority in at least some districts.

Congress has had to exercise its authority to provide for the eventuality that a state government may neglect to enact a redistricting measure despite changes in its allotment of seats. When such an impasse occurs, either of two processes follows: If the state's quota of congressmen is increased, the additional number of seats (beyond those already districted) are elected at large. Alternatively, where a state loses seats and fails to redistrict, *all* of the representatives must be elected at large. Following the 1961 reapportionment, eight states failed to redistrict after their allotments were changed and had to elect among them a total of 15 seats at large. Excluding the five Congressmen elected at large from the states with only one seat apiece, this left the overwhelming balance of 415 seats to be elected by single-member districts.

Congress long tried to regulate the way the states laid out district boundaries by requiring that they be composed of *contiguous* and *compact* territory. The intent was to reduce 'gerrymandering,' i.e., the partisan manipulation of district boundaries to include or exclude voters in order to insure favorable distributions. *Contiguity* would prevent inclusion in the same district of nonconnected areas. (For a flagrant example, see the map of the former 23rd district of Ohio—note the portion contained as an island entirely surrounded by the 20th district.) *Com-*

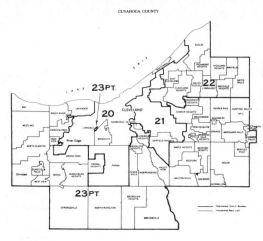

*The Twenty-third Congressional
District of Ohio long contained
noncontiguous territory: Note the
town of Linndale, a voting part
of the Twenty-third, is wholly
contained within the Twentieth
Congressional District.*

pactness would limit the twistings and turnings of boundary lines into 'salamander' and other irregular shapes.

Congressional regulations were never effective and, since 1929, the contiguity and compactness requirements have been deleted altogether from the national apportionment statutes. The upshot is that, although Congress has constitutionally apportioned congressional seats *among* the states upon a population basis, no national statute required a state to apportion the districts *within* that state on a population basis. Consequently, the states produced some grossly inequitable congressional districts.

For example in 1962, Michigan had both the nation's *smallest* district, and the nation's *third largest* district: Michigan's 16th district, with 802,994 people, contained more than four and one half times as many residents as its 12th district with only 177,431 people. Similarly Texas, with the *largest* congressional district, also had the *fifth smallest* in the nation: The 5th district, with 951,527 inhabitants, contained almost four and one half times as many people as the adjoining 4th district with a population of 216,371.[7]

Problems of Fair Representation

As a practical matter it is impossible to arrange legislative district boundaries to achieve a mathematically perfect distribution of population. Professional experts accept variations of up to 15 per cent from the ideal as sufficiently equitable. Forty-one per cent of the 430 districts (from states entitled to plural seats) in the Eighty-eighth Congress varied

[7] Figures are from U.S. Bureau of the Census, *Congressional District Data Book* (*Districts of the 88th Congress*) (Washington: U.S. Government Printing Office, 1963).

by more than 15 per cent from an ideal population distribution. The grossest disparity was in the 5th district of Georgia with a 208.9 per cent variation from the ideal.[8] Three times the number of people lived in the 20 most populated districts than in the 20 least populated. Each district, however sparsely or densely populated, elects one congressman. Consequently voters in different parts of the country have for many years had significantly unequal influence over decisions of the House, despite the plain fact that it is supposed to represent the people according to number. Such disparities led one writer to rename the lower chamber a "House of Unrepresentatives."[9]

Redistrictings following the 1960 census left intact the long-established pattern of malapportionment of districts within the states. Rural areas remained heavily overrepresented at the expense of urban areas, with the new suburban areas the most underrepresented. Undoubtedly, many rurally dominated state legislatures deliberately produced this situation. The problem has been cumulative. State legislatures themselves have been strongly weighted in favor of rural areas, and this in turn led them to apportion congressional districts in favor of the same interests and areas. Thus reapportionment, within the states, of both state legislative and congressional districts has been intertwined.

What justification could there be for thus drastically departing from the population basis in constructing congressional districts? Some state legislators have argued the need to protect rural and small-town interests from being swamped in a national sea of big-city votes. The Senate, they say, cannot be depended on for this protection. Senatorial elections are statewide; since there are now urban majorities in most states, senators have become increasingly sensitive to 'big-city interests.' Thus, they conclude, the House of Representatives is the only remaining source of national protection for rural and small-town interests. Another argument is that sparsely populated districts, in order to equal the population of even the smallest city district, must cover a huge territory. This puts the rural area dwellers at a great disadvantage because their congressman is physically less accessible to them, and hence less able to represent them. Thus, it has been argued, the physical size of an area is a necessary ingredient of fair representation.

On the other side, proponents of equal-population districts base their arguments mainly on democratic principles of majority rule and of political equality—'one man, one vote.' Malapportioned districts, they argue, result in minority rule in the legislatures of both state and nation. Area as such is not a proper criterion for representation. In an age of

---

[8] This condition was challenged in an ultimately successful suit requiring Georgia to reapportion her congressional districts so that "as nearly as is practicable one person's vote in a congressional election is to be worth as much as another's." *Wesberry v. Sanders* 376 U.S. 1 (1964).

[9] Gus Tyler, "House of Unrepresentatives," *New Republic*, CXXX (June 21, 1954), 8–11; CXXX (June 28, 1954), 14–15; CXXXI (July 5, 1954), 13–14.

Father of the bride.

jet-propelled travel and instantaneous communication, the modern member of Congress is readily accessible to the most distantly located of his constituents. Moreover, they emphasize, disproportionate minority representation in the House of Representatives—the popular chamber—is unconstitutional.

Judicial Answers to Political Questions

Legislators are understandably reluctant to commit political suicide, and have long resisted changing the very apportionments by which they themselves were elected. Proponents of legislative reapportionment, frustrated by the difficulty of gaining legislative support, turned to the courts. For many years these efforts were unavailing, and the judges seemed intent on avoiding what Justice Frankfurter called a "political thicket." Judicial self-restraint was imposed in 1946 in *Colegrove* v. *Green*[10] when the Supreme Court, in a four to three decision, refused to intervene in an Illinois suit to compel reapportionment. For 45 years, the Illinois state legislature had left congressional districts unchanged despite enormous population shifts. Some districts contained

---

[10] 328 U.S. 549.

nine times the number of people as others in the state. But Justice Frankfurter held that the issues posed were "political questions" and not justiciable. "There is not under our Constitution a judicial remedy for every political mischief." Rather relief "must come through an aroused popular conscience that sears the conscience of the people's representatives."

Despite the *Colegrove* decision not to review and invalidate the Illinois congressional apportionment, the Court was closer to entering the "thicket" than even the bare majority vote indicated. The majority *decision* had been expressed in two separate *opinions*. One was Frankfurter's opinion, on behalf of himself and two other justices, that apportionment was a "political question." The other was a single concurring opinion, which supported the decision to refuse jurisdiction *in this particular case,* but *not* on the ground that apportionment was not justiciable *in principle*. This concurring justice together with the dissenting minority formed a 'hidden majority' willing to submit legislative apportionment questions to judicial review. In 1962 the hidden majority became the actual majority, and in *Baker* v. *Carr*[11] the Supreme Court affirmed the right of citizens of Tennessee to challenge the failure to reapportion their state legislature in the federal courts. Many cases were then pressed before the courts, and in two historic cases the Supreme Court upheld the equal-populations principle of districting for both houses of bicameral state legislatures[12] and for the United States House of Representatives.[13] The former decision was based on the Fourteenth Amendment's equal-protection clause, the latter on the requirements of Article I. "Legislators," the Court majority maintained, "represent people, not trees or acres. Legislators are elected by voters, not farms or cities or economic interests." Sensitive to claims that they were treading on political matters beyond their proper judicial purview, the Court responded: "We are cautioned about the dangers of entering into political thickets and mathematical quagmires. Our answer is this: a denial of constitutionally protected rights demands judicial protection. . . ."[14]

Apportionment and Objectivity: A Prognosis

The precise standards of reasonableness by which specific legislative apportionments are to be judged were left to the lower courts. Considerable litigation remains before long-established patterns are altered to accord substantially with the Supreme Court's principles. This is a highly complex undertaking.

Congress has ample power under the Constitution to determine the boundaries of congressional districts within the states, or at least to

---

[11] 369 U.S. 186.
[12] *WMCA* v. *Lomenzo*, 377 U.S. 633 (1964).
[13] *Wesberry* v. *Sanders*, 376 U.S. 1 (1964).
[14] *Reynolds* v. *Sims* (1964), as printed in *New York Times*, June 16, 1964, p. 28.

reestablish minimal standards for the states to follow. The automatic reapportionment machinery which has worked so well since 1929 in distributing seats *among* the states conceivably could be extended to apportioning districts *within* the states. Some hope that statisticians, demographers, and other professional experts of the Census Bureau might overcome the narrow partisanship that now characterizes the process. However, it is far easier to know when an unfair allocation of seats has been made among the states than it is to know the fairness of district boundaries within states. Simple arithmetic can be applied in the former case because the state boundaries are permanently fixed. But it is highly doubtful that anyone can devise a comparably objective procedure for state districting because there it is the boundaries themselves that are in question. And every geographical arrangement is fraught with political consequence. Bureaucratic gerrymandering is likely to be as ugly as that produced by legislatures acting as avowedly political agencies of government. It is difficult, indeed, to take the politics out of politics.

Nonetheless, the difficulty of the task should not obscure what even imperfect and imprecise standards of reasonableness can reveal. Some congressional districts violate even the most minimal requirements of compactness and contiguity. The differences between gross distortions and borderline suspicions of gerrymandering which can be known by common sense should not be repudiated as a guide simply because perfect professional standards are not available. Congress could require reasonable standards of compactness and contiguity of district territory as well as equality of population. The federal courts have demonstrated their readiness to apply such standards to cases of gross malapportionment. Great changes in the apportionment of state legislatures and Congress—tilting the political balance between rural-urban-suburban and farm-business-labor interests—are underway. And the "appointments" have, indeed, been "materially affected."

Nominations

The hugeness of the political community, which necessitates the election of representatives, similarly makes necessary a system of advance nomination of candidates for public office. Consider how the total number of eligible persons is reduced to manageable electoral alternatives. For example, there are perhaps seventy million persons who now meet the constitutional qualifications for the Presidency. Imagine the voter's hopeless task if only a blank ballot were supplied. Which one of the millions of possible names should he write upon the ballot? Only a statistical miracle could lead to sufficient agreement so that somehow a single name would emerge across the country as the majority's choice. Reduction of choice to manageable proportions is regularly achieved by the nominating process which identifies the few actual candidates long before election day.

At the same time, the power to name the candidates effectively determines the practical range of electoral choices. Influence over nominations, therefore, is eagerly sought by political activists, and control over major party labels—which identify the major candidates—is a key ingredient of political party power.

Evolution of Nominating Techniques

The nominating process is an elemental feature of politics. It arises in private and informal ways wherever a grouping of persons agree in advance to support a candidate in common, and may be everywhere witnessed in all manner of associations. In Anglo-American politics an informal partisan combination is often called a *caucus*. An early example was described in a 1763 journal entry by John Adams:

> This day learned that the Caucus club meets at certain times in the garret of Tom Dawes, the Adjutant of the Boston regiment. . . . There they smoke tobacco till you cannot see from one end of the garret to the other. There they drink flip, I suppose, and they choose a moderator who puts questions to the vote regularly; and selectmen, assessors, collectors, firewards, and representatives· are regularly chosen before they are chosen in the town.

The 'smoke-filled room,' where the *slate* of nominees is picked, was originally condemned as conspiratorial. Gradually, such groups became so common that they achieved relative respectability. They had to become common. The meeting of 'king-makers' is as old as politics. But democratic forms of election, even more than other systems less dependent on broad electorates, cannot do without some means of carrying out the nominating function. The Constitution, however, does not establish a specific procedure for nominating candidates for elective office. Yet the "times, places and manner of holding elections" clause was known to entail such procedures, and the states and Congress were generally empowered to provide such regulation as they wished. However, nominating practices were little regulated until the twentieth century, being long regarded as essentially private and extra-governmental partisan activities.

The Legislative Caucus. The natural statewide meeting place for politicians was the state legislature. Legislative caucuses were already organized to advance partisan interests in each session; they soon came to consider potential candidates as well as legislative matters. The caucuses were ready-made places to consider candidates for governor and other statewide offices. The national Congress functioned similarly in the nominations of presidential candidates until 1824. The convenience of this regularly gathered national meeting of prominent politicians was an inducement to active nominating politics. Moreover, the method of electing the President and Vice President gives Congress a potentially powerful role. Prior to the fuller development of national party organization, it was reasonable to have expected that presidential elections would frequently be decided in the House. Congressmen, therefore, had a strong sense of involvement in presidential nominating politics, and the congressional caucuses provided the clearest early embodiment of national party structures.

Legislative caucus nominations soon aroused increasing dissatisfaction. Some critics were opposed in principle, arguing that 'King Caucus' was subject to wire-pulling by political bosses and was unrepresentative of general party opinion. And quite apart from principle, factional groups which unsuccessfully backed particular candidates in the caucus looked to other forms of nomination as possible ways to increase their intra-party power. The strength and prestige of the caucuses eroded under these assaults. By 1830 the caucus form persisted mainly at the local level; most statewide candidacies were certified by state conventions. In 1824 the seriously weakened national congressional caucus of the dominant Democratic-Republican party invited final disaster by rejecting the immensely popular Andrew Jackson. In 1832 the victorious Jacksonian Democrats inaugurated the first major party national nominating convention—which has been the basic presidential nominating device ever since.

Nomination by Convention

American nominating conventions have always provided flamboyant spectacles. Thousands of delegates march with banners, stamp their feet, cheer and boo, and in general provide a milling and often inattentive forum for innumerable and repetitive orations. They have been hailed as an uniquely American folk pageant and condemned as frivolous and degrading circuses. Some see in them a great expression of democracy in action, others a mass puppet show manipulated by machine politicians. Whatever their merits or demerits, they remain instruments of enormous political power. Behind the outward show is an intricate process controlling the way the nation chooses candidates for its most responsible governmental position—the President of the United States.

Here we concentrate chiefly on the formal details of that process—the apparatus and regulations by which the parties select delegates and organize the conventions, postponing to the next chapter much of the dynamic interplay of candidates, interest groups, and party factions as they seek to influence the outcome.

Apportioning the convention. The apportionment of convention votes within the national parties provides a problem of political representation reminiscent of legislative apportionment itself. Indeed, for a considerable time the parties merely applied the national congressional apportionment as the basis for their own national conventions. Each state delegation was given the same number of votes as the state had electoral votes for President (the number of representatives plus senators). But this made *general population* the basis for reaching party decisions irrespective of the proportion of *party supporters* represented by those delegates. On this basis, Southern Republicans, who never won elections, nonetheless had considerable power in the Republican national conventions and were much wooed (and bribed with patronage) by candidates. Similarly, Democrats from rock-ribbed Republican states carried disproportionate weight at the Democratic conventions.

Republicans used the electoral-vote basis of apportioning their convention votes until 1916; Democrats continued until 1944. Since then, the apportionment formulas give bonus votes to delegations from states having won party victories in national or state elections. But as in legislative apportionment, it is not easy to eliminate malrepresentation. For example, the twelve most populous states were still underrepresented at both national party conventions in 1956. As it happened, these states had provided 65 per cent of each party's total votes, yet in each case they received only 47 per cent of the total votes at the nominating conventions.

The allocation of convention votes *among the states* is made by the party national committees. There is no governmental regulation of that apportionment. The delegate distribution *within the states,* however, is commonly regulated by state laws. Four methods are variously employed and combined to select delegates within the states: (1) state party committees; (2) state party conventions; (3) district conventions or district caucuses at state conventions; (4) some form of state-conducted popular (direct primary) elections. The statewide convention system is strongly favored; 35 states elect most of their delegates to the Democratic national convention this way, 37 in the case of the Republicans. The second most prevalent method is direct popular election; 16 states elect some or all Democratic delegates, 14 in the case of the Republicans. Few states turn the selection of any delegates over to the state party committees; six states for the Democrats, three for the Republicans. The district selection of delegates (as distinct from selection at large) is by far a Republican usage: Twenty states select such Republican delegates at district conventions or caucuses, only four do so in the case of the Democrats.[15]

Organizing the convention. Conventions require complicated preliminary organization and preparation. The party national committees issue the official calls to the conventions, appoint arrangements committees long in advance, and seek to drum up a rising crescendo of publicity. Merely arranging the physical facilities requires prodigious preparatory efforts. Thousands of delegates, alternates and observers must be housed; clerks and pages must be hired; committee and caucus sessions must be accommodated; a vast communications network must be organized; the amphitheatre has to be planned for 'traffic flow,' (i.e., aisle demonstrations), and arranged and decorated suitably for the television cameras.

The convention delegates are self-governing; they can legally establish their own rules and reject prior arrangements made in their name.

---

[15] Consult the *Congressional Quarterly, Convention Guide* (supplement), June 12, 1964.

But the leadership function is inescapable in preparing physical facilities, the agenda (schedule) of the proceedings, the selection of speakers (their order, topics, and time allotment), and the preliminary choice of convention officials. Yet conventions have on occasion exerted their sovereignty. For example, a bitter contest at the 1952 Republican convention over the seating of certain delegates established the dominance of the Eisenhower forces over the Taft-controlled national committee. However, it requires equivalent advance preparation and organization by an opposition with broad national support to challenge what has been done by the national committee. Leadership functions have to be undertaken, no matter by whom, as a condition of readying the convention for its work and as a condition of political control.

When assembled, a convention is more like a mass rally than a deliberative body. Division into committees is essential for converting this huge assembly into working units. Here too, the work must begin in advance of the formal convention. Committee members are chosen by the state delegations (usually one member from each delegation). Preparatory meetings are held and the committees continue to meet after the convention opens, readying their reports while oratory, 'floor shows,' and politicking occupy the rest of the delegates. There are four major standing committees: Credentials, which settles disputes over the seating of delegates; Permanent Organization, which names the slate of permanent officers (usually confirming the national committee's advance selection, but occasionally becoming a battleground between contending factions); Resolutions, which mainly prepares the platform; and Rules, which compiles the official rules governing convention procedure.

Within these committees and sometimes on the floor there are occasionally battles over organizational issues. As so often happens, the procedural issues can have substantive consequences or implications. Two typical ones are the 'Loyalty Oath' and the 'Fair Play' amendment.

The Loyalty Oath was adopted as part of the rules by the 1952 Democratic convention; no delegates were to be seated who did not pledge to support the party ticket. The object was to prevent repetition of the use of the Democratic party label to elect presidential electors not pledged to the national party's candidates. Four southern states had used this device to back the Dixiecrat candidate instead of President Truman in 1948. The oath was rendered ineffective in 1952 when delegates of three states were seated despite their refusal to comply. In 1956 the oath was replaced with a rule merely proclaiming it the "understanding" of the convention that a state party organization sending a delegation would support the convention nominees in the ensuing election.

The Fair Play amendment originated in 1952 when a Republican battle (between Taft and Eisenhower forces) over southern delegate credentials resulted in a rule disqualifying challenged delegates from voting on all questions unless they had been placed on the temporary roll by a two-thirds vote of the national committee. The Democrats merely require challenged delegates to refrain from voting on the question of their own seating.

The roll call of states. Most Americans are familiar with the roll call of the states, and have been gripped by the excitement of seeing the race for the presidential nomination reach its climax. *"Alabama!"* And the roll call goes alphabetically through the list of states and territories, the first time for entering names in candidacy. This is accompanied by nominating and seconding speeches ritually making no mention of the candidate's name until the very conclusion, and thereby triggering great demonstrations in the aisles. Then, once more through the roll of states, this time for the crucial counting of votes. Each time through the entire alphabetical listing is one 'ballot.' In 1964, Lyndon B. Johnson and Barry Goldwater were each nominated on the first ballot, as had been John F. Kennedy and Richard M. Nixon in 1960. However, deep divisions in the parties sometimes produce prolonged and exhausting balloting. In 1880 it took the Republicans 36 ballots to nominate James A. Garfield. The longest Democratic impasse was at the 1924 convention, which finally chose 'dark-horse' John W. Davis on the 103rd ballot! The 1924 Democratic convention was deadlocked by the two-thirds rule which was eventually eliminated in 1936. Both party conventions now require a simple majority to nominate and lengthy deadlocks are infrequent.

Contests over the vice-presidential nomination are rare; typically the convention abides by the presidential candidate's preference. Normally, an effort is made to 'balance the ticket' so that some additional group within the party or within the electorate may be won over. However, the Democratic vice-presidential nomination was vigorously contested in 1956. Senator Estes Kefauver narrowly defeated Senator John F. Kennedy when presidential candidate Adlai Stevenson surprisingly declared it an open race.

The climax of the convention comes with the personal appearance of the successful candidates, and their acceptance speeches seek to rally the party and win the nation. This reveals an important function of the convention beyond its nominating activity. The leaders utilize the national convening of thousands of party activists to unify the diverse factions and to gird the party workers for the hard campaigning ahead.

Direct Primaries

The convention system for nominating *congressional* and *state-level* candidates eventually succumbed to much the same criticisms as did the legislative caucus form. Political bosses were said to control delegate selection and convention nominations by manipulation of patronage and sometimes by even less savory methods. Popular and distinguished personages were sometimes defeated by little known 'machine' candidates. The turn of the century Progressive movement won wide support for nominating party candidates directly by the electorate in state-conducted primary elections (hence the term *direct* primaries). Wisconsin led the way in 1903, and by 1917 all but four states had adopted similar processes for nominating state and congressional candidates.

Nominations by direct primary are generally required only for major party candidates. Minor parties usually place their candidates on the *general election* ballot by circulating petitions to be signed by a specified proportion of the voters. Candidates seeking nomination on a major party ticket typically get on the *primary nominating* ballots by a similar petition route. Collecting numerous signatures, usually by door-to-door soliciting, is hard work. Similarly, getting out a favorable vote in a primary is much like the organizational effort needed to win a general election. Since the party organizations specialize in just such activity, they are not much more eliminated by the direct primary nominating process than they were by the convention method.

There are two important varieties of direct primaries: open and closed. The difference concerns voter eligibility to participate in choosing a particular party's candidates. A *closed primary* is officially closed to voters who are not avowed supporters of that party. How such support is required to be demonstrated differs considerably among the states. Public advance registration of partisanship is a common method and perhaps the most effective way to limit a party's primary ballot to its regular partisans. Alternatively, an *open primary* is officially open to all voters, irrespective of partisanship. Even in open primaries, however, voters must restrict their choices to one or the other party. The lone exception is the state of Washington. There, a so-called 'blanket' ballot form is used, and voters may select among the primary candidates of *both* major parties (though the voter is limited to one party per office). When the primary is open to the general public, Democrats, say, are able if they choose to swing the balance in a Republican primary. Many oppose the open primary as destructive of party responsibility and discipline.

Sixteen states (plus the District of Columbia) used some form of *presidential primary* in 1964. There are two main types: those where the voters elect delegates to the party national conventions, and those where the voters only express preferences among known presidential contenders. There are combinations of these, so that some states require would-be convention delegates to pledge their support to a particular presidential candidate, and some states require such delegates to vote as pledged for at least one convention ballot.

At one time there was far more enthusiasm for presidential nominating primaries than today, though there continue to be strong advocates of a national presidential primary to replace the convention form of nomination altogether. However, criticism of the national party conventions, which made primaries seem desirable, has waned considerably. The weakening of patronage-based organizations, with the growth of civil service merit systems, has weakened the old-style political machine—it may well have shouted its "Last Hurrah"![16]

There is also somewhat less enthusiasm for direct primary nominations of state and congressional candidates. It is argued that primaries do not and cannot eliminate 'bosses'—a word all too frequently meaning merely the other faction's leaders. Leadership and organization are inherent in an election system and primaries simply add additional elections requiring additional organization. Moreover, the electorate is burdened by the multiplicity of elections. Hence, voter participation in primaries is usually very low, and a united party leadership can usually control enough votes to carry the primary.

Further, ordinary voters choose nominees without consideration of the best overall ticket. A convention or a caucus can work out compromises between groups and balance a ticket between them so as to make the slate of party candidates broadly appealing. For example, prior to the introduction of the direct primary in Massachusetts, Boston Democrats were given about 25 per cent of the slots on the ticket by state party conventions. The higher turnout of Bostonians in the primary now results in about 80 percent of the nominees coming from Boston.[17]

The unifying function of party conventions has been noted; the direct primary, by contrast, tends to bring intra-party schism into full public view. Bitterness in primary battles between party factions is quite common, and frequently the breach is not healed in time for the ensuing general election. The strain on candidates in terms of time, energy, and financial expenditures has also been assailed. The mounting cost of campaigning threatens to make public office a preserve of the wealthy or those too closely tied to powerful interest groups.

The primary system is strongly entrenched, however, and it suits well the average American's somewhat negative view of party politics. And although it has been far less than the panacea for all political ills imagined by its original proponents, the direct primary has enabled dissident groups within the parties more effectively to challenge an entrenched leadership. Meanwhile, the leadership process continues in organizing the campaigns for contesting primary elections as it does in the general elections. *Preprimary conventions* are utilized in a few states to ameliorate the harshness of factional warfare and to provide a 'balanced ticket,' hoping it will be ratified by the voters in the subsequent primary. In most states, *postprimary conventions* are held to write the party platform, promote unity, and ready the party workers for the election campaign still to be waged.

---

[16] For an interesting account of old-style politics, see the novel *The Last Hurrah*, by Edwin O'Connor (Boston: Little, Brown, 1956).

[17] V. O. Key, Jr., *State Politics*, pp. 154–56.

INSTRUCTION BALLOT
Kent County, Michigan
General Election, November 3, 1964

INSTRUCTIONS—To vote a straight party ticket make a cross (X) in the circle under the name of your party. Nothing further need be done. To vote for a candidate not on your party ticket, make a cross (X) in the square ☐ before his name. Candidates for president and vice-president must be voted for as a unit, and the vote cannot be split. If two or more candidates are to be elected to the same office, and you desire to vote for candidates not on your party ticket, make a cross (X) in the square ☐ before the names of the candidates for whom you desire to vote on the other ticket, and strike out an equal number of names on your party ticket, for that office. If you do not desire to vote any party ticket, do not make a cross (X) in the circle at the head of any ticket, but make a cross (X) in the square ☐ before the name of each candidate for whom you desire to vote. If you wish to vote for a candidate not on any ticket, write or place the name of such candidate on your ticket opposite the name of the office. Before leaving the booth, fold the ballot so that the face of the ballot is not exposed and so that the numbered corner is visible.

NAMES OF OFFICES VOTED FOR:	DEMOCRATIC PARTY	REPUBLICAN	SOCIALIST WORKERS PARTY	SOCIALIST LABOR PARTY	FREEDOM NOW PARTY
PRESIDENTIAL — Electors of President and Vice-President of the United States	Lyndon B. Johnson / Hubert H. Humphrey	Barry Goldwater / William E. Miller	Clifton DeBerry / Edward Shaw	Eric Hass / Henning Blomen	
STATE GOVERNOR AND LIEUTENANT GOVERNOR	Neil Staebler / Robert A. Derengoski	George Romney / William G. Milliken	Frank Lovell / Harriet Tanin	James C. Horvath / W. Clifford Bentley	Albert B. Cleage, Jr. / James Jackson
SECRETARY OF STATE	James M. Hare	Allison Green	Jan Garrett	Ralph W. Muncy	Loy A. Cohen
ATTORNEY GENERAL	Frank J. Kelley	Meyer Warshawsky	Robert Pink	William Walbridge	Allen Bibb
CONGRESSIONAL — UNITED STATES SENATOR	Philip A. Hart	Elly M. Peterson	Evelyn Sell	James Sim	Ernest C. Smith
REPRESENTATIVE IN CONGRESS, 5th District	William G. Reamon	Gerald R. Ford			
LEGISLATIVE — STATE SENATOR, 31st District	Richard W. Blake	Robert Vander Laan			
REPRESENTATIVE IN STATE LEGISLATURE, 91st District	Tony Brouwer	Thomas G. Ford			
STATE BOARDS — MEMBERS OF THE STATE BOARD OF EDUCATION (TWO YEAR TERM) VOTE FOR NOT MORE THAN TWO	Leon Fill	Karla Parker			Henry L. Hill
	Donald M. D. Thurber	Ellen M. Solomonson			Margaret Willis
MEMBERS OF THE STATE BOARD OF EDUCATION (FOUR YEAR TERM) VOTE FOR NOT MORE THAN TWO	Carmen L. DelliQuadri	Joyce Hatton			Helen Kelly
	Marilyn Jean Kelly	Bourke Ledewyk			Clara Maravin
MEMBERS OF THE STATE BOARD OF EDUCATION (SIX YEAR TERM) VOTE FOR NOT MORE THAN TWO	Thomas J. Brennan	Robert F. Briggs			Mattie E. Mays
	Peter Oppewall	John C. Kreger			Constance Diane Mulette
MEMBERS OF THE STATE BOARD OF EDUCATION (EIGHT YEAR TERM) VOTE FOR NOT MORE THAN TWO	Charles E. Morton	Alvin M. Bentley			Ella Mae Perryman
	Edwin L. Novak	James F. O'Neil			John R. Thomas
MEMBERS OF THE BOARD OF TRUSTEES OF MICHIGAN STATE UNIVERSITY VOTE FOR NOT MORE THAN TWO	Frank Hartman	Paul D. Bagwell		Theos A. Grove	Grace Lee Boggs
	Clair White	John S. Pingel		Albert Mills	Eugene S. McGuire
MEMBERS BOARD OF GOVERNORS WAYNE STATE UNIVERSITY VOTE FOR NOT MORE THAN TWO	William B. Hall	Wilber M. Brucker, Jr.		Charles Fraser	Helen Nuttall Brown
	Benjamin M. Rose	Charles Gershenson		Lowell E. Miller	Louis J. Cleage
COUNTY — PROSECUTING ATTORNEY	Edward George Szpindewski	James K. Miller			
SHERIFF	Thaddeus A. Nowak	Arnold O. Pigorsh			
COUNTY CLERK	Walter A. Barnes	Jack Bronkema			
COUNTY TREASURER	Jane K. Denney	Henry Romyn			
REGISTER OF DEEDS	Carol L. Booker	Ruth E. Webber			
DRAIN COMMISSIONER		Frank W. Bouma			
SURVEYOR	Clayton S. Hay	Wilfred B. Williams			

Printed by Authority of County Election Commission

Above: Michigan Party-Column Ballot (Indiana type).

Opposite: Massachusetts Office-Block Ballot (Massachusetts type).

STATE ELECTION

OFFICIAL BALLOT
FOR

FALL RIVER
Ward 7
Precinct C

Tuesday, November 3, 1964

Kevin H. White

SECRETARY OF THE COMMONWEALTH
OF MASSACHUSETTS

To vote for a Person, mark a Cross X in the Square at the right of the Party Name or Political Designation.

ELECTORS OF PRESIDENT AND VICE PRESIDENT.

To vote for Electors of President and Vice President under any one of the following Party Name or Political Designations, mark a Cross X in the Square at the right of such Party Name or Political Designation.

Vote for ONE

GOLDWATER and MILLER — Republican	
HASS and BLOMEN — Socialist Labor	
JOHNSON and HUMPHREY — Democratic	
MUNN and SHAW — Prohibition	

To vote for a Person, mark a Cross X in the Square at the right of the Party Name or Political Designation.

SENATOR IN CONGRESS
Vote for ONE

EDWARD M. KENNEDY — of Boston — Democratic	
HOWARD WHITMORE, Jr. — of Newton — Republican	
LAWRENCE GILFEDDER — of Maynard — Socialist Labor	
GRACE F. LUDER — of Waltham — Prohibition	

GOVERNOR
Vote for ONE

FRANCIS X. BELLOTTI — of Quincy — Democratic	
JOHN A. VOLPE — of Winchester — Republican	
FRANCIS A. VOTANO — of Lynn — Socialist Labor	
GUY S. WILLIAMS — of Auburn — Prohibition	

LIEUTENANT GOVERNOR
Vote for ONE

JOHN W. COSTELLO — of Boston — Democratic	
ELLIOT L. RICHARDSON — of Brookline — Republican	
EDGAR E. GAUDET — of Lynn — Socialist Labor	
PRESCOTT C. GROUT — of Peabody — Prohibition	

ATTORNEY GENERAL
Vote for ONE

EDWARD W. BROOKE — of Newton — Republican	
JAMES W. HENNIGAN, Jr. — of Boston — Democratic	
WILLY N. HOGSETH — of Quincy — Socialist Labor	
HOWARD B. RAND — of Merrimac — Prohibition	

SECRETARY
Vote for ONE

KEVIN H. WHITE — of Boston — Democratic	
WALLACE B. CRAWFORD — of Pittsfield — Republican	
FRED H. INGERSOLL — of Lynn — Socialist Labor	
JULIA B. KOHLER — of Boston — Prohibition	

TREASURER
Vote for ONE

ROBERT Q. CRANE — of Boston — Democratic	
WARREN C. CARBERG — of Malaya — Republican	
ARNE A. SORTELL — of Randolph — Socialist Labor	

AUDITOR
Vote for ONE

THADDEUS BUCZKO — of Salem — Democratic	
ELWYNN J. MILLER — of Newton — Republican	
JOHN CHARLES HEDGES — of Newton — Prohibition	
ETHELBERT L. NEVENS — of Lynn — Socialist Labor	

To vote for a Person, mark a Cross X in the Square at the right of the Party Name or Political Designation.

CONGRESSMAN
Tenth District
Vote for ONE

JOSEPH WILLIAM MARTIN, Jr. — of North Attleborough — Republican	
EDWARD F. DOOLAN — of Fall River — Democratic	

COUNCILLOR
Vote for ONE

CHRIS BYRON — of Wareham — Democratic	
NICHOLAS W. MITCHELL — of Fall River — Democratic	

SENATOR
First Bristol District
Vote for ONE

MARY L. FONSECA — of Fall River — Democratic	

REPRESENTATIVES IN GENERAL COURT
Seventh Bristol District
Vote for TWO

JOHN J. LONG — of Fall River — Democratic	
JAMES A. O'BRIEN, Jr. — of Fall River — Democratic	

To vote for a Person, mark a Cross X in the Square at the right of the Party Name or Political Designation.

CLERK OF COURTS
Vote for ONE

WILLIAM P. GRANT — of Fall River — Democratic	

REGISTER OF DEEDS
Fall River District
Vote for ONE

JOSEPH E. HANIFY, Jr. —	

COUNTY COMMISSIONERS
Vote for TWO

CHARLES J. FRATES — of — Democratic	
PATRICK H. HARRINGTON — of — Democratic	

To vote on a Question, mark a Cross X in the Square at the right of YES or NO.

QUESTION NO. 1

PROPOSED AMENDMENT TO THE CONSTITUTION

	YES
	NO

QUESTION NO. 2

PROPOSED AMENDMENT TO THE CONSTITUTION

	YES
	NO

QUESTION NO. 3

THE CONSTITUTION

	YES
	NO

QUESTION NO. 4

THE CONSTITUTION

	YES
	NO

QUESTION NO. 5

VE PETITION

	YES
	NO

QUESTION NO. 6

LAW SUBMITTED UPON REFERENDUM AFTER PASSAGE

	YES
	NO

QUESTION NO. 7

A. Shall licenses be granted in this city or town for the sale therein of all alcoholic beverages (whisky, rum, gin and all other malt beverages, wines and all other alcoholic beverages)?

	YES
	NO

B. Shall licenses be granted in this city or town for the sale therein of wines and malt beverages (wines and all other malt beverages)?

	YES
	NO

C. Shall licenses be granted in this city or town for the sale therein of all alcoholic beverages in packages, so called, not to be drunk on the premises?

	YES
	NO

Election Machinery

The question of election machinery involves: (1) types of ballots by which voter preferences may be indicated and recorded; (2) the single-member district common in the United States; (3) the machinery for electing Presidents; and, finally, (4) the problem of administering elections with accuracy, fairness, and competence.

Types of Ballots

An ancient form of voting is conducted orally and publicly. *Viva voce* (live voice) voting continues to be used in many legislative divisions and in balloting at party conventions. The word ballot derives from the tiny colored balls once used for secret voting; blackball, i.e., a negative vote, is a related term. The modern paper ballot was initially introduced for public elections as a printed 'ticket' supplied by the political parties. This was not calculated to ensure privacy of choice, since each party's tickets were distinctively colored. Party watchers stood by as votes were publicly cast with these visibly partisan ballots, noting friends and opponents. Secret voting was used in a number of places in the colonial period, and state officials were elected by secret ballot in New York as early as 1788. But effective procedures to protect the anonymity of a voter's choices were a late nineteenth-century product.

Numerous scandals over corrupt practices in election administration and the need for secret balloting stimulated a movement of electoral reform. It culminated in widespread adoption of the Australian ballot (so called because it originated there in 1856). Its essential ingredients are its design to ensure the privacy of each voter's selections and the elimination of all ballots other than those officially supplied by government election officials. There are two major types of Australian ballots used presently to elect congressmen and presidential electors:

The party-column ballot is used in 33 states. Commonly called an Indiana ballot, it lists vertically all candidates of one party under that party's name and symbol. In all but six of these states, a circle or box is printed at the head of each party's column to be marked if the voter wishes to vote a straight ticket, i.e., to vote for all of that party's candidates with only one marking. (On voting machines, a single lever is provided to accomplish the same thing.) Obviously, straight-ticket voting is thereby greatly facilitated, but tickets can be split by separately marking each candidate for different offices in their respective party columns.

The office-block ballot is used in 17 states. This so-called Massachusetts ballot groups the candidates by the office sought instead of by parties. The order of names within each group does not necessarily follow the same party sequence, though party identifications accompany each name. The typical Massachusetts ballot requires voters to mark each candidate they intend to support. Thus, straight party voting is rendered more difficult. This sometimes reduces the amount of votes cast to decide minor contests, since less educated and interested voters often quit after marking the blocks for major offices such as President or Governor.

All congressional and presidential ballots include party identifications of the candidates. Nonpartisan ballots, however, are used for some state and local offices in this country, and that very embodiment of strong party government, the British Parliament, is elected on such a ballot. British voters, however, have little difficulty knowing the party affiliation of the candidates since they have only the one office on the ballot in parliamentary elections.

Congressional Elections

Representatives are usually elected by plurality votes in single-member districts. In discussing apportionment problems of the single-member district system, we noted how gerrymandering and malapportionment can prevent statewide majorities from winning a majority of the state's congressional seats. But even when congressional seats have been perfectly apportioned and districted according to population, some electoral anomalies remain possible because of the otherwise satisfactory single-member district system. Especially, it is possible that the party with the most votes in the state as a whole may actually win fewer legislative seats than the party with the smaller statewide total of votes. This can result where the major party has its supporters heavily concentrated in a few districts. Imagine a state with ten single-member districts, each with 100 votes to cast. If party *A* wins four districts by margins of 80:20, and party *B* wins six districts with margins of 60:40, party *B* with a statewide total of 440 votes will win six seats whereas party *A* with a larger total of 560 votes will win only four seats.

The fact that single-member district election does not perfectly distribute legislative seats to parties in proportion to votes stimulated reformers to design alternative plans, the most notable being that of an English mathematician, Thomas Hare, in 1859.[18] The Hare system of Proportional Representation (P.R.) utilizes *multi*-member districts for representatives and *preferential* ballots for voters. Voters indicate an order of preference by numerically ranking the candidates—1 for first choice, 2 for second choice, 3 for third choice, and so on. An alternative was later developed requiring the voter merely to choose a single *party list* of candidates, each party then obtaining seats for a proportion of its list equal to the proportion of all votes received.

The Hare system of P.R. won many fervent adherents and was adopted in many localities. All have since abandoned it as overly complicated and destructive of the two-party pattern because it awards

---

[18] Cf. C. G. Hoag and G. H. Hallett, *Proportional Representation* (New York: The Macmillan Company, 1926).

some electoral success to even very weak parties. Many European countries continue to elect their parliaments by P.R., but fragmentation of the party system, and consequent cabinet instability, has reduced the enthusiasm and number of its supporters.[19]

Presidential Elections

Article II, section 1 provides that "each State shall appoint, in such manner as the legislature thereof may direct, a number of electors, equal to the whole number of Senators and Representatives to which the State may be entitled in the Congress. . . ." The candidate with a majority in the Electoral College thus selected becomes President. If no candidate wins a majority of electors, the election goes to the House of Representatives. The House then votes by states, each state delegation having one vote. The House chooses (only a plurality is required) from among the three candidates with the highest votes in the Electoral College. Only three elections—1796, 1800, and 1824—have ever gone to the House.

A flaw was soon revealed in the constitutional design. Each elector was required to vote for two persons, but there was no way to designate which vote was intended for President and which for Vice President. The Vice President was simply the next most favored candidate. This led to absurd difficulties. The 1796 election produced a *Federalist* President and a *Republican* Vice President; and in 1800 it was possible that the Republican vice-presidential candidate Aaron Burr would be chosen over Republican presidential candidate Thomas Jefferson. A remedy was devised in the Twelfth Amendment (adopted in 1804), and the presidential electoral process is still controlled by the original provisions as thus amended: Electors cast separate ballots for President and for Vice President. If no presidential candidate has a majority the election goes to the House as above described. The Vice President must also obtain a majority of electoral votes, failing which the Senate chooses from the top two candidates.

The electoral system contains important *federal* elements: the apportionment of electoral votes among the states so that more weight is allotted the smaller states than population alone justifies, and voting by states as units in the House when there is no majority in the Electoral College. These federal elements have been buttressed by state action. All the states now choose their electors by statewide popular elections, and the electors are everywhere bound by party pledges to vote for the people's choice. This was an early achievement; by 1824 all but four states and by 1832 all but one state chose electors by popular elections. The elections are now everywhere conducted on a *statewide at-large* basis, and voters must vote for an *entire slate* of party-pledged presidential electors as one package; ticket-splitting among electors is rarely permit-

[19] See the attack on P.R. by F. A. Hermens in *Democracy or Anarchy* (Notre Dame, Ind.: Notre Dame University, 1941).

ted. Thus each state casts all of its electoral votes for a *single* candidate. The vice-presidential candidates are not presented independently on the state ballots, but are coupled with the candidates for President; all the state's electoral votes simultaneously go as a unit for the winning candidate and his vice-presidential running mate. Typically the electors are not even listed on the ballot; only the names of the presidential and vice-presidential candidates to whom they are pledged appear before most of the voters.

The Constitution is consistent with this system, but does not require it. The states prefer it because casting all their votes for one candidate maximizes their political weight in the Electoral College. This immensely increases the importance of the state as the decisive unit of the political system. The states could choose to hold presidential elections on a district basis, indeed districts were utilized in some states at the outset. This enabled a statewide minority party to win some districts, as in the election of congressmen, and thus obtain a portion of the state's electoral votes for its national candidates. All the states abandoned district election of electors by 1832, and it is unlikely that any state would now readopt districting and thus voluntarily weaken itself in the Electoral College.

However, efforts have been made to use national authority to require district election. Urban-centered groups have strongly opposed these efforts, claiming that malapportionment and gerrymandering would sully presidential politics. Also, the largest metropolitan areas enjoy a substantial advantage from the electoral college system as presently conducted. While some metropolitan areas contain only slightly more than half of a state's voters, they can swing the state's entire electoral vote. This gives an advantage to the Democrats who are strong in the big cities. It also tends to favor the large ethnic minorities concentrated in the major cities of the North and West. Organized labor follows a similar geographic distribution. As a result many liberals strongly oppose abandoning statewide at-large election of electors; and they have restrained what might otherwise be their enthusiasm for abandoning the Electoral College. An irony of history finds them allied with the small-state representatives who fear that a direct national popular election would dilute their influence even more than the present system. That leaves very few interests to favor a fundamental constitutional change.

A general public interest persists, however, in the desire that no candidate be elected President with fewer popular votes than his opponent. Three factors make such an outcome possible: (1) The federal element—each state, no matter how sparsely populated, has a minimum of three electoral votes; (2) The block-voting system—even the thinnest plurality of popular votes obtains all the state's electoral votes; and (3) No matter how few persons actually vote, all of a state's electoral votes are counted in the election. '

Despite this, instances in which a candidate won the people but lost the Electoral College are extremely rare. Only three Presidents did not lead all their opponents in popular votes. In 1824, when the two-party system had temporarily broken down into four major candidacies, the House chose John Quincy Adams, the second-ranking of three leading candidates in the Electoral College. The second example, in 1876, involved disputed election returns rather than distortion by the Electoral College. As Professor Pritchett pithily notes: "The Democrats stole the election in the first place, and the Republicans then stole it back."[20] The only pure case, entirely due to the indirect process of filtering popular votes through the Electoral College, occurred in 1888. President Cleveland lost his bid for reelection though he led his opponent, Harrison, by nearly 100,000 popular votes. Cleveland had his second term, however, defeating President Harrison in an 1892 rematch. It is interesting to note that even in these three cases the electoral college system never rejected a candidate for the Presidency who had an *undisputed majority,* rather than simply a *plurality,* of popular votes.

Efforts have been made to reform the Electoral College. But neither a simple national popular election nor a district-based system has won sufficient support. The Lodge-Gossett compromise proposal to divide each state's electoral votes among the candidates in proportion to their popular vote and thus obtain a closer approximation of the electoral to the popular vote attracted some support in the 1950s. But too many interested groups feared possible adverse effects of any change and the whole issue has faded from public attention. A major overhauling of the presidential election system awaits the kind of public clamor which only an actual frustration of the people's choice by the Electoral College might supply.

The Administration of Elections

Authority for administering elections derives mostly from state and local laws, but some national regulations also bind election officials. The Constitution, of course, must be adhered to with respect to suffrage and equal protection of the laws. National power is further extended by the Civil Rights, Corrupt Practices, and the Hatch acts. (The latter limits partisan electoral activity of national civil servants and regulates campaign money contributions generally.) Congress has used its power under the "times, places and manner" clause to require that a single day—the first Tuesday after the first Monday in November—be used uniformly for electing senators, representatives, and presidential electors. However, the statute permits states by constitutional provision to fix another day; Maine long maintained an earlier date, but all states now use the November date. A secret ballot has been required by congressional statute since 1872.

These few details almost exhaust the scope of national regulation, though Congress has ample constitutional authority to extend its con-

---

[20] C. Herman Pritchett, *The American Constitution* (New York: McGraw-Hill Book Company, 1959), p. 287.

trol.[21] By contrast, state laws are extremely numerous and complex. Their common object is to ensure uniformity of practice throughout the state and to promulgate standards of fairness and efficiency.

Most states designate the secretary of state as chief election officer. Typically, special boards or election commissions are provided by law for each county or city. They coordinate and supervise the tiny voting districts and precincts where the actual balloting is conducted. National election authority and administration is thus a remarkably decentralized activity, with minimal supervision and control exercised by the national government.

Advance registration. Advance registration is designed to screen out the ineligible voters by limiting the suffrage on election day to persons previously enrolled on an official list of qualified voters. Only three states have no system of advance registration. Typically, preelection registration sessions are scheduled, and personal application must be made by prospective voters. With advance registration, officials and party workers can investigate the qualifications of voters prior to the hectic rush of election day. And on election day they can compare recorded identification data (e.g., signatures and physical description) with applicants for ballots to forestall fraudulent voting.

There are two major forms of advance voter registration—*periodic* and *permanent*. Periodic registration requires voters to register at recurring intervals. Permanent registration requires a new voter to appear only once to establish his qualifications; thenceforth he need appear only to vote. Frequent periodic reregistration, in some cases prior to each election, tends to reduce participation in elections. The things that limit actual voting, like illness or bad weather, take a double toll when advance personal registration is additionally required. Indifference, a common basis for failure to vote, is also increased when registration periods occur too far in advance of an election for the excitement of the campaign to stir the less interested to register. This does not always affect the parties equally, and there has been much speculation concerning partisan advantages of registration systems. For this reason, some reformers have tended to favor permanent registration lists.

The trend strongly favors permanent voter lists. Thirty-three states require such throughout the state. However, eleven other states provide permanent registration for only a portion of the state—typically the rural and small town districts—and require periodic registration only in the larger cities. Supporters of this distinction argue that larger cities are more prone to corruption and need more frequent review of voter qualifications to prevent 'cemetery voting' (using the names of deceased voters) and other frauds. Needless to say, this is viewed quite differently in the affected places, and the issue has become part of a general political conflict between big-city and small-town interests.

---

[21] Voting rights for Negroes has been the subject of much recent congressional legislation (see p. 457–60).

Election Day procedure. The first Tuesday after the first Monday in November can be a busy time for the officials who operate the polls. They are variously named election judges or inspectors, and their assistants are clerks. Generally their selection is bipartisan by law, with the majority party getting a larger share of appointments. The work is obviously temporary and strenuous, but it is something of a patronage reward to the party faithful, even if minimally remunerative and prestigeful.

Order and decorum are enforced (with the aid of police)—a value in democratic elections not be taken for granted. No electioneering is permitted within the polling place, neither is liquor (taverns and package stores are closed). The security of ballots requires procedures comparable to handling bonds or currency. Packages of ballots, or seals on voting machines, may be broken only at the proper time and by authorized personnel. Sequential numbers on the ballots (later detached), used for control against counterfeiting and other frauds, must be in order; the tabulating numbers on the voting machines should start from zero. Applicants for ballots are asked to identify themselves and are checked against registration rolls. Occasional challenges require a special oath to be administered as a matter of record for subsequent criminal proceedings if a fraudulent vote is then cast. When the voter receives his paper ballot, or is admitted to the machine, his registration record is duly noted (one vote per customer). Private booths are provided for marking ballots; machines are also screened off. Ballots are deposited through a slot in a sealed box after identifying numbers are removed. The number of ballots in the box should equal the number of identification tabs. Every ballot, used or unused, must be accounted for.

Also present during the polling operation are party 'watchers' in formal partisan role. They help keep things honest on the competitive principle—the two parties' watchers watch each other. They also watch the voters—to offer challenges where they suspect 'ringers' (unqualified voters) brought in by the opposition. The watchers also run a last-minute bring-in-the-vote campaign. In well organized precincts, the watcher keeps a list of party supporters and checks off the faithful as they vote. In due time, before the polls close, the party 'runners' set out on the double to contact the delinquent potential supporters. ("We think the vote's going to be awfully close, and we hope you haven't forgotten this is the day to vote. Do you need a baby-sitter or a ride to the polls?"). This kind of organization won't beat an Eisenhower or a Johnson, but when the race is close the pros know it can make the difference between winner and also-ran.

When the results have all been canvassed and centrally accumulated, usually all that remains is to certify the winners and officially notify them of their election. That will take several days, but unofficial results are quickly released to the communications media on election day. The official results may be challenged as erroneous or fraudulent, and the courts appealed to for redress. Laborious investigation and recounting may en-sue. Finally, each house of Congress is constitutionally made "the judge of the elections, returns and qualifications of its own members. . . ." (Art. I, sec. 5.) Congressional candidates have the right to appeal election disputes directly to Congress, irrespective of state laws. Congress has exercised its supreme authority on the whole with commendable restraint.

Corruptions and reforms. Corruption of the voting process is as old as its history, but conditions have been vastly improved by the Australian ballot and corrupt practices regulatory legislation. Four major perversions of balloting procedures command attention:

(1) Voting the ineligible: Padding the register by including on registration rolls names of the deceased, the no-longer resident, and fictional names to be voted by repeaters.

(2) Intimidating the eligible: Order is an essential of fair elections; eligible voters must not be kept from the polls by fear of violence or other reprisals. The problem was once widespread where hoodlums kept guard around polling places; it continues to be a serious problem for many southern Negroes.

(3) Stuffing the ballot box: There were many illegal schemes. One old sophisticated fraud is chain-voting, more gaily known as the 'Tasmanian dodge' (around the Australian ballot). A blank ballot is illegally obtained and marked for the 'right' candidates. The first corrupted voter then is supplied this previously marked ballot before he enters the polling place and upon leaving he gives the party worker the blank one that he legally receives. The party worker then marks this ballot and the same process continues throughout the day. The aim, of course, is to ensure that corrupted voters actually vote as they promise to do. Since the number of the ballot that the voter casts is necessarily different from the one he is legally given, the chain is easily detected if the identification tab system is used and administered scrupulously.

(4) Short-counting and over-counting: Tallying frauds are sometimes ingenious and may be expedited by gross collusion of officials. For example, a package of previously marked counterfeit ballots can be substituted for bona fide ballots. If the 'cooperation' is really good, the tallying sheets themselves can be doctored. A total of 1,000 can easily become 1,600 by a tiny line added to the first zero—much easier than getting 600 voters to the polls! Finally, the destruction of ballots is not unknown; a senatorial investigating committee majority reported that 13,000 ballots were burned in the New Mexico senatorial election of 1952.

Another object of election reform is the problem of nonvoting. The large number and frequency of elections are thought to reduce voter turnout. This is more of a problem on the state and local levels, but off-year (mid-presidential term) congressional elections are also affected. The solution proffered is unpopular: increase the term of congressmen to four years, reduce the term of senators correspondingly, and elect all national legislators during the quadrennial presidential elections. This would probably greatly increase presidential and national party control over Congress. The function of staggered elections as part of the system of checks and balances is generally deemed more valuable than an increased voter turnout.

To encourage greater voter turnout, polling places have been opened for longer periods to enable workers to vote more easily. Twenty-nine states have time-off-for-voting laws and some require employers to compensate workers for a free period on election days. Sunday has been urged by the more secular-minded as a ready-made free day. An annual national voting holiday has been proposed to provide free time and patriotic emphasis; but it might well become just one more vacation day, like the Fourth of July, and actually increase nonvoting.

Reactions to such reforms vary between the traditional view that voting is a duty of citizenship and the view that uninformed voting is no service to democracy. Some are content to calculate the partisan impact of increased turnout, and act in accordance with party interest. Some contemporary social scientists claim that moderate turnouts are actually a healthy sign in democracies, betokening popular satisfaction. High voting turnouts may signify discontent and sharp schism in a nation. However, in many nations with good democratic credentials, a far greater proportion of the citizenry vote than in the United States. Moreover, there is no necessary inconsistency between seeking greater voter turnout and raising the level of voter information and awareness. Indeed, the former may be a means of stimulating interest and motivation for the latter.

A major reform of state elections was achieved by the Progressives at the turn of the century: They introduced the *initiative, referendum,* and *recall.* By petition, the initiative places substantive legislative proposals directly before the voters for decision. The votes on such policy questions are termed referenda. Special elections may also be initiated by petition enabling the voters to recall an elected official prior to the expiration of his full term. These instruments of direct democracy have not won acceptance on the national level. There is no national initiative process at all. There are minor approximations to referenda elections in the agricultural subsidy programs. But major referenda, for example, the effort to require a national referendum before a declaration of war, have failed to attract much support. There is no voter recall process whatsoever in the case of national office.

The recent trend has been away from the idea that the cure for deficiencies in popular government is to make it more *directly* democratic, or that the cure for democracy's ills is in general still more democracy. There has been renewed positive appreciation of the existing constitutional structures. In effect there has been a return to the principles of *representative* democracy as the necessary instrument of large-scale popular government. And this has necessarily entailed renewed belief that responsibility for government should be borne by *party leaders* who are supported or rejected by the people in free elections.

BIBLIOGRAPHICAL NOTE

A useful collection of readings on legislative apportionment, including guidance for research and essays, is Glendon Schubert (ed.), *Reapportionment* (1965). Older, but valuable, is the symposium edited by R. Kramer (ed.), on "Legislative Reapportionment," in *Law and Contemporary Problems*, (Spring, 1952). The theory of representation is considered in Alfred de Grazia, *Public and Republic* (1951); cf. the same author's *Apportionment and Representative Government* (1963). Arguments pro and con reapportionment are summarized in Herbert Garfinkel and Leonard J. Fein, *Fair Representation: A Citizen's Guide to Legislative Apportionment in Michigan* (1960). An important argument is analyzed in Robert B. McKay, *Reapportionment and the Federal Analogy* (1962). Another dimension is treated in Gordon E. Baker, *Rural Versus Urban Political Power* (1955). Texts of judicial opinions are reproduced in National Municipal League, *Court Decisions on Legislative Apportionment* (10 vols.; 1962–64). Basic data are presented in U.S. Department of Commerce, Bureau of the Census, *Congressional District Data Book* (1961), plus supplements.

Presidential nominating machinery is examined in Paul T. David, R. M. Goldman and R. C. Bain, *The Politics of National Party Conventions* (1960). Valuable data are compiled in Richard C. Bane, *Convention Decisions and Voting Records* (1960). A useful *Convention Guide* is published quadrennially as a supplement to the *Congressional Quarterly Weekly Report*. One among numerous case studies is Abraham Holtzman, *The Loyalty Pledge Controversy in the Democratic Party* (1962). State nominations and elections are ably presented in V. O. Key, Jr., *American State Politics* (1956). Still standard is Charles E. Merriam and Louise Overacker, *Primary Elections* (1928).

Presidential election procedures are reviewed in Lucius Wilmerding, *The Electoral College* (1958). Cf. Subcommittee of the Senate Committee on the Judiciary, Hearings, *Nomination and Election of President and Vice-President*, 84th Congress, first session (1955). More general are Joseph P. Harris, *Election Administration in the United States* (1934); and John B. Johnson and Irving J. Lewis, *Registration for Voting in the United States* (rev. ed. 1946).

Among many case studies, see: Harold Gosnell, *Machine Politics: Chicago Model* (1937); James Reichley, *The Art of Government: Reform and Organization Politics in Philadelphia* (1959); and Frank J. Sorauf, "State Patronage in a Rural County," *American Political Science Review* (December, 1956).

Chapter 12

Campaigns
and
Voting Behavior

DEMOCRATIC AND REPUBLICAN LEADERS HAVE A COMMON TASK: A CON-
tinuous search for support by popular majorities. The two major parties
are the great majority-seeking organizations forging the link in every
election at every level between the thousand-voiced public and the majority of votes which gives office. More precisely, they seek those Madisonian "coalitions of a majority" by which American elections are won.

Such winning coalitions are difficult to form on any level. They are
most difficult to piece together nationally, as Madison anticipated, "among
the great variety of interests, parties, and sects" which the "extended
republic" embraces. But the national prize is the greatest elective office
in the world and we have never wanted for aspirants to the office where
Washington, Jefferson, and Lincoln sat.

The Making of a President: Nominating Campaigns

The presidential nominating process begins long before the conventions and long before the primaries. Actually, it has no single beginning
point, but is a continuous process. The party 'king-makers' and the mass
media are constantly alert to new personages who have the 'right look'
and appear at the right time and place on the political scene. Frequently,
a 'natural' comes along. And when nature's bounty fails, politicians in-
ventively improve on nature. There are always hopefuls and their cohorts
who strive to create the right look and to control timing and other strategic factors so they will be 'discovered.' The cycle begins anew every
four years. Each presidential campaign always leaves a residue of by-
passed, but still hopeful, front-runners who will spend the next four years
improving their chances at the next national convention. And the experienced eye can spot many less prominent hopefuls whose activities
have for some time been but a prelude to conventions four or eight years
in the offing.

But how does one get to be a front-runner or even a long-shot 'dark horse'? What marks the likely contenders?

Presidential 'Availability'

In American political parlance, availability has little to do with a prospect's willingness to accept nomination. Rare indeed is the American who will withdraw unequivocally from consideration for President in the classic manner attributed to General Sherman in 1884: "If nominated I will not accept; if elected I will not serve." Acceptance is taken for granted; availability refers rather to qualities deemed likely to increase the chances for electoral victory. When politicians discuss availability, they are sizing up the potential candidates to see who has the makings of a winner.

The attributes of availability are merely generalizations or averagings of past experience. They describe the men who previously won the Presidency. But the past need not repeat itself, and, as to all such generalizations, there are exceptions. Men have often been nominated and elected who lacked one or more of these qualities. But the chances are usually remote for a candidate substantially lacking in these traditional attributes of presidential availability.

One attribute is of course absolutely necessary; the constitutional qualifications must be met.[1] The other attributes may be noted under seven headings.

Large pivotal states. The right place for a candidate to be from is a major 'swing' state—one whose large bloc of electoral votes frequently shifts between the parties. The practical politicians theorize that a native son has some advantage in carrying his home state, and it makes sense for a party to take this assumed advantage in as large a doubtful state as possible. From 1868 to 1964 more than half the nominees came from New York or Ohio (27 out of 50). Of the remainder, most came from other relatively large swing states. The most famous exception, Democrat William Jennings Bryan of Nebraska, was nominated three times and lost three times. The most recent exception was Barry Goldwater of Arizona who in 1964 barely carried his home state, and it was the sole nonsouthern state that he did carry for the Republican ticket. However, native sons have been beaten in their home states and candidates have won who lacked this attribute of availability. Still, other things being equal, politicians prefer candidates from the large pivotal states.

Prior governmental experience, governors and senators preferred. Only two major candidates have ever been nominated directly from

---

[1] 'No person except a natural born citizen, or a citizen of the United States, at the time of the adoption of this Constitution, shall be eligible to the office of President; neither shall any person be eligible to that office who shall not have attained to the age of thirty-five years, and been fourteen years a resident within the United States.' Article II, section 1.

private life without previously serving as elected or appointed public (or military) officials. Horace Greeley, editor of the *New York Tribune,* was Democratic nominee in 1872, and Wendell Willkie, a utility corporation lawyer, was Republican nominee in 1940. Neither was successful. No business, labor, agricultural, or professional leader ever moved directly from such career posts into the· White House.

There has been a substantial preference for state governors, though in 1960 the front-runners, other than Governor Rockefeller, were all based in the Senate, as was the Republican candidate in 1964. Governors are favored for several reasons. As state party chief and most important native son, they often control their state's convention delegation. Unlike congressmen and senators, who have had to vote on many specific national issues, governors may have alienated fewer voting groups. And there is the debatable notion that gubernatorial executive experience is the best preparation for the White House. The increasing availability of senators may reflect a changing view of the Presidency that now emphasizes the functions of legislative and diplomatic leadership.

Evident popularity. Four ways of demonstrating popularity may be noted: (1) A proven vote-getter in a large state is bound to be sized up, particularly if he can lead his ticket or win in the face of his party's general defeat. Thus Republican Governor George Romney's presidential availability zoomed with his 1964 reelection in the face of a Johnson landslide. (2) State presidential primaries may be entered to demonstrate broad appeal to the electorate. (3) A great military hero sometimes can convert personal popularity or respect into political popularity. (4) Public opinion polls can provide advance soundings of national popularity.

Presidential 'look.' A candidate must have what the politicians call 'heft.' An ideal combination is a dignified and sincere manner, lucidity of speech and adroitness in fielding questions, and a physical appearance of vigorous maturity as well as manly handsomeness. These qualities must come through to the voting public via the modern mass media of communication. Television with its cosmetics and complex lighting techniques raises new problems regarding the presidential 'look,' and greatly widens the public base of this appraisal. Physical and psychic stamina, it should be added, are needed for more than appearance's sake. The strain of a presidential candidacy, not to say the Presidency, is enormous.

'WASPM' preference. An almost iron rule of American politics is that a President must be a white, Anglo-Saxon, Protestant male. The single but significant exception was the election in 1960 of a Roman Catholic, John F. Kennedy. The extraconstitutional religious test remains, though it may now read Christian rather than Protestant. Governor, and later Senator, Herbert H. Lehman of New York would surely have been available except for his Jewish faith. The Anglo-Saxon preference is remarkably strong and reflects the country's British origins. Of the 35 men who have been President, 28 were of predominantly British descent.

Although candidates typically come from a relatively narrow stratum of the population, they must appear free of racial or religious prejudice. If the minorities cannot obtain the Presidency for one of their own race or faith, they have in effect a veto over bigoted but otherwise available aspirants. To give deep offense to a minority concentrated in large pivotal states is to court political suicide. Indeed it is increasingly necessary for candidates to go beyond mere tolerance and to champion civil rights for racial and religious minority groups. And as high government posts are increasingly opened to minorities and to women, it is likely that their presidential availability will improve.

Family man. The most common public relations picture of a candidate is a family scene. And not only should the candidate have a family, but it is increasingly necessary that they campaign with him. Mamie Eisenhower and Pat Nixon helped the Republican cause in 1952 and 1956, while Adlai Stevenson's divorced status hurt him.[2] Public distaste for divorced candidates is thought to be lessening as divorce becomes more common and as female roles change. But in 1964 Nelson Rockefeller's excellent chance for the Republican nomination was destroyed by public reaction to circumstances involved in his then recent divorce and remarriage.

Moderate views. The factors that moderate the major parties' policy views tend also to produce moderate rather than extreme candidates. Fundamental consensus on what we have termed the basic 'regime questions,' the great multiplicity of interests in a large heterogeneous nation, the looseness of party discipline and organizational decentralization, all ordinarily require candidates of moderate views who can produce the necessary coalition of a majority.

Presidential Primary Campaigns

Sometime prior to January of each presidential election year, nearly a year before the election, aspirants must make a difficult decision.[3] Shall they undertake the journey to the nominating conventions chiefly via the arduous, expensive, and politically hazardous direct primary route? Or shall they chiefly politick behind the scenes and line up state delegations through contacts with influential party leaders? Candidates who are strong with primary voters cannot neglect the many states where there are no primary elections; and candidates who are strong with party activists and leaders rarely can completely ignore the challenge of the primaries. Typically, they choose a mix—that combination of primaries and behind-the-scenes politicking favorable to their candidacy. For this

---

[2] Angus Campbell, et al., *The American Voter*, p. 58.
[3] The early date derives from the legal filing deadlines and the practical need to determine one's support prior to the filing dates in each of the primary-conducting states. See the schedule in "Presidential '64," *Congressional Quarterly*, Supplement to January 17, 1964, p. 106.

reason, primaries remain important even though they have steadily declined in number since their zenith in 1916. Fortunately for the wear and tear on campaigners, about half the primaries are usually preempted by unopposed favorite son candidates—a governor or other state leader who can thus keep his delegation united, uncommitted, and under his control until the convention.

In the presidential primaries candidates have four major objectives:

Demonstrate broad vote-getting power. Since the only national elections are for President, there is no prior *interstate* test of a prospective candidate's vote-getting power other than the primaries. Primary campaigns are an excellent way to demonstrate availability as a vote-getter and also a means of obtaining national attention. Already-famous candidates may well prefer not to risk the primaries, resting on their established reputations. Specific unavailability handicaps may also be overcome with a carefully selected primary victory. Roman Catholic John F. Kennedy greatly helped his nomination bid by beating Protestant and liberal Hubert Humphrey in West Virginia, an overwhelmingly Protestant and strongly New Deal state.

Stake a moral claim to the nomination. Not only can vote-getting in the primaries help a candidate to impress the coming national convention; it also gives him a claim upon the convention. This is particularly important to presidential hopefuls opposing a favorite of the party regulars. Winning the popular primary contests fair and square creates a claim of democratic legitimacy to counter the legitimacy of party regularity. Thus, in 1952, General Eisenhower had not only to display vote-getting ability, but to counter the claim to legitimate succession of "Mr. Republican" Robert A. Taft. This was the very intent of the reformers who pioneered the direct primary in rebellion against nomination by convention bosses in smoke-filled rooms. Nonetheless, success in the primaries as the people's choice only buttresses a case and may be frustrated in the end. Senator Estes Kefauver of Tennessee swept the 1952 Democratic primaries from New Hampshire to California. But incumbent President Truman successfully managed the nomination for the reluctant dark horse, Illinois Governor Adlai E. Stevenson. Thus, the primaries are commonly deemed *elimination* rather than *nomination* contests. A bad showing is generally fatal, whereas a good showing enhances the candidate's position but does not guarantee a favorable outcome.

Demonstrate campaign prowess. The primaries pretest the candidate in campaign action. It is a kind of tryout for the presidential election in the Fall. Leaders and convention delegates watch for evidence of skill with sharply probing reporters, charm with crowds, appeal to party activists and amateurs. Evidence is needed of presidential *stature*, and increasingly of sheer *stamina*, in innumerable and widely scattered personal appearances and televised speeches. Thus, Governor Harold Stassen by vigorous campaigning beat noncampaigning Dewey in early 1948 Republican primaries, and began to look like a strong candidate.

Dewey had to abandon his pose of unchallengeable front-runner and met Stassen head-on in Oregon. Stassen was "so utterly out-classed"[4] in a major radio debate with Dewey that he never recovered his stature as presidential 'timber.'

Win delegate votes. Some primaries are called mere beauty contests because they have no binding effect upon the selection of convention delegates. But some primaries do take the form of actual delegate selection and sometimes of obliging the delegates to cast a first-ballot vote for the candidate to whom they were pledged in the primary.[5] These primaries produce guaranteed votes at the convention. For example, in the 1960 Democratic Convention, Senator John F. Kennedy had 196.5 of the 533 primary pledged votes. Most of the others were committed to favorite sons.

Presidential primary campaigns are not only preparation for the nominating conventions; they are an aspect of the general campaign for the Presidency. A candidate in a state presidential primary simultaneously creates a national, not merely a state, nor purely a party, image. Aspirants use the primary campaigns to experiment with issues and strategies for the main campaign to come. Also they must raise huge sums of money[6] and put together effective campaign machinery in each of the contested primary states. This will be the organizational nucleus for the imminent general election campaign.

Finally, the substantial temptations to use tactics narrowly directed to primary victories are checked by the omnipresence of the full presidential context. Successful primary contenders must avoid wrecking their own party in the wake of these limited victories; they may well need the later support of their factional opponents. More broadly still, the narrow appeals to narrow interests that might win a state primary contest are tempered in anticipation of the full burden of the Presidency which will descend on the successful candidate before the year is out. That responsibility weighs heavily and reaches down even into factional warfare in the presidential primaries.

Winning the Convention Battle

The nomination campaign and the actual election campaign converge during the hectic national party conventions. Three considerations about the ensuing election dominate the nomination decision: (1) Which contender has the best prospect over the opposing party's nominee? (2) Which contender best reflects the party's general viewpoint on issues? (3) Which candidate would be the best compromise among the rival

---

[4] Wilfred E. Binkley, *American Political Parties* (New York: Alfred A. Knopf, 1959), p. 400.

[5] No state or national legal penalties enforce the primary or other pledges. They are deemed a moral obligation, as with the Electoral College vote for President.

[6] The 1952 Eisenhower nominating campaign alone cost 2.5 million dollars. See Paul T. Davis, et al, *The Politics of National Nominating Conventions*, p. 286.

factions to keep the party intact as an effective campaign instrument? Victory, policy agreement, party harmony—these are what each convention seeks.

Intrinsically difficult, the task must be undertaken under the relentless glare of national publicity and pressure from powerful interest groups. Delegates are buttonholed in the lobby, pickets demonstrate outside the hall; letters, telegrams, and long-distance calls urge support for particular platform planks, resolutions, and candidates. Moreover, the delegates themselves have more than a simple national party interest; they seek platform wording and nominees able to help carry the local ticket. Many delegates are themselves candidates for state or congressional office; others are interest-group representatives as well as party activists. The delegates must balance these numerous considerations as they go about their major business of choosing the national party ticket.

While common elements can be discerned, each convention is an unique phenomenon. Innumerable factors determine whether a convention shall be a public brawl (many claim this to be a Democratic specialty) or a closely managed public performance. When an incumbent President is to be renominated (e.g., Johnson in 1964) or when nomination of a practically unchallenged front-runner is assured (like Nixon in 1960), the convention is largely a giant preelection rally and campaign-planning session. But when several leading contenders do battle, with numerous compromise hopefuls waiting for the leaders to 'kill' each other off, then there is an open convention. There one finds the full drama and excitement generally associated with the politics of American national party conventions.

The opening line-up. As thousands of delegates and alternates arrive, some are primary-pledged to a particular contender, at least for one ballot. Most delegates were selected at state, territorial, or district conventions, and were lined up for a candidate during the months of preconvention politicking. Some, despite contrary personal preference, are bound to unit-rule agreements within their delegations. Some arrive uncommitted. Thus even before the convention opens there are shrewd estimates of the relative strength of rival contenders. Generally the convention is made up of blocs of delegates rather than free-wheeling individuals. The federal system is evident in the basic groupings, the state delegations sitting together under state standards on the convention floor and meeting in state caucuses for deliberation and action. Other caucus groupings reflect various factional alignments, regional and specialized interests (such as southerners, conservatives, or labor union delegates). The delegations and interest blocs present a profile of the party, reflecting its basic composition, its sources of strength and patterns of internal division. These are the groups that contenders for the nomination will have to keep in line or win over as the convention proceeds.

Some delegates are 'more equal than others.' The cheerful pan-

demonium of a major convention gathering confuses the viewing public—
and not a few of the delegates. More than half are likely to be at their
very first national party convention. With so many novices, the leadership
process looms especially large. Contact between delegation and caucus
leaders and caucus leaders and top candidates is the major communication
linkage. The natural spokesmen and negotiators of the caucuses are the
prominent figures at home: party leaders, public officials, and candidates.
The 'most equal' and the most sought-after delegates at the convention
are such leaders of the key delegations. (Key delegations are those able
to deliver the most convention votes and which are not too firmly sewed
up.) Delegation votes, unlike state electoral votes, may usually be split,
and intrastate party decentralization facilitates such splits. Rival leaders
within delegations can crack a state delegation's preconvention alignment.
(Thus, Governor Brown, although officially the favorite son candidate,
could not control his 1960 California delegation to the Democratic national convention.)

Individual delegates are not altogether neglected. Individual waverers
and mavericks, especially in a tight race, are stones not to be left un-
turned. The leading contenders extend hospitality to all delegates; they
maintain hotel suites where delegates may visit, enjoy refreshments, and
feel valued for their individual voting power. Nonetheless, the convention
communication process is preponderantly a leadership process. The leaders are the persuasive voices in the group and caucus infighting. It is
mainly through them that preconvention commitments have been obtained and through them that realignments of candidate commitments
can be effectuated.

The convention finale. The basic strategy for front-runners is to
create and maintain a 'bandwagon psychology.' They enter the convention as national celebrities, often fresh from primary election triumphs.
Everything is directed to sustaining and increasing that momentum. They
have a twofold leverage on the delegates: the intense desire to come up
with a winning ticket, plus the important gamesmanship of joining the
winning camp while it still counts. Every delegate knows that a contender's prenomination backers are likely to be highly valued; where
better to look for loyal and sympathetic members of a new Administration?

Dark-horse hopefuls pursue an opposite strategy. If any of them are
to be nominated, the bandwagon must be stopped before its momentum
becomes overpowering. Essentially theirs is a tactic of temporary coalition.
The lesser contenders must combine forces, piecing together a convention majority united merely in opposition to the front-runner. If such a
coalition can hold out for one or two ballots, it may be able to shake
loose enough supporters from the leading contender to allow a new bandwagon to start rolling.

All this takes place in a frenzy of activity: endless caucusing, noisy
demonstrations, passionate arguments, numerous speeches, and even

1964 Republican running mates Goldwater and Miller acknowledge the cheers of the convention delegates who nominated them.

semiformal debates.[7] And the expertise of political brokerage is continuously applied, even after the actual balloting has begun.

As soon as the nomination is made, the election campaign is underway. Indeed, it begins even prior to formal completion of the final ballot. Delegations seek recognition to change their recorded votes to the emerging victor, and all but a few diehards join this public display of party unity. The convention typically ratifies the presidential candidate's selection of his running mate. This too is an aspect of the election campaign more than of intraparty considerations. The selection reflects much the same availability criteria applied to the presidential nominee, but with a desire to balance regional, age, ethnic, or other appeals of the national ticket. Finally, the candidates and their families are triumphantly presented to the convention and the nation. Cheering and demonstrating delegates convert the days of convention strife into a gigantic election campaign rally. The candidates' acceptance speeches, usually carefully scheduled to get the largest TV audience, fire the opening blasts in the now officially launched campaign.

The Requisite of Victory—270 Electoral Votes

Campaign strategies are designed to secure a majority—presently 270 votes—in the Electoral College. Five related facts condition this quadren-

---

[7] Then-senators John F. Kennedy and Lyndon B. Johnson appeared together to argue their respective claims to the 1960 Democratic presidential nomination before their home-state Massachusetts and Texas delegations. It was one of the very dramatic televised features of the convention.

nial exercise in presidential arithmetic: (1) each state gets a quota of electoral votes; (2) these quotas reflect the relative size of a state's population; (3) each state's entire quota almost always is awarded as a unit; (4) these go to the winner of a statewide plurality of popular votes; and (5) a majority of electoral votes is required, or the House of Representatives, voting by states, chooses the President from the three candidates with the most electoral votes.

Thus the fundamental political unit in presidential elections is the state. All other units—individual voters, small-scale voting precincts, cities, and counties—can help elect a President only as they can be combined to carry a whole state. Electoral votes come packaged in state-sized containers. Consequently, presidential campaign strategists seek statewide popular pluralities in a combination of states that adds up to a majority of electoral votes.

Campaigning State by State

The states are not equal building blocks for achieving victory. Some states are bigger prizes with many electoral votes. Also, the rival parties begin with different geographical centers of strength and weakness, providing different opportunities in particular places. Campaigns are organized to take advantage of these differences in the political characteristics of the states.

Safe and hopeless states. Some states have voted for the same political party in most presidential elections. From the Civil War up to (but not including) 1964, Vermont consistently voted Republican, and Georgia just as consistently Democratic. These are extreme examples of one-party dominance, but several other states repeatedly favor one party. Thus each party begins its campaign with some states considered practically 'in the bag' and some practically hopeless. Taking any one for granted is always a risk, and historical patterns may not hold in a particular election. But national campaign managers must play the odds. They cannot afford to devote major energy and resources to states where either victory or defeat seems a highly probable outcome.

Swing states are those politically uncertain and unsafe for either party. By definition, there is considerable interparty competition,[8] but swing states are not necessarily prime presidential campaign targets. The ones with negligible quotas of electoral votes are simply not worth major effort by the candidate personally.

Key states are those that both swing between the parties and have substantial blocks of electoral votes. The twelve most populous states can name the President irrespective of how the other thirty-eight and the District of Columbia might vote. Indeed the largest eleven plus any other state, however small, would suffice. Actually, such a sweep of key

---

[8] Cf. Joseph A. Schlesinger, "A Two-Dimensional Scheme for Classifying the States According to the Degree of Inter-Party Competition," *American Political Science Review*, Vol. XLIX (December 1955), pp. 1120 ff.

STATES WITH MOST ELECTORAL VOTES

States	Elect. Votes 1964	Party victory for Pres. in						No. of times party won, 1856-1964*		
		1944	1948	1952	1956	1960	1964	Other	Dem.	Rep.
New York	43	D	R	R	R	D	D	0	11	17
California	40	D	D	R	R	R	D	1	10	17
Pennsylvania	29	D	R	R	R	D	D	1	6	21
Illinois	26	D	D	R	R	D	D	0	10	18
Ohio	26	R	D	R	R	R	D	0	7	21
Texas	25	D	D	R	R	D	D	1	22	3
Michigan	21	D	R	R	R	D	D	1	5	22
New Jersey	17	D	R	R	R	D	D	0	15	13
Massachusetts	14	D	D	R	R	D	D	0	9	19
Florida	14	D	D	R	R	R	D	1	19	7
Indiana	13	R	R	R	R	R	D	0	8	20
No. Carolina	13	D	D	D	D	D	D	1	23	3

*Totals for Texas, Florida, and North Carolina vary because Confederate states did not participate in elections during the Civil War.

states is seldom achieved, though Roosevelt succeeded in 1936, Eisenhower got all but one, and Johnson succeeded again in 1964. The election is likely to hinge on the outcome in ten key states.[9] It is difficult to win nationally while losing any substantial number of them, and campaign strategists usually concentrate on them as the most rewarding targets.

Sectional Patterns

Common political interests arising from common needs and cultural background have long dominated certain states and regional groupings of states. In some notable cases these political interests found partisan expression preponderantly in one political party. As with the safe states, each national party has had the benefit of relatively 'safe sections.' Thus New England has had a long history of Republican dominance. Even in 1936, the greatest electoral vote sweep since the Civil War, Maine and Vermont stood alone for the Republican candidate. The Midwest farm belt was the birthplace of the Republican party and long a happy hunting ground for its presidential candidates. And of course the Solid South was the sectional bedrock for a century of Democratic presidential campaigns. The states have always tended to divide between the parties in sectional groups rather than at random.

But industrial and urban expansion has weakened political section-

---

[9] Of the twelve largest, all but Indiana and North Carolina may presently be classified as *key* states, being simultaneously large and shifting between the parties.

alism. Fewer states have distinguishing dominant interests; increasingly, each has a mixture of agriculture, manufacturing, and commerce, and a mixture of peoples and cultures. As the states become more varied internally, they become more like each other throughout the nation. "The changes of time" have had the "assimilating effect" which Madison foresaw.[10] Maine and Florida, Vermont and Texas, North and South (although the South remains our most distinctive regional culture) are not nearly so dissimilar as they once were. Democratic governors, congressmen, and senators have recently been elected throughout New England; Republican congressmen represent Alabama and Mississippi; Florida went Republican for President in three successive elections (1952, 1956, 1960); and Republican Goldwater received all his electoral votes outside Arizona from southern states in 1964.

Thus the presidential candidates no longer begin their campaigns with regional blocks of electoral votes safely in hand. Both parties necessarily take a more national view and have increased their campaigning in all geographical sections. (Note the regional distribution of the key states in the table.) In 1964, the Republicans extended their southern assault even though the Democratic nominee was a Southerner, while President Johnson concentrated on the new Democratic party bedrock, the huge metropolitan population centers of the North and the West.

Urban and Suburban Trends

The industrial-urban transformation of the nation has created giant metropolitan areas with a distinctive political orientation. These were the areas of expanding population—from higher birth rates outstripping rural and small-town growth, and from the large concentrations of immigrants and in-migrants. As the frontier shrank, the cities absorbed the bulk of the American population explosion. And the city dwellers were markedly different from country folk. Catholics, Jews, Irish, Italians, eastern and central Europeans, Latins, and Negroes overwhelmed the older native stock and revolutionized our politics.[11]

These huge population centers are located in the key states and frequently swing close elections. That is why metropolitan voters are so important to presidential campaign arithmetic: It is difficult to win nationally without the large cities. That has been a major difficulty for the Republican party; big-city voters tend to favor the Democrats. With the catastrophic depression of the thirties as catalyst, the New Deal formed an electoral coalition that managed to reconcile the Old South and its white supremacist core with the ethnic and religious minorities of the urban North. Needless to say, their agreement was not on civil rights; rather, it was based on a mutual need for economic welfare. But the

---

[10] *Federalist* 56, p. 349.
[11] Samuel Lubell, *The Future of American Politics* (New York: Anchor Books, 1956).

coalition has been strained to the breaking point as economic conservatism grew in the South and civil rights became a dominant national issue.

Suburbanization has been an additional trend, intensified since World War II. Metropolitan core-city population has remained stationary or even declined while surrounding suburbs have grown. Moreover, suburban voters have been less inclined to the Democrats than are central city residents.[12] And they are less keen on racial integration. Many fled the central city tenements, not only for a 'yard for the kids,' but to escape integration of the old-city neighborhoods. Goldwater Republicans, in 1964, sought unsuccessfully to build a new majority coalition by combining southern, suburban, and some urban opposition to federal racial integration with general social and economic conservatism. This did not entail, of course, taking a white-supremacist position. It sufficed that Goldwater, more moderate on behalf of civil rights than the liberal Democrats (and liberal Republicans), urged the primacy of the state governments and a preference for a slow educational rather than rapid legislative approach. The strategy backfired, however, when the expected northern metropolitan 'white backlash' failed to develop, and when greatly aroused Negro voters flocked to the polls in sufficient numbers to help carry the bulk of southern and border states for the Democrats.

Voting Behavior

The political patterns that characterize regions, states, and districts result, of course, from tendencies and acts of individuals. Voters' attitudes, opinions, interests, and voting decisions are analyzed both by campaign strategists hoping to influence elections and by political scientists hoping for a deeper understanding of the political system.

Voting Studies

Aggregate data analysis. The behavior patterns of individual voters once had to be inferred from *aggregate* data; i.e., statistics showing the dominant characteristics of a *whole* county or similar voting jurisdiction. To know how rich people voted, analysts can contrast voting records of wealthy and poor sections. Similarly Catholic and Protestant, Negro and white voting tendencies can be studied by comparing election outcomes in places where these groups are concentrated.

But aggregate data analysis has four major shortcomings: (1) Some important factors such as age and sex are insufficiently grouped by voting

---

[12] For example, Kennedy in 1960 carried the core of the New York–New Jersey metropolitan area with 62.9% of the vote, but lost the surrounding suburbs with 47.6%. The combined metropolitan vote, however, was 55.5% Democratic enabling New York and New Jersey's electoral votes to go to Kennedy. See Hugh A. Bone and Austin Ranney, *Politics and Voters* (New York: McGraw-Hill Book Company, 1963), pp. 47–49.

jurisdictions; there are few wholly male or female voting precincts. (2) Neither voting records nor other aggregate data can reveal such factors as individual personality traits; e.g., there are no voting jurisdictions made up of the same kind of neurotics. (3) Changes in a district's voting pattern may falsely be attributed to the dominant group, whereas the change may have resulted from atypical residents of the area. (4) The method is largely limited to analyzing single factors, but voting reflects a combination of factors requiring comparisons, say, of young, wealthy Catholics with old, poor Catholics. Yet, within these limits, many fine studies have been made and it is by no means an outmoded research technique.[13] Indeed it is the sole method for studying elections held prior to the collection and storage of modern polling data.

The shortcomings, however, led social scientists to devise the methods of public opinion polling that freed electoral analysis from its dependence on aggregate data. Since voters are individually interviewed, their social, economic, and personality traits can be identified and linked directly to their political views and candidate preferences.

Public opinion polls. Before the advent of modern opinion polls, journalists conducted straw votes to satisfy the public's avid desire for election forecasts. The *Literary Digest* magazine's national reputation and circulation zoomed with the accuracy of its predictions, but in 1936 both reputation and circulation were lost in a classic miscalculation. A huge but unrepresentative sample had been drawn from telephone subscription and automobile registration lists. Especially in the Depression, these were scarcely universal utilities. On the basis of this biased sample, which included a disproportionately large number of wealthier and older persons, the *Literary Digest* predicted that Republican Governor Landon would defeat President Roosevelt. The magazine became a laughingstock when Roosevelt won in the greatest electoral landslide of modern times.

That very year, the public opinion polls blossomed. Gallup, Crossley, and Roper correctly predicted Roosevelt's reelection and loomed into prominence as beneficiaries of the *Literary Digest's* debacle. Dr. Gallup and his fellow pollsters obtained their data from small but representative samples of the national population. Their surveys were designed to reflect the true proportions in the population of rich and poor, Protestants and Catholics, men and women, young and old, rural and city dwellers, etc.— the relevant influences upon voting behavior. Journalistic interest expanded election polling into regularly featured surveys of public opinion on a wide variety of governmental policy issues.

Flushed with initial success, pollsters made extravagant claims that public opinion polling was "the most useful instrument of democracy

---

[13] An outstanding example is V. O. Key, Jr., *Southern Politics* (New York: Alfred A. Knopf, 1949). Cf. Austin Ranney, "The Utility and Limitations of Aggregate Data in the Study of Election Behavior," in Ranney (ed.), *Essays on the Behavioral Study of Politics* (Urbana: University of Illinois Press, 1962).

Year	Actual Dem. Vote (%)	Gallup Poll Pred.	Gallup Poll Error	Roper Poll Pred.	Roper Poll Error	Literary Digest Pred.	Literary Digest Error
1936	60.2	53.8	−6.4	61.7	+1.5	40.9	−19.3
1940	54.7	52.0	−2.7	55.2	+0.5		
1944	53.8	51.5	−2.3	53.6	−0.2		
1948	49.5	44.5	−5.0	37.1	−12.4		
1952	44.5	46.0	+1.5	43.0	−1.5		
1956	42.0	40.5	−1.5	40.0	−2.0	Harris Poll	
1960	49.7	49.0	−0.7	47.0	−2.7	Pred.	Error
1964	61.0	64.0	+3.0	....	.....	64.0	+3.0

ever devised."[14] Despite later hedging, the initial claims rested implicitly on a theory of direct democracy fundamentally opposed to representative forms of democracy. By this view, the polls "helped speed up the processes of democracy" enabling representatives to *know*, rather than having merely to *guess*, their constituents' desires, and thus enabling them speedily to implement those desires.

> The speed with which sampling *referenda* can be completed for the entire nation is such that public opinion on any given issue can be reported within forty-eight hours if the occasion warrants. Thus the goal has nearly been reached when public opinion can be ascertainable at all times.[15]

But Dr. Gallup wrongly regards such 'quickie' responses as meaningful opinion. Public *opinion* is the outcome of political debate, of interest groups and opinion leaders informing and arousing the public, of government officials seeking to defend their policies, of newspaper reporting and editorials—in short, the normal process of democratic politics. Democracy requires government to respond to the majority opinion that results from such deliberations, and not from the snap responses and misinformation which polling measures. Ironically, Dr. Gallup can claim that his polls speed things up only because they are not taken too seriously. If representatives really viewed the polls as binding referenda, interested groups would insist on their right to campaign for public support, time would be needed to inform and interest the public, safeguards would be needed to protect the anonymity of respondents and the honesty of the count, and the whole process would have to come under public regulation. If taken seriously, the polls would have to resemble a not particularly speedy, old-fashioned referendum.

There are also technical problems besetting public opinion measurement. Among the most difficult is designing objective questions of unambiguous meaning. For example, the Gallup poll asked white re-

---

[14] George Gallup, quoted by Paul B. Sheatsley, "Public Opinion," *Encyclopedia Americana*, XXII, 773.

[15] George Gallup, *A Guide to Public Opinion Polls* (Princeton: Princeton University Press, 1944), p. 4. Italics supplied.

In 1948 President Harry Truman defeated the polls as well as Dewey. He enjoyed displaying the famous premature headline announcing his defeat.

spondents: "Do you think the Kennedy administration is pushing integration too fast, or not fast enough?"[16] But the phrasing, "pushing integration," may well encourage negative responses. Compare the sound of "protecting civil rights." "Pushing" is particularly loaded in reference to minority groups which are often stereotyped as 'pushy' (pushing themselves into places where they aren't wanted). Techniques developed by social scientists for detecting biased questions are too often ignored in hasty journalistic polling procedures.

In 1948 the pollsters fell victim to the general conviction that Dewey would beat Truman—which everyone except President Truman seemed to share. Elmo Roper stopped polling on September 9 as a waste of further effort, and Gallup declared confidently: "We have never claimed infallibility, but next Tuesday the whole world will be able to see down to the last percentage point how good we are."[17] It was a good lesson in humility when Truman won. However, the election was very close, and Gallup's statistical margin of error in wrongly predicting Truman's defeat was actually *better* than when he won public acclaim in 1936 for rightly predicting Roosevelt's victory.

The Social Science Research Council ascribed the pollsters' failure to three primary faults: (1) A last-minute shift to Truman went undetected because the pollsters quit interviewing too soon; (2) An unusually large

---

[16] *Los Angeles Times*, September 11, 1963, p. 2.
[17] Quoted by Lindsay Rogers, *The Pollsters* (New York: Alfred A. Knopf, 1949), p. vi.

SOME DEMOGRAPHIC CORRELATES OF VOTING

(figures = % of major party preferences; minor parties excluded)

Demographic Characteristics	1948 D	1948 R	1952 D	1952 R	1956 D	1956 R	1960 D	1960 R	1964 D	1964 R
Religious										
Protestant	47	53	36	64	36	64	37	63	63	37
Catholic	66	34	52	48	45	55	83	17	79	21
Jewish	100	0*	74	26	77	23	89	11	89	11
Race										
White	53	47	40	60	39	61	47	53	64	36
Negro	65	35	82	18	67	33	72	28	100	0*
Education										
Grade School	69	31	49	51	42	58	55	45	80	20
High School	54	46	43	57	44	56	53	47	69	31
College	24	76	26	74	31	69	36	64	54	46
Age										
34 and younger	63	37	45	55	41	59	52	48	72	28
35 to 44	61	39	45	55	42	58	51	49	68	32
45 to 54	47	53	42	58	39	61	55	45	69	31
55 to 64	43	57	35	65	33	67	44	56	70	30
65 and over	50	50	36	64	44	56	38	62	55	45
Sex										
Male	57	43	43	57	44	56	53	47	65	35
Female	53	47	40	60	37	63	46	54	69	31
Household Head's Occupation										
Professional and Managerial	19	81	32	68	31	69	45	55	58	42
White Collar	50	50	35	65	40	60	48	52	65	35
Skilled and Semi-skilled Workers	77	23	52	48	45	55	59	41	77	23
Unskilled Workers	74	26	68	32	47	53	59	41	83	17
Farm Operators	64	36	37	63	46	54	33	67	64	36
Union Membership										
Labor Union Families	82	18	56	44	52	48	64	36	84	16
Non Union Families	44	56	36	64	35	65	44	56	62	38
Income										
Lower	65	35	42	58	45	55	47	53	74	26
Lower Middle	69	31	46	54	43	57	46	54	71	29
Upper Middle	49	51	42	58	41	59	55	45	71	29
Upper	38	62	26	74	35	65	46	54	56	44
Community Size										
Metropolitan Areas	60	40	43	57	45	55	58	42	72	28
Cities (over 50,000)	..	..	52	48	33	67	50	50	67	33
Towns (2,500-49,999)	48	52	37	63	37	63	40	60	61	39
Rural (under 2,500)	67	33	39	61	42	58	48	52	69	31

Source: Data from Survey Research Center, University of Michigan. Definitions of some categories varied slightly in different election year studies and are only generally comparable.
*Fewer than 1% of respondents favored the Republican candidate in these instances.

number of undecided respondents did not divide evenly as expected, but were incipient Truman supporters; (3) In trying to distinguish probable voters from nonvoters, the pollsters overweighted their samples with college-educated respondents (who are more likely to turn out and vote), but this overrepresented upper-class Republicans, whereas a surprisingly large number of persons with only a grade-school education actually turned out to vote for Truman.[18] Subsequently, methods have been improved and preelection polls are a standard feature of American politics.[19]

Social Science Survey Research. The basic concern of social scientists is not with election forecasting, except as a test of accuracy, nor with reporting particular opinions as an end in itself. They use polling techniques to learn *why* people vote as they do, not simply for whom they did or will vote.

Initially, in investigating this difficult question, a preponderant emphasis was placed on socio-economic status and similar demographic (i.e., population differentiating) variables: religion, urban or rural residence, and similar factors. These social background characteristics seemed to predispose people to vote in a predictable way. As one study then put it, "a person thinks, politically, as he is, socially."[20] However, in later elections, seemingly well-established correlations between social factors and political behavior broke down as new personalities and political controversies emerged. Thus, urban Catholics were much less likely to vote Democratic in the Eisenhower elections than usually. Negro voters, once solidly Republican, are now solidly Democratic and they could shift again. Social correlates of voting are not permanently fixed relationships. It was necessary to find "a supplementary theoretical structure . . . that would bring politics into the study of electoral behavior."[21]

More recent survey research voting studies have included political as well as demographic and socio-psychological variables in their basic design. We shall draw upon this developing literature in summarizing the major influences on American voting behavior.

Influences on Voting Behavior

Party identification: Republicans and Democrats. Four out of five Americans are more or less favorably inclined toward one of the two major

---

[18] See Frederick Mosteller, *et al.*, *The Pre-Election Polls of 1948* (New York: Social Science Research Council, Bulletin No. 60, 1949), particularly pp. 299–303.

[19] The performance of state and national 1964 presidential election polls is recorded in *Congressional Quarterly Weekly Report*, November 20, 1964, p. 2710.

[20] P. F. Lazarsfeld, B. Berelson, and H. Gaudet, *The People's Choice* (2nd ed.; New York: Columbia University Press, 1948), p. 27.

[21] V. O. Key, Jr. and F. Munger, "Social Determinism and Electoral Decision: the Case of Indiana," in E. Burdick and A. Brodbeck, eds. *American Voting Behavior* (Glencoe: Free Press, 1959), p. 282. Cf. the response to this criticism by S. M. Lipset, *et al.*, "The Psychology of Voting: An Analysis of Political Behavior," in Gardner Lindzey (ed.), *Handbook of Social Psychology*, Vol. 2 (Cambridge, Mass.: Addison-Wesley, 1954), pp. 1112 ff.

political parties, and they usually vote for their favored party's candidates. Thus, "the most potent factor differentiating responses is not economic status, social milieu, or variation in deep-seated temperament, but quite simply the political party. . . ."[22] Even in the Eisenhower landslides, where the victor appealed broadly across party lines, the single most important influence on voting was the individual's attachment to his political party.[23] These feelings of party identification are long-enduring; even when voters stray from their party's choice, they nonetheless retain their sense of party identification. Thus the proportions of Democrats to Republicans in the electorate—about three to two—remained remarkably constant right through the Eisenhower era; even while voting for Eisenhower, many still considered themselves Democrats.

What are the sources of these enduring partisan predispositions? As with attachment to a religion, many more people are 'born and bred' Democrats or Republicans than deliberately select the 'party of their choice.' The first political lessons are learned at home. Children become Democrats or Republicans and acquire the basic political viewpoints which characterize the parties. And once established in the family, party identifications are reinforced and sustained by shared interests and loyalties typical of peer, socioeconomic, and other groups. Thus, since the New Deal, Democrats have been found in greater proportion than Republicans among lower-income, union-membership, ethnic and religious minority, and large-city groups.

More than three fourths of the voters never change their party preference. But the remaining fourth do change; there is a continuous process of individual switches in party identification as innumerable factors influence particular persons. And critical transformations occur from time to time, involving great numbers of voters. Such was the emergence of the Republican party out of the critical pre-Civil War period, and the new dominance of the Democratic party as an outcome of the Great Depression. The bearers of these historical changes tend to be the youth, whose political habits are least fixed. Thus, the generation which came of voting age during the Depression broke with their parents' predominantly Republican ties. But their children have been reared as Democrats with the result that there is presently an "overwhelming Democratic to Republican ratio among . . . those under 25 years of age."[24]

While party identification is the most important single influence upon voting behavior, it is by no means the sole influence. If it were, the Republicans could not have elected Eisenhower, nor come as close to winning with Dewey or Nixon. Election outcomes have varied in response to three additional influences upon voting behavior: issues, candidates, and voter turnout.

---

[22] Angus Campbell, Philip E. Converse, Warren E. Miller, and Donald E. Stokes, *The American Voter* (New York: Wiley, 1960), p. 292.

[23] *Ibid.*, p. 139.

[24] Warren Miller, "The Political Behavior of the Electorate," *American Government Annual, 1960–61* (New York: Holt, Rinehart and Winston, 1960), p. 52.

The influence of issues. Although all campaigns begin with a residue from the past, each election is an unique event. Each has its own specific policy issues and in each the electorate has different interests. Changing circumstances dictate these issues and interests. Nothing could keep the depression out of the 1932, nor the Korean war out of the 1952, campaign.

The impact of particular issues on voting behavior is twofold. First, the issue conflict rallies the party faithful. Certain kinds of issues recur and the parties' basic positions on them are widely known. This is especially true of economic issues like recession, inflation, depressed areas, and labor-management relations. Conflict over such issues, in which the basic party positions are expressed, is the way party predisposition—habitual attachment to a party and its point of view—is converted into actual votes. Although most voters never grasp the particulars, the slogans and headlines filter down and summon up the basic party loyalties. Foreign-policy issues have become increasingly prominent in elections since the Cold War began, but Republicans and Democrats differ less persistently on foreign than on domestic matters. Accordingly, foreign-policy conflict is less influential in mobilizing party regulars.

Issue conflict has a second impact on voting behavior. Issues arise in every election which especially affect particular interests and groups. Voters thus affected frequently feel so strongly about such an issue that they may vote contrary to their basic party identification. By stressing such issues, presidential candidates can appeal across party lines and win votes ordinarily belonging to the opposing party, or make special gains among independent voters. In the Fifties, for example, Republicans hammered away at the loss of eastern Europe to Russia; thousands of voters of eastern European descent, ordinarily big-city Democrats, voted for Republicans in consequence of this single issue. In 1948, many rural areas were depressed, and thousands of ordinarily Republican midwestern farm votes went to President Truman, who campaigned strenuously on his agricultural program. Another example is President Eisenhower's famous 1952 campaign pledge, that he would "go to Korea," implying his special ability to end that prolonged and dispiriting war. Thousands of troubled voters turned to him on this issue, regardless of their basic party allegiance.

Survey data demonstrate that most voters cannot identify the campaign issues and the candidates' conflicting stands on them. This fact has sometimes wrongly been interpreted to imply that voting behavior is little affected by campaign issues. But the decisive fact is that, variously, 10 to 50 per cent of the voters—that is, millions of voters—are adequately aware of the issues; and those especially responsive to particular issues are keenly aware of them. Accordingly, more than enough voters to decide most elections can be switched from their ordinary party loyalties by competent campaigning on issues.

The influence of candidates. The candidates' personal attributes seem to influence voters decidedly less than either party identification or issue orientation. However, candidate appeal would probably be a more important election variable were it not for the fact that both parties usually nominate attractive candidates, which tends to cancel out this factor. Nonetheless, the switch of even a small percentage of the electorate can decide an election. A candidate's personal reputation, appearance, speech, style, and family has an independent impact on the electorate. General Eisenhower in 1952 was an outstanding example. War hero, 'above politics,' buoyantly charming, he powerfully attracted voters. In 1956, as incumbent President, his personal appeal was so great that he captured 57 per cent of the presidential vote while the Democrats were winning both houses of Congress. Such a split had not occurred for 108 years.

Voter turnout. Presidents are not elected by citizens who prefer them, but only by those who turn out to vote on election day. Even in presidential elections some 40 million out of 100 million American adults usually do not exercise their franchise. (Nonvoting is proportionately much larger than in other democracies.) However, far from all nonvoters are simply apathetic about politics. Many are people on the move and temporarily disqualified by residence and registration requirements. Some are ill, some are in jail. Inevitably, each election day, some families suffer a death, a burned-down house, a deserting husband; such calamities discourage even the most politically inclined from voting. Large numbers of southern Negroes are deliberately barred. Given the usual near-certainty of the outcome, Southerners, white or Negro, have lacked much incentive to vote in general elections. (Outside the South the voting rate is about 75 per cent; in Mississippi, by contrast, it is about 22 per cent, in Louisiana about 35 per cent.)

Still, an immense number—estimated at 15.5 million persons—[25] lack these reasons and simply neglect to vote. This would have little political significance, despite the huge numbers, if their political preferences were not characteristically different from those who did vote. (Election outcomes would remain the same, only the totals would change.) But nonvoters, compared with voters, tend to divide quite differently politically.

Partisans turn out to vote more than self-styled independents. Actually there are few genuine independents, i.e., people of such independent political judgment that they refuse to be limited in their consideration of alternatives by the standard party alignments. Those who call themselves independents when interviewed by survey procedures also admit to much less interest in politics generally and are less likely to have voted than respondents with definite party identifications. Feeling strongly about the differences between the parties is closely linked with feeling that the campaign issues and candidates are worth voting about.

But partisanship can be diluted. Ironically, the campaign itself makes some potential voters stay away from the polls. They begin with their usual party preferences, but then may be reached by the other party with

---

[25] Clinton Rossiter, *Parties and Politics in America* (Ithaca: Cornell University Press, 1960), p. 31.

RELATIVE VOTER TURNOUT OF VARIOUS GROUPS

HIGHER TURNOUT compared with LOWER TURNOUT

HIGHER TURNOUT	LOWER TURNOUT
men	women
middle-aged (35-55)	younger and older
whites	Negroes
Catholics and Jews	Protestants
urban	rural
North	South
partisans	independents
Republicans	Democrats
organizational joiners	non-joiners
upper socio-economic status	lower socio-economic status
professional and businessmen	unskilled workers
skilled workers	farm laborers
union member workers	non-union workers
more formal education	less formal education

particular issues or candidates. They are thus subject to *cross-pressures,* torn between normal party loyalty and the other party's particular appeals. This may lead to splitting one's ticket, or to indecision and nonvoting.

Another kind of cross-pressure is important. Most people have a harmonious pattern of group involvements and corresponding political values. For example, a person of lower socio-economic status, with a wife of the same class, joins his union, associates with union workers at lunch, goes bowling and exchanges social visits with a similar group of acquaintances. Such a harmonious pattern tends to a single partisan direction. But when a worker is promoted to foreman or opens his own shop, or a Republican woman marries a Democrat, then there are cross-pressures pulling in opposing political directions which sometimes produce indecision and nonvoting.

Two major correlates of nonvoting are low socio-economic status and low educational attainment. These are obviously related factors, even with mass educational opportunities, and usually operate with combined force. But they vary independently as well in influencing voting turnout. For example, better-educated workers are more likely to be voters than are less-educated workers. Similarly, other demographic categories are interrelated. About 80 per cent of Southerners with some college study usually vote compared with 50 per cent of those who finished only grade school. (The comparable Northern figures are 92 per cent and 68 per cent.) [26] Education is a massive independent variable influencing turnout. It is related to a person's capacity to confront political issues and complexities with reasonable comprehension. By contrast, less educated people are

---

[26] *American Voter,* p. 478.

commonly less aware of political happenings, lack information on issues and candidate stands, and generally feel impotent vis à vis government.[27]

But high socio-economic status and high educational attainment—massive factors in influencing high voter turnout—are not evenly distributed between the parties. Rather, as we have seen, these are more characteristic of Republicans than of Democrats. Thus, 24 per cent of 'strong' Democrats but only 8 per cent of the 'strong' Republicans in a sample survey reported not having voted in 1952. This significantly affects the parties and poses a strategic campaign problem, particularly for the Democrats. They must design campaign efforts to get their more apathetic fellow party identifiers to the polls. At the same time, however, a high turnout does not always assure a Democratic victory, as the unusually large turnout in the 1952 Eisenhower victory demonstrated.

The Making of a President: Campaigning

From nomination in early summer to the first Tuesday after the first Monday in November, presidential candidates campaign strenuously to become the people's choice. An effective campaign strategy must be designed to utilize limited time and resources efficiently: Voting behavior patterns have been closely studied to extract current issues which might tilt the balance of voter turnout and preferences; national, state, and local organizations—party and interest groups—are spurred into action; press and television interviews, speeches, and propaganda materials, from 'planted' news features to buttons and badges, eat away at energies and funds; and, finally, there is the long and hard campaign trail with each candidate expected to appear personally in a barnstorming swing through the nation.

Campaign Strategy

Campaigning affects voting in three ways: (1) Predominantly, the campaign whips up sufficient enthusiasm to *reinforce* and *reactivate* those who are probable supporters if only they can be gotten to the polls on election day. (2) Some opponents may be *neutralized* into indecision and apathy by the right combination of candidate and issue appeals. (3) There is less hope that outright opponents can be *converted* into supporters, though in some critical elections major transformations of previous patterns of party identification have been effected. A campaign strategy is the manner by which party leaders plan to perform these functions of activation, neutralization, and conversion of voters.

The basic principle is to emphasize and dramatize issues and candidate qualities most favorable to one's own candidacy and to avoid or

---

[27] The latter factor has been studied by the Survey Research Center by means of a series of questions comprising a scale of "political efficacy." See *The American Voter*, pp. 103 ff.

minimize unfavorable matters. Campaign strategies dangerously incline toward mere expediency, toward bending, and sometimes twisting, program and principle. But there are important constraints on such expediency. Expediency itself requires that a candidate operate within the limits of his party's general orientation and history. He cannot—in order to woo his opponent's normal supporters—twist program and principle so far that he weakens or loses his own following. Another limit on a candidate's flexibility are his own talents and attributes. An obviously youthful contender, like Kennedy in 1960, can scarcely campaign as an experienced elder statesman. He appeals rather to "new frontiers" to conquer and the need for youthful vigor in "getting the country moving again." A candidate's personal qualities and views thus restrict his range of appeals.

And beyond expediency, the sense of imminent presidential responsibility for the national security and welfare looms ever larger as the campaign nears its climax. This responsibility is concretely manifested in the fact that the incumbent President—specifically to minimize rash campaign promises dictated by narrow partisan considerations—now offers to brief his major party opponent on secret military and diplomatic matters. (But, on the other hand, challengers are wary of accepting the offer, for fear that their hands may be excessively tied by such briefings.) Thus, there is a balance between the temptation to raise any issue to attract votes and considerations of principle and the public interest.

Moulding the issues. Each campaign develops its own decisive issues, its own special character and tone. But there are recurring characteristics. For example, different roles usually distinguish the ins and the outs. An incumbent President seeking reelection can count on his opponent's shooting at the Administration's record, probing for failures and unpopular policies. But the presidential office is equipped with powerful defences. The incumbent may manage to take the offensive as Harry S. Truman did in 1948. Accepting the nomination, he electrified the Democratic convention and millions of TV viewers by challenging the opposition-controlled Congress to enact the recently drafted *Republican* platform. For this purpose, he announced, the President was calling the "do-nothing Republican 80th Congress" back into special session. The Republicans counterattacked this use of presidential constitutional authority as a political maneuver, which it no doubt was, but it proved an effective maneuver throughout that memorable campaign.

Both parties typically emphasize or deemphasize certain campaign issues and candidate qualities in accord with the strategic implications of persistent voting behavior patterns. Democrats tend to benefit when economic welfare issues are most salient. Republicans have more often benefited from a foreign policy emphasis. Thus Democrats tried to minimize the impact of the Korean War in 1952 by stressing economic issues. Economic prosperity was celebrated as a Democratic accomplishment—'Don't let them take it away,' was a favorite Democratic slogan. The theme was: 'Remember Hoover and the Republican depression, don't be taken in by Republican sweet talk, they opposed every reform benefitting the poor man, and had to be dragged kicking and screaming into the twentieth century.' Democratic partisan identifications outnumbering Republicans in the population, the strategy was to pin Eisenhower down as a Republican and saddle him with his party's relative unpopularity on economic issues.

The Republicans responded by underplaying economic issues, though they made fear of inflation a minor theme. Their major strategy was to hold the Democratic Truman administration responsible for 'Communism, Corruption and Korea.' Above all, and especially above party,[28] there was Ike Eisenhower, the attractive national hero who would "clear up the mess in Washington" and who would "go to Korea" to resolve that "sorry mess" as well. He would end Communist infiltration into high governmental positions, influence-peddling by corrupted governmental officials, and the killing of American boys in a futile war in a far-off land. Adlai Stevenson attracted an ardent following, but he faced an unbeatable combination of candidate, situation, and campaign strategy.

The Democrats countered the charge of corrupt influence-peddling by publicizing a private fund (which they labeled a 'millionaires' club') maintained over the years in support of Republican vice-presidential candidate, Richard Nixon. This rebuttal sought to tie the Republican ticket to rich businessmen, and, above all, to shift the target from the invulnerable Eisenhower to the less popular and more partisan figure of Nixon. However, in a skillful televised appeal to the public, Nixon emerged with a net gain. The country remained predominantly Democratic and the Democrats continued to be favored on economic issues, but the 1952 election issues were perceived by the bulk of the public in primarily noneconomic terms—precisely the aim, if not altogether solely the result, of the successful Republican campaign strategy.

Key states and key groups. Candidates dare not obviously slight any geographical or group interests. Considerable campaigning is thus directed to the whole national audience through the mass media of communication. At the same time, however, candidates must concentrate their major efforts—quantitatively and thematically—on those states and groups deemed decisive for victory. Increasingly, both parties have had to emphasize the same key states. For example, in 1960, the seven largest states were identified as prime campaign targets by both the Kennedy and Nixon strategists.[29]

Three main tactics are employed in appealing to voters in these pivotal states: (1) The candidate and his ablest supporting speakers, including the vice-presidential candidate, schedule more personal appearances in

---

[28] Eisenhower had been approached by leaders of *both* major parties with offers of nomination for the Presidency, so successfully had the General steered clear of partisan identification prior to 1952.

[29] See p. 386, table. Kennedy listed the two next ranking states as well; see Theodore H. White, *The Making of the President 1960* (New York: Atheneum, 1961), pp. 295, 318.

these key states. (2) When possible, issues of greatest interest to voters within these states are emphasized. (3) Organizational energies and resources are strategically concentrated rather than spread evenly across the fifty states. While no area can be left wholly uncared for, these priorities are unavoidable in the selection of prime campaign targets and appeals.

Similarly, key groups are given special attention. It is now traditional for the Democratic candidate officially to kick off his barnstorming campaign with a Labor Day speech in Detroit's Kennedy (formerly Cadillac) Square, symbolizing organized labor's importance to the Democratic electoral coalition. Care is taken in campaign scheduling to have the candidate extend recognition to all the important groups by a speech or at least a brief visit. The vice-presidential running mate can be a great help here. In 1960, Republican Henry Cabot Lodge brought his recent status as American ambassador to the United Nations to the campaign for support by the more recently arrived ethnic minority groups of the Northeast. Then Democratic vice-presidential candidate, Lyndon Johnson of Texas devoted his efforts to salvaging the South for Kennedy. Selected to balance the presidential ticket, the running mate focuses his campaign efforts on the specific groups his candidacy was meant to appeal to.

Campaign strategists recognize the need to adapt their advance planning to changing conditions during the course of the campaign. Some openings may be left in the candidate's schedule to take advantage of later opportunities. New situations may be turned to advantage in the heat of the campaign. For example, the jailing of Negro leader Martin Luther King, Jr. during the 1960 campaign enabled Kennedy to symbolize his sympathetic responsiveness on civil-rights issues. Negroes, especially King's wife, feared that King would be taken from his Georgia jail cell and lynched. John F. Kennedy personally phoned Mrs. King to reassure her, while Robert Kennedy phoned the Georgia judge urging that King be released. These were 'private' calls, but Mrs. King happily informed the Negro community, and King's father—a Baptist minister who had earlier supported Nixon on religious grounds—publicly switched to Kennedy: "I've got a suitcase full of votes, and I'm going to take them to Mr. Kennedy and dump them in his lap.[30] As it turned out Negro voters were a crucial element in Kennedy's close margin of victory.

On the Campaign Trail

Barnstorming through the country is an old presidential campaign tradition. The candidate shows himself to the public, shakes millions of hands, demonstrates his oratorical skills, creates local headlines and, he hopes, national ones as well. The strain on all participants—the candidate,

---

[30] Quoted by White, *ibid.*, p. 387.

John F. Kennedy on the campaign trail in the 1960 presidential election.

frequently his family, staff, and accompanying reporters—is enormous. The candidate makes fantastic numbers of daily appearances with little time for sleep, and none for relaxation, and has to repeat stock phrases in stock speeches before jaded reporters—yet somehow in an ever lively, persuasive, and sincere manner. It is frequently said that the Presidency is a man-killing job. The first blows surely are felt on the campaign trail even prior to election. Here is a candidate's typical campaign day as recorded by an astute first-hand observer:

Kennedy had had four hours' sleep each of the two previous evenings, and now, in Detroit, he was allowed six and a half hours' sleep before he was woken to the first of his three breakfasts. The first breakfast at seven o'clock was . . . with his personal staff. . . . The second breakfast, unannounced, was brief: with John Swainson, . . . Democratic candidate for Michigan's governorship—Swainson and his young men would be taking over leadership from the older Williams-Staebler group if elected, and Kennedy wanted to know them. Then the third, public, breakfast at eight, with Wayne County CIO leaders. Then, at nine o'clock, a full hour of picture taking with all Congressional candidates, statewide candidates and other dignitaries who must be flattered with pictures of the Presidential candidate in conversation with them; then another half hour of greeting and two-minute chats with labor leaders and party leaders all of whom, forever after, would be able to refer to their talk with "Jack." One half hour of work revising his speech followed, and then out to Cadillac Square in the brilliant sun to address the cheering mass, then back, five minutes late to honor Walter Reuther with a personal conversation; then a hasty meal with his own staff . . . picture taking again—a picture with "Mudcat" Grant, Negro pitcher of the Cleveland Indians, to please his Civil Rights Division; another picture with the Lennon Sisters, several more pictures with various Detroit judges. Then, . . . a motor tour through Michigan.

The Michigan State Fair first, for five minutes; then the Labor Day Picnic at Pontiac, Michigan (where he received a ceremonial Indian headdress); then the long drive to Flint, Michigan, and another Labor Day Picnic and another speech (along the way he hastily read, then approved, a statement blasting the State Department on the situation in the Congo); then an airplane flight in the dusk (he had now switched to his own Convair, the "Mother Ship" in which he was to remain for the rest of the campaign) to Muskegon airport; a seven-mile drive through a defile of cheering people holidaying on Labor Day to Pere Marquette Park, where he addressed another Labor Day Picnic, his voice hoarsening by now. Running about an hour behind schedule, he ate a rushed dinner alone in a hotel room . . . found time for a telephone call to Hyannisport to speak to his wife, and then on to the Dew-Drop Inn of Muskegon to give the Democratic candidate of Michigan's Ninth Congressional District a lift. A short speech—mainly historical, intertwining Michigan's history with the history of the Democratic Party—and then out to the airport, taking off at eleven in the evening and arriving in Pocatello, Idaho, at two in the morning. (There would be five hours' sleep in Pocatello that night before he must rise for more breakfasts, more speeches, more flights, briefings on the situation in Idaho, in Tacoma, in Spokane, in Seattle.)

It was to be this way for both candidates from the first week in September until the day of voting. . . .[31]

The candidate goes out to rally the people, but he can scarcely appear in person, even fleetingly, before more than a tiny fraction of the public. Barnstorming, more importantly, is a device to stimulate mass-media

---

[31] White, *ibid.,* pp. 302–303.

reporters and group and organizational opinion leaders through whom much of the campaign is mediated in communicating with the electorate. Especially important are the local party leaders and candidates. The national and local campaigns are closely interdependent. Accordingly, when the presidential caravan pauses at a 'whistle stop,' the national campaign must dovetail with these local political interests. Candidates for congressman, governor, and mayor, among others, ride a short distance on the train and are publicly greeted and photographed with the presidential candidate.[32] Party workers are hand-shaked and pep-talked to spur increased organizational efforts. Private consultations with state and local leaders yield reactions and suggestions concerning campaign strategy. These personal contacts give top-level recognition to the lower ranks of campaign workers.

Campaign Organization

Not only must the candidate and his retinue perform on the campaign trail, but he and his aides also comprise the campaign's top command. Save for a few inept men, candidates have personally dominated campaign planning and organization. For the top organizational level they choose confidants of many years standing. Lyndon B. Johnson used as key aides many who had long associated with him in the Senate. President Kennedy, before him, drew heavily on members of his family for aides. This highly personal general staff then coopts the party national chairman and national committee organization to its campaign operations.

Below this level, there is no clear chain of command, no neat table of organization. The normal confusion of American politics, with its thousands of important political actors, inescapably asserts itself—though there is tighter discipline in presidential campaigns than at other times. Campaign organization is complex for three major reasons: First, the sheer magnitude of effort is enormous; so much must be done in so short a time by thousands of people spread over a huge territory. Second, the decentralized party structure hampers efficient national direction of state and local efforts. Third, diverse campaign functions and particularized appeals to a wide variety of voters and groups generate unmanageably numerous specialized and auxiliary organizational entities.

Thus, national campaign management must operate through many autonomous groupings of leaders and activists. In addition to the candidate's immediate staff, four types of organizational structures require coordination: (1) the geographically organized national, state, and local regular party machinery; (2) specialized party and nonparty auxiliary committees directed at particular groups—Negroes and other 'ethnics,' women, lawyers, movie stars, veterans, farmers, etc. (For example, The

---

[32] Embarrassing problems may arise. Senatorial candidate Joseph McCarthy rode the Eisenhower campaign train in Wisconsin despite the General's considerable discomfiture.

Healing Arts Committee for Nixon and Lodge aimed its appeal at physicians, dentists, nurses, and pharmacists.) (3) nonparty, interest-group sponsored electioneering organizations, like the AFL-CIO Committee on Political Education (COPE); and (4) nonpartisan electioneering groups which lure independents and party defectors willing to work for the candidate but not under his party's auspices. The classic example is the highly successful Citizens for Eisenhower. All these organizational units raise funds, schedule speakers, obtain publicity, distribute leaflets, posters, and automobile bumper stickers, and hold all kinds of meetings, from mass rallies down to 'coffee hours' in neighborhood homes where small groups meet the local candidates and discuss campaign issues.

Financing the Campaign. An old saying has it that 'it takes money to make money'; a new one might be, 'it takes money to get votes.' Actually, this has always been so, though modern election campaigns are extremely expensive. About fifty million dollars is spent on each side in a presidential contest.[33] The impact of that figure is lessened when we realize that it costs four times as much merely to advertise each year's new crop of automobiles. Nor, despite common belief, has the amount or relative importance of campaign expenditures been steadily rising. Even though modern campaigning involves heavy expenditures for new modes of electioneering like television and other public relations techniques, costs have not increased during the last generation beyond the general rise in living costs. Indeed the impact of money on elections may well be less than in the past. Until the victories of Franklin Roosevelt and Harry Truman, every presidential election from 1904 through 1928 went to the candidate, Republican or Democrat, who spent the most money. That correlation no longer holds in presidential elections. But money has probably become more vital to nominating campaigns.

Millions of people contribute rather than only a few 'fat cats.' Tens of thousands give several hundred dollars each. In 1964 the Republicans raised over 7 million dollars in donations of one hundred dollars or less.[34] Contrary to their underdog image, Democrats get a substantial share of big-business givers, although Republicans get even more of this money. And contrary to another stereotype, trade unions' cash donations are but a small proportion of the Democratic total; however, contributions of top-level union staff and man-hours of precinct and other campaign workers have substantial additional value. The difference between the parties is moderate, but in general Republicans have raised and spent more than the Democrats.

No doubt campaign contributions are frequently made with a *quid pro quo* in mind. But political money-giving is also a means of furthering

---

[33] This includes expenditures on all organizational levels—national, state, and local. *Cf.* Alexander Heard, *The Costs of Democracy* (Chapel Hill: University of North Carolina Press, 1960), pp. 7 and 372. This section on campaign finance relies on this authoritative source.

[34] *Congressional Quarterly Weekly Report*, January 8, 1965, p. 49.

general political beliefs and policies, of identifying with one's party and, like voting, is a mark of civic virtue. Sordid practices are uncovered from time to time,[35] but there is no ground for the naive cynicism that grossly oversimplifies political motives. Major politicians are seldom for sale to the highest bidder if only because they "prize votes more than dollars."[36] Politicians cannot afford to accept donations tied to vote-losing policies. Moreover, modern corrupt-practices regulations and congressional investigations exert fairly strong controls. But the regulation of contributions and expenditures has also imposed some dubious requirements on campaign organizers. The 1940 Hatch Act limits donors to five thousand dollars for a national candidate. This leads to an unseemly pursuit of legal loopholes, and places an onus on a necessary financial ingredient of democratic elections. Many donors are also discouraged by the "public disclosure" requirement; names and addresses of all giving one hundred dollars or more must be filed with the Clerk of the House of Representatives. Finally, the Hatch Act limits any one national organization to collecting or spending no more than three million dollars. This has probably not reduced total receipts or expenditures, but it has greatly increased the number of campaign organizations, making accountability and management more difficult. Reforms have been urged, ranging from governmental subsidies to income tax deductions for campaign contributors. No remedies can be found without public recognition of the legitimate functions of campaign organizations. These functions are unavoidably expensive, and the costs of democracy must be borne by public or private means.

PR on James Madison's Avenue. Public relations is now a standard aspect of large business firms and increasingly of political campaign organizations.[37] The rise of the 'PR man' coincides with the development of modern mass-communications media—newspapers, magazines, radio, and television. His main expertise lies in using the mass media to obtain a desired public response. Within quite broad limits, that skill is for hire by anyone or anything needing an improved public image: movie stars, bankers, labor leaders, milk, soup, or soap. Using sample survey research techniques to explore consumer attitudes and motivations, Madison Avenue PR agencies plan and organize entire marketing programs. Making trade names into household words and purchases has become a multimillion dollar industry.

Catchy slogans, sex appeal, status appeals, the singing commercial, all were designed to sell any product—why not statesmen? Inevitably, election campaigners turned to the PR specialists for help. They began by teaching the politicians the camera tricks of television as candidates

---

[35] Cf. U.S. Senate Special Committee to Investigate Organized Crime in Interstate Commerce, *Hearings* (Washington: Government Printing Office, 1951); popularly known as the Kefauver Crime Committee. Cf. Heard, *op. cit.*, pp. 154–68.

[36] Heard, *op. cit.*, p. 6.

[37] *Cf.* Stanley Kelley, Jr., *Professional Public Relations and Political Power* (Baltimore, Md., Johns Hopkins University, 1956).

sought to master the new medium. Then, in the 1950s, they devised elaborate TV spectaculars blending politicians with documentary style news clips and Broadway and Hollywood stars. Some candidates turned their entire election campaign over to PR agencies, which practically dictate to the candidate the choice of main campaign themes, issues, speeches, and slogans as well as techniques for using the mass media. Almost all major candidates now bring PR men into their top policy-making staff so that PR considerations receive constant emphasis in managing the campaign.

The dominant PR consideration is: Find out what the people want— that is, what sells best—and give it to them in a more effective package than anybody else. To the extent that such thinking dominates a campaign, one vital aspect of representative democracy is utterly destroyed. The educative function of democratic leadership is abdicated. Candidates who should be leading public opinion become merely its clever lackeys. A more remote—and opposite possibility—is that PR techniques will someday 'brainwash' the voters into wanting whatever the candidate wants them to want. In any case, excessive use of toothpaste-type commercials to peddle public policies cheapens the democratic deliberative process. True, campaigning always involved some cheap slogans, demagogy, and propaganda techniques. But the systematic reduction of political communication to what can be conveyed in a jingle on a thirty-second TV 'spot' carries new dangers—especially when PR specialists come to command entire campaign strategies. It remains to be seen whether James Madison's Constitution will be dangerously undermined by James Madison's Avenue.

Elections are won in the precincts. Despite the inroads of PR-managed campaigning, politicians continue to persuade their hard-core activists that effective precinct work can spell the difference between victory and defeat.[38] Abraham Lincoln described the process to his fellow Whigs:

The whole State must be so well organized that every Whig can be brought to the polls. So divide the county into small districts and appoint in each a committee. Make a perfect list of the voters and ascertain with certainty for whom they will vote. . . . Keep a constant watch on the doubtful voters and have them talked to by those in whom they have the most confidence. . . . On election days see that every Whig is brought to the polls.[39]

---

[38] The general view is that precinct work has declined, but comparative figures are hard to obtain. The Survey Research Center of the University of Michigan reported that 12 per cent of its national sample were visited by party workers during the 1952 campaign. By extension, that is the equivalent of about 7.5 million voters— enough to swing almost all presidential elections. See Angus Campbell, Gerald Gurin, and Warren E. Miller, *The Voter Decides* (Evanston, Ill.: Row, Peterson and Company, 1954), p. 33.

[39] Quoted in Chamber of Commerce of the United States, *Action Course in Practical Politics* (Washington, D.C.: Chamber of Commerce of the United States, 1959), No. 3, p. ii.

Precinct workers are a door-to-door political collection agency. They are out to collect the party faithful and, if possible, to reclaim the waverers. The basic technique requires periodic house-to-house canvasses (surveys) of the voting area mainly to supply up-to-date lists of likely supporters. These canvasses are utilized in two related operations: a preelection phase and an election-day phase. The preelection operation ensures that all eligible supporters are registered and able to vote. The canvassers uncover potential new voters—those just come of age or new residents who meet the legal qualifications—and also determine which friendly voters will be unable to appear at the polls on election day, requiring absentee ballots. (Many elections have been won in the voting booths only to be lost when the absentee ballots were added to the totals.) An accurate canvass is essential to the next phase. On election day, party runners identify likely supporters who have neglected to vote. The last few hours before the polls close are a frenzy of activity in which the maximum number of friendly voters are rounded up.

Many political organizations became so efficient at this mode of electioneering that the term 'political machine' entered the American language to designate the smoothness of their operations. Mainly, the term is used pejoratively because of the great reliance on patronage-rewarded 'professional' precinct captains (also called committeemen) and the consequent deemphasis of issues and principles as determinants of political activity and voting. But, in close elections, efficient campaign organization is a decisive factor. In the American democratic republic, the road to the White House, no less than to the Congress, unavoidably runs through the voting precincts.

Campaigning for Congress

Much of what we have considered about presidential campaigns applies as well at the congressional level. The serious candidates are almost always Democrats or Republicans. Congressmen face the same sorts of campaign problems—fund-raising, precinct-canvassing, PR huckstering. But the profound political localism of the American national-and-federal system distinguishes congressional campaigning. Congressional election campaigns are not a single, unified national phenomenon. Every two years there are 435 individual elections to the House of Representatives and 30-some-odd to the Senate. No single one is typical; each varies with peculiar local, state, and regional characteristics. To every generalization about congressional campaigns, some valid and significant exception can be found.

Reduction in Scale

The most obvious difference between congressional and presidential elections is the difference in scale. Even the election of a senator from a huge state like California or New York is a small affair compared with a presidential election. House districts are smaller still, embracing but a portion of a state, or even a small area of a densely populated city. Two related differences arise from this reduction in scale: first, a state or a congressional district lacks that great multiplicity of interests which characterizes presidential elections; second, the state or district may have some dominant parochial interest at variance with the national interest.

A dominant interest within the district. Each congressional district ordinarily having less "multiplicity of interests and sects," it is easier for a small number of powerful groups to form a majority among themselves. Because they can fairly easily dominate their district, these few groups have less need to moderate their demands; that is, the canceling-out of narrow self-interest, which often happens in the national coalition of a presidential majority, is less likely to happen at the congressional level. Often one economic, religious, or ethnic group interest dominates; and one newspaper and one TV station monopolizes the public channels of information. Within such narrow confines, a congressional candidate must communicate his views to the public and obtain organizational endorsements and financial backing. Too often, against his own best judgment and against the welfare of the whole district, the candidate is obliged to yield to the dominant interest groups.

A parochial interest of the whole district. Very often, however, it is not a question of one interest group dominating over all others within the district. Rather it is a question of the parochial interest of the whole district. Many districts and states have a distinctive interest conflicting with that of other regions or with the national interest. The interests of California and Arizona conflict over Colorado River water. Texas congressmen and senators vie with those from Massachusetts and Michigan for defense contracts. This is commonly deplored, but other things being equal the 'homefolks' quite properly expect *their* representative in Congress to champion *their* vital interests as against those of other regions. The conflict with the national interest, however, poses graver problems. Districts sometimes demand what representatives know is harmful to the country. But harmful or not, parochial issues can so dominate a congressional campaign that, while the rest of the country debates momentous issues like racial strife or Administration policy in Southeast Asia, the election in district X may well turn on the most minute—but locally dominant—issue. The parochialism of congressional elections is where the congressman's dilemma regarding his two constituencies (see pp. 166–68) begins. He is elected from a *locality* with all of its parochial concerns, but he must serve in a *national* legislature.

Getting Nominated

Congressional 'availability' criteria are not nearly so clear as those for the Presidency. Here too, of course, availability means winning qualities, but a greater variety of men and *women* have been elected to Congress. This includes a variety of religious and ethnic types reflecting local and state diversity in populations. Where party organization is strong, candidates for the House of Representatives are likely to be reliable party men, well-known to the local party leaders. But 'reliable' does not refer to national party program—it refers to local issues and to local party matters. Assure constituents of fidelity on these matters and, so to speak, you may be a statesman on everything else.

The dominant mode of selecting major party nominees is by direct primary, but the outcome is usually a foregone conclusion. The big exception is the South, where primaries are frequently the real contest for election. But, elsewhere, the vital decision is likely to be made prior to the primaries. For one thing, most incumbents seek reelection. (In 1964, 34 of the 35 senators with expiring terms sought renomination; an almost equally high proportion obtained for House incumbents.) Incumbents infrequently face serious challenge in the primary. Renomination is usually easy because the congressman is on the job continually with paid staff, mail franking privileges and funds, making his the best-organized political office in most districts.

Where there is no House incumbent seeking reelection—which is always the case for at least one party in every district—serious primary contests are somewhat more frequent. Only somewhat because in districts with strong party organizations the party leadership determines who shall be the regular organization's candidate, and he usually wins the primary. Obtaining the nomination often comes down to convincing that leadership—ward committeemen, county chairmen, and sometimes state bigwigs—that one is the most available man among the prospective candidates. In districts where the party is poorly organized, would-be candidates know who the local community powers are and whose support is indispensable. They try to prove to these leaders that they have the abilities, the group support, and the funds (a candidate's ability to raise or supply his own money is often vital) to wage an effective campaign.

Another reason why there are relatively few primary contests is that the parties sometimes have trouble getting one decent candidate willing to be led to probable slaughter, let alone enough for a primary battle. This of course occurs in districts where the party has little chance of winning. Obtaining the nomination here consists largely in having the will, the funds, and the energies. In some places, the prospects are so hopeless that the field is left wide open to eccentrics and publicity seekers.

Nonetheless, the primary system means that the final decision rests with the voters. Whenever interests and issues press hard enough, a primary battle can erupt. One type is likely to be more common in the 1960s and 1970s when legislative reapportionments stimulated by judicial decisions and the 1970 census produce *two* incumbents fighting for a single collapsed new district. In general, primary warfare emerges from the familiar sources of political controversy: liberals versus conservatives, new- versus old-resident ethnic groups in demographically changing districts, 'young Turk' reformers versus older entrenched leaders, a surfeit of ambitious candidates.

Senatorial nominations are generally the preserve of leading party figures. They are everywhere prized and often sharply contested: To be senator from a large state is highly prestigeful, and in a small state it is *the* political plum. Senator Goldwater, prior to any presidential consideration, was always a more prominent figure than any governor of Arizona. Retiring governors, former national cabinet members, prominent businessmen, and ambitious lesser state officials wage expensive and arduous campaigns for the high senatorial office. Sometimes the exhausted factional contestants are unable to pick up the organizational pieces effectively to engage the opposing party's candidate.

Getting Elected

Campaigning for Congress in a presidential year differs radically from mid-term elections. When the presidential candidate heads the ticket, congressional campaign strategy is frequently to clutch the presidential coattails, hoping to ride into office on the national candidate's popularity. Then, the national campaign issues are likely to be an important part of the state or district campaign. But when the presidential candidate is deemed a liability—say Michigan's liberal Republican Governor Romney vis à vis conservative Republican Goldwater's 1964 presidential campaign—local issues and independence of the national ticket are emphasized. Most campaigns are blends of these alternatives. In practice it is seldom possible to remain completely aloof. When the presidential caravan comes through one's state or district, a complete snub is very unlikely. And there is always some obligation for candidates to square their views as much as possible with the national candidate and platform, particularly where no locally crucial matters need be sacrificed.

The mid-term election. Mid-term elections are substantially different. As the very name implies, it is a time when the presidential focus is at its low point. A sure sign of this is the greatly lower participation and interest of voters in mid-term compared with presidential elections. Nonetheless, Presidents try to use their popularity to secure party victories in Congress. However, presidential coattails are extremely weak in mid-term. That is the reason generally given to explain why the President's party almost always loses rather than gains congressional seats in mid-term elections.[40] Presidents seem little able to wield their personal popularity when they themselves are not in danger of personal defeat. The

---

[40] Exceptions, since the Civil War, are 1934 and 1962. Cf. V. O. Key, Jr., *Politics, Parties and Pressure Groups*, pp. 519 ff.

centrifugal influences within the system become most pronounced. Though national concerns are always present to some extent, and on occasion may even be decisive, parochial influences predominate. And, as we have noted, the congressional incumbent or challenger is subject to few disciplinary controls by the decentralized party organizations. There is fullest range for independency of view—parochial or national. When efforts were made to establish a common platform for the 1942 mid-term congressional elections, Senator Robert A. Taft, the leading Republican in the Senate, declared: "The party National Committee clearly has no authority. . . . I see no reason why each Senator should not run on his own foreign policy."[41]

Without the unifying influence of the actual presidential candidacy, party schism is greatly increased—between the factions and on programmatic issues. The moderating influence of seeking a national majority is removed, and dozens of local candidates are free to be their more obstreperous selves and ride their more extreme ideological hobbyhorses.

Organization: national and local. Despite decentralization and localism, there is more national organizational apparatus involved in congressional campaigns than may be appreciated. Each of the parties in each house of Congress maintains its own national campaign organization. Though the independence of these congressional and senatorial campaign committees is jealously guarded, they operate in close relation to the party national committee structure during presidential campaigns. They are, of course, most important in the mid-term election when not overshadowed by the presidential campaigns. They maintain permanent headquarters and staff and supply candidates with a variety of campaign aids: a speaker's bureau, stock speeches, photographic studio, film strips, news stories, leaflets, pamphlets, and limited financial assistance. Based on analyses of the electoral situation, resources are disbursed to places where party gains can be made—the marginal rather than the safe or hopeless districts.

Nonetheless, congressional campaign organizations are fundamentally local rather than national. Often they are separate and independent even of city, county, and state party structures. For example, the official headquarters for New York Senator Lehman's 1950 campaign was The Independent Citizen's Committee for the Reelection of Herbert H. Lehman. Again, as in primary campaigns, incumbents make heavy use of their own office staffs. Administrative and legislative assistants and clerical workers readily convert into campaign aides. For House members, particularly, this involves little changeover from regular functions. With a harrowingly short term, the campaign is practically continuous. Much time between elections is spent on 'case work' or 'keeping the home fences

---

[41] Quoted in Committee on Political Parties of the American Political Science Association, *Toward a More Responsible Two-Party System* (New York: Rinehart, 1950).

In his unsuccessful 1950 reelection campaign, conservative Democratic Senator Millard Tydings of Maryland was smeared by a fake photo depicting him as friendly with Communist party leader Earl Browder. This widely circulated picture was composed from unrelated cropped pictures. The smear campaign was apparently in retaliation for Tydings' exoneration of the State Department after investigating Senator Joseph McCarthy's charges of Communist infiltration.

mended,' as congressmen refer to the multitude of services regularly performed for their constituents.

Congressional campaign techniques differ little from many employed in presidential campaigns, though the reduced scale again is consequential. Speeches to local groups, press releases, publicity, fund raising, 'coffee hours' are standard. However, because of much lower turnouts in mid-term congressional elections, precinct canvassing operations can produce a much greater payoff: The lower the turnout, the more weight attached to each voter gotten to the polls by precinct workers. The road to Washington—White House, Senate, or House of Representatives does indeed run through the voting precincts.

"Toward a More Responsible Two-Party System"?

We have explored numerous tensions in the American political system: between central discipline and local anarchy, middle of the road
vacuity on issues and extremity of viewpoint; debate of issues and
huckstering reductions to sloganeering; tensions between narrow group
interest and the national public interest. Every aspect of American
politics—parties, groups, presidential nominations, party platforms, congressional elections—is the product and expression of such tensions.
Inevitably, critics of the system have wanted to resolve the tensions in
one or another direction.

At one time, political machines and bosses were attacked as the major
threat to democracy. A variety of reforms ensued: civil service to end
the spoils system; the Hatch Act to end electioneering and other narrowly
partisan activities by government employees; initiative, referendum, and
recall to obtain direct democratic short-cuts past unresponsive legislatures; proportional representation to obtain partisan division of legislatures proportioned to partisan divisions among the voters; direct
primaries to take nominations out of boss-dominated caucuses and conventions and place them directly in the voters' hands.

Such reforms generated partial remedies, but also new problems:
If civil service employees were 'hatched,' parties and candidates became
more dependent on interest groups for election workers; initiatives and
referenda overburdened the electorate by lengthening and compli-
cating the ballot; proportional representation produced multi-party fragmentation and extremism; direct primaries indiscriminately reduced
party leaders' power, including their ability to moderate differences with
balanced tickets. This is a common difficulty in designing political solutions. Improving one part of a system may well entail unintended and
unwanted consequences for another part.

All these reforms had an essentially anti-party spirit. Democracy
was to be perfected by decentralizing party controls and by freeing
candidates from dependence on party leaders. More recently, a committee of eminent political scientists[42] proclaimed the same ultimate objective—perfecting democracy—but by the opposite route of more
centralized and disciplined parties.

The Case for 'More Responsible Parties'

Historical and other factors have caused the American two-party system
to operate as two loose associations of state and local organizations, with
very little national machinery and very little national cohesion. As a
result, either major party, when in power, is ill-equipped to organize its

---

[42] *Ibid.*

members in the legislative and executive branches into a government held together and guided by the party program. Party responsibility at the polls thus tends to vanish.[43]

This indictment is derived by contrasting American parties with an idealized model of a 'democratic, responsible, and effective' party system. Four ideal requisites emerge: In a responsible party system: (1) the parties provide clear, coherent programs spelling out the policies to be enacted on assuming office; (2) two programmatically opposed parties compete so that the voters have a meaningful choice; (3) internal party discipline obliges candidates to fulfil the party pledges on taking office; (4) party organization is sufficiently centralized so that government fragmentation (federalism, separation of powers, etc.) is overcome in the interest of effective government. Thus, the ideal is two parties clearly differentiated on philosophy and policies, each capable of implementing its program when in power. The underlying theory is that only such a party system is fully democratic because only through such 'responsible parties' can government be held accountable to majority rule.

Disclaiming panaceas and denying the need for constitutional amendment or congressional legislation, the APSA Committee pretty much leaves it up to the parties to undertake their own reform. The parties are urged to hold mid-term, as well as quadrennial presidential, national conventions. Between the biennial conventions, a new national party council would become the highest party organ. Bridging the national committee and congressional and senatorial campaign committee structures, it would formulate party policy, propose a platform to the convention, and provide official interpretations of the platform between conventions. And "as it gained respect and prestige," the Party Council would endorse prospective congressional candidates, loyal to the national platform, for ratification in the state primaries. The hoped-for consequence would be to increase party unity, bridge the separation of powers, and thus loosen the dangerous "deadlock of democracy."[44] Thus equipped with "responsible parties," American democracy could more effectively confront its "grave problems of domestic and foreign policy in an era when it is no longer safe for the nation to deal piecemeal with issues that can be disposed of only on the basis of coherent programs."[45]

Rebuttal: Defense of the Existing Party System

The idealized responsible parties model may sound attractive, but it is unrealistic and dangerous. Its proponents implicitly assume that their recommended changes would remove only certain unwanted features

---

[43] *Ibid.*, p. v.

[44] Cf. James M. Burns, *The Deadlock of Democracy* (Englewood Cliffs, N.J.: Prentice-Hall, Inc., 1963).

[45] APSA Committee on Political Parties, *op. cit.*, p. v.

of the existing party-group system. Gone will be vacuous platforms, dominant localism, parochial interests, and recalcitrant congressmen. Yet somehow retained unaltered will be all the good things—major parties of moderate viewpoint, peaceful succession to office, the defeated opposition's loyalty, and a two-party system. Programmatic differences will not spiral and become sharper with each succeeding election; the philosophically differentiated parties will never become bitterly divided enemy camps. Only moderates become major party leaders. Somehow, 'responsible parties' will never be successfully formed by racists, religious bigots, isolationists, Communists, and Fascists. Yet, as noted in Chapter 9, this has happened in most nations with sharply differentiated, doctrinally cohesive, centralized, and disciplined party systems.

Responsible-party advocates make these cheerful assumptions, in part, because they believe that is what happened in Britain.[46] In some respects, British parties are indeed like the ones recommended for America, and Britain has long had decent and moderate government. But did the party system of itself produce those desirable features in Britain, and would centrally-disciplined parties produce the same beneficent results in the United States? The key fallacy is to view British party forms as the primary and sufficient cause of the British virtues. As we have seen, American parties are substantially responses to the whole constitutional-governmental-social order. So too the British parties are products of centuries-old traditions of British constitutionalism, parliamentarism, and an entire political culture. Where constitutional institutions are strong, parties are more the creature than master of a constitutional system. Thus it is expecting the wheels to power the engine to expect the American parties first to transform themselves and then to transform the Constitution, all without formal amendment.

But let us suppose that the Republican and Democratic parties managed to become sharply differentiated and disciplined parties without formal constitutional change. Would they in fact bridge the continuing separation of powers as the proposed reform intends? Yes, when the voters give one party control of both houses of Congress and the Presidency. But suppose the voters persevere (as is likely) in their present untidy habits; House, Senate, and Presidency would then be divided between programmatically disciplined parties with a resulting deadlock worse than anything yet seen. Politics could easily become a stalemated war, with entrenched rivals sniping away from constitutional ramparts such as separation of powers, staggered elections, fixed terms, and powerful state governments.

Another unintended consequence of party reform without constitutional reform involves the two-party question. The 'responsible-party' advocates simply assume that the two-party pattern would continue. To quote Gilbert and Sullivan, they assume

---

[46] The APSA Committee report skirts this issue on p. 35.

That Nature always does contrive . . .
That every boy and every gal
That's born into the world alive
Is either a little Liberal
Or else a little Conservative!

The expectation is that the Democrats will become the liberal party, absorbing all liberal Republicans, and the Republicans the conservative party, absorbing all conservative Democrats. But why must party differentiation occur only on the broad (and really rather amorphous) lines of liberalism and conservatism? Party fission need not stop with the liberal and conservative molecules; parties can split into numerous factions along the lines of many other philosophies and policies. Again, it is probably the British experience which is misleading. Yet nothing in the logic of the responsible-parties model insures obtaining Britain's roughly two-party pattern rather than Europe's multi-party fragmentation.

The British model is misleading in still another respect. British parties never were so clearly differentiated in practice as the theoretical model implies.[47] And recently they have been becoming even more alike. British Conservatives and Labourites relate to each other more and more the way Republicans and Democrats do—overlapping, moderate, aiming for the programmatic center, with doctrinaire socialism and conservatism both falling by the wayside. Thus, even if the British party system could be transplanted in the United States, no remarkable transformation could be expected in the political system.

Apart from all these weaknesses in the logic and realism of the responsible-parties model, the indictment of the American party system is itself questionable. It scants the good things in the system and exaggerates the bad.

In Chapter 9 we examined the party traits which moderate economic and social antagonism, and traced their intimate connection with the general constitutional design. The features of that design, disliked by the critics because they produce 'irresponsible' parties, are the very same constitutional and party features which produce the things they admire. Yet the critics scant their importance and too willingly risk losing the baby with the bathwater. But most Americans are sensibly loath to risk the moderation and substantial national consensus of their party system. Such qualities are too rare in the world to be jeopardized for less than the most convincing reasons.

Moreover, the 'bathwater' is not so bad as the critics make out; the existing major parties are more differentiated and disciplined than the critics acknowledge. In Chapter 9 we saw the differences of hue which distinguish Democratic and Republican party platforms, the muted regime questions from which major policy issues are drawn, and the sig-

[47] Cf. David Butler, "American Myths about British Parties," *Virginia Quarterly Review*, Vol. XXXI (Winter 1955).

nificant degree of party cohesion and discipline in Congress.[48] These are substantial enough to supply partisans in the electorate with real controversy over real issues. The politically interested are fully at liberty to engage in political struggle—to form groups or even minor parties— over narrow interest or broad principle. Democratic accountability to majority rule is sufficiently satisfied by the not-so-irresponsible American party system. But political battles are regularly constrained within a constitutional system that prevents an excess of party spirit from abusing the liberty from which parties and factions arise.

This is not, however, to view with complacency; moderation, liberty, and democratic accountability are splendid, but still not enough. Competent government is equally necessary. Leadership to think through sound principles, devise wise policies and enforce them vigorously, and guide and rally popular opinion—these remain staples of competent government. Such leadership was never more necessary nor less automatically guaranteed—by the American Constitution or any other system. But the American system may be vindicated on balance as one good way to cope with modern problems. And what the system as a system cannot supply will have to be found where it must always be found—in the efforts of good men and in the workings of fortune.

BIBLIOGRAPHICAL NOTE

Changing notions of presidential "availability" may be traced in William B. Brown, *The People's Choice: The Presidential Image in the Campaign Biography* (1960). An extensive study of the nominating process is Paul T. David, Malcolm Moos, and Ralph Goldman (eds.), *Presidential Nominating Politics in 1952* (5 vols., 1954). A case study of a presidential primary contest is Harry W. Ernst, *The Primary that Made a President: West Virginia, 1960* (1963).

Arthur N. Holcombe studied the waning of sectional influences in *The New Party Politics* (1933). Specific regional patterns are analyzed in V. O. Key, Jr., *Southern Politics in State and Nation* (1949); Duane Lockard, *New England State Politics* (1959); and John H. Fenton, *Politics in the Border States* (1957). A related work is Robert Wood, *Suburbia* (1958). On modern voting trends, see Samuel Lubell, *The Future of American Politics* (1960).

Public opinion is introduced in Robert E. Lane and David O. Sears, *Public Opinion* (1964). More advanced is V. O. Key, Jr., *Public Opinion and American Democracy* (1961). George Gallup's "town meeting" view is expressed in his *Public Opinion in a Democracy* (1939). Cf. the attack by Lindsay Rogers, *The Pollsters: Public Opinion, Politics and Democratic Leadership* (1949). And see John C. Ranney, "Do the Polls Serve Democracy?" *Public Opinion Quarterly* (Fall, 1946).

Major voting behavior studies are examined by Peter H. Rossi, "Four Landmarks in Voting Research," in Eugene Burdick and Arthur J. Brodbeck (eds.),

---

[48] See also pp. 138–42.

American Voting Behavior (1959). Two renowned studies are Bernard R. Berelson, P. F. Lazarsfeld, and W. N. McPhee, *Voting: A Study of Opinion Formation in a Presidential Campaign* (1954); and Augus Campbell, P. Converse, W. Miller, and D. Stokes, *The American Voter* (1960). See the criticism by Walter Berns, "Voting Studies," in Herbert J. Storing (ed.), *Essays on the Scientific Study of Politics* (1962).

On presidential campaigns, see James J. Reston, "Our Campaign Techniques Reexamined," *New York Times Magazine* (November 9, 1952); and Stanley Kelley, Jr., *Political Campaigning* (1960). For case studies, see Theodore H. White, *The Making of the President, 1960* (1961); *The Making of the President, 1964* (1965), and Harold Faber (ed.), *The Road to the White House: The Story of the 1964 Election* (1965). A difficult question is posed in Harold F. Gosnell, "Does Campaigning Make a Difference?" *Public Opinion Quarterly* (Fall, 1950).

For congressional elections, see Cortez A. M. Ewing, *Congressional Elections, 1896–1944* (1947); and William N. McPhee and William A. Glaser (eds.), *Public Opinion and Congressional Elections* (1962). The tie between congressional and presidential elections is examined in Malcolm Moos, *Politics, Presidents, and Coattails* (1952); and Charles Press, "Voting Statistics and Presidential Coattails," *American Political Science Review* (December, 1958).

The American party system is criticized in Committee on Political Parties, American Political Science Association, *Toward a More Responsible Two-Party System* (1950); Stephen K. Bailey, *The Condition of Our National Political Parties* (1959); and James M. Burns, *The Deadlock of Democracy: Four-Party Politics in America* (1963). Generally supportive of the present system are Pendleton Herring, *The Politics of Democracy* (1940); Herbert Agar, *The Price of Union* (1950); Austin Ranney, *The Doctrine of Responsible Party Government* (1954); and Julius Turner, "Responsible Parties: A Dissent From the Floor," *American Political Science Review* (March, 1951). Discussion from both points of view is provided in Robert A. Goldwin (ed.), *Political Parties, U.S.A.* (1964).

Part Five

GOVERNING

Chapter 13

Government
and
Personal Freedom

*. . . in Order to . . . secure the Blessings of Liberty to our-
selves and our Posterity. . . .*

PREAMBLE TO THE CONSTITUTION

PEOPLE ARE UNDERSTANDABLY PRONE TO THINK OF POLITICAL LIBERTY SIMPLY
as freedom from governmental oppression because the most enduring
and widespread political oppression has resulted from men tyrannically
exercising the authority of government. The best-known struggles for
liberty are of men opposing their governments: the Magna Carta, the
British Petition of Right, the French Declaration of the Rights of Man,
the American Declaration of Independence. It is easy, particularly in the
American tradition, to conceive of individual freedom as endangered
solely by government. By this view, liberty expands when governmental
power contracts. But this is to ignore the most fundamental fact about
political liberty: It exists *through* government, not merely *against* government; and, indeed, it is sometimes positively furthered *by* government
programs.

Liberty *through* government: law and order. Liberty is meaningful
only in political community. It is a relationship between men living in
society under government. In the absence of government, an individual's
freedom—if freedom really applies to men apart from political community
—depends upon his personal ability to defend himself. But *civil* rights
and liberties are enjoyed in the *city* (both *civil* and *city* have a common
Latin derivation); they are rights and liberties ensured through law
and the power of government. Accordingly, liberty does not necessarily
expand when the power of government contracts—on the contrary, it
may decline. Government must have sufficient power in all sorts of
circumstances to achieve the degree of law and order within which
liberties can flourish.

423

Liberty *against* government: individual rights. Law and order are a necessary but insufficient condition for securing liberty. Liberty requires also that the polity honor and protect certain rights of individuals against government itself.

> The powers which it is necessary for government to possess in order to repress violence and preserve order cannot execute themselves. They must be administered by men in whom, like others, the individual are stronger than the social feelings. And hence the powers vested in them to prevent injustice and oppression on the part of others will, if left unguarded, be by them converted into instruments to oppress the rest of the community. That by which this is prevented, by whatever name called, is what is meant by *constitution.* . . .[1]

Constitutional governments thus are those in which the ruler's necessary authority is not arbitrary or boundless, but is circumscribed by the fundamental law which rulers and ruled alike are duty-bound to respect. Much of what we examine in this chapter concerns various means by which the authority of American government is constitutionally circumscribed with respect to personal freedom.

Liberty *by* government: programs and policies. But government is not the only threat to liberty. Liberty is also threatened by private groups and persons who intimidate and deprive others of the free exercise of their rights. Government is indispensable to protecting the liberty of the weak from the private aggressions of the strong. Protecting alleged criminals against lynchings or street corner speakers against hostile crowds are common examples of government securing liberty by maintaining order. But more positively, government can use its power to expand liberty through programs aimed at adjusting the balance of power among groups and individuals. Thus, the Wagner National Labor Relations Act proclaimed and protected labor's right to organize and bargain collectively, and the later Landrum-Griffin Act protected some rights of individual workers within their unions. Other examples are the President's Committee on Equal Employment Opportunity and other civil-rights agencies. The "quest for a sword"[2] on behalf of civil rights is a highly controversial question regarding the extent to which government can properly seek to expand individual liberties.

Conceived in Liberty

Whatever are its complex philosophical implications, liberty was unquestionably given a preeminent place in the polity that, in Lincoln's phrase, was "conceived in liberty." The Declaration of Independence held

---

[1] John C. Calhoun, *A Disquisition on Government* (New York: Liberal Arts Press, 1953), p. 7 (emphasis in original).

[2] The phrase is from Robert K. Carr, *Federal Protection of Civil Rights* (Ithaca: Cornell University Press, 1947).

that the rights of individuals to "life, liberty, and the pursuit of happiness" are "unalienable" because these rights derive from nature, are endowed by the Creator, and inhere in every man since all are "created equal." In this natural-rights view, liberties are not gifts bestowed by governments and thus cannot legitimately be denied by government or the community.

Equally influential in the origin of the American republic was the heritage of liberty forged in England's critical seventeenth-century struggles. America was founded when the English love of liberty was at high tide and the Anglo-Americans laid claim to their rights as Englishmen. We have seen how English liberty was developed under American conditions, but the common source is what makes both England and the United States nations that stress civil liberties and rights.

A third significant influence on the American commitment to liberty was the education of the leading constitutional Framers. They were imbued with the Renaissance-revived classical learning, an outstanding political-historical lesson of which was the repeated destruction of liberty by a demagogue-led populace in the Greek city-states and in Rome.

The combination of these strands of thought and practice—natural rights, English tradition, and classical views of the relation of liberty and democracy—strongly influenced American democracy. The resulting view of liberty became a part of the fundamental law inscribed in the Constitution. Upon the basis of the Constitution, the American polity places great emphasis upon individual liberty enforced through law and the judicial element of government.

Civil Liberty in the Constitutional Order

The Nature of Civil Liberty and its Protection

The "blessings of liberty" are not secured by any single device or process; that is a task for the entire polity. Liberty has therefore been an aspect of everything we have considered thus far. But now we consider liberty when it is not merely an aspect but is *the* problem.

What are the specific civil liberties? To whom and under what conditions are they available? How and to what extent are they protected? What are the boundaries beyond which protection does not extend? How are they reconciled with the other needs, interests, and values of the polity?

How problems of civil liberties arise. As we have seen, government always contains danger to civil liberties. Supreme power may fall into the hands of men who simply have a taste for oppression. Oppression may take place by accident or by the malice or blundering of lesser officials. Or the authorities may honestly feel that the public goal being pursued is so overwhelmingly important as to justify whatever harsh measures against individuals may seem necessary; this is common in times of crisis, or when effective, competent government seems to be at stake. Or the problem of civil liberties may arise—and this especially poses the issue of democratic rule versus liberty—when an interest group or a class, having won some majority support, uses the power of government to pursue its factional ends. For example, a local majority gets its religion into the public schools; a legislature in the South enacts discriminations against Negroes; an influential employers' group procures passage of a city ordinance restricting picketing by trade unions.

Always there are competing claims—by officials, groups, and individuals, who appeal to government and to public opinion with all the devices of the political struggle. The inevitable result is a political dimension whenever government and civil liberties meet, and on occasion virtually all the political forces come flooding in and virtually all the political processes come into play.

The uses of law and the judicial. How to cope with these thronging problems and these potent forces? Most polities make some use of law and the judicial element of government; the American does so in a high degree. We have seen how much Americans tend to legalize and constitutionalize, to argue politics and policy as issues of constitutional law, how much American governing finds its way into the courts, and how much judicial statesmanship and judicial politics there are in the American system. In civil liberties the system explicitly gives law and the judicial a major voice.

Law and the judicial have some important virtues here. Civil-liberties problems usually appear as specific issues in specific fact situations: Should this man be allowed to do this? Should that law be enforced against that man? Law and the judicial deal well with specifics. Civil-liberties problems are often sharp and heated; law and the judicial can be conveniently long-handled and insulated tongs. And they have the common-law skill in picking up problems still small and new, in single cases, and in working out broad policies and fundamental solutions step by prudent step through precedent.

But law and the judicial have their limitations. Courts can only decide cases, can only do what litigants ask; they are passive, and cannot actively and affirmatively go out and do justice on their own initiative as can the legislative and executive. Litigation is usually slow, expensive, cumbersome, and inflexible, especially when conflicts are hot and difficult constitutional questions are involved. Courts' powers are not absolute; see the widespread evasion in the South of judicial decisions on the rights of Negroes.[3] In short, courts and the law are vital and powerful but they are only part of the governmental processes, and here they are dealing with problems that ramify out far beyond ordinary law and ordinary litigation.

---

[3] For official documentation, see the continuing studies of the United States Civil Rights Commission and many opinions of the federal courts.

The Judicial Equipment: The Sources of Constitutional Doctrine

To what does an American appeal when he decides that 'they can't do that to me,' and asks law and the courts to protect him? What do his lawyers say? What terms, concepts, and modes of thought do they and the judges use? What does the American dialogue about the law of civil liberty actually sound like?

An inventory. An inventory of the intellectual equipment used by law and the courts in dealing with civil liberties could well include all the constraints on governmental power discussed in Chapter 4 and most of the characteristics of the judiciary discussed in Chapter 7. It would especially emphasize many of the constitutional limitations reviewed in Chapter 4. Some of these are in the Constitution proper. Most however are in the Bill of Rights and the Fourteenth Amendment. The Bill of Rights contains principally the 'First Amendment freedoms,' restraints on procedure in criminal and quasi-criminal matters, some protections for property, and the broad and vital provision that no person may be "deprived of life, liberty, or property, without due process of law." The Fourteenth Amendment contains its own due process clause and the clause forbidding any state to deny to any person "the equal protection of the laws."

What do the protective provisions mean? Like the powers granted by the Constitution, so also are the limitations subject to the processes of judicial construction, whereby much doctrine is drawn from a few words. This is especially so with provisions—e.g., due process and equal protection—that entail broad standards of fairness, rationality, and justice. In the hands of the courts due process has developed a double aspect that has been the subject of much judicial construction. *Procedural* due process addresses itself to procedure, to the methods whereby governmental power is exercised against the individual, and *substantive* due process addresses itself to the content and effect of the power itself. (See pp. 126–27.)

The contents and the applications of these and the other protective clauses are always developing and changing. This is natural and proper. The Constitution is intended to endure for ages to come[4] as a protection of rights as well as a grant of powers, and out of its classic language new doctrine must be evolved as change and growth bring to the courts new cases bearing new needs and new problems.

The question of 'inherent' rights. The constitutional provisions, as developed and expounded by judicial construction, are what the Constitution says about civil liberties. But is there more, beyond these boundaries—perhaps rights that are 'inherent' in, or natural to, the in-

---

[4] This famous phrase of Mr. Chief Justice Marshall's has been quoted several times in this book: "a constitution intended to endure for ages to come, and, consequently, to be adapted to the various crises of human affairs." *McCulloch v. Maryland,* 4 Wheat. 316 (1819).

dividual by virtue of divine grant or of his nature, rights that human society and human law do not create but are bound to respect? It is sometimes asserted that there are, and that the Constitution recognizes and somehow enforces them.

Certainly the idea of natural rights has been vital in American government and politics; indeed the American 'credo' rests upon the Declaration of Independence's appeal to "unalienable rights." And certainly the idea of natural rights has always been present in American constitutional law, but chiefly in a subterranean way. The courts and other official agencies have occasionally expressly referred to such inherent rights and perhaps in a few instances have relied upon them. But that is not the usual way. In some very recent cases, for example, the Court seems to be talking natural rights language but the actual holdings in the technical sense were not based upon it.[5] As important as the general idea of natural rights is in the American polity, the great mass of the constitutional law of civil liberties is grounded in the actual provisions of the Constitution.

The Federal Problem and 'Incorporation' of the Bill of Rights in the Fourteenth Amendment

The federal element is important in civil liberties as in most aspects of American government. In a unitary system the basic question would be: May *the* government do this to that person? In our system a more complicated question arises: *What* may *which* government, state or national, do to *whom?* That is, we do not have a uniform national law, but rather the law applicable to actions by the national government and that applicable to actions by the states. Given the familiar tensions of our federal-national compound, the question inevitably arises: How far has the protection of civil liberty been 'nationalized'? That is, what protections does the national law give as against actions by the states? A central problem is the extent to which the Bill of Rights, the basic charter of liberties as against the national government, has been 'incorporated' into the Fourteenth Amendment and thus made applicable against the states. By its terms the Fourteenth Amendment applies only to the states: "No State shall. . . ." The question is what detailed content is to be given to the three general limitations of Section 1 of the Amendment, due process, equal protection, and privileges or immunities. This is commonly spoken of as the question of how many of the specifics of the Bill of Rights are 'incorporated' into them.

---

[5] Two of the recent cases, *Aptheker* v. *Secretary of State*, 84 S. Ct. 1659 (1964), and *Zemel* v. *Rusk*, 85 S. Ct. 1271 (1965), involve the right to travel abroad, interestingly, a necessarily basic right in the modern natural rights philosophies of Hobbes, Locke, and Rousseau. For an account of the natural rights idea in American constitutional law, see Charles Grove Haines, *The Revival of Natural Law Concepts* (Cambridge: Harvard University Press, 1930).

The historical evidence indicates that the Bill of Rights was intended to apply only to the national government, and in 1833 in the case of *Barron* v. *Baltimore*[6] the Supreme Court so held. But the adoption of the Fourteenth Amendment obviously raised new problems. Its broad protective clauses (including an exact reproduction of the Fifth Amendment's due-process language) created national authority to protect some liberties as against the states. But which liberties? For a long time it was generally thought that few of those in the Bill of Rights were covered. One ingenious argument in support of this view was the "economy of language" argument:[7] the phrase "due process of law" appears in the Fifth Amendment as *part* of the Bill of Rights so it at least, therefore, cannot mean the *whole* Bill of Rights; hence, the argument continued, the same phrase in the Fourteenth Amendment likewise cannot mean the whole Bill of Rights. But due process was 'such a fellow' as not long to be so narrowly constrained.

The courts gradually developed Fourteenth Amendment due process as a very broad protection of the rights of property against state regulatory legislation that affected business, and gradually there seemed to be less and less reason not to give the Amendment a similarly broad reading as to civil liberties generally. The Supreme Court took a decisive step in the 1925 case of *Gitlow* v. *New York*[8] in which it "assumed" without "deciding" that the First Amendment freedoms were covered. Since then the Court has followed a somewhat variable policy of picking and choosing, on the basis of standards never fully defined, among the Bill of Rights provisions, incorporating some in the Amendment and rejecting others. The formula the Court has most often used is that the Amendment incorporates those Bill of Rights protections which are "of the very essence of a scheme of ordered liberty" or are based upon "a principle of justice so rooted in the traditions and conscience of our people as to be ranked as fundamental."[9]

By today many, perhaps most, of the important protections of the Bill of Rights have been incorporated. Critics argue that by not adopting a clear policy or formula on inclusion and exclusion, the Court allows itself too wide a discretion and creates confusion and instability in the law. Supporters reply that the Court is using statesmanlike common sense in striving to profit from experience while adapting case by case to changing times in a difficult and changing subject.

When we study specific civil liberties, as we now shall, we must consider whether and to what extent each has been incorporated into the Fourteenth Amendment as a limitation on the states as well as on the national government.

---

[6] 32 U.S. (7 Pet.) 243 (1833).
[7] Accepted at one time by the Supreme Court, *Hurtado* v. *California*, 110 U.S. 516 (1884), but quietly abandoned later.
[8] 268 U.S. 652 (1925).
[9] *Palko* v. *Connecticut*, 302 U.S. 319 (1937).

Government and Religion

Congress shall make no law respecting an establishment of religion, or prohibiting the free exercise thereof. . . .

The First Amendment protects freedom of religion by two provisions. The first, the establishment clause, forbids any "law respecting an establishment of religion." The second, the free exercise clause, forbids any law "prohibiting the free exercise" of religion.

The language is absolutely prohibitory in form: "*no* law." Should such absolute language be given its literal meaning? The problem comes up repeatedly throughout the law of civil liberty. Some commentators, and some Supreme Court justices, say it should be.[10] They point out that the Framers could use qualified language when they wanted to (e.g., the Fourth Amendment prohibits only "*unreasonable* searches and seizures") and that hence we can assume they meant absolute language to be absolute. But most commentators, and most justices,[11] have disagreed. First, they argue, there is always a potential conflict with values other than liberty; e.g., on occasion a liberty must be limited to protect national security. Second, liberties can conflict and must be limited to accommodate to each other; e.g., an absolutely free exercise of religion in proselyting might involve the invasion of the Fourth Amendment right of privacy. Third, different persons can conflictingly claim the same liberty; e.g., two speakers cannot use the same street corner at the same time. Hence some laws must be passed dealing with these matters.

The Court therefore has developed the policy and practice of weighing, or balancing, the interests involved when a constitutional liberty is asserted. The difficulty and uncertainty of the constitutional law of civil liberty—and its flexibility, feasibility, and capacity for development—are largely due to this policy.

A related problem is that of 'strict' versus 'liberal' construction (see pp. 113–15). Should the constitutional provisions be read narrowly, limited to their specifics and to fact situations the Framers probably had specifically in mind, or broadly, as declarative of general policy and freely applicable to all similar or analogous situations? Partly under the influence of Chief Justice Marshall's famous maxim,[12] the Supreme Court has inclined in recent years toward liberal, broad constructions, just as it long has in interpreting the national powers.

---

[10] Notably Mr. Justice Black. See his famous lecture, "The Bill of Rights," 35 *N.Y.U.L. Rev.* 865 (1960).

[11] The name of Mr. Justice Frankfurter is especially associated with this position, termed 'relativist,' as opposed to the 'absolutist' position of Mr. Justice Black.

[12] ". . . we must never forget, that it is a constitution we are expounding. . . ." See note 4.

Establishment: Separation of Church and State

The Court has recently been giving the establishment clause an almost absolute construction, holding that the clause forbids not only "establishment of religion" in the strict sense of adoption by government of an official religion but also almost any aid or support to any particular religion or to religion generally. Thus construed, the clause requires a "wall of separation between church and state."[13] And even though the United States is happily free from the deepest cleavages over questions of religion and government that plague many European countries,[14] the Court has recently faced issues of substantial importance; the future may well bring more.

Religion and education. Several of these issues have revolved around religious education. The Court has spoken most clearly on religious exercises in the public schools; the prohibition there seems virtually absolute and has been fully applied to the states through the Fourteenth Amendment. A state may not require, or even encourage, daily recitation in its classrooms of a short nondenominational prayer devised by the public authorities, nor classroom reading aloud of verses from the Bible and recitation of the Lord's Prayer,[15] even though in neither case is any student required to participate or even be present. However, public sentiment for religious instruction is sufficient, and various groups are sufficiently active in urging it, that the Court's rulings have been widely disregarded; prayer continues in many public schools in many states. As we have remarked, the judiciary is not omnipotent.

The Court has been somewhat less clear, but perhaps more widely obeyed, on 'released time,' the policy of releasing children, upon parental request, for part of the day to attend church schools. The Court's position seems to be that if the religious instruction takes place off school property and if public school personnel and facilities are not involved released-time programs are constitutional.[16]

Still less clear, partly because the problems and the fact situations are most complex, is the area of public assistance to private schools having religious affiliation. Many religious denominations, e.g., the Roman Catholic, maintain extensive educational systems, from parochial schools up to universities; and about 15 per cent of all school children attend parochial schools. This entails a substantial expense for the parents, who

---

[13] The phrase is Thomas Jefferson's. It was given modern currency by its use in the Court's opinion in *Everson* v. *Board of Education*, 330 U.S. 1 (1947).

[14] The "multiplicity of sects" that can flourish in a large republic (see p. 80) help moderate in advance the constitutional conflicts that come to the courts; and at the same time the constitutional provisions undergird the tendency to religious diversity.

[15] *Engel* v. *Vitale*, 370 U.S. 421 (1962); *School District* v. *Schempp*, 374 U.S. 203 (1963).

[16] *Zorach* v. *Clauson*, 343 U.S. 306 (1952). But see *McCollum* v. *Board of Education*, 333 U.S. 203 (1948).

also must pay the ordinary taxes for the support of public schools. Some people regard this as unfair double taxation. A related financial question has arisen acutely with regard to state and federal aid to education. The Court is not likely to uphold as constitutional direct subsidies to parochial schools out of public funds, state or national, although some indirect assistance such as tax exemptions has been upheld. A major line of development is the 'student benefit approach'; e.g., the states have been allowed to supply free textbooks and bus rides to parochial school children on the ground that the benefit was being conferred upon the student, not upon religion.[17] The 1965 aid to education acts are carefully drafted to avoid constitutional difficulties, and rely substantially on the child-benefit theory. There will no doubt be further exploration of the potentialities of this approach.

Religion by government. What of religion by government, either actual religious activity or favorable recognition of religious activity? Some issues have come up and more are likely to. The Supreme Court has held that a sabbath may not be established by a city for religious purposes but may be if the purpose is to provide a general day of rest.[18] The national government has long provided chaplains for Congress and for the armed forces; the Supreme Court opens its proceedings each day with an invocation of the assistance of Divine Providence as do many other public bodies; the phrase 'in God we trust' appears on coins; and so on. Are any of these open to constitutional doubts? We do not know, because the Court has not spoken, and prediction is difficult because these are borderline questions. Relations between religion and government are not simple and no doubt will be subject to continuing revision and working out.

Freedom of Religion

Like the establishment clause, the free exercise clause is given by the Court in many respects a nearly absolute construction, and has been fully incorporated in the Fourteenth Amendment.

The law is settled that government may not forbid religious activities of any of the usual sorts, nor may it force members of the public to participate in any religious activities or in certain activities clearly contrary to recognized religious scruples. An example of the last is that public school children may not be required to salute the flag if this offends their religion. Indeed government apparently cannot even require members of a religious sect to get a license before going from door to door proselyting and soliciting funds.[19] There are limits, however.

---

[17] *Everson* v. *Board of Education*, see note 13.

[18] See for example *McGowan* v. *Maryland*, 366 U.S. 420 (1961) and *Braunfeld* v. *Brown*, 366 U.S. 599 (1961).

[19] *West Virginia Board of Education* v. *Barnette*, 319 U.S. 624 (1943); *Cantwell* v. *Connecticut*, 310 U.S. 296 (1940).

The clause does not necessarily excuse a person from the ordinary law. For example, polygamous marriages are forbidden and punished even though authorized by a religion; states validly apply child labor laws to children engaged in religious work;[20] the law has acted against religious practices, such as snake cults and flagellation cults, that gravely offend general community standards, and also against religious activities, such as excessively loud or boisterous services, that simply disturb the peace or constitute a 'nuisance' at law. And no doubt practioners of a religion requiring human sacrifice would be subject to homicide prosecutions.

But there remain numerous questions that are unsettled or so far unexplored. The state's 'police power'[21] authorizes some kinds of public health and therapeutic measures under some circumstances (e.g., compulsory vaccination of school children for purposes of protecting the public generally) but not others, in the face of religious objection.[22] Children are involved in another unsettled question. The state's traditional special concern with the welfare of children has been held on some occasions but not on others to justify the overriding of parental religious scruples respecting medical treatment of children. The purpose here is not as in mass vaccination to protect the public generally but to protect a particular child against the parents. This protection has its roots in the long-established rule of equity that the court can overrule or even replace the parents of a child if they neglect or abuse him. But it remains unsettled (if it ever can be) where precisely the line is to be drawn between the parents' religious rights and the court's view of the child's physical well-being. Another unsettled problem involves the rights of persons who refuse on religious grounds to perform military service. Still other unsettled questions involve public control of educational curriculum and qualifications of teachers in parochial schools and tax treatment of the incomes and expenditures of religious organizations. The constitutional law of religious liberty is in truth an ever-changing thing.[23]

---

[20] *Reynolds* v. *United States,* 98 U.S. 145 (1878); *Davis* v. *Bacon,* 133 U.S. 333 (1890); *Prince* v. *Massachusetts,* 321 U.S. 158 (1944).

[21] Usually defined as the state's inherent governmental power to legislate for the health, safety, welfare, and morals of its people.

[22] *Jacobson* v. *Massachusetts,* 197 U.S. 11 (1905).

[23] An example of how changing circumstances may raise religious liberty questions in unanticipated areas (and of the conflict of competing rights) is the following: Modern trade unions often sign 'union shop' contracts with employers that make union membership a condition of continued employment. Section 14(b) of the 1947 Taft-Hartley Act permits states to enact legislation prohibiting such contracts; there has since been sharp conflict over proposals to repeal this section and over proposed state 'right to work' laws. A religious factor unconnected with the labor-management problem has complicated the conflict. Several religious groups, e.g., the Seventh Day Adventists, have religious scruples against union membership or mandatory dues payment, and they demand exemption from 'union shop' contracts. It is entirely conceivable that this novel and unanticipated question may some day come to the courts in the name of our original constitutional freedom of religion.

Freedom of Expression

Congress shall make no law . . . abridging the freedom of speech or of the press. . . .

All civilized societies, for various motives, allow some degree of freedom of expression. Some such freedom at least for some persons is admitted to be essential to full human development and dignity. Further, it has recognized values for the society; without some degree of freedom, the society is deprived of the achievements of its most talented individuals, and art, literature, history, philosophy, the social sciences, much of the physical sciences, and many other branches of creation and learning can hardly exist. Another value is political; any regime, but democracy especially, requires at least some communication about politics. The American polity is especially committed to liberty. The final and most eloquently stated aim of the Constitution, given in the Preamble, is to "secure the blessings of liberty to ourselves and our posterity."

The First Amendment language quoted above is the principal express pronouncement of the Constitution on the subject.

Norman Thomas, American socialist leader, was pelted with eggs when he defied Mayor Hague's ban by speaking at a street meeting in Jersey City, N.J., 1938. The police forcibly expelled Mr. Thomas from the city, but the resulting court challenge produced a victory for freedom of speech.

The General Law and Its Boundaries

As with religion, the constitutional language is absolutely prohibitory in form. Some modern authorities argue that it should be read as absolute, and that literally no law abridging the freedom is constitutional. Others arrive at an absolutist position for at least *political* expression on the ground that self-government requires that all citizens have access to *all* facts and arguments relevant to politics and hence to self-government.[24]

The orthodox position is a good way short of these absolutes, however, and the Supreme Court, though it has in recent years protected extensive freedom of expression, continues to find limits to it, and to balance the public interest in it with other aspects of the public interest, such as preserving order, punishing libel and slander, controlling obscenity, and repressing subversion and political conspiracies. A famous statement by a great justice of the Court catches the spirit of the better-reasoned limits: "The most stringent protection of free speech would not protect a man in falsely shouting fire in a theatre, and causing a panic."[25]

The Standard Tests: 'Bad Tendency' and 'Clear and Present Danger'

Free expression obviously can bring about substantive evils such as sedition, rioting and disorder, injury to the reputations of innocent individuals, and so on. Government can of course do some things quite apart from free expression issues to prevent such evils; e.g., it can arrest and punish conspirators preparing an armed coup to overthrow the Constitution. But to what extent can government constitutionally limit or punish free expression in order to prevent these or other evils—e.g., mere seditious *talk* as compared to revolutionary *action?*

The Court's principal doctrine has been the *clear and present danger* test. The first modern case was that of a criminal conviction for obstructing the draft by sending to men subject to it a leaflet urging them, in impassioned language, to oppose it. The Court admitted that in many places and in ordinary times the First Amendment might apply but, it went on to say,

> The question in every case is whether the words used are used in such circumstances and are of such a nature as to create a clear and present danger that they will bring about the substantive evils that Congress has a right to prevent. It is a question of proximity and degree.[26]

So saying, the Court determined that the evil involved—obstruction of the national effort under the government's constitutional war powers—was one that Congress was entitled to prevent, and that under the circum-

---

[24] A leading statement of this position is Alexander Meiklejohn, *Political Freedom* (New York: Harper & Brothers, 1960).

[25] Mr. Justice Holmes, for a unanimous Court, in *Schenck v. United States,* 249 U.S. 47 (1919).

[26] *Ibid.*

Freedom of expression, even at the White House gates . . .

stances the danger that the expression would cause this evil was sufficiently clear and present. It therefore upheld the conviction.

The other doctrine is that of *bad tendency*. This allows expression to
be limited or punished if it simply has a tendency to produce a substantive evil. The danger of the evil need not be clear and need not be present.

The clear and present danger test can be made so narrow, by requiring more and more clarity and more and more immediacy, that almost *no*
expression can be restrained. The bad tendency test on the other hand
can be made so broad, by requiring less and less badness and less and
less immediacy, that almost *any* expression can be checked. Over the
years the Court has developed much law on the problem, in general
adhering to the clear and present danger test though at times coming
close to making it a bad tendency test in reality.[27] Recently, however,
decisions have inclined to be critical of most limitations.

---

[27] The opinion of Mr. Chief Justice Vinson in *Dennis* v. *United States*, 341 U.S. 494
(1951), is frequently cited as an instance of this.

. . . *contrasts with retaliations for Negro protests against segregation in Birmingham, Alabama.*

Sedition and Related Problems

The most important and most hotly debated problems are those of political expression. Here lie the greatest needs for control; e.g., a society has to be able to protect itself against seditious conspiracies by unscrupulous minorities. Here also lie the greatest dangers; e.g., it is all too easy for officials and dominant political groups to strike at democratic freedom and their political opponents by such controls. As might be expected in so large, difficult, and highly charged a subject, the constitutional law is neither simple nor completely settled.

One important theme of the law, especially in recent years, is that controls are to be strictly and narrowly construed, that thorough proof is required before a violation of them is found, and that although free expression is not absolute it does occupy a "preferred position"[28] relative to other constitutional provisions.

---

[28] *Kovacs* v. *Cooper,* 336 U.S. 77 (1949).

As to federal action, the rule seems to be that serious limitation is constitutionally allowable only when national security quite clearly requires it. The 1951 *Dennis* case is the furthest the Court has gone in allowing punishment of speech and opinion. The Court there upheld the convictions of the leaders of the Communist Party for conspiring to form a party to teach and advocate the overthrow of the government by force and for conspiring to advocate that such overthrow was right and necessary. This is a distance from any very clear or very present danger; the defendants were not charged with actually conspiring to overthrow or even of actually advocating overthrow. Later cases suggest that the Court might no longer go this far. Further, less extreme political opinion and expression have received a fairly wide range of protection.[29]

The states have attempted more control of political expression than has the national government. The Court's decisions on these attempts are not all clear nor easily reconciled, but it seems that the Court looks at state controls more critically than at national ones, the states not being the final guardians of the national interest and security.[30]

Nonseditious Expression: Domestic Tranquillity and the Public Convenience

The states (and to a limited extent the federal government) have also imposed limitations in situations less dramatic and compelling than sedition and political conspiracy. Currently the most significant concern limitations to preserve domestic tranquillity by preventing riots and disorders. Some decisions are not very clear. For example, the Supreme Court upheld a conviction in a case where a soapbox orator was convicted of disorderly conduct under a city ordinance for persisting in provocative talk that was apparently leading to some disorder in the crowd; but in another and somewhat puzzling case the Court overturned a conviction where a speaker in a hall was convicted on a similar charge for even more provocative talk that in fact did lead to violent action by opponents of his in the crowd outside.[31]

A little more clarity appears in the decisions where the limitation was imposed for the public convenience. Here the rule seems to be that the interference with public convenience must be substantial and the convenience involved important (although again we cannot be entirely clear). For example, a conviction under a city ordinance forbidding any use whatever of sound trucks without a permit was reversed, but another

---

[29] *Dennis* v. *United States,* see note 27. In *Yates* v. *United States,* 354 U.S. 298 (1957), the Court explained that mere advocacy or teaching of overthrow as an abstract doctrine is constitutionally permissible free speech, whereas advocacy or teaching directed at promoting actual unlawful action is not, and that *Dennis* involved the latter.

[30] A good case is *Pennsylvania* v. *Nelson,* 350 U.S. 497 (1956).

[31] *Feiner* v. *New York,* 340 U.S. 315 (1951); *Terminiello* v. *Chicago,* 337 U.S. 1 (1949).

under an ordinance forbidding "loud and raucous" sound trucks was upheld.[32]

Picketing in labor disputes is in part protected by the right of free expression. It frequently raises just such problems of disorder and the public convenience. In general, the boundary is that the picketing may be forbidden if it is for an "unlawful objective."[33] Here, as with the public convenience and tranquillity cases generally, the Court seems inclined to look closely at the specific fact situations rather than to rely on clear general rules.

Nonseditious Expression: Art and Literature

At one time constitutional law may have allowed the authorities a nearly free hand in forbidding or punishing the dissemination of works of art and literature (or alleged art and literature) that seemed offensive, or obscene, or sacrilegious, or otherwise undesirable as judged by the authorities according to some supposed community standards or their own personal standards. Today the situation seems nearly reversed; only the extraordinarily obscene may be restrained or punished and even then the procedures must be reasonable and fair.[34] The law seems about the same for the national and state governments—that is, the protection has been fully incorporated into the Fourteenth Amendment.

A continuing troublesome problem, however, is that of *prior restraint.* This is censorship *per se;* dissemination is forbidden unless approval is obtained from the authorities in advance. An example is that of censorship of motion pictures; various states and localities require motion pictures to be reviewed and licensed by some official authority before being shown to the public. This is a peculiarly severe form of restraint because the work in question is denied to the public by official action in advance. This would be extremely serious if applied to political expression; e.g., the party in office could gravely cripple the campaign activities of its opponents. Therefore even at common law (and the common law was not nearly as tolerant of freedom of expression as we have become) censorship or prior restraint on publication of books and newspapers was frowned on. The Supreme Court has considerably strengthened this disapproval, although it has not quite forbidden all forms of prior restraint in all situations, even in the field of political expression.

Special difficulties arise, moreover, when the expression is not political and when dissemination by mass media is involved. It is argued that sometimes reasonable prior restraint on, for example, motion pictures,

---

[32] *Saia v. New York,* 334 U.S. 558 (1948); *Kovacs v. Cooper,* 336 U.S. 77 (1949).

[33] *International Brotherhood of Teamsters v. Vogt,* 354 U.S. 284 (1957).

[34] *Roth v. United States,* 354 U.S. 476 (1957); *Manual Enterprises Inc. v. Day,* 370 U.S. 478 (1962); *Kingsley International Pictures Corp. v. Regents,* 360 U.S. 684 (1959).

news-stand materials, and public art exhibits is justified if the matter is obscene or otherwise clearly objectionable, since otherwise many people will be subjected to revolting experiences before they can protect themselves, and immature or disturbed or otherwise vulnerable persons may be seriously harmed before they can be protected. On the other hand, it is contended that any power of prior restraint is so likely to be abused that other means of protection should be employed. Recently the Supreme Court upheld, in a very close case, a city requirement that motion pictures be licensed before public showing.[35]

Freedom of Association

> Congress shall make no law . . . abridging . . . the right of the people peaceably to assemble, and to petition the Government for a redress of grievances.

Politics is in large measure a phenomenon of groups, of relationships among persons, organizations, and governments. Free politics therefore requires not only free expression but also some freedom to form groups, to organize, to communicate, and to exchange expression—including freedom "peaceably to assemble, and to petition the Government for a redress of grievances." This freedom of association has been most discussed recently in connection with protest movements on behalf of the Negro, and with extremist political groups, notably those of the far left.

The Supreme Court has developed a substantial body of constitutional law and is developing more. Broadly speaking, the Court applies about the same rules to the national government and to the states; the First Amendment's freedom of association has been incorporated into the Fourteenth Amendment.[36]

The General Law and the Boundaries

In general the Supreme Court has given substantial protection to freedom of association. Peaceful meetings are upheld even when the subject, or the participants, or both are highly unpopular; authorities are to preserve order by protecting the meeting from disturbance rather than by taking the often easier and more popular course of forbidding or breaking up the meeting to forestall hostile disorders aimed at it. In March 1961 a large group of Negro high school and college students held a meeting on the grounds of the South Carolina state house, an area open to the

---

[35] *Times Film Corp.* v. *Chicago*, 365 U.S. 43 (1961). The basic case on prior restraint is *Near* v. *Minnesota*, 283 U.S. 697 (1931). See also *Lovell* v. *Griffin*, 303 U.S. 444 (1938). A leading case on censorship of movies is *Joseph Burstyn, Inc.* v. *Wilson*, 343 U.S. 495 (1952). A leading case on censorship of books is *Kingsley Books, Inc.* v. *Brown*, 354 U.S. 436 (1957).

[36] Robert A. Horn, *Groups and the Constitution* (Stanford: Stanford University Press, 1956).

public, to protest to the state legislature and to the public generally against racial discrimination. The meeting was peaceful, although the students did march and sing. A large crowd of hostile onlookers gathered. The police determined that law and order were threatened, although no violence was occurring and the statements by the students were well within their rights of free speech. The police ordered the students to disperse, and when they refused to do so arrested all of them. One hundred and eighty-seven of them were convicted of breach of the peace. These convictions were reversed by the Supreme Court, with the statement "The Fourteenth Amendment does not permit a State to make criminal the peaceful expression of unpopular views."[37]

Similarly, peaceful groups that seek simply to exercise other constitutional freedoms are protected, even though they were extremely unpopular with the authorities. Several Southern states have tried to prevent the National Association for the Advancement of Colored People from operating or even existing within their boundaries. These attempts have been very ingenious, based upon many lines of argument and various state powers, but the Court has struck them all down. The states have been so determined to evade the Court's orders, however, that their practical success has been considerable.[38]

Even groups whose doctrines and objectives are of very dubious legitimacy—the Ku Klux Klan, for example, and such hate groups as the American Nazi Party—are protected if they refrain from criminal action. There are limits, however. An association which is in fact a conspiracy to commit crimes may be treated as such; the American Nazi Party would be subject to prosecution to the extent that it is a conspiracy to desecrate religious buildings and commit assaults upon people it dislikes.

Nonpolitical Association

Freedom of association is concerned most fundamentally with association for political purposes, and to some extent with association for the exercise of other constitutional freedoms. Many associations are not involved with politics or with free expression and hence are not entitled to the freedom of association protected by the First Amendment. Thus, the normal activities of the ordinary business corporation can be regulated much as government sees fit without infringing freedom of association; for example, association to fix prices or monopolize in violation of the antitrust laws can certainly be forbidden. But the lobbying association for the corporation's industry might well be protected as involving political expression. Similarly, in labor-management relations, some aspects of picketing and union activity and some aspects of man-

---

[37] *Edwards* v. *South Carolina,* 372 U.S. 229 (1963).
[38] A well-known series of such episodes involved the NAACP and the state of Alabama. See for example the case of *NAACP* v. *Alabama ex rel. Flowers,* 377 U.S. 288 (1964).

agement publicity and antiunion activity are protected by the rights of freedom of expression and association, while other aspects (e.g., incitement to violence and association for purposes of violence) are subject to regulation. It is not easy to say where the right of association ends; the richness and variety of associational life in America and the pervasiveness of politics combine to raise questions of the constitutional freedom of association in many unexpected places.

Further, we may be seeing, in the increasing governmental regulation of the internal affairs of unions, corporations, and other organizations, the beginnings of government efforts to foster by affirmative action freedom and justice in intra-associational matters. Constitutionally and conceptually this is quite a different thing from the First Amendment interdiction of government interference with freedom of political association, but in some ways it is inspired by the same ideal, that association should be available to all men for legitimate purposes.

The Great Problem: Subversive and Seditious Associations

One of the hardest problems that any government that respects individual freedom has to face is that of freedom for those opponents who profoundly reject the regime and seek to subvert it. One of the hardest problems of constitutionally guaranteed civil liberties in the United States today is that of their application to Communism, to individual Communists, to Communist ideas and expression, and to associations that are Communist or Communist-tinged. Communism beyond doubt is antagonistic to the American political system. Should not the system be entitled to defend itself against its enemies by any means necessary? We can understand how hard it is for a free polity to answer that question by contemplating the famous statement of Justice Holmes:

> But when men have realized that time has upset many fighting faiths, they may come to believe even more than they believe the very foundations of their own conduct that the ultimate good desired is better reached by free trade in ideas—that the best test of truth is the power of the thought to get itself accepted in the competition of the market, and that truth is the only ground upon which their wishes safely can be carried out. That at any rate is the theory of our Constitution. It is an experiment as all life is an experiment. . . . While that experiment is part of our system I think that we should be eternally vigilant against attempts to check the expression of opinions that we loathe and believe to be fraught with death, unless they so imminently threaten immediate interference with the lawful and pressing purposes of the law that an immediate check is required to save the country. . . .[39]

Profound affirmation of liberty though this statement is, the problem

---

[39] Mr. Justice Holmes, dissenting, in *Abrams* v. *United States*, 250 U.S. 616 (1919).

still remains: When may checks constitutionally be applied? We have already seen how hard it is to draw the line in our discussion of freedom of expression. The problem may seem easier in connection with freedom of association: Let them talk, but do not let them organize. But some degree of association is, as we have seen, a necessary part of freedom of expression. Again, where to draw the line?

The basic federal statute is the Smith Act, passed in 1940. The "membership" provisions of this Act make it a crime knowingly to belong to an organization that advocates the overthrow of the government by force.[40] Before 1940 the Court had overturned some convictions under state acts against subversive or seditious organizations and had sustained others, and had sustained substantially all convictions under temporary federal wartime statutes. In 1952 the Court sustained the convictions of the leaders of the American Communist Party under the Smith Act, but not on grounds of simple membership. In 1961 the Court upheld the conviction under the Act of a person who was an *active* member of the Communist Party and knew of the party's illegal advocacy of violent overthrow.[41]

Also in 1961 the Court decided a case involving the next major federal statute, the Subversive Activities Control Act of 1950. The Communist Party had been ordered, under the Act, to register and to disclose its membership lists and finances. The Court upheld the constitutionality of the order.[42]

In 1954 Congress enacted still another statute, the Communist Control Act. It purports to deprive the Communist Party of all "rights, privileges, and immunities attendant upon legal bodies created under the jurisdiction of the laws of the United States or any political subdivision thereof." This Act has not been definitively interpreted by the Court as yet and the law of the Constitution remains uncertain in this whole vexing area. The reconciliation of the needs of freedom with those of security is not any easier for judges than for statesmen and philosophers.

The Rights of Persons Accused of Crimes

The Problem and the American Record

The very first civil liberty is simply the safety of life, limb, and property within the political community. Government must therefore be able to guard against and punish those who criminally violate that

[40] 54 Stat. 671 (1940); 18 U.S.C. 11.
[41] *Dennis* v. *United States, supra.* The indictments were under the conspiracy provisions of the Act, section 3. *Scales* v. *United States,* 367 U.S. 203 (1961).
[42] *Communist Party* v. *Subversive Activities Control Board,* 367 U.S. 1 (1961). The Party's officers then declined to file the required registration statement, on the ground that if they did so they would be incriminating themselves, contrary to the Fifth Amendment. In view of the very drastic language of existing statutes against Communist activity the courts were compelled to uphold this contention.

safety, the achievement of which is the precondition of political existence. But one mark of a civilized government is that it requires its law enforcement officials to give humane treatment to persons in their hands and assures some justice and fairness in its criminal and quasi-criminal proceedings. Among the blackest crimes of the German Nazi regime were the bestial abuses of human beings that it allowed (indeed encouraged) its police to commit, and the travesties it made of its criminal trials. Communist countries are rightly condemned as often little better. Such regimes are in fact commonly termed, with contempt, 'police states.' Unfortunately, many otherwise honorable governments have similarly degraded themselves, violating their own professed standards. In contrast, one of the acknowledged distinctions of Great Britain is that with few exceptions her police are fair and humane and her courts and officials just.[43]

Unhappily America cannot match the British record. We can claim some honors in this field, but we have to acknowledge very many misdeeds as well, some of them most grim and disgraceful. A large share have been against Negroes, against poor people, against the weak, the helpless, the disadvantaged, and the unpopular. Things have improved, but maltreatment of the accused and convicted is a continuing grave problem. Negroes especially are still frequently subjected to harsh discrimination and police brutality. Lynchings with police connivance or indifference, principally but not only of Negroes, have declined from hundreds annually fifty years ago to a very few today; but other grave violations of the rights of accused persons are all too common in the South and in most of the North as well.

Prosecuting attorneys have intentionally used false evidence and suppressed truthful evidence, and perjury and the distortion or manufacture of evidence by police and other officials have been exposed. Confessions have been illegally forced from defendants. Some have been denied the help of a defense attorney. Some have had their witnesses and supporters harassed and intimidated by police and officials. The list could be lengthened shockingly.

Nor are abuses limited to persons involved in criminal proceedings. Many extend to persons not seriously suspected of any crime, to persons victimized by unscrupulous legislative investigating committees, to persons subject to immigration and naturalization procedures, to persons entangled in the various government loyalty and security programs, and to people touched in other ways by officialdom.

The Constitution and the law grant various rights to all such persons. But these are often unavailable in practice. Unless the person has ex-

---

[43] For a perceptive account of the contemporary administration of criminal justice in Europe see Sybille Bedford, *The Faces of Justice* (New York: Simon & Schuster, 1961). A standard treatment of Soviet judicial administration may be found in Harold J. Berman, *Justice in the U.S.S.R.* (rev. ed.; Cambridge: Harvard University Press, 1963).

ceptional resources, his formal rights are often a sad mockery. The great task is to make our practices conform with our constitutional principles. There is however some ground for a little guarded and cautious hope of future improvement; opinion—even some official opinion—is becoming more concerned with the problems, and the Supreme Court is taking substantial remedial steps within its rather limited powers.

The Court can, in appropriate cases, do some things to require compliance by federal courts and officials with the Bill of Rights and by state courts and officials with the Fourteenth Amendment. It also has, as head of the national court system, some limited general supervisory power over the federal courts. But it can act only in "cases or controversies," because it is only to these that "the judicial power of the United States shall extend. . . ." Further, it can act only in cases that reach it. So it can do nothing directly, and very little indirectly, about abuses that do not get into cases, and into cases that get before it. Further, its power even in these cases is usually only to reverse the criminal judgment of conviction and send the case back for further proceedings.

But should it so reverse when the defendant is clearly guilty, and the reversal will allow him to go unpunished? There is widespread belief in informed quarters that officials take advantage of this dilemma. Certainly some of them criticize the Court unscrupulously and bitterly when it reverses illegally obtained convictions—even of guilty defendants. It may well be doubted that such demagogic criticism discloses any real attachment to the principles of the Constitution. Grave as is the modern problem of crime and disorder, the solution should not be at the expense of elementary constitutional liberties and decencies.

The Framework: Judicial Supremacy and Lay Participation

The basis of our discussion is the actual criminal proceeding, since most constitutional provisions relevant to the rights of persons accused of crimes explicitly concern this. But we must note that these provisions have major applications to other proceedings as well. We start with the framework within which the specific rights find their place.

Habeas corpus. The writ of *habeas corpus* is the foundation, because it establishes the supremacy of law and of the *judicial enforcement of law* over the other powers of government. By the writ a court of competent jurisdiction can (with the usual fringe of exceptions) inquire into the lawfulness of any detention of any person by any official authority, including the states.[44] So official detention is subject to judicial surveillance,

---

[44] The name of the writ is from the Latin *habeas corpus*, "You must have the body [of . . .]," these being the operative words of the writ in its original form. Similar words of command appear in the usual forms of the writ as employed today. Upon being served with the writ, duly issued by the court, the official detaining the person must bring him, literally his body, into the presence of the court at the time and place the writ sets forth, and the judicial inquiry is thereupon conducted.

and ultimately judicial control. The writ protects the first and most basic right—*access* to law and the courts.

The right to jury trial. Article III, section 2, provides that "the trial of all crimes, except in cases of impeachment, shall be by jury." This locates all trials for crime in the *judicial branch.* Further, it takes part of the actual trial from the power even of the judicial personages themselves and puts it in the hands of the jury of laymen; not even judicial officialdom is to be trusted fully. Compare, for example, Soviet Russia, where administrative and police authorities can make some determinations of criminal guilt, and those European countries where the jury is a rather recent innovation and is almost dominated by the judges who are career civil servants and tend much more to think of themselves as employees responsible to government than do English and American judges, with their tradition of utter independence and of membership in the guild of lawyers.

The upshot in America is the supremacy of law and the judiciary, and ultimately of the lay jury. As to the states, the Supreme Court has not held jury trial to be required by the Fourteenth Amendment. But no doubt any attempts by a state to abolish or drastically limit it (there have been none) would be severely scrutinized. And there is no doubt that the supremacy of law and of effective judicial control are both constitutionally required of the states by the Fourteenth Amendment's due process clause.

The specifics of jury trial. Article III, section 2 establishes the general principles of jury trial in criminal matters. The Sixth Amendment goes further, perhaps as far as a constitution feasibly can go, to make sure that the right is not evaded, or stultified, or made a nullity by any official scheming. By it, the right is given to the accused *as a right,* not left as a general direction to the courts as the provision in Article III might conceivably be claimed to do. The trial is to be speedy; the accused is not to be kept until it suits the convenience or advantage of the authorities to try him. The trial is to be public; he can have his friends around him, and have the proceedings of the officials, even of the judicial officials, subject to the sovereign remedy of public scrutiny. The jury is not to be just any jury; it must be an impartial one. And he is to be tried either on his home grounds or where the deed was done; he cannot be taken away to some distant place to his disadvantage.

The Mechanics of the Judicial Process

Of the mass of particulars within the framework, we will deal with some of the major ones, roughly in the order in which they might present themselves in a typical proceeding.

Search and seizure, and self-incrimination. Searches of an individual's person, house, papers, and effects, and compulsions to force him to incriminate himself, are dealt with in different amendments but should be considered together. They first become important to him at the same time, early in the proceeding when the officials are looking for evidence against him. Also they both relate to the means available to these officials for getting such evidence.

Since it is inconceivable to forbid all searches and seizures, the Fourth Amendment forbids only "unreasonable" ones. Obviously, much depends upon what the courts, in changing circumstances, interpret unreasonable to mean. (E.g., does the amendment prohibit modern wire-tapping, which requires no physical entry of a suspect's premises? The matter is not yet wholly settled.) The prohibition against unreasonable searches and seizures is now enforced by the courts in the only just and practicable way— evidence obtained by an unlawful search cannot be used in court.

The Fifth Amendment provides, among other things, that nobody, whether he is innocent or guilty, "shall be compelled in any criminal case to be a witness against himself." This is construed to mean to provide *any* evidence against himself.[45] The prosecution must prove its own case. This construction goes beyond a strictly literal reading of the provision. However, it is undoubtedly well within the Framers' intention. It seems broad only because so many ingenious attempts have been made to circumvent the basic common-law policy of the provision. These attempts have necessitated an appropriate breadth of construction to achieve the provision's intended aim.

Some have criticized the courts violently for giving these rights even such scope as they have, although hitherto it has not been very broad. Indeed the very principles of both amendments have been attacked. Thus we sometimes hear that anyone who 'takes the Fifth Amendment' is necessarily admitting his guilt of whatever misdeed he may be charged with, and that an innocent person 'has nothing to hide' and should willingly submit to whatever inquiries or searches any official agency wishes to make, and that any objection to any inquiry or any assertion of a constitutional right is a confession of guilt. However, attacks upon these rights, like attacks upon other parts of the Constitution, may be regarded with caution. The Constitution has served America well, and we have learned to appreciate many of the Framers' shrewd precautions. They had small regard for officialdom as officialdom; they granted constitutional rights against official excesses because they believed (and experience bears them out) that men in high places can be officious, can be wrong, can be tyrannical.

Presentment or indictment by a grand jury. Everybody with experience of the subject agrees that the power to bring a prosecution, to make some private individual a defendant in a criminal proceeding and put him on trial, is an enormous and dangerous one. Further, law en-

---

[45] For a survey of the subject and the literature, see Erwin N. Griswold, *The Fifth Amendment* (Cambridge: Harvard University Press, 1955). A different point of view is given in Sidney Hook, *Common Sense and the Fifth Amendment* (Chicago: Henry Regnery Company, 1963).

forcement officers, investigators, and prosecutors, even with the best will in the world (let alone the many unhappy cases of malice or other unworthy motives), can become prey to enthusiasm or single-minded but unwise dedication, and will bring prosecutions that should not have been brought.

Accordingly, civilized judicial systems provide that allegations by prosecutors and police are reviewed by some more impartial agency before an actual prosecution is brought. The traditional Anglo-American device is the grand jury, a group of citizens chosen annually in each jurisdiction to pronounce judicially upon prosecutions that officials propose and to decide which have sufficient merit to be carried further. The Fifth Amendment requires this in all federal prosecutions. The Supreme Court has held that the Fourteenth Amendment does not require it of the states; however, the states that do not voluntarily use it use other reviewing procedures.[46]

Confrontation, witnesses, and counsel. The Sixth Amendment provides detailed and specific constitutional provisions concerning the actual machinery of trial. The model is that of the common law, but decisively improved. The Amendment's logic is straightforward and sensible. The trial is to be a rational inquiry; therefore the defendant must be informed of the nature of the accusation, so that he can put forward a rational defense if he has one and, by trying to help himself, help the court reach a reasonable and informed decision. He must be confronted with the witnesses against him; they must tell their stories in open court before an impartial jury, and must submit to his cross-examination. The truth, the whole truth, and nothing but the truth (the old formula whereby a witness is still sworn) is best discovered in open confrontation, not in the whispers of secret informers nor in the tales of investigators who confidentially report to their eager superiors what they claim to have found—which is all too often what they wish they had found; these whispers and tales will not survive severe hostile questioning and the scrutiny of a dispassionate tribunal.

And the accused is to have compulsory process for obtaining witnesses in his favor. The prosecutor and the police have all the might of the government at their backs. The accused here has a little of it at his, turned against government's immediate self but in favor of its true self; for, when its tribunal sits in judgment, the true interest of the government is not that the wishes of its officials be granted but that justice be done. A regime whose criminal prosecutions cannot face open

---

[46] *Hurtado* v. *California*, 110 U.S. 516. One common reviewing procedure is the preliminary hearing. Before a person can be put on trial in the general trial court for a felony, a hearing—a 'preliminary hearing'—must have been held before a magistrate on the complaint alleging the offense, at which the prosecution must have put on sufficient evidence to convince the magistrate that the crime was committed, and that there is 'reasonable ground' for believing the defendant committed it. At the hearing the defendant has in essence all the procedural rights he would have at the trial.

dispute with a defendant armed with some resources for his own defense by the discovery of the truth stands self-confessed of being in this respect a despotism.

Hence the defendant's right to have the assistance of counsel, the right that is the *sine qua non* of them all. Against an almost literally overwhelming array of officialdom, bent by the nature of things on his destruction because that is their job, the accused can hardly hope to compete single-handed, uninformed, and inexpert.[47] American constitutional law therefore gives him the slim but vital privilege of employing a qualified advocate. He can get a good one, or more than one—if he can afford them.

But what if he cannot afford one? Until 1938, he usually had to do without. But the Court has since interpreted "the right . . . to have the assistance of counsel" to mean that every defendant in a federal criminal case must be provided with an attorney if he cannot afford to hire one.[48] The indigent accused gets what he is given, which may not be much. Commonly, this has meant that lawyers in private practice are appointed by the judge in the particular case to serve without fee or even payment of their expenses, simply as a personal contribution to the administration of justice. Recently, very belatedly, Congress has started to supply some statutory authority, and a little money, to create at least a rudimentary system of public defenders, but this is hardly more than a beginning.[49] Recently the Supreme Court has also held that indigent defendants in major criminal prosecutions by the states must be supplied counsel.[50] Some states were already doing so. Others, incredibly, were doing nothing at all.

Other Rights

The Bill of Rights contains other protections for the defendant in a criminal proceeding. Some are quite specific, e.g., the right that excessive bails not be required, nor excessive fines imposed, nor cruel and unusual punishments inflicted. Some, especially the implied ones, are much broader; e.g., the right to appeal from the trial court's rulings

---

[47] It was a very conservative and very experienced justice speaking for the Court over thirty years ago who pointed out the fundamental fact: Every person accused of a crime "requires the guiding hand of counsel at every step in the proceeding against him." Mr. Justice Sutherland, speaking for the Court in *Powell* v. *Alabama*, 287 U.S. 45, 77 (1932).

[48] *Johnson* v. *Zerbst*, 304 U.S. 458 (1938).

[49] The statutory authority is the Criminal Justice Act of 1964, 78 Stat. 552 (1964).

[50] *Gideon* v. *Wainwright*, 372 U.S. 335 (1963). Previously the rule (since 1942) had been that the state was constitutionally required to provide counsel only when not doing so would result in a trial "offensive to common and fundamental ideas of fairness and right." *Betts* v. *Brady*, 316 U.S. 455 (1942). The rule was much criticized when it was announced and ever after. Eventually most informed opinion came to agree it was inadequate, and the Court overruled *Betts* in *Gideon*. In *Gideon* twenty-two states argued that *Betts* should be overruled; only three supported it.

has been inferred from the general common-law character of the Constitution, appeal being available at common law. Some are general. Of these the greatest is the right to due process. This, in its dual form of procedural and substantive due process, gives the courts, and ultimately the Supreme Court, a broad range of authority to require that procedure in criminal matters be fair and that the criminal statutes be rational and nonarbitrary.

Other Applications

We have so far spoken of the application of the protections in the ordinary criminal proceeding in the courts. This is their traditional field. But there are other fields in which government power is exercised upon the individual. He applies for a passport. The government seeks to cancel his citizenship. The Securities and Exchange Commission passes on his request to sell stock in a corporation he is forming. The Federal Aviation Agency flunks him when he takes its examinations for a private pilot's license. The Bureau of Customs charges him duties on the souvenirs he brings back from a trip to Europe. The Internal Revenue Service audits his income tax return and determines that additional tax is due. The list is endless. What rights and what protections—if any—does he have?

There is no simple answer. The law is developing. For example, the applications of the Bill of Rights protections in administrative proceedings are being developed in the large and specialized subject of administrative law.[51]

The Rights of Property

The American political tradition has always held that justice and good government require that, in addition to the various rights we have discussed so far, the individual must also have some rights as to his property, his private agreements, and his ordinary economic and social activities, against government interference and against government abuse of its legitimate powers.

As with the other rights, profoundly difficult questions are encountered in formulating these, and in achieving the proper balance between individual freedoms and the needs of the whole polity as represented by government acting in the public interest. Here the questions arise primarily when government power is being brought to bear upon business and economic activities; accordingly, they are given principal treatment in the next chapter which deals with government and the economy. However it is important to remember that the American system regards such questions as in a profound sense matters of individual rights and

---

[51] For administrative law see the authoritative work in this field, Kenneth Culp Davis, *Administrative Law Treatise* (4 vols.; St. Paul: West Publishing Co., 1958). It is kept up to date with annual pocket parts.

freedoms. The individual's rights to property and his liberties in his business and economic activities are seen as important components of his freedom, and it is felt that he is freer when he has these than he ever can be under a regime where they are drastically limited or nonexistent. As to the important place of private property in the American polity in general, consider only how central to the whole scheme is the idea of an extended *commercial* republic.

Civil Rights: An Irrepressible Problem

I have a dream that one day this nation will raise up and live out the true meaning of its creed: "We hold these truths to be self-evident, that all men are created equal."

The American Dream and the American Dilemma

Speaking from the steps of the Lincoln Memorial to hundreds of thousands who had 'marched on Washington' for civil rights, Negro leader Martin Luther King, Jr. dreamed the American dream of liberty and justice for all. But, he protested, despite the "magnificent words of the Constitution and the Declaration of Independence . . . the Negro finds himself an exile in his own land."

King was conjuring up the perennial "American Dilemma"[52]—the clash between the democratic creed and heritage and the exclusion of Negroes, first by slavery and then by discriminatory practices, from the American dream. The Civil War and the Thirteenth, Fourteenth, and Fifteenth Amendments affirmed the Negro's equality, but the dilemma remained; the constitutional promise was not readily fulfilled.

The creed and its constitutional affirmation are intrinsically hard to live up to. The American system seeks to govern a deep-rooted human propensity of group to oppress group in the name of racial or religious superiority. This is the source of the dilemma, not just neurotic bigotry and hatred but universal human frailty. Moslems and Hindus have slaughtered and African tribes have enslaved each other; and the gap between profession and practice is evidenced in the treatment of African students and Jews in Russia, Pakistanis and West Indians in England, untouchables in India, and dark-skinned Yemenite Jews in Israel.

The American Dilemma has affected Jews, Catholics, Orientals, and other ethnic and religious minorities. But the problem of the Negro is the massive and irrepressible form of the American civil-rights problem.

The Negro Protest

The Negro struggle for civil rights is today at the center of America's national politics. But for most of its history after the Civil War, it was

---

[52] Cf. Gunnar Myrdal, *An American Dilemma* (New York: Harper & Bros., 1944).

a forlorn cause of relatively few Negro and white leaders. After the Reconstruction period, the Negroes' situation became desperate. The Supreme Court narrowly construed the Civil War Amendments, substantially invalidating protective measures like the 1875 Civil Rights Act.[53] White America largely turned its back on the emancipated slaves, and white supremacist Democrats triumphed throughout the South. State 'Jim Crow' laws enforced a pattern of segregation—two worlds, segregated from maternity hospitals to cemeteries. Negroes were restricted to the most menial occupations. And numerous lynchings intimidated Negroes who might claim their rights as free men.

Booker T. Washington and W.E.B. DuBois. In these trying circumstances two great leaders arose, each with a different strategy for achieving Negro equality. Booker T. Washington became the most renowned Negro spokesman of his day. Washington advocated not organized political protest but individual self-improvement. He deliberately narrowed Negro demands, believing that a struggle for full equality was then hopeless and even harmful. He sought to placate the white South with a carefully modest style of speech and by arguing that "agitation of questions of social equality is the extremest folly." Instead of combating segregation, he counseled Negroes to concentrate on the manual arts and to lead exemplary lives. With patience, "the time will come when the Negro in the South will be accorded all the political rights which his ability, character and material possessions entitle him to."[54]

Washington's strategy thus depended wholly on qualified Negroes receiving their due "in time." But too few whites did their part. Negro patience waned as it became increasingly clear that they were to be not only socially segregated but kept inferior in every respect. This was revealed in unequal Negro schools, libraries, hospitals, railway coaches, and other public facilities. The Supreme Court upheld segregation as conforming to the Fourteenth Amendment's "equal protection" clause, so long as facilities were equal as well as separate.[55] In practice, separation was perfect, equality rare.

W. E. B. DuBois, Massachusetts-born and -bred and a Harvard Ph.D., challenged Booker T. Washington's strategy. In 1905 he formed the Niagara Movement[56] to demand immediate enforcement of the Civil War Amendments. Dr. DuBois emphasized the need for training intellectuals, the "talented tenth," from which a competent Negro leadership could emerge. This contrasted with Washington's educational emphasis on farming and the manual arts. And the Niagara Movement reasserted the

---

[53] *Civil Rights Cases*, 109 U.S. 3 (1883).

[54] *Up from Slavery* (New York: Bantam Books, 1959), p. 165. Detractors often overlook the fact that Washington never yielded up the claim to political equality but subtly affirmed it while emphasizing corollary responsibilities of Negroes and whites.

[55] *Plessy* v. *Ferguson*, 163 U.S. 537 (1896).

[56] So named for the place of its founding conference; unable to obtain lodgings on the American side, delegates met on the Canadian side of the falls.

primacy of political equality. To DuBois, "manly self-respect is worth more than land and houses." Furthermore, "a disfranchised working class in a modern industrial civilization is worse than helpless."[57] It was this Negro movement that combined with a revitalized white abolitionist and reformist spirit to form the National Association for the Advancement of Colored People (NAACP) in 1909.

The immediate stimulus was an incident in 1908 in which a white mob in Springfield, Illinois killed and wounded scores of Negroes and drove thousands from the city. White consciences were especially shocked that this riot occurred in the land of Lincoln. On Lincoln's birthday, 1909, white reformers initiated the formation of the NAACP, and it has remained an interracial organization.[58] The NAACP functioned primarily as an intellectual vanguard, rather than a mass membership organization. Its weapons were propaganda, lobbying, and, above all, litigation.

The NAACP and the school segregation cases: triumph and frustration. Carefully selecting test cases and patiently preparing innumerable briefs, the NAACP launched a half century of litigation. Problem areas ranged widely, from suits against "grandfather clause" deprivations of voting rights to "restrictive covenants" forbidding real-estate sales to Negroes.[59] But the ultimate and major concern was to obtain the Supreme Court's reversal of its *Plessy* "separate but equal" doctrine. Until that construction of the Fourteenth Amendment could be revoked, state-enforced segregation would continue and Negroes would remain second-class citizens under the Constitution.

The segregated public schools and colleges were a prime target. A major development occurred in the late 1930s when the *equal* element in the *Plessy* v. *Ferguson* "separate but equal" formula began to be applied with increasing stringency. Previously all-white professional and graduate schools were required, by increasingly demanding criteria, to admit Negroes—first, because there were no similar Negro schools at all, then because the hastily created segregated graduate schools (lacking research facilities, reputation, etc.) were held to be, for all practical purposes, incapable of supplying equal graduate training.[60] Finally, a unanimous Supreme Court overruled *Plessy*, holding that "separate educational facilities are inherently unequal" under the Fourteenth Amendment's equal-protection clause as to the states, and under the Fifth Amendment's due process clause as to the national District of Columbia.[61]

---

[57] Quoted in Rayford W. Logan, ed., *What the Negro Wants* (Chapel Hill: University of North Carolina Press, 1944), p. 99.

[58] The National Urban League was formed shortly after, in 1911, to aid the new Negro urbanites, as the race problem moved northward and into the cities.

[59] *Guinn* v. *United States*, 238 U.S. 347 (1915); *Shelley* v. *Kraemer*, 334 U.S. 1 (1948).

[60] Cf. *Missouri ex rel. Gaines* v. *Canada*, 305 U.S. 337 (1938); *McLaurin* v. *Oklahoma State Regents*, 339 U.S. 637 (1950); *Sweatt* v. *Painter*, 339 U.S. 629 (1950).

[61] *Brown* v. *Board of Education*, 347 U.S. 483 (1954); *Bolling* v. *Sharpe*, 347 U.S. 497 (1954).

The 1896 *Plessy* opinion had denied that racial segregation "stamped" a "badge of inferiority" on Negroes. This was rejected in the 1954 school-desegregation opinion: "To separate [school children] from others of similar age and qualifications solely because of their race generates a feeling of inferiority as to their status in the community that may affect their hearts and minds in a way unlikely ever to be undone." Technically the new rulings applied only to schools, but the principle was soon extended and the constitutional basis for legally enforced racial segregation was shattered.

Initially a relatively compliant spirit prevailed as some seven hundred previously all-white school districts, mainly in border states, admitted Negroes within two years of the decision. But hard-core southern resistance soon developed. Several states resurrected the doctrine of nullification, claiming a right to 'interpose' their authority between the national government and the people. Some laws, cleverly designed to circumvent the decision, made extensive additional litigation necessary. Open defiance of court orders by Governor Faubus of Arkansas finally led President Eisenhower to employ military force to escort Negro pupils past white rioters into Little Rock's Central High School. Similar riots have required armed national intervention at state universities in Alabama and in Mississippi. A period of intense racial discord began, first in the South but then in the North as well, as the Negro protest took a new turn.

Satyagraha in America. Martin Luther King, Jr., then a 27-year-old Baptist minister from Montgomery, Alabama, told the 1956 NAACP con-

1957: A Negro girl is jeered as she attempts to enter high school in Little Rock, Arkansas.

1963: A Negro girl attends class at Little Rock's Hall High School; she is also a member of the school's chapter of a national honor society.

vention: "There is a brand-new Negro in the South, with a new sense of dignity and destiny." For an entire year, Negroes in Montgomery had walked rather than ride the public buses, demanding that the indignity of segregated seating be abolished. The Montgomery Movement spread to other cities and became the Southern Christian Leadership Conference. Adapting the Gandhian doctrine of *satyagraha*—that passive resistance and love can conquer hatred and injustice—Dr. King made nonviolent civil disobedience a major weapon of American Negro protest.

Southern 'sit-ins,' 'wade-ins,' and 'kneel-ins' erupted into headline-catching and televised spectacles. In the North, too, there were 'lie-ins' to block bulldozers on construction jobs where discriminatory hiring practices and trade union policies excluded Negroes. New organizations and leaders competed with each other and the established NAACP; the Committee on Racial Equality (CORE), the Student Nonviolent Coordinating Committee (SNCC), and others entered the fray, and demonstrations proliferated. The nation (and to America's embarrassment, the world) saw remarkably well-disciplined passive demonstrators subjected to indignities and violence. Negro students sitting at lunch counters had catsup poured on them and were pummeled by white toughs. Demonstrators were subjected to high-pressure water hosings and police dogs. Medgar Evers, Mississippi's NAACP field secretary, was shot dead from ambush; Negro children attending Sunday school were killed in one of several bombings and burnings of Negro churches; four civil-rights workers were kidnapped and murdered during voter registration drives.

Nonviolent *satyagraha* might yet beget tolerance and fraternity, but the drive for 'Freedom Now' in the 1960s engendered anything but interracial harmony.

Political coalition. Although interracial harmony has decreased in many local communities, Negro political power in the nation has steadily increased. By 1965, six Negroes sat in the United States House of Representatives, and Negro voters hold the balance of power in some fifty congressional districts in the North and West. Negroes form a vital part of the liberal-labor minorities voting coalition that has made the Democratic party the dominant national majority since the New Deal. Underlying this is a great exodus of Negroes from the South, where they could not vote, to the North and West where they could. Moreover, Negro migrants are not randomly scattered but have relocated in the nation's largest cities, where *de facto* segregation of neighborhoods produces concentrated power at the polls.

Negroes retained their Republican party loyalties longer than any comparable lower-class or minority group, predominantly supporting Hoover over Roosevelt in 1932. But their historic ties to the party of the Great Emancipator were largely severed by 1936. Undoubtedly, the greatest strain was the economic depression which gave Negroes a mammoth stake in the relief and welfare measures of the New Deal. At the same time, many highly placed New Dealers—most prominently, Eleanor Roosevelt, the President's wife—befriended the Negro cause. And the rise of industrial unions, unlike the exclusive skilled craft unions of the American Federation of Labor (AFL), brought great numbers of Negroes into the Congress of Industrial Organizations (CIO) with its strongly Democratic partisanship. Negro organizations joined in political alliance with other ethnic groups—Irish, Jews, Poles, Czechs, Italians, Greeks—as "the old minorities have become the new majority."[62] Out of these elements was forged the modern coalition of liberal, labor, and ethnic groups that has supported civil rights.

Governing for Civil Rights

When, after many years, the movement for national civil-rights legislation began to develop strength, anti-lynching and anti-poll-tax bills were filibustered to death in the Senate or permanently pigeon-holed by the House Rules Committee. Greater progress was made with the Presidency where concentrated voting power in the major cities, and hence in the key states, made Negroes an increasingly important political factor.

Executive orders. In 1941, partly in response to a threatened march on Washington unless Negroes got a fair share of the new wartime pros-

---

[62] Samuel Lubell, *The Future of American Politics* (New York: Doubleday Anchor Books, 1956), p. 87.

General Graham, commanding officer of the Alabama National Guard (note Dixie emblem on uniform) is shown acting under a presidential order to enforce court-ordered admittance of Negro students to the state university. Alabama's Governor Wallace (microphone around neck) symbolically blocked entry, yielding only to the national show of force.

perity, President Roosevelt established the Fair Employment Practices Commission (FEPC). This was done by the first executive order concerning Negro rights since Lincoln's Emancipation Proclamation. Every President has since maintained similar executive agencies to promote equal employment opportunity in the federal civil service and by private government contractors.

President Truman exercised his authority as commander-in-chief to end racial discrimination in the armed forces. This had particularly galled Negro servicemen during wars 'to save the world for democracy' and against Nazi racism. Another Truman order created the President's Committee on Civil Rights as a fact-finding and policy-proposing body; the committee effectively argued the necessity of legislation "to secure these rights."[63]

Legislation. After a decade of legislative struggle, Congress passed and President Eisenhower signed into law the first national civil-rights statute since 1875. The Civil Rights Act of 1957 sought mainly to ensure

---

[63] U.S. President's Committee on Civil Rights, *To Secure These Rights* (Washington: U.S. Government Printing Office, 1947), pp. 149–73.

the voting rights of huge numbers of prospective Negro voters who were kept from registering in many southern states by devices ranging from discriminatory application of literacy tests to economic and physical intimidation. The 1957 Act authorized the national government to seek court orders enjoining illegal interference with voting rights in federal elections (although the Fifteenth Amendment applies equally to state and local elections). Failure to comply entailed contempt-of-court penalties, which gave the Act real teeth, but jury trials were required if heavy fines or jail sentences were imposed in criminal contempt proceedings. (Many civil-rights proponents opposed the jury trial provision, arguing that southern white juries usually failed to convict white offenders against Negro rights. But southern congressmen, unable to defeat the bill in toto, found enough other congressmen who were convinced that the right to trial by jury is vital to liberty. Thus the jury trial provision was a crucial compromise in securing passage of the bill.) As an aid to enforcement, the Act established a Civil Rights Division within the Department of Justice, and created an additional Assistant Attorney General to head the division. Finally, the United States Commission on Civil Rights was created as a bipartisan fact-finding executive agency.

The Civil Rights Act of 1960 provided additional safeguards for voting rights after serious difficulties were encountered in enforcing the 1957 Act. Some state officials refused to permit national investigators to examine voter registration records; an Alabama statute permitted local registrars to destroy their records; some registrars resigned and their positions were deliberately left vacant to frustrate court orders to register eligible applicants. The Civil Rights Commission reported: "Some method must be found by which a Federal officer is empowered to register voters for Federal elections."[64] The 1960 Act authorized the Federal courts to appoint referees to grant voting certificates binding on election officials under penalty of contempt proceedings, and required state election officials to preserve their records for at least 22 months following primary or general elections, permitting Justice Department inspection. The 1960 Act went somewhat beyond voting rights to make obstruction of federal court orders by "threats or force" (e.g., in school integration cases) a federal crime. It is also made it a federal offense to transport explosives, or to move from one state to another to escape prosecution for attempting to bomb or otherwise desecrate churches or synagogues.

The Civil Rights Act of 1964 is the strongest and most comprehensive civil-rights legislation since Reconstruction. As to voting rights, the Act provides federal regulation of state literacy testing. Tests must be given in written form, not orally, and to all applicants or none, and a sixth grade education (in English) is made a presumption of literacy (a state wishing to disqualify such an applicant has the burden of proving illiter-

---

[64] United States Commission on Civil Rights, *With Liberty and Justice for All* (Washington: U.S. Government Printing Office, 1959), p. 95.

acy in a federal court). But the 1964 Act went far beyond voting rights. The greatest legislative breakthroughs were in public accommodations, school integration, and fair employment practices.

Equal access to public accommodations is guaranteed, assuring the right of all persons to be served in hotels, theatres, restaurants, gasoline service stations and similar establishments catering to transients and the general public. Although perhaps not the most urgent need, the dramatic student sit-ins had made this "the symbolic focal point of the Negro protest movement."[65] The regulation is limited to accommodations where interstate commerce or travel is involved, and "Mrs. Murphy's boarding house" (any place with no more than five rooms for rent) is excluded.

By requiring the United States Office of Education to assist local authorities to desegregate, the Act implicitly endorses the Supreme Court's school desegregation decision.

Fair employment practices, the prime legislative target of the civil-rights movement for twenty years, were also given congressional sanction. "Equal employment opportunity" is required of employers (of 100 or more in 1965, and after 1968 of 25 or more) who are engaged in or whose businesses affect interstate commerce; labor unions and employment agencies must also comply. The equal-opportunity provision prohibits employment discrimination because of race, color, sex, religion, or national origin, except where such is a legitimate occupational qualification. A Federal Equal Employment Opportunity Commission hears complaints by aggrieved parties or initiates complaints in the courts. Primary reliance for enforcement is placed on investigatory powers and on conciliation. The ultimate sanction is a court order with contempt penalties for non-compliance.

Among the miscellaneous provisions, the tenure of the Commission on Civil Rights is extended; the Census Bureau is directed to collect registration and voting statistics; the Attorney General is authorized to intervene in private suits involving alleged denial of the equal protection of the laws; and a Community Relations Service is established in the Department of Commerce to aid communities to resolve disputes and to promote harmonious intergroup relations.

The 1965 Voting Rights Act strikes mainly at two obstacles frustrating prior efforts to protect Negro suffrage. Discriminatory literacy tests and similar qualifying procedures were suspended in any state or county where less than 50 per cent of the voting-age population could vote as of November 1, 1964.[66] And the Act empowers the Attorney General to send federal examiners into any county, armed with authority to register persons who meet state requirements of age, residency, and lack of a criminal record. Subsequently, federal poll watchers may be appointed to ensure

---

[65] *Congressional Quarterly*, June 19, 1964, p. 1205.
[66] Six southern states fit this category: Alabama, Georgia, Louisiana, Mississippi, South Carolina, and Virginia. Also affected are 26 counties in North Carolina, and one county each in Arizona, Idaho, and Maine.

that federally registered voters are permitted to cast ballots in elections. Other provisions direct the Attorney General to file suits challenging the constitutionality of poll tax prerequisites to voting in state and local elections.[67]

Prognosis

Unquestionably, great progress has been made, even if more slowly and in lesser degree than Negro demands. Substantial governmental instruments are now available, and Negro political power will assure a

The Southern Moderate

—as he looks to SOUTHERN RACIAL EXTREMISTS...

—as he looks to the NAACP...

—as he looks to OTHER SECTIONS OF THE U.S. ....

—as he looks to the PUBLIC SCHOOL TEACHERS

—as he looks to the POLITICIAN...

no such animal

—as he looks to the CITIZENS COUNCILS

—as he sees himself...

reasonable measure of administrative implementation. Increased Negro voting in the South is very likely to produce fundamental improvements in civil rights as elected officials respond realistically to their changing constituencies. A fairer administration of justice and removal of the grossest indignities of racial segregation in public facilities and accom-

---

[67] Affected states were Alabama, Mississippi, Texas, and Virginia.

modations are foreseeable in the not-too-distant future. Negro-white relations in the South will increasingly approximate those in the North.

De jure (sanctioned by law) segregation is thus fading from American life—which still leaves the hard kernel of the race problem, *de facto* segregation. Informally maintained residential discrimination restricts Negro housing throughout the nation. Wherever boundaries burst and Negroes move into formerly all-white territory, white property owners and renters depart en masse rather than accept Negroes as neighbors. This pattern underlies racial segregation of public schools in the North. Frustrated in its efforts to integrate neighborhood housing, the northern civil-rights movement has attacked the principle of neighborhood-based schools as too often a subterfuge for perpetuating *de facto* segregation, and, at best, as a secondary principle that must yield to the superior value of inter-racial education. Negro boycotts, demonstrations, and more conventional tactics have pressured educators to promote increased racial integration in the public schools. Various plans have been instituted, including transporting Negro and white pupils between different neighborhood schools. Such measures provoked widespread opposing pressures, including counter-boycotts and counter-demonstrations by northern white groups.

Negro protest and white 'backlash' reciprocally engender and enflame each other so that moderate leaders find it difficult to control hot-heads and resist militant demands for 'direct action.' Some demonstrations have been converted into riots, degenerating into violence, looting, and wanton destruction. Leaders like Roy Wilkins of the NAACP and Martin Luther King, Jr. have strongly condemned these disgraceful outbreaks. The problem for white and Negro moderates alike is a perennial political problem of controlling the spirit of faction—not to let the struggle over the pace and direction of civil-rights progress degenerate from a constitutionally restrained political endeavor into a physical battle among rioting mobs. The need is for responsible leadership. Negro leaders have to continue their dual task of effectively organizing the drive toward racial equality while simultaneously aiding and stimulating Negroes to avail themselves of the many opportunities already won in education and employment. White leaders—in government, commerce, education, religion, professions, and mass media—must seek moderate courses of action, but such 'gradualism,' if it is to avoid hypocrisy, must move decisively toward specific progress in confirmation of the American Dream.

BIBLIOGRAPHICAL NOTE

Most of the materials on law and the courts described in the bibliographical notes to Chapters 4 and 7 are useful for the present chapter as well.

Current developments in civil liberties and civil rights are reported in the various publications of such organizations as the American Civil Liberties

Union and the National Association for the Advancement of Colored People. Current information on legal aspects is found in the *Race Relations Law Reporter*, published by the Vanderbilt University School of Law, and in *United States Law Week*, published by the Bureau of National Affairs. Several agencies of the U.S. government provide information, e.g., the continuing studies of the U.S. Commission on Civil Rights and the U.S. Department of Justice press releases describing the Department's activities.

The greatest source of legal and constitutional information and analysis is found in the law reviews and some other scholarly journals. The *Index to Legal Periodicals* indexes virtually the whole of this large literature under a detailed classification system, and is kept current within a very few weeks; the ILP also indexes all book reviews appearing in the periodicals it covers.

The ILP provides another valuable service. Most law reviews publish case notes. These are summaries, and normally also detailed background and critical discussions, of major current judicial decisions. These are indexed under the case's name in the ILP.

In general, consult T. I. Emerson and D. Haber, *Political and Civil Rights in the U.S.* (1959); R. E. Cushman, *Civil Liberties in the U.S.* (1956); and Milton R. Konvitz, *Fundamental Liberties of a Free People* (1957). Classical writings include: John Milton, *Areopagitica* (1644); John Locke, *Letter Concerning Toleration* (1689); and John Stuart Mill, *On Liberty* (1859). See also A. J. Carlyle, *Political Liberty: a History of the Conception in the Middle Ages and Modern Times* (1963). An important controversial theoretical work is Walter Berns, *Freedom, Virtue, and The First Amendment* (1957). C. Herman Pritchett, *Civil Liberties and the Vinson Court* (1954) gives a close-up view of Supreme Court decisions in this area.

On religious liberty, see Leo Pfeffer, *Church, State, and Freedom* (1953); free expression, Z. Chafee, Jr., *Free Speech in the U.S* (1941); censorship, R. McKeon, *et al*, *The Freedom to Read* (1957); loyalty problems, E. Bontecou, *The Federal Loyalty-Security Program* (1953); due process and fair trial, A. Barth, *Law Enforcement Versus the Law* (1963) and Sir Patrick Devlin, *Trial by Jury* (1956).

The classic work on American civil rights and the Negro remains Gunnar Myrdal, *An American Dilemma* (1944). A useful collection is E. T. Thompson and E. C. Hughes (eds.), *Race: Individual and Collective Behavior* (1958). These last two books contain extensive bibliographies. Also see: St. C. Drake and H. R. Cayton, *Black Metropolis* (1945); J. H. Franklin, *From Slavery to Freedom* (1956); H. Garfinkel, *When Negroes March* (1959); L. Kesselman, *Social Politics of FEPC* (1948); L. Lomax, *Negro Revolt* (1962); A. Westin, (ed.), *Freedom Now* (1964); and C. Vann Woodward, *The Strange Career of Jim Crow* (1955).

Chapter 14

Governing the Economy

The Polity and The Economy[1]

ECONOMICS—HOW MEN MAKE THEIR LIVING, HOW THEY PRODUCE AND distribute goods and services—always and everywhere is deeply involved with politics, both domestic and international. The contemporary example that leaps to mind is the Cold War: Economics is obviously central to that great political confrontation. Echoing the original Marxian idea that Communism is the economic order destined by history to supersede capitalism, Nikita Khrushchev promised that Communism would 'bury us' by virtue of its economic superiority. Thus at the very heart of the contemporary conflict there has been the rivalry of the economic systems of the western democracies and the Communist countries. The profound link between economy and polity is revealed in the way that each claims that its economic system is the indispensable foundation of a truly democratic political order.

This great political-economic rivalry coincides with the historic emergence of the new Asian and African nations. It thrusts upon them their most fundamental question: Whether a free market economy in the western style is the road for them to economic development, or whether they should choose Communist collectivism. So profoundly are polity and economy linked that how the new nations choose will influence their political careers for generations, and will have immense consequences for the entire world.

But the linking of politics and economics is by no means limited to the Cold War or the emergence of the new nations. Modern national econ-

---

[1] For a striking use of this phrase and an analysis of an author highly relevant to understanding American capitalism, see Joseph Cropsey, *Polity and Economy: An Interpretation of the Principles of Adam Smith* (The Hague: Martinus Nijhoff, 1957).

omies have innumerable involvements with each other; trade flows across the world at an astonishing rate. And government must superintend those involvements and that trade.

Moreover, international political-economic relationships affect political-economic relationships within the United States. American foreign policy employs many economic instrumentalities—Marshall Plan direct economic aid, influence in international monetary organizations, tariff policies, price support of strategic commodities on the world markets, etc. Manipulating the economy for such foreign-policy purposes obviously has domestic consequences, not least by engendering party and group conflict. For example, a tariff reduction that helps an ally (and aids American consumers) adversely affects some business and labor groups who promptly oppose it. A proposal to permit an American firm to sell a synthetic rubber plant to Communist Rumania (on the theory that this would encourage Titoism, i.e., independence of Russia) produces pressure group and congressional protest that this is appeasement.

But the questions raised so far, dramatic and important as many are, all derive from international problems and thus only lead toward the primary concern of this chapter—domestic political-economic relationships.

The Influence of Government on the Economy

The primeval fact is that the very existence of government and of civil society depends in one simple and ultimate sense on economics in that man must eat before he can do anything else. And if the economy is to be much more than the berry-picking of a naked solitary in John Locke's "state of nature," it requires and is influenced by political organization. Government must at a minimum maintain some degree of order and internal stability so economic activity can go on, must defend it against incursions from outside, must protect economic assets from destruction, and must regulate relationships among members of the political community. In primitive societies, and in parts of some present-day underdeveloped countries, government does little more than these minima, and indeed often does not do even these very well. If an economy is to grow, government must do much more, until we reach the immensely large and complex economies—and governments—of the modern industrial nations.

Men soon learn that government can be explicitly and directly used to affect economic matters; by it society as a whole can affect the economy and by it politically influential groups can get more economic benefits than other groups. Indeed, much political history is a history of struggles to obtain and use political power for economic purposes. The inevitable outcome is that in societies developed beyond the primitive stage the economy and its distribution of goods and services are largely the creations of and are controlled by government and politics.

Regimes and Economies

The most fundamental polity-economy relationship concerns the very nature of the regime itself. So important are the mutual influences and interactions of government and economics that political regimes are customarily characterized largely according to their various stances toward

"Phew! That's a nasty leak. Thank goodness it's not at our end of the boat."

the economy, that is, how each society produces its goods and services and who are its chief beneficiaries. The very first chapter of Aristotle's *Politics*, for example, deals with matters we now call economic—with "property and the art of acquiring it"—and the question of whether the poor or rich predominate is central to Aristotle's famous classification of regimes. At the very center of John Locke's *Two Treatises of Government* is a chapter entitled "Of Property." And the reader of this book needs little reminder how important the idea of an extended *commercial* republic was to James Madison.

Thus we commonly speak of socialist regimes, communist regimes, capitalist regimes, and of these regimes at various stages of economic development or mixture. Within the familiar history of capitalism, we distinguish a variety of regimes based upon their mixture of economic and political factors. There are some where business and industrial wealth exercise so much political influence that the regime can fairly be described as plutocratic (a term of opprobrium in contrast with aristocracy, because hardly anyone has considered mere wealth a sufficient claim to rule). Some regimes in late medieval western Europe can only be understood as mixtures of nascent capitalism and essentially aristocratic orders. Nineteenth-century Britain similarly blended aristocratic institutions but with a full blown system of laissez faire capitalism.[2] And in America today we speak of democratic capitalism, a term we shall consider later.

Economic Transformations

A thumbnail sketch of capitalist and earlier polity-economy relationships in western Europe will serve three purposes. First, it emphasizes the importance of economic change and transformation. History is marked by great economic transformations that occurred so imperceptibly as to be visible only to the most discerning contemporaries; yet these changes immensely affect the polity. Second, by showing the course of earlier economic development, the sketch may clarify the directions the economies and polities of the modern world are likely to take. And, third, it supplies a background for understanding the basic American polity-economy relationship.

Perhaps the greatest transformation—and the most mysterious—is the eruption of civilization out of unpromising stagnation, difficult to distinguish from apparently similar circumstances where other peoples languish without change for ages. Western European history begins with just such an emergence of classical Greece and Rome from among the agricultural, almost primitive, societies of the Mediterranean world. Some of the primitive parts of the earth today seek to achieve similar 'take-offs,' to borrow a term popular in the economics of development.[3]

At its height in, say, 300 A.D., the Roman empire was an immense and largely unified political order; it was also an equally immense and unified economy, albeit one that was nonindustrial, largely agricultural, but with an important commercial sector. This ancient commerce, however, was minuscule compared with modern commerce. Ancient Mediterranean trade was largely between countries of similar climate and state of economic development—hence with relatively little worth exchanging. (Consider how little trade there has been among the innumerable villages of Asia, each producing the same few sorts of things.) Above all, ancient commerce did not vitally affect the lives of everyone, and therein lies the great difference with modern commerce. Raised to an immense scale by the forces of modern technology, modern commerce is all-pervasive; it is, so to speak, democratized commerce so that everyone is drawn fully into the orbit of the market.[4] It was this sort of commerce that Madison envisaged for the large republic.

---

[2] The catchphrase laissez faire is widely used to characterize economic theories which urge that the economy be allowed to act on its own, without substantial government regulation or control.

[3] In economic development a central problem is how an underdeveloped economy acquires enough capital and other resources plus a sufficiently effective technology, manpower, and organizational structure so it can begin to generate a self-sustaining increase in production—can take off into growth.

[4] A classical account of ancient commerce and of modern changes is Montesquieu, *The Spirit of Laws*; see especially Volume I, Book XX, and Volume II, Book XXI.

Ancient commerce was stilled when first the barbarians and later the Moslems disrupted the Roman empire and the Mediterranean system. After centuries of quiescent 'Dark Ages' and early medievalism, another major period of economic and political change began. Towns and commerce revived; feudal localism and the complicated feudal system of correlative rights and duties were replaced by the nation-state and monarchical sovereignty, and the period of capitalism dawned. A new aggressive spirit of acquisitiveness combined with a rapidly developing technology (based on the new scientific view that nature existed to be conquered) produced three centuries of unparalleled commercial and then industrial development.

The late nineteenth century saw the noon of high capitalism. This was an economic order that was industrialized, productive, and expansive, brutally exploitative on occasion, deeply embroiled in imperialist and colonial adventures, laissez faire in the Anglo-American world and some other places, and neomercantilist in much of Europe. The same general period was also the noon of the political order and political philosophy of nineteenth-century constitutionalism. But both of these imposing systems contained seeds that twentieth-century world wars, revolutions, and social and economic change have helped grow into vast problems that now confront us.

Enormous advances in the western capitalist countries (and Japan) since World War II, Soviet Russia's technological accomplishments, the dawn of ultra-modern technology, the population explosion, the end of colonialism and the emergence of the underdeveloped nations, are part of the great economic-political changes occuring today. In what general directions are the economies and polities of the world likely to move: toward the Communist pattern; toward socialist economics and authoritarian government; toward some evolved form of contemporary liberal and democratic regulated western capitalism; back toward neomercantilism in economics and classic absolutism in politics; back toward the laissez faire capitalism and cautious constitutionalism of nineteenth-century Britain; or toward what? Dozens of countries today are embroiled in deciding just such fundamental questions. The inevitable consequence, when profound issues are debated, is the political turbulence so characteristic of this generation.

Polity and Economy in America

In comparison with many other countries, Americans are fundamentally agreed on the gravest economic questions as we have seen them to be on political questions. That is to say, they are agreed on the nature of their regime, which necessarily involves both political and economic principles. Nonetheless, the fundamental question that faces others—a free versus a controlled economy or a mixture of the two—underlies American political disputes. Great issues often lurk just beneath the surface of consensus. Still the dominating fact is that the American political system includes a decision about the economy. The decision rests on the belief that democratic political institutions find support in significantly free economic institutions, and that a free economy generates long-run economic growth. Capitalism—however qualified, regulated, or democratized—is the economic premise most Americans see as necessary to and implicit in their political order.

Thus in this chapter we examine the problem of governing the economy, not primarily regarding the basic form of polity and economy, but as the economy is governed within the basically accepted American system. With an awareness of the great issues, we are concerned to learn as well the daily problems of governing the economy, the institutions and processes by which it is governed, and the relatively serious conflicts over how it shall be governed.

The Transformations of the American System

America began amid speculative economic schemes. Most of the colonization was undertaken in the hopes of making money and aimed at cheap land, new resources, the ever-alluring mirage of gold, new markets, and trading advantages. "The adventurous spirit, which distinguishes the commercial character of America"[5] (and which the constitutional design presupposed), was at work from the outset. And active commerce has been one of the mainsprings of American life ever since, to an energetic extent and in ways few other countries can match. Inevitably these enterprising economic forces thrust demands and problems upon government and politics.

We have seen how the Revolution and the Founding Decade must be understood partly in terms of economic forces and issues (see e.g., pp. 57–59). The new government was hardly launched when these continuing economic forces and problems led to a grand confrontation on vitally central issues of government policy toward the economy. This confrontation, associated with the names of Hamilton and Jefferson, permanently affected the course of policy, and their views have been a primary source of American ideas and rhetoric on polity-economy relations ever since.

Hamiltonianism and Jeffersonianism

At the heart of Hamilton's political thought was a view of the proper relationship between government and the economic system. His overarching aim was a powerful American empire that would win the respect of the world and bring lasting fame for its founders and leaders. This required that the ample constitutional powers of the national gov-

---

[5] *Federalist* 11, p. 85.

ernment be used to help create an expanding and powerful economy. Such an economy, being manifestly national in scope and functioning, would in turn justify the exercise of the national powers. And, further, he expected self-interested businessmen to support both a powerful government and the political party—Hamilton's—that was their benefactor.

The Hamiltonian view asserts (we can speak in the present tense because the view is still very much alive) that government should support, sustain, assist, and aid the forces of private business, and particularly the expanding aspects of private business. This positive support and encouragement of private business is regarded as a not only legitimate but also vitally desirable function of government. And at every stage in American history there have been those, Hamiltonians in some ultimate inspiration, who have urged that the government foster—in private hands—economic growth, development, expansion, and in general all movements out into new fields of large-scale economic activity.

Hamilton's policies. Hamilton obtained enactment of so complex and comprehensive a program of government aids for business that he has been deemed the architect of the national economy. Most prominently, he organized the new government's monetary and financial system. His program had two main features: establishing the first Bank of the United States (considered in another connection on pp. 113–14), and handling the national debt.

Article VI of the Constitution expressly provided that "all debts contracted and engagements entered into, before the adoption of this Constitution, shall be as valid against the United States under this Constitution, as under the Confederation." This provision may too readily be accepted as merely routine by those habituated to fiscal responsibility and contractual fidelity. But when there is a change of basic regimes—and the establishment of the Constitution was nearly such a change—the grave question almost always comes up: Is the new regime responsible for the debts of the old (and usually discredited) regime?[6] But, revealingly, the question never arose in 1787; Americans were already so committed to some sort of commercial society that they accepted the resultant necessity of fulfilling financial obligations and maintaining the national credit. But the method by which to handle the national debt was something else again.

There were two key questions: How to manage the payment of the national debt, and Whether the national government should assume the indebtedness of the states. Hamilton proposed to assume the state debts and to fund the entire indebtedness at face value. This would enrich speculators who had bought 'certificates of indebtedness' at greatly depreciated prices. But in the process, the national guarantee of commercial

---

[6] For example, Aristotle considers the question so characteristic of regime changes that he begins his discussion of regimes with it; see *Politics*, Book III, chs. 1, 3. A recent important example of the problem was the repudiation of Czarist debts by the Soviet government after the 1917 Bolshevik Revolution.

transactions would be aggressively asserted; and a vast quantity of credit and capital would be pumped into the economy in the hands of emboldened men who would multiply its effects in new economic activities. This is a perfect example of Hamilton's basic idea of government aid to the expanding forces of the private economy.

Hamilton's proposals provoked bitter opposition, led by Jefferson[7] and Madison, who broke with Hamilton over this issue. But Hamilton largely carried the day, and his principle of government aids to an expanding capitalist economy was embodied in long-range national policy. The transformation of America from an agricultural to a vigorous capitalist economy was well begun.

In his famous *Report on Manufactures,* Hamilton proposed further means to foster manufacturing and industrial activity. One means—the protective tariff—became the subject of intermittent controversy for nearly a hundred and fifty years. This device of levying a duty on foreign imports was to provide a wall behind which American industry could grow through exploitation of the domestic markets thus secured to them. Such relief from the rigors of open competition, whatever it may have cost the consumers of the country, was often a politically effective device. (It attached powerful special interests to Hamiltonian policies, while the general consumer interest was usually weak and diffuse. For one thing, economic interests that benefitted from a tariff benefitted greatly, and thus had far more motive to become effective pressure groups than consumers generally, who had no natural organizational ties and only a small economic interest in any single tariff.) Tariffs continued in use—the highest in history were enacted around 1930—long after the nation's industries had emerged from the 'infant' state which Hamilton had urged as their principal justification.

Hamiltonianism was advocated in various forms before the Civil War. The major example is Henry Clay's "American system," which proposed "internal improvements" by way of road, canal, and harbor developments at federal expense, coupled with the tariff and other measures directly aimed at aiding business enterprise, especially established enterprise. After the Civil War, the economy expanded enormously, almost entirely in the hands of private business. But there was important encouragement in the Hamiltonian mode. Perhaps the most spectacular was the program of land grants and other aids to railroads, especially in the West. The necessity or temptation to settle the West was a standing invitation to government support of economic activity. Government land policies encouraged rapid settlement; subsidies were granted to stagecoach companies and to the Pony Express, often as payment for postal services. In later years, maritime shipping and airlines sought and received similar subsidies. Other business aids with a Hamiltonian stamp have included loans, tax advantages, and informational and research services.

---

[7] For a fascinating but utterly one-sided account of Hamilton's "phalanx of the Treasury," see Jefferson's "The Anas," in *The People Shall Judge,* I, 395–400.

The Jeffersonian alternative. Jefferson thought that Hamilton's idea of an expanding commercial and industrial economy spurred by a powerful national government doomed America to plutocracy, monarchism, and all the corruptions of the Old World. He proposed instead a kind of democratic agrarian Arcadia because he believed that republican virtue lay in agricultural pursuits and yeomen farmers. Government should encourage agriculture (and commerce as its handmaid), and thus maintain a simple republican society that could be governed under a quite strictly federal (in the old sense) system of limited central powers strictly construed. His policy was a kind of agrarian laissez faire.

A wise and frugal government, [he said in his first Inaugural Address] which shall restrain men from injuring one another, shall leave them otherwise free to regulate their own pursuits of industry and improvement, and shall not take from the mouth of labor the bread it has earned. This is the sum of good government. . . .

Because this national policy was essentially negative, while Hamilton's was strongly positive, the Jeffersonians were almost always on the defensive. They were always trying to undo some Hamiltonian damage. A good example is Andrew Jackson's war against the second Bank of the United States. In the Jeffersonian spirit, the Jacksonians blamed "constitutional impiety, consolidated national power, aristocratic privilege, and plutocratic corruption" on this "bad seed of Hamilton's first Monster."[8]

But there was a tension implicit in Jeffersonianism or between it and the underlying economic forces of the time. The Jeffersonian agrarian simplicities were doomed by the economic forces released by Jeffersonian laissez faire. Allowed to go its own way, American society was being "drawn fatally . . . to the revolutionizing ways of acquisition, emulative consumption, promotion, and speculation."[9] The dilemma was especially clear in Jackson's time; the Jacksonians tried to achieve a Jeffersonian union of "the simple yeoman values with the free pursuit of economic interest, just as the two were splitting hopelessly apart.[10]

Industrialism and Finance at Full Career

The Civil War and its aftermath launched into full career the industrialism and finance that led to the modern economy. One immediate consequence was that Jeffersonian agrarianism was rendered palpably infeasible as an economic alternative. A now irrevocably capitalistic

---

[8] Marvin Meyers, *The Jacksonian Persuasion* (New York: Vintage Books, 1960), p. 11.
[9] *Ibid*, p. 15.
[10] *Idem.*

economy was expanding at an enormous rate[11] under the double thrust of full blast industrialization and exploitation of the western continent. This expansion was almost entirely in the hands of private business, vigorous, often colorful, self-confident, more than a little unscrupulous on occasion—and immensely effective.

Laissez Faire and 'Social Darwinism.' As in England, this was the heyday of laissez faire—unfettered capitalism proceeding by unregulated competition. Leading economists, like those of the Manchester School, argued that the market mechanism, operating in a setting in which the acquisition and use of private property were virtually unlimited by government, would automatically bring about the optimum allocation of resources, optimum level of economic activity, and optimum rate of growth. Further, they argued (e.g., against socialist proposals) that *only* the market mechanism could do so.

For a long time, American public opinion substantially accepted the consequences of such a market economy—its extremes of wealth and poverty, hardship falling on those who for whatever reason fail in the competitive struggle, and much waste, injustice, and privilege—if only the end of economic expansion and wealth-creation was served. One extreme version of this view was 'social Darwinism.' Darwinism as then conceived argued that in nature there is a struggle for survival, and that the 'survival of the fittest' leads to evolutionary progress. This supposed law of nature was applied to society to justify the harsh consequences of laissez faire and to condemn proposals for welfare measures as preserving the unfit.

Hamiltonianism and Jeffersonianism transformed. The industrial transformation of the economy transformed also the way Hamilton's and Jefferson's ideas were used.[12]

Hamilton's idea of government aid to private business, of course, remained congenial to business interests; they used their dangerously great political power to obtain much positive action by government, laissez-faire protestations to the contrary notwithstanding. Similarly, the primacy in the polity that Hamiltonianism assigned to commercial and industrial interests remained wholly congenial; in this spirit business interests opposed limiting the political power of economic groupings and the tactics they can use in their pursuit of productivity and gain.

But these latter-day Hamiltonians were distinctly hostile to one vital Hamiltonian idea, broad interpretation of the national powers. Great industrial and financial corporations were now the established institutions; they now had more to fear from a government that, after all, was con-

---

[11] Despite numerous violent economic crises and fluctuations, the Gross National Product was doubling every decade or so; per capita real income rose from about $240 per year around 1870 to about $550 around 1910, and in the 1890s the United States became the greatest industrial producer in the world.

[12] See especially ch. 7 of Merrill D. Peterson, *The Jefferson Image in the American Mind* (New York: Oxford University Press, 1960), which presents a general account of Jeffersonian 'transformation.'

genitally vulnerable to popular pressures than they had to seek from it. They did not want to have broad national powers constitutionally available for regulating the economy. Accordingly, Hamiltonianism was shorn of the constitutional theory of energetic government that was its hallmark and vital spirit.

Ironically, the surgery on Hamilton was performed with Jeffersonian ideas and rhetoric, but these also had to be truncated in order to serve. Jeffersonianism had to be shorn of its simple agrarian republicanism in order to make it justify an urban industrial capitalism Jefferson would have detested. But thus shorn, Jeffersonian laissez faire, states' rights, and strict construction perfectly suited the purposes of entrenched economic interests, and the restraining spirit of Jeffersonianism could be used for purposes very different from those Jefferson had in mind. For example, strict construction was used to hold unconstitutional many reforms of which the populist side of Jeffersonianism might well have approved.[13] The latter-day Hamiltonians willingly accepted government aid to business and drastic federal intervention on behalf of business in its conflicts with the early labor movement. But they simultaneously used Jeffersonian ideas to oppose government intervention that interfered with profit-making. This included such seemingly reasonable interventions as securing minimum wages and maximum hours for women and children working in industrial plants; assuring that industrial products (even food and drugs) will not be dangerous or fraudulent; setting minimum standards of honesty in selling stocks and bonds and minimum standards of efficiency and fairness in running railroads and other public utilities; in dealing with the nation's natural resources, and in innumerable other matters where the pursuit of private gain has struck across some public interest.

New alternatives. A long time passed before a viable major alternative to latter-day Hamiltonianism[14] really formed. Many ideas were advanced and, especially on the emerging 'left,' it was a time of beginnings and ferment. The South developed political devices, rooted in the Democratic party and Southern representation in the Senate, for protecting its agrarian economy against the industrial North. Protesting farmers in the West and parts of the South, badly squeezed by the railroads, the financial system, and other forces of the new capitalism, pursued the self-help and lobbying Granger movement and populism. Populism had the long-run significance that it was interested in grand new reforms of the economic system, including panaceas such as the free coinage of silver, which was expected to break the supposed grip of the eastern financial

---

[13] See p. 115–16 on dual federalism for one narrow constitutional doctrine characteristic of this period.

[14] For an entirely different Hamiltonianism, see Herbert Croly, *The Promise of American Life* (New York: Capricorn Books, 1964). Written in 1909, Croly's book influenced the Progressive movement and showed how Hamiltonianism could support a quasi-socialist view. This book is an interesting example of how much American politics and rhetoric is conducted within the Hamiltonian-Jeffersonian polarities.

powers. Various grand schemes of social reform, including those of the socialist movement that seemed to be growing rapidly in the early 1900s, were widely debated. The labor movement emerged through various experiments and stormy episodes. Ideas of direct government regulation of business and means to put these ideas into effect began to be developed. In general, the concept of what may be called positive government in the economic sphere crystallized; it began to be argued that government could be used, and should be used, as an instrument whereby society could deliberately and affirmatively act to rearrange the economy and—always crucial—the distribution of its benefits.

Various governmental policies to regulate economic activity or to ameliorate its effects were actually put into effect. State regulation of railroads began in the 1870s and the federal Interstate Commerce Commission was established in 1887 and given some regulatory powers. Some legal control of monopolistic abuses of competition appeared (e.g., the Sherman Antitrust Act of 1890). Progressivism just after the turn of the century and the 'New Freedom' of Woodrow Wilson urged considerable regulation and reform. But by and large, laissez-faire and business-oriented views and policies remained dominant on into the 1920s.

The Modern Economic World

Depression. The modern economic world dawned abruptly in America. The first event was the Great Depression of 1929. The laissez-faire capitalist system seemed to have broken down in America and, indeed, throughout the world. By 1933, in America, the volume of business and the level of the Gross National Product were half what they had been in 1928–1929, and about a third of the labor force was unemployed. Further, the system seemed to show few signs of recovering, either on its own or with the traditional kinds of government aid attempted by the Hoover Administration. A new economic theory came to the fore, associated mainly with the English economist John Maynard Keynes and his extraordinarily influential book, *The General Theory of Employment, Interest and Money*.[15] The older economics had said that a market economy left to itself would recover from depression and move toward full employment and toward expansion and growth. The new economics said, and the evidence of the times seemed to agree, that an economy left to itself could stabilize at much less than full employment and that consumer spending and business investment could simply stagnate at unendurable depression levels.

But the new economics had not just a melancholy diagnosis of the economy, it also had a politically explosive, because profoundly anti-laissez-faire, prescription. The theory argued that it was up to government to pull the economy out of the depression, because during a

---

[15] (New York: Harcourt, Brace and Company, 1936).

depression only government could spend and invest on a scale sufficient to galvanize the economy. This argument gave rise to the 'deficit financing' or 'compensatory spending' policies that made 'Keynesianism' a loaded political term for a generation.

The new economics triumphed and, from the New Deal on, the result was a profound change in policy. The society decided, in effect, that the risks of government inaction were too great and that government must undertake responsibility for the general management of the economy. There is frequent conflict on important details, but this view is now the cornerstone of American policy on economic matters. Public opinion and the national leadership of both political parties have largely accepted it. And it has been written into public law in the declaration of policy and provisions of the Employment Act of 1946.

World war. The second event was World War II. The kinds of controls that had been so controversial during the New Deal suddenly seemed beyond question necessary for conducting the war effort. The economy was fully mobilized and managed under government direction, and with extraordinary effectiveness. The old laissez-faire idea that a developed industrial economy could not be effectively managed by government seemed to be overthrown. The depression had thrust upon government the responsibility for the general performance of the economy; now during the war experience, the national government developed the skills and knowledge necessary for the job. Habituated to a managed economy, by the remarkable economic success of the war years, it seemed natural to many Americans that the government should in peacetime prevent stagnation and lead the economy toward effectiveness and growth.

Postwar reconstruction and the Soviet challenge. The third great event was the task of the postwar reconstruction of Europe and the challenge of Soviet Russia and of Communism. The immediate task of reconstruction was direct American economic aid to help the European nations to survive and, more difficult, to rebuild their own economies. The immediate impact of the Communist challenge was military; it abruptly became necessary to consider the mobilization of the economic, military, and other capacities of the country against a grave threat of politico-military aggression.

But both problems had long-range consequences that shaped the modern economic world and American participation in it. Reconstruction involved living in an increasingly close-knit and interdependent economic world with the very successfully revived European economies. The interdependence results from the sheer magnitude of American economic relations with these economies, and also from the close connection between economic relations and diplomatic purposes. Thus the American economy no longer could go its own way, as it had for decades, in comparative isolation from the other economies of the world, with such relations as there were being regulated by quasi-automatic means or by nongovernmental institutions. The economy is now geared to the

European and to the world economies; and while the free play of private international commerce remains important, government must now actively superintend international economic relations. The government must control economic relations with the European Common Market, manage the dollar on the world market, deal with balance of payment and gold outflow problems, and function in many international organizations, such as the Economic and Social Council of the United Nations and the International Monetary Fund.

The Communist challenge has also become a long-range economic problem. Some economists had long pointed out that Soviet Russia was growing economically at an extraordinary rate. Their alarm had been discounted; indeed some quarters had contended that Russia was not only a stagnant society but one doomed to internal collapse. But Russian space accomplishments and some other economic successes made it ominously clear that these comfortable beliefs were very wrong. Brilliant as has been the postwar performance of the American economy (and of the capitalist or quasi-capitalist western European and Japanese economies), the United States faces in Communism a system that offers competition in the economic sphere.

The fourth great event is only now unfolding. It is the necessity America seems to feel to exercise a substantial degree of world economic leadership, particularly with respect to undeveloped and emergent nations. It is deemed necessary to our own safety and development and, also, partly a duty to the world, that we aid the underdeveloped nations, and that in some measure we influence and guide international economic affairs.

Economic Pressure Groups and the American Political Process

"The most common and durable source of factions," Madison observed, "has been the various and unequal distribution of property." This has certainly been true in America. From that source, Madison continued, greatly varied interests "grow up of necessity in civilized societies." By that measure America stands at the apex of civilization. Perhaps the most distinguishing characteristic of American economy-polity relationships is the proliferation of specialized economic interests and their intense and varied political activity. Property—constitutionally protected, democratized, specialized, aggressively pursued property—generates factions. A free political order allows them access to politics to pursue their interests. Almost inevitably, then, "the regulation of these various and interfering interests forms the principal task of modern legislation and involves the spirit of party and faction in the necessary and ordinary operations of government."[16]

These factions or, in neutral modern terms, these economic interest

---

[16] All quotations in this paragraph are from *Federalist* 10, p. 79.

groups, are intensely affected by public policy. In turn, the number and variety of demands concerning the economy that are urged upon government, and of the groups that urge them, are both extraordinary.

Business, Labor, and Agriculture

Despite this variety, it is customary to emphasize three major groupings—business, labor, and agriculture. This tends to underestimate the importance of many other important groups, such as the various professions, consumers, high-level government employees, state and local government entities (which in a sense function as economic interest groups). But if it is remembered that there are these other groups, and that there are immense differences within the three major categories themselves, then it is reasonable and convenient to use this familiar division of economic groupings.

Business. Business and businessmen have always been concerned with government. Hamiltonianism forged enduring links between the two. The importance of private business in American society has given them a special place. For seven or eight decades after the Civil War, the outlook and activities of business, especially of successful large-scale business, nearly dominated American life. And even now, in the continuous daily work of governing, business stands first in importance among the economic interest groups.

But does business really form a political entity? Is there really a business community such as to produce cohesion and unity in business interest group activities? Many argue that, if the answer is negative, it is at least true that business is the most cohesive of the three major groups. There are intra-business conflicts of interests and many specific interests not widely shared, but there has long been a significant central core of shared interests and opinion.

Business is extensively organized in state and national trade associations on industry lines and into local associations on locality lines (the local Chambers of Commerce, of course, but also groups like the Rotary or Kiwanis, where businessmen usually predominate). These associations form the basis of the two comprehensive nationwide organizations that are the principal spokesmen for business as a whole, the National Association of Manufacturers and the Chamber of Commerce of the United States. Contributing greatly to business's political solidarity is the fact that American business, especially in industry and finance, has some elements of centralization (although much less so than in many European countries) and is influenced by a rather small number of very large firms and by hierarchical corporation structures.

Labor. Labor at first glance presents an even greater picture of unity, since most trade unions are part of the AFL-CIO. Unfortunately for labor's political influence, however, a good deal of the seeming solidarity is limited or illusory.

Modern labor organization dates from the success of the American Federation of Labor in the late nineteenth century. The cautious, conservative, but tough, craft unionism of the A.F. of L. won out over groups like the grandiose and, in some ways, more radical Knights of Labor, and thoroughly subdued socialist forces within the trade unions.

Both in its efforts to organize workers into unions and in its political activity, labor has been handicapped by damaging divisions and rivalries within its ranks. These rivalries often result from conflicting interests among the specialized crafts and industries of the complex American economy; craft union rivalries are a perfect example of the fragmentation of faction envisaged by James Madison (see e.g., p. 79). Labor's influence has also been weakened by recurrent extremist groups, e.g., the semi-anarchist Industrial Workers of the World of the 1910s and 1920s and the troublesome Communist infiltration into some unions and locals, especially when the Congress of Industrial Organizations was growing in the 1930s and 1940s. In general, labor has had difficulty achieving full public respectability and acceptance as a legitimate and responsible part of political life.

But perhaps the greatest handicap has always been the lack of any real belief among American working people that they belong to a 'working class' with strong interests separate from the rest of society. Never more than a quarter of them have joined unions. They do not 'vote labor' in a solid bloc on election day. They do not uniformly and energetically support labor political causes and activities. For example, Ohio Republican Senator Robert A. Taft won reelection in 1950 despite intense union opposition because of the 1947 Taft-Hartley Act that labor had dubbed 'a slave labor act'; voting data showed that union members simply did not vote as expected. There are labor political devotees and diligent volunteer political workers, but there are also many labor Republicans and very many political apathetics.

In the light of all these handicaps, however, labor has a remarkable record of political effectiveness. In alliance with various 'liberal' organizations it has, especially in recent years, offered vigorous and frequently successful competition to politically organized business and other groups whose demands on government it opposes, or competes with, or wants to modify. Much welfare legislation that unions support has been enacted in recent years. Labor is fully entitled to the status customarily given it of second among the great configurations of American political interest groups, even though its power and effect are often overstated.

Agriculture. Agriculture is in many respects the most obscure and puzzling of the big three. Today it is politically represented chiefly by three different organizations. The largest is the American Farm Bureau Federation which began as the association of local groups organized to cooperate with governmental programs of technical aid to farmers. The Federation is also the most active and most closely allied with business, and is in the usual sense the most 'conservative.' The Grange is the oldest, and now least political. Its roots are deep in the traditions of farmers' fraternal and self-help organizations, of the lodge type, and of the solidarities of country life some generations ago. The Farmers' Union is heir to what survived of the agrarian populism of the 1880s and 1890s. Accordingly its politics are the most radical of the three in language, but it stands firm in devotion to the idea of the family farm.

Farmers and farming as an industry are today distinctly a minority activity. Scientific agricultural productivity has increased astoundingly enabling a constantly decreasing fraction of the labor force to supply the agricultural wants of the nation. (The American record here is immensely superior to that of the Communist countries where recalcitrant farmers and agricultural production is a perennial problem.) About one twelfth of the country's population lives on farms, and only a small portion of the national income now comes from farming. Yet agriculture is still exceedingly powerful in politics. Why? One reason is history and tradition; agriculture has always been highly respected in American life, hallowed in the Jeffersonian tradition, and, despite their devotion to economic progress, Americans are a politically nostalgic people. Another is constitutional; farm states have two senators apiece just like the vast industrial states (and rural areas have been somewhat overrepresented in the House). Two others are political. Farm leaders tend to be very adroit political actors. And some of the farm organizations, notably the Farm Bureau, tend to represent large-scale industrialized agriculture (rather than the traditional family farm) and very successfully and effectively to make common cause with the large business interest groups with which they thus share many values.

How Economic Pressure Groups Operate

It has already been emphasized that the convenient classification into the three main categories of business, labor, and agriculture can obscure the actual fragmentation of American economic interests into thousands of organized groups. Business, labor, and agriculture are not economic monoliths; each contains a vital multiplicity of internal differentiations and conflicts. That classification, which oversimplifies the actual economic diversity, also suggests a misleadingly simple picture of the American political process. If government really were dealing mainly with three great, coherent interests, then the political process would likewise tend to be simple and coherent; presumably, a clear-cut, unified political authority would deal unambiguously and directly with the three great economic powers. That is precisely what does *not* happen.

In emphasizing 'economic multiplicity,' we must at the same time emphasize the 'governmental multiplicity' in the American political order. Economic diversity is, so to speak, the reciprocal of the diversity of the American political authorities that deal with economic problems. The two multiplicities reinforce each other. In simpler political systems, where political decisions are made by fewer and more unified decision-making bodies, economic groups must unite in a comparably massive and tight-knit way in order to be politically effective. That is, centralization discourages economic groups from differentiating themselves politically. But American governmental multiplicity has the opposite effect of inducing such fragmentation; economic groups subdivide and seek political influence for narrow economic interest in all the nooks and crannies where political influence is to be found in the American political order. (See pp. 302 ff) for an account of this relationship as it affects the decentralization of American political parties). And, in turn, the diversity of organized economic groups preserves the political multiplicity. The independent centers of political authority preserve their independence, in part, precisely because of the volume of specific economic demands pressed upon them; the economic groups whose well-being they can affect become sources of political strength—money, manpower, and votes.

What is this political multiplicity which is the framework within which economic groups function and polity-economy relationships are conducted? In a word, it is the entire constitutional system; the multiplicity results from the operation of the leading constitutional principles such as federalism, enumeration of powers, separation of powers, and bicameralism.

Federalism, with its concomitant division of powers and responsibilities between nation and states, means that there are differences in the economic affairs and situations that fall within the two purviews. Drawing these boundaries and preserving substantially separate spheres for state and national action continues to be among the great problems of polity-economy relationships and becomes especially difficult in an economy as developed, complex, and closely interrelated as ours.

Economic matters have historically provided major problems for the constitutional doctrine of enumerated powers. The question of how far the enumerated national powers reach has been the framework for an extraordinary volume and variety of public controversy, politicking and lobbying, debate, and action in Congress and the executive, and, of course, for litigation in the courts and the exercise of judicial review. On the whole, the constitutional doctrines applied to the economic problems of federalism are the same as those that we saw in Chapter 4 applied to problems of federalism generally. The national constitutional powers are now interpreted broadly so as to allow them to serve their purpose of acting broadly upon all matters of national scope and concern. And within their sphere, the national powers are plenary and supreme. But the result is to be federal not unitary; and cooperative rather than competitive, or dual federalism. And despite inevitable conflicts and overlaps—in which, for example, some specific business firm engaged in a single activity can be maddeningly and expensively subject to national and state (and local) power—the conflicts and overlaps do usually get worked out, and the system preserves an adequately federal balance.

Quite apart from the question of boundaries—whether drawn to enhance or diminish the national powers—the essential political fact has been the existence of two sets of political authorities engaged in governing the economy. Economic policy is made, and economic groups must lobby and politick, in fifty state governments as well as in Washington, D.C. *State* water policies may have far more economic impact for thousands of farmers than national policy; *state* utilities commissions affect enormous economic interest; *state* licensing policies are crucial for most professions and crafts. Complex and interrelated modern economy notwithstanding, federalism still profoundly decentralizes economic regulation and, accordingly, pressure group activity. And within the states, political-economic relations are further decentralized to the level of county, city, and specialized district. Here are settled innumerable daily questions of zoning, taxation, building inspection, etc., that affect countless business enterprises. And here the distinctive American multiplicity of economic and political units is greatest.

What federalism and local decentralization accomplish as between levels of government, separation of powers (and bicameralism) does at the national level. There is no point in rehearsing here the main points developed earlier. The briefest recapitulation suffices.

By virtue of separation of powers, national authority over the economy is neither vested in a single all-embracing governmental authority, nor is it the exclusive province of any of the three branches. The economy is governed—as is the country in all important matters—by the conflict and cooperation of the three separated branches of government. Thus, when we examine any program of economic regulation, we need to know not only what the statutes say and what Congress thinks, but also what the policies of the White House on its execution are, how the administrative system functions, and what the courts think.

Thus economic policy is made and its execution is influenced in all three branches, in the administrative system where Congress and President contend and cooperate, and in all the interstices of Washington politics. Accordingly, those who make economic demands upon government tend to subdivide, make their demands narrow and precise, and fan out through all the national, state, and local institutions and processes to make themselves more effective.

Government and Programs

The *U.S. Government Organization Manual* requires hundreds of pages to describe, even in very brief and general terms, some of the major agencies and activities by means of which the economy is governed. There is hardly a major agency or program of the national government that does not affect economic matters in some way. Even something as seemingly remote as the American Battle Monuments Commission has its impact on the affairs of certain business- and property-owners, and on occasion is the subject of some lobbying.

In a brief presentation of the major government activities affecting the economy there is a serious problem of categorization. The activities can be categorized by the agencies that administer them; thus, we could simply study what is done by each department, by the Civil Aeronautics Board, the Federal Communications Commission, the Interstate Commerce Commission, and so on. They can also be categorized by the industries they affect, by the ends they seek, by their historical origins, or by any of a number of other principles. Since this book is concerned with government and politics rather than with the substantive content of the activity, the present chapter employs a categorization based on the primary *political function* the activity performs.

These political functions fall under six major headings: government as lawgiver and judge, monetary and fiscal activities, the government's own economic activities, government as protector of the market economy, government as regulator, and the sphere of 'positive government.'

Government as Lawgiver and Judge

Perhaps the most basic function is the oldest and most traditional one, that of lawgiver and judge. Any government affects its economy in innumerable ways by the system of law it provides and the arrangements it supplies for enforcing the system. Law touches property, land-holding, resource utilization, commercial and financial transactions, employment, and all the rest, and touches them everywhere. Thus, in America, the fact that the federal courts are an efficient and modern system of tribunals broadly open to litigation on many business matters undoubtedly has substantial effects on the economy. The U.S. Court of Appeals for the Second Circuit, for example, has long been a most distinguished one, staffed by some of the ablest and most highly respected judges in the country. Its territory embraces the great commercial state of New York, and some economically important parts of New England as well. Under the important 'diversity jurisdiction,' the federal district courts of the circuit are open to a very large portion of the enterprises doing business in the area, and many of these major enterprises operate more vigorously and effectively because of their confidence that should litigation arise their rights would be well protected by law.

Another important aspect of the way the general law affects economic activity is found in the federal income-tax law. One well-known example is the 'depletion allowance.' Under it taxpayers operating oil wells and some other kinds of extractive businesses where the asset is subject to being depleted are allowed very substantial reductions in the amount of federal income tax they would otherwise have to pay. This has greatly stimulated interest in the oil-production industry and the utilization of petroleum resources, and is responsible for a good part of the legendary wealth of Texas. Businesses everywhere make decisions, otherwise economically ludicrous, which become profitable or necessary because of the complications of tax laws.

Monetary and Fiscal Activities

Governments have long known that their monetary and fiscal activities greatly affect an economy. For example, the comparatively stable and reliable coinage system of the Roman empire was one of the principal bases of its success.

The American government has always used fiscal and monetary measures to affect its economy; recall, for example, the great emphasis given the issue of monetary and fiscal policy by Hamilton. As the scale of the government's monetary and fiscal operations has increased, they have become one of the most crucial single factors for the economy.

One standard instance of the effect of monetary and fiscal policy concerns the supply of money. The government can increase the available supply of money by appropriate monetary and fiscal action, such as monetary action by the Federal Reserve System and fiscal action (e.g., deficit spending) by the government generally. In the right circumstances this will tend to have an upward effect on the general level of economic activity. By opposite measures the government and the Federal Reserve, perhaps when they fear a disastrous inflation, can reduce the supply and cause a depressing or restrictive effect.

The two central institutions are the Treasury Department and the Federal Reserve. The Treasury has principal responsibility for fiscal policy, i.e., policy concerning taxes, government spending, and the national debt. The Federal Reserve System (and its presiding agency, the Board of Governors) deals primarily with monetary matters; it is largely independent of the President and Congress both by reason of its statutory design (when it was created in 1913–14 such independence was regarded as highly desirable, to 'keep it out of politics') and by reason of its traditionally close links with the world of banking and finance.

Examples of fiscal policy in action were the general reduction in income taxes in President Kennedy's administration and the reduction in excise taxes in President Johnson's. The income-tax cut was intended to stimulate the economy by reducing the amount of money the government took out of it, thus leaving more for consumers to spend and businesses to invest. The excise-tax cut was intended to have the same general effect and also the specific one of reducing what purchasers had to pay for articles subject to excise taxes (e.g., automobiles) and hence of increasing their tendency to buy. Both tax cuts seemed to serve their purpose well.

An example of monetary policy in action is the Federal Reserve's 'open market operations.' Suppose the Board decides there is danger of a slowdown in economic activity. It buys large quantities of government bonds in the open market, offering attractive prices for them. Banks are large holders of government bonds, and they respond to the attractive prices by selling bonds to 'the Fed.' This increases their 'reserves' (in this case, their accounts with the System). With increased reserves they are permitted by law to make more loans to businesses. Businesses then have more money in their accounts with their banks and, since bank accounts are in effect as much 'money' as dollar bills, the supply of money has been increased. The increase will in turn tend to encourage business to invest and spend more, and hence stimulate the economy.

Monetary devices are effective, but they have limitations. For example, banks may decide not to make more loans, or business may decide not to apply for more despite the increases in reserves, with the result that no stimulating effect takes place. This occurred during the darker days of the Great Depression. Government powers, including these and other regulatory powers, are not omnipotent; in the case of the Depression, fiscal measures such as deficit spending turned out to be more effective than monetary measures. But even they were not completely successful, as the long life of the Depression attests.

The Government's Own Economic Activities

Only rather recently has the importance of the government as a major, direct *participant* in economic activities begun to emerge and to be recognized. Traditionally, government has been conceived as an umpire with respect to the economy, but it has clearly become an economic player as well. This is perhaps most obvious in government's role as over-whelmingly the most important single *customer,* buying goods and serv-ices of almost every conceivable sort and in enormous quantities and from almost every important source of supply. The government is also a *producer* of goods and services on a gigantic scale. Thus, it operates substantial business enterprises itself, especially in manufacturing and transportation. Its Military Air Transport Service has at times been one of the country's largest air transportation undertakings. Through the Ten-nessee Valley Authority (TVA), the government is a major producer of electric power. The postal service is an enormous business enterprise whose services are indispensable to the private economy, and whose decisions (e.g., regarding rates for the mailing of newspapers, periodicals, and advertising matter) vitally affect many industries.

As a participant on such a scale it naturally has influence. Thus, as a customer, the government's procurement policies are among the most important facts in the world for at least a half dozen major industries— for example, aerospace and defense. The government's activities as pro-ducer make it a major employer whose labor policies affect those of private industry, and involve it in a network of relationships with thou-sands of private firms who buy the government's products and who perform as subcontractors for the national government. It should never be forgotten that the national government spends in the neighborhood

THE GOVERNMENT DOLLAR

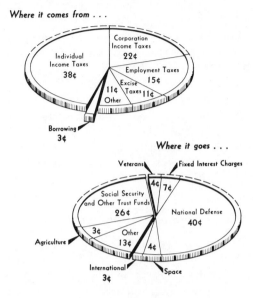

Where it comes from . . .

Individual Income Taxes 38¢

Corporation Income Taxes 22¢

Employment Taxes 15¢

Excise Taxes 11¢

Other 11¢

Borrowing 3¢

Where it goes . . .

Veterans 4¢

Fixed Interest Charges 7¢

Social Security and Other Trust Funds 26¢

National Defense 40¢

Agriculture 3¢

Other 13¢

Space 4¢

International 3¢

Fiscal Year 1966 Estimate

Includes Trust Funds

of a hundred billion dollars a year, and that the Gross National Product runs to a bit more than six hundred billion; government's voice can be proportionately loud.

Besides being a customer and producer, the government is also the *holder of the national domain.* Immense resources belong to it simply as its property—grazing lands, forests, minerals, and more. All the lands west of the thirteen original states once belonged to it, of course. Much of this empire was sold or given away. But much remains. Indeed, in some western states the national government remains the owner of more than half the land area. Over other great economic resources—for example, fisheries and water power—it exercises a general control in the nature of a trusteeship.[17] Government policies concerning these multitudinous re-

---

[17] Its powers in both these instances depend upon its constitutional "admiralty and maritime jurisdiction," which the Supreme Court has in effect held to cover not only all navigable waters but all waters that can be made navigable. The Court, following the constitutional concept that national powers are plenary and Chief Justice Marshall's policy of giving to the national government every facility for making the economy a fully *national* one, has construed other powers similarly broadly to expand national authority in this area.

sources inevitably exercise great influence upon their utilization and hence upon the resource base of the whole economy.

To some extent, all governmental policies affecting the economy have always been made and executed with consciousness of their political significance. One classic example is the way late-nineteenth century Republican administrations granted continental tracts of the public lands of the West—to railroads, land speculators, and, to a lesser extent, homesteaders and colleges—in fashions calculated to generate political support. The use of monetary and fiscal policies for political purposes has become increasingly sophisticated; so too has the use of government's direct participation in the economy. What the government does as a customer, producer, and resource-holder is increasingly the subject of artful use by politicians in Congress and the administration and of ferocious lobbying by interests concerned; it is a major factor on the American economic scene.

Government as Protector of the Market Economy

The American economy is based fundamentally on the system of competition, on the operation of private enterprise in the open market. If the competitive processes are crippled, if the functioning of the market is distorted or rendered impossible, then the whole basis of the system evaporates. Many forces exist in an economy of private capitalism which can, if allowed to operate unchecked, produce this disastrous result.

The general danger is that of any kind of *restrictive practices*. Business firms, understandably anxious to escape the often-painful rigors of free competition, are often tempted to devise with each other various kinds of agreements or customs not to compete.[18] A remarkable example of this came to light a few years ago involving the great firms that manufacture heavy electrical equipment, including some of the most famous and respected names in American industry. Government prosecutors discovered that officials of several companies had engaged in a sweeping and highly effective conspiracy to divide up the market and fix prices. Their pretended 'competitive' bidding for government contracts, for example, was made simply a sham, and government and other purchasers were badly overcharged. These conspirators were punished, but it is hard to make the punishment sufficient to inhibit this very profitable crime, and it is hard to secure satisfactory evidence that such illegal collusion, often extremely informal, is taking place.

Such arrangements are obviously incompatible with the idea of a market economy. Others, smaller in scope or more in the public interest

---

[18] It is natural that, while a man may believe in a competitive system in general, he is not too keen on very much competition with *his* trade or business. The leading theorist of capitalism was perfectly aware of the tendency toward restrictive practices. "People of the same trade seldom meet together, even for merriment and diversion, but the conversation ends in a conspiracy against the public or in some contrivance to raise prices." Adam Smith, quoted in *The People Shall Judge*, I, 378.

in their nature, are not detrimental, and in fact may even be desirable (e.g., the owners of the two pharmacies in a small town agree to alternate in staying open on Sundays). The danger is that dense networks of restrictions can develop, so that the competitive system remains such in appearance only, with the reality quietly strangled by understandings and accommodations among the supposed competitors. The ultimate danger is monopoly, where a single firm or a close-knit combination of firms achieves such dominance that it can exclude its competitors and can charge what it sees fit, thus rendering the market mechanism nugatory.

The problem first became publicly recognized in the 1870s and 1880s with the appearance of the 'trusts.' One of the most famous was the vast Standard Oil combine, which by 1879 controlled about 95 per cent of the oil-refining industry and much else besides. Another was the 'sugar trust,' which in the early 1890s controlled nearly 98 per cent of its industry. Both, and many others, made enormous profits and engaged in some remarkably unscrupulous practices. The trusts and other forms of combination and restrictive agreements over a period of several decades in many instances interfered seriously with the effective operation of the competitive system.

It has long been agreed that the government, as the umpire of a free market economy, should take some measures to preserve competition. A good many have been taken, with varying degrees of effectiveness, using most of the familiar tools of government. Government regulation began with attempts at control by the classic tool of prohibitory statutes, to be enforced in the courts. The first and still most basic of these was the Sherman Act of 1890. It forbade, as to interstate commerce, agreements "in restraint of trade." Further, it forbade "monopolizing" whether by agreement or otherwise. It is enforced by lawsuits in the courts, either by government prosecuting attorneys or by private persons injured by violations of it. Both methods were used against the recent electrical-equipment conspiracy. The Antitrust Division of the Department of Justice conducts a vigorous program of investigation and litigation.

The Act and litigation under it proved only partially adequate to the problem, however, and public policy has gone on to establish extensive programs of control by means of another tool, the administrative agency clothed with broad investigative and regulatory powers. The principal agency in this field, the Federal Trade Commission, was created in 1914. Today many statutes contain provisions forbidding restrictive practices in various specific lines of commerce, and most of the regulatory agencies and programs have responsibilities for acting against such practices.

Government as Regulator

When the government is acting as protector of the market economy, it is, so to speak, standing outside the actual processes of the economy;

Child labor, before the Fair Labor Standards Act of 1938 forbade the employment of children under sixteen.

as umpire its limited role is simply to see to it that the participants abide by the general rules of the game. Over the years the American national government has taken on a considerably more active duty, that of *regulator* of many of the actual processes of the economy in considerable detail.

Laissez-faire economics, from Adam Smith down through the Manchester School, argued that competition—"the obvious and simple system of natural liberty"—was enough by itself to achieve nearly ideal functioning of an economy. However, some exceptions were almost always recognized. One concerned 'natural monopolies,' in which competitive relationships among participating firms could not exist, so that not just umpiring but some government regulation was necessary and proper. There was, of course, always recognition that, to a rather ill-defined extent, force, fraud, and overreaching should be prevented by government authority. There was also a rather hazy and unstable recognition that there was some class of businesses "affected with a public interest" which could appropriately be regulated. And social and humanitarian considerations were allowed to justify some degree of government regulation of such things as industrial dangers, child labor, and impure foods and drugs. But the central reliance was on merely umpiring private competition, not on government regulation.

However, as the record of the grim side of the industrial age which accompanied its productivity piled up, as economic life became increasingly complex, and as specific problems emerged that the system of natural competitive liberty seemed unable to deal with, the exceptions began to be expanded and additional grounds discovered for moving toward policies of regulation. The movement began at least as early as regulation of the railroads by the states in the 1870s and has continued ever since. However, its development has been slow and irregular and marked by periods of retreat. For example, the Supreme Court for most of the period 1890 to 1910 rigorously applied narrow views of the constitutionally permissible scope of regulatory power, both state and federal, and invalidated literally hundreds of regulatory statutes, and the Republican administrations of the 1920s dismantled substantial parts of those regulatory programs that had survived the Court.

The necessities of the Great Depression and of World War II brought regulation into prominence. Although regulation today is vastly less than it was during wartime (e.g., when wages and prices were regulated in considerable detail and many commodities were rationed), it is a prominent part of government activity.

Regulatory agencies and programs are used for all manner of purposes; the *U.S. Government Organization Manual* is full of them, in almost bewildering scope and variety. A few examples illustrate. Some agencies regulate entire industries, and under broad programs of cooperative support and overall direction; e.g., the Civil Aeronautics Board and the commercial air transportation industry. Some regulate specific activities under programs aimed only at preventing specific abuses. For example, the Securities and Exchange Commission regulates the issuance and sale to investors of corporate securities. But its statutory powers authorize it only to insure that all the facts about an issue are available to prospective buyers; it has no power to regulate the quality of the issue (indeed, even to comment on this quality), or to set prices. Some agencies regulate a broad economic area to effectuate a considerable array of public policies concerning it. An example is the Atomic Energy Commission. It is concerned with nearly all aspects of the development and use of atomic energy and, among other things, is authorized to promote research, encourage participation by private business in development and use, license atomic energy production installations for safety, and produce atomic energy itself. The list could be continued almost indefinitely; regulation and regulatory agencies are one of the great tools of modern governing.

"The General Welfare" and Social Justice: Positive Government

The foregoing categories of activities lead up to the one which is perhaps the most rapidly developing today and is certainly the most debated.

Ever since the Great Depression it has been firmly settled in American public policy that the national government must accept the responsibility that such a catastrophe does not happen again. This is given statutory recognition, as we saw in our discussion of the Council of Economic Advisers in Chapter 6, in the Employment Act of 1946. The national government is therefore profoundly involved in the maintenance of general prosperity and health in the economy as a whole, and with fostering growth and development in that economy. In this whole vital area it is in a real sense seeking to carry out the purpose announced in the Constitution's Preamble, to "promote the general welfare."

But general economic prosperity and growth, and a broad concern with the welfare of the nation at large, is only the beginning. Within this framework the government is also engaged in a mass of more specific activities aimed at bettering the conditions of economic life in the nation. These are associated with such phrases as 'social justice,' 'the welfare state,' and 'positive government.'

Today the national government has programs dealing with social security, unemployment pay, labor-management relations, minimum wages and hours, industrial safety, and with many other matters of concern to workers. It also has many programs dealing with support for agriculture and various industries, technical aid, the fostering of economic activity in specific regions, and innumerable other matters of concern to farmers and businessmen. And it has still other programs—for example, support for housing and urban renewal, medical care for the aged, inspection of foods and drugs, research on new economic resources and technologies—that are of economic concern to consumers, to the general public, to everybody. Everywhere in the economic sphere we find today activities by government that intervene in the free play of economic forces, intended to ameliorate what are thought to be injustices and to aid specific groups in their economic position. In many areas government has moved far from its classic negative role of umpire, far even from its role of regulator, into a strongly positive role of promoter and, partly, distributor of the general welfare.

Democratic Capitalism and the Welfare State

'Big government' has grown big through the programs and policies with which Americans have sought to remedy their economic and attendant social problems. Many ardently support these programs and policies and would even increase the pace and scope of governmental responsibility for economic welfare; others, equally ardent, warn that we are thus moving steadily down the road to socialism. Much recent American politics has been fought along these 'liberal' and 'conservative' lines.

Capitalism, Socialism, and Democracy

At the two extremes of this liberal-conservative debate on the extent of 'positive' government are the radical socialists and the proponents of laissez faire. Those who hold these conflicting extreme views join in contending that a democratic political system can survive only when coupled with a particular kind of economy. Each side holds that only its mode of governing the economy can provide the crucial prerequisites for liberty and popular sovereignty.

Many socialists have argued that "whatever the forms of state, political power will, in fact, belong to the owners of economic power."[19] Accordingly, they view democratic capitalism as a sham that conceals a plutocratic reality. They share Anatole France's scorn for a political-legal equality which prohibits poor and rich alike from sleeping in the park on a cold winter's night. True equality and hence true political democracy, they argue, require economic equality. The promise of political democracy cannot be fulfilled unless citizens enjoy an equality of economic means whereby they can actually take advantage of their legal rights and opportunities. Common ownership of the means of production and substantial economic equality are necessary to prevent political privilege from accruing to a private ownership (capitalist) class. Thus is socialism claimed to be a necessary condition for democracy.

Laissez-faire advocates agree that economic power entails political influence. That is precisely why they deem it crucial to separate political and economic power, to minimize this influence. Socialism—state ownership of industry and central economic planning—would combine political and economic power in the same hands, and would inevitably result in tyranny. Laissez-faire capitalism by contrast, they argue, secures liberty by fragmenting and separating economic and political power. Individual freedom to accumulate private property, to contract for goods and services at a free-market determined price, and the least possible government interference with the economy—i.e., 'free enterprise'—is thus said to be the only kind of economic environment within which political democracy can flourish.

The common premise of these otherwise antagonistic views—that political democracy must be coupled with a particular kind of economy— is challenged by many democratic theorists. Democracy, they argue, is simply a *procedure* for settling disputed proposals for governmental action and entails no *substantive* economic content or underpinning.[20] This procedural view of democracy accepts a great variety of economic policies as consistent with political democracy; socialist democracies, laissez-faire democracies, and in-between democracies are all equally legitimate and possible according to this view.

There is more merit in the procedural view of democracy than in the dogmatic assertions of socialism and laissez faire. Unlike the latter two, the procedural view can at least account for some of the most obvious facts of recent history. For example, nineteenth-century America was substantially laissez-faire capitalist and yet (socialist cavilling notwith-

---

[19] Harold J. Laski, *Liberty in the Modern State* (New York: Harper, 1930), p. 8.
[20] "The democratic method is that institutional arrangement for arriving at political decisions in which individuals acquire the power to decide by means of a competitive struggle for the people's vote." Joseph A. Schumpeter, *Capitalism, Socialism, and Democracy* (2nd ed.; New York: Harper & Brothers, 1947), p. 269.

standing) was unquestionably a democratic regime; on the other hand, modern Britain and Scandinavia have gone far in the direction of a socialist economy and yet (conservative lamentations notwithstanding) have manifestly remained democratic.

The proceduralists are right in arguing that democracy is compatible with a far greater range of regulatory and welfare policies than either socialist or laissez-faire dogmatists admit. Neither increases nor decreases in such policies—within limits—necessarily add to or subtract from the democratic character of a regime. But the proceduralists err in making democracy wholly neutral with respect to the economy. *Within limits*: That is the key. It is extremely unlikely that, despite socialist and laissez-faire claims, democracy can long survive either total socialism or total laissez faire. The overwhelming evidence of our time is that democracy, in any recognizable form, has perished under the total socialization of the Communist kind. Equally convincing is the fact that democratic majorities everywhere have rebelled against the harsh inequalities of uncontrolled capitalism and have demanded ameliorative governmental measures. Total socialism destroys democracy and democracy destroys total laissez faire; neither is the suitable economic mate of political democracy.

Modern democracy seems to require a 'mixed economy'—a mixture of capitalism and some policies derived from socialism. In order to be a democracy wherein liberty can flourish, it needs the diversity or pluralism which capitalism contributes[21]; and the capitalist mode of private property creates a citizenry inclined to the free political institutions within which capitalism flourishes. On the other hand, the equalitarian side of democracy and the principles of democratic justice require regulatory and welfare measures of the kind socialists were among the first to propose.

The American Welfare State: A Mixed Economy

Modern America has neither a socialist nor a laissez-faire economy, but a 'mixed economy,' or 'welfare state' as it is often called. The welfare state may perhaps be a form of 'creeping socialism,' as many conservatives charge, but this presumes that the economy will continue to be transformed in a wholly socialist fashion. But in the American economy, as it now stands and seems likely to remain, private ownership remains dominant, and goods and services are mainly produced and distributed in a significantly competitive market. The essential qualities of capitalism

---

[21] Those who argue that democracy is economically neutral usually subscribe at the same time to the theory that democracy (or at least a free or liberal democracy) needs 'social pluralism.' The underlying argument is that in a plural society each of its many groups will recognize that the security of its own liberty requires a system of liberty for all. But procedural theorists necessarily fail to acknowledge the extent to which capitalism is a vital source of the diversity upon which the theory of pluralism relies. It should be noted in passing that questions about the economic or social 'prerequisites' of democracy are really questions about the prerequisites of *liberty* in a democracy.

have proved far more compatible with the massive increases in regulatory and welfare programs than most observers believed possible. The spirit of American life remains vigorously capitalistic. Those who glumly predict capitalism's imminent demise do not adequately appreciate the vitality of the economic principle they cherish.

Not only have capitalist economics been substantially preserved under the welfare state, but capitalism has continued to be a source of political freedom. It makes its contribution to freedom of speech, press, and association, and to competitive elections, as much as ever. And the decentralized political institutions and processes, so valuable to liberty and so intimately connected with capitalism, have also been substantially preserved.

The continuing economic and political successes of capitalism have confounded not only its laissez-faire partisans; even more, these successes have confounded capitalism's socialist critics. Increasing impoverishment of the proletariat, elimination of the middle class, continual and worsening economic crisis, intensified class antagonisms—all of which Karl Marx had prophesied would lead to proletarian revolution and socialism—have simply not occurred. American political democracy proved much more than the sham that Marxists believed it to be. Under the pressure of democratic majorities, new economic theories and tools have been devised that have enabled the government to modify the economy in a far more equalitarian way than capitalism's critics believed possible. A mixed economy has been emerging to the consternation of the purist ideologists of socialism and laissez-faire alike.

A major question regarding the future of the mixed economy is whether it will stay mixed or whether it will indeed creep to a socialist or some other kind of bureaucratized and stifling conclusion. To argue that great increases in regulatory and welfare measures have *thus far* preserved the valuable features of capitalism is *not* thereby to approve of every existing or future measure.

Some programs are wasteful, fail even to achieve their objective, do things private enterprises could better perform, kill incentive and initiative, harass business, increase bureaucracy, and stifle freedom and economic energy. But simple ideological answers will not suffice; each measure will have to be judged on its individual merits. It is a task of American statesmanship pragmatically to maintain a balance among the capitalist and welfarist elements of the emerging mixed economy.

Outstanding reasons for American eclecticism in choosing a middle way to govern the economy include: (1) the profound attachment of American public opinion to the basic ideas of capitalism; (2) the American constitutional-democratic political system which tends to require moderate policies in forming the majority coalitions needed to win political power; (3) American pragmatism—the tendency to reject grandiose blueprints in favor of piecemeal solutions. Partly by commitment, partly by design, and partly by temperament—Americans have confronted their economic problems with a combination of economic policies and programs adding up over time into the modern welfare state.

Prognosis

Social security, fair labor standards, fiscal regulation and many other reforms—all have contributed to social and economic welfare. The desperate problems of the 1930s are substantially controlled, if not fully solved. Not surprisingly, however, continuing problems are exposed, old reforms develop flaws, and new reforms are demanded as each generation applies itself to the effort to harness governmental power to political interests and ideals, and as new conditions engender new problems.

Automation is a new version of the problems caused by technological advances outmoding preexisting occupations. In the long run these changes may well prove economically wise, but dislocated workers suffer severely in the short run. It is argued that the costs of retraining those affected should be borne socially since the benefits redound to the good of the entire society. As fully automatic factories increase in number this problem will become intensified; the problem of the leisured masses may be on mankind's agenda for the first time in history.

The technological revolution—space exploration as well as automation —places enormous strain on educational institutions. Our efforts to overtake the Russians, since the shock of the first sputniks, have emphasized the need for scientists, mathematicians, and engineers in far greater quantity and quality than produced in the past. Federal aid to education has increased somewhat over recent years, but we have yet to invest national resources in public education on a scale commensurate with this problem. Meanwhile, concern for locally controlled education as a prime value of American society balances the pressure for centralizing further the distribution of governmental power within the welfare state.

The transformation of America into an urban-dwelling people has raised to urgent proportions such problems as water and air pollution, slums, crime, and a multitude of social problems. Consequent pressure has prompted an urban affairs post in the President's cabinet and the expansion of urban renewal and other metropolitan area programs.

Labor-management relations are remarkably different from the time when union organizations were illicit conspiracies under the common law. But problems continue over compulsory union membership, racketeer-run unions, lack of internal democracy in the government of unions, and the general apathy of many union members for whom union dues are merely one more payroll tax and membership more an imposition than a valued economic and political interest-group affiliation. The right to organize public employees, and to bargain collectively with government on behalf of a growing portion of the total work force poses additional problems for the future of industrial and labor relations.

Another important problem is a continuing form of the age-old affliction of poverty. The form it takes in the midst of American affluence involves relatively few people, and even these underprivileged have a much higher standard of living than the poor of other lands. This is acknowledged even as the charge is leveled that poverty is a continuing feature of the American welfare state.

> To be sure, the other America *is not impoverished* in the same sense as those poor nations where millions cling to hunger as a defense against starvation. This country has escaped such extremes. That does not change the fact that tens of millions of Americans are, at this very moment, maimed in body and spirit, existing at levels beneath those necessary for human decency. If these people are not starving, they are hungry, and *sometimes fat with hunger, for that is what cheap foods do.* They are without adequate housing and education and medical care.[22]

That Americans do not view their accomplishments complacently is revealed in the current governmental 'war on poverty.' Yet, a reasonable degree of satisfaction is nonetheless appropriate. Political power as organized under American constitutional-democratic forms has impressively tamed economic power. The remarkable record of the past thirty years is that American government has greatly reduced the discrepancy between rich and poor, regulated the pendular arc of the business cycle, reduced plutocratic political privilege, and generally civilized our economic life.

BIBLIOGRAPHICAL NOTE

One of the great sources of facts on the history of the American economy is U.S. Bureau of the Census, *Historical Statistics of the United States: Colonial Times to 1957* (Washington: Government Printing Office, 1960). A comprehensive nine-volume series of books on the principal periods in American economic history is published by Holt, Rinehart and Winston. The volumes for the periods since 1815 are Paul W. Gates, *The Farmer's Age: Agriculture, 1815–1860* (1960); George R. Taylor, *The Transportation Revolution, 1815–1860* (1951); Edward C. Kirkland, *Industry Comes of Age: Business, Labor, and Public Policy, 1860–1917* (1961); Fred A. Shannon, *The Farmer's Last Frontier: Agriculture, 1860–1917* (1945; Harold U. Faulkner, *The Decline of Laissez Faire, 1897–1917* (1951); George Soule, *Prosperity Decade: From War to Depression, 1917–1929* (1947); and Broadus Mitchell, *Depression Decade* (1947).

On many aspects of polity-economy relationships the *Encyclopedia of Social Sciences* contains articles that remain valuable. There are numerous general textbooks on economics. Two standard ones, both published in current editions, are George Leland Bach, *Economics: An Introduction to Analysis and*

---

[22] Michael Harrington, *The Other America* (New York: Macmillan, 1962), p.1–2 emphasis added.

Policy (1963), and Paul A. Samuelson, *Economics: An Introductory Analysis* (1964).

Two histories of economic thought are Erich Roll, *A History of Economic Thought* (rev. and enl. ed., 1950), and Leo Rogin, *The Meaning and Validity of Economic Theory: A Historical Approach* (1956).

A text on government regulation is Merle Fainsod, Lincoln Gordon, and Joseph C. Palamountain, Jr., *Government and the American Economy* (3rd ed., 1959). One by a political scientist is Emmette S. Redford, *American Government and the Economy* (1965). One by an economist is Clair Wilcox, *Public Policies Toward Business* (1955). Extensive suggestions for further reading on many specific subjects may be found in these volumes.

Among books dealing with contemporary controversy over polity-economy relationships, see Friedrich A. Hayek, *The Road to Serfdom* (1944); Barbara Wootton, *Freedom Under Planning* (1945); Ludwig von Mises, *Human Action* (1949); John Kenneth Galbraith, *American Capitalism: The Concept of Countervailing Power* (1952); Robert A. Dahl and Charles E. Lindblom, *Politics, Economics, and Welfare* (1953); Harold W. Chase and Paul Dolan, *The Case for Democratic Capitalism* (1964).

Chapter 15

The Conduct of Foreign Affairs

THE VERY WORD *FOREIGN*—FROM THE LATIN *FORANUS*, MEANING OUTSIDE THE doors—suggests the basic difference between foreign affairs and domestic politics. Politics normally concerns the questions: What ought *we* to do? What kind of country shall *we* be? Conflicting opinions arise and men seek to impose upon each other, through the accepted authority of government, policies for the whole polity. Politics thus concerns primarily the quality of life *within* the polity—so to speak, within the city walls. Foreign affairs, on the contrary, deal with all the other polities outside the city walls—not with how things shall be among us, but with how things shall be between *us* and all of *them*. This is the basic fact that makes the affairs *foreign*. Politics in the ordinary sense are the relations among citizens; foreign affairs concern the relations between one political community and all others.

The Relations among Nations

There is no common authority over nations in the way there is government over fellow citizens. A government or regime requires underlying common principles regarding the kind of life to be lived under that government. Countries differ over these underlying principles and thus live different ways of life under separate governments. Thus the primal fact of international relations is the relative absence of the unifying and moderating forces that make a country a political community.

The relations among nations tend easily to conflict. While all politics involves conflict, domestic partisanship is normally moderated by ultimate common interest; the conflicting partisans are of one political community, drawn together by their mutual separation from all others. In addition to the underlying sense of community, the tradition and force of government tend to produce habitual compliance. Few such institutions moderate conflict among nations.

The stakes are greater in international relations. Shame, servitude, and extinction are more normally the outcomes of foreign than of domestic affairs. (Domestic revolutionary crisis is, of course, the exception that proves the rule; during revolutionary crisis the political community has disintegrated.) Defeat in war or failure to secure vital national objectives ordinarily has more terrible consequences than the outcome of domestic political contest. To state it simply: Failure in the conduct of foreign affairs today can mean either succumbing to Communist tyranny or nuclear holocaust.

Conflict among nations tends to be ruthless. Considerations of justice and morality are fragile enough in conflict between citizens within the political community. They tend to be even more readily sacrificed in conflict among nations. In defense of the national interest men are taught to do what would be regarded as abominable if done within their country. Lying, espionage, subversion, and massive violence are readily accepted as necessities of the conduct of foreign affairs and the national defense. The extent of this tension between the demands of justice and the needs of the national interest has always troubled statesmen and scholars, and is a distinguishing feature of the conduct of foreign affairs.

Transnational Factors

To this point, cleavage and conflict in international relations have been emphasized. But this is not to suggest that men live only within their city walls, that no interests and forces draw them together amicably across national boundaries, or that justice is irrelevant to international relations. Certainly there is cooperation as well as conflict.

Common interests lead nations to form alliances. 'My enemy's enemy is my friend' is an ancient principle that leads nation *A* to join *B* against *C*; France, for example, long sought eastern European alliances against Germany. Regional interests can draw nations together for specific purposes; Canadian-American amicable sharing of the St. Lawrence River is an outstanding example. But rivers are sources of regional contention as well as of cooperation. Despite the fact that the Jordan River could thus be used more efficiently, the Arab nations have refused joint control with Israel, and the river has been another source of Middle Eastern controversy.

Nations share many practical interests, and public and private international organizations have been formed to superintend them. A familiar example is the Universal Postal Union (founded in 1874 and now a specialized agency within the United Nations system) which establishes international postal procedures and standards. Similarly, by universal custom the ships and planes of all nations carry a red light on the port side and a green light on the starboard; no nation has an interest in zigging when everybody else is zagging.

Beyond such routine interests, more powerful interests draw men together. Commerce, industry, and finance are more international today than ever before. International business creates innumerable links from which transnational interests develop. The men who share these interests strive within their own countries for advantageous foreign policies. Religion has often powerfully transcended the political community. Moslems of any tribe or nation have had some sense of community with all other Moslems, Roman Catholics of diverse nationality consider themselves members of a universal church, and Jews have some sense of kinship with Jews in other countries and in Israel.

Obligations of brotherhood or of justice obtain among human beings no matter what the relations of nations are. These obligations are often expressed in individual and governmental acts of generosity. Especially in modern times (with America leading the way), the people of one country offer food and medicine to another people during time of natural disaster or to distressed nations after a war. More enduringly, principles and practices of international law have developed over centuries (albeit often violated during crisis) to institutionalize the obligations among nations. And at a still grander level, there have always been visions of a time when the political separation of men would end, when interhuman relations would supplant international relations. Pacifists, socialists, world federalists, each in different ways, today seek to create that kind of world community. And it is no vision to affirm that there is a universal human interest in survival when modern weaponry seriously places that question on the agenda.

In short, the 'we' of each country is by no means a monolithic body unaffected by transnational forces. Indeed most of the forces which can unite men within a political community can also be sources of community beyond the city walls. There are we Catholics, we scientists, we financiers, we socialists, we artists; but important as these bonds are, they have been and are inferior in strength to the we of the political community. The most common and durable community has been the political community, be it city-state, feudal kingdom, or nation. It is this primacy of the political community which gives to the conduct of foreign affairs its distinctively harsh character.

Requirements of Foreign Affairs

Governments conduct foreign affairs so as to secure the well-being or advantage of their respective countries. The most fundamental fact is that these national interests clash—and in practically limitless ways. Burgeoning population, economic rivalry, desire to dominate a strategic territory or waterway, the need for food or other economic resources, or sheer imperialistic exuberance, are only some familiar examples. It is apparently the irresistible impulse or need of countries to expand their trade, their religion, their beliefs, or simply to extend their might over the land. The successful conduct of foreign affairs amid such complexity, intensity, and fatefulness of conflict places immense strains upon any political system. In the American system, where the aim is to achieve a free and competent government upon the basis of democracy, the strain is perhaps especially acute. War and diplomacy make secrecy necessary; for example, tactics of bluff or 'brinkmanship' may necessitate 'managing the news,' that is, deliberately deceiving the domestic press so as to deceive the foreign opponent. The full disclosure of facts, indispensable to intelligent democratic discussion, can be fatal in time of international crisis. Further, the need to summon up the national resources and unity challenges the complicated system of American government. War and diplomacy require speed of decision and execution, and speed is no friend of due process or of liberties in general. And the stuff of foreign affairs demands knowledge and instincts that a democratic citizenry cannot possess so well as they can in domestic affairs. These inescapable necessities of war and diplomacy are bad enough; worse still are the dangerously persuasive arguments they offer to those who wish to subvert liberty or democracy under cover of the national interest.

It is a terrible question whether a political system compoundly federal and national, which stresses individual liberties and which relies greatly upon the opinions of majorities, can muster the special competences necessary to the skillful conduct of foreign affairs. Always relevant, this question now has a special urgency when the stakes are greater and more precariously wagered than ever before. What the United States does with its immense power now involves not only its own freedom and survival but perhaps that of the whole world as well.

Having considered some fundamental aspects of the relations among all nations, this chapter turns next to some persistent themes in American involvement in international relations, after which it will consider the world situation today—the Cold War, the framework within which foreign affairs have been conducted for a generation; the strain upon constitutionalism which arises from the conduct of foreign affairs in such a context; and the politics and administration of diplomacy and defense. The chapter will conclude by considering a few of the gravest and most revealing contemporary international problems.

The American Posture in World Affairs

Countries frequently have characteristic postures in foreign affairs—a compound of basic and enduring objectives, policies, and techniques. This characteristic posture is the product of many things, and it persists or changes as the things that cause it persist or change. A country's physical situation and internal resources profoundly influence its economic and military needs and possibilities. Insular England, for example, long inclined to emphasize naval power. Switzerland's mountainous isolation made reasonable her traditional policy of neutrality. Countries whose well-being depends upon some port or land route make control of that port or route a dominant objective. Religion may persistently incline a country to crusades and struggles which its situation might not otherwise recommend. Ideology may grip a country in the same way, as is so visibly the Communist case. Also a country's political system and domestic politics influence the style and substance of its conduct of foreign affairs.

The 'American Mission'

Considerations of power and interest enter the foreign policy of all nations. Indeed, nations often pursue their interest to the limit of their power with little attempt to justify what they are doing. More often, perhaps, nations believe or pretend to believe that their national interest coincides with some transcendent purpose, with the justifiable cause of a civilization, a race, a religion, or a political system. Of no nation—with the possible exception of the Soviet Union—has this been more true than of the United States. The unusual persistence, emphasis upon, and specific content of the American version of transcendent purpose make the 'American Mission' a distinguishing feature of American conduct of foreign affairs.

The Founding Fathers' general sense of novelty and universal purpose carried over into the realm of foreign policy. The entire founding generation probably shared the view expressed by Washington in his First Inaugural Address:

> The preservation of the sacred fire of liberty and the destiny of the republican model of government are justly considered as deeply, perhaps as finally staked, on the experiment entrusted to the hands of the American people.

Republican government was not, he suggested, exclusively for the benefit of Americans; they were responsible for it to all mankind. This notion that American government was uniquely significant for the entire world deeply influenced the American posture in foreign affairs. From the very outset, American foreign policy was rationalized, discussed, formulated, and administered, not alone with regard to what would profit and secure the nation, but also with an eye to the American Mission—the responsibility somehow to advance the cause of republicanism everywhere.

Coincidence of National Interest and Mission: The First 50 Years

The physical situation and national interests of the United States long coincided with the concept of mission, and this coincidence strengthened the distinctive American habit of approaching foreign affairs with the twin considerations of national interest and universal purpose. But from 1776 to the 1820s, America was hardly in a position actively to carry any mission to the world. Her own survival was in question. Europe was where danger lay, and successful policy required agile manipulation of conflicting European interests in order to fend them off. American independence depended in the first place on the fact that France, for her own purposes, wanted to weaken England. Later the Napoleonic Wars continued the drain upon English power and absorbed other European military energies that might have threatened the new nation. It is within this context that Washington's famous Farewell Address is to be understood. It was American policy to avoid any permanent entanglement in European affairs because such entanglement would give European powers excuse or opportunity to intervene in America. But all this did not mean 'isolationism' or inactivity in foreign affairs. On the contrary, all the Presidents of this period were men experienced in foreign affairs, and their administrations were marked by frequent conflicts over foreign policy. The national interest dictated three fundamental objectives. First, by means of temporary agreements and a flexible diplomacy, every effort was made to prevent the emergence of any European power likely to harass America. Second, policies were pursued, e.g., freedom of world commerce and navigation, that furthered America's aim of self-development. Third, the energetic expansion into the American continent continued unabated.

What normal national interest considerations dictated—noninvolvement in Europe's broils—was paralleled by reasoning about the republican mission. America's unique and isolated republic, many believed, could maintain an uniquely just foreign policy. The argument ran as follows: Because America was republican she ought not engage in the kind of wars Europe's rival monarchies waged; such nations pursued glory and domination, while America could peacefully pursue republican happiness. Remote from all others, America could be above the battle. She could negotiate and trade impartially with all others and be neutral in their quarrels, and thereby maintain herself intact as an example of republicanism for others to follow.

But the republican element in American foreign policy could be said to imply more than neutrality. Many argued that America was obliged to befriend actively the cause of republicanism everywhere, to give diplomatic and military aid to republican revolutionaries. The idea of the positive republican mission inevitably conflicted with a policy of republican neutrality. The issue of neutrality versus involvement on behalf of republicanism marked many quarrels over American foreign policy. Indeed an intense conflict arose immediately over whether America ought to support the French Revolution against its enemies. The decision was for neutrality, but the appeal of the French revolutionaries was only the first in a long series of such appeals to American humanitarian and republican instincts. The modern idea that America has special responsibility to the cause of freedom thus has deep roots.

The idea of the American Mission has, of course, often been used for purposes of self-glorification and hypocritical justification of what was manifestly being done for national advantage or the gain of some particular interest group. But it is equally true that the sense of mission has sometimes led America to actions not dictated by normal considerations of private or national interest. It would be naive folly to pay attention only to the noble words in which American foreign policy is typically conducted and not to recognize when there are underlying elements of power and profit. But it would be cynical folly not to appreciate the importance of the concept of mission in the basic American posture toward foreign affairs.

The Ninteenth Century: Hemisphere and Continent

The Monroe Doctrine (originally a policy announced by President Monroe in his annual message to Congress in 1823) marked a departure in American foreign policy. It asserted in effect that, with survival now assured, new and broader horizons must be considered regarding both the national interest and the national mission. The blend of interest and ideals is perfectly exemplified in the Monroe Doctrine.

The primary national interest of the previous half-century had been to avert European intervention in the United States or along its borders. Now there was an opportunity to extend the range of American policy to the whole of the Western Hemisphere. Revolution had weakened Spanish power in South America, but the European powers (the Holy Alliance, Quadruple Alliance, and the other combinations of anti-republican European monarchies) threatened to reestablish Spain (or themselves) in the Western Hemisphere. Monroe dramatically proclaimed that the United States would regard any such attempt "as dangerous to our peace and safety"; war against South America would be treated as war against the United States herself. Henceforward, no European power was to be permitted new military bases in the new world.

This was a particularly ambitious and shrewd piece of work, since America did not then have even remotely the power to exclude Europe. The Doctrine tacitly relied upon the British navy (Britain had her own imperial reasons for opposing other European ambitions in South America), but without paying the price of the formal entangling alliance that Britain wanted. But the Doctrine was not entirely a matter of power and national interest. Republican idealism also suggested the doctrine. American public opinion was on the side of the new South American republics. The aged Jefferson expressed the common sentiment: While Europe is "the domicile of despotism, our endeavor should be to make our hemisphere that of freedom."[1] *Our* hemisphere, but a *free* one—exactly the blend of national interest and mission. But public opinion divided over how to make the hemisphere free—by missionary activism or by a form of neutrality. Henry Clay favored active assistance to all the Latin-

---

[1] Letter to James Monroe, October 24, 1813, printed in *The People Shall Judge*, I, 508.

American revolutionaries. But Secretary of State John Quincy Adams' formulation of the Monroe Doctrine preserved the policy of neutrality. It pledged to repel new European intervention in the hemisphere (while leaving existing colonies alone), and in return promised that the United States would stay out of European affairs. But even in the guise of neutrality, the Doctrine was expected to advance the cause of republicanism. President Monroe emphasized that his doctrine permanently excluded not only European military power but also the monarchical "political system" from the Western Hemisphere. The idea was deeply reinforced that those who aspired to the blessings of republican liberty had some kind of special claim upon the American people, especially in our hemisphere.

Although the Monroe Doctrine proclaimed an enlargement of America's horizon in foreign affairs, American involvement in foreign affairs subsequently diminished. Throughout the nineteenth century, there were few major European military threats within the Western Hemisphere. British manipulation of the European balance of power contributed to American security. America was able aggressively to turn her energies to continental expansion. The shrewd and flexible diplomacy of the first half-century hardened into dogma and habit. America began luxuriously to consider herself forever detached and distant from the ordinary vicissitudes of foreign statecraft.

America as a World Power

At the close of the nineteenth century, America—in both national interest and mission—began to turn outward again, and in new ways. American energies were no longer totally absorbed in the great tasks of continental expansion. And above all, the world situation had changed; new directions were opening in foreign affairs.

Britain's dominance was coming to an end. Germany, Japan, and the United States herself were emerging as new world powers. There was a great scramble for colonies, markets, and spheres of influence. Americans began to invest hundreds of millions of dollars abroad; investors demanded protection and America moved vigorously into 'dollar diplomacy.' Dozens of interests—oil, shipping, fruit (in the well-named 'banana republics')—pressed for and often got favorable foreign policies and Marine protection.

As military technology enlarged the reach of all the great powers, the old bases of American national security were no longer adequate. Security required an enlargement of military and diplomatic power. Moreover, leading Americans like Theodore Roosevelt and Henry Cabot Lodge shared the late-nineteenth-century European sense that the western powers were entitled to dominate the world, and they had a taste for glory and the exercise of power.

A Senate debate after the Spanish-American War shows how the characteristic blend of national interest and missionary considerations persisted as America began its career as a world power. Successfully defending the imperialistic annexation of the Philippines and the crushing of the native revolt, Senator Albert Beveridge claimed that it was America's duty to become "the arbiter, under God, of the destinies of mankind. . . . He has marked the American people as His chosen nation to finally lead the regeneration of the world. This is the divine mission of America."[2] Arguing against annexation, William Jennings Bryan drew very different implications from the American mission. We have a "grander destiny," he argued, than to employ the ordinary means of statecraft and imperialistic expansion. "American civilization will, by the influence of example, excite in other races a desire for self-government."[3] As America began to extend the range of its foreign policies far beyond the Western Hemisphere and more aggressively into it, every new issue was marked by variations of the Beveridge-Bryan conflict: Should America increasingly involve itself in world affairs and expand its power (imperialistically or otherwise), or should it preserve itself intact and withdrawn, an honorable example of republican government?

The question arose sharply over America's entry into both world wars. Most Americans initially regarded World War I as a shocking example of precisely those European 'broils' to be avoided. Woodrow Wilson was reelected in 1916 on the slogan, 'He kept us out of war.' But Wilson and other leaders came increasingly to fear that Germany would emerge as a dangerously dominant European power. Yet, from the point of view of national interest alone, there was no irresistible necessity for America's involvement when she entered the war. In the welter of conflicting arguments and ethnic and business pressures, the American sense of mission probably tipped the scales. Increasingly, Germany came to seem the embodiment of overweening autocracy and the Western Allies increasingly the champions of democracy. German U-boat warfare and the 'Zimmerman note' finally turned public opinion overwhelmingly against Germany and, under the missionary slogans, 'Making the world safe for democracy' and 'A war to end all wars,' America embarked on her crusade.

After the war, Americans were disillusioned to learn that the victorious Allies were not what wartime propaganda had made them out to be, but, rather, were pursuing traditional national interests. Disillusionment dominated the literature and intellectual life of the next decades in America (and Europe as well). America concluded that it had just proven to itself at bitter cost how wise was Washington's injunction to avoid entanglements in European affairs. One important outcome was that, after a dramatic and complicated political struggle, the treaty that would have made America a member of the League of Nations failed to secure the necessary two-thirds vote of the Senate.

[2] *The People Shall Judge,* II, 301–2.
[3] *Ibid.,* p. 305.

But it was impossible for America, now genuinely a world power in fact as well as aspiration, to withdraw entirely from world affairs. The dominant effort of the 1920s was to seek an explicitly formulated balance of power. For example, under American stimulation, the great nations in a series of treaties committed themselves to maintain the ratio of existing naval strength, a ratio which it was hoped would make it unprofitable for any country to start a war.

But the parchment provisions proved entirely inadequate. Such treaties rested upon the assumption that the great powers could be frozen into a balance of power. But five nations were growing in power and ambition at a rate that shattered the balance—the United States, Russia, Italy, Japan, and Germany—especially the last two. The 1930s were dominated by the triumphs of Fascism, Naziism and Japanese militarism, by the Berlin-Rome Axis (and then by the German-Italian-Japanese Anti-Comintern Pact). American opinion divided along the familiar lines—to use the pre-World War II terms—of isolationism and interventionism. Policies of neutrality and isolationism initially predominated, but the World War I pattern repeated itself. The Stalin-Hitler Pact, the staggering Nazi conquests in Europe, and the enormous appeal of Churchill-led Britain rapidly swung American opinion overwhelmingly against the Axis powers. And this time American ideals and interests were indeed profoundly jeopardized. America became, first, the 'arsenal of democracy,' and then the dominant military power in the war. From that moment America's involvement in world affairs was profoundly transformed. America became inescapably a 'superpower' at the center of world affairs.

The Contemporary Framework: The Cold War

In any given generation, there is a constellation in world affairs, a pattern of forces, aspirations, and ambitions within which the problems of that generation arise. The Cold War—the apt phrase created by common-sense language—has been for this generation that great constellation. World affairs and American foreign policy have revolved around the central fact of the Cold War: the profound conflict between the two superpowers, America and Russia. But frameworks modify or change. And the uncertain shape of the future already shows itself in possible changes within Russia, and in the emergence of Communist China as a world power, bitterly hostile to the United States and—to an extent impossible as yet to determine—in conflict with Russia as well.

Development of the Cold War

Franklin Roosevelt's genius had brought America into full opposition to Nazi Germany and Japan, and he had superbly summoned up the immense energies of America into a bold conduct of the war. But he miscalculated the peace. Roosevelt and the American military, like other

American leaders before them, neglected to conduct war with a sufficient consideration of its political aftermath. The most efficient military means to achieve unconditional surrender of the enemy was the overriding objective; political opportunities of the kind Churchill recommended to limit Russia's influence in Europe were neglected. An outstanding example was General Eisenhower's decision on purely military grounds not to take Berlin with British or American troops but rather to leave its capture to the Russians.

In general, Roosevelt was too confident of his personal ability to deal with Stalin after the military victory and of the ability of the United Nations to achieve world order.

> [But] the history of the next few years was to show that a Communist Russia had become the heir of Nazi Germany in Central and Eastern Europe; . . . that the Western democracies, for all their sacrifices, had succeeded in rolling back the tide of totalitarianism only from the Rhine to the Elbe. The struggle for Europe was not yet over; it had merely entered a new phase with a new protagonist, more dangerous perhaps than the old because less reckless and more calculating.[4]

Even before the end of the war, Stalin's Communist and Russian imperialist aims had become clear. Betraying pledges made at the 1945 Yalta Conference, he liquidated the Polish non-Communist underground leaders and began to establish a Communist satellite Poland. The Russians began to detach and communize their zone of occupied Germany. It became perfectly clear that Stalin intended to further Communist ideological and Russian imperial designs. He reiterated the Leninist view that wars were inevitable so long as capitalism persisted, thereby making clear that no diplomatic plans for world order could hope for serious Russian acceptance. The international organization of Communist parties embarked upon militant campaigns to seize power in the prostrate European countries.

Russia's legitimate national interests—e.g., her need to be influential in eastern and central Europe and thus prevent renewed danger from Germany—would have led to some conflict with the interests of her former allies. But such conflict might well have been negotiable and on a limited scale. In any event, when aggressive Russian imperial expansionism linked with ideological world Communism was added to these national interests, conflict began to achieve the full dimensions of the Cold War.

As early as 1946 there was a confrontation over Iran. Although British troops withdrew according to a wartime agreement, the Russians refused to withdraw theirs and, instead, set up a separatist puppet Communist government in the Iranian province of Azerbaijan. President Truman and the British government threatened military reprisal, and the Russians withdrew. In 1947 Communist-inspired civil war was raging in Greece;

---

[4] Chester Wilmot, *The Struggle for Europe* (New York: Harper Colophon Books; 1963), p. 708.

simultaneously Stalin was demanding naval bases and the cession of a large land area from Turkey. Again, Truman responded firmly. In a speech to Congress, he laid out a program (which came to be called the Truman Doctrine) of economic and military aid to the two endangered countries. Again, the stiff policy prevailed. Immensely aided by the quarrel between Yugoslavia's Tito and Stalin (Tito had been a main source of arms for the Greek Communist insurrectionaries), the Greeks were able to defeat the Communists and form a relatively stable government, and Stalin backed down from his threats to Turkey.

Two basic elements of American policy for the next decade were foreshadowed in the Truman Doctrine—the Marshall Plan and 'containment.' That is, on the one hand, economic aid to help countries restore internal stability, and military resistance where necessary to save countries from internal or external Communist attack. The Marshall Plan was an imaginative, generous, and remarkably successful conception. It supplied large-scale American economic aid to the European countries. And it drew these countries into a general system of European recovery, thereby continuing the alliance of the western powers and laying the basis for possible European unity.

Two years after the Greek-Turkish crisis, the Cold War became more deeply fixed. American public opinion and leadership, and Europe's as well, were shocked in 1948 by the Communist coup in Czechoslovakia, hitherto a model of liberal democracy in central Europe. Hard on the heels of Czechoslovakia came the first great Berlin crisis. Berlin, the seat of the four occupying powers' Allied Control Council for Germany, was an enclave located one hundred miles within Communist East Germany. Stalin sought to drive the western Allies out by blocking all land routes to Berlin. But under American leadership, the now-famous Berlin airlift ferried supplies to the occupying forces and the free Berliners. Russia backed down, but repeated harassment and dangerous conflict is the unfinished story of isolated Berlin and divided Germany. Then came Korea. In June, 1950, the North Korean Communist regime invaded and nearly conquered South Korea. President Truman, in an example of the lonely authority of the Presidency, made the decision to fight. It became a United Nations' 'police action' but in fact America bore the brunt of the heavy fighting.

The Cold War Today

Characteristically, America had demobilized after World War II with undue haste. The whole country was—understandably, but mistakenly—feverishly anxious to 'bring the boys home' and withdraw from the enormous commitments of the war. Korea irrevocably ended the withdrawal. From that moment, America has been involved in a titanic program of military preparedness. In consequence, managing the defense establishment occupies a huge portion of the federal budget and personnel. Military considerations and military staff are involved in the highest levels of foreign policy debate and formulation. And, ominously, an almost unbelievably sophisticated and deadly military technology has resulted.

But conflict is by no means merely military. A staggering range of quasi-military and nonmilitary problems have been drawn into the Cold War context. To name only a few, racial conflict and the rise of the non-white peoples, anticolonial struggles and the emergence of dozens of new nations, aiding or resisting revolution, forging alliances, rivalry in space, world trade, the unity of Europe. The range and difficulty of these problems and the endless skills required to deal with them make the burden of foreign affairs almost unbearable. Not least is the frustration of public opinion as it contemplates a world in which solutions never catch up with the problems that arise constantly and from places one never heard of.

Yet the difficulties of daily crisis do not exhaust the burden. There is the difficulty of sensing fundamental changes in the basic pattern of international relations. Such changes can and do occur. And government and public opinion must adapt to change when it does indeed occur. Some now claim to see such fundamental change—and the need for new policies—because of the 'liberalization' process in Russia and because of the Sino-Soviet conflict.

Continued American Cold War adamancy, they argue, would slow or stop Russian domestic liberalization and would draw together the Russians and Chinese. They therefore propose new approaches—for example, recognizing Communist East Germany or selling wheat to Russia without political strings—which, they argue, would strengthen the forces of moderation within Russia and draw her farther away from China and toward the West. But others question this reasoning; they argue that, even if Russian liberalization is more than skin-deep and even if the Sino-Soviet conflict is severe, the proposed softening of Cold War policies does not logically follow. A Communist Russia less tyrannically harsh to Russians, they argue, might be just as determined to 'bury' the West. If Russia and China permanently split, Russia need not turn to the West in friendship. America cannot woo Russia away from China or into altering her internal order; forces beyond American control will help determine those outcomes. And to the extent that American power can shape the outcome, major concessions to Russia now would seem an invitation to precisely the feared Russian intransigence. What reason, they ask, would she have to moderate her demands if aggression secures them?

Whatever the future may hold, the Cold War is not over and its basic policies remain relevant. The term itself suggests those basic policies: There is a *war* between liberal democracy (however imperfect) in the West and Communist tyranny, Russian or Chinese. But it must be kept *cold*; the conflict must be waged so as to lessen the likelihood of nuclear war. But to assert that the basic policies must persist is not to deny that, after a generation, the Cold War is changing in important ways. During

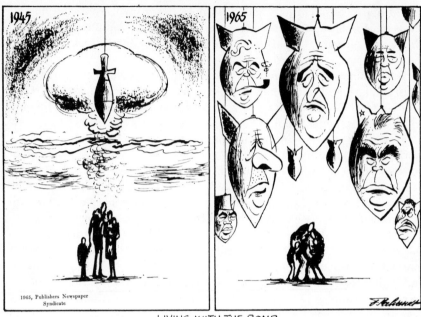

LIVING WITH THE BOMB.

that generation modern war has become terribly more destructive. Under Khrushchev the Russians had affirmed that world war is neither necessary nor in anyone's interest (unlike the Chinese who cling to the opposite Lenin-Stalin conception of war as inevitable). Although Russia and America remain the superpowers, the rest of the world is no longer economically and militarily insignificant. The European powers (including West Germany) have made giant economic strides and have increasing military potential. Many countries have a generation of expertise in playing off America and Russia to their own advantage. The system of alliances, both western and Russian, is no longer rigid. The world is still divided, but the lines are no longer as clear. It remains America's task to further this nation's interests and to advance the cause of liberal democracy wherever possible. But the task is harder than ever, and the prospect of perfect and permanent achievement as remote as ever.

Strains upon Constitutionalism

Speed, secrecy, efficiency, vigorous enforcement, discretionary authority in individual hands, national unity, long-range calculation—these are the special urgencies of the conduct of foreign affairs and the national defense. And they are precisely what is least compatible with the spirit of the American democratic constitutional system. Constitutionalism implies, above all, limits and restraints, while the imperatives of diplomacy and defense thrust toward unlimited and unrestrained action.

Pacifism is not enough.

The necessity for full-bodied power, especially with regard to diplomacy and defense, was unambiguously and persuasively stated by The *Federalist*.

> It is impossible to foresee or to define the extent and variety of national exigencies, and the correspondent extent and variety of means which may be necessary to satisfy them. The circumstances that endanger the safety of nations are infinite, and for this reason no constitutional shackles can wisely be imposed on the power to which the care of it is committed.[5]

Publius is saying that the Constitution must grant the government, ultimately, the power to do anything in any way that the unforeseeable future may make necessary for national survival. But this argues not only against "constitutional shackles," but by implication points to an utterly unrestrained power in the government. There is a profound problem here. The constitutionally granted power necessary to cope with all "national exigencies" is inevitably power sufficient also to destroy the liberties the Constitution was established to preserve. On the other hand, fidelity to the restrictive side of the Constitution can fatally enfeeble government. The problem is to find the mean, a path of sound constitutionalism without falling over into either extreme.

But in the American system, which constitutionalizes its politics and its rhetoric, it is not enough only to find a prudent path. It becomes

---

[5] *Federalist* 23, p. 153. Italics omitted. *Cf. Federalist* 31, p. 194.

necessary for the Supreme Court to pronounce explicit constitutional formulations. And therein lies a rub.

The Problem in the Court

The case of *Missouri* v. *Holland*[6] reveals some of the difficulties of express formulation. It turned on a question of federalism. It was inevitable, after all, that the compoundly federal and national character of the American political system would be drawn into the question. Does the existence of the states and the constitutional division of governing power between them and the national government limit what can be done? *Missouri* v. *Holland* makes clear that in foreign affairs and defense the national authority is least encumbered by the federal element in the system.

The specific issue in *Missouri* v. *Holland* concerned the regulation of migratory birds. Conservationists, then growing in numbers, feared that under existing state-by-state regulation, or lack of it, migratory birds would be destroyed. In 1913 Congress enacted regulatory legislation for their protection, but the courts ruled the statute an unconstitutional exercise of power not granted to the national government. Subsequently, the United States undertook by treaty (with Great Britain) to protect the wildlife jointly with Canada. To implement the treaty, Congress enacted new legislation more stringently regulatory than the invalidated 1913 statute. The constitutionality of the new treaty-based legislation was promptly challenged. The Court recapitulated the argument that opponents of the legislation had made:

> It is said that a treaty cannot be valid if it infringes the Constitution, that there are limits, therefore, to the treaty-making power, and that one such limit is that what an act of Congress could not do unaided, in derogation of the powers reserved to the states, a treaty cannot do.

The Court rejected this argument and upheld the constitutionality of the new law:

> It is obvious that there may be matters of the sharpest exigency for the national well-being that an act of Congress could not deal with, but that a treaty followed by such an act could, and it is not lightly to be assumed that, in matters requiring national action, "a power which must belong to and somewhere reside in every civilized government" is not to be found.

For present purposes, the vital point is how far the opinion goes toward making the treaty power the source of unlimited government power to deal with "exigencies." Although the opinion held—and this is extremely important—that treaties "must not contravene any prohibitory words to be found in the Constitution," little else seems to be denied;

---

[6] 252 U.S. 416 (1920).

what is not expressly prohibited is assumed to be permitted. This is dramatically different from the situation in domestic affairs. There it is not enough that the government not contravene constitutional prohibitions; it must act upon the basis of constitutionally granted powers, either stated or implied. This is precisely what *Missouri* v. *Holland* denies with regard to the treaty power; it makes the treaty power one source of that constitutionally unshackled "variety of means" which Publius pronounced necessary.

The Court had little alternative to interpreting the treaty power so broadly; the necessities of war and diplomacy do indeed demand such breadth. But in the process, the Court revealed the difficulty in finding constitutional formulations that adequately consider the necessities of power while holding firm the constitutional constraints.

U.S. v. *Curtiss-Wright Export Corporation*[7] further reveals the Court's difficulty in this area. In 1934 Congress empowered the President to prevent Americans from selling arms to Paraguay and Bolivia, then fighting the protracted Chaco War. In upholding both the national authority and Congress's right thus broadly to delegate power to the President, the Court employed the doctrine of *inherent power.* This doctrine expressly dispenses with the necessity of grounding a national exercise of power in any particular constitutional grant at all. It asserts instead that authority in certain crises inheres in the very idea of government, and thus in American government, the silence of the Constitution notwithstanding:

> That the Federal government can exercise no powers except those specifically enumerated in the Constitution, and such implied powers as are necessary and proper . . . is categorically true only in respect of our internal affairs. . . . The powers to declare and wage war, to conclude peace, to make treaties, to maintain diplomatic relations with other sovereignties, *if they had never been mentioned in the Constitution,* would have vested in the federal government . . . . [because powers of this kind are] *inherently* inseparable from the conception of nationality [emphasis added].

This is an extreme formulation from which most judicial authorities now prefer to retreat.[8] But that the Court went so far (the same 'conservative' Court was then striking down New Deal domestic legislation as exceeding the national powers) reveals the difficulty of denying to defense and diplomacy the breadth of power they manifestly require.

Missouri v. *Holland* and *Curtiss-Wright* show how hard it is to square the requirements of both power and constitutionality in this area. But the Court, while it is preeminently the formulator of constitutional doctrine, is by no means the sole factor in the constitutionalization

---

[7] 299 U.S. 304 (1936).
[8] Cf. *Reid* v. *Covert*, 354 U.S. 1 (1956).

of power in foreign affairs. We turn now to an effort in which the legislative branch took the initiative.

The Bricker Amendment Controversy

The problem—constitutionally enfeebled government or unshackled power—became the basis of the mid-1950 controversy over the 'Bricker Amendment.' The controversy involved the danger of the treaty power to the constitutional system in general and of the executive agreement to the rights of the Senate in particular.

Untrammeled as the treaty-making power tends to become, still more so does the executive agreement. An *executive agreement* is an agreement made by the President with other heads of state. The key fact is that this agreement does not have to be ratified by the Senate like a treaty; it can be made by the President entirely on his own authority. Otherwise, these agreements resemble treaties and may cover any of the subjects of treaties. Although it is not expressly provided for in the Constitution, this great power has long been held to be a necessary incident of executive responsibility in foreign affairs.[9] As a matter of fact, most executive agreements are not made solely upon executive authority, but rather are usually authorized by prior congressional statute or prior treaty provision. Thousands of such agreements have been made, by far the greater number during the last half century. Most deal with routine diplomatic, commercial and, now, military matters. But some immensely important actions have been taken by executive agreement—and solely upon executive authority—e.g., the Lend Lease agreement of 1940 which committed America to the Allied cause in World War II.

The executive agreement has obvious advantages to which nearly all would agree: efficiency in conducting minor and routine matters, secrecy and speed in handling the most vital matters. But the executive agreement always tempts a strong President to avoid submitting his best laid plans to harsh senatorial scrutiny. This is just what brought the treaty power and the executive agreement under their sharpest attack.

Bitter disillusionment as the Cold War developed, the disclosure of numerous World War II diplomatic commitments (many of which were made by executive agreement and some of which proved unwise), retrospective Republican hostility to Presidents Roosevelt and Truman—all contributed to bring the matter to a head in 1954. Senator John Bricker, an Ohio Republican, proposed an amendment to guard the constitutional system from treaties and executive agreements. There were two key provisions, one directed in effect against the decision in *Missouri* v. *Holland,* the other against the executive agreement:

> Section 2. A treaty shall become effective as an internal law in the United States only through legislation which would be valid in absence of treaty.

[9] *Cf. B. Altman & Co.* v. *United States,* 224 U.S. 583 (1912).

Section 3. Congress shall have power to regulate all executive and other agreements with any foreign power or international organization. All such agreements shall be subject to the limitations imposed on treaties. . . .

The aim was to bring the treaty power under the constraints of federalism and to limit presidential authority in favor of congressional. But this was to impose on the national conduct of foreign affairs precisely the sort of shackles against which the *Federalist* had warned and which the Constitution avoided.

Although the amendment had powerful Democratic support, the primary force behind it was Republican. Nonetheless, Republican President Eisenhower responded, so to speak, presidentially; his administration led the fight against the amendment. The amendment was first watered down and then finally fell one vote short of the required two-thirds majority. However, the strength of sentiment in favor of the amendment may have prompted President Eisenhower not to join in several United Nations conventions by executive agreement.

The Bricker Amendment controversy shows how difficult it is to formulate acceptable limitations on the national power in foreign affairs. But it shows also, despite its defeat, how public opinion and congressional leadership serve as restraints upon executive discretion. If constitutional shackles cannot be imposed by formulation, still the workings of the system tend to hold the conduct of foreign affairs within constitutional bounds. Nonetheless, the constitutional situation in sum is that defense and diplomacy enjoy somehow a privileged breadth of power; the national government is little encumbered constitutionally by the presence of the states, and the President as the chief organ of the nation in foreign affairs has far-reaching authority.

The Conduct of Foreign Affairs: The Political Context

The government's broad powers in diplomacy and defense are partially constrained by the need for political unity in their exercise. Because foreign affairs involves the politics of all of 'us' against all of 'them,' unity is more necessary than in domestic affairs. And indeed there usually is more ultimate agreement on what foreign policy should be, and certainly far more rallying of the whole nation in the execution of foreign policy. Republican Senator Arthur Vandenberg of Michigan observed that "partisan politics cease at the water's edge." By this maxim he emphasized the bipartisan unity necessary in the conduct of foreign affairs; and, from having been an isolationist, he himself supplied that unity to Democratic administrations during and after World War II. But this is not to say that all of us are perfectly united in the conduct of foreign affairs and that diplomacy and defense are immune from partisan politics and the political process generally. Far from it. Politics enters inevitably and, moreover, is desirable in many respects.

Value and Necessity of the Political Context

In a democracy, foreign affairs should be conducted within the context of the political process because, whatever else it is, democracy is the political system that rests emphatically upon widespread public opinion. And politics is the mode whereby that opinion influences policy. First of all, then, politics is how you find out who is a majority on what; only through politics can majorities direct the course government takes. Foreign policy thus frequently and properly becomes a central election issue. The League of Nations question in the 1920 presidential election is a famous example, and the problem of the Korean War in 1952 is another.

Second, if foreign policy were immune from politics, it would thereby also be relatively immune from effective criticism. It is all well and good for the President to discuss things with his subordinates and to have them channel criticism to him. But in this process the rough edges are all too often smoothed away. Yet effective criticism usually means criticism by adversaries. And that in practice means democratic politics. For all its confusions and melodramatics, politics is the means whereby criticism is made and heard. This is not to suggest that the President must sway with the winds of criticism. Indeed he must not, and his office was designed to give him great independence. Nonetheless both he and the nation need to hear the criticism. So long as the American Congress retains its character this need will be more than amply satisfied.

Third, quite apart from the constructive value of the criticisms, another benefit accrues from conducting foreign affairs within the context of politics. It is only when complaint and criticism have had an opportunity to be uttered that the Administration can estimate the public mood, estimate what the country will put up with, and thus determine what is in the long run feasible for policy. This is not a sufficient, but it is an indispensable, condition for the formulation of policy in a democratic republic.

There are, of course, offsetting disadvantages. The vulnerability of every political system lies in the peculiar incapacity of its ruling element. Democracy's problem lies always in the ignorance of the majority. That ignorance is perhaps greatest and certainly most dangerous in foreign affairs. Ignorant opinion, packaged, sloganized, and impassioned by demagogic leaders, is one of the hazards of democratic foreign policy. But criticisms of mass public opinion can be overdone. It should be emphasized that in recent decades, mass opinion has at least recognized the enemy; even if uninformed or foolish regarding tactics and strategies, most American people recognized first in Naziism and subsequently in Communism their true enemy. And on the whole they have shouldered the resulting heavy burdens steadfastly.

But whatever the judgment must be of democratic public opinion, two factors lessen its force in the conduct of foreign affairs. First, the bulk of the public tends to be relatively apathetic about specific foreign policy issues; most people are not visibly affected in their narrow interests by such issues and, also, cannot be well-informed about them. Consequently, second, while many interest groups press for favors or special foreign policies, generally the pressure is less than the thrust, say, of farm, labor, business, or civil-rights groups in domestic matters. Hence, the President and Congress have the greatest degree of independence from mass opinion in the formulation and execution of foreign policy.

The Political Context at the Level of Government

Whether desirable or not, politics inevitably deeply affects foreign-policy decision-making. For one thing, politics enters by the familiar path of separation of powers. The competition of President and Congress is a natural vehicle for American political conflict and affects the conduct of foreign affairs perhaps as keenly as it does domestic affairs. Professor Corwin points out that the Constitution leaves it "for events to resolve" whether President or Congress "shall have the decisive and final voice." The Constitution

is an invitation to struggle for the privilege of directing American foreign policy. . . . [T]he power to determine the substantive content of American foreign policy is a *divided* power with the lion's share usually falling to the president, though by no means always.[10]

The constitutional overlapping of executive and legislative is a logical expression of the natural links between the two. Executive-initiated foreign policy requires enabling legislation and appropriations. Congress is thus inevitably drawn—perhaps more accurately, inevitably thrusts itself—into the conduct of foreign affairs. And all the forces of American politics, as we saw in Part Three of this book, make their way into the arena where President and Congress collaborate and compete.

In addition to the logical link between congressional legislation and oversight and foreign policy, there is the general connection between domestic and foreign affairs. These are not in separate compartments. Defense and diplomatic decisions, for example, affect the domestic economy in innumerable ways, and the affected interest groups bring pressures to bear on foreign affairs. Similarly, the demands of purely domestic politics carry over, sometimes wholly inadvertently, into foreign affairs. It may make no difference whatsoever to the national defense whether a military installation or a weapons contract is located in congressional district *A* or congressional district *B*. But from the point of view of the 'pork-barrel,' defense establishments are no different than post offices, dams, or any other federal project that benefits a local economy and ingratiates the congressman with his constituents. Similarly, the 1964 legislation authorizing sale of grain to Russia had an inadvertent but com-

---

[10] E. S. Corwin, *The President: Office and Powers* (New York: New York University Press, 1941), 2nd. ed.; pp. 200–1, emphasis in original.

pelling political connection with the desire of midwestern farmers—a majority of whom ordinarily denounce such deals with Communism—to dispose of their surplus wheat profitably.

Practically every aspect of foreign policy—save for those significant and spectacular instances of solitary presidential decision regarding war in Korea or confrontation over Cuba by naval quarantine—must make its way through the whole machinery of Congress. Presidents increasingly have drawn leading senators and congressmen into regular consultation and into participation as quasi-diplomatic representatives at international conferences. It has become increasingly important to the President that the congressional leadership on both sides of the aisle work closely with him. Democratic Senate Majority Leader Lyndon Johnson was indispensable to Republican President Eisenhower, as Republican Senate Minority Leader Everett Dirksen became to Democratic President Johnson. This extent of congressional involvement is an important constraint upon executive discretion in foreign policy.

Foreign policy—like domestic policy—must make its way through the complicated machinery of government and the welter of political forces which make the machinery run.

Politics of Foreign Affairs among the Electorate

Parties naturally take full advantage of general foreign-policy issues during all campaigns, especially presidential campaigns. In 1952 Eisenhower took advantage of the national frustration over the Korean war. In 1960 Kennedy hammered away at an alleged 'missile gap' dangerous to American security. In 1964 Cuba and South Vietnam became campaign issues. The prolonged frustrations and difficulties of the Cold War have tended to make 'hard' versus 'soft' policies toward Communism an issue. On the whole, Republicans have tended to criticize the Democrats for allegedly congenital softness. But this did not prevent Democrat Kennedy from seizing the issue in 1960; he criticized the incumbent Republicans for insufficient militancy regarding Cuba.

Partisan politics also links foreign and domestic political factors for reasons peculiar to the American electorate. America's ethnic, religious, and racial diversity impinges upon foreign policy. For more than a century, differences between Americans of English stock and Americans of Irish and German stock exacerbated foreign-policy conflict. Many Polish Roman Catholics deserted the Democrats because of President Roosevelt's policy at the Yalta Conference in 1945. American policy in the Middle East reflects in part the concern of millions of American Jews with the fate of Israel. The fact that there are twenty million American Negroes and the fact that color is a great issue in world affairs closely connect American foreign policy with a vital domestic question. While the importance of world public opinion has been sentimentalized and exaggerated, it is nonetheless true that what America does about civil rights domestically has some bearing upon America's situation in the world. What is done here affects, say, Japanese public opinion, which in turn limits what Japanese governments can do in support of American foreign policy.

Regarding the impact of such factors upon American foreign policy, suffice it to conclude with this observation: Were there many more Americans of Greek or Turkish descent, the Cyprus crisis would have been a major issue in the 1964 presidential campaign. Note well that this does not warrant merely cynical inferences about the political process. Quite apart from considerations of power politics, American diversity has probably made America more sensitive to injustice—the oppressed elsewhere have support from some segment of the electorate—and has supported the concept of the American Mission.

Finally, we must note a somewhat tenuous but probably important connection between domestic and foreign affairs which affects the context within which the latter are conducted. The nature of its political order supplies a country with natural affections and hostilities. The link between domestic polity and foreign policy is especially close in a country like America, where a sense of mission has so often influenced foreign policy. Thus it never was—nor should have been—possible that the American people would actively befriend either Nazi or Communist tyranny. America has often supported dictatorial regimes, especially recently under the pressures of the Cold War. Sometimes this has been done to secure military objectives regarded as vital, sometimes to stave off a feared Communist-led overthrow of a dictatorship, and sometimes because the dictator has sufficiently ingratiated himself with powerful American religious or economic interests that profit from his regime. American aid to nondemocratic regimes is a difficult question. But whatever the answer, this much is clear: Such aid has never had the character of firm, consistent, deeply popular friendship. That has been reserved for the victims of dictatorship and aggression. Thus Franklin Roosevelt could rally American feeling for the cause of beleaguered England and defeated France—feeling far different from that which supports our aid for expedient reasons to regimes democratic Americans do not admire.

Administration of Foreign Affairs and Defense

The Department of State

The Secretary of State[11] has always been the administrative official next in dignity to the President. On the whole, he appears to have been

---

[11] Secretary derives from the same Latin root as the word secret. In England it came to mean a high official and confidant of the crown. "State" refers here to matters of grave public importance. The term Secretary of State is an American contraction of the title used for the similar official in England, the Secretary of State for Foreign Affairs.

the Cabinet member with the greatest intellectual equipment and training. In no other Cabinet post have so many distinguished Americans
served. Thomas Jefferson was the first Secretary, and for a time it was
the stepping stone to the Presidency; Secretaries of State Madison, Monroe, and John Quincy Adams were heirs-apparent and succeeded to the
Presidency. The various statutes establishing succession to the Presidency
have all placed the Secretary of State first in line among the Cabinet.

The invariable custom that the Secretary sit immediately at the
President's right at Cabinet meetings symbolizes the fact that foreign
affairs is peculiarly the province of the President. The original statute
establishing the Secretaryship fully acknowledged this: "The Secretary
of State shall perform such duties . . . respecting foreign affairs as the
President . . . shall assign to the department and he shall conduct the
business of the department in such a manner as the President shall direct." Each President is thus free to determine the kind of Secretary of
State he wants to have—retiring or aggressive. Some Presidents choose,
as the phrase goes, to be their own Secretary of State in effect (in England the Prime Minister may choose actually to be the Foreign Minister
as well), while other Presidents leave the area largely to their Secretaries.
However, the basic functions of all Secretaries can be seen as falling into
five groups.

First, and perhaps above all, the Secretary formulates foreign policy
for the President's approval and is usually his chief foreign-affairs advisor
and source of information. In this capacity he must have frequent, private,
and sometimes instantaneous access to the President.

Second, the Secretary must speak for his Department and for the
President within the Cabinet, the National Security Council, and the
many other White House and interagency committees on foreign affairs
and defense. If he is close to the President and enjoys his confidence (if
he is what the press calls a 'strong' Secretary), he will be able to see to it
that the President's decisions are being complied with throughout the
enormous administrative system. Otherwise he will be but one voice
among many.

Third, the Secretary himself authoritatively decides and carries out
matters not needing presidential approval or execution. The dividing
line between needing and not needing approval depends upon the relations between each President and each Secretary; but ordinarily this
function gives the Secretary authority on some extremely important matters and adds to his political weight. He is also the chief negotiator of
treaties and international agreements and he himself maintains high-
level diplomatic contacts. Indeed improved transportation has led Secretaries into perhaps too much direct conduct of diplomacy, thereby
depreciating the standing of the ambassadorial staff.

Fourth, the Secretary is ordinarily the President's chief foreign-affairs
spokesman to Congress and the public. Like all other department heads,
he is accountable to Congress, subject to its inquiries and solicitous of

DEPARTMENT OF STATE

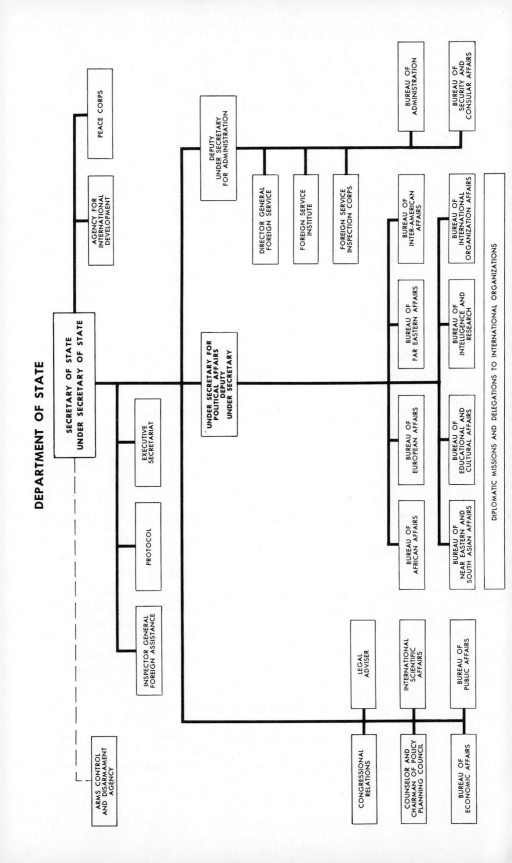

SECRETARY OF STATE
UNDER SECRETARY OF STATE

ARMS CONTROL AND DISARMAMENT AGENCY

AGENCY FOR INTERNATIONAL DEVELOPMENT

PEACE CORPS

INSPECTOR GENERAL FOREIGN ASSISTANCE

PROTOCOL

EXECUTIVE SECRETARIAT

DEPUTY UNDER SECRETARY FOR ADMINISTRATION

DIRECTOR GENERAL FOREIGN SERVICE

FOREIGN SERVICE INSTITUTE

FOREIGN SERVICE INSPECTION CORPS

BUREAU OF ADMINISTRATION

BUREAU OF SECURITY AND CONSULAR AFFAIRS

UNDER SECRETARY FOR POLITICAL AFFAIRS
DEPUTY UNDER SECRETARY

BUREAU OF INTER-AMERICAN AFFAIRS

BUREAU OF INTERNATIONAL ORGANIZATION AFFAIRS

BUREAU OF FAR EASTERN AFFAIRS

BUREAU OF INTELLIGENCE AND RESEARCH

BUREAU OF EUROPEAN AFFAIRS

BUREAU OF EDUCATIONAL AND CULTURAL AFFAIRS

BUREAU OF AFRICAN AFFAIRS

BUREAU OF NEAR EASTERN AND SOUTH ASIAN AFFAIRS

DIPLOMATIC MISSIONS AND DELEGATIONS TO INTERNATIONAL ORGANIZATIONS

LEGAL ADVISER

INTERNATIONAL SCIENTIFIC AFFAIRS

BUREAU OF PUBLIC AFFAIRS

CONGRESSIONAL RELATIONS

COUNSELOR AND CHAIRMAN OF POLICY PLANNING COUNCIL

BUREAU OF ECONOMIC AFFAIRS

its appropriations. With Congress's great and frequently hostile involvement in foreign affairs since World War II, congressional liaison is becoming an increasingly important function of the Secretary. Similarly, he is usually the Administration's chief spokesman on foreign affairs to the American public. When he is a strong figure and has the President's confidence (as in the case of John Foster Dulles under Eisenhower), the Secretary of State's public utterances and press conferences will receive newspaper and television coverage second only to those of the President's.

Fifth, the Secretary heads an executive department with over 25,000 employees and a complex organizational structure. He must manage effectively the several dozen senior officials upon whom he must depend to keep departmental machinery in running order. These include career officers who were there before the Secretary and who will be there after he is gone. He must win their loyal support; this requires in turn that he to some extent represents them. He must make their needs and their opinions known to the President if he is to get them loyally to carry out his and the President's program.

Perhaps above all a Secretary must succeed in winning the confidence of the President. But, as was pointed out in the discussion of presidential roles, success or failure in any single function strengthens or saps ability in the performance of the others. A Secretary of State, too, neglects any of his functions only at peril to all the others.

State Department organization. The Department of State is one of the smallest of the executive departments because, unlike most of the other departments, it performs few regulatory functions, produces few products, and especially, has no vast establishment throughout the nation. Nonetheless the pressure of contemporary foreign affairs produces an enormous burden of business. And departmental organization is inevitably complex because of the scope and subtlety of foreign affairs, and because of the great degree of specialization necessary for dealing with all the countries of the world.

The Secretary of State

> sits amidst 2 Under Secretaries and 2 Deputy Under Secretaries, 13 Assistant Secretaries or their equivalent in charge of 13 Bureaus, over 30 Deputy Assistant Secretaries, more than 60 area and other Office Directors, and over 90 Country Desk Officers, together with assorted advisers and special assistants, counselors and inspector generals, and emissaries from the agencies that lie only partly within the Secretary's jurisdiction.[12]

No wonder that Secretary Dean Rusk observed "that inside of the Department our principal problem is layering."[13] The vital opinion of a Country Desk Officer may well have to go through eight "layers" of

---

[12] U.S. Congress, Senate, Committee on Government Operations, *Administration of National Security*, 88th Cong., 2nd sess., 1964, p. 5.

[13] *Idem.*

administrative structure to reach the Secretary: Deputy Office Director, Office Director, Deputy Assistant Secretary, Assistant Secretary, Deputy Under Secretary for Political Affairs, Under Secretary for Political Affairs, Under Secretary. Only one thing would be worse than this red-tape layering which stands between 90 Desk Officers and the Secretary—the lack of it. The Secretary would otherwise drown in a sea of reports that he ought never to be bothered with. Sound administration requires constant maintenance of the right amount and permeability of 'layering.'

The field staff. Field personnel are divided into two staffs—*consular* and *diplomatic*. No clear line of division is possible because the functions of the two overlap. But on the whole the consular staff performs the more routine, almost subpolitical, duties. Most nations accord each other's travelers, businessmen, and resident aliens certain reciprocal civilities. Within this tradition, the consular service is engaged in the routine protection of American lives and interests abroad. They administer American law in foreign ports insofar as it is applicable, aid seamen, students, and tourists, and issue visas for entry into the United States. The consular service protects American commercial and financial interests and actively seeks to promote trade. There are four grades within the consular service: in ascending order—consular agent, vice-consul, consul, consul-general. The higher grades are assigned to the more important areas and tasks.

In contrast with consular commercial duties, diplomatic personnel protect American political interests abroad. These more responsible duties usually involve much more ceremony in their performance. The often-mocked diplomatic pomp and ceremony express the dignity sovereign states and rulers claim for the persons who represent them. Protocol—the elaborate etiquette of diplomatic procedures—has long grated on American sensibilities. Many Americans regard this as 'cookie-pusher' stuff. Be that as it may, protocol serves useful functions. By supplying an objective and internationally agreed-upon procedure, protocol eliminates the necessity for choice—and thus possible controversy—in each new instance. The long tradition in these matters is revealed in the somewhat archaic titles of diplomatic posts: ambassador, papal legate or nuncio, envoy, minister resident, chargé d'affaires, diplomatic agents. Most of these actually perform similar functions; as in the case of consuls, the title usually indicates the importance of the area or task. The higher the title the more elaborate the diplomatic rituals; for example, ambassadors are received by the President upon their arrival, ministers by the Secretary of State.

Diplomatic personnel are substantially exempt from local law, their papers and effects are presumed to be exempt from local seizure, they are guaranteed safe conduct during war. In general, embassies are accorded extra-territorial status; they are regarded essentially as extensions of the nation they represent. From this fact arises the tradition of asylum. During upheavals fugitives take refuge in embassies; Cardinal Mindszenty, for example, has resided for years in the American Embassy in Communist Hungary.

Embassies (where the senior official is an ambassador, legations where he is a minister) perform many functions. Three important ones are obvious: communication, information, and propaganda. Ambassadors were formerly the chief communication link between countries. Modern communication and transportation technology—a dramatic instance is the telephone 'hot-line' directly linking the American and Russian chiefs of government—have made it possible for foreign ministers and heads of state to deal with each other directly. But ambassadors continue to perform an important communication function. Second, it is the embassy's job to know what is going on in the country and to keep the State Department promptly and accurately informed. Some 1,500 cables reach Washington daily as part of the voluminous reporting from the diplomatic field staff. Third, the embassy supplies information to interested foreigners and interprets America to them in the best light. Much of this function is performed through the United States Information Agency which conducts a variety of public information programs (e.g., libraries, films, press releases). Diplomats perform a host of miscellaneous functions in superintending American interests (exchange of persons, cultural programs, extradition, visas, etc.), many of which overlap those of the consular service.

Both diplomatic and consular personnel belong to the Foreign Service. This is the Department's professional service organization of both field and Washington personnel. The Foreign Service was originally plagued by spoils-system problems and was once a jealously guarded enclave within the State Department. It was integrated into the Department and professionalized under the Foreign Service Act of 1946. Foreign Service appointments are highly regarded by college students among whom recruitment is actively pursued. Admission to the service is by rigorous examination; about one thousand try annually and about one hundred succeed. Men are frequently shifted in the field as part of their training, and promotion is determined by merit. The highest diplomatic posts however, are frequently a preserve of presidential patronage; it has always been convenient to reward a loyal politician or large contributor with an honorific foreign post. In fact, many of these 'political' appointees have been men of the highest ability, suggesting that diplomatic skill is the product of more backgrounds than narrow professional diplomatic training. But in recent years, many of the most important posts have gone to career officers, and this has served as incentive to maintain the Foreign Service at a high level.

Department of Defense

In striking contrast to the situation during most of the country's history, the Department of Defense is now by far the largest of the executive departments. Until World War I the national military establishment had traditionally been puny, smaller in proportion to population

DEPARTMENT OF DEFENSE

SECRETARY OF DEFENSE
DEPUTY SECRETARY OF DEFENSE

ARMED FORCES POLICY COUNCIL

DIRECTOR OF DEFENSE RESEARCH AND ENGINEERING

ASSISTANT SECRETARY OF DEFENSE (COMPTROLLER)

ASSISTANT SECRETARY OF DEFENSE (MANPOWER)

ASSISTANT SECRETARY OF DEFENSE (INSTALLATIONS AND LOGISTICS)

ASSISTANT SECRETARY OF DEFENSE (INTERNATIONAL SECURITY AFFAIRS)

GENERAL COUNSEL OF THE DEPARTMENT OF DEFENSE

ASSISTANT SECRETARY OF DEFENSE (PUBLIC AFFAIRS)

ASSISTANT SECRETARY OF DEFENSE

ASSISTANT TO THE SECRETARY (LEGISLATIVE AFFAIRS)

ASSISTANT TO THE SECRETARY (ATOMIC ENERGY)

DEPARTMENT OF THE ARMY
SECRETARY OF THE ARMY
UNDER SECRETARY AND ASSISTANT SECRETARIES OF THE ARMY
CHIEF OF STAFF, ARMY

DEPARTMENT OF THE NAVY
SECRETARY OF THE NAVY
UNDER SECRETARY AND ASSISTANT SECRETARIES OF THE NAVY
CHIEF OF NAVAL OPERATIONS
COMMANDANT OF MARINE CORPS

DEPARTMENT OF THE AIR FORCE
SECRETARY OF THE AIR FORCE
UNDER SECRETARY AND ASSISTANT SECRETARIES OF THE AIR FORCE
CHIEF OF STAFF, AIR FORCE

DEFENSE SUPPLY AGENCY

JOINT CHIEFS OF STAFF
CHAIRMAN, JOINT CHIEFS OF STAFF
CHIEF OF STAFF, ARMY
CHIEF OF NAVAL OPERATIONS
CHIEF OF STAFF, AIR FORCE
COMMANDANT, MARINE CORPS

THE JOINT STAFF

DEFENSE INTELLIGENCE AGENCY

DEFENSE COMMUNICATIONS AGENCY

DEFENSE ATOMIC SUPPORT AGENCY

ALASKAN COMMAND

ATLANTIC COMMAND

CONTINENTAL DEFENSE COMMAND

EUROPEAN COMMAND

PACIFIC COMMAND

SOUTHERN COMMAND

STRIKE COMMAND

STRATEGIC AIR COMMAND

Source: U.S. Government Organization Manual

than perhaps that of any other major nation, and it again lapsed into near-puniness during the 1920s and 1930s. But similar demobilization after World War II was abruptly halted by the onset of the Cold War. Not only is the military establishment now enormous, but military considerations pervasively affect public policy and the operations of government in a way unparalleled in our history. Although successful military men have often risen in American politics, perhaps never have there been so many before—Eisenhower, Marshall, MacArthur, Lucius Clay, Walter Bedell Smith, Maxwell Taylor—in so many important posts.

Defense Department functions. The Department's functions may be considered under five heads: daily maintenance, military planning, sharing in overall policy and administration, research, and a set of domestic functions. First, the Department is responsible for the daily maintenance of the armed forces; it recruits, feeds, shelters, equips, and stations the entire military establishment, and this requires an enormous and expensive administrative apparatus. Second, the Department formulates basic military policy and plans strategy and tactics. These are the two most traditional defense functions. Third, the President depends upon the Department for the military considerations that overlap diplomatic and other executive matters. American participation in NATO, for example, is jointly a military and diplomatic matter. Economic aid to allies and nations whom the government is wooing is often as much a military as a diplomatic question, and planning and administering foreign military aid has become a major departmental activity. Fourth, the Department supports an astonishing range of research activities, some barely recognizable as military. But then, under modern circumstances, it is hard to tell where peace begins and war leaves off. Research includes such varied activities as space science, basic research in physics and chemistry, engineering, and social science investigations of how to govern occupied territories and conduct psychological warfare.

Fifth, the Department has some responsibilities not connected with defense against enemies abroad. Under the President, the military forces can be called upon to help enforce national law, as when a President has federalized the National Guard in race relations crises in Arkansas and Alabama. Similarly the national armed forces may be called upon to maintain law and order in civilian disaster areas or, in exceptional circumstances, to impose martial law. The Department has other domestic responsibilities which barely involve its military character. The Army Corps of Engineers works on improving navigable waters, building dams, and maintaining flood control. And military personnel may be used simply to help out in purely civilian ways in flood, fire, earthquake, or other natural disasters.

Defense Department organization. Even with the most perfect and frictionless administrative structure, the Defense Department's task would still be nearly unmanageable by virtue of sheer bulk of personnel and quantity and variety of tasks to be performed in the Pentagon, the huge establishments throughout the United States, and military missions all over the world.

But the administrative structure is not frictionless. After an intense struggle, the opposition of the separate armed forces to unification was finally overcome and the Department of Defense was created in 1949. The newly unified department was intended to eliminate duplication of functions and extreme rivalry among the branches of the armed forces, and to end their separate politicking and lobbying with Congress and the White House. But no method of organization could instantly and completely still such powerful sources of controversy. Despite unification, each service still has its own privileges and interests, and has its own characteristic way of regarding the national security. All agree that the defense program should be balanced, but each service tends to think that such balance requires more money and manpower concentrated in the weaponry and operations in which it specializes; and all compete for control of the new modes of warfare, for control over missile, orbital, and space weaponry. The Secretary must preside over these powerful rivalries while performing all the other functions of his immensely difficult job.

The Secretary of Defense has duties similar to those of the Secretary of State—advisor to the President, spokesman within the Cabinet, the inter-agency committees, and throughout the administrative systems, decider of subpresidential matters, liaison with Congress and public, and head of a large and complex department.

In addition, the Secretary must maintain the American tradition of civilian control over the military. Most of the secretaries of the new Defense Department (and before them the secretaries of War and Navy) have been civilians rather than professional military men. The job of maintaining civilian supremacy while giving military experts the support and authority they need has never been more difficult. A number of recent novels and movies—*Dr. Strangelove, Fail-Safe, Seven Days in May*—are nightmare fantasies of the Neurotic General pushing The Button. The facts are more reassuring than the fantasy; even after a generation of Cold War, civilian control is still strong. But this is not to depreciate the danger or disparage entirely those who warn of possible consequences. One of President Eisenhower's last official pronouncements warned the American people against danger to liberal democracy from a combined military and industrial elite. But the solution cannot be to destroy The Button, junk The Bomb, or dispense with generals or admirals; they are indispensable in the present state of world affairs. Thus, American constitutional government, which in general has held strong during the last generation, must continue to be relied on. But not even such institutions can suffice indefinitely. Checks and balances are not enough. Never were decency, wisdom, and courage in high places more necessary to the democratic Republic.

Some Great Problems

Regulating the economy, justly reconciling conflicting economic and sectional interests, distinguishing between civil liberties and license, dealing with crime and disorder, and, always, instructing public opinion—all these tax the resources of statesmanship. But in foreign affairs, although the problems are not necessarily more profound, the difficulties are perhaps even greater. Problems erupt 'out there.' The intentions and capacities of opponents are less knowable than in domestic politics. Foreign opponents are not subject to the ordinarily moderating forces of domestic polity. There are no common political principles to which to appeal. The stakes are huge and the problems apparently endless.

It is impossible here even barely to touch on all the important modern problems of foreign affairs. Moreover, these problems are constantly changing. Crises come and go, sometimes in weeks; and the shape of even the enduring problems is constantly changing. Thus no attempt is here made to survey all the great problems. Rather, three areas have been selected for consideration because they illustrate well some of the most important contemporary problems and thus serve as a guide to the understanding of other problems.

The United Nations

What should be American policy toward the United Nations? Should we be 'loyal' to it, make furtherance of its ends our fundamental end? Should we make it the chief instrument for effectuating our foreign policy? Should we at least submit all our disputes to it? Or should we rather consider it as just one more arena within which to prosecute foreign policy, using or bypassing it as it suits our vital interests? Or should we ignore it entirely, indeed get out of it as soon as we can?

The answer to what we should do depends largely upon what the U.N. is, because that determines what can be achieved there. Is it an alliance or a confederation or a world government in embryo or just a utopian hope? The nature of the U.N. conforms to no neat answer, but its origin and aspirations shed some light.

The phrase 'United Nations' was a coinage of President Roosevelt's and its initial emphasis was on unity against a common foe.[14] But from the outset the U.N. was more than just a World War II alliance of the nations united against the Axis Powers. It was intended to become some sort of permanent confederation to superintend the peace. Yet confederations are voluntary associations of a particular group of countries united for their own domestic benefit and for defense against all others. In contrast, the U.N. was intended in time to embrace the whole world and

---

[14] H. G. Nicholas, *The United Nations as a Political Institution* (New York: Oxford University Press, 1963), p. 2.

THE UNITED NATIONS AND RELATED AGENCIES

THE UNITED NATIONS

INTER-NATIONAL ATOMIC ENERGY AGENCY

UNITED NATIONS OPERATIONS IN THE CONGO

UNITED NATIONS EMERGENCY FORCE

UNITED NATIONS RELIEF AND WORKS AGENCY FOR PALESTINE REFUGEES

UNITED NATIONS SPECIAL FUND

UNITED NATIONS CHILDREN'S FUND (UNICEF)

OFFICE OF UNITED NATIONS HIGH COMMISSIONER FOR REFUGEES

REGIONAL ECONOMIC COMMISSIONS

FUNCTIONAL COMMISSIONS

ADMINISTRATIVE COMMITTEE ON COORDINATION

TECHNICAL ASSISTANCE BOARD

SECURITY COUNCIL

GENERAL ASSEMBLY

TRUSTEESHIP COUNCIL

ECONOMIC AND SOCIAL COUNCIL

INTERNATIONAL COURT OF JUSTICE

SECRETARIAT

MILITARY STAFF COMMITTEE

DISARMAMENT COMMISSION

UNITED NATIONS ADMINISTRATIVE TRIBUNAL

UNITED NATIONS SCIENTIFIC ADVISORY COMMITTEE

SCIENTIFIC COMMITTEE ON EFFECTS OF ATOMIC RADIATION

COMMITTEE ON THE PEACEFUL USES OF OUTER SPACE

COMMITTEE ON INFORMATION FROM NON-SELF-GOVERNING TERRITORIES

INTERNATIONAL LAW COMMISSION

ADVISORY COMMITTEE ON ADMINISTRATIVE AND BUDGETARY QUESTIONS

COMMITTEE ON CONTRIBUTIONS

OTHER SUBSIDIARY BODIES OF GENERAL ASSEMBLY

THE SPECIALIZED AGENCIES

INTERNATIONAL FINANCE CORPORATION

INTERNATIONAL BANK FOR RECONSTRUCTION AND DEVELOPMENT

INTERNATIONAL TRADE ORGANIZATION General Agreement on Tariffs and Trade

INTERNATIONAL DEVELOPMENT ASSOCIATION

INTER-GOVERNMENTAL MARITIME CONSULTATIVE ORGANIZATION

WORLD METEOROLOGICAL ORGANIZATION

WORLD HEALTH ORGANIZATION

INTERNATIONAL TELECOMMUNICATION UNION

UNITED NATIONS EDUCATIONAL, SCIENTIFIC AND CULTURAL ORGANIZATION

UNIVERSAL POSTAL UNION

FOOD AND AGRICULTURE ORGANIZATION OF THE UNITED NATIONS

INTERNATIONAL CIVIL AVIATION ORGANIZATION

INTERNATIONAL LABOUR ORGANISATION

INTERNATIONAL MONETARY FUND

to achieve not the advantage of a group of nations but certain universal purposes.

These purposes expressed the deep longing of mankind for enduring peace and democracy and freedom, in the name of which (despite the irony that Stalin's Russia was an ally of the West) the second terrible war in a generation had just been fought. Its Charter proclaims that the U.N. seeks:

> To maintain international peace and security. . . . [To suppress] acts of aggression. . . . [To achieve] respect for the principle of equal rights and self-determination of peoples. . . . To achieve international coopera- tion in solving international problems of an economic, social, cultural, or humanitarian character, and in promoting and encouraging respect for human rights and for fundamental freedoms for all. . . . To be a centre for harmonizing the actions of nations in the attainment of these common ends.[15]

The nature of the U.N. (and thus the consideration of what American policy should be toward it) lies in these grand aspirations *and* in the way it has failed to achieve them. The U.N. aspired to go beyond the tradi- tional confederal form. Yet precisely because it sought to be a universal association, it proved more wholly voluntary and less united than many ordinary confederations of the past.

The U.N. depended entirely upon the continuing unity of its members, upon their having common postwar objectives. It depended especially upon the 'concert' of the major wartime allies, each of whom had the power (and no intention to relinquish it) individually to block the U.N.'s universal purposes. This fact was given legal recognition in the now famous veto power. Along with six rotating members, the Big Five (Britain, China, France, U.S.A., U.S.S.R.) were made permanent mem- bers of the U.N. Security Council, the body to which the U.N.'s major functions are entrusted. The veto operates because the Security Council cannot legally perform any major function to which one of the five per- manent members object; thus the Security Council could not function save by their unanimity. But with the onset of the Cold War, the pre- requisite unity ended; the great threats to peace came precisely from the disunity between Russia and the rest of the Big Five regarding post- war objectives. Thus, almost from the start, U.N. realities confounded the organization's original premise. To exist, the U.N. had to develop in un- anticipated ways, and America's U.N. problems and policies have reflected these developments.

At first, American leaders were enthusiastic about the U.N. The Senate thrust aside traditions of neutrality and isolation and overwhelmingly (89–2) made America the first signatory to the U.N. Charter. When Russia repeatedly vetoed American-led U.N. majority actions, American

---

[15] From Chapter I, Article I, of the U.N. Charter, quoted in Nicholas, *op. cit.*, p. 197.

spokesmen paraded our devotion to the U.N. in contrast with Russian churlishness. The devotion was partly genuine and reasonable (no other major power has tried as hard to help the U.N.), but there was also something of either hypocrisy or folly; American devotion rested at least in part on being able to win General Assembly and Security Council majorities based on western European and Latin-American countries. Both to take advantage of its General Assembly majority and to evade the Russian Security Council veto, America in 1950 secured passage of the controversial Uniting for Peace Resolution which enlarged the powers of the General Assembly, where the veto does not operate.

But this change, which seemed shrewd when America commanded General Assembly majorities, has come to seem less unquestionably wise now that the U.N. has grown from 50 to 114 member nations. Each country is endowed by the Charter with an equal vote in the General Assembly without regard to population or power. And the politics of this vastly enlarged General Assembly—with its new Asian and African countries, its less closely united western European countries, and its neutralist and 'third force' blocs—makes it highly problematical which way the majority will go. Related to the growing independence of the General Assembly is still another change—the development of the office of the Secretary-General, which has moved toward the authority of an independent executive.

Given these changes, America is now, as Russia has long been, in a situation where she could lose on a vital issue. And when this happens, America, like the Russians earlier, almost certainly would have recourse to the veto. It can be hoped that America will use the veto on behalf of juster causes; but the exercise of the veto by a major power must be viewed as legitimate both under the Charter and in the present state of international relations.

The United States simply cannot rely primarily upon such a U.N. to achieve its major foreign policy goals, practically all of which have had to do with containing or dealing with Communist Russia and international Communism.[16] Communism cannot be contained by an organization in which Russia exercises a veto, in which the politics of the majority are uncertain, and in which an unpredictable Secretariat exercises independent influence. Regimes threatened by Communism cannot be bolstered primarily through the U.N.; Truman's Greek-Turkish policy and the Marshall Plan could not have been executed through the U.N. Deterring major power aggression—and thus world war—is basically beyond the capacity of the U.N.; that is the task of America's arms and those of her allies. And control of nuclear arms must presently be approached by the nuclear powers directly; none of them will now accept the uncertain authority of the U.N.

---

[16] Cf. Lincoln P. Bloomfield, The United Nations and U.S. Foreign Policy (Boston: Little, Brown and Company, 1960), p. 248.

The questions asked at the outset are now nearly answered. The U.N. is not an alliance, not a confederation, and most surely not a world government. But it exists. Millions look to it. It is not so much a thing as a place; it is a new place where the nations of the world talk. Its international staff numbering more than four thousand and its numerous agencies perform some useful international functions. Still more, when Russian and American interests do not vitally conflict, it can help 'police' small conflicts and keep them from 'escalating.' And by an accident (Russia had 'walked out' of the Security Council), it performed valuably in the Korean conflict. Moreover, no man can say what the future holds; the terror of modern warfare and the human adventure in space may someday force developments now inconceivable. The U.N. might then prove of still greater value. It would thus be folly to 'Get the U.N. out of the U.S. and the U.S. out of the U.N.'

But statesmen must live in the present. And for the present the U.N. can only be deemed one of the many arenas for the prosecution of American foreign policy. It is a place to pursue policies in the American national interest, with such fidelity to the development of U.N. institutions as its Charter requires and as vital American interests permit. Not more. But that is still very much indeed.

Making and Keeping Alliances

The U.N. proving no substitute for traditional diplomacy and defense, the United States has resorted to a major power's classical policy—a system of alliances. Traditional elsewhere, it is a novel foreign policy for America. The kind of alliances America now builds are precisely the permanent and "entangling" kind George Washington warned against. With one difference. Washington warned against alliances that would entangle the weak new republic in the quarrels of others, which by a policy of neutrality we could avoid. The situation is now turned around: As a world power we want to entangle others in our quarrels. And one more difference: Washington warned against "interweaving our destiny . . . [with unjust] European ambition, rivalship, interest . . . or caprice." Our contest with Russian and Chinese Communism is not primarily a matter of selfish ambition, mere rivalship, narrow national interest, or caprice. The struggle against Communism is indispensable to our own security, but also to the security and freedom of others as well. But however just our cause, we nonetheless are engaged in the business of entangling others in a struggle in which we take the leading part.

First and foremost in our alliance system has been cooperation with Britain in particular and western Europe in general. While American and British interests and views sometimes clash (e.g., recognition of Communist China, the "Suez War"), Anglo-American unity has been firm on the major question of resisting Communist expansion; and British support has been indispensable in building the larger alliance with western

Europe. This general alliance commenced in the Marshall Plan for European economic recovery. But as the Cold War intensified, it was feared that an economically rebuilt Europe would nonetheless fall to direct Russian military aggression or, more likely, to internal subversion combined with the Russian military threat. The result was the formation in 1949 (despite criticism that it would worsen tensions and bankrupt Europe) of the historic North Atlantic Treaty Organization (NATO) which partly coordinated the military strength of 14 countries.

From the American point of view, NATO was a profound break with tradition. It is America's first peacetime permanent alliance, as against temporary wartime alliances; and by the provision that an attack on any member nation is to be treated as an attack on all, NATO formally linked American destiny with that of western Europe. The enormous scale of NATO and its weak but still partially supranational features (e.g., its permanent multinational coordinating bodies and its supranational command structure) make it a remarkable alliance from any point of view.

The outstanding success of America's postwar foreign policy has been the halting of Communist expansion into Europe, so threatening in 1947, and the general restoration of western Europe. But during two decades, the problems of keeping NATO intact have been difficult, frequent, and ever-changing. An alliance is seldom very much more than the present reasons the partners have for continuing to cooperate. The interests and views of (17 in 1965) very different countries have constantly had to be reconciled. Entirely understandable fears of Germany have had to be dealt with in bringing German divisions and officers into NATO. (This was only one of many complications, for example, in deciding how to equip NATO with nuclear weapons. Who could be happy about having to rearm Germany less than a generation after World War II?) As European countries regained strength and pride—France, for example—they have understandably been less willing to follow American leadership. Centrifugal forces within the alliance have become stronger as the partial 'thaw' within Russia and the Sino-Soviet conflict have lessened the common fear of the U.S.S.R. While NATO remains the most important alliance, the center of conflict has shifted away from Europe for the time being.

America has built an elaborate system of alliances throughout the world, many modeled on NATO but most of them far less effectual. There is ANZUS (Australia, New Zealand, and the U.S.), CENTO (Central Treaty Organization), SEATO (South East Asia Treaty Organization), and many important pacts with individual countries. On the whole these alliances are valuable, not as viable organizations, but because through them American officials have constant opportunity to try to strengthen the economic, social, and military links of these countries with America. Far more than NATO, the reality underlying these alliances is America's own power. Their greatest value is that they supply an established basis for American intervention when necessary to block Communist aggression.

Alliances of the Free World? America speaks of all these arrangements as alliances of the Free World. Is the claim just? In fact, America is now allied or linked with some nations whose forms of government are unfree, dictatorial, feudal, or corrupt. And one consequence of the alliance with America usually is that the unsatisfactory regime is thereby strengthened.

Nonetheless the claim is just in the broadest sense: The alliances help preserve the free nations of the world (and some dictatorships) from Communist expansion. 'Realists' in foreign affairs argue correctly that, unfortunately, allies are where you can find them. What counts is whether they can supply air, naval, or missile bases, materiel, troops, or ships. If a dictatorship is strong or strategically located, it may well be an indispensable ally, form of government notwithstanding. Indeed in an unstable country a dictatorship may have temporarily to be propped up as the sole practical way to maintain a vital military objective. But the 'idealists' are right to be troubled by such unsavory allies. We should at least treat them coolly; it is possible to do business with a dictator without falling over into friendship. Especially considering the tradition of an American Mission, full friendship should be reserved for allies like Britain and France (quarrels with de Gaulle notwithstanding) where ties are based upon some common fundamental principles as well as merely strategic considerations.

A War but a Cold One

Problems erupt in endless ways and places and demand rapid and varied responses. The task is to respond competently in such a way that the grand objectives of foreign policy are served. This requires what it is easier to state than to achieve. A competent administrative system must anticipate trouble, and be able rapidly to pull together the knowledge, hunches, and alternative proposals of State Department desk officers, embassies, the Central Intelligence Agency (not just cloak-and-dagger stuff, but also scholarly reports on economics and politics), the military branches, and bureaus scattered throughout the executive departments. And more than knowledge and plans are necessary. The wherewithal to execute policy must be available—a Seventh Fleet detachment in the Gulf of Tonkin to respond to crisis in Vietnam, planes available for a Berlin airlift, men, money, and supplies for use wherever necessary.

But above all a President is needed who understands the nation's grand objectives and who can respond to specific crises with specific policies appropriate to the long-range goals. These grand objectives or goals must be seen in the context within which every President since the end of World War II has had to act—the Cold War against Communist aggression be it Russian or Chinese. As we have seen, the term itself suggests what American policy, despite important differences among rival statesmen, has been and must be. The policy has been to 'win' the Cold War—but to win only in the limited sense of halting the spread of Communism and weakening it, thus achieving a world sufficiently free and secure for the American republic to endure. But the policy is also to keep the war cold if humanly possible; modern nuclear war is so awesomely destructive that anything less than utter sobriety in contemplating it is contemptible folly. It is with these two grand imperatives in mind that we can consider briefly some specific crises and problems of the last generation.

Burundi is our business? The conflict over the Congo is a good example of the kinds of problems America now encounters. It illustrates the immense range of American involvement in foreign affairs, the confusion and complexity of each specific problem, and the overall framework within which such problems must be faced.

Initially utterly unable to govern itself, the Congo was a standing invitation to crisis after the hasty grant of independence by Belgium in 1960.

> [T]o other African states their new-found independence seemed at stake in the fate of the Congo; to the U.S.S.R. this was a heaven-sent opportunity to intervene in the name of anti-colonialism; to Belgium and to a lesser degree other Western states a valuable economico-strategic interest was involved in the big copper mines of the *Union Minière* of the province of Katanga.[17]

A further complication was the intervention of a U.N. military force into the Congo crisis. Hoping to prevent the Congo from becoming a new battleground of the Cold War (and later out of a determination to prevent the 'secession' of the relatively wealthy and stable Katanga province), the U.N. found itself embroiled in a costly and bloody operation for which only scant justification could be found in its Charter. Although the United States supported it, the U.N.'s Congo policy brought severe criticism from the U.S.S.R., France, Belgium, and from many Americans.

What business is all of this of the United States? Traditionally, little more would have had to be done than protect American lives and property. But the Cold War makes all the difference. America had to have a general Congo policy because Russia had one. Russia was achieving ominous influence through the policies of Patrice Lumumba who was then the Congo's strongest leader. America had to become deeply involved because a Russian-dominated Communist base in the heart of Africa would have been very dangerous. It is possible to argue whether America should have supported the U.N. or whether, as critics urged, it should have backed Moise Tshombe's Katanga government, but it is hard to see how America could have avoided taking some stand on the Congo crisis.

The U.N. intervention, Russian clumsiness, and the murder of Lumumba all helped dissipate the Soviet threat. But in 1964 a new complication was introduced. Rebel guerrillas, aided and partially led from the neighboring country of Burundi, threatened to overthrow the Congolese

---

[17] H. G. Nicholas, *op. cit.*, p. 63.

government. Well what of that? Why not let the Burundis and Congolese fight it out and be done with it? Unfortunately, the Chinese Communists had entered the picture. By sending economic aid, technicians, and military advisers, the Chinese had gained a foothold in newly independent Burundi and were influencing the Congolese rebels. Had the rebels succeeded, Burundi and the Congo could well have become bases for Chinese-led Communist subversion throughout Africa. Perhaps a portent of the future, the original Cold War factor in the Congo crisis had yielded to one stemming from the Sino-Soviet conflict. But the decisive fact was the continued threat of Communist aggression. Difficult as it is to bring American force or wealth to bear in so chaotic and remote a situation, the Congo and Burundi thus inescapably become America's business.

Crises and 'hot spots.' Berlin, Korea, Vietnam, France and Algeria, Cuba, the Dominican Republic, Egypt and Israel, India and Pakistan, India and China, Greece and Turkey—each crisis or 'hot spot' has been or is a special problem with its own peculiar intractibilities, nuances, and dangers. But some generalizations about these conflicts and American responses to them are possible.

First, some conflicts are relatively uninvolved in the Cold War. There are territorial disputes, anticolonial struggles, the thrust of nationalism, economic rivalries, religious bitternesses—the things that have inflamed the relations among nations for centuries. Even if Russia and America did not exist, Greece and Turkey would still clash over the island of Cyprus with its Greek (and Orthodox Catholic) majority and its Turkish (and Moslem) minority. India and Pakistan would still clash over religious and territorial issues in Kashmir. The Arab nations would still clash with Israel. And quite apart from the Cold War, America would in traditional ways be obliged to execute policies with regard to these clashes. American nationals are involved, there are American oil interests in the Middle East and commercial interests almost everywhere, American citizens have ties to countries of their national origin, and like many modern civilized nations America could not stand by without making some effort to prevent the slaughter and misery of millions of human beings. As always the difficulties are great; every policy has costly consequences. To help, say, Algeria in its struggle for independence against France, is to ignore the claims of a traditional ally and to jeopardize long-standing relations with France. To help India is to lose ground with Pakistan. (Russia appeared to have the same sort of problem in the China-India border war.) And, finally, while these conflicts are *relatively* uninvolved with the Cold War, there is always its shadow. To fail to help Algeria may be to lose ground among other newly emerging nations in Africa whose support may someday be vital. Greece and Turkey are NATO members who happen to be in close proximity to Russia; a full-fledged war between them would weaken the major western alliance.

Second, there are some hardy perennials of the Cold War. For example, West Berlin and the two Germanys are unfinished business of World

War II; East-West conflict has been recurringly acute in West Berlin, isolated within Communist East Germany and always vulnerable to Russian pressure. The Congo, as we have seen, is an area where crisis is always ready to flare up. Another such area is Southeast Asia, where Chinese political and military pressure is greatest and where America is deeply involved in South Vietnam. Another is Cuba where Castro, firmly within the Communist camp, seeks throughout Central and South America to cause the unrest and disorder calculated to open the way to new Castro-like regimes; fear of Castro vastly complicated American problems in the Dominican Republic internecine conflict in 1965.

Third, apart from *ad hoc* responses to crisis, there are longer-range programs aimed at effecting permanent changes in the world balance of forces. This consists fundamentally in trying to strengthen the countries of the Free World along the lines of the restoration of western Europe. The only enduring defense against Communist subversion is stable self-government resting upon an adequate economy. But it is infinitely easier to restore than to create free or stable institutions. The western European countries had political and economic traditions and institutions upon which to rebuild. Similarly, in Asia, America helped restore Japan's stability and strength. But in most parts of the world no such traditions and institutions exist to be restored. Without any great success as yet, for example, America has worked through the regional Organization of American States and through the controversial Alliance for Progress (a long-term program of economic aid) to foster greater stability in Latin America. And America has provided special assistance to countries like Venezuela where the recent Betancourt regime, under bitter onslaught from Castro, nonetheless made progress in a democratic and liberal direction.

The 'brink of war' and 'limited war.' John Foster Dulles, Secretary of State under Eisenhower, argued that America had to be prepared to go to the very brink of war to resist the thrust of Communist expansion. This 'brinkmanship' was immediately sharply criticized, and the criticism was just if Dulles meant a truculent readiness to oppose every Communist move with instant military show-down. But if, as is more likely, the policy meant being prepared to meet vital Communist challenges with force even at risk of war, it is hard to see how it can be gainsaid. A classic example of 'going to the brink' occurred during the Cuban missile crisis of 1962. In October of that year, aerial reconnaissance of Cuba revealed that Russian military personnel were rapidly completing a major nuclear missile base on the island. This was an intolerable threat to American security and a daring attempt by the Russians to change the military balance of the Cold War. President Kennedy ordered a naval quarantine to prevent Russian ships then on the high seas from delivering further materiel. After several tense days the Russian ships turned back, and steps were taken to dismantle the missile establishment (but not to remove the Russian military presence). There was no guarantee that the Russians would back down; President Kennedy had taken the country—and the world—to the brink. But any other course would have been fatal to American interests and those of the free world. Had America backed down from the Russian missile challenge in Cuba, neither Russia nor America's allies could believe that she would ever really stand fast anywhere. The ability to face the gravest consequences in meeting grave threats is indispensable to American foreign policy.

And not only has America gone to the brink during a generation of Cold War, she has actually been to a 'shooting war' in Korea. Sometimes called 'Truman's War,' it was also 'Truman's Victory': Communist aggression was repelled. But it was victory of a new (and less satisfying) kind in a rather new kind of war—limited war.

Limited war is a peculiarly modern concept. In earlier ages there were incidents, skirmishes, little wars, and big wars, but not really limited wars. It took two uniquely modern things to conjure the concept into being— the existence of the U.S.A. and the U.S.S.R. as *superpowers* with *superweapons*. Limiting war means limiting conflicts in which the U.S.A. and the U.S.S.R. are actually or potentially engaged in two ways. First, it means keeping them from deepening their involvement and thus drawing their respective allies and thus the whole world into the conflict—i.e., limiting the spread of the war. Second, it means limiting the use of weapons—i.e., keeping conventional warfare from 'escalating' into thermonuclear war. Much thought is presently being given to ways to make limited war possible in preference to total war. The assumption is that world law and order is far from a present reality, and that wars will in fact break out. As it were, men are now trying to make war safe for the world, to permit the eruption of conflict while keeping it from profoundly impairing human civilization.

The burden these realities place upon statesmanship is enormous. A President must be able to recognize the truly grave threats, and he must be able to choose actions that stay within the range of 'limitation.' An example was President Johnson's response in August, 1964 to two North Vietnamese torpedo boat attacks upon American destroyers in the Gulf of Tonkin. His reply was immediate, precise, and limited—carrier-based planes bombed the North Vietnam torpedo boat bases. As the attack was in progress, President Johnson publicly announced precisely what was being done and made clear that nothing more was presently being contemplated. Effort was made to keep the military reply limited and to prevent conflict from escalating beyond the necessities of the situation. Subsequently, as Viet Cong attacks mounted in South Vietnam, American aerial bombardment of North Vietnam was greatly increased and American troops directly entered the conflict. But this was still limited warfare. The aim was not destruction and conquest of the enemy and traditional victory; rather it was limited application of force to oblige the Communists to reduce their attacks in South Vietnam.

The Burden upon Democratic Government

The conduct of foreign affairs under such constraints and amid nearly constant crisis places a burden not only upon statesmanship, but upon public opinion and the democratic form of government. Tocqueville warned that

> foreign politics demand scarcely any of those qualities which are peculiar to a democracy; they require, on the contrary, the perfect use of almost all those in which it is deficient. . . . [A] democracy can only with great difficulty regulate the details of an important undertaking, persevere in a fixed design, and work out its execution in spite of serious obstacles. It cannot combine its measures with secrecy or await their consequences with patience. These are qualities which more especially belong to an individual or an aristocracy.[18]

This would seem to pronounce doom upon democracy in an age of permanent international crisis. But as in all of Tocqueville's *Democracy in America,* he is here speaking of the *tendency* of democratic nations. It is the test of men and nations and systems of government whether they can prevent their unworthy tendencies from becoming their actual conduct. The whole of American government is an attempt to conquer the adverse tendencies of democracy with respect to liberty and the competence of government. Once again a great crisis is testing whether a system of government thus conceived can produce citizens and statesmen who, largely because they deserve to, will long endure.

BIBLIOGRAPHICAL NOTE

Hans J. Morgenthau, *Politics Among Nations* (3rd ed., 1960) and Quincy Wright, *The Study of International Relations* (1955) are general introductions to the field. Robert A. Goldwin (with Ralph A. Lerner and Gerald Stourzh), ed., *Readings in World Politics* (1959) will lead the student to many important writings. Primarily concerned with modern aspects of international relations, and differing in point of view, are Raymond Aron, *On War* (1959), John H. Herz, *International Politics in the Atomic Age* (1959), and Henry A. Kissinger, *Nuclear Weapons and Foreign Policy* (1957).

Standard introductions to the history of American foreign relations are Samuel F. Bemis, *A Diplomatic History of the United States* (4th ed., 1955) and Julius W. Pratt, *A History of United States Foreign Policy* (2nd ed., 1965). For an account of modern developments, see William G. Carleton, *The Revolution in American Foreign Policy* (1957) and George F. Kennan, *American Diplomacy: 1900–1950* (1951). Three works which consider from different points of view the problem of 'realpolitik' and the American Mission are Hans J.

---

[18] Tocqueville, *op. cit.*, I, 243–44.

Morgenthau, *In Defense of the National Interest* (1951), Robert E. Osgood, *Ideals and Self-Interest in America's Foreign Relations* (1953), and Frank Tannenbaum, *The American Tradition in Foreign Policy* (1955). Standard histories of American constitutional law discuss the constitutional basis of the conduct of foreign affairs and give bibliographic guidance. See especially Edward S. Corwin, *The President: Office and Powers* (1948) and *Total War and the Constitution* (1947).

Walter Lippmann, *Essays in the Public Philosophy* (1954) deals with problems of conducting foreign affairs in a democracy. Robert A. Dahl, *Congress and Foreign Policy* (1950), Daniel S. Cheever and H. Field Haviland, Jr., *United States Foreign Policy and the Separation of Powers* (1952), and H. Bradford Westerfield, *Foreign Policy and Party Politics* (1955) deal with the political process and foreign policy. Public opinion in relation to foreign policy is treated in Gabriel A. Almond, *The American People and Foreign Policy* (1950). For the administration of foreign affairs see James L. McCamy, *The Administration of American Foreign Affairs* (1950) and Arthur W. Macmahon, *Administration in Foreign Affairs* (1953). The military in the American political system is considered in Samuel P. Huntington, *The Soldier and the State* (1957), Jerome G. Kerwin, *Civil-Military Relationships in American Life* (1948), Walter Millis, Harvey C. Mansfield, H. Stein, *Arms and the State* (1958).

For World War II and the beginnings of the Cold War see Chester Wilmot, *The Struggle for Europe* (1963). Fuller accounts of the Cold War are John Lukacs, *A History of the Cold War* (1961), Hugh Seton-Watson, *Neither War nor Peace* (1960), and D. F. Fleming, ed., *The Changing Cold War*, a special issue of *The Annals*, January, 1964; Hugh Ross, *The Cold War: Containment and its Critics* (1963) is a short collection of documents on the problem. Analysis of the Soviet Union in international relations and guidance to further reading is to be found in Robert A. Goldwin (with Gerald Stourzh and Marvin Zetterbaum, eds.), *Readings in Russian Foreign Policy* and Zbigniew K. Brezezinski, *The Soviet Bloc: Unity and Conflict* (1960).

It is obviously possible to mention only a few works on specific contemporary problems. The literature is vast and proliferating. The titles of the following indicate their subject matter; further guidance to readings can be found in each. Inis L. Claude, Jr., *Swords into Plowshares: The Problems and Progress of International Organization* (1956); Clark M. Eichelberger, *U.N.—The First Fifteen Years* (1960); George G. Taylor and Ben Cashman, *The New United Nations* (1965); Bernard Brodie, *Strategy in the Missile Age* (1959); and Robert A. Goldwin, (ed.), *America Armed: Essays on United States Military Policy* (1964); George Liska, *The New Statecraft: Foreign Aid in American Foreign Policy* (1960); Tang Tsou, *America's Failure in China*, 1941–50 (1963); Theodore Draper, *Castro's Revolution* (1962); Robert E. Osgood, *Limited War* (1957).

APPENDIX

APPENDIX

THE DECLARATION OF INDEPENDENCE—1776[1]

In Congress, July 4, 1776

THE UNANIMOUS DECLARATION OF THE THIRTEEN UNITED STATES OF AMERICA

WHEN in the Course of human events, it becomes necessary for one people to dissolve the political bands which have connected them with another, and to assume among the powers of the earth, the separate and equal station to which the Laws of Nature and of Nature's God entitle them, a decent respect to the opinions of mankind requires that they should declare the causes which impel them to the separation.—We hold these truths to be self-evident, that all men are created equal, that they are endowed by their Creator with certain unalienable Rights, that among these are Life, Liberty and the pursuit of Happiness.—That to secure these rights, Governments are instituted among Men, deriving their just powers from the consent of the governed,—That whenever any Form of Government becomes destructive of these ends, it is the Right of the People to alter or to abolish it, and to institute new Government, laying its foundation on such principles and organizing its powers in such form, as to them shall seem most likely to effect their Safety and Happiness. Prudence, indeed, will dictate that Governments long established should not be changed for light and transient causes; and accordingly all experience hath shown, that mankind are more disposed to suffer, while evils are sufferable, than to right themselves by abolishing the forms to which they are accustomed. But when a long train of abuses and usurpations, pursuing invariably the same Object evinces a design to reduce them under absolute Despotism, it is their right, it is their duty, to throw off such Government, and to provide new Guards for their future security.— Such has been the patient sufferance of these Colonies; and such is now

---

[1] Reprinted from the facsimile of the engrossed copy of the original manuscript in the Library of Congress.

the necessity which constrains them to alter their former Systems of Government. The history of the present King of Great Britain is a history of repeated injuries and usurpations, all having in direct object the establishment of an absolute Tyranny over these States. To prove this, let Facts be submitted to a candid world.—He has refused his Assent to Laws, the most wholesome and necessary for the public good.—He has forbidden his Governors to pass Laws of immediate and pressing importance, unless suspended in their operation till his Assent should be obtained; and when so suspended, he has utterly neglected to attend to them.—He has refused to pass other Laws for the accommodation of large districts of people, unless those people would relinquish the right of Representation in the Legislature, a right inestimable to them and formidable to tyrants only.—He has called together legislative bodies at places unusual, uncomfortable, and distant from the depository of their public Records, for the sole purpose of fatiguing them into compliance with his measures.—He has dissolved Representative Houses repeatedly, for opposing with manly firmness his invasions on the rights of the people.—He has refused for a long time, after such dissolutions, to cause others to be elected; whereby the Legislative powers, incapable of Annihilation, have returned to the People at large for their exercise; the State remaining in the mean time exposed to all the dangers of invasion from without, and convulsions within.—He has endeavoured to prevent the population of these States; for that purpose obstructing the Laws for Naturalization of Foreigners; refusing to pass others to encourage their migration hither, and raising the conditions of new Appropriations of Lands.—He has obstructed the Administration of Justice, by refusing his Assent to Laws for establishing Judiciary powers.—He has made Judges dependent on his Will alone, for the tenure of their offices, and the amount and payment of their salaries.—He has erected a multitude of New Offices, and sent hither swarms of Officers to harrass our people, and eat out their substance.—He has kept among us, in times of peace, Standing Armies, without the Consent of our legislatures.—He has affected to render the Military independent of and superior to the Civil power.—He has combined with others to subject us to a jurisdiction foreign to our constitution, and unacknowledged by our laws; giving his Assent to their Acts of pretended Legislation:—For quartering large bodies of armed troops among us:—For protecting them, by a mock Trial, from punishment for any Murders which they should commit on the Inhabitants of these States:—For cutting off our Trade with all parts of the world:—For imposing Taxes on us without our Consent:—For depriving us in many cases, of the benefits of Trial by Jury:—For transporting us beyond Seas to be tried for pretended offences:—For abolishing the free System of English Laws in a neighbouring Province, establishing therein an Arbitrary government, and enlarging its Boundaries so as to render it at once an example and fit instrument for introducing the same absolute rule into these Colonies:—For taking away our Charters, abolishing our most valuable Laws, and altering fundamentally the Forms of our Governments:—For suspending our own Legislatures, and declaring themselves invested with power to legislate for us in all cases whatsoever.—He has abdicated Government here, by declaring us out of his Protection and waging War against us.—He has plundered our seas, ravaged our Coasts, burnt our towns, and destroyed the lives of our people.—He is at this time transporting large armies of foreign mercenaries to compleat the works of death, desolation and tyranny, already begun with circumstances of Cruelty & perfidy scarcely paralleled in the most barbarous ages, and totally unworthy the Head of a civilized nation.—He has constrained our fellow Citizens taken Captive on the high Seas to bear Arms against their Country, to become the executioners of their friends and Brethren, or to fall themselves by their Hands.—He has excited domestic insurrections amongst us, and has endeavoured to bring on the inhabitants of our frontiers, the merciless Indian Savages, whose known rule of warfare, is an undistinguished destruction of all ages, sexes and conditions. In every stage of these Oppressions We have Petitioned for Redress in the most humble terms: Our repeated Petitions have been answered only by repeated injury. A Prince, whose character is thus marked by every act which may define a Tyrant, is unfit to be the ruler of a free people. Nor have We been wanting in attentions to our Brittish brethren. We have warned them from time to time of attempts by their legislature to extend an unwarrantable jurisdiction over us. We have reminded them of the circumstances of our emigration and settlement here. We have appealed to their native justice and magnanimity, and we have conjured them by the ties of our common kindred to disavow these usurpations, which, would inevitably interrupt our connections and correspondence. They too have been deaf to the voice of justice and of consanguinity. We must, therefore, acquiesce in the necessity, which denounces our Separation, and hold them, as we hold the rest of mankind, Enemies in War, in Peace Friends.—

WE, THEREFORE, the REPRESENTATIVES of the UNITED STATES OF AMERICA, in General Congress, Assembled, appealing to the Supreme Judge of the world for the rectitude of our intentions, do, in the Name, and by Authority of the good People of these Colonies, solemnly publish and declare, That these United Colonies are, and of Right ought to be FREE AND INDEPENDENT STATES; that they are Absolved from all Allegiance to the British Crown, and that all political connection between them and the State of Great Britain, is and ought to be totally dissolved; and that as Free and Independent States, they have full Power to levy War, conclude Peace, contract Alliances, establish Commerce, and to do all other Acts and Things which Independent States may of right do.—And for the support of this Declaration, with a firm reliance on the protection of

Divine Providence, we mutually pledge to each other our Lives, our Fortunes and our sacred Honor.

JOHN HANCOCK.

New Hampshire
JOSIAH BARTLETT,
WM. WHIPPLE,
MATTHEW THORNTON.

Massachusetts Bay
SAML. ADAMS,
JOHN ADAMS,
ROBT. TREAT PAINE,
ELBRIDGE GERRY.

Rhode Island
STEP. HOPKINS,
WILLIAM ELLERY.

Connecticut
ROGER SHERMAN,
SAM'EL HUNTINGTON,
WM. WILLIAMS,
OLIVER WOLCOTT.

New York
WM. FLOYD,
PHIN. LIVINGSTON,
FRANS. LEWIS,
LEWIS MORRIS.

New Jersey
RICHD. STOCKTON,
JNO. WITHERSPOON,
FRAS. HOPKINSON,
JOHN HART,
ABRA. CLARK,

Pennsylvania
ROBT. MORRIS,
BENJAMIN RUSH,
BENJA. FRANKLIN,
JOHN MORTON,
GEO. CLYMER,
JAS. SMITH,
GEO. TAYLOR,
JAMES WILSON,
GEO. ROSS.

Delaware
CAESAR RODNEY,
GEO. READ,
THO. M'KEAN.

Maryland
SAMUEL CHASE,
WM. PACA,
THOS. STONE,
CHARLES CARROLL of Carrollton.

Virginia
GEORGE WYTHE,
RICHARD HENRY LEE,
TH. JEFFERSON,
BENJA. HARRISON,
THS. NELSON, JR.,
FRANCIS LIGHTFOOT LEE,
CARTER BRAXTON.

North Carolina
WM. HOOPER,
JOSEPH HEWES,
JOHN PENN.

South Carolina
EDWARD RUTLEDGE,
THOS. HEYWARD, JUNR.,
THOS. LYNCH, JUNR.,
ARTHUR MIDDLETON.

Georgia
BUTTON GWINNETT,
LYMAN HALL,
GEO. WALTON.

NOTE.—Mr. Ferdinand Jefferson, Keeper of the Rolls in the Department of State, at Washington, says: "The names of the signers are spelt above as in the facsimile of the original, but the punctuation of them is not always the same; neither do the names of the States appear in the facsimile of the original. The names of the signers of each State are grouped together in the facsimile of the original, except the name of Matthew Thornton, which follows that of Oliver Wolcott."—*Revised Statutes of the United States,* 2d edition, 1878, p. 6.

THE CONSTITUTION OF THE UNITED STATES[1]

We the People of the United States, in Order to form a more perfect Union, establish Justice, insure domestic Tranquility, provide for the common defence, promote the general Welfare, and secure the Blessings of Liberty to ourselves and our Posterity, do ordain and establish this Constitution for the United States of America.

Article. I.

Section. 1.   All legislative Powers herein granted shall be vested in a Congress of the United States, which shall consist of a Senate and House of Representatives.

Section. 2.   The House of Representatives shall be composed of Members chosen every second Year by the People of the several States, and the Electors in each State shall have the Qualifications requisite for Electors of the most numerous Branch of the State Legislature.

No person shall be a Representative who shall not have attained to the Age of twenty five Years and been seven Years a Citizen of the United States, and who shall not, when elected, be an Inhabitant of that State in which he shall be chosen.

Representatives and direct Taxes shall be apportioned among the several States which may be included within this Union, according to their respective Numbers, which shall be determined by adding to the whole Number of free Persons, including those bound to Service for a Term of Years, and excluding Indians not taxed, three fifths of all other Persons. The actual Enumeration shall be made within three Years after the first Meeting of the Congress of the United States, and within every subsequent Term of ten Years, in such Manner as they shall by Law direct. The Number of Representatives shall not exceed one for every thirty Thousand, but each State shall have at Least one Representative; and until such enumeration shall be made, the State of New Hampshire shall be entitled to chuse three, Massachusetts eight, Rhode-Island and Providence Plantations one, Connecticut five, New-York six, New Jersey four, Pennsylvania eight, Delaware one, Maryland six, Virginia ten, North Carolina five, South Carolina five, and Georgia three.

When vacancies happen in the Representation from any State, the

---

[1] Reprinted from a literal copy of the engrossed Constitution as signed. The original is in four sheets, with an additional sheet containing the resolutions of transmittal. The note indented at the end is in the original precisely as reproduced here.

Executive Authority thereof shall issue Writs of Election to fill such Vacancies.

The House of Representatives shall chuse their Speaker and other Officers; and shall have the sole Power of Impeachment.

Section. 3.   The Senate of the United States shall be composed of two Senators from each State, chosen by the Legislature thereof, for six Years; and each Senator shall have one Vote.

Immediately after they shall be assembled in Consequence of the first Election, they shall be divided as equally as may be into three Classes. The Seats of the Senators of the first Class shall be vacated at the Expiration of the second Year, of the second Class at the Expiration of the fourth Year, and of the third Class at the Expiration of the sixth Year, so that one third may be chosen every second Year; and if Vacancies happen by Resignation, or otherwise, during the Recess of the Legislature of any State, the Executive thereof may make temporary Appointments until the next Meeting of the Legislature, which shall then fill such Vacancies.

No Person shall be a Senator who shall not have attained to the Age of thirty Years, and been nine Years a Citizen of the United States, and who shall not, when elected, be an Inhabitant of that State for which he shall be chosen.

The Vice President of the United States shall be President of the Senate, but shall have no Vote, unless they be equally divided.

The Senate shall chuse their other Officers, and also a President pro tempore, in the Absence of the Vice President, or when he shall exercise the Office of President of the United States.

The Senate shall have the sole Power to try all Impeachments. When sitting for that Purpose, they shall be on Oath or Affirmation. When the President of the United States ∧ is tried, the Chief Justice shall preside: And no Person shall be convicted without the Concurrence of two thirds of the Members present.

Judgment in Cases of Impeachment shall not extend further than to removal from Office, and disqualification to hold and enjoy any Office of honor, Trust or Profit under the United States: but the Party convicted shall nevertheless be liable and subject to Indictment, Trial, Judgment and Punishment, according to Law.

Section. 4.   The Times, Places and Manner of holding Elections for Senators and Representatives, shall be prescribed in each State by the Legislature thereof; but the Congress may at any time by Law make or alter such Regulations, except as to the Places of chusing Senators.

The Congress shall assemble at least once in every Year, and such Meeting shall be on the first Monday in December, unless they shall by Law appoint a different Day.

Section. 5.   Each House shall be the Judge of the Elections, Returns and Qualifications of its own Members, and a Majority of each shall constitute a Quorum to do Business; but a smaller Number may adjourn from day to day, and may be authorized to compel the Attendance of absent Members, in such Manner, and under such Penalties as each House may provide.

Each House may determine the Rules of its Proceedings, punish its Members for disorderly Behaviour, and, with the Concurrence of two thirds, expel a Member.

Each House shall keep a Journal of its Proceedings, and from time to time publish the same, excepting such Parts as may in their Judgment require Secrecy; and the Yeas and Nays of the Members of either House on any question shall, at the Desire of one fifth of those Present, be entered on the Journal.

Neither House, during the Session of Congress, shall, without the Consent of the other, adjourn for more than three days, nor to any other Place than that in which the two Houses shall be sitting.

Section. 6. The Senators and Representatives shall receive a Compensation for their Services, to be ascertained by Law, and paid out of the Treasury of the United States. They shall in all Cases, except Treason, Felony and Breach of the Peace, be privileged from Arrest during their Attendance at the Session of their respective Houses, and in going to and returning from the same; and for any Speech or Debate in either House, they shall not be questioned in any other Place.

No Senator or Representative shall, during the Time for which he was elected, be appointed to any civil Office under the Authority of the United States, which shall have been created, or the Emoluments whereof shall have been encreased during such time; and no Person holding any Office under the United States, shall be a Member of either House during his Continuance in Office.

Section. 7. All Bills for raising Revenue shall originate in the House of Representatives; but the Senate may propose or concur with Amendments as on other Bills.

Every Bill which shall have passed the House of Representatives and the Senate, shall, before it become a Law, be presented to the President of the United States; If he approves he shall sign it, but if not he shall return it, with his Objections to that House in which it shall have originated, who shall enter the Objections at large on their Journal, and proceed to reconsider it. If after such Reconsideration two thirds of that House shall agree to pass the Bill, it shall be sent, together with the Objections, to the other House, by which it shall likewise be reconsidered, and if approved by two thirds of that House, it shall become a Law. But in all such Cases the Votes of both Houses shall be determined by yeas and Nays, and the Names of the Persons voting for and against the Bill shall be entered on the Journal of each House respectively. If any Bill shall not be returned by the President within ten days (Sundays excepted) after it shall have been presented to him, the Same shall be a Law, in like Manner as if he had signed it, unless the Congress by their Adjournment prevent its Return in which Case it shall not be a Law.

Every Order, Resolution, or Vote to which the Concurrence of the Senate and House of Representatives may be necessary (except on a question of Adjournment) shall be presented to the President of the United States; and before the Same shall take Effect, shall be approved by him, or being disapproved by him, shall be repassed by two thirds of the Senate and House of Representatives, according to the Rules and Limitations prescribed in the Case of a Bill.

Section. 8.   The Congress shall have Power To lay and collect Taxes, Duties, Imposts and Excises, to pay the Debts and provide for the common Defence and general Welfare of the United States; but all Duties, Imposts and Excises shall be uniform throughout the United States;

To borrow Money on the credit of the United States;

To regulate Commerce with foreign Nations, and among the several States, and with the Indian Tribes;

To establish an uniform Rule of Naturalization, and uniform Laws on the subject of Bankruptcies throughout the United States;

To coin Money, regulate the Value thereof, and of foreign Coin, and fix the Standard of Weights and Measures;

To provide for the Punishment of counterfeiting the Securities and current Coin of the United States;

To establish Post Offices and post Roads;

To promote the Progress of Science and useful Arts, by securing for limited Times to Authors and Inventors the exclusive Right to their respective Writings and Discoveries;

To constitute Tribunals inferior to the supreme Court;

To define and punish Piracies and Felonies committed on the high Seas, and Offenses against the Law of Nations;

To declare War, grant Letters of Marque and Reprisal, and make Rules concerning Captures on Land and Water;

To raise and support Armies, but no Appropriation of Money to that Use shall be for a longer Term than two Years;

To provide and maintain a Navy;

To make Rules for the Government and Regulation of the land and naval Forces;

To provide for calling forth the Militia to execute the Laws of the Union, suppress Insurrections and repel Invasions;

To provide for organizing, arming, and disciplining, the Militia, and for governing such Part of them as may be employed in the Service of the United States, reserving to the States respectively, the Appointment of the Officers, and the Authority of training the Militia according to the discipline prescribed by Congress;

To exercise exclusive Legislation in all Cases whatsoever, over such District (not exceeding ten Miles square) as may, by Cession of particular States, and the Acceptance of Congress, become the Seat of the Government of the United States, and to exercise like Authority over all Places purchased by the Consent of the Legislature of the State in which the Same shall be, for the Erection of Forts, Magazines, Arsenals, dock-Yards, and other needful Buildings;—And

To make all Laws which shall be necessary and proper for carrying into Execution the foregoing Powers, and all other Powers vested by this Constitution in the Government of the United States, or in any Department or Officer thereof.

Section. 9. The Migration or Importation of such Persons as any of the States now existing shall think proper to admit, shall not be prohibited by the Congress prior to the Year one thousand eight hundred and eight, but a Tax or duty may be imposed on such Importation, not exceeding ten dollars for each Person.

The Privilege of the Writ of Habeas Corpus shall not be suspended, unless when in Cases of Rebellion or Invasion the public Safety may require it.

No Bill of Attainder or ex post facto Law shall be passed.

No Capitation, or other direct, Tax shall be laid, unless in Proportion to the Census or Enumeration herein before directed to be taken.

No Tax or Duty shall be laid on Articles exported from any State.

No Preference shall be given by any Regulation of Commerce or Revenue to the Ports of one State over those of another: nor shall Vessels bound to, or from, one State, be obliged to enter, clear, or pay Duties in another.

No Money shall be drawn from the Treasury, but in Consequence of Appropriations made by Law; and a regular Statement and Account of the Receipts and Expenditures of all public Money shall be published from time to time.

No Title of Nobility shall be granted by the United States: And no Person holding any Office of Profit or Trust under them, shall, without the Consent of the Congress, accept of any present, Emolument, Office, or Title, of any kind whatever, from any King, Prince, or foreign State.

Section. 10. No State shall enter into any Treaty, Alliance, or Confederation; grant Letters of Marque and Reprisal; coin Money; emit Bills of Credit; make any Thing but gold and silver Coin a Tender in Payment of Debts; pass any Bill of Attainder, ex post facto Law, or Law imparing the Obligation of Contracts, or grant any Title of Nobility.

No State shall, without the Consent of ^the Congress, lay any Imposts or Duties on Imports or Exports, except what may be absolutely necessary for executing it's inspection Laws: and the net Produce of all Duties and Imposts, laid by any State on Imports or Exports, shall be for the Use of the Treasury of the United States; and all such Laws shall be subject to the Revision and Controul of ^the Congress.

No State shall, without the Consent of Congress, lay any Duty of Tonnage, keep Troops, or Ships of War in time of Peace, enter into any Agreement or Compact with another State, or with a foreign Power, or engage in War, unless actually invaded, or in such imminent Danger as will not admit of delay.

Article. II.

Section. 1.   The executive Power shall be vested in a President of the United States of America. He shall hold his Office during the Term of four Years, and, together with the Vice President, chosen for the same Term, be elected as follows

Each State shall appoint, in such Manner as the Legislature thereof may direct, a Number of Electors, equal to the whole Number of Senators and Representatives to which the State may be entitled in the Congress: but no Senator or Representative, or Person holding an Office of Trust or Profit under the United States, shall be appointed an Elector.

The Electors shall meet in their respective States, and vote by Ballot for two Persons, of whom one at least shall not be an Inhabitant of the same State with themselves. And they shall make a List of all the Persons voted for, and of the Number of Votes for each; which List they shall sign and certify, and transmit sealed to the Seat of the Government of the United States, directed to the President of the Senate. The President of the Senate shall, in the Presence of the Senate and House of Representatives, open all the Certificates, and the Votes shall then be counted. The Person having the greatest Number of Votes shall be the President, if such Number be a Majority of the whole Number of Electors appointed; and if there be more than one who have such Majority, and have an equal Number of Votes, then the House of Representatives shall immediately chuse by Ballot one of them for President; and if no Person have a Majority, then from the five highest on the List the said House shall in like Manner chuse the President. But in chusing the President, the Votes shall be taken by States, the Representation from each State having one Vote; A quorum for this Purpose shall consist of a Member or Members from two thirds of the States, and a Majority of all the States shall be necessary to a Choice. In every Case, after the Choice of the President, the Person having the greatest Number of Votes of the Electors shall be the Vice President. But if there should remain two or more who have equal Votes, the Senate shall chuse from them by Ballot the Vice President.

The Congress may determine the Time of chusing the Electors, and the Day on which they shall give their Votes; which Day shall be the same throughout the United States.

No Person except a natural born Citizen, or a Citizen of the United States, at the time of the Adoption of this Constitution, shall be eligible to the Office of President; neither shall any Person be eligible to that Office who shall not have attained to the Age of thirty five Years, and been fourteen Years a Resident within the United States.

In Case of the Removal of the President from Office, or of his Death, Resignation, or Inability to discharge the Powers and Duties of the said Office, the Same shall devolve on the Vice President, and the Congress may by Law provide for the Case of Removal, Death, Resignation or Inability, both of the President and Vice President, declaring what Officer shall then act as President, and such Officer shall act accordingly, until the Disability be removed, or a President shall be elected.

The President shall, at stated Times, receive for his Services, a Compensation, which shall neither be encreased nor diminished during the Period for which he shall have been elected, and he shall not receive within that Period any other Emolument from the United States, or any of them.

Before he enter on the Execution of his Office, he shall take the following Oath or Affirmation:—"I do solemnly swear (or affirm) that I will faithfully execute the Office of President of the United States, and will to the best of my Ability, preserve, protect and defend the Constitution of the United States."

Section. 2.   The President shall be Commander in Chief of the Army and Navy of the United States, and of the Militia of the several States, when called into the actual Service of the United States; he may require the Opinion, in writing, of the principal Officer in each of the executive Departments, upon any Subject relating to the Duties of their respective Offices, and he shall have Power to grant Reprieves and Pardons for Offences against the United States, except in Cases of Impeachment.

He shall have Power, by and with the Advice and Consent of the Senate, to make Treaties, provided two thirds of the Senators present concur; and he shall nominate, and by and with the Advice and Consent of the Senate, shall appoint Ambassadors, other public Ministers and Consuls, Judges of the supreme Court, and all other Officers of the United States, whose Appointments are not herein otherwise provided for, and which shall be established by Law: but the Congress may by Law vest the Appointment of such inferior Officers, as they think proper, in the President alone, in the Courts of Law, or in the Heads of Departments.

The President shall have Power to fill up all Vacancies that may happen during the Recess of the Senate, by granting Commissions which shall expire at the End of their next Session.

Section. 3.   He shall from time to time give to the Congress Information of the State of the Union, and recommend to their Consideration such Measures as he shall judge necessary and expedient; he may, on extraordinary Occasions, convene both Houses, or either of them, and in Case of Disagreement between them, with Respect to the Time of Adjournment, he may adjourn them to such Time as he shall think proper; he shall receive Ambassadors and other public Ministers; he shall take Care that the Laws be faithfully executed, and shall Commission all the Officers of the United States.

Section. 4.   The President, Vice President and all civil Officers of the United States, shall be removed from Office on Impeachment for, and Conviction of, Treason, Bribery, or other high Crimes and Misdemeanors.

Article III.

Section. 1.   The judicial Power of the United States, shall be vested in one supreme Court, and in such inferior Courts as the Congress may from time to time ordain and establish. The Judges, both of the supreme and inferior Courts, shall hold their Offices during good Behaviour, and shall, at stated Times, receive for their Services, a Compensation, which shall not be diminished during their Continuance in Office.

Section. 2.   The judicial Power shall extend to all Cases, in Law and Equity, arising under this Constitution, the Laws of the United States, and Treaties made, or which shall be made, under their Authority;—to all Cases affecting Ambassadors, other public Ministers and Consuls;—to all Cases of admiralty and maritime Jurisdiction;—to Controversies to which the United States shall be a Party;—to Controversies between two or more States;—between a State and Citizens of another State;—between Citizens of different States,—between Citizens of the same State claiming Lands under Grants of different States, and between a State, or the Citizens thereof, and foreign States, Citizens or Subjects.

In all Cases affecting Ambassadors, other public Ministers and Consuls, and those in which a State shall be Party, the supreme Court shall have original Jurisdiction. In all the other Cases before mentioned, the supreme Court shall have appellate Jurisdiction, both as to Law and Fact, with such Exceptions, and under such Regulations as the Congress shall make.

The Trial of all Crimes, except in Cases of Impeachment, shall be by Jury; and such Trial shall be held in the State where the said Crimes shall have been committed; but when not committed within any State, the Trial shall be at such Place or Places as the Congress may by Law have directed.

Section. 3.   Treason against the United States, shall consist only in levying War against them, or in adhering to their Enemies, giving them Aid and Comfort. No Person shall be convicted of Treason unless on the Testimony of two Witnesses to the same overt Act, or on Confession in open Court.

The Congress shall have Power to declare the Punishment of Treason, but no Attainder of Treason shall work Corruption of Blood, or Forfeiture except during the Life of the Person attainted.

Article. IV.

Section. 1.   Full Faith and Credit shall be given in each State to the public Acts, Records, and judical Proceedings of every other State. And the Congress may by general Laws prescribe the Manner in which such Acts, Records and Proceedings shall be proved, and the Effect thereof.

Section. 2.   The Citizens of each State shall be entitled to all Privileges and Immunities of Citizens in the several States.

A Person charged in any State with Treason, Felony, or other Crime, who shall flee from Justice, and be found in another State, shall on Demand of the executive Authority of the State from which he fled, be delivered up, to be removed to the State having Jurisdiction of the Crime.

No Person held to Service or Labour in one State, under the Laws thereof, escaping into another, shall, in Consequence of any Law or Regulation therein, be discharged from such Service or Labour, but shall be delivered up on Claim of the Party to whom such Service or Labour may be due.

Section. 3. New States may be admitted by the Congress into this Union; but no new State shall be formed or erected within the Jurisdiction of any other State; nor any State be formed by the Junction of two or more States, or Parts of States, without the Consent of the Legislatures of the States concerned as well as of the Congress.

The Congress shall have Power to dispose of and make all needful Rules and Regulations respecting the Territory or other Property belonging to the United States; and nothing in this Constitution shall be so construed as to Prejudice any Claims of the United States, or of any particular State.

Section. 4. The United States shall guarantee to every State in this Union a Republican Form of Government, and shall protect each of them against Invasion; and on Application of the Legislature, or of the Executive (when the Legislature cannot be convened) against domestic Violence.

Article. V.

The Congress, whenever two thirds of both Houses shall deem it necessary, shall propose Amendments to this Constitution, or, on the Application of the Legislatures of two thirds of the several states, shall call a Convention for proposing Amendments, which, in either Case, shall be valid to all Intents and Purposes, as Part of this Constitution, when ratified by the Legislatures of three fourths of the several States, or by Conventions in three fourths thereof, as the one or the other Mode of Ratification may be proposed by the Congress; Provided that no Amendment which may be made prior to the Year One thousand eight hundred and eight shall in any Manner affect the first and fourth Clauses in the Ninth Section of the first Article; and that no State, without its Consent, shall be deprived of it's equal Suffrage in the Senate.

Article. VI.

All Debts contracted and Engagements entered into, before the Adoption of this Constitution, shall be as valid against the United States under this Constitution, as under the Confederation.

This Constitution, and the Laws of the United States which shall be made in Pursuance thereof; and all Treaties made, or which shall be made, under the Authority of the United States, shall be the supreme

Law of the Land; and the Judges in every State shall be bound thereby, any Thing in the Constitution or Laws of any State to the Contrary notwithstanding.

The Senators and Representatives before mentioned, and the Members of the several State Legislatures, and all executive and judicial Officers, both of the United States and of the several States, shall be bound by Oath or Affirmation, to support this Constitution; but no religious Test shall ever be required as a Qualification to any Office or public Trust under the United States.

Article. VII.

The Ratification of the Conventions of nine States, shall be sufficient for the Establishment of this Constitution between the States so ratifying the Same.

The Word, "the," being interlined between the seventh and eighth Lines of the first Page, The Word "Thirty" being partly written on an Erazure in the fifteenth Line of the first Page, The Words "is tried" being interlined between the thirty second and thirty third Lines of the first Page and the Word "the" being interlined between the forty third and forty fourth Lines of the second Page.

Attest WILLIAM JACKSON Secretary

done in Convention by the unanimous Consent of the States present the Seventeenth Day of September in the Year of our Lord one thousand seven hundred and Eighty seven and of the Independance of the United States of America the Twelfth In witness whereof We have hereunto subscribed our Names,

G⁰ WASHINGTON—Presidᵗ

and deputy from Virginia

New Hampshire	{ JOHN LANGDON NICHOLAS GILMAN }
Massachusetts	{ NATHANIEL GORHAM RUFUS KING
Connecticut	{ W^M SAM^L JOHNSON ROGER SHERMAN
New York	ALEXANDER HAMILTON
New Jersey	{ WIL: LIVINGSTON DAVID BREARLEY. W^M PATERSON. JONA: DAYTON
Pensylvania	{ B FRANKLIN THOMAS MIFFLIN ROB^T MORRIS GEO. CLYMER THO^S FITZSIMONS JARED INGERSOLL JAMES WILSON GOUV MORRIS
Delaware	{ GEO: READ GUNNING BEDFORD jun JOHN DICKINSON RICHARD BASSETT JACO: BROOM
Maryland	{ JAMES M^CHENRY DAN OF S^T THO^S JENIFER DAN^L CARROLL
Virginia	{ JOHN BLAIR— JAMES MADISON JR.
North Carolina	{ W^M BLOUNT RICH^D DOBBS SPAIGHT HU WILLIAMSON
South Carolina	{ J. RUTLEDGE CHARLES COTESWORTH PINCKNEY CHARLES PINCKNEY PIERCE BUTLER.
Georgia	{ WILLIAM FEW ABR BALDWIN

Amendments to the U.S. Constitution

AMENDMENT I.

[Ratification of the first ten amendments was completed December 15, 1791]

Congress shall make no law respecting an establishment of religion, or prohibiting the free exercise thereof; or abridging the freedom of speech, or of the press; or the right of the people peaceably to assemble, and to petition the Government for a redress of grievances.

AMENDMENT II.

A well regulated Militia, being necessary to the security of a free State, the right of the people to keep and bear Arms, shall not be infringed.

AMENDMENT III

No Soldier shall, in time of peace be quartered in any house, without the consent of the Owner, nor in time of war, but in a manner to be prescribed by law.

AMENDMENT IV

The right of the people to be secure in their persons, houses, papers, and effects, against unreasonable searches and seizures, shall not be violated, and no Warrants shall issue, but upon probable cause, supported by Oath or affirmation, and particularly describing the place to be searched, and the persons or things to be seized.

AMENDMENT V

No person shall be held to answer for a capital, or otherwise infamous crime, unless on a presentment or indictment of a Grand Jury, except in cases arising in the land or naval forces, or in the Militia, when in actual service in time of War or public danger; nor shall any person be subject for the same offence to be twice put in jeopardy of life or limb; nor shall be compelled in any criminal case to be a witness against himself, nor be deprived of life, liberty, or property, without due process of law; nor shall private property be taken for public use, without just compensation.

AMENDMENT VI

In all criminal prosecutions, the accused shall enjoy the right to a speedy and public trial, by an impartial jury of the State and district wherein the crime shall have been committed, which district shall have been previously ascertained by law, and to be informed of the nature and cause of the accusation; to be confronted with the witness against him; to have compulsory process for obtaining witness in his favor, and to have the Assistance of Counsel for his defence.

AMENDMENT VII

In Suits at common law, where the value in controversy shall exceed twenty dollars, the right of trial by jury shall be preserved, and no fact tried by a jury, shall be otherwise re-examined in any Court of the United States, than according to the rules of the common law.

AMENDMENT VIII

Excessive bail shall not be required, nor excessive fines imposed, nor cruel and unusual punishments inflicted.

AMENDMENT IX

The enumeration in the Constitution, of certain rights, shall not be construed to deny or disparage others retained by the people.

AMENDMENT X

The powers not delegated to the United States by the Constitution, nor prohibited by it to the States, are reserved to the States respectively, or to the people.

AMENDMENT XI [January 8, 1798]

The Judicial power of the United States shall not be construed to extend to any suit in law or equity, commenced or prosecuted against one of the United States by Citizens of another State, or by Citizens or Subjects of any Foreign State.

AMENDMENT XII [September 25, 1804]

The Electors shall meet in their respective states and vote by ballot for President and Vice-President, one of whom, at least, shall not be an inhabitant of the same state with themselves; they shall name in their ballots the person voted for as President, and in distinct ballots the person voted for as Vice-President, and they shall make distinct lists of all persons voted for as President, and of all persons voted for as Vice-President, and of the number of votes for each, which lists they shall sign and certify, and transmit sealed to the seat of the government of the United States, directed to the President of the Senate;—The President of the Senate shall, in the presence of Senate and House of Representatives, open all the certificates and the votes shall then be counted;—The person having the greatest number of votes for President, shall be the President, if such number be a majority of the whole number of Electors appointed; and if no person have such a majority, then from the persons having the highest numbers not exceeding three on the list of those voted for as President, the House of Representatives shall choose immediately, by ballot, the President. But in choosing the President, the votes shall be taken by states, the representation from each state having one vote; a quorum for this purpose shall consist of a member or members from two-thirds of the states, and a majority of all the states shall be necessary to a choice. And if the House of Representatives shall not choose a President whenever the right of choice shall devolve upon them, before the fourth day of March next following, then the Vice-President shall act as President, as in the case of the death or other constitutional disability of the President.—The person having the greatest number of votes as Vice-President, shall be the Vice-President, if such number be a majority of the whole number of Electors appointed, and if no person have a majority, then from the two highest numbers on the list, the Senate shall choose the Vice-President; a quorum for the purpose shall consist of two-thirds of the whole number of Senators, and a majority of the whole number shall be necessary to a choice. But no person constitutionally ineligible to the office of President shall be eligible to that of Vice-President of the United States.

AMENDMENT XIII [December 18, 1865]

Section 1. Neither slavery nor involuntary servitude, except as a punishment for crime whereof the party shall have been duly convicted, shall exist within the United States, or any place subject to their jurisdiction.

Section 2. Congress shall have power to enforce this article by appropriate legislation.

AMENDMENT XIV [July 28, 1868]

Section 1. All persons born or naturalized in the United States, and subject to the jurisdiction thereof, are citizens of the United States and of the State wherein they reside. No State shall make or enforce any law which shall abridge the privileges or immunities of citizens of the United States; nor shall any state deprive any person of life, liberty, or property, without due process of law; nor deny to any person within its jurisdiction the equal protection of the laws.

Section 2. Representatives shall be apportioned among the several States according to their respective numbers, counting the whole number of persons in each State, excluding Indians not taxed. But when the right to vote at any election for the choice of electors for President and Vice President of the United States, Representatives in Congress, the Executive and Judicial officers of a State, or the members of the Legislature thereof, is denied to any. of the male inhabitants of such State, being twenty-one years of age, and citizens of the United States, or in any way abridged, except for participation in rebellion, or other crime, the basis of representation therein shall be reduced in the proportion which the number of such male citizens shall bear to the whole number of male citizens twenty-one years of age in such State.

Section 3. No person shall be a Senator or Representative in Congress, or elector of President and Vice President, or hold any office, civil or military, under the United States, or under any State, who, having previously taken an oath, as a member of Congress, or as an officer of the United States, or as a member of any State legislature, or as an executive or judicial officer of any State, to support the Constitution of the United States, shall have engaged in insurrection or rebellion against the same, or given aid or comfort to the enemies thereof. But Congress may by a vote of two-thirds of each House, remove such disability.

Section 4. The validity of the public debt of the United States, authorized by law, including debts incurred for payment of pensions and bounties for services in suppressing insurrection or rebellion, shall not be questioned. But neither the United States nor any State shall assume or pay any debt or obligation incurred in aid of insurrection or rebellion against the United States, or any claim for the loss or emancipation of any slave; but all such debts, obligations and claims shall be held illegal and void.

Section 5. The Congress shall have power to enforce, by appropriate legislation, the provisions of this article.

AMENDMENT XV [March 30, 1870]

Section 1. The right of citizens of the United States to vote shall not be denied or abridged by the United States or by any State on account of race, color, or previous condition of servitude.

Section 2. The Congress shall have power to enforce this article by appropriate legislation.

AMENDMENT XVI [February 25, 1913]

The Congress shall have power to lay and collect taxes on incomes, from whatever source derived, without apportionment among the several States, and without regard to any census or enumeration.

AMENDMENT XVII [May 31, 1913]

The Senate of the United States shall be composed of two Senators from each State, elected by the people thereof, for six years; and ach Senator shall have one vote. The electors in each State shall have the qualifications requisite for electors of the most numerous branch of the State legislatures.

When vacancies happen in the representation of any State in the Senate, the executive authority of such State shall issue writs of election to fill such vacancies: *Provided,* That the legislature of any State may empower the executive thereof to make temporary appointments until the people fill the vacancies by election as the legislature may direct.

This amendment shall not be so construed as to affect the election or term of any Senator chosen before it becomes valid as part of the Constitution.

AMENDMENT XVIII [January 29, 1919]

Section 1. After one year from the ratification of this article the manufacture, sale, or transportation of intoxicating liquors within, the importation thereof into, or the exportation thereof from the United States and all territory subject to the jurisdiction thereof for beverage purposes is hereby prohibited.

Sec. 2. The Congress and the several States shall have concurrent power to enforce this article by appropriate legislation.

Sec. 3. This article shall be inoperative unless it shall have been ratified as an amendment to the Constitution by the legislatures of the several States, as provided in the Constitution, within seven years from the date of the submission hereof to the States by the Congress.

AMENDMENT XIX [August 26, 1920]

The right of citizens of the United States to vote shall not be denied or abridged by the United States or by any State on account of sex.

Congress shall have power to enforce this article by appropriate legislation.

AMENDMENT XX [February 6, 1933]

Section 1. The terms of the President and Vice President shall end at noon on the 20th day of January, and the terms of Senators and Representatives at noon on the 3d day of January, of the years in which such terms would have ended if this article had not been ratified; and the terms of their successors shall then begin.

Sec. 2. The Congress shall assemble at least once in every year, and such meeting shall begin at noon on the 3d day of January, unless they shall by law appoint a different day.

Sec. 3. If, at the time fixed for the beginning of the term of the President, the President elect shall have died, the Vice President elect shall become President. If a President shall not have been chosen before the time fixed for the beginning of his term, or if the President elect shall have failed to qualify, then the Vice President elect shall act as President until a President shall have qualified; and the Congress may by law provide for the case wherein neither a President elect nor a

Vice President elect shall have qualified, declaring who shall then act as President, or the manner in which one who is to act shall be selected, and such person shall act accordingly until a President or Vice President shall have qualified.

Sec. 4. The Congress may by law provide for the case of the death of any of the persons from whom the House of Representatives may choose a President whenever the right of choice shall have devolved upon them, and for the case of the death of any of the persons from whom the Senate may choose a Vice President whenever the right of choice shall have devolved upon them.

Sec. 5. Sections 1 and 2 shall take effect on the 15th day of October following the ratification of this article.

Sec. 6. This article shall be inoperative unless it shall have been ratified as an amendment to the Constitution by the legislatures of three-fourths of the several States within seven years from the date of its submission.

AMENDMENT XXI [December 5, 1933]

Section 1. The eighteenth article of amendment to the Constitution of the United States is hereby repealed.

Sec. 2. The transportation or importation into any State, Territory, or possession of the United States for delivery or use therein of intoxicating liquors, in violation of the laws thereof, is hereby prohibited.

Sec. 3. This article shall be inoperative unless it shall have been ratified as an amendment to the Constitution by conventions in the several States, as provided in the Constitution, within seven years from the date of the submission hereof to the States by the Congress.

AMENDMENT XXII [February 26, 1951]

Section 1. No person shall be elected to the office of the President more than twice, and no person who has held the office of President, or acted as President, for more than two years of a term to which some other person was elected President shall be elected to the office of President more than once. But this Article shall not apply to any person holding the office of President when this Article was proposed by the Congress, and shall not prevent any person who may be holding the office of President, or acting as President, during the term within which this Article becomes operative from holding the office of President or acting as President during the remainder of such term.

Sec. 2. This article shall be inoperative unless it shall have been ratified as an amendment to the Constitution by the legislatures of three-fourths of the several States within seven years from the date of its submission of the States by the Congress.

AMENDMENT XXIII [March 29, 1961]

Section 1. The District constituting the seat of Government of the United States shall appoint in such manner as the Congress may direct: A number of electors of President and Vice-President equal to the whole number of Senators and Representatives in Congress to which the District would be entitled if it were a State, but in no event more than the least populous State; they shall be in addition to those appointed by the States, but they shall be considered, for the purposes of the election of President and Vice-President, to be electors appointed by a State; and they shall meet in the District and perform such duties as provided by the twelfth article of amendment.

Section 2. The Congress shall have power to enforce this article by appropriate legislation.

AMENDMENT XXIV [January 23, 1964]

Section 1. The right of citizens of the United States to vote in any primary or other election for President or Vice-President, for electors for President or Vice President, or for Senator or Representative in Congress, shall not be denied or abridged by the United States or any State by reason of failure to pay any poll tax or other tax.

Section 2. The Congress shall have the power to enforce this article by appropriate legislation.

Illustrations

Index

[A question which is complicated, shall, [at the request of any member, be divided, and put separately on the propositions, of which it is compounded.

The determination of a question altho' fully debated, shall be postponed, if the deputies of any State desire it until the next day.

A writing which contains any matter brought on to be considered, shall be read once throughout for information, then by paragraphs to be debated, and again, with the amendments, if any, made on the second reading; and afterwards, the question shall be put on the whole, amended, or approved, in its original form, as the case shall be.

Committees shall be appointed by ballot; and the members who have the greatest number of ballots, altho' not a majority of the votes present, shall be the Committee. When two or more members have an equal number of votes, the member standing first on the list in the order of taking down the ballots, shall be preferred.

A member may be called to order by any other member, as well as by the President; and may be allowed to explain his conduct or expressions supposed to be reprehensible. And all questions of order shall be decided by the President without appeal or debate.

Upon a question to adjourn for the day, which may be made at any time, if it be seconded, the question shall be put without a debate.

When the House shall adjourn, every member shall stand in his place until the President pass him.]